The Political Economy of
Communist China

The Political Economy of Communist China

JAN S. PRYBYLA

Professor of Economics
The Pennsylvania State University

INTERNATIONAL TEXTBOOK COMPANY

an **Intext** *publisher*
Scranton, Pennsylvania 18515

International's series in

ECONOMICS

HC
427.9
P75

ISBN O 7002 2257 X(cloth)
ISBN O 7002 2319 3 (paper)

To my father and the memory of my mother

Preface

This book is the result of many years' interest in the political economy of communism and comparative communist economic systems. It follows a number of studies published in professional and other journals over nearly two decades, but it is not a simple repetition or collection of those earlier articles. It ranges farther afield and tries to bring together and weave into a pattern the knowledge and, hopefully, the insight acquired as one goes along.

I have tried to be fair and to approach the subject with the objectivity and detachment one reads about in prefaces to books about Communist China. I do, however, have certain reservations about totalitarian systems as vehicles of human advancement and about progressive ends justifying regressive and repressive means. How far I have succeeded in giving a workably balanced picture of China is for the reader to judge.

Professors Chu-yuan Cheng of the University of Michigan and Chi-ming Hou of Colgate University were kind enough to read the manuscript and offered valuable suggestions. I wish here to record my sincere thanks to them. It goes without saying that the responsibility for any errors, omissions, and other defects is mine alone. My wife has for years, patiently and with good grace, put up with Mao and a houseful of counterrevolutionaries, rightists, leftists, mountain-toppists, black hands, and special agents of China's No. 1 person in authority taking the capitalist road. Our invisible guests have taken over much of what otherwise might have been diverting social conversation. My students have had their fill too. To all of them my thanks.

J.S.P.

University Park, Pennsylvania
May 1970

Contents

1 | Introduction

The book deals with the development of China's economy during the first two decades of communist power in the whole country. In the communist world economics was and remains political economy in the literal meaning of that phrase. In spite of occasional attempts to construct a science of economics, sovereign, objective, and independent of the ruling political philosophy, economic reasoning and the implementation of economic policies are matters of State power, branches and tributaries of politics. The conduct of economic life hinges on the extent to which those in whose hands rest the reigns of political power succeed in enforcing their writ both within society at large and in the narrow circle of power holders.

The story of Communist China's effort to subdue nature—that is, to adequately feed, clothe, house, and keep in good health a population which increases by over 200 million every fifteen years—and to remold man into a collective being responsive to the ideals of Marxism-Leninism and Mao Tse-tung's thought is here traced through its many ups and downs and sharp turns that have marked the communist tenure of power since October 1949. The story is told in chronological order and divided into periods which roughly correspond to the shifts in the power balance at the top and the corresponding changes in economic policy within the body politic.

The frequent shifts and, indeed, contradictions in Chinese Communist strategy of economic development call for an explanation. As usual, a combination of documented fact and informed guesswork will have to do until such time as the archives of the Chinese Communist Party and government become available for inspection, which is not likely to be tomorrow or the day after. But even now it is possible to list certain assumptions and dispel some myths about the twists and turns of economic policy during the first two decades of communist rule.

First, it is important to recognize that "strategy" is largely an ex post concept. Hindsight reveals a pattern of conduct, a fairly consistent trend hidden from the observer of current policies. This underlying consistency of conduct is nowhere as great as the official ideology makes it out to be, but it is there. What it adds up to is a series of social experiments tending in a certain direction and geared to a

1

few broad and general beliefs concerning what its holders think is the best possible society. It is not a set of rigid recipes for strategy and tactics laid down once and for all, and followed unswervingly by all concerned. Not even "Stalinism," which was supreme in Russia from 1929 to 1953, could be reduced to such simple accounting precision.

Second, a good part of any "strategy" consists of responses to urgent and persuasive circumstances of the moment. These may be domestic or foreign in origin, but the pressure which they exert is often such as to significantly narrow down the range of alternatives open to decision makers.

Third, no leadership, however closely knit, has ever been absolutely monolithic, thinking and acting as one, and having its writ run smoothly through society. Although those in positions of authority may share the same general conviction on how mankind is to be saved, there are bound to be among them differences in background and temperament tending to give rise to differing interpretations of events, divergences of views on remedies to be applied, and on emphases to be given to this or that course of action. In the claustrophobic atmosphere at the top of the totalitarian pyramid, personal and policy rivalries are common. There are factions and quarrels, feats of individual chameleonism, enmities and grievances lovingly nursed, none the less real for being hidden from the masses on whose behalf power is being wielded. Occasionally they surface as purges, confessions by the losers, or power stalemates. Leadership rifts— opposition within oppositionless one-party states—is a basic datum too often overlooked, forgotten, or denied. It is of special relevance to Communist China. One may perhaps assert that without taking it into account, little sense can be made of the country's economic history since 1949.[1] It is of course easier to recognize the existence of factions than to identify their membership and platforms, but even the latter is possible. The important first step is to rid oneself of the misleading myth of the totalitarian monolith.[2]

[1] Factional struggles were a regular feature of the history of the Communist Party of China before 1949 as well. See Guy Wint, *Common Sense About China* (New York: Macmillan, 1961); Chun-tu Hsueh, *The Chinese Communist Movement 1921-1937* and *The Chinese Communist Movement, 1937-1949* (Stanford, Calif.: Hoover Institution Press, 1967).

[2] For the regime stability-*cum*-monolith error, see A. Doak Barnett, *Cadres, Bureaucracy, and Political Power in China* (New York: Columbia U. P., 1967). The subject must be handled with extreme care. Many of the allegedly treacherous and revisionist or right-opportunist statements (as well as left deviations) attributed to high Party and government officials at various times, but especially during the purge years 1966-69, seem to be taken out of the political context of the time at which they were made. There is much distortion and no right or possibility of reply by the accused. For an instructive, well-reasoned discussion of this problem, see John Gittings, "The Crimes of China's K," *Far Eastern Economic Review* (*FEER*) (April 16, 1968), pp. 176-179.

In the chapters that follow, frequent reference will be made to frictions between the radical, left-wing elements of the Party leadership, and the more right-inclined, relative moderates. This classification is convenient and broadly indicative of the main leadership groupings, but it has to be interpreted carefully. In the first place, the leadership divisions are certainly more complex and subtle than the classification suggests. No doubt there is much nervous shifting of positions, many ways of being moderate, many shades of radicalism, and a fair share of "mountain-topism" ("sitting on top of the mountain and watching the tigers fight").[3] Secondly, terms such as "liberal" or "moderate" should not be understood in a Western democratic sense. In China's communist context, the moderates have tended to be recruited from the entrenched one-Party and governmental bureaucracy—that is, the power elite. They are men whose job it is to run the country day by day. By virtue of this function, they are more inclined to be sensitive and responsive to the complexities and nuances of social life, and hence relatively cautious and disinclined to rock the boat. The totalitarian "liberals" are practitioners of *Realpolitik*. They range from market socialists to hard-line Stalinists. Their understanding of Western-type parliamentary processes and of the meaning of individual freedom is marginal at best. They are moderate in the sense that they curb their emotional responses to events in a more disciplined way than their more heady colleagues. In fact, the leftists of Communist China often reveal Trotskyite proclivities (for example, in their insistence on the permanence of revolution) and anarchic (hopefully, from their standpoint, controlled-anarchic) trends. The moderates, on the other hand, are characteristically believers in the totalitarian *apparat*, proponents of unquestioned obedience to Party commands and the sanctity of the Party's edicts.[4] Perhaps the rift between the left wing radicals and the totalitarian moderates ("liberals") is better described by such appelations as romantics versus pragmatists, hotheads versus coolheads, ideologues versus apparat-men. Both are total-

---

[3] For a tentative classification of the "radical" and "moderate" positions on major issues, see Chapter 8.

[4] As a badly rattled Liu Shao-ch'i once put it: "The Leftists may undergo changes during and after the movement. Those who are Leftists at the beginning may not be Leftists at mid-stage. Those who are Leftists at mid-stage may not be Leftists in the last stage. In one movement, some people are Leftists; in another movement, they may not be Leftists. . . . On one point, they are not Leftists; but on another point, they may be Leftists." Liu Shao-ch'i, "Talk to the Great Proletarian Revolution Corps" (August 3, 1966), in *Collected Works of Liu Shao-ch'i, 1958-1967* (Hong Kong: Union Research Institute (*URI*), 1968), p. 337. Taken from a Red Guard publication. In his self-criticism of October 23, 1966 (*ibid.*, p. 360), Liu allegedly admitted that "In 1962 I committed the mistake of being Right-inclined. In 1964 I was superficially 'Left,' but actually Right-inclined."

itarian, tough, authoritarian. George F. Kennan's appraisal of the victims of Stalin's purges applies with equal force to China's communist
moderates: ". . . Many of the leading victims of these persecutions
owed their sufferings to no moral scruples of their own about the
methods of the regime: but for the vicissitudes of politics in an
authoritarian political organization, they would themselves have been
sitting, without pangs of conscience, among the judges, jailers, camp
commanders, or hangmen."[5] It is, as the dialecticians say, the same
but opposite.

Finally, it should be recognized that there is many a slip between
command and the execution of command. Assuming that orders
from the top are consistent both at a point in time and over time,
their implementation may be both inconsistent and far removed
from what the original command was intended to achieve. The reverse may also be true. The faltering of leaders can be, to an extent,
neutralized by society which quietly goes its own way amid loud
protestations of allegiance and submission, "agreement by mouth,
but disagreement at heart," as the saying goes. To a degree, the
alterations which any order issued at the top undergoes in the process of execution is due to the fact that "whereas the characteristics
of the state are authority, unity and habitual obedience, those of
society are diversity, internal contradictions and pluralism,"[6] even
though, as has been argued above, the authority, unity, and habitual
obedience of the state machine are relative. The centralizing forces of
the state are likely to meet with opposition or passive resistance from
the pluralistic forces of society at large. Local interests and short-
time horizons may clash with the larger interests and longer-range
views of the center. Hard realities at the operational level may alter
in practice the theoretical blueprints elaborated in planning offices.
There will be difficulties of communication between those who make
the plans and those who carry them out; control may turn out to be
lax or spotty, commands meant to achieve a given end may have
unforeseen side effects, and so on. The lesson to be drawn from all

[5] George F. Kennan's review of Robert Conquest's *The Great Terror:
Stalin's Purge of the Thirties*, in *New York Times Book Review* (October 27,
1968), p. 2. ©1968 by The New York Times Company. Reprinted by permission. The limits of Chinese Communist liberalism and moderation have been
defined by Liu Shao-ch'i: "You have heard me say that the minority should be
protected. (Audience interrupted: 'We've heard.') We should primarily protect
the good people. It is possible we may protect the bad people for a short period
of one to three months, or even up to a year. When we have collected sufficient
data on them, we will draw our conclusions. We may arrest some of them, but
still leave the majority free." Liu Shao-ch'i, *Collected Works, op. cit.*,
pp. 337-338.

[6] Ghita Ionescu, *The Politics of the European Communist States* (New
York: Praeger, and London: George Weidenfeld & Nicholson Ltd., 1967), p. 1.

this is that paper strategies and what actually goes on may not always coincide, and that to know what course of action was followed one has to look not only to the official documents and instructions, but to what actually happened down at the farm and on the factory floor.

SOURCES OF INFORMATION

The Chinese Communists have been less than generous in giving the outside world (or their own people, for that matter) reliable and comprehensive information about the economy. The degree of secretiveness and reliability has varied from period to period, as also presumably have the reasons.[7] Such information as we have is gathered from official statistics, the Chinese national and provincial press, books, monographs, and reports published in China (many of which are available in English), monitoring of mainland radio broadcasts, accounts by travelers (tourists, foreign students, businessmen, technicians, residents of Hong Kong who are occasionally allowed to visit their relatives in China), reports from foreign correspondents stationed in Peking, and interviews with refugees. Although the physical volume of this information is imposing, the quality is, on the whole, questionable. Travelers and foreign correspondents are not normally allowed to roam through the country at will; their accounts tend, therefore, to be partial and frequently not very perceptive. Few eyewitnesses, for example, noticed the deep rifts which for many years divided the apparently monolithic leadership of the Chinese Communist Party and government. There was practically no hint from those who visited China in 1965 of the impending upheaval known as the Great Proletarian Cultural Revolution (Chapters 11 and 12). Refugee accounts contain a bias which it is not always easy to pinpoint. The

---

[7] Among the reasons are (1) the absence of a national statistical network and shortage of trained technical personnel (1949-52); (2) the staggering magnitude of the task of collecting and processing data in a vast and populous country; (3) distortions at the reporting level (plant and farm) traceable to a particular system of "success indicators" for managers and others and to a relatively modest "arithmetical literacy" of lower level cadres; (4) a desire at the top to conceal weaknesses, errors of judgment, policy failures, and other shortcomings, and its converse—the wish to convey the impression of dynamism, success, and progress ("Statistics," Lenin had said, "are the weapon of the proletarian State."); (5) the breakdown of statistical services during periods of political euphoria (1958-60, 1966-69); (6) a "military secrets" mentality, broadly interpreted to cover much of the economy, fairly typical of totalitarian societies, especially in periods of early economic development (cf. the Soviet statistical drought from 1936 through the mid-1950's). See Leo Orleans, "Troubles with Statistics," *Problems of Communism* (January-February 1965), pp. 39-47. For the comparable Soviet experience, see Jan S. Prybyla, "How Statistics Are Made," *Problems of Communism* (January-February 1962), pp. 50-53.

reading of official publications calls for special skills: at first sight, all Chinese newspapers seem to say the same thing, right down to the use of standardized, officially sanctioned vocabulary.[8] On the other hand, journals and newspapers (next only to the telephone, provincial radio broadcasts, and actual meetings) are an important link between the central leadership and the leaders' staff in the field ("cadres"). This suggests that articles in the press must deal with real life problems on which the cadres seek guidance. No doubt, it is particularly true of the provincial press, and helps to explain why the export abroad of provincial newspapers has been banned in recent years.

The statistical situation was never quite satisfactory. It deteriorated after 1959 to the point of complete blackout. Before 1952 the figures released by the Chinese authorities were fragmentary and often not comparable from year to year. After the establishment of the State Statistical Bureau in 1952, and with Soviet and East European technical aid (which was cut off in mid-1960), the situation improved for a time. This improvement ended abruptly in 1958 when statistical reporting became a political weapon pure and simple, with every trace of professional integrity removed for the duration of the Great Leap Forward. The first and only Chinese Communist statistical manual, a rather slender, retrospective job entitled *Ten Great Years*, was published in September 1959. Although fundamental to the study of China's economy, it bears the marks of exaggeration characteristic of the Great Leap period. The figures for 1958 which it contains, are probably worthless. After 1959 no statistical information of any meaningfulness was released. Occasional references to percentage production increases in invididual plants, municipalities, counties, and regions are useless for any systematic study of the economy. The statistically great ten years were followed by ten silent years during which China went first through a period of reconstruction and then through another upheaval. The statistical blackout which descended on the country after 1959 has no precedent in the history of any modern nation—even the secretive Albanians have been more communicative. Compared with this great wall of silence, the meager Soviet statistics of the late 1930's, 1940's, and early 1950's appear generous. The phenomenon is probably traceable to

[8] Three exceptions to this rule should be noted: (1) until 1966 professional journals sometimes carried "discussion articles" in which individual experts were allowed to float suggestions regarding economic theory and policy; (2) unorthodox views on many matters were published during a brief period in 1957 (see Chapter 7) and, in an allegorical form, in 1961-65 (see Chapter 11); (3) in the early stages of the Cultural Revolution of 1966-69, wall posters put up by contending factions carried news which, with due allowance for youthful exuberance, was often unavailable elsewhere.

two causes: unwillingness to publicize the harmful effects on the economy of the Great Leap policies, and later the disorganization of the statistical apparatus (and possibly of all planning worthy of the name).

All the difficulties, however, are not of Chinese making. There is a cultural gap between China and the West, an ethnocentrism which is not the exclusive property of the Chinese. A great effort of understanding is needed on both sides if the mistrust and hostility that have marked China's relations with the West (and Russia) are not to degenerate into disastrous conflict in the future. The spadework for implanting such understanding is being done in the West, albeit slowly. In spite of all obstacles, Western knowledge of China is gaining ground. In the last ten years a number of highly competent studies of China's economy, her political system, and social structure have appeared in the United States and elsewhere. Together they give a fairly comprehensive picture of the land and its people and of the policies of China's leaders. The details can be filled in later, when the veil of secrecy surrounding China's experiment in communism is lifted, as it is bound to be.[9]

[9] The most comprehensive collection of Chinese Communist figures is Nai-Ruenn Chen (ed.), *Chinese Economic Statistics: A Handbook for Mainland China.* A monograph of the Committee on the Economy of China of the Social Science Research Council (Chicago: Aldine, 1967). The main communist source is *Ten Great Years: Statistics of the Economic and Cultural Achievements of the People's Republic of China* (Peking: Foreign Languages Press [hereafter referred to as *FLP*], 1960). See also Helen and Y. C. Yin, *Economic Statistics of Mainland China, 1949-1957* (Cambridge, Mass.: Harvard U. P., 1960); Choh-ming Li, *The Statistical System of Communist China* (Berkeley: U. of California Press, 1962); Alexander Eckstein, "A Brief Note on the Quality and Reliability of Chinese Communist Statistics," Appendix A of *Communist China's Economic Growth and Foreign Trade* (New York: McGraw-Hill, 1966); Helen W. Yin, *The Industrial Statistics Reporting System of Communist China, 1949-1958,* Ph.D. dissertation, Columbia University, 1966 (microfilm). Figures on Communist China's foreign trade are compiled monthly by the *Far Eastern Economic Review (FEER),* Hong Kong, and published in mimeographed form in *China Trade Report.* An instructive general source on the economy is the *Quarterly Economic Review: China, Hong Kong, North Korea* issued by The Economist Intelligence Unit in London. A good reference is *Union Research Service* (hereafter referred to as *URS*) a biweekly bulletin published by the Union Research Institute in Hong Kong. It contains translations from the mainland press, each issue being devoted to a particular subject. *The China Mainland Review* published in Hong Kong was a useful source of analytical articles. It ceased publication in 1967. English translations of articles appearing in the Chinese Communist press are also available in *Survey of China Mainland Press* and *Extracts from China Mainland Magazines (SCMP, ECMM)* published by the U.S. Consulate General in Hong Kong. These are part of the general Joint Publications Research Service *(JPRS)* series, and are available either in mimeographed or microfilm form. Other China sources include the *Peking Review* (weekly), the Hsinhua News Agency (New China News Agency or *NCNA) Daily News Release,* the *Hsinhua Selected News Items, China Pictorial,* and *China Reconstructs.* See also *China News Analysis* (Hong Kong), *China Quarterly* (London), *Asian Survey*

A NOTE ON CHINESE LAW

In the pages that follow, reference will occasionally be made to legal texts promulgated by China's Communist leaders. As with economic statistics, there is here a serious problem of reticence. But the difficulty is really more intractable. It lies in the paucity of Chinese law and the sweeping provisions of the few laws that have been enacted. "Up to now," writes a Soviet commentator, "neither a civil nor a criminal code, nor any codes in other areas of law have been adopted in the Chinese People's Republic, nor have procedural norms been defined." [10] This fact is confirmed by Western students of Chinese jurisprudence: a collection of the fundamental laws of the Chinese People's Republic (constitution and programs, organic laws, other formal laws) takes up only 603 pages of rather large print. [11] The Chinese, for their part, claim that there are "4,000 laws and ordinances" which some 2,700 of their courts can busy themselves with. Most of these laws and ordinances are probably administrative decisions of limited scope and applicability. On balance, it would appear that the body of law in Communist China is extremely emaciated. Chou En-lai, in what surely must be regarded as a monu-

---

(Berkeley), *Journal of Asian Studies, Problems of Communism* (Washington, D.C.: United States Information Agency). A useful reference guide is Peter Benton and Eugene Wu *Contemporary China: A Research Guide* (Stanford, Calif.: Hoover Institution Press, 1967). Also, Nai-Ruenn Chen, *The Economy of Mainland China 1949-1963: A Bibliography of Materials in English* (Berkeley, Calif.: Committee on the Economy of China, Social Science Research Council, 1963).

[10] F. Kalinychev, "Democracy and Legality," *Izvestia* (February 12, 1967), p. 4.

[11] Albert P. Blaustein (ed.), *Fundamental Legal Documents of Communist China* (South Hackensack, N.J.: Rothman, 1962) and Tao-Tai Hsia, *Guide to Selected Legal Sources of Mainland China* (Washington, D.C.: Library of Congress, 1967). For a genesis of Chinese Communist law, see *Fundamental Laws of the Chinese Soviet Republic*, with an introduction by Bela Kun (New York: International Publishers, 1934). Other recommended sources are: J. A. Cohen, "The Criminal Process in the People's Republic of China," *Harvard Law Review* (January 1966), pp. 469-533, his "The Criminal Process in China," in Donald W. Treadgold (ed.), *Soviet and Chinese Communism: Similarities and Differences* (Seattle: U. of Washington Press, 1967), pp. 107-143, and "The Party and the Courts, 1949-1959," *The China Quarterly* (April-June 1969), pp. 120-157; S. C. Leng, "The Lawyer in Communist China," *Journal of the International Commission of Jurists* (Summer 1962); Luke T. Lee, "Chinese Communist Law: Background and Development," *Michigan Law Review* (February 1962), pp. 308-340; David Finkelstein, "The Language of Communist China's Criminal Law," *Journal of Asian Studies* (May 1958), pp. 503-521; Stanley B. Lubman, *The Nature and Role of Law in Communist China*, J.S.D. dissertation, School of Law, Columbia University (1968); George Ginsburgs and Arthur Stahnke, "The People's Procuratorate in Communist China: The Institution Ascendant, 1954-1957," *China Quarterly* (April-June 1968), pp. 82-132.

mental understatement, admitted in June 1957 that "the legal system in our country is not all it should be,"[12] but denied that, as some critics had suggested, "there [was] no law to go by."

The reasons for this situation, unusual even for a totalitarian system in which arbitrary decisions of the leadership are an important substitute for due process of law, may be summed up as follows:

1. The Chinese society's attitude to law. The Chinese traditionally make no clear distinction between enacted law and customary norms of behavior. Over most of its history, the country has been administered more by reliance on a multitude of subtle ways of transmitting commands than by precisely defined, duly enacted and published legal texts.[13] Under the Ch'ing Dynasty, for example, the General Code of Laws stipulated that it was a criminal offence to "do what you ought not to do." A Western correspondent in Peking was rebuked by his Chinese hosts for suggesting that China was not a prosperous country. In answer to his query whether this was not true, he was told that it was not polite, and that consequently how could it be true if it was not polite?[14]

2. The last example points up a related problem: the Chinese attitude to words. One student of China puts it this way: "Words are regarded as symbolic counters, to be moved about the chessboard of life in order to produce the desired effect. This leads to reservations and subtleties of expression and action which need to be interpreted within the framework of the Chinese environment and which a stranger might not understand. There commonly lacks a sense of an obligation for words and beliefs, or words and actions, to correspond. While this phenomenon is certainly present in other cultures, it is not normally so strong as in China."[15] Thus, in the area of jurisprudence, jotted-down laws may be one thing, legal rights quite another.

3. This trait has become more sharply defined under the communists. The Party—or, more exactly, the dominant faction within the Party—is law unto itself, no matter what the legal texts may say. The Party, insofar as it manages to resolve its internal dissentions, is presumed to have a monopoly on the sense of the direction which history is taking. No laws, not even those which it itself has dictated, are binding on it if "objective circumstances" seem to warrant a change. All laws are politically determined, the particular correct

---

[12] *NCNA* (June 26, 1957).

[13] Audrey Donnithorne, *China's Economic System* (New York: Praeger, and London: George Allen & Unwin, 1967) pp. 23-24. Cf. Amaury de Riencourt, *The Soul of China* (New York: Coward-McCann, 1968), pp. 91-93.

[14] Jacques Marcuse, *The Peking Papers* (New York: Dutton, 1967), p. 131.

[15] Audrey Donnithorne, *op. cit.*, p. 508.

politics of the moment being that actually practiced by the dominant
Party leadership faction. This tendency of the Party to be both
lawgiver and to stand above the law may lead to a nihilistic attitude
toward law "consisting of the premise that stable and firm legislation
'is out of tune with the spirit of permanent revolution and is un-
suited to revolution and construction.'" [16] The Chinese Communists
seem to concur, although not quite in those terms. There is, they
believe, little point in becoming overly legalistic and thorough about
a situation which is undergoing rapid and profound social transformation.

[16] F. Kalinychev, *loc. cit.*, p. 4.

2 | Reconstruction and Reform, 1949–52: Methods and Instruments

On October 1, 1949, before a delirious crowd gathered in Peking's Tien An Men square, Mao Tse-tung, Chairman of the Communist Party of China and at that time also Chairman of the Chinese People's Government, announced the establishment of the People's Republic of China. On November 30 the Nationalist Government of Chiang Kai-shek retreated to Taiwan (Formosa). By the end of the year the whole mainland was under communist control. After more than three decades of devastating civil upheaval and foreign wars, the country settled down under a new dynasty and braced itself for the job of rebuilding.

This gigantic task had two aspects: physical reconstruction and institutional reform. The communist revolution was not at that stage a palace affair;[1] its aim was not merely to patch up shattered physical assets; rather, it was to restructure Chinese society and introduce a new political, cultural, and economic order. The new order was to be built from blueprints drafted by Marx, Engels, Lenin, Stalin, and most importantly Mao himself, and tested by the communists in Kiangsi (1931-34), northern Shensi (1935-47), the rural areas of Manchuria (1946-49), and other communist-controlled regions of China.[2]

In this book we shall be concerned primarily with institutional reforms carried out by the communists during their tenure of power, especially with the reshaping of China's economy. This will involve reference to physical repair work and construction. But the stress throughout will be on the remolding of man-made institutions and the reshaping of men's minds.

---

[1] But see Chapter 11, below.

[2] On the Chinese Communists' practical experience of government before 1949, see J. M. H. Lindbeck, "Transformations in the Chinese Communist Party," in Donald W. Treadgold (ed.), *Soviet and Chinese Communism: Similarities and Differences* (Seattle: U. of Washington Press, 1967), pp. 80-82; Robert Goldston, *The Rise of Red China* (Greenwich, Conn.: Fawcett, 1967); Mark Hofheinz, *The Peasant Movement and Rural Revolution: Chinese Communists in the Countryside, 1923-27* (Unpublished Ph.D. dissertation, Harvard University, 1966).

THE METHODS OF INSTITUTIONAL REFORM

Mao Tse-tung[3] sees human history as a recurring clash of contradictions within society, a permanent revolutionary confrontation of
opposing class forces. Although the nature of these contradictions
may change once socialism is reached, conflict persists right through
the various Marxist historical stages until the advent of full communism.[4] "Marxist philosophy holds that the law of the unity of
opposites is the fundamental law of the universe. This law operates
universally, whether in the natural world, in human society, or in
man's thinking. Between the opposites in a contradiction there is at
once unity and struggle, and it is this that impels things to move and
change. Contradictions exist everywhere, but they differ in accordance with the different nature of different things. In any given
phenomenon or thing, the unity of opposites is conditional, temporary and transistory, and hence relative, whereas the struggle of opposites is absolute."[5] The resolution of contradictions through mass
confrontation of those who move with history, as defined by Marx,
and those (reactionaries, counterrevolutionaries, enemies of the
people) who obstinately oppose the forward thrust of history, takes
the form of mass campaigns, drives, or *yün-tung*. These apocalyptic
struggles pit the mass line elaborated by the communists (a sort of
running translation of the Laws of History discovered by Marx)
against all those whose ideological blindness and political obtuseness
make them reluctant or unable to join the progressive forces. The
outcome of the struggles is preordained: the mass line always wins in
the end, though not without much prodding by the enlightened vanguard of the proletariat, the Communist Party. The mass campaign to
implement the mass line and so bring this Greeklike tragedy to its
finale is the communist substitute for the due process of law: profound changes in the makeup of society are launched, not legis-

[3] On Mao Tse-tung, see Stuart Schram, *Mao Tse-tung* (Baltimore: Penguin
Books, 1967); Robert Payne, *Mao Tse-tung* (New York: Weybright & Talley,
1969).

[4] See Mao Tse-tung, "On Contradiction" (August 1937), *Selected Works of
Mao Tse-tung* (Peking: FLP, 1964), Vol. I, pp. 311-346, and *On the Correct
Handling of Contradictions Among the People* (Peking: FLP, 1957). The reader
is also urged to consult the Introduction (pp. 3-89) of Stuart Schram's excellent
The Political Thought of Mao Tse-tung (New York: Praeger, 1963). An instruc-
tive source on the dialectical underpinnings of Maoist philosophy is Benedetto
Croce, *Essays on Marx and Russia* (New York: Ungar, 1966). Somewhat tougher
but well worthwhile is Erich Fromm, *Marx's Concept of Man* (New York: Ungar,
1961). If the reader's curiosity is sufficiently aroused, he should proceed to
Robert Freedman (ed.), *Marx on Economics* (New York: Harcourt, 1961). Cf.
Chapter 7 below.

[5] Mao Tse-tung, *On the Correct Handling of Contradictions Among the
People* (February 27, 1957), pocket ed., 1957, p. 18.

lated.[6] A law may formalize an already unleashed campaign, but the law's existence is incidental to the process of change.

The Marxist-Maoist view of the world is thus characterized by absolutism of thought, a conviction that violence is the most powerful agent of change, a "jerky moving staircase" conception of history (sequence of ever higher stages successively reached by revolutionary jumps), optimism[7] regarding man's destiny (at the end of the road there is the promise of full communism, the qualitatively highest stage of all), and a propensity to view men in the aggregate, as members of given social classes rather than as atomistic units, each endowed with a personality and will of its own. Nothing on a micro-human scale is to be allowed. Depersonalized life is to be made larger than life itself. Man's salvation hinges on his conscious submission to inexorable laws of history, the accurate perception of which is reserved for the most progressive section of the most progressive class: the leadership of the Communist Party.

Such a view of man's story and of the very human striving for a better life now implies a state of alternating tension and relaxation, a wavelike movement made more pronounced by disagreements within the narrow circle of the elect about the feasibility, timing, length, extent, and intensity of the campaigns.[8]

In the period 1949-52 the mass line was implemented through several mass campaigns, which may be classified as follows:

Land Reform: The land reform campaign.

[6] An interesting eyewitness account of some Chinese mass drives is to be found in Mikhail A. Klochko, *Soviet Scientist in Red China* (New York: Praeger, 1964), Chapter 5.

[7] This includes a certain indifference to present evils. There is inherent in Marx's conception of history as a progression from darkness to light, an acceptance of present wrong seen as the necessary ingredient of future justice and equality. The industrial hardships which capitalism brought in its train were to Marx preferable to the virtues of the feudal order. To his Leninist successors, the abuses of socialism personified in Stalin were better than the best that mature capitalism had to offer. The "means" of each historical stage justified the "end" of the next. There is implicit in all this a tendency to see the affairs of men primarily in long-range perspective.

[8] Mao's reference to such disagreements may be found in his statement to a *New China News Agency* correspondent and published in the Party theoretical journal *Hung-ch'i*, No. 10, 1958. Note also the relative moderation which frequently surfaces in Liu Shao-chi's *Report on the Draft Constitution of the People's Republic of China* [September 15, 1954] (Peking: *FLP*, 1955): "We must proceed step by step in the light of the experience and political consciousness of the masses and in accordance with what is possible in the actual situation. . . . It is of primary necessity that the transitional forms we adopt be flexible and varied." On the general problem of the place, role, and vicissitudes of ideology in the Chinese Communist movement, see Benjamin I. Schwartz, *Communism and China: Ideology in Flux* (Cambridge, Mass.: Harvard U. P., 1968), and Lloyd Eastman, "Mao, Marx, and the Future Society," *Problems of Communism* (May-June 1969), pp. 21-26.

Industrial and Commercial Reform: The 3-Anti and 5-Anti movements.

Financial Reform: The campaign to sell government bonds and coax voluntary savings out of the citizens.

Social Reform: Campaigns to implement the Marriage Law, the drive for ideological remolding, and the health campaign against the "four evils."

Political Reform: Domestically, the hunt for counterrevolutionaries, and the campaign to subordinate minority nationalities and religions to communist state power; externally, the "Resist America, Aid Korea" campaign, and the campaign for friendship with the Soviet Union.

Each of these is discussed in Chapter 3. The exact manner in which a mass campaign unfolds will be examined in connection with the land reform movement. At this point, however, it may be helpful to list the features common to all mass drives. They are eight in number.

(1) Any given campaign is usually given a trial run in some out-of-the-way locality. (2) The experience gained there is then summed up in the form of a "model campaign case." (3) The model case is thereupon given official blessing in the press and other mass media. (4) Orders go out to government and Party organs, and mass organizations (sometimes ad hoc formations outside the Party—see Chapter 11) to unleash the campaign throughout the country. (5) These agencies hold mass meetings, struggle sessions,[9] parades, demonstrations, and so on, to ensure the proper carrying out of the drive. Somewhere along the way (6) the campaign may be formalized by the issuance of an appropriate law, but this is optional. (7) At some point, the leadership may openly call a halt to the drive, reverse it, or simply take the heat off cadres [10] and others, and allow the campaign to gradually taper off. The various inspirational heroes and symbols conjured up during the drive may never be heard of again, or they may reemerge years later. (8) There follows a prolonged period of

[9] We shall meet with the "struggle session" phenomenon again and again in the pages of this book. At this early stage it would be helpful to read an eyewitness account of one such session, reported by B. Reece in "A Struggle Meeting," *Far Eastern Economic Review* (*FEER*) (April 4, 1968), p. 22.

[10] "Cadres" means officials in responsible positions. See Walter E. Gourlay, *The Chinese Communist Cadre: Key to Political Control* (Cambridge: Russian Research Center, Harvard University, 1952); A. Doak Barnett, *Cadres, Bureaucracy, and Political Power in Communist China* (New York: Columbia U. P., 1967). "Quite a few ignoramuses who cannot even read simple documents without difficulty have been appointed to positions of leadership. Such, I am told, is the Party's policy for cadres." Ch'en Yang-chih, *Kuang Ming Daily* (June 5, 1957), quoted in Roderick MacFarquhar, *The Hundred Flowers Campaign and the Chinese Intellectuals* (New York: Praeger, and London: Stevens & Sons Ltd., 1960), p. 68.

stock-taking during which the results of the drive are analyzed and lessons are drawn for future campaigns.[11]

THE INSTRUMENTS OF INSTITUTIONAL REFORM

The mass line elaborated by the top Party leadership is put into effect by (until 1966) four main agencies of communist power: the Communist Party, the government apparatus (including security forces), mass organizations, and the People's Liberation Army (PLA).[12] These four agencies were also, at least until 1966, the principal channels of social mobility for those aspiring to leadership positions.

THE COMMUNIST PARTY[13]

Since 1929, when Stalin fashioned his formidable juggernaut, communist parties have been characterized by

(a) an elite, militant leadership periodically purging itself, armed

[11] See Richard L. Walker, *China Under Communism: The Early Years* (New Haven: Yale U. P., 1955), pp. 77-100. The "model case" (2) is sometimes symbolized in a real or imaginary hero, farm, or factory labor brigade, which everyone is urged to emulate. On this see Mary Sheridan, "The Emulation of Heroes," *The China Quarterly* (January-March 1968), pp. 47-72, and Chapter 10. The campaign is frequently expressed in easy-to-remember numbers (often representing ideographs relevant to the drive) which can be plastered on the walls or flashed on the screen, producing instant mass response.

[12] This was generally true from 1949 to 1966. After 1966 the existing Party apparatus, much of the governmental structure, and most of the mass organizations were shattered. See Chapter 11.

[13] On this general subject consult Carl J. Friedrich and Zbigniew K. Brzezinski, *Totalitarian Dictatorship and Autocracy* (New York: Praeger, 1965), and Zbigniew K. Brzezinski, *Ideology and Power in Soviet Politics* (New York: Praeger, 1962). Good general sources are R. N. Carew Hunt, *The Theory and Practice of Communism* (New York: Macmillan, 1958), and Joseph M. Bochenski and Gerhart Niemeyer (eds.), *Handbook on Communism* (New York: Praeger, 1962). On the Soviet Communist Party, see John S. Reshetar, Jr., *A Concise History of the Communist Party of the Soviet Union* (New York: Praeger, 1964), and Panas Fedenko, *Khrushchev's New History of the Soviet Communist Party* (Munich: Institute for the Study of the USSR, 1963). The last should be read in conjunction with N. S. Khrushchev's Special Report to the 20th Congress of the Communist Party of the Soviet Union (the "secret" report), which is available under the title *The Crimes of the Stalin Era* (annotated by B. I. Nicolaevsky), *The New Leader* 1956. On the Chinese Communist Party, see Robert C. North, *Chinese Communism* (New York: McGraw-Hill, 1966), and his *Moscow and the Chinese Communists* (Stanford, Calif.: Stanford U. P., 1953, 1963); Franklin W. Houn, *A Short History of Chinese Communism* (Englewood Cliffs, N.J.: Prentice-Hall, 1967); Benjamin I. Schwartz, *Chinese Communism and the Rise of Mao* (New York: Harper Torchbooks, 1967), and Conrad Brandt, Benjamin Schwartz, John K. Fairbank, *A Documentary History of Chinese Communism* (New York: Atheneum, 1966); John Wilson Lewis, *Leadership in Communist China* (Ithaca, N.Y.: Cornell U. P., 1963). On the transformation of the Communist Party of China after 1965, see Chapter 11 below.

with the revolutionary theory of Marxism-Leninism (Doctrine of the Elect);

(b) a highly centralized and disciplined organization involving conscious submission, willing or enforced, by the rank and file ("Democratic Centralism");

(c) an orthodoxy, or unity of views, imposed from above. This unity concerns programs, tactics, and organization. Opposition groups within the Party (factionalism) are promptly and thoroughly purged so that the leadership, whatever its internal divisions, can speak out with one voice, which is the only "correct" voice (Freedom to Conform). [14]

To this list the Chinese Maoists have added:

(d) heavy involvement with peasant masses, particularly with the poorest peasant strata (Agrarian Communism);

(e) nationalism often verging on chauvinism (National Communism);

(f) great emphasis on the power of correct political faith (Romantic Communism);

(g) an impressive body of military doctrine based on the concept of guerrilla and mobile warfare waged in the rural hinterland of underdeveloped countries, and involving the martial qualities of responsiveness to discipline, disdain for material discomfort, and an idealization of asceticism (Military Communism).

These additional characteristics were present in some degree in other communist parties, but the Chinese have endowed them with special importance. A few brief comments on each of these additions may be helpful.

Agrarian Communism. [15] The Chinese Communist emphasis on involvement with the peasant masses makes sense in the setting of a vast underdeveloped country in which the peasants constitute about 80 percent of the population. Grass-roots activity in the countryside and the Party's early identification with peasant grievances was an important element in the communists' final success. Moreover, after 1927 the communists, having lost their urban bases, retreated to inaccessible rural areas from which they did not emerge until total victory in 1949. It was in this isolated rural setting that the Party's philosophy was formed, Marxist propositions were agrarianized, ad-

[14] But see Chapter 11 for the special Chinese case.

[15] Useful references are Chalmers A. Johnson, *Peasant Nationalism and Communist Power: The Emergence of Revolutionary China, 1937-1945* (Stanford, Calif.: Stanford U. P., 1962); the dissertation by M. Hofheinz already cited (note 2); James Harrison, *The Communists and Chinese Peasant Rebellions* (New York: Atheneum, 1969); Shanti Swarup, *A Study of the Chinese Communist Movement* (Oxford: Clarendon Press, 1966).

ministrative experience gained, and membership conscripted. In 1949 peasants constituted about 80 percent of Party membership. This proportion had been somewhat reduced by 1952.

National Communism. The emphasis on national aspirations was also reasonable. Chinese communism is a product of the national revival of the turn of the century. At first the communists were merely the radical minority of a broad nationalist movement, united for a time with the majority Nationalist Party (Kuomintang) by bonds of common antipathy toward foreign intervention in Chinese affairs and a desire to assert China's rights through modernization. Much of the support among the population which the communists gained over time is traceable to a steadfast adherence to the doctrine of national self-confidence and a continuing belief in the inner strength and vitality of the Chinese people.

Romantic Communism. The romantic streak in Chinese communism is due in some measure to the communists' success in surmounting what seemed like overwhelming odds, the movement's isolation from the intellectual currents in the great cities, and the outward relative stability (until 1966) of the top leadership. The belief in the titanic strength and irresistibility of firmly held convictions summed up in the thoughts of one leader (the charisma of Mao Tse-tung's thought) go beyond Lenin's insistence on the importance of conscious political activity. As will be shown (Chapters 8, 11, and 12), the romantic outpouring of organized sentiment, at times turned into political revivalism of an excessive kind; a noisy, in many ways pathetic, deification of the leader and his thoughts.

Military Communism. "The seizure of power by armed force," Mao has said, "the settlement of the issue by war, is the central task and the highest form of revolution. . . . Experience tells us that China's problems cannot be settled without armed force. . . . All things grow out of the barrel of a gun. . . . Whoever wants to seize and retain state power must have a strong army." [16] Perhaps the most immediately relevant cause of the communists' success in China was the identification of the Party with the gun, the militarization of communism, the establishment and maintenance in a weak polity of a strong, disciplined army which until the seizure of state power was almost identical with the Party. In 1945, for example, out of a total Party membership of 1.2 million, 1 million members were under a

---

[16] Mao Tse-tung, "Problems of War and Strategy" (November 1938), *SW*, (Peking: *FLP*, 1965), Vol. II, pp. 219, 222, 225. See also his *On the Protracted War* (May-June 1938) (Peking: *FLP*, 1960), and Samuel B. Griffith, *Mao Tse-tung on Guerrilla Warfare* (New York: Praeger, 1961). These should be read in conjunction with Cuba's Che Guevara, *Guerrilla Warfare* (New York: Monthly Review Press, 1961).

"military supply system" working without pay and under barracks-type discipline. In 1949 army men and women made up about 22 percent of the party membership of 4.5 million.[17]

By June 1951 the membership had reached 5.8 million; 6 million by 1953; 10.73 million in 1956 (69 percent peasants, 14 percent workers, 1.25 percent intellectuals), 13.96 million in September 1958, and 17 million in June 1961.[18]

Chinese society after 1927 provided few institutional channels for the expression of minority views. The communists' a priori preference for the resolution of contradictions by strong-arm methods, thus found a ready-made rationalization in the actual state of Chinese society. The Party's military tradition continued to exercise a significant influence on the thinking and behavior of many Party members after seizure of state power.

Figure 2-1 summarizes the organizational structure of the Communist Party of China during the Party's early years as ruler of the Mainland. The diagram pretends to be no more than a simplified representation of reality. It is based on the Party's constitution which was adopted only in 1956. The constitution, however, reflected the actual organization which the communists had built up over the years and which they extended to the whole territory of China in the years 1949-52. It is probably true that during the period of reconstruction and reform, with which we are concerned here, the Party apparatus was not fully in place and that much of what later was done by Party organs was at that early time carried out by the People's Liberation Army, individual cadres, and the mass organizations. Given all these warnings and reservations, the diagram does show the direction in which the organizational efforts of the communists were tending in the period 1949-52 and the essentially totalitarian nature of the enterprise.[19]

Nominally, the ultimate authority rested with the *National Party Congress*, which under the Party Constitution (adopted in 1956, but in actual, if somewhat spotty, use before that time) was to have been convened once a year by the Central Committee. The Congress could be postponed "under extraordinary conditions." In fact, this basic provision has been ignored. The first Party Congress after seizure of power (eighth in the history of the Party) was convened in Septem-

[17] J. M. H. Lindbeck, *op. cit.*, pp. 75-78, 90. About 73 percent of the Party's members in 1949 were working in various localities; 5 percent were employed at the center.

[18] *Jen-min Jih-pao* (*People's Daily*), July 1, 1951, Sept. 14, 1956, Sept. 28, 1959, July 1, 1961. See *URS*, Vol. 44, No. 8 (July 26, 1966).

[19] The Party's post-April 14, 1969, constitution may be found in the Appendix. The full text of the 1956 constitution may be found in *The Constitution of the Communist Party of China* (Peking: *FLP*, 1965).

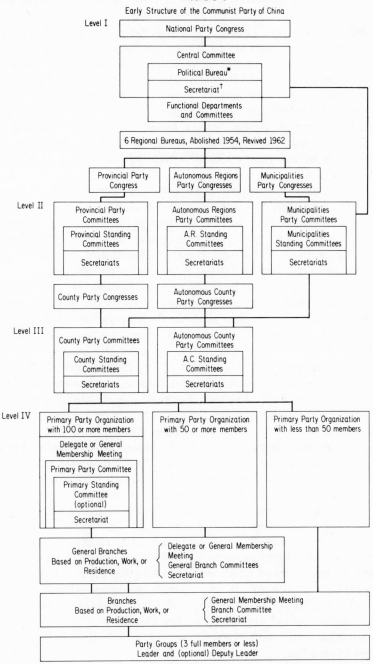

FIGURE 2-1

Early Structure of the Communist Party of China

Level I

National Party Congress

Central Committee
Political Bureau*
Secretariat†
Functional Departments and Committees

6 Regional Bureaus, Abolished 1954, Revived 1962

Provincial Party Congress | Autonomous Regions Party Congresses | Municipalities Party Congresses

Level II

Provincial Party Committees
Provincial Standing Committees
Secretariats

Autonomous Regions Party Committees
A.R. Standing Committees
Secretariats

Municipalities Party Committees
Municipalities Standing Committees
Secretariats

County Party Congresses | Autonomous County Party Congresses

Level III

County Party Committees
County Standing Committees
Secretariats

Autonomous County Party Committees
A.C. Standing Committees
Secretariats

Level IV

Primary Party Organization with 100 or more members
Delegate or General Membership Meeting
Primary Party Committee
Primary Standing Committee (optional)
Secretariat

Primary Party Organization with 50 or more members

Primary Party Organization with less than 50 members

General Branches Based on Production, Work, or Residence
{ Delegate or General Membership Meeting
General Branch Committees
Secretariat

Branches Based on Production, Work, or Residence
{ General Membership Meeting
Branch Committee
Secretariat

Party Groups (3 full members or less)
Leader and (optional) Deputy Leader

*A Standing Committee of the Politbureau was set up by the First Session of the Eighth National Party Congress in September 1956.

†The post of Secretary General was established in 1956 (it had previously been abolished in 1935).

ber 1956; the second (ninth since the Party's formation) in April 1969. The Party Congress has long been regarded in the West as a rubber-stamp affair. However, developments since 1966 indicate that the Congress may be used in intraparty power struggles, if one of the contending factions manages to keep its hold on the Party's lower level organizations which send delegates to the Congress. Hence, perhaps, the reluctance of the Maoist faction to convene a ninth Congress (finally held in April 1969), a hesitation even more understandable in view of the post-1965 stalemate in the Central Committee. (See Chapter 11.)

The *Central Committee* was supposed to meet in plenary session at least twice a year. It was to have been elected by the Party Congress for a five-year term. Both these provisions have been honored in the breach. Effective policy-making power within the Party rested until 1966 with the *Political Bureau* (Politbureau) picked by the Central Committee, and more especially with the *Bureau's Standing Committee*, a narrower circle of power holders. Members of the Politbureau concurrently occupied key posts in the government machinery, mass organizations, and the military command. Mao Tse-tung was chairman of the Party and of the People's Government, and head of the People's Revolutionary Military Council. Liu Shao-ch'i was vice-chairman of the Central Committee and of the Politbureau, one of the vice-chairmen of the government, and of the People's Revolutionary Military Council. He also held the post of honorary chairman of the All-China Federation of Trade Unions, was president of the Sino-Soviet Friendship Association, and a ranking member of other mass organizations. Chou En-lai besides being a member of the Central Committee and the Politbureau, was Premier of the Government Administration Council (the top provisional government organ) and Minister for Foreign Affairs. The same type of interlocking directorate applied to the other members of the Politbureau: Chu Teh, P'eng Chen, Ch'en Yun, Kao Kang, Tung Pi-wu, and Lin Tsu-han, and to most members of the Central Committee. Government and Party leadership was, so to speak, a family affair. These men had worked together for the better part of twenty years and gave the impression of an unassailable, monolithic directorate. By 1967 Liu Shao-ch'i, Chu Teh, and P'eng Chen had been branded by the Maoists as infiltrators who were allegedly leading China down the capitalist path, and Kao Kang had killed himself after being accused of anti-Party conspiracy in 1954-55.

The *departments and committees* under the Secretariat were the principal control organs of the whole vast undertaking. The main departments were those of Organization (the Party's personnel office was at this time headed by Jao Shu-shih who was to be involved with

Kao Kang in the 1954-55 conspiracy), Propaganda (comprising several offices, e.g., Theoretical Affairs, Scientific Affairs, Higher Education, Literary and Art Affairs, Newspapers and Publication), Social Affairs, United Front (charged with relations with the so-called democratic parties, noncommunist personalities, national minorities, and overseas Chinese), Liaison (relations with foreign Communist Parties), Economy (Rural Work, Urban Work, Industry, Finance and Trade, Communications, Planning), Culture and Education, Political and Legal Affairs, and Political Security Affairs. The Department of Social Affairs was probably in charge of the secret police and espionage. The main committees under the Secretariat were those for Party Organs Directly Subordinate to the Central Committee (dealing with Party personnel at the central level), Committee for Central State Organs (dealing with government personnel at the central level), Women's Work, Trade Unions, Youth, Party press, and Party school.[20]

The totalitarian character of this organization is evident from the chain of command running from the top to the bottom levels, the pyramidlike structure of each level (reproducing exactly the pattern set at the top), and the pervasiveness of the organization. No activity, however trivial, escaped the Party's watchful eye, no action eluded formal structuring. Although unprecedented in its thoroughness, the Party organization was not without chinks and failures of communication. Regionalism and localism continued to exert their traditional influence, making the actual exercise of command from the top something less than the organizational chart suggests.[21] These centrifugal forces inherent in Chinese society became particularly insistent when the early unity of the Politbureau finally fell apart in 1966. (Chapter 11.)

GOVERNMENT APPARATUS

A network of government organs spanning the length and breadth of the country and reaching from the top leadership down to

[20] Ellis Joffe, "Levers of Power," *FEER* (March 2, 1961), pp. 364-365.

[21] Another version of the Party's structure was given during the Hundred Flowers interlude by Liu Pin-yen of the Editorial Department, *Chinese Youth Newspaper*, a Party member since 1944. According to a *People's Daily* account published during the antirightists campaign that followed the Hundred Flowers (see Chapter 7), Liu allegedly described the Party's hierarchy in the following terms: ". . . The top consisted of a number of conservative forces—the 'privileged class' of ranking cadres—the middle was in the hands of a group of outwardly submissive but inwardly rebellious 'local emperors'—the leading Party cadres at provincial and municipal levels—and the bottom was a crowd of unsuspecting and ignorant 'fools.' " Quoted in Roderick MacFarquhar, *op. cit.*, p. 73. Liu's analysis was not without relevance to the events of 1966-69 (see Chapters 11 and 12).

the tiniest hamlet was, next only to the Party machine, the means by which the communists proposed to unify and control the country and discharge the day-to-day tasks of civil rule.

The problem can be tackled in two steps. First it is necessary to take a brief look at the theory underlying the formation of governmental organs in the period 1949-52, a theory which went under the name of "new democracy," and second, to examine the various instruments of government themselves.

The theory of new democracy. [22] Basing himself on the Marxist view of history as a succession of stages (beginning with the lowest tribal-communal stage, rising through "slavery," "feudalism," "capitalism," and "socialism" to fully fledged "communism"), Mao declared those parts of pre-1949 China not under communist control as being "semifeudal, semicolonial." The qualification "semi" implied the embryonic existence in China of the next higher stage, "capitalism," and a measure of national self-determination. The revolution which Mao and his companions led, was spearheaded, according to this argument, against domestic feudalism (represented primarily by "die-hard" sections of the landlord class and their agents, the "bureaucrat capitalist" officials, and foreign colonial imperialism [23]—represented at home by the urban, big, comprador, and "capitulationist" bourgeoisie). Negatively, the aim was to uproot feudalism and foreign (colonial) imperialism by annihilating the landlords and the big bourgeoisie as a class.

Positively, the aim was to replace semifeudalism and semicolonialism not with capitalism and parliamentary bourgeois democracy [24] (represented in China by rich peasants and middle or national bourgeoisie), but with a system of national or "new democracy." In China the Marxist historical progression was to take the form: semifeudalism $\longrightarrow$ new democracy $\longrightarrow$ socialism $\longrightarrow$ communism, instead of the orthodox feudalism $\longrightarrow$ capitalism $\longrightarrow$ socialism $\longrightarrow$ communism. [25] What this meant, in essence, was that the capitalist stage (with its political counterpart of parliamentary democracy) was to be skipped, and that an underdeveloped country could pass from a neo-

[22] On the various Maoist-Marxist categories (poor peasants, rich peasants, national bourgeoisie, etc.), see Chapter 3.

[23] I.e., "international capitalism."

[24] Or as Mao puts it, "bourgeois dictatorship."

[25] On the relationship of Mao's new democracy to the Eastern European construct of the "people's democracy" and the Soviet idea of a "national democratic" state in underdeveloped countries, see Donald S. Carlisle, "The Changing Soviet Perception of the Development Process," and Roger E. Kanet, "The Recent Soviet Reassessment of the Development Process in the Third World," in Harry G. Shaffer and Jan S. Prybyla (eds.), From Underdevelopment to Affluence: Western, Soviet, and Chinese Views (New York: Appleton, 1968), pp. 112-142.

feudal stage into the new-democratic antechamber of socialism. For the record, to show that the Marxist sequence had not really been violated, it was argued that China had experienced a capitalist stage of sorts (implicit in the other half of "semifeudalism"), but that was the end of it. The communists did not wage a long and bitter war in order to inaugurate an era to which they were fundamentally opposed. The removal of semifeudalism and semicolonialism was not intended to usher in the rule of rich peasants, and national capitalists. They could be associated in the work of new democracy, won over to the communists' point of view, but on no account were they to be granted even the shadowy semblance of power. Mao's new democracy was, in other words, a transitional stage during which preparations were made for the introduction of socialism. It was to be dominated throughout by the Communist Party. Other classes (with the exception of most landlords and big bourgeois) were to cooperate with the communists in this task, in what the theory called a "united front," but only on condition that they submitted to communist leadership. The united front of Maoist conception was a front of "all those who could be united," of all those, that is, willing to go along with the communists toward socialism. Others would be relegated to the dustheap of history and classed as "people outside the people."[26]

A number of so-called "democratic parties" totally submissive to the Communist Party were allowed to exist not only during the new democratic but also during the subsequent socialist stage. These united front organizations were composed of remolded or semiremolded bourgeois intellectuals, businessmen, experts, and so on. After the transformation of the Chinese People's Political Consultative Conference (see below, p. 26) into the National People's Congress in 1954, the democratic parties' central forum assumed the name of Chinese People's Political Consultative Conference (CPPCC). In 1962 and 1964, for example, the CPPCC met at the same time as the National People's Congress and had about as much to say in the formulation of policy—that is, very little.

The most important of these democratic parties were:[27]

The China Democratic League. Founded in 1941, the League had supported the communists before 1949. Its membership consisted mostly of intellectuals in the areas of education and culture.

[26] On the United Front, see Lyman P. Van Slyke, *Enemies and Friends: The United Front in Chinese Communist History* (Stanford, Calif.: Stanford U. P., 1967); Li Wei-han, *The Struggle for Proletarian Leadership in the Period of the New Democratic Revolution in China* (Peking: *FLP*, 1962).

[27] Colina MacDougall, " 'Bourgeoisie'—A Sigh of Relief?" *FEER* (May 10, 1962), p. 263.

Revolutionary Committee of the Kuomintang. This was a Kuomintang (KMT) splinter group formed in 1948. Its main object was to reeducate former KMT officials and other upper- and middle-class elements who formerly had close ties with the Kuomintang.

China Democratic National Construction Association. Founded in 1944, the Association was composed primarily of former industrialists and businessmen. Its main object was to remold its members in a socialist direction and organize them in a compact and easily controlled group.

Chinese Peasants' and Workers' Democratic Party was also a KMT splinter group formed in 1928. Its membership was composed of scientists, medical men, and intellectuals.

China Chih Kung Tang. This was the organization of overseas Chinese, founded in San Francisco in 1925.

The Chiu San—September 3 Society. Founded in 1944, its purpose was to organize scientists and technicians.

Taiwan Democratic Self-Government League. A front organization which was resurrected each time the Taiwan question came up for discussion in international forums. The League on such occasions would send telegrams and make statements in support of the Chinese government's position in a display of national unity *cum* pluralism.

The new democratic revolution led by the proletariat through a Maoist-type Communist Party embraces the broad masses of the "people"—the urban proletariat, the poor and middle peasants (see Chapter 3), the petty bourgeoisie, some vagrants, and temporarily at least (i.e., during wars against foreign imperialism) some rich peasants, the national bourgeoisie, and even a section (the malleable section) of the landlord and big bourgeois classes. Membership in this communist-led alliance is determined more by one's attitude toward foreign intervention and the Communist Party than by one's relation to the means of production (except in the case of landlords and the big bourgeois, but even here some tactical flexibility was permitted in times of stress). In other words, at the stage of new democracy one's patriotism and national consciousness, as evaluated by the communists, are all-important. At the same time one tends to be more surely patriotic and ideologically trustworthy if one happens to stand in the correct Marxist relation to the means of production.

The argument is practical. Capitalism and its ruling classes must not be allowed to seize power alone, not even for an instant. International capitalism's influence over the underdeveloped world must be ended, and domestic feudalism and bureaucrat capitalism (feudalism's officialdom) must be replaced by the communist-led united front. In that united front the communists are the only decision-making and armed group. Once power is seized in this manner, the united front can be gobbled up, and the transition to socialism can begin. As Lenin had so clearly seen and so steadfastly practiced, one morsel of state power in hand is worth two promises of power in the bush. The communists must be in on it from the very beginning and at every stage. The rest is dialectical calisthenics, the flexing of old ideological muscles to fit new circumstances. Under the banner of patriotism the communists can get through the precarious early period of power and push on toward the promised land. They need the energies and brains of noncommunists in the task of reconstruction, and cooperation of nonbelievers in the job of reform. But they do not need advice, much less direction, in the matter of the future shape of society.[28]

The new democratic stage in the whole of China officially lasted from 1949 to 1952.

Instruments of Government

The communists were not novices to government. There was, however, a difference between administering backward, isolated, rural areas and the relatively rich, populous regions (including a number of large cities) that fell into communist hands by the end of 1949.

Initially, the task of government devolved, by and large, on the People's Liberation Army. It was modelled on the administrative experience acquired by the communists in the "old liberated areas" with due adjustments for new circumstances. The basic unit of government was the "military control commission," a provisional body set up in newly conquered localities by the military command which happened to be on the spot. Military control commissions were charged not only with establishing order, screening former officials, punishing political undesirables, and so on, but also with the organization of more permanent "local people's governments." At first this was done by appointing army personnel trained in civil administration to people's government posts at the basic levels (rural district or *hsiang*, market town or *chen*, district or *ch'ü*, and county or *hsien*). Concurrently the top communist leadership set to work organizing the higher levels of government (province or *sheng*, special municipalities, i.e., the larger towns or *t'e-pieh shih*, autonomous regions or *tzuchih ch'ü*—these in 1952, municipalities under provinces or autonomous regions, and special districts or *chuan ch'ü*). Until June 1954 the top leadership also made use of six Great Regional Admin-

---

[28] The main communist source is Mao Tse-tung, "On New Democracy," (January 1940), *SW* (Peking: *FLP*, 1965), Vol. II, pp. 339-384. A concise summary of the arguments for a new democratic revolution may be found in Chen Po-ta, *Mao Tse-tung on the Chinese Revolution* (Peking: *FLP*, 1953), pp. 14-30.

istrative Councils the duty of which was to supervise, on behalf of the leadership, the work of provincial people's governments in their respective regions.

The two-pronged movement to establish a new administrative structure in the whole of China was formalized in September 1949 by the Chinese People's Political Consultative Conference (CPPCC) convened in Peking. The CPPCC was the predecessor of the National People's Congress set up in September 1954. It consisted of 662 delegates drawn from the Party and its satellite formations, the regions, army, and mass organizations, and included seventy-five "specially invited personalities" (e.g., Mme. Sun Yat-sen and members of the Kuomintang peace delegation who had gone over to the communist side). The Conference adopted the Organic Law of the CPPCC (the "starting point of the domestic and foreign policy of the new China")[29], elected a 180-member National Committee of the CPPCC, produced the Organic Law of the Central People's Government, nominated the members of that government, and passed a number of resolutions on such diverse subjects as the country's capital city, flag, national anthem, and calendar. In conformity with the theory of new democracy, the CPPCC and the Central People's Government Council contained some noncommunist formations which made the system into what the theory said it was: a united front under communist leadership and control.

The CPPCC and its successor, the National People's Congress, gave to the new administrative structure a semblance of popular participation. In December 1949, this democratic illusion was extended by a government decision to establish "all-circle people's representative conferences" at the provincial, municipal, and county levels. On paper, the conferences were granted rather extensive powers over their respective local governments, but like their Russian equivalents, the "soviets," they remained in practice atrophied and impotent. Like their parent stem, the CPPCC, the conferences' membership was elected from among mass organizations and satellite political parties and included some independent personages. The principal function of the representative conferences was to act as a sort of geographically based trust of mass organizations. Their purpose was to serve, not instruct the local government organs; to carry out orders, not give them.

[29] Liao Kai-lung, op. cit., p. 116. The documents mentioned here may be found in A. P. Blaustein, op. cit., pp. 34-53, 96-103, 104-114, 180-192. See also F. W. Houn, op. cit., pp. 135-140, and T. Shabad, China's Changing Map (New York: Praeger, 1956).

Figure 2-2 gives an idea of what the governmental structure looked like toward the end of the period of reconstruction and reform.

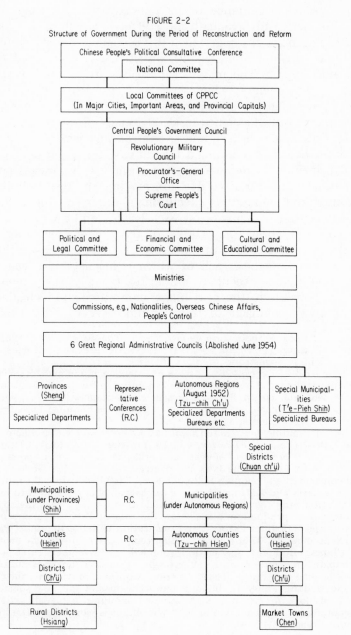

FIGURE 2-2

Structure of Government During the Period of Reconstruction and Reform

MASS ORGANIZATIONS

A totalitarian state, whether of the Right or the Left, demands not just passive acceptance of its philosophy and policy by the people, but active involvement and collective worship, so to speak. One of the agencies through which this is assured under communism is the "mass organization" set up, directed, and controlled by the central authority. [30] The mass organizations are tailored to specific interests within society. They serve as transmission belts for the authority's revealed preferences, as sounding boards, agencies for the actual carrying out of assigned tasks (especially of the recurrent mass campaigns discussed earlier), and as control organisms in areas which might otherwise elude command from the center. Their basic organizational principle is "democratic centralism," which means popular participation and centralized decision making, the responsibility for the prompt and meticulous execution of orders resting with each level of executors. Discussion at each level is on how best to carry out orders, not about the validity of the orders themselves. Mass organizations rely heavily on grass-roots activity exercised through local cells and branches, each of which is headed by a leader and administered by an executive committee (usually Party members) directly responsible to the next higher committee and its leader, and so on up to the pinnacle of the pyramid. [31] As of early 1953, the

[30] See A. Doak Barnett, *Communist China: The Early Years, 1949-1955* (New York: Praeger, 1966), pp. 29-44. On the Soviet prototype of mass organizations, see John A. Armstrong, *Ideology, Politics, and Government in the Soviet Union* (New York: Praeger, 1962), pp. 58-61. Membership in mass organizations is nominally voluntary. However, as Miss Donnithorne has pointed out in a nice understatement (*op. cit.*, p. 39): "in present circumstances in China, voluntariness is an elusive concept." On the fate of Chinese communist mass organizations after 1965, see Chapter 11.

[31] See for example *The Trade Union Law of the People's Republic of China* (June 29, 1950) (Peking: *FLP*, rev. ed., 1951). Among the duties of the trade unions (Article 9) are (1) to "educate and organize the masses of workers and staff members to support the laws and decrees of the People's Government in order to consolidate the people's State power . . ." (2) "educate and organize the masses of workers and staff members . . . to observe labor discipline, to organize labor emulation campaigns and other production movements in order to ensure the fulfilment of production plans." On the role of Party members in mass organizations, see Chapter IX of "The Constitution of the Communist Party of China" (September 26, 1956), in A. P. Blaustein, *op. cit.*, p. 95. The main tasks of the Chinese Buddhist Association founded in November 1952 were to (1) participate in land reform, (2) struggle against counterrevolutionaries, (3) play a leading role in the Resist America, Aid Korea movement, and (4) recognize the Buddhist duty to build a new religion and the new society. See Richard L. Walker, *op. cit.*, p. 188. A Chinese Communist explanation of "democratic centralism" may be found in John Wilson Lewis (ed.), *Major Doctrines of Communist China* (New York: Norton 1964), pp. 219-220.

Chinese Communists had created a number of such organizations, the names and membership of some of which are given in Table 2-1.

TABLE 2-1
Some Mass Organizations as of Early 1953*

Name	Membership (millions)
Trade Unions	10.2
China New Democratic Youth League (linked directly to the Communist Party of China, i.e., the "Party's assistant")	9.0
Young Pioneers...............................	(?)
All-China Students' Federation	3.4
All-China Educational Workers' Conference	(?)
All-China Federation of Literary and Arts Circles	(?)
Conference of Scientists.......................	(?)
Association of Journalists......................	(?)
All-China Democratic Women's Federation	76.0
Sino-Soviet Friendship Association	69.0
Chinese Buddhist Association	(?)
Peasants' Associations of the Four Greater Areas (East, Center-South, Southwest, Northwest)	88.0
Rural Supply and Marketing Cooperatives	148.0

*Source of membership figures: Liao Kai-lung, *From Yenan to Peking* (Peking: *FLP*, 1954), p. 155.

THE PEOPLE'S LIBERATION ARMY[32]

The Chinese Communist army which, as we have seen, was for a considerable time almost identical with the Communist Party, has often been described by the Chinese Communists as an army "of a new type." In the two decades preceding seizure of state power, and in the years with which we are dealing here, this newness consisted in the army's political content, peasant class base, guerrilla and mobile-warfare strategy and tactics, and the combination of military service with economic, administrative, and educational work.

The military strategy and tactics (guerrilla and mobile warfare)

[32] The literature on this subject is listed in Edward J. M. Rhoads, *The Chinese Red Army, 1927-1963: An Annotated Bibliography* (Cambridge: East Asian Research Center, Harvard University, 1964). See also Robert B. Rigg, *Red China's Fighting Hordes* (Harrisburg, Pa.: The Military Service Publishing Company, 1951, 1952); F. F. Liu, *A Military History of Modern China* (Princeton, N. J.: Princeton University Press, 1956); Samuel B. Griffith, "The Military Potential of China," in Alastair Buchan, *China and the Peace of Asia* (New York: Praeger, 1965), pp. 65-91.

cannot be discussed here, even though they are of compelling interest. On this subject the reader is referred to the sources given earlier (footnotes 16 and 32 on pp. 17 and 29).

The revolutionary army, so goes the Maoist argument, is different from other armies. Political organization and class origin are important. The Red revolutionary army is a politicized army: military strategy, training, tactics, equipment, and so forth are significant, but politics is in command. "Military affairs are only one means of accomplishing political tasks [a quite important one, as we have seen].... The Chinese Red Army is an armed body for carrying out the political task of the revolution.... The Red Army fights not merely for the sake of fighting, but in order to conduct propaganda among the masses, organize them, and help them to establish revolutionary political power [i.e., it is essentially an armed mass organization]. Without these objectives, fighting loses its meaning and the Red Army loses the reason for its existence." [33] The purely military viewpoint, which we shall encounter later on in connection with the movement to professionalize the armed forces, is according to Mao, quite alien to a truly revolutionary army. It is born of low political consciousness, mercenary mentality, absence of confidence in the strength of the masses, and the Party's failure to attend to and discuss military work in its relation to ideology. The failure must be remedied whenever it occurs. It can be corrected by appropriate political organization of army units and attention to the class origin of recruits. Army units, like government bureaus, should have attached to them Party representatives. The ratio of Party to non-Party members in the army should typically be 1:3.

Among the early attractions of Mao's revolutionary army were the removal of the age-old Chinese mercenary system and the equitable, though not always equal, distribution to the men of grain, money for cooking oil, salt, firewood, vegetables, and a little pocket money. Although discipline was strict and the justice meted out ruthless and swift, the practice of officers' beating their men, a method of argument deeply rooted in the Chinese mercenary tradition, was abolished. Rules of correct conduct vis-à-vis the civilian population were laid down and applied to the letter, exceptions being tolerated only where "people who were outside the people" (ideologically nonreformable elements) were concerned.

The specific conditions in which the Chinese Communist army took shape presented the leadership with the problem of a sizable army living for long periods of time in the midst of a working popu-

[33] Mao Tse-tung, "On Correcting Mistaken Ideas in the Party" (December 1929), *SW* (Peking: *FLP*, 1964), Vol. I, p. 106.

lation. Armed forces of "the old type" typically lived off the land, a way of marching on their stomachs which did not endear them to the peasants. "A situation in which such a large number of personnel, divorced from production, depends solely on the people . . . for supplies, certainly cannot last long and is very dangerous. Therefore, all army units and government organs must take part in production when not fighting or doing their regular work, except for those field armies which are concentrated and charged with major military actions." [34] This principle of combining military duties with economic tasks, fighting with labor, is an elaboration and extension of the Marxist-Leninist insistence on the unity of theory and practice. As will be seen later, it was applied not only to the army, Party, and government workers, but above all to the intellectuals. As the early revolutionary, communist-controlled "base areas" expanded, the turning of the army into a working force became even more important. It also met with considerable opposition from professional military circles. "The People's Liberation Army is always a fighting force. . . . The People's Liberation Army is also a working force. . . . With the gradual decrease in hostilities, its function as a working force will increase. . . . We must look upon the field armies . . . as a gigantic school for cadres." [35] Thus wrote Mao on the eve of the seizure of power in March 1949.

*   *   *

In the period of reconstruction and reform (1949-52), to the detailed examination of which we now turn, the method of mass campaigns was used by all four agencies of communist power. Interlocked as they were, the Party, the government, the mass organizations, and the PLA, worked together in apparent harmony, in spite of frictions within each and despite muted jurisdictional disputes. Mao Tse-tung headed both the Party and the government, and was the undisputed leader of the army. The period also saw a blending of agrarian, national, romantic, and military communism. In later years the many contradictory elements of this blend began to assert themselves, culminating in the destruction of the Party and government structures, the dissolution of the old mass organizations and their replacement by new agencies of Maoist and anti-Maoist power in the

[34] Mao Tse-tung, "Build Stable Base Areas in the Northeast" (December 28, 1945), *Selected Works of Mao Tse-tung* (Peking: FLP, 1961), Vol. IV, p. 84.

[35] Mao Tse-tung, "Report to the Second Plenary Session of the Seventh Central Committee of the Communist Party of China" (March 5, 1949), *SW* (Peking: FLP, 1961), Vol. IV, pp. 362-363. Cf. "The army is not only a fighting force, it is mainly a working force. All army cadres should learn how to take over and administer the cities." Mao Tse-tung, "Turn the Army into a Working Force" (February 8, 1949), *ibid.*, Vol. IV, p. 337.

cauldron of the Great Proletarian Cultural Revolution (Chapter 11). From this cataclysmic revamping of the instruments of communist power, only the army emerged relatively unscathed—but even it was shaken. At different times in the unfolding story of Communist China the various characteristics of Chinese Communism also struggled for supremacy. By 1966 agrarian communism had been overshadowed by the peculiar Maoist brand of romantic pragmatism and chauvinism, depending for survival on the loyalty of the army and its military version of communism.

3 | Reconstruction and Reform, 1949–52: Main Areas of Reform

LAND REFORM

LAND REFORM AND AGRICULTURAL REFORM

The term "land reform" (or "agrarian reform") might conveniently be used to denote the broadening of land ownership, the replacement of large by small holdings. The concept, while not without economic implications, is primarily political and psychological. By itself, land reform need not necessarily result in better productivity and efficiency because many agricultural operations are not susceptible to subdivision without a temporary or permanent loss of output per man or per acre, or without a reduction in the marketed portion of output, and the incentive effect of broadened land ownership may be neutralized by the absence of the needed technical know-how, or capital, or both on the part of the new owners. Where there are grounds for the beneficiaries of the reform to suspect that property titles bestowed on them run a good risk of being revoked in the future, "equalization of ownership" may have few economic incentives to begin with.

"Agricultural reform" is primarily a technical and economic concept. It means advances in productive efficiency, diversification and rotation of crops, improvement in plant strains, water conservancy and irrigation systems, introduction of chemical fertilizers, pesticides, and insecticides, the raising of the educational level of the agricultural labor force, and so on.[1]

THE SITUATION AT THE OUTSET

1. Land Tenure

Communist literature has made much of the "feudal" relations which existed in China's countryside and of the class hatred that had

[1] See Committee for Economic Development, *How Low Income Countries Can Advance Their Own Growth* (New York: C.E.D., 1966), pp. 42-44. Cf. T. Lynn Smith (ed.), *Agrarian Reform in Latin America* (New York: Knopf, 1965), p. 46.

built up over the centuries because of the exploitation of poor peasants and farm laborers by landlords and richer peasants. Lopsided land tenure was held responsible for the backwardness and weakness of the country.

According to the communists, Chinese rural society consisted of five major classes:

1. Landlords—that is, those who owned land but did not engage in labor, or engaged only in supplementary labor, and who depended on exploitation for their livelihood. Exploitation took chiefly the form of land rent, but also of money lending, the hiring of labor, or the simultaneous carrying on of industrial or commercial enterprises.

2. Rich peasants who generally owned land, "better" means of production, and some floating capital. As a rule they were dependent on exploitation for a part or the major part of their means of livelihood. This exploitation took chiefly the form of hiring long-term laborers, but also rent from surplus land let out, money lending, and the carrying on of industrial or commercial enterprises.

3. Middle peasants either owned all or only a portion of the land which they cultivated, or owned no land at all. In the latter case, they rented land from others. They depended for a living wholly or mainly on their own labor. In general, they did not hire labor nor did they hire out their own labor to others. They normally owned a certain number of farm implements.[2]

4. Poor peasants in general had to rent land for cultivation and were exploited by others through rent and/or loan interest. They hired labor to a limited degree (i.e., for limited periods of time). Their farm implements were inadequate.

5. Workers (including farm laborers) generally had neither land nor farm implements. They depended wholly or mainly on the sale of their labor for their living.[3]

This division of rural society into five classes was primarily ideological and political. Ideologically it expressed the Marxist proposition that presocialist societies are torn by antagonistic contradictions between those who own and those who do not own means of production. In this particular instance the contradiction was between

---

[2] The category middle peasants is usually divided into "upper-middle" and "lower-middle," the latter being generally considered allies of the rural and urban proletariat. To remain so classified, "upper middle" peasants could not earn more than 5 percent of their income from "exploitation." In some cases (e.g., large family but small number of working members), the maximum exploitation income could go as high as 30 percent of total income.

[3] "How To Analyze Class Status in The Countryside," *The Agrarian Reform Law of the People's Republic of China* (Peking: FLP, 1950, 1951), pp. 19-24. Cf. Mao Tse-tung, "Analysis of Classes in Chinese Society" (March 1926), *SW* (Peking: FLP, 1964), Vol. I, pp. 13-21.

landlords and rich peasants on the one hand, and middle peasants, poor peasants, and landless laborers on the other, but especially the last two. The degree of exploitation resulting from the tenure system was quantified by the communists in the way shown in Table 3-1 (left-hand column).

TABLE 3-1
Land Tenure in China Before Land Reform

Communist Version	Noncommunist Versions
Landlords and rich peasants constituted less than 10 percent of the population. They owned from 70 to 80 percent of the land. Poor peasants, middle peasants, and farm laborers constituted over 90 percent of the population. They owned 20 to 30 percent of the land.	1. 54.2 percent of peasants owned all the land they worked. 39.9 percent of peasants were part owners. 5.9 percent of peasants were tenants. 28.7 percent of cultivated land was rented. For the country as a whole, 75 percent of land was owned by those who worked it. 2. "Middle class" households (i.e., those owning between 0.8 and 16 acres of land) accounted for 63.5 percent of total households. Their land holdings represented 75.4 percent of total land area.

Sources: Communist: Liu Shao-ch'i, "On the Agrarian Reform Law," a Report presented at the Second Session of the National Committee of the Chinese People's Consultative Conference, Peking, June 14, 1950 in *The Agrarian Reform Law of the People's Republic of China* (Peking: FLP, 1950, 1951), pp. 75-76. Cf. Mao Tse-tung, "On the Present Situation and Our Tasks" (December 25, 1947), *SW* (Peking: *FLP*, 1961), Vol. IV, p. 164. *Noncommunist:* 1. J. L. Buck, *Land Utilization in China* (Chicago: The U. of Chicago Press, 1937, ©1937 by the University of Chicago), p. 194. The data are based on a survey of 16,787 peasant holdings in 168 localities in 154 *hsien* (counties) of 22 provinces, between 1929 and 1933. 2. A survey of more than 1.75 million peasant households in 16 provinces carried out by the Land Commission of the Nationalist Government, cited in Cheng Chu-Yuan, *Communist China's Economy, 1949-1962* (South Orange, N.J.: Seton Hall U. P., 1963), p. 5. Audrey Donnithorne in her *China's Economic System* (New York: Praeger, 1967), p. 36, points out that the richer peasants, especially landlords, constituted a higher percentage of rural population than of rural households. Their higher income enabled them to support the extended family of Chinese tradition, or a stem family. The poorer peasants, on the other hand, more typically supported only the nuclear family. See also Franklin L. Ho, "The Land Problem of China," *Annals*, American Academy of Political and Social Science, No. 276 (July 1951), pp. 6-11.

It is possible that war and civil strife (1937-49) contributed to some concentration of land ownership, although it is unlikely that any great changes occurred. In any event, the communist figures are supposedly based on a survey published in 1936 by an Institute of Rural Economic Research, the identity and very existence of which are in doubt.[4] The actual land tenure situation in pre-1949 China was certainly more complex, the shadings more subtle than the picture presented in the left-hand column of Table 3-1. An important problem, for example, was the fragmentation of small private holdings. The average number of fragments per farm found by Buck in a 1929-33 survey of 16,700 farms was 5.6.

The "10 percent of population owning 80 percent of the land" version of China's pre-1949 rural troubles, should perhaps be seen as a way of mathematizing a fairly realistic belief that most Chinese peasants were far from happy with things as they were and that they aspired to a better life. The economic arithmetic is incidental and probably false; the sociological insight is not. The figures in the left-hand column of Table 3-1 are analytically less trustworthy than those in the right-hand column. But the figures in the right-hand column seem, on historical evidence, to have understated the depth of peasant disaffection and the opportunities which the land tenure system offered to a determined, organized, and ruthless minority to turn this disaffection into a revolutionary situation. The landlords and rich peasants of pre-1949 China were certainly not estate owners in the pre-1917 Russian sense as far as the acreage which they owned was concerned: the land they possessed was typically only a little bigger than that of their poorer neighbors. Their status in the village was, however, vastly superior to that of other farmers. The income differential between the "rich" and the poor may not have been very great, but it was the difference between security and subsistence, some little ease and much hardship.[5] This income gap, filled by rent and interest on loans, was therefore a highly political phenomenon. The communist classification of Chinese rural society and the crude mathematics associated with it addressed themselves to the politics of this income and status gap.

[4] See Richard L. Walker, *China Under Communism: The First Five Years* (New Haven, Conn.: Yale U. P., 1955), pp. 131-132.

[5] J. L. Buck's surveys reveal the very small average size of Chinese farms in 1929-33. The mean size in 22 provinces surveyed was 1.7 hectares, the median 1.3 hectares, and the mode 1.6 hectares. See Audrey Donnithorne's discussion of this problem in her *China's Economic System*, p. 31. Another survey cited by Miss Donnithorne revealed that the difference in farm size between owners and part-owners was small. However, tenants had on the average about 17 percent less land than owners and part-owners.

The better-off farmers (rural gentry), especially those within a relatively short distance of market towns, were much more a part of the monetized economy and responded more keenly to market signals than poorer farmers who, because of their modest marketable surpluses, tended to consume on the farm an important portion of their output. According to a Chinese Communist source (referring to the year 1955), rich farmers marketed 43.1 percent of their grain, middle peasants 25.2 percent, and poor peasants 22.1 percent.[6]

The better-off farmers had more reserves than their poorer neighbors. This enabled them to react to changes in the general level of agricultural prices and respond to fluctuations in relative prices. They had better storage facilities, which lessened the pressure on them to sell their output immediately after harvest.

The richer farmers profited from rising rents in the first half of this century. The precise rent situation in pre-1949 China is not very clear, and communist data on this subject are open to question.[7] Rent usually took one or other of three forms: fixed cash or produce, share of the main crop (normally 40 percent, but often much higher), and rent deposits on entry into tenancies.

The more prosperous farmers were also able to supplement their earnings by money lending and, in some instances, from shopkeeping. In the mid-1930's some 80 percent of rural credit was supplied by them, most of it for nonproductive purposes.[8] They were able, up to a point, to parry the thrusts of middlemen and tax collectors.

The fact that richer farmers tended to maintain extended family ties, whereas poorer farmers' families were usually of the household type, made the influence of the former more pervasive and widespread. The landlords, in particular, had more access to sources of political power and constituted a link between the state and the village.

All this does not inevitably imply that class conflict in the countryside was as sharp and clear-cut as the communists say. Social

[6] Tung Ta-lin, *Agricultural Cooperation in China* (Peking: *FLP*, 1959), p. 23. Figures based on a survey of 13,245 households in 18 provinces. See also the discussion of this problem in Dwight H. Perkins, *Market Control and Planning in Communist China* (Cambridge, Mass.: Harvard U. P., 1966), Chapter III, and G. W. Skinner, "Marketing and Social Structure in Rural China" (Parts I, II, III), *Journal of Asian Studies* (November 1964, February 1965, May 1965). See also Nai-Ruenn Chen and Walter Galenson, *The Chinese Economy Under Communism* (Chicago: Aldine, 1969) pp. 2-10.

[7] For example, Chen Po-ta, *A Study of Land Rent in Pre-Liberation China* (Peking: *FLP*, 1958). 1958, as was pointed out in the Introduction, marked a low in Chinese Communist statistical reliability.

[8] Audrey Donnithorne, *op. cit.*, p. 32. These "nonproductive purposes" included consumption, weddings, birthdays, funerals.

mobility, though easier at the top of the rural income ladder, was not altogether absent at the bottom. Ties of kinship and economic cooperation were at least as important as resentment, jealousy, and suspicion. Even the communists had to admit that the situation was more complex and fluid than their a priori scheme of five classes made it out to be.[9] China's rural community was held together by bonds of tradition and established rules of behavior which gave it stability and a capacity to weather natural and man-made storms. Within the limits set by tradition, Chinese ingenuity and hard work found scope to make themselves felt: the land was intensively and carefully cultivated, dikes and irrigation ditches were built and repaired, the produce of the soil was distributed. Agricultural practices were pushed to the limits permitted by traditional knowledge, but no farther. The situation, however, had explosive potentialities: it made progress slow and sluggish. The communists made use of these weaknesses to the full; they awakened discontent where it was dormant, created it where it was nonexistent.

2. Policy Constraints

At the very start of land reform (1950), the range of choice open to the communists was circumscribed by past commitments (i.e., by the long-standing promise to distribute land to the tillers) [10] and, more importantly, by urgent pressures of the moment. These pressures may be listed as follows:

(i) Disruption of food production brought about by thirteen years of war and civil conflict, and a bad flood in 1949.

In 1950 total food production was roughly two-thirds of the pre-1949 peak. The 1949 flood was said to have affected 8 percent of China's cultivable area. The severity of the disaster was no doubt traceable in large measure to wartime damage inflicted on water control systems.

[9] In their "Decisions Concerning Some Problems Arising from Agrarian Reform," published in August 1950 for the guidance of cadres charged with the task of carrying out land reform, they further subdivided the various classes into "well-to-do middle peasants," "reactionary rich peasants," "bankrupt landlords," "poor odd-jobbers," "intellectuals," "idlers," "workers from rich peasant and landlord families," and "religious practitioners." The latter were frequently assimilated with "superstitious practitioners" (clergymen, priests, monks, Taoists, lay Taoists, geomancers, fortune tellers, and diviners). See *The Agrarian Law of the People's Republic of China* (Peking: *FLP*, 1950, 1951), pp. 25-56.

[10] "The republic will take certain necessary steps to confiscate the land of the landlords and distribute it to those peasants having little or no land, carry out Dr. Sun Yat-sen's slogan of 'Land to the Tiller,' abolish feudal relations in the rural areas, and turn the land over to the private ownership of the peasants." Mao Tse-tung, "On New Democracy" (January 1940), *SW* (Peking: *FLP*, 1965), Vol. II, p. 353.

(ii) A chaotic rural market situation coupled with a sharp decline in the marketed portion of output.

In 1950 less than one-fifth of agricultural output was marketed. This compares with an estimated 50 percent in the 1920's.

(iii) Shortage of trained cadres to initiate, lead, and supervise the land reform movement.

About 180,000 cadres had to be quickly trained to help carry out the reform. Under cadre direction, thousands of students and intellectuals were drafted into work teams and sent to the countryside to remold their thoughts and raise their revolutionary consciousness by taking part in "bitter class conflict."[11]

(iv) The magnitude of the task.

Liu Shao-ch'i's June 1950 report on the agrarian reform law indicates the following (Table 3-2):

TABLE 3-2
The Status of Land Reform
(As of June 14, 1950)

Population (millions) living in areas in which:			
Land reform had been completed		Land reform had yet to be carried out	
Total population	Rural population	Total population	Rural population
160	145	310	264

The figures suggest that for the communists, land reform was at that time certainly not a beginner's exercise, even though the conditions in the east, central-south, and south, which had just then come under communist control, differed in many respects from those which prevailed in previously occupied areas. In the latter, land reform had been in force for years. The task, nevertheless, was formidable.

(v) Policy disagreements within the leadership.

Although the leadership responded to the land reform challenge collectively and with one voice, differences in emphasis could be detected within this apparently unanimous response. Some of these were made public during the campaign against Liu Shao-ch'i in 1967-68. It is retrospectively clear that Mao Tse-tung and some members of his entourage saw land reform as just another military-political operation, a matter of working up revolutionary zeal, a psychological mobilization of the masses. Others, probably those to

[11] See Theodore H. E. Chen, *Thought Reform of the Chinese Intellectuals* (Hong Kong: Hong Kong U. P., 1960), pp. 21-24; Ou-yang Tsai-wei, "Intellectuals and Land Reform," *People's China*, Vol. II, No. 3 (August 1, 1950).

whom fell the responsibility of day-to-day administration, were inclined to be more cautious and less hasty. The factions were probably more fluid, numerous, and diversified than is suggested by this dichotomy of revolutionary zealots and pragmatic moderates. The classification used here is, however, realistic enough, provided it is understood that it simplifies a complex and shifting spectrum of opinion. The differences in stress, often bordering on disagreements of substance, may tentatively be summarized as follows.

(a) Bitter class struggle and mass revolutionary zeal versus controlled orderliness and strict adherence to orders from the Party and government center.

For all its revolutionary gong-beating, Liu Shao-ch'i's report on the agrarian reform law emphasizes the need for orderly process. "We must not be impetuous," "agrarian reform must be carried out under our guidance, in a planned and orderly way," and other admonitions of like kind recur in the report. "To sum up, chaotic conditions must not be allowed to occur and no deviation or confusion may be allowed to remain uncorrected for long in our agrarian reform work in the future." If chaotic conditions arise, reform in the affected areas "should be held up." [12] This was particularly likely to happen in regions inhabited by national minorities. China's entry into the Korean War (October 1950) strengthened the hand of the more militant faction within the leadership. It injected into the land reform movement an element of urgency, heightened the feeling of suspicion, and encouraged the radicals to press on with their hunt for spies, secret agents, saboteurs, class enemies, counterrevolutionaries, and other "suspected elements." The net outcome of the contending forces was that the reform was carried out in piecemeal fashion, with considerable variations from place to place, and with much violence.

(b) Liu's insistence on orderly process and deemphasis of political revivalism reflected an administrator's preoccupation with the repercussions of the reform on production. While the restoration of output to at least prewar levels occupied the thoughts of both leadership factions, the revolutionary left was more concerned with the reform's political objectives. "The basic aim of agrarian reform," Liu warned in his report, "is not purely one of relieving the poor peasants. It is designed to set free the rural productive forces . . . in order to develop agricultural production and thus pave the way for China's industrialization." [13]

(c) This same preoccupation with production made Liu and others who shared his views, take literally Mao Tse-tung's dictum that after the reform "a rich peasant economy will be allowed in the

---

[12] Liu Shao-ch'i, *op. cit.*, pp. 73-75.

[13] *Ibid.*, pp. 78-79. Cf. "The basic reason for and the basic aim of agrarian reform are intended for production." (p. 79.)

rural areas." [14] For the Maoists a rich peasant economy was first and foremost a political concept fraught with dangers. If it had to be allowed, it was with regret and for tactical reasons. The Maoists were inclined to look upon the transitional stage, during which private farming and rich peasants were in evidence (the stage of new democracy), as one of short duration, an uncomfortable interlude to be liquidated as soon as possible. Their stress was on permanent revolution rather than on the gradual maturation of revolutionary stages as originally envisaged by Marx. Liu, on the other hand, saw in the development of a rich peasant economy the condition *sine qua non* of future socialist construction. For him and others it was a strategy, the duration of which had to be determined empirically. In 1967, when Liu was branded by the Maoist press as "China's biggest ambitionist, schemer, and top Party person in authority taking the capitalist road," [15] this alleged deviation from Mao's line was dug out and exhibited as proof of his treachery. According to the charges, Liu ("China's Khrushchev who shared the same pair of pants with the landlords and rich peasants and sat on the same bench with them") [16] tried to promote the so-called "Four Major Freedoms": freedom for individual peasants to lend money at interest, hire labor, sell land, and run private enterprises. The peasants, he thought, should be encouraged to get rich: "hiring farm hands and individual farming should be left to take their own course. Let them own three horses and a plough." [17] If this enrichment of the peasants carried with it the danger of exploitation, it was ideologically justified as an objective stage in the historical progression toward socialism. In January 1950 Liu was alleged to have said that "to prohibit exploitation is dogmatism. At present we must have exploitation and welcome it." [18] "He purposely distorted Chairman Mao's policy toward the treatment of the rich peasant economy by alleging that 'protecting the rich peasant economy is a long term policy.' " [19] Collectivization was to be introduced only after the full development of a healthy

[14] Mao Tse-tung, "On New Democracy" (January 1940), *SW* (Peking: *FLP*, 1965), Vol. II, p. 353.

[15] *Rural Youth* (Shanghai), September 10, 1967 in *URS*, Vol. 49, No. 17 (November 28, 1967), p. 226. The article had this to say about Liu's wife: "His present wife, Wang XX, is a bourgeois stinking apparition."

[16] *Rural Youth*, September 10, 1967 in *URS*, Vol. 49, No. 18 (Dec. 1, 1967), p. 242.

[17] *Nung-yeh Chi-hsieh* (Agricultural Machinery Technique) (Peking), No. 5 (August 1967) in *URS*, Vol. 49, No. 4 (October 13, 1967), p. 51. Cf. "Some [peasants] thought that they might become wealthy from the small peasant economy; they expected to live with '30 *mou* of land, an ox, a wife, some children, and a comfortable bed' and thought that the revolution had come to an end." "Is It Good Enough To Have Thirty *Mou* of Land and an Ox?" *Chung-kuo Ching-nien*, April 6, 1963 in *URS*, Vol. 32, No. 7 (July 23, 1963), p. 128.

[18] *Agricultural Machinery Technique*, *loc. cit.*, in *URS*, *loc. cit.*, p. 51.

[19] *Rural Youth*, *loc. cit.*, in *URS*, *loc. cit.*, p. 238.

individual peasant economy. According to Liu, only when 70 percent of peasant households owned those three horses and a plough, was it possible to set up collective farms "in the future." [20] In July 1955 Mao said: "In agriculture, under the conditions of our country, there must be collectivization first, before large machinery can be employed." [21] In June 1950 during the conference at which Liu presented his report on the agrarian reform law, he allegedly remarked: "Only when conditions are so mature that a large amount of machinery can be employed for farming in the countryside, will the existence of the rich peasant economy become unnecessary. However, it will be a fairly long time in the future before we can achieve this." [22] He characterized the belief that collectivization could be based on mutual aid and tilling teams as "a kind of Utopian socialism" which he considered erroneous. [23]

The charges leveled against Liu by the Maoists in 1967 were probably exaggerated. Liu's words were put in a distorted context. However, there can be little doubt that Liu's approach to land reform was substantially different from that of the more radical faction, and that disagreements at the top were in part responsible for the fits and starts, and the contradictions of actual policy.

OBJECTIVES AND EXECUTION OF LAND REFORM

From what has been said it should be apparent that the objectives of land reform were to radically transform the social and political power structure in the countryside so as to make some 120 million peasant households more amenable to central direction, and to restore production to at least the peak prewar levels. The first was to

---

[20] *Agricultural Machinery Technique, loc. cit.*, in: *URS, loc. cit.*, p. 51.
[21] *Ibid.*, p. 52.
[22] *Ibid.*, p. 51. In his report (*op. cit.*, p. 79) Liu said: "Precisely because of this basic reason and aim, [to promote production] the Central Committee of the Communist Party of China has proposed that rich peasant economy be preserved and protected from infringement in future agrarian reform. This is because the existence of a rich peasant economy and its development within certain limits is advantageous to the development of the people's economy in our country. It is, therefore, also beneficial to the broad peasant masses." This was, at the time, interpreted as merely an elaboration on Mao's statement that "a rich peasant economy will be allowed in the rural areas. . . . In general, socialist agriculture will not be established at this stage, though various types of cooperative enterprises developed on the basis of 'land to the tiller' will contain elements of socialism." Mao Tse-tung, "On New Democracy," *op. cit.*, p. 353.
[23] *Agricultural Machinery Technique, loc. cit.*, in *URS, loc. cit.*, p. 50. As has been pointed out in the Introduction (note 2), the accusations made against Liu Shao-ch'i and others after 1965 must not be taken at face value. Even the most innocuous and "orthodox" statements were turned against them out of factional spite. Where truth is relativized and becomes a weapon in the class struggle, anything goes.

be a prelude to the socialist transformation of agriculture (collectivization) and the integration of this sector in a planned, command-type economy. The second was regarded as an essential condition for future industrialization and growth. The first implied class struggle in conformity with the Party's definition of social classes. It meant the tearing down of established institutions seen as politically outmoded and dangerous, the frequent use of the stick, and at least temporary disorder. [24] The second objective called for orderliness, resort—where necessary—to old-type institutional arrangements (e.g., the market), and even to such ideological taboos as the profit motive.

Stripped to its barest essentials, the radical transformation of the social and political fabric in the countryside (i.e., the first objective) meant four things.

1. Confiscation of "surplus" land, draught animals, farm implements, houses, and grain of landlords (that is, of assets "in excess of those needed by landlords and their families," presumably to stay alive), and of land belonging to rich peasants but not worked by them.

2. Distribution of the confiscated assets to poor peasants and workers (landless laborers).

3. Confiscation and distribution to be carried out in such manner as to make the landlords lose face in the eyes of their humbler neighbors, and thus destroy, once and for all, the awe in which they had been held by the poor, and the prestige which once attached to their station in life.

4. Establishment of cooperative arrangements (credit cooperatives, mutual aid teams) intended to help the poor and middle peasants face up to their new obligations as owners of land, animals, implements, and buildings. [25] Some members of the communist leadership saw in these arrangements the nucleus of a not too distant socialist transformation (collectivization) of the countryside.

Confiscation, distribution, humiliation, and reconstruction—these were the cornerstones of land reform seen as an ideological and political weapon. They added up to the elimination, as a class, of those most opposed to communism in the countryside.

The restoration of production to at least the prewar peak (second objective) meant:

1. Establishment of incentives for peasant owners to produce and market increasing amounts of grain and other products.

[24] "In the first revolutionary period, intervention into economic processes by political force plays a decisive role." Oskar Lange, "The Political Economy of Socialism," *Publications on Social Change*, No. 16 (The Hague: Institute of Social Studies, 1957), p. 16.

[25] *Mutual Aid and Cooperation in China's Agricultural Production* (Peking: FLP, 1953).

In the period 1950-52 this meant, in effect, the restoration of order in and reliance on the market mechanism. The use of the market, while ideologically and politically repugnant to the communists (especially to the left wing), was a necessity at this early stage. Alternative arrangements of an administrative command character were still in their infancy. Thus, for example, there were few agricultural producer cooperatives (collective farms) in 1950 and 1951. In 1952 only 0.1 percent of peasant households were members of "lower-level" producer cooperatives. [26] Mutual aid teams (i.e., the pooling together by several households, seasonally or permanently, of labor, draught animals, and implements, ownership of the pooled assets being retained by the individual households) accounted for 10.7 percent of peasant households in 1950, 19.2 percent in 1951, and 39.9 percent in 1952. [27] Again, in 1950 the state commercial network controlled only 10 percent of purchases from agriculture, and under 25 percent in 1951. [28] A central planning apparatus was in the process of being set up but was not yet in a position to issue orders that would be internally consistent, or to supervise their execution.

Reliance on the market mechanism to spur production and marketing implied the halting of hyperinflation and prompt restoration of an adequate flow of industrial (mainly handicraft) consumer goods to the countryside. The output value of consumer goods (1949 = 100) reached 214.8 in 1952. [29] Above all, resort to the market meant allowing individual peasant households to respond to material incentives (i.e., grow rich), something that many in the leadership viewed with anxiety.

2. Inducing the peasants to concentrate on expanding the production and sale to the state of products used for export and as raw materials for industry.

An adequate supply of such products as cotton, silk, rice, and tea was essential to the recovery of industrial production and for paying one's way in foreign trade. The method adopted consisted of the setting of centrally determined (incentive) purchase prices, and the

---

[26] Agricultural producer cooperatives (collective farms) mean the pooling of land, labor, draught animals, and farm implements. Ownership of these assets is vested in the collective (except as below). In "lower-level" cooperatives, a share of the harvest is paid out as dividend on the land pooled to individual member households, the share of each being based on the amount of land contributed. The remainder of the crop is distributed according to labor contribution. In "higher-level" cooperatives all payments are made according to labor. The ownership of all assets (land included) is vested in the collective. Where land is nationalized (i.e., belongs to the state), it is leased to the collectives in perpetuity.

[27] *Ten Great Years* (Peking: *FLP*, 1960), p. 35. Cf. Table 2, Chapter 5.

[28] Dwight H. Perkins, *op. cit.*, p. 31.

[29] *Ten Great Years*, p. 88.

institution of advance purchase contracts, the intent of which was to protect the producer from adverse price movements between planting and harvest.

3. Supplying credit to the farmers.

The immediate effect of the elimination of landlords was a reduction in the availability of rural credit (see p. 49). Credit cooperatives had to be established to fill this gap, especially since the so-called "equalization of ownership" resulting from the reform left many peasant households with nonviable pieces of land, inadequate draught power, storage facilities, implements, and reserves. For example, in 1949 there were about 400 tractors (in terms of standard makes of 15 hp) to be shared by some 105 million households. By 1952 the number of tractors had risen to 2,000, a mere drop in the bucket.[30] As with some types of draught animals, the additional tractors tended to be owned by mutual aid teams and lower-level collectives. Apart from this trend, the use of cooperative arrangements to stimulate the political consciousness of the masses in the direction of socialism was checkmated at this stage by the more immediately compelling need to secure increased output from individuals.

4. Assuring revenues to the state without adversely affecting agricultural production and marketing.

To secure revenue and grain to feed the army, the communists introduced an agricultural tax. This tax was normally payable in grain, two times a year, at designated collection centers to which the payer had to deliver the grain. In exceptional circumstances payment was accepted in other products or cash. In newly occupied areas the tax was progressive, estimated at between 7 and 30 percent of the "normal" yield of different localities. In formerly occupied areas (north, northwest, and northeast) the tax was a fixed proportion of the yield. The net effect of this method of collecting revenue appears to have been to encourage the peasants to grow more grain so as to discharge their fiscal liabilities.[31]

The executive organs of agrarian reform were:

Land reform *cadres*, usually sent down from nearby towns. Their task was to select *active elements* from among the peasants to serve as the core of local *peasants' associations*. The associations were to

---

[30] *Ibid.*, p. 135. It has been suggested that 100,000 "standard units" = 50,-000 physical units. This would mean that in 1949 China had about 200 tractors, and 1,000 in 1952.

[31] On this subject see Audrey Donnithorne, *op. cit.*, Chapter 13; Dwight H. Perkins, *op. cit.*, pp. 42-48; George Ecklund, *Taxation in Communist China, 1950-1959* (Washington, D.C., 1961); *Agrarian Policy of the Chinese Communist Party* (New Delhi: Asia Publishing House, 1960); George N. Ecklund, *Financing The Chinese Government Budget: Mainland China 1950-1959* (Chicago: Aldine, 1966).

be class pure (i.e., no landlords or rich peasants were to be admitted to membership). The active elements in the village were also to serve as the nucleus of a *people's militia* or citizens' police totally submissive to central direction. To help them investigate the class status of the villagers, cadres and active elements made use of *informers* recruited from among poor peasants and landless laborers. These revealed to the authorities attempts by landlords and rich peasants to dissimulate their status by, for example, having poor relatives occupy a part of their land during the reform. [32] Subversives, despots, secret agents, local bullies (real or imagined) [33] were to be tried by *people's tribunals*. These were in effect, general meetings of former landless and poor peasants and others who jumped on the bandwagon out of conviction, opportunism or fear. In the background, at all times, stood the five million-strong People's Liberation Army (PLA).

The process of land reform in a locality went typically through several stages. [34]

A few cadres (usually young people with high school education) would arrive in the village and seek out one or two "active elements" (theoretically activists from among poor peasants and landless labor-

[32]The following extract from Mikhail A. Sholokhov's new trilogy, *They Fought For Their Country* (published in five installments in *Pravda* in 1969) gives a vivid description of the role of informers in fanning class war in the Russian countryside under Stalin in the early thirties. The account was published in the *New York Times* on March 16, 1969, p. 30. "Suppose Ivan's pig crashes into Peter's vegetable garden. Peter, without talking it over, takes a pencil, licks it, and writes to the G.P.U. [secret police] about Ivan: 'Look, Ivan, my neighbor, served with the Whites and committed atrocities against the families of Red Army soldiers.' So the G.P.U. invites Ivan by taking him by the collar, and a month later you may find him in Siberia. Then Ivan's brother informs against Peter, and Peter gets arrested. So a relative of Peter's starts licking his pencil and informs against the brother. And so on. They all finally had one another arrested in the village, and only a few men are left. The village people are called scribblers. They live like dogs. They develop a taste for sending one another to jail. They have all become politicians. There was a time, if you were insulted, you'd slug the other person, and that would be the end of it. Now all is different." ©1969 by The New York Times Company. Reprinted by permission.

[33]In communist parlance a "local bully" was the head of an armed gang which terrorized the village and fleeced the peasants. Frequently the bully engaged in opium traffic and gambling enterprises. He may or may not have been a landlord or rich peasant, but—according to the communists—was allied with those classes. Normally he did not himself engage directly in banditry, but merely pulled the strings. In the course of the Revolutionary War (1927-49) many such bullies were absorbed into the communist ranks and remolded along Party lines.

[34]This outline draws heavily on an eyewitness account, in C. K. Yang, *A Chinese Village in Early Communist Transition* (Cambridge, Mass.: The Technology Press, M.I.T., Harvard U. P., 1959), Chapters IX-XIV. See also *New York Times*, February 7, 1951, p. 4, and February 17, 1951, p. 2; Thomas P. Bernstein, *Soviet and Chinese Organizational Policies in Preparation for and as a Factor in the Collectivization of Agriculture: A Comparison.* Ph.D. Dissertation, Department of Public Law and Government, Columbia University, 1968; Ezra Vogel, "Land Reform in Kwangtung 1951-1953: Central Control and Localism," *China Quarterly* (April-June 1969), pp. 27-62.

ers, but often quite simply those among the middle peasants who had been active in village affairs and were willing to throw in their lot with the communists for reasons best known to themselves).

The cadres and active elements would then pick out a few poor peasants and landless laborers and coax them into telling stories of their past suffering at the hands of landlords. The process known as "woe-pouring" or "spitting-out stories of bitterness" (*t'u k'u*), or "struggle dispute" (*tu ch'eng*) unrolled during accusation meetings, and was designed to encourage others to do likewise (*ch'uan lien*). The idea behind it was to suscitate class hatred in the countryside, put the landlords and other "exploiters" on the defensive, and place them in a psychologically untenable position.

Concurrently the military authorities and the newly formed people's militia collected all firearms in the village and meted out swift punishment to anyone who tried to conceal arms.

When, as a result of *t'u k'u*, *tu ch'eng*, and *ch'uan lien* the number of villagers with worked-up grievances was large enough, the peasants' association was formed around them. This was made up of the more obvious poor peasants, landless laborers, and some middle peasants, the last being as a rule barred from the leadership of the association.

The association then proceeded to harass the landlords economically by demanding a refund of rent deposits and of excessive portions of rent. The usual way was to go in a noisy group to the landlord's house, loot his grain and implements, and rough him up if he objected to this process of democratic consultation.

Any serious resistance put up by the landlord was dealt with by dragging the man before the people's tribunal. The same treatment was administered to local bullies. Where local bullies did not exist, a suitable substitute was manufactured. As a rule, the accused was shoved and beaten through the village street, made to kneel, his hands bound, his head lowered before his massed accusers. The exact number of landlords killed during the reform is, of course, not known. [35] An estimated 35 million people were labeled "exploiters"

---

[35] Some sources have cited figures ranging from 1.5 to 2 million, but this may be exaggerated. See Richard L. Walker, *op. cit.*, p. 137, and Arthur G. Ashbrook, Jr., "Main Lines of Chinese Communist Economic Policy," in *An Economic Profile of Mainland China*, Joint Economic Committee, Congress of the United States (Washington, D.C.: Government Printing Office, 1967), Vol. I, p. 19. "When the landlords, rich peasants, counterrevolutionaries, capitalists, and bad elements are arrested," said a beleaguered Liu Shao-ch'i in 1966, "they should also be reformed. When you have successfully reformed them, then you can emancipate yourselves. If you shoot them, there are still their children. Their children will avenge their death. And if the children fail, then their grandchildren will do it. Were not a batch of them shot in the past? But their children are still living, and carrying on fairly well!" Liu Shao-ch'i, "Talk to Cultural Revolution Corps," *Collected Works of Liu Shao-ch'i, 1958-1967* (Hong Kong: URI, 1968), p. 338.

and "class enemies" and consigned to "controlled residence" (i.e., surveillance by peasants' associations and the militia) or to labor reeducation camps.

Landlords and local bullies having been terrorized into submission or killed off, the cadres (with or without the help of the peasants' association) proceeded to determine the exact class status of all individuals in the locality. This work was completed by early 1951 and the lists of remaining landlords, rich, middle, and poor peasants, and workers were displayed on village walls.

The land reform cadres thereupon proceeded to confiscate the land of landlords and some surplus land of rich peasants. Those subject to confiscation (and still around) were ordered to move their belongings out of their houses and surrender any surplus buildings. These and the land were then pooled and redistributed among laborers and poor peasants. The process led to frictions among the peasants, but apparently all attempts at factional, clan-based opposition were nipped in the bud by the threat of swift and merciless punishment.

The farms which emerged from land reform were, for the most part, economically nonviable. The average area of land per person after the reform works out at about one third of an acre, but this takes into account only the 300 million peasants to whom land, according to the communists, had actually been given. This figure should probably be raised by about 50 million to include state functionaries and their families, members of the armed forces and of mass organizations who also benefited from the reform.[36] Moreover, in the densely inhabited agricultural areas, the average land per person was probably much less than one-third of an acre. Shortly after the completion of land distribution, mutual aid teams were set up in many villages. The transition was made easier not only by the objective need for some pooling of land, capital, and labor, but also by the fact that aid among families as a way of getting at external economies was a long-standing tradition in China's countryside. It had also been a form of rural organization used by the communists in the areas occupied by them before 1949.[37] Already in 1951, the Shansi Provincial Party Committee proposed to transform the province's mutual aid teams into advanced collective farms. The proposal was criticized by Liu Shao-ch'i and dropped. During the Cultural Revolution (see Chapters 11 and 12) Liu's opposition to such accelerated collectivization was cited as one of the points of accusation drawn up against him by the Maoists.

---

[36] Cheng Chu-Yuan, *op. cit.*, p. 27.

[37] John Wong, "Mutual Aid Cooperation in China's Agricultural Collectivization," *China Mainland Review* (Hong Kong, June 1967), pp. 373-382.

RESULTS OF LAND REFORM

There can be little doubt that by 1952, when land reform was substantially completed, the old power structure in the countryside had been broken and the groundwork had been laid for future collectivization. Thus it can safely be said that the first objective of the reform was achieved almost in toto. The qualification "almost" is inserted as a reminder that it is not possible to gauge with any certainty the thought processes of Chinese peasants. Outward conformity, synthetic mass enthusiasm, and the apparent acquiescence of the rural masses in what the new masters were doing, were not necessarily signs of a radical transformation of the peasants' innermost thoughts or evidence that patterns of traditional conduct were as thoroughly altered as the communists would have others believe or sometimes believed themselves. Subject to this reservation, it is true that politically, from the communist standpoint, the reform was a success.

The economic objectives of the reform (increase in production and marketing) were also attained. Here, however, the picture calls for even more qualification. First, the communist figures on production successes in the period 1950-52 (Table 3-4) cannot be taken at face value. Some of the improvement in output which they reveal was probably due to an improvement in statistical coverage in 1952 compared with 1950. Second, it is known that a serious credit shortage hit the countryside in 1951 and 1952 in consequence of the communist campaign against usury. Cooperative credit was apparently quite modest and unable to fill the void left by the disappearance of private lending. Third, the transfer of an important part of surplus farm produce (which formerly took the form of rent paid to landlords) from those whose marginal propensity to consume was relatively low (landlords) to those whose propensity to consume was high (poor peasants), resulted in a sharp grain crisis in 1953. Fourth, the economic position of the poor does not seem to have been substantially improved by the reform, although the Maoists perhaps made more of this than the facts warranted, thus buttressing their argument for early collectivization. In 1955 Mao Tse-tung said that with all the land reform "people are still in a state of poverty because they lack the means of production. Many have gone into debt. Others have sold or rented their land."[38] More importantly, from

[38] Mao Tse-tung, "On the Question of Agricultural Cooperatives," *People's China* (November 1, 1955), p. 17. A 1953 survey in one *hsiang* of Kiangsu Province showed that of 50 households which sold their fields, 33 were poor peasant households, 17 were middle peasant. Among the 52 households buying land, 37 were middle peasant, 13 were households of private merchants, and 2 were households of landlords. *Chung-kuo Ching-nien Pao* (April 3, 1963) in *URS*, Vol. 32, No. 7 (July 23, 1963), p. 132.

the Maoist standpoint, "not only were the old rich peasants not put under restriction, but new rich peasants made their appearance. Many well-to-do middle peasants did their best to climb up and become rich peasants. Among the poor peasants, some had incurred debts and tried to make repayment by labor; others sold their land and houses."[39] In one county of Shansi Province there were reportedly 1,792 land sales in 1951, 10,505 in 1952, and 16,578 in the first ten months of 1953. Most of the sales were apparently due to the inability of the owners to cope with natural calamities, pay for illness in the family, marriages, and burials.[40] The antiprivate enterprise campaign in the towns (see pp. 76-79) narrowed the peasants' opportunities for part-time employment, and so aggravated their shortage of floating capital. One bright side after 1949 was good weather, always a matter of the greatest import in Chinese agricultural history. Also, the vesting of land ownership in formerly landless and poor peasants must have brought to the surface much talent and ability which in the past had little scope for expression.

Table 3-3 shows the distribution of land and other means of production per household after land reform. It is based on a survey of 15,432 rural households in 23 provinces carried out in 1954 and published in the July 20, 1965 issue of *Ching-chi Yen-chiu* (Economic Research), p. 13.

TABLE 3-3
Per Household Holdings of Land, Draught Animals, Plows, and
Water Wheels After Land Reform
(ca. 1954)

	Land		Draught Animals		Plows		Water Wheels	
	Mou	Index	Head	Index	Unit	Index	Unit	Index
Average	15.25	100	0.64	100	0.54	100	0.10	100
Poor peasants and laborers	12.46	82	0.47	73	0.41	76	0.07	70
Middle peasants	19.01	125	0.91	142	0.74	137	0.13	130
Rich peasants	25.09	165	1.15	180	0.87	161	0.22	220
Landlords	12.16	80	0.23	36	0.23	43	0.04	40
Others	7.05	46	—	—	—	—	—	—

Source: John Wong, "Mutual Aid Cooperation in China's Agricultural Collectivization," *The China Mainland Review* (June 1967), p. 384. Table VII based on *Ching-Chi Yen-Chiu* (July 20, 1965), p. 13.

[39] *Rural Youth* (Shanghai), No. 17 (September 10, 1967), in *URS*, Vol. 49, No. 18 (December 1, 1967), p. 241.
[40] *URS, ibid.*, p. 129.

It will be seen that even after the land reform the rich peasants had markedly more land, draught animals, plows, and water wheels than the poor peasants. In fact, the landholdings of the poor were so small that the full use of labor on them was not practicable. Both because of that and to gain knowledge and experience in the cultivation of the soil, the poor peasants and laborers often hired themselves out to work on rich peasants' land. The preferred communist alternative was the mutual aid team in which poor and middle peasants joined forces. Note also that in terms of landholdings the former landlords had been reduced to the level of poor peasants. In terms of their ownership of draught animals, plows, and water wheels, they were worse off than the poor peasants and agricultural laborers.

A sample survey carried out by the communists in 1954 showed that the land reform had pushed former landlord gross earnings to a level below that of the poor peasants. The former landlord earned (gross) 226 yuan, the poor peasant 244 yuan, and the rich peasant 432 yuan. Per capita gross income (i.e., taking account of the number of members in household) was 118.4 yuan for former landlords, 116.4 for poor peasants, 209.2 for rich peasants, and 154.8 for lower-middle and upper-middle peasants. While the average number of persons in poor peasant and former landlord households was the same (4.2), the average number of *working* members was 2 in the poor peasant households and 2.2 in the former landlord households. The average number of persons in rich peasant households was 6.2,

TABLE 3-4

Agriculture During the Land Reform Period, 1950-52

	Prewar Peak	1950	1952
Gross output value of agriculture index (1949 = 100)		117.7	148.5
Grain crops index (prewar peak = 100) . .	100		111.3
Wheat (million catties)	46,600	29,000	36,200
Rice, unhusked (million catties)	114,700	110,200	136,900
Cotton (thousands of tan)	16,980	13,850	26,070
Soya beans index (1949 = 100)			187.2
Cured tobacco index (1949 = 100)			516.8
Tea index (1949 = 100)			200.7
Big draught animals (thousands of head). .	71,510		76,460
Sheep and goats (thousands of head)	62,520		61,780
Pigs (thousands of head)	78,530		89,770
Increase in irrigated area (thousands of mou)		12,040	40,180

Source: Ten Great Years (Peking, *FLP*, 1960), pp. 118, 119, 120, 124, 126, 130, 132. 1 catty = 1.1023 pound; 1 tan = 0.0492 long ton; 1 mou = 0.1647 acre.

and the average number of working members in those households was 3.[41]

According to one source, the rehabilitation of China's water conservancy works (dikes, irrigation canals, drainage ditches, reservoirs) involved during this period the moving of 1.7 billion cubic meters of earth, equivalent to digging 10 Panama Canals or 23 Suez Canals.[42] The army was often used on these projects. The marketed portion of farm output (calculated from communist raw data) rose from 17 percent of gross agricultural output in 1950 to 27 percent in 1952.[43] Up to the end of 1952, over 340,000 new-type farm tools were reportedly adopted (including 240,000 walking plows).[44]

All in all, one would not be far wrong in concluding that the communist claim to agricultural rehabilitation during this period was justified. The revival was probably due more to the reestablishment of a degree of order and stability after years of war and physical destruction (and especially to the communists' undoubted success in halting inflation) than to the land reform measures themselves. For all its local upheaval, the process of land reform never quite eluded central direction and control. Its violence was, with local variations, choreographed by the cadres, and the cadres, with local exceptions, responded to directions from the center.

INDUSTRIAL, COMMERCIAL, AND HANDICRAFT REFORM

In the matter of industry, domestic commerce, and handicrafts the objectives of the communists were:
1. Rehabilitation of existing industries followed by rapid industrialization on a predetermined pattern (stress on capital goods industries—see Chapter 4).
2. Transformation of the ownership structure of industry, trade, and handicrafts.

REHABILITATION AND INDUSTRIALIZATION

Before 1949 Chinese industry was characterized by the following.[45]

[41] Victor C. Funnell, "Social Stratification," *Problems of Communism* (March-April 1968), p. 19, Chart 2. The information is derived from an unpublished dissertation by P. Shran, "The Structure of Income in Communist China," University of California, Berkeley, 1961, and based on *T'ung-chi Kung-tso* (Statistical Work), May 29, 1957, pp. 31-32. Cf. Chapter 5.

[42] Liao Kai-lung, *From Yenan to Peking* (Peking: FLP, 1954), p. 163.

[43] Dwight H. Perkins, *op. cit.*, p. 41.

[44] "Outline of Struggle," *URS*, Vol. 53, Nos. 5-6, p. 54.

[45] A useful reference is J. K. Fairbanks et al., "Economic Change in Early Modern China—An Analytical Framework," *Economic Development and Cultural Change* (October 1960). See also Nai-Ruenn Chen and Walter Galenson, *The Chinese Economy Under Communism* (Chicago: Aldine, 1969), Chapter 1.

1. Dual Structure

A relatively "modern" (capital intensive) sector coexisted with a "traditional" or handicraft sector using little or no mechanical power and located mostly in homes and small workshops. Modern industry and handicrafts were sometimes complementary, more often not competitive. While modern industry dominated the machinery, chemical, metal processing, electrical, and public utilities sectors, handicrafts predominated in the production of simple tools, artistic goods, services, as well as goods, and services ancillary to the activities of modern industry. Handicraft output accounted for just over two billion (1933) yuan of an estimated 1933 net domestic product of 28.86 billion yuan. In that year, 72 percent of the net value added to manufacturing originated in the handicraft sector, which employed 18 million persons out of an estimated total employment of about 259 million.[46] In 1952 (1952 prices) handicrafts (individual, cooperative, and factory) accounted for roughly 36 percent of the net value added to industry (or about 62 percent if 1933 prices are used).[47]

2. Smallness of the Industrial Sector

In the 1930's the contribution of industrial output (modern industry and handicrafts) to national income was about 10 percent. The exclusion of handicrafts would bring this down to about 3 percent. However, there was during this period a slow increase in the importance of the contribution of industrial output to national income. At least up to the early 1940's the modern industrial sector expanded relatively more quickly than national product. The average rate of growth of this sector's output before the war was 8-9 percent per year (Manchuria included), belying the impression of long-term stagnation made popular by the communists. The industrial advance was, however, sporadic.[48] According to the communists the proportion of the gross output of industry (handicrafts presumably included) to the combined gross output value of industry and agriculture was 30.1 percent in 1949 and 41.5 percent in 1952.[49] In 1952 net value added in Chinese modern factories, mining, and utilities was 6.2 percent of the net domestic product (compared with 3.4 per-

---

[46] Nai-Ruenn Chen and Walter Galenson, *The Chinese Economy Under Communism* (Chicago: Aldine, 1969), pp. 10-15; Ta-chung Liu and Kung-chia Yeh, *The Economy of The Chinese Mainland: National Income and Economic Development 1933-1959* (Princeton, N. J.: Princeton U. P., 1965); Y. L. Wu, F. P. Hueber, and M. M. Rockwell, *The Economic Potential of Communist China* (Menlo Park, Calif.: Stanford Research Institute, 1963).

[47] Audrey Donnithorne, *op. cit.*, p. 219.

[48] John K. Chang, "Industrial Development of Mainland China, 1912-1949," *Journal of Economic History* (March 1967), pp. 56-81.

[49] *Ten Great Years*, p. 80.

cent in 1933, both contributions valued in constant 1933 prices). If 1952 prices are used, the proportion was 11.5 percent. [50]

During the years 1949-52 the industrial sector (both modern and traditional) was rehabilitated and expanded, the expansion being particularly noticeable in the modern subsector. The number of industrial workers during this period rose from about 3 million to just under 5 million. [51]

3. Emphasis on Light Industry Producing Consumer Goods and Modest Development of Heavy Industry

The prewar industrial structure of China was biased toward such industries as cotton textiles, food processing, paper manufacturing, and printing. Machine tools, metallurgy, mining, utilities, as well as transportation were relatively undeveloped. According to communist sources, before the war 70 percent of industrial output was accounted for by light industry producing consumer goods and 30 percent by heavy industry manufacturing means of production. [52] Noncommunist sources agree with the general view of the prewar Chinese economy's consumer goods orientation, but differ on the degree of the bias. One study suggests that in 1933 consumer goods output accounted for 81.8 percent of modern industrial production (manufacturing, mining, utilities), while heavy industry contributed 18.2 percent. [53] A somewhat narrower tabulation of industrial output into consumers' goods, coal, ferrous metals, other mining products, and electric power, comes up with 41.4 percent of total net value added for the first, and 53.7 percent for the rest (the balance being accounted for by cement and crude oil.) [54] The textile industry in the early 1930's employed one-fourth of the factory labor in China. Three-fourths of the workers were between the ages of 11 and

[50] T. C. Liu and K. C. Yeh, *op. cit.* (Princeton: Princeton U. P., 1965), Table 8, p. 66.

[51] *Ten Great Years*, p. 183. Gross output value of handicrafts rose from 3.24 billion yuan in 1949 to 7.31 billion yuan in 1952. Gross output value of modern industry rose from 7.91 billion yuan to 20.05 billion yuan. *Ibid.*, pp. 91, 94.

[52] *Ten Great Years*, p. 79.

[53] Ta-chung Liu and Kung-chia Yeh, *op. cit.* (Santa Monica, Calif.: 1963), pp. 215-217 and Appendix H, quoted by Yuan-li Wu, *The Economy of Communist China: An Introduction* (New York: Praeger, and The Pall Mall Press, London, 1965).

[54] John K. Chang, *op. cit.*, p. 68, Table 5. Chang's consumer goods cover cotton yarn and cotton cloth, his ferrous metals include iron ore, pig iron, and steel, and other mining products cover antimony, copper, gold, mercury, tin, and tungsten.

25. Children and women represented 47 percent of total textile labor force.[55] The working day was frequently twelve hours, wage rates were low, and there were no appropriate labor protection regulations.

It should be pointed out that the prewar consumer orientation of industry did not imply the ability to produce domestically a broad range of finished goods. On the contrary, China relied heavily on the importation of a wide variety of consumer products to bridge domestic gaps and fill bottlenecks, a phenomenon known in development literature as the "conversion problem."[56] A leading producer of tungsten, China before the war imported electric bulbs. Apparel and other consumer goods were bought abroad both because they were readily available and because their quality was better than that of the domestic product.[57]

The picture of a consumers' goods oriented Chinese industry before the war should be qualified also in another respect. Although basically correct, the picture did undergo change if looked at geographically and according to different subperiods. During their occupation of Manchuria the Japanese pushed forward the development of heavy industries, especially mining and metallurgy. A similar trend was discernible in the southwestern areas of China under Nationalist control. In general, the years 1940 through 1945 were marked by a decline in consumers' goods production and a stress on the production of ferrous metals, electric power, machinery, and chemicals. The wartime heavy industry gains in Manchuria were largely undone by Soviet pillage of the area in 1945. According to a Western estimate the Soviets removed $900 million worth of industrial assets in a brief span of time from under the noses of both the Chinese Nationalists and the communists. The Soviets later admitted that they had seized as reparations only $97 million in industrial and other equipment.[58]

One final note. The technical level of Chinese prewar industry was low. A good part of the so-called heavy industry consisted, in

[55] H. D. Fong, *Cotton Textile Industry in China* (Shanghai, 1934) in Teh-wei Hu, *The Development of the Cotton Textile Industry and Its Influence Upon the Chinese Economy (1890-1937)*. Unpublished paper (1969).

[56] Yuan-li Wu, *op. cit.*, p. 114.

[57] See Jan S. Prybyla, "Red China in Motion: A Non-Marxist View," in Harry G. Shaffer (ed.), *The Communist World: Marxist and Non-Marxist Views* (New York: Appleton, 1967), pp. 153-154.

[58] Edwin W. Pauley, *Report on Japanese Assets in Manchuria to the President of the United States* (Washington, D.C.: U.S. Govt. Printing Office, 1946). See also Marshall I. Goldman, *Soviet Foreign Aid* (New York: Praeger, 1967), p. 10; *New York Times*, February 16, 1951, p. 4, and February 17, 1951, p. 14.

fact, of rather antiquated repair facilities and assembling plants. [59] There was also a shortage of skilled scientific, engineering, and managerial personnel. Before 1949 it was not unusual for the government to assign officers to manage factories, a procedure repeated by the communists both in 1949-52 and again after 1965 (see Chapter 11). In the period 1928-29 to 1947-48 a total of 29 million natural and agricultural scientists were graduated from Chinese institutions of higher learning. This compares with 13.8 million graduated in the three years 1948-49 to 1951-52. [60] At the end of the period of reconstruction and reform (1952) China had a total of 164,000 engineering and technical personnel. [61]

The predetermined pattern of industrialization to which reference was made at the beginning of this discussion consisted of (i) stepping up the rate of capital accumulation, (ii) channeling investments, even at this early period, primarily into heavy industry, and (iii) within the modern industrial sector, stressing the development of heavy industry. This strategy of resource allocation was inspired by the Soviet Stalinist model, and became much more sharply defined in the subsequent period (Chapter 4). Taking $1950 = 100$, the index of total investment in capital construction reached 384 in 1952. In the latter year, industry received 38.8 percent of total investments, transport and communications 17.5 percent, and agriculture, forestry, water conservation, and meteorology 13.8 percent (of which water conservation was 9.4 percent). In 1952 investment in heavy industry represented 76 percent of total industrial investment, or an investment ratio of light to heavy industry of 1:3.2. Taking $1949 = 100$, the index of the gross output of modern industry was 278.6 in 1952 and the percentage value of modern industry to total gross output of industry was in that year 64.2 (56.4 percent in 1949). The index of gross output value of handicrafts ($1949 = 100$) was 225.9 in 1952. [62]

4. Geographical Concentration

The modern industry of prewar China was concentrated in a few centers, especially along the coast. In the mid-1930's the main indus-

[59] According to the communists, in Shanghai before 1949 there were only 18 machine plants employing more than 100 workers each, and most of them could only assemble and repair, but not make machinery. Of the more than 1,000 machine plants in that city, only seven were complete in all processes, and of the 443 knitwear mills, only 2 percent were complete. Kuan Ta-tung, *The Socialist Transformation of Capitalist Industry and Commerce in China* (Peking: FLP, 1960), pp. 24-25.

[60] Cheng Chu-yuan, *Scientific and Engineering Manpower in Communist China, 1949-1963* (Washington, D.C.: National Science Foundation, 1965), p. 119, Table 19.

[61] Cheng Chu-yuan, *loc. cit.*, p. 111, Table 15.

[62] *Ten Great Years*, pp. 55, 59, 61, 91, 94.

trial concentrations were to be found in Shanghai and Manchuria. After 1937, Manchuria and North China as well as the Nationalist-controlled areas of southwest China emerged as the more significant industrial centers, and the relative importance of Shanghai declined. Railway development paralleled these spatial characteristics.

In 1933 Shanghai accounted for more than 50 percent of the country's modern industrial output and Manchuria for another 12 percent.[63] At the end of World War II the cities of Shanghai, Tientsin, Tsingtao, Peking, and Nanking had 90.7 percent of China's total industrial motive power (Shanghai had 57.7 percent), employed 85.5 percent of the total industrial labor force, and had 85.6 percent of all factories.[64] In 1948 only 18 cities in China had enough manufacturing capacity to be considered (modest) "industrial centers."[65] That year east China had just under 70 percent of total modern manufacturing industry in terms of motive power, employment, and number of factories.[66] From 1918 to 1930, 84.5 percent of spindles were in six main cities; Shanghai alone accounting for 55.8 percent of the total. Almost half the labor force in Shanghai was employed in the textile industry.[67]

The reasons for this lopsided spatial pattern were (i) the importance of foreign capital in China's industrial development, which meant the establishment of industries in treaty ports and in a few inland river ports (external economies) and the promotion of extractive industries in the geologically explored areas of Manchuria and elsewhere along the eastern seaboard, (ii) the accelerated development of Manchurian industry by the Japanese occupation authorities, and (iii) the parallel establishment of wartime industries by the Nationalists in the southwest. What was clearly lacking was a locational policy geared to the concept of regional division of labor and to the objective of developing remote and backward areas of the country.

Even in the early years of reconstruction, the communists incorporated the regional and developmental concepts into their locational philosophy. In addition, they introduced into their industrialization policy the concept of national defense (i.e., military-strategic considerations). In the years 1949-52 investment in capital construction in the so-called "national minority areas" (most of them hither-

[63] Yuan-li Wu, *op. cit.*, p. 116 quoting Wang-foh Sheng, *China's Industrial Production, 1931-46* (Nanking: Institute of Social Sciences, 1948), p. 4. See also E. B. Schumpeter *et al.*, *The Industrialization of Japan and Manchukuo, 1930-1940* (New York: Macmillan, 1940).

[64] Yuan-li Wu, *The Spatial Economy of Communist China* (Hoover Institution Publications; New York: Praeger, 1967), p. 11.

[65] *Ibid.*, p. 8.

[66] *Ibid.*, p. 11.

[67] Kung Tsien, *Outline of Modern Industry Development History in China* (Shanghai, 1933), cited by Teh-wei Hu, *op. cit.*

to undeveloped) represented 7.1 percent of total investment. [68] The extent of industrial relocation in this and subsequent periods should not, however, be overstressed. The general impression is of a movement away from the coast but not exclusively or even mainly toward the less developed regions. The common denominator of the communists' locational policy seems to have been the further development of already developed industrial centers away from the immediate coastal regions. [69]

5. Importance of Foreign Ownership and of the Private Sector

Before World War II a significant part of China's modern industry was owned by foreigners, especially British, French, Japanese, and American investors. In fact, the modernization of Chinese industry is directly traceable to foreign investments in treaty port manufacturing industries and in Manchuria. In 1933, for example, one half of the industrial workers in Shanghai were employed by foreign-owned firms. [70] The communists claim that before the war with Japan (1937-45), foreign capital controlled 70 percent of China's coal production, over 95 percent of her iron output, and 73 percent of her shipping tonnage (83.8 percent of this being oceangoing), and by far the greater share of her public utilities. In the mid-1930's, more than half of the country's textile industry was foreign owned. Moreover, foreigners exercised influence over China's banking, insurance, and foreign trade. [71] During the pre-1937 period, industries owned by domestic capital were typically small and relatively less efficient.

[68] *Ten Great Years*, p. 63.

[69] During the First Five Year Plan period (1953-57) the proportion of investment in capital construction going to the minority areas remained the same as during 1949-52. In absolute amounts, however, the 1957 investment in those areas was about double that of 1952.

[70] Yuan-li Wu, *The Economy of Communist China: An Introduction, op. cit.*, p. 117. See also Chi-ming Hou, *Foreign Investment and Economic Development in China, 1840-1937* (Cambridge, Mass.: Harvard U. P., 1965).

[71] Hsueh Mu-ch'iao, Su Hsing, and Lin Tse-li, *The Socialist Transformation of the National Economy in China* (Peking: FLP, 1960), pp. 1-2. Hsueh Mu-ch'iao, Director of the State Statistical Bureau was relieved of his office in 1959. Wang Ching-yu, "Why Old China Could Not Be Industrialized," *Jen-min Jih-pao* (May 21, 1953) gives the following shares for 1933 (foreign-owned industries): coal, 39 percent; pig iron, 82.5 percent; shipbuilding, 48.2 percent; cotton yarn, 29.1 percent; cotton cloth, 61.5 percent. See Chu-yuan Cheng, *op. cit.*, pp. 4-5. Before 1937 the greater part of China's foreign commerce was controlled by Western and Japanese corporations. After that date governmental participation grew substantially, displacing foreign control. See G. C. Allen and A. Donnithorne, *Western Enterprise in Far Eastern Economic Development* (London, 1954).

Professor Teh-wei Hu, [72] gives the following reasons for the failure of domestic control over China's important textile industry during the fifty-odd years of that industry's development (1890-1937): (i) the unsettled political situation in China since 1890, (ii) shortage of capital, which in part was responsible for high interest rates as compared with foreign countries; this raised production costs and contributed to business failures, (iii) shortage of managerial skills which resulted in high costs of production relatively to foreign countries, (iv) the heavy and complicated tax structure for domestic textile products made it difficult for the industry to compete with foreign textiles. At that time China could not resort to tariffs to protect domestic industries since she was a defeated power.

After 1937, and especially during World War II (1939-45), there took place an expansion of state-owned industry in the Nationalist controlled areas. The spread of the (Nationalist) state sector was enhanced by postwar (1945-46) confiscation of Japanese owned industries in China. Thus in 1946 the state sector in industry was said to have comprised 67.3 percent of total industrial capital. [73] It was not unusual for the government to encourage the process of industrial development, and for the private sector to supply the capital. In 1949 the private sector in industry accounted for 55.8 percent of the gross output value of industry, private commerce for 85 percent of total retail sales and about 76 percent of wholesale sales. [74]

From the communist standpoint the post-1937 shift in the ownership structure of industry meant simply that the larger portion of Chinese industry was thenceforth owned by "bureaucrat capital," a vassal, as they put it, of "international capitalist imperialism." [75] This bureaucrat capital, represented by the "four big families" of Chiang-Kai-shek, T. V. Soong, H. H. Kung, and the Chen Ko-fu and Chen Li-fu brothers, was, on communist theory, opposed to the small "national capitalists" (i.e., the remaining 32.7 percent of industrial capital as of 1946). During the period of reconstruction and reform the national capitalists were to be allowed to continue their operations under communist supervision, provided they did not engage in sabotage and other illegal activities. They were, on the whole,

[72] Teh-wei Hu, *The Development of the Cotton Textile Industry and Its Influence Upon The Chinese Economy, 1890-1937.* Unpublished paper (1969).

[73] Yuan-li Wu, *The Economy of Communist China: An Introduction,* op. cit., *p. 117,* quoting a Chinese Communist source. *Cf.* Nai-Ruenn Chen and Walter Galenson, *op. cit.,* pp. 15-22, and Yu-Kwei Cheng, *Foreign Trade and Development of China* (Washington, D.C.: University Press, 1956).

[74] *Ten Great Years,* pp. 38, 40, and Kuan Ta-tung, *op. cit.,* p. 42.

[75] See Hsu Ti-hsin, "The State Monopoly Capitalism of Old China," *Peking Review* (March 3, 1961), pp. 9-15.

listed among those who "could be united." Bureaucrat capital, on the other hand, was to be the raw material of nationalization, the foundation of "socialist industry."

TRANSFORMATION OF THE OWNERSHIP STRUCTURE OF INDUSTRY, TRADE, AND HANDICRAFTS

The transformation of ownership structure or "property relations," is a key component of the Marxist view of progress. [76] During the new democratic period of reconstruction and reform (1949-52) the communists proceeded to change the basic property relations in China's industrial, commercial, and handicraft economy in three steps: (1) confiscation of Chinese bureaucrat and foreign capital and its transformation into "socialist capital" (this applied mainly to industry and trade); (2) the association of national capital in the task of reconstruction, i.e., its toleration so long as it strictly adhered to the communist line; and (3) restriction and gradual liquidation of the private sector (national capital) in industry, trade, and handicrafts. The means used to take the last of these three steps included the so-called "Three-Anti" and "Five-Anti" campaigns (see pp. 76-79).

1. Confiscation of Chinese Bureaucrat and Foreign Capital and its Transformation into Socialist Capital

Industry

Enterprises owned by the Nationalist government were taken over by the communist state and became the foundation of the state sector in industry (as well as in banking, see pp. 83-85). This confiscation put into communist hands a significant, in some cases dominant, portion of China's heavy industry, e.g., 90 percent of iron and steel output, 67 percent of electric power, the whole petroleum and non-ferrous metals industries, railroad, modern highway, and air transport, and 45 percent of cement output. [77] It also meant state control of important segments of light industry, especially textiles. The communist state secured in this way the "commanding heights" of China's industrial economy. These could be, and in fact were, used to dominate the remaining private enterprises.

As of the end of 1949 the number of industrial firms confiscated was 2,677 employing 753,000 production workers. Fourteen of the confiscated enterprises employed 189,000 production workers. [78]

[76] For a historical parallel see Jan S. Prybyla, *Reflexions on the Third Sector: Private Initiative in a Changing "Socialist" Economy—The Example of Poland* (Bern: Osteuropa Bibliothek, 1958).

[77] Hsueh Mu-ch'iao et al., *op. cit.*, pp. 27-28.

[78] Nai-Ruenn Chen, *Economic Statistics of Mainland China, op. cit.*, p. 181, Table 4.1. The state in 1952 owned 8.6 thousand of China's 27.5 thousand large industrial establishments.

A more subtle form of confiscation was applied to foreign owned industries. Although at first permitted to continue operations, they were subjected to discriminatory taxation and discrimination in matters of inputs, financing, and marketing. As a result many of them were obliged to close down or to surrender their operations to the state. Outright confiscation of the remaining foreign enterprises began in December 1950 (U.S. companies) and continued through 1952 (British and French companies). The last few foreign firms (Danish, Norwegian, Swiss, and French)—most of them shipping concerns—were liquidated in 1960-61.[79]

In 1949 and 1950 the communists pursued a flexible, and on the whole liberal policy with regard to the employment of the old managerial and technical personnel in bureaucrat and foreign capital firms. The only thing asked of these people was that they stay on at their posts and not engage in economic sabotage. Beginning in late 1950, however, the former Nationalist managers and technicians as well as foreign personnel were decreed subversive and subjected to intensive remolding as part of the hunt for counterrevolutionaries and the Five-Anti movement (pp. 76-79). Thousands of them were imprisoned or sent to labor camps, others—the foreigners—were expelled from the country. At the same time the system of factory

[79] Estimated Number of Foreign Residents in Shanghai, 1937 and 1962.

	1937	1962
Japanese (and in 1962 Koreans)	19,000	100–200
British (in 1962 also Commonwealth		
except Indians).	11,000	40
Russian emigrés.	10,000	40
Americans	3,500	3
Portuguese	1,800	0
French.	1,600	6
Germans	1,500	7
Danes	350	0
Italians	350	3
Poles	350	"Some"
Spaniards	250	0
Swiss	220	2
Dutch	200	0
Greeks	200	1
Norwegians	160	3
Czechs	150	0
Others	200	0
Soviets.	0	50
Stateless*	0	"Several"
Iraqi	0	3
Indians	0	35
Belgians	0	3

*Between 1939 and 1945 there were also some 20,000 Jewish refugees from Germany and Austria. From "Foreigners in Shanghai," *FEER* (November 22, 1962), p. 410.

management was changed so as to conform to the political system of democratic centralism (Chapter 2).

The expansion of the socialist (state) sector of modern industry in the years 1949-52 may be seen from Table 3-5.

TABLE 3-5
Percentage of Gross Output Value of Modern Industry
Accounted for by Socialist Industry

1949	1950	1951	1952
34.7	45.3	45.9	56.0

Source: Ten Great Years, p. 38.

Domestic Trade[80]

The war with Japan, Japanese occupation, and the civil conflict drastically reduced the role of foreign merchants in China's domestic trade. The foreigners' involvement in China's internal trade was the result of their control over a large part of the country's external commerce, and was limited to a few commodities (cigarettes, oils, dyes). When Nationalist China became cut off from overseas commercial contacts, the foreign-dominated domestic trade network in those commodities came to an end, never to be revived. The disappearance of foreign commercial capital was accompanied by the emergence of Nationalist government trade companies. These companies dealt in such key commodities as food, fuel, and cotton. On coming to power in 1949 the communists thus found very little foreign capital to expropriate in the domestic trade sector. The Nationalist government's trading companies (commercial "bureaucrat capital") were replaced by communist bureaucrat capital (*state wholesale bureaus* run by the Ministry of Commerce and *state trading corporations*). Within two years of coming to power the communists controlled through these bodies about 60 percent of wholesale and 18 percent of retail sales.[81] State trading corporations increased their number of outlets and purchasing points from 8,000 in 1950 to 31,444 in 1952, and 97,405 in

[80] A good reference source is Audrey Donnithorne, *China's Economic System, op. cit.,* Chapter 11.

[81] *New China Fortnightly* (September 6, 1956), p. 46, "Wholesale is an important link in commodity exchange. It serves as a bridge between industry, commerce, and agriculture as well as between the socialist, capitalist, and individual sectors of the national economy. The state must control it before it can successfully implement the plan for national economic construction, guarantee a stable market and strengthen the leadership of the socialist sector over the capitalist and individual sectors of the economy to facilitate their socialist transformation." Kuan Ta-tung, *op. cit.,* p. 65.

1955. Employment in state trading corporations rose from 216,000 in 1950 to 535,000 in 1952, and 1.1 million in 1955.[82]

TABLE 3-6
Percentage of Wholesale and Retail Sales Accounted for
by State Commerce

	1950	1952
Wholesale sales	23.2	60.5
Retail sales	9.7	18.2

Source: New China Fortnightly (September 6, 1956), p. 46.

Another state commercial organ introduced during this early period was the *supply and marketing cooperative* which had been tried out in the old communist controlled areas before 1949. Although nominally a collective and listed as such in statistical reports ("cooperative commerce"), the supply and marketing cooperative is hardly distinguishable from state commercial organs with which, however, it not infrequently competes. At the local level the cooperatives seem to depend for their supplies on the state trading companies and were organizationally dependent on the state wholesale bureaus.[83] Supply and marketing cooperatives operate mainly in rural areas: over 90 percent of their membership consists of peasants, every peasant household being represented in the cooperatives by at least one member. Since 1954 the cooperatives have been supervised and regulated by a central body—the All-China Federation of Supply and Marketing Cooperatives with a membership of 150-160 millions. Lower level organs include provincial and *hsien* federations. The cooperatives through their retail outlets and purchase points in the countryside (and to a lesser extent in urban areas) sell bazaar-type goods and simple equipment to the peasants and buy from them—on behalf of the state—agricultural commodities of all kinds. In 1950 there were some 44,000 such retail outlets and purchasing points; 113,000 in 1952, and 236,000 in 1955. They employed 166,-000 people in 1950; 711,000 in 1952; and 1.1 million in 1955.[84] By 1953 the cooperatives accounted for 75 percent of total state purchases and almost 100 percent of state purchases of the main agricultural products.[85]

[82] Nai-Ruenn Chen, *op. cit.*, p. 385, Table 7.1. The local offices of the state trading corporations were controlled at the *hsien* level by a "*hsien* commercial department."

[83] P. H. M. Jones, "Get Out and Sell," *FEER* (November 25, 1965), pp. 371-375. The cooperatives at the basic level (market town, commune, brigade, team) apparently dealt primarily in local produce and bazaar type goods.

[84] Nai-Ruenn Chen, *op. cit.*, p. 385, Table 7.1.

[85] Audrey Donnithorne, *op. cit.*, p. 279.

The growth of supply and marketing cooperatives may be seen from Table 3-7.

TABLE 3-7

Percentage of Wholesale and Retail Trade Accounted for by
Cooperative Commerce (Supply and Marketing Co-ops)

	1950	1952
Wholesale sales	0.6	2.7
Retail sales	6.7	23.8

Source: *New China Fortnightly* (September 6, 1956), p. 46.

2. Association of National Capital in the Task of Reconstruction

"The number of industrial enterprises run by national capital in 1949 was 123,165 employing over 1,640,000 workers and other employees and producing a total value of over 6,800 million yuan in that year. In 1950 the number of commercial establishments, including the vast number of private, individual small merchants, was about 4,020,000; there were 6,620,000 people (of whom over 960,000 were employees) engaged in the trades; and the sales totaled over 18,200 million yuan."[86] In 1952 the number of private trading establishments was 4,300,000. There were 6,768,000 merchants (of whom 917,000 were workers and employees), and sales totaled 19,170 million yuan.[87]

Since the overwhelming majority of private merchants in China were small traders and peddlers carrying their capital on their backs, so to speak, they could hardly be classed with the national bourgeoisie and treated as such in the process of socialization.[88] The communists were uneasily aware of this: "They were not capitalists, but individual working people engaged in commercial transactions. As a rule, they possessed only a meager amount of capital, operated a small shop, a stand or stall, or traveled while peddling their wares. Only a very few employed assistants and the overwhelming number depended upon their own labor entirely. . . . They were laborers."[89] The need to remold them in a socialist direction arose from their potential for mischief: they "were often inclined toward spontaneous capitalist development and speculation. Quite often they were a strong enough force to upset the equilibrium of the market, the

---

[86] Kuan Ta-tung, *op. cit.*, p. 24.
[87] Nai-Ruenn Chen, *op. cit.*, p. 385, Table 7.1.
[88] In 1955, 96 percent of the total number of private commercial establishments were of the small trader and peddler type. They accounted for 65 percent of the total value of transactions handled by private commerce. Hsueh Mu-ch'iao et al., *op. cit.*, p. 159.
[89] *Ibid.*, pp. 159-160.

state's supply and marketing plan and price policy. In the course of socialist transformation, it was necessary to make provisions for them and to remold them in a suitable manner." [90] The suitable manner did not much differ from the manner adopted in remolding national capitalists. The special features of the process as it was applied to the small traders and peddlers will be noted in the course of the discussion of elementary and advanced state capitalism (below, pp. 68-70).[91]

Until 1951 the national capitalists were allowed to join the ranks of those who, under communist guidance and supervision, worked for reconstruction. However, they were never viewed as reliable allies, and the projected span of their class life was short. "The national bourgeoisie," Mao had written, "is a class which is politically very weak and vacillating. But the majority of its members may either join the people's democratic revolution or take a neutral stand, because they, too, are persecuted and fettered by imperialism, feudalism and bureaucrat-capitalism. They are part of the broad masses of the people but not the main body, nor are they a force that determines the character of the revolution. . . . Because they are important economically . . . it is possible and necessary for us to unite with them . . . to win over the majority of the national bourgeoisie and isolate the minority. To achieve this aim we should be prudent in dealing with the economic position of this class, and in principle should adopt a blanket policy of protection. Otherwise we shall commit political errors." [92] The association of national capitalists with the communist revolution was thus a tactical alliance dictated by economic necessity. It was that at least in the mind of Mao, although some of Mao's companions may have interpreted the maneuver as one of somewhat greater depth and duration. Liu Shao-ch'i, for example, was quoted in the *People's Daily* of April 15, 1967, as having remarked to the Shanghai capitalist Sung Fei-ching in the spring of 1949: "The more factories you build, the more workers you exploit, the better. . . . Exploitation by capitalists is a historical service, and not a single communist will blot out the services performed by the capitalists. . . . Of course, there is also a bit of crime in it, but the service is great, while the crime is small. Today capitalism in China is in its youth, and it is precisely the time to develop its historical,

[90] *Ibid.*, p. 160.

[91] There were also large numbers of unlicensed hawkers, some 20,000 in Peking alone (1957). They kept popping up year after year, making their profits from local price differentials in state and cooperative commerce. See Audrey Donnithorne, *op. cit.*, pp. 279-280.

[92] Mao Tse-tung, "On the Question of the National Bourgeoisie and the Enlightened Gentry" (March 1, 1948), *SW* (Peking: *FLP*, 1961), Vol. IV, pp. 208-209. Cf. "The Dual Character of the National Bourgeoisie," Kuan Ta-tung, *op. cit.*, pp. 29-34.

active role." [93] Assuming that Liu actually said this, and that words have not been put in his mouth ex post by his Maoist detractors, the sentiment would still make good orthodox Marxism, while revealing poor political horse sense. One should at any rate be careful in blaming the national capitalists for falling for a rather obvious communist ruse, especially since the options open to them in 1949-50 were exiguous. The fact is that most of them went along with the communist offer and cooperated or stayed neutral.

The national capitalists, contrary to Mao Tse-tung's characterization of them, were a hardy breed. As we shall see soon, they cashed in on the Korean War, and after being crushed, cashed in again on Mao buttons and other devotional articles, eighteen years later. [94] They did so, however, as scattered individuals. As a social class they had been liquidated by 1955. A few showcase capitalists were officially exhibited to selected Western tourists as late as 1967. Their usefulness to the communists was purely histrionic; their social, economic, and political influence was nil. [95]

The association of modern private industry and commerce in the work of reconstruction (or as the communists were later to put it, their "use") in 1949-52 took three forms: private firms were sometimes allowed to produce and market a portion of their total output without any government control (free production and sales); elementary state capitalism; advanced state capitalism. Handicraft production presented a special case. It is discussed separately.

Free Production and Sales

A portion of the output of modern industry was at this time produced and sold by private enterprises themselves without direct state instructions, i.e., for the market and in response to market signals, and the same was true of private trade in so far as part of total distribution was concerned. It should however be remembered that this market was increasingly influenced by the state through its fiscal and monetary policies and its ownership of the economy's commanding heights. The share of this type of activity in the total

[93] Dick Wilson, "The China After Next," *FEER* (February 1, 1968), p. 192. Cf., the attacks on Liu cited earlier in this book. In 1967 Liu was described as "a bad egg of countless crimes." His major crime was disobedience to Mao. "Man obeys Chairman Mao, and earth obeys man," was then the rule. See "Hold Aloft the Great Red Banner of Mao Tse-tung's Thought and Topple Completely China's Khrushchev," *Rural Youth* (Shanghai) No. 17 (September 10, 1967) in *URS* (November 28, 1967), p. 229.

[94] See *China News Analysis*, No. 695 (February 9, 1968), p. 3, and Dick Wilson, *loc. cit.*, pp. 192-193.

[95] Jan S. Prybyla, "The Soviet View of Mao's Cultural Revolution," *The Virginia Quarterly Review* (Summer 1968). These few surviving capitalists were of the "advanced state capitalism" type (see below, pp. 70-71).

gross output of industry and in retail and wholesale commerce can be seen from the data in Table 3-8.

TABLE 3-8

Percentage of Gross Output Value of Modern Industry and of Retail and Wholesale Sales Accounted for by Free Production and Sales by Private Firms

	1949	1950	1951	1952
Industry (percentage of total gross output value of modern industry)..	55.8	36.9	28.7	17.1
Retail commerce (percentage of total retail sales)................		85.0 (83.5)	75.5	57.2 (57.8)
Wholesale commerce (percentage of total wholesale sales)..........		76.1	65.4	36.3

Sources: Ten Great Years, pp. 38, 40; Kuan Ta-tung, *op. cit.*, p. 66; the figures in parentheses for retail trade from *New China Fortnightly* (September 6, 1956), p. 46. In 1950 private traders accounted for 32 percent of China's exports and imports. This share fell to 8 percent in 1952. In this area, private enterprise was progressively displaced by governmental foreign trade corporations. The remnants of private foreign trade enterprises were transformed into joint state-private (advanced state capitalist) undertakings before 1956. A Ministry of Foreign Trade was set up in 1952.

Quite clearly, whatever the occasional infusion of stimulants into the private sector by a state anxious to keep it alive in perilous times, use went hand in hand with restriction. The closing of the Shanghai stock exchange and the takeover of banks (pp. 83-85 below) resulted in a sharp curtailment of private sector activity in the first half of 1950. Since the state needed the goods and services produced by private industry and distributed by private trade, if only to help contain inflation, measures were taken in the second half of 1950 to keep private enterprise afloat. The method used was known as "elementary state capitalism." In proper dialectical fashion, elementary state capitalism both helped the private sector stay alive in a communist state in the short run, and enabled the state to liquidate private business in the long run.

Elementary State Capitalism

Elementary state capitalism in industry meant that (a) the socialist sector, mainly the state trading companies, supplied private factories with raw materials and semifinished products, and instructed them to process these according to certain specifications (quantity, quality, time). The state trading corporations then took the finished products and paid the private factories a sum of money for the job. The payment covered costs of production, including business tax and "a reasonable" profit. After fulfilling the state order, the private factories could produce the same goods with their own materials and sell them on the market. (b) The socialist sector placed orders with private factories for specified commodities. As a rule, in this instance, the factories fended for themselves so far as raw materials were concerned, although the state might in some cases supply part of the raw materials and advance part of the selling price as a deposit. (c) In some instances the state might market the whole output of private factories at "appropriate" prices. This applied to certain key industrial products. In such cases the state trading corporations were given the exclusive right of purchase i.e., the private contractor was not allowed to sell the same commodities on the market, as under (a) above. (d) The state trading corporations might market all finished products of private enterprises. The difference between this and (a) and (b) was that products in excess of the agreed-on quota resulting from improvements in production could not be marketed independently but had to be sold to the state.

Elementary state capitalism in commerce meant that (a) private stores acted as retail distributors for the state trading companies. The goods supplied by the state companies had to be paid for in cash and sold at the retail level at prices set by the corporations. Usually the prices set were such as to leave a margin of profit to the private retailers. The private retailers could also buy the same commodities for which they acted as state distributors from the free market. The same procedure was applied to private wholesale commerce. In the case of some less important commodities, private retail stores acting as distributors for the state, were allowed to purchase the whole stock of such commodities from the free market and sell them at prices approved by the state corporations. (b) In some cases private trading enterprises acted as commission agents for the state, i.e., they deposited a certain sum of money with the state trading corporations or supply and marketing cooperatives as guarantee, and sold the goods on a commission basis according to the state plan and at retail prices set by the state corporations. Purchase of the same commodities on the free market was not permitted. The same procedure was applied to private wholesale traders and to private import and export concerns.[96]

Since, as we have seen, over 90 percent of private commercial enterprises were one-man peddler-type operations with the capital consisting of a stall or at best a tiny store in the front of the house, the retail distribution and commission business had to be handled in a special way. The description just given in (a) and (b) would fit

[96] The process is well described by Kuan Ta-tung, *op. cit.*, Chapter 5, pp. 59-71.

without qualification the larger private commercial establishments only. These as we have seen handled about 45 percent of the private trading business as late as 1955. In the case of small traders and peddlers the distributing and commission business was handled on their behalf by cooperative groups under the supervision of supply and marketing cooperatives and/or state trading corporations. Selling was still the responsibility of the individual members of the group who also accounted for their own profits and losses via some rather loose accounting carried in their heads. The purpose of the group was simply to keep track of the traders and simplify the state's task of using them as distributors and commission agents.

"The whole problem," as Lenin had said, ". . . [was] to find the correct methods of directing the inevitable (to a certain degree and for a certain time) development of capitalism into the channels of state capitalism; to determine what conditions to hedge it around with, how to ensure the transformation of state capitalism into Socialism in the not distant future."[97]

The development of elementary state capitalism in industry and trade during 1949-52 may be seen from Table 3-9.

TABLE 3-9
Percentage of Gross Output Value of Modern Industry and of
Retail and Wholesale Sales Accounted for by State Capitalist
Enterprises of the Elementary Type

	1949	1950	1951	1952
Industry (percentage of total gross output value of modern industry)...	7.5	14.9	21.4	21.9
Retail commerce (percentage of total retail sales)*	. . .	0.1	0.1	0.2
Wholesale commerce (percentage of total wholesale sales)*	. . .	0.1	. . .	0.5

*Covers state-capitalist and cooperativized commerce.
Sources: Ten Great Years, pp. 38, 40; New China Fortnightly (September 6, 1956), p. 46.

At first sight the restriction of private commerce appears much less than the shrinkage in private industry. However, the share of retail sales and wholesale trade by elementary state-capitalist commerce during this period should be related to the decreasing share of private trade on the free market (Table 3-8) and the growing share of state commerce (Table 3-6).

[97] V. I. Lenin, Selected Works (2 vols.) (Moscow: Foreign Languages Publishing House, 1952), Vol. II, Part 2, p. 544. Cf. Liu Shao-ch'i's statement: "The socialist transformation of capitalist industry and commerce by the state will be gradually realized over a relatively long period of time through various forms of state capitalism." [Emphasis added.] Liu Shao-ch'i, Report on the Draft Constitution of the People's Republic of China (Peking: FLP, 1954), p. 29.

Advanced State Capitalism

Advanced state capitalism in China was synonymous with joint state-private enterprises. "A joint state-private enterprise is one in which the state invests and to which it assigns personnel to share in management with the capitalists. In such an enterprise, there are state shares (public shares); personnel are appointed by the state (to represent the state shares) and capitalists or their agents (to represent the private shares). But the relationship between these two groups is not the same as that in a capitalist joint-stock company. It cannot be one of ordinary partnership. It is one between the leader and the led. . . . [State appointed] representatives are in a leading position in the joint enterprise. . . . The socialist sector has placed the capitalist sector under its direct supervision and control." [98]

The essential difference between elementary and advanced state capitalism was that whereas in the first case private firms were still managed by individual businessmen within a framework of contracts and controls set up by the government, in the second case the enterprises were managed by state appointees. The private shares in an advanced state-capitalist enterprise received a part of the dividend on net income and interest on the original investment. The private partner was, however, deprived of any significant say in the running of the business. It was a sort of united front arrangement, an industrial application of the political theory of new democracy. Table 3-10 shows the process of expansion of advanced state capitalism in modern industry during 1949-52.

TABLE 3-10
Percentage of Gross Output Value of Modern Industry Accounted
for by State Capitalist Enterprises of the Advanced Type

1949	1950	1951	1952
2.0	2.9	4.0	5.0

Source: Ten Great Years, p. 38.

Advanced state capitalism in commercial, catering, and personal service establishments was not developed before 1955. At the end of 1954, only 137 such establishments were jointly managed in this way. In the case of small traders and peddlers, advanced state capitalism was to take the form of cooperative stores whereby individual operations would become collective ones. The stores were to consolidate the "capital" of their members, account for profits and losses, and distribute profits among the members. Their distributive and

[98] Kuan Ta-tung, *op. cit.*, pp. 75-76.

commission operations for the state were to be supervised by state trading corporations or supply and marketing cooperatives. They could also engage in some independent trading on their own. The project apparently never quite took hold.

Handicrafts

Handicrafts in China have been defined as those methods of production which used manual rather than mechanical power, employed simple implements and tools, and made use of traditional production processes.

At the time of the communist takeover, handicraft production comprised subsistence handicrafts, private individual handicrafts, and small privately owned handicraft workshops. Subsistence handicrafts were domestic sideline activities requiring a low degree of skill, few and simple implements, and little specialization. This type of production was carried on by peasant families for their own use and included the preliminary processing of farm produce. For statistical purposes subsistence handicrafts have been classified by the communists with agriculture and their output has been included under agricultural output. Private individual handicrafts were characterized by a somewhat higher level of skill, some specialization of labor, greater amount and complexity of tools and implements, production for the market, and the regular spending of a part of one's time in handicraft production (i.e., away from agricultural occupations *sensu stricto*). This type of activity involved the private ownership of tools and implements by the individual and/or his family. The work was normally done in the craftsman's home, by himself or with the help of his relatives. Frequently the individual craftsman would employ an apprentice or a journeyman. Privately owned handicraft workshops ("capitalist handicraft workshops" in communist parlance) were a little above individual handicrafts from the standpoint of capital requirements, degree of skill, specialization, and regular time spent on this activity. Privately owned handicraft workshops were owned and run by peasant craftsmen with the help of their families and with some hired wage labor. Whereas private individual handicraft establishments normally had less than four gainfully employed persons, including the owner and members of his family, a "capitalist handicraft workshop" would have at least four and less than ten gainfully employed persons, including the owner, family helpers, and wage laborers. Statistically, capitalist handicraft workshops were classified under industry and their output under industrial output. The statistical category "individual handicrafts" usually covered more than privately owned individual handicrafts, although the usage has been far from consistent. For statistical purposes "individual handicrafts" included—as a rule—some elementary forms of handicraft cooperation, such as supply and marketing groups and supply and marketing cooperatives (see below). In 1958 the category "handicrafts" was eliminated from official statistics in line with the movement to transform handicrafts into "factories" run by local state organs or the people's communes (see Chapters 8 and 9).[99]

In 1952 handicrafts accounted for 62 percent of the net value added in industry (calculated in 1933 yuan) and roughly 37 percent if 1952 prices are used. Their contribution to net national product at current prices was 7 percent. Their importance in supplying the countryside with articles of daily use and with simple tools was greater than these figures suggest. In the period 1949-52 the communists were concerned not to disrupt the operations of the handicraft sector through hasty collectivization since about 70 percent of the goods needed in the countryside (plows, harrows, water wheels, furniture, kitchen utensils, etc.) were supplied by rural part-time craftsmen. The pressure on craftsmen to join handicraft cooperatives of various kinds began to be exerted in all seriousness in 1953-54, and reached its peak in 1955-56 (See Chapter 5). In 1954 independent craftsmen were said to have numbered about 8 millions and peasant part-time craftsmen some 12 millions.

From the standpoint of Marxist property relations, China's handicrafts were classified in the following way.

Private individual handicrafts. These were regarded as "a form of commodity production" (i.e., production for the market). The means of production were owned privately, and as a rule, work was carried out in the home, with perhaps a store at the front of the house. Accounting was often of the in-the-head type. In comparison with peasants working on their own (i.e., private farming) individual craftsmen were said by the communists to have maintained closer connections with commercial and credit establishments and with customers (especially in the case of service trades). In other words, production and trade were combined over a wide segment of individual handicrafts. Because in the communist view individual craftsmen worked for the market and had to be supplied through the market,

[99]The whole statistical picture regarding handicrafts is beset with enormous difficulties. Definitions have been switched without warning or explanation. It is quite likely that such statistics as have been released refer primarily to full-time handicraftsmen rather than to the whole handicraft sector (i.e., inclusive of peasant part-time craftsmen). As a rough rule of thumb, one can venture the following suggestion: full-time craftsmen numbered about 5-8 million in the 1950's and 1960's, while part-time peasant craftsmen numbered an additional 20 million or so. More than half the full-time craftsmen lived in urban areas.

"their socialist transformation had to be started by organizing the supply of raw materials and the marketing of their products."[100] Private individual craftsmen were not classified by the communists with capitalists because the tools they used were rather simple and because the apprentices whom they hired tended to become independent producers soon after they learned their trade. The means of production which these craftsmen used were in the communist view means of labor rather than means of exploitation. "But quantitative change leads to qualitative change. If the economic status of such independent handicraftsman improved so that he finally hired more workers, and his own labor gradually became of secondary importance, then he would have become a small proprietor or even a capitalist" [i.e., owner of a "capitalist handicraft workshop" whose output would statistically fall under industry, and whose political fate would be linked to that of the national bourgeoisie].[101]

Small supply and marketing groups. The immediate purpose of these groups was to buy raw materials from the state trading organizations and the supply and marketing cooperatives (trading cooperatives), sell handicraft products to them, and accept orders for processing goods. The group, in other words, seized control of the channels through which inputs and outputs of the private individual handicrafts had to pass—that is, of the handicrafts' "strategic heights." The members' means of production remained privately owned, and each member of the group continued to engage in independent production, accounting for his own profits and losses. Apprentices and hired hands as well as family helpers were not eligible for membership. In time the groups began to accumulate some collectively owned property. "Spontaneous trends toward capitalism" apart, the complaint voiced in official circles against the small supply and marketing groups was that sometimes they sold their inferior products to the state trading agencies, while marketing the good ones on their own. "When the market was brisk, some would request freedom to produce and sell on their own, but when the market was dull, they would ask for processing and purchasing orders from state enterprises."[102]

Looked at from the vantage point of Marxist property relations, the next higher form of handicraft organization was represented by supply and marketing cooperatives organized (under appropriate state pressure) by individual craftsmen and supply and marketing groups. At the beginning these cooperatives were responsible only for

---

[100] Hsueh Mu-ch'iao, et al., *op. cit.*, p. 147.
[101] Hsueh Mu-ch'iao, et al., *op. cit.*, p. 141.
[102] *Ibid.*, p. 149.

obtaining raw materials and marketing products, leaving the production process alone. "The members contributed shares, but retained ownership of their tools and equipment. As production expanded and the collective consciousness of the members was raised, certain processes of production became centralized. . . . Thus a simple supply and marketing cooperative gradually turned into one for production."[103] In 1955-56 (see Chapter 5) this gradualness completely broke down. Whereas in 1955, 73.1 percent of craftsmen were classified as being "individual handicraftsmen" (a category, which it will be remembered, covered private individual handicrafts, supply and marketing groups, and supply and marketing cooperatives), a year later the percentage of craftsmen in that category dropped to 8.3.[104] The supply and marketing cooperative was entitled to make deductions from its profits and buy common means of production. A part of the means of production owned by the members could also be turned into common property. Membership was open not only to the head of the family, but to family helpers, apprentices, journeymen and assistants.

The *handicraft producers' cooperatives.* These were full socialist handicraft enterprises based on the collective ownership of the means of production and collective labor of their members either in central workshops or in members' homes. Management was unified as was the calculation of profits and losses. The cooperatives' capital funds came from membership shares, accumulation (including membership fees), depreciation reserves, and special reserves (cultural, educational reserve funds, reserves for awards and public welfare), and loans from the People's Bank. The income of the cooperatives, net of deductions for taxes, accumulation, depreciation, and special reserves was distributed to the members in the form of wages and work bonuses on the principle of "to each according to his work" (i.e., on a piecework basis). In the case of peasant craftsmen who spent part of their working week in agricultural tasks of their collective farm and another part in handicraft pursuits within the handicraft producers' cooperative, the system of remuneration was somewhat more complex, involving the commutation of labor for cash. Since this system was revived in the period 1961-65 after a lapse of two or three years, it will be described in Chapter 9. Handicraft producers' cooperatives

---

[103] Hsueh Mu-ch'iao et al., p. 149. A description of such a cooperative in Shanghai is given in *FEER* (December 6, 1962), p. 512: "Many shops have their interior walls removed and one large shop made from several small ones. Large groups of workers work in the enlarged shop as they would in a factory, every man concentrating on his particular job, while others attend to administrative affairs, interview customers, obtain the materials needed for work, keep accounts, etc."

[104] *Ten Great Years*, p. 36.

were regarded by the communists as a stage in the transition to "ownership by the whole people." From 1949 to 1957 this was understood to mean state ownership (i.e., state-owned handicraft factories). For a time, during the Great Leap Forward of 1958-60 (Chapter 8), it also came to mean ownership by the rural or urban people's communes.

An intermediate step in the development of the producers' co-operatives has also been mentioned by the communists. This was the elementary handicraft producers' cooperative in which private means of production were rented to the cooperative or pooled for its common use as shares. The cooperative paid dividends or rent to the members out of its income according to the amount of the means of production put to common use. "But unlike the land-owning peasants working on their own, the independent handicraftsmen depended mainly on the skill of their hands for their living. The means of production they owned were comparatively simple. It was, therefore, easier to turn them into common property than it had been with the peasants. This explains the reason why this elementary form of cooperative did not develop extensively during the socialist transformation of handicrafts."[105]

The final step was the transformation of handicraft producers' cooperatives into *state owned factories*. This transition was originally scheduled to take place in the distant future—that is, after a substantial technical development of the producers' cooperatives. In fact, during the Great Leap Forward (see Chapter 8) many handicraft producers' cooperatives were turned into factories "owned by the whole people"—owned by local state authorities or the people's communes,

TABLE 3-11

Gross Value Output of Handicraft Cooperatives and Individual
Handicrafts at 1952 Prices

Year	Grand Total (millions of yuan)	Handicraft Cooperatives (thousands of yuan)				Individual Handicrafts (thousands of yuan)
		Total	Producers' Co-ops	Supply and Marketing Co-ops	Production Teams	
1949	3,237	15,000	15,000			3,222,000
1950	5,062	40,000	40,000			5,022,000
1951	6,141	134,360	134,360			6,006,640
1952	7,312	255,140	246,405	7,406	1,326	7,056,860

Source: Reprinted from Nai-Ruenn Chen, *Chinese Economic Statistics* (Chicago: Aldine, 1967). Copyright © 1967 by the Social Science Research Council, p. 233, Table 4.59.

[105] Hsueh Mu-ch'iao et al., *op. cit.*

or into cooperative factories nominally under the Federation of Handicraft Cooperatives.

The growth of the handicraft cooperative sector may be seen from Tables 3-11 and 3-12.

TABLE 3-12
Number of Persons Engaged in Handicrafts (by Form of Ownership)*

Year	Total	Cooperative Handicrafts† (thousands)	Individual Handicrafts (thousands)	Percentage Cooperative Handicrafts†	Percentage Individual Handicrafts
1949		89			
1952	7,364	228	7,136	3.1	96.9

*Part-time peasant craftsmen not included.
†Handicraft producers' cooperatives, supply and marketing groups, and supply and marketing cooperatives.
Sources: Ten Great Years, p. 36; *NCNA*, Peking, December 16, 1957.

3. Restriction and Gradual Liquidation of the Private Sector (National Capital) in Industry and Trade

We have already dealt with some of the ways in which private industry and commerce were restricted by the communists in 1949-52 while being used to spur the process of reconstruction. The pace of restriction was stepped up in 1951 and 1952 in the course of two terror campaigns: the so-called "Three-Anti" and "Five-Anti" mass movements. Restriction, it should be remembered, was always related to the concurrent expansion of the state and cooperative sectors. The Three-Anti and Five-Anti campaigns were similarly related to the campaign against counterrevolutionaries discussed under the heading "Political Reform." (See below, pp. 95-97).

It seems that the unleashing of the Anti campaigns is explainable in four ways. First, it is likely that the more radical faction within the leadership had by the end of 1950 prevailed, if only for a while, over the more pragmatic group. The state of war in which China found herself at that time may help explain the more militant tone of the collective leadership and the upper hand which the radicals gained in the councils of Party and state. Second, the state's need for supplies during the Korean conflict helped transform the domestic market into one favorable to the sellers of goods and services. As a result there was a revival of what the communists described as "capitalist tendencies," particularly in industry and trade, accompanied by price instability. With a costly war on its hands, the communist leadership found it increasingly difficult to apply effective economic restraints on individual market activities and therefore resorted to strong-arm police methods. Third, by 1951 the communists felt that their political position was sufficiently entrenched to permit them to deal harshly with capitalist tendencies without running an undue risk of nationwide revolt. Fourth, the campaigns may be seen as a particularly ruthless and thorough housecleaning operation in preparation for a new central planning era which the communists proposed to inaugurate in 1953.

Having transformed the capitalist "base" of society, the communists proceeded to remold the capitalists' "superstructure" of ideas. The "Three-Anti" movement (*su fan*) was launched in northeast China in August 1951 and extended to the whole country by December. The targets of the campaign were corruption, waste, and bureaucratism, provincial regionalism included. The basic assumption was that the bourgeoisie was at the origin of these failings, and consequently this class became the object of organized mass wrath. The Three-Anti movement soon merged with the Ideological Remolding Campaign (see pp. 88-90) sweeping through the universities. The Five-Anti movement (*wu fan*) began in earnest in January 1952 and was directed against the "Five Evils" of bribery, tax evasion, cheating on government contracts, theft of state property, and theft of economic information from government sources for speculative purposes. The principal targets were the bureaucrats on the one hand and private industrialists and merchants on the other. The ground for this reign of terror was laid in the course of 1951 by the campaign against counterrevolutionaries, the Three-Anti movement, and the campaign for ideological remolding. The atmosphere was thick with fear. Within days of the launching of the Five-Anti campaign, tens of thousands of breast-beating victims appeared as if by magic. The head of China's secret police, for example, announced on January 16 that 80 percent of his administrative personnel were corrupt in various degrees.[106] There were "little graft-ridden tigers" (who had allegedly misappropriated less than $50 each), "medium tigers" and "big tigers." The tiger hunt involved the use of a sliding scale of penalties from "residence under the supervision of the masses" to summary execution.[107] Names of picked victims were blared out over public address systems ordering the accused to report immediately to prescribed "confession centers." Special post office boxes were opened in the larger cities for use by informers ("collection of data from the masses") to protect those who denounced others "from revenge and intimidation."[108] At a mass meeting in Tientsin, broadcast by radio

[106] *New York Times* (February 4, 1952), p. 3, quoting *Jen-min Jih-pao* of January 17, 1952.
[107] *New York Times*, March 15, 1952, p. 2, and January 2, 1952, p. 2.
[108] *Ibid.*, January 6, 1952, p. 5.

to an estimated one million listeners, 34,000 persons confessed to corruption and waste or denounced others for these crimes. In Peking, on the same day, six officials were denounced by their wives before a huge crowd sitting in judgment over the victims.[109] In special concentration camps set up earlier in the course of the campaign against counterrevolutionaries, a general reeducation curriculum was worked out: prisoners were divided according to "senior," "intermediate," and "elementary" levels of political consciousness. The different groups were not allowed to speak to each other. Graduation from the elementary to the senior level, and eventually to supervised residence could be achieved by showing oneself to be "progressive." Those who did not make it were shot or sent to stricter "labor reeducation" camps. In a camp near Mukden in Manchuria, 14,000 prisoners wearing on their backs a number and the yellow characters *Tze Hsin Jen* ("reeducated man") were subjected to this routine combined with hard labor. Suicides were a daily occurrence. Heavy fines were levied on most private businesses following inspections carried out by cadres. In Peking, for instance, investigating teams found that 40,000 out of the 50,000 private enterprises were guilty of breaking the law, which, incidentally, was not formally promulgated until April 1952.[110] In the so-called Greater Northern Wilderness (northeast China) where temperatures in winter go down to - 45 degrees Centigrade, labor reform farms called *Hsin Kai Ho* or "New Life Farms" were set up side by side with military reclamation farms and projects run by army production and construction corps. In 1960 the total population of this region was estimated at 300,000 people, one-third of them soldiers or ex-servicemen (including veterans of the Korean War), the rest political prisoners. A former prisoner, a cadre with a sixteen-year Party membership, sentenced to six years of labor remolding for rightist deviations in 1957, testified that in 1955 he was sent to interrogate 93 prisoners in the Northern Wilderness. He could see only 19, all of them under forty years of age. The others were listed as having perished.[111]

All "this gave the capitalists a profound education in patriotism and the observance of law. They learned to know through practical experience the tremendous strength of the working class. . . . Changes in class alignments in the country brought about the

[109] *Ibid.*, February 1, 1952, p. 2.

[110] *New York Times*, March 4, 1951, p. 8, January 15, 1952, p. 4, and March 7, 1952, p. 2. For the text of the "Statute on Penalties for Corruption," see Blaustein, *op. cit.*, pp. 227-233. (Cf. Chapter 1, "A Note on Chinese Law.")

[111] Tang Chuan-hsin, "Labor Reform Farms in the Greater Northern Wilderness Are Hell on Earth," *Kung Sheung Daily News* (Hong Kong), October 1, 1964, p. 12. Cf. "Police-Security-Forced Labor: The Collapse of a System," *China News Analysis*, No. 742 (January 31, 1969).

emergence of a group of progressives among the capitalists. These progressives expressed their readiness to accept socialist remolding."[112] The progressives marched through the streets of Shanghai and other cities, banging away at gongs and cymbals, shouting with unalloyed joy, petitioning the people's power to let them be absorbed by the state sector, or, at the very least, to become advanced state capitalists.[113]

FISCAL AND MONETARY REFORM

More than Chiang Kai-shek's demoralized armies, dissident warlords, bandits, real and imagined class enemies, saboteurs, and counterrevolutionaries, hyperinflation was in 1949 the obstacle to the restoration of economic order. According to Chou En-lai, writing a decade later, "in the twelve years from the outbreak of the anti-Japanese war in July 1937 to May 1949, the volume of currency issued by the reactionary Kuomintang government increased over 140,000 million times, while commodity prices rose over 8,-500,000 million times."[114] In the first three weeks of October 1947, the wholesale commodity price index in Shanghai rose from 74,367 to 108,357 (1931=1).[115] Monthly interest rates on loans to Shanghai merchants rose from 24-30 percent in June 1949 to 70-80 percent in December.[116] Inflation aggravated the sense of insecurity and further alienated the people from their government. One of the first steps which the communists had to take was to stabilize the currency, and to this they gave at once their undivided attention.

[112] Hsueh Mu-ch'iao et al., *op. cit.*, pp. 229-230. "Never treat a person as if he were worse than dog's excreta one moment and regard him as worth ten thousand ounces of gold the next. The intellectuals cannot stomach the ice cold, nor can they swallow the piping hot." Professor T'an Ch'i-hsiang, Department of History, Futan University, *Kuang Ming Daily* (May 11, 1957), quoted in Roderick MacFarquhar, *op. cit.*, p. 66.

[113] As has been pointed out in the Introduction, the genuineness and sincerity of yesmanship among even the "progressives" is difficult to determine. Surely, there was fear and outward conformity. There was no alternative to submission. Suspicious and uneasily aware of the duality of the citizens' public and private face, the Party went over the same ground again and again. More than other communists, the Chinese wanted not just a planned economy, but planned thought, and felt that they were missing out on the latter. If it is true that the people feared the Party's anger, it is equally certain that the Party feared the people's thoughts: the "redness" of the people's words and the suspected "whiteness" of their minds. On May 29, 1968, sixteen years after the first round of remolding, the *Honan Province Daily* complained that some officials "ostensibly obey but inwardly defy, say one thing and mean another. They say nice things to your face, engage in nasty business behind your back."

[114] Chou En-lai, *A Great Decade* (Peking: FLP, 1959), p. 2.

[115] A. Doak Barnett, *China on the Eve of Communist Takeover* (New York: Praeger, 1963), p. 20.

[116] Alexander Eckstein, *Communist China's Economic Growth and Foreign Trade* (New York: McGraw-Hill, 1966), p. 27.

The basic reason for the inflation was the Nationalist government's sizeable budgetary deficit (caused by rising war expenditures and a narrowing tax base as the territory under the government's control shrank day by day)[117] financed by resort to the printing press. Subsidiary reasons were corruption in the state apparatus and wrong-headed economics. Chiang's economists believed prices to be cost-determined. Since interest rates were considered to be an important component of production costs, the attempt was made to stall price increases by pegging interest rates charged by banks at a low level, a policy which, of course, had the opposite effect from that intended. The banks found themselves unable to attract any voluntary savings. For their lending operations they made recourse to the central bank of issue, which allotted to them their quota funds out of the press.[118] Note issue in November 1947 was estimated at CNC $40 billion per day.[119]

Hyperinflation is the supreme expression of a people's loss of confidence in the economic system and the authority behind it. The restoration of confidence is a complex problem, but it does involve at least three things: (1) establishment of fiscal order (i.e., putting the government's expenditures and income in order), (2) setting up controls over the banking system, and (3) reactivation of commodity markets.

1. FISCAL ORDER[120]

Restoration of fiscal stability meant, in the circumstances, the balancing of governmental revenues and expenditures. This was done by the end of 1951 through an initial (early 1950) reduction in governmental disbursements, reorganization of the tax system[121] and centralization of fiscal powers. These measures were aided by the

---

[117] According to Barnett, *loc. cit.*, p. 260, the 1947 budget of the Sinkiang Province government was CNC $49 billion, of which only CNC $18 billion was covered by current income from taxes. The balance was made good by a central government subsidy, most of which came from the printers. See also Chang Kia-ngau, *The Inflationary Spiral: The Experience in China 1939-1950* (New York: Wiley, 1958); Chou Shun-hsin, *The Chinese Inflation, 1937-1949* (New York: Columbia U.P., 1963); Arthur N. Young, *China's Wartime Finance and Inflation* (Cambridge, Mass.: Harvard U.P., 1965).

[118] See S. C. Tsiang, "Money and Banking in Communist China," in *An Economic Profile of Mainland China, op. cit.*, Vol. 1, p. 325. How much voluntary saving could be extracted from a disintegrating and impoverished economy (high interest rates or not) is another question.

[119] A. Doak Barnett, *op. cit.*, p. 20.

[120] An interesting account of China's fiscal policy (1950-54) may be found in E. F. Szczepanik, "Four Years of Fiscal Policy in Communist China," *Contemporary China*, I, 1955, *op. cit.*, pp. 68-82.

[121] Before 1949 China's peasants were subjected to about 200 taxes of various kinds.

extension of communist political control over the whole mainland and the cessation of civil war. The sharp increase in governmental expenditures brought about by China's entry into the Korean War (October 1950) was covered by current income and special levies directed especially against private firms which had profited from the boom.

The overall situation from 1950 through 1952 is summarized in Table 3-13.

A few comments on the items in Table 3-13 would seem to be in order.

On the revenue side the item "Taxes" includes the agricultural tax (*kung-liang*), at least part of which represented rent formerly paid to landlords and rich peasants, as well as urban taxes on enterprises, turnover commodity taxes, salt taxes, and customs duties. The importance of revenues from the agricultural tax relatively to income from the profits of state enterprises decreased between 1950 and 1952. In 1950 the agricultural tax accounted for 29.3 percent of total revenues, while income from state enterprises contributed only 13.3 percent of total revenues. In 1952 the respective shares were 15.4 percent and 32.6 percent. Taxes on private business amounted to 1,910 million yuan in 1950, 3,312 million yuan in 1951, and 3,458 million yuan in 1952, or respectively 39, 40.8, and 35.4 percent of all taxes.[122] In addition, the column "Other" almost certainly includes income from fines imposed on private enterprise, particularly during the Five-Anti campaign, in other words, a capital levy on the private sector. The item "Credits" refers in part to the issue of "People's Victory Real Unit Bonds," first launched in December 1949. These were expressed in real units (commodity basket values) consisting of a bundle of 3 kilograms of rice, 0.75 kilogram of wheat flour, 1.33 meters of white cotton muslin, and 8 kilograms of coal. The conversion rate between these commodities and the bonds was apparently calculated every ten days on the basis of the weighted average of the combined wholesale prices of the bundle commodities in six major cities.[123] The bonds (which in 1950 are known to have amounted to 260 million yuan) carried an annual interest rate of 4 percent, repayable in currency at the latest real unit conversion rate, over five years ending in 1956. The degree of voluntariness in subscribing to the bonds was minimal, especially where private traders and other bourgeois were concerned. From the very beginning the revenue side of the state budget thus served not only to contain inflation and enable the government to discharge its day-to-day func-

---

[122] Nai-Ruenn Chen (ed.), *Chinese Economic Statistics, op. cit.*, p. 441, Table 10.1. The 1951 figures for "credits" should include a 2,174-million yuan foreign (Soviet) loan, noted by another Chinese Communist source.

[123] S. C. Tsiang, *op. cit.*, p. 327.

TABLE 3-13
State Budget
(Millions of yuan)

Revenue

Year	Taxes	Percent	Income from State Enterprises	Percent	Credits and Insurance	Percent	Other	Percent	Total
1950	4,900	75.1	870	13.4	330	5.0	420	6.5	6,520
1951	8,110	62.6	3,050	23.5	570	4.4	1,230	9.5	12,960
1952	9,770	55.6	5,730	32.6	190	1.1	1,870	10.7	17,560

Expenditure

Year	Economic Construction	Percent	Social, Cultural, Educational	Percent	National Defense	Percent	Government Administration	Percent	Other	Percent	Total
1950	1,740	25.5	750	11.1	2,830	41.5	1,310	19.3	180	2.6	6,810
1951	3,510	29.5	1,340	11.3	5,060	42.5	1,750	14.7	240	2.0	11,900
1952	7,630	45.4	2,280	13.6	4,370	26.0	1,730	10.3	780	4.7	16,790

Total Revenue and Expenditure

Year	Revenue	Expenditure	Balance
1950	6,520	6,810	– 290
1951	12,960	11,900	+1,060
1952	17,560	16,790	+ 770

Source: Ten Great Years, pp. 21–24. In 1952 the state budget accounted for 27.6 percent of national income. On the reliability of the data, see Cheng Chu-yuan, Communist China's Economy, 1949–1962 (South Orange, N.J.: Seton Hall U. P., 1963), p. 182.

tions, but as a social reform weapon as well. Notice also the rapid absolute increase in income from state enterprises and its rising contribution to total revenues. This subject is discussed in greater detail in Chapter 6.

The social policy function of the budget is even clearer from the expenditures side. As the size of the budget grew both absolutely and relatively to national income, state finance was increasingly used to give shape to the new economy. Thus outlays on "economic construction" (i.e., on building a command-type economy) rose from 25.5 percent of total state expenditures in 1950 to 45.4 percent in 1952. The Korean War does not seem to have significantly interrupted this trend, except perhaps in late 1950 and the first few months of 1951. State investment was about 4 percent of the gross national product in 1950, rising to about 12 percent in 1952. Note that the increase of 2,230 million yuan in outlays on national defense between 1950 and 1951 (caused by the Korean emergency) was matched almost exactly by a 2,212-million yuan rise in revenue from taxes on private enterprise and in the yield of the item labeled "Other" (i.e., mostly fines on private business). Among the structural changes operated during this time was the readjustment of the ratio of output of capital to consumer goods. In 1949 capital goods accounted for 26.6 percent of the gross value of industrial output and consumer goods for 73.4 percent. In 1952 the respective shares were 35.6 and 64.4 percent.

The successful execution of the anti-inflationary fiscal policy was due in no small measure to the effective centralization of key fiscal management functions formerly delegated to local authorities.

2. CONTROLS OVER THE BANKING SYSTEM

Centralization meant not only the vesting of control over governmental revenue and expenditure in the state treasury, but tighter control and eventual liquidation of China's 450 odd major private banks. This was done in five main steps.[124]

(a) The establishment in 1948 in the communist-controlled areas of the People's Bank of China (central bank) through the merger of previously created communist government banks, and the extension of its authority to the whole country in 1949.[125] Government funds previously deposited with the private banking system were withdrawn and placed under the control of the People's Bank. The result

[124] For an excellent analysis of these steps, see Cheng Chu-yuan, *op. cit.*, pp. 62-64, and his *Monetary Affairs of Communist China* (Hong Kong: URI, 1954).

[125] The People's Bank of China replaced the Nationalist Central Bank, but its powers and range of duties were much wider than those of its predecessor.

of this operation was the disappearance within six months of about half the then existing private banking institutions.

(b) Private banks owned by "bureaucrat capital" (family members of the former Nationalist regime) and by foreigners were confiscated.

(c) The remaining private banks were then ordered to substantially increase their capitalization. Many were unable to do this, and went out of business.

(d) The survivors were then ordered to merge into five groups, each under a unified administration, most members of which were appointed by the People's Bank.

(e) Finally, in November 1952 the five groups were merged into a single unit, most of the directors of which were again appointed by the People's Bank. As of that date, private banking in China ceased to exist for all practical purposes.

The institutional centralization of the banking system was accompanied by measures intended to attract voluntary savings and so hopefully mop up a part of the purchasing power in the hands of private persons. This was done in two steps.[126]

(a) In the latter part of 1949, government banks were authorized to open "real goods savings deposits," which, like the real unit bonds already discussed, consisted of a basket of staple commodities. As in the case of bonds, the conversion rate between the money value of the deposits and the equivalent commodities was calculated every ten days on the basis of the goods' wholesale prices, and withdrawals in cash were valued according to the latest real unit conversion rate. Apparently the combined impact of the real unit savings, real unit bonds, and fiscal restraint was to severely contract the currency in circulation. By March 1950 the rise in the general price level was stopped. In fact, wholesale prices began to fall sharply, threatening a decline in general prices, and a shrinking of voluntary savings calculated on the basis of wholesale commodity prices. This could have had serious repercussions on the commodity markets, at that time still imperfectly controlled by the government.

(b) The threat of deflationary pressures was countered in May 1950 by the institution of "double guarantee savings deposits." The DGS deposits' cash value was to go up if the composite price of the commodities in terms of which the cash value was expressed went

---

[126] See S. C. Tsiang, *op. cit.*, pp. 326-329. On the economics of mopping up purchasing power through savings deposits, see *ibid.*, pp. 328-329. Professor Tsiang ascribes the communists' desire to attract savings to an exaggerated importance which they attached to the store of value function of money. This may be so, but perhaps more than this, the communists viewed money in the hands of private persons as a potentially dangerous aspect of *political* countervailing power eluding central control.

up; if, however, the composite commodity price went down, the cash value of the deposits was to remain at its original level. The depositors were in this way protected against (both inflationary and deflationary) adverse effects on the money value of their savings.[127]

3. REACTIVATION OF COMMODITY MARKETS

In the absence of extensive physical controls over production and distribution, the communists during this period relied heavily on market incentives to reactivate the production and exchange of agricultural and industrial goods. A key element was price stabilization, the achievement of which depended to a very large extent on the restoration of fiscal and monetary order, i.e., (1) and (2) above. Many of the steps taken to put order into commodity markets have been dealt with in the sections on Land Reform and Industrial-Commercial Reform (pp. 49-52 and 60-79). To this pciture one need only add the rebuilding of the country's transportation system, the economic importance of which was equalled by its political function as a unifier, and by its military significance. Communist sources reveal a determined effort carried out by the army, prison labor, and conscripted peasant labor to repair and extend the transportation network (Table 3-14).

TABLE 3-14
Transportation

	1949	1952
Length of railways (kilometers)	21,989	24,518
Length of highways (kilometers)	80,768	126,675
Civil air routes (kilometers)	—	13,123
Total goods carried (thousands of tons)	67,130	168,590
Total freight turnover (millions of ton-kilometers)	22,980	71,540
Passengers carried (thousands of persons)	134,940	240,350
Total length of postal routes (thousands of kilometers)	748	1,290

Source: Ten Great Years, pp. 144, 146, 148, 150, 157. See also Yuan Li-wu, *The Spatial Economy of Communist China* (New York: Praeger, 1967).

There can be little doubt that the objectives which the communists set out to attain were, in fact, achieved in a surprisingly brief span of time. Money interest rates for loans authorized by the People's Bank declined from 65.5 percent per month in December

[127]It should be added that severe penalties were meted out for "undermining the State monetary system." See "Provisional Statute on Penalties for Undermining the State Monetary System" (adopted by the State Administrative Council, April 19, 1951), in Blaustein, *op. cit.*, pp. 233-236.

1949 to 2 percent per month in June 1951.[128]   The stabilization of the price level can be seen from Table 3-15.

TABLE 3-15
Price Indices

	1950	1951	1952
Wholesale price (1950 = 100)	100	117.9	118.1
Wholesale price (March 1950 = 100)		92.4	92.6
Retail price in eight big cities (1950 = 100) . . .	100	111.9	112.9
Retail price in eight big cities (March 1950 = 100)			
Two sets of communist data available		94.6	93.7
		88.0	88.8
Industrial products sold in rural areas			
(1950 = 100)	100	110.2	109.7

Source: Reprinted from Nai-Ruenn Chen, *Chinese Economic Statistics* (Chicago: Aldine, 1967). Copyright © 1967 by the Social Science Research Council, p. 409, Table 8.1.

SOCIAL REFORM

MARRIAGE LAW

On May 1, 1950, the communist government promulgated its Marriage Law,[129] thus fulfilling an old promise. The intent of the measure was to sweep away ancient customs whereby marriages were arranged between families, a ceremonial price being paid before the ceremony by the bridegroom's family to the family of the bride. The law stipulated freedom of marriage for both men and women (i.e., free consent of both partners)[130] freedom to divorce,[131] and equal

[128] S. C. Tsiang, *op. cit.*, p. 329. See also Ronald Hsia, *Price Control in Communist China* (New York: Institute of Pacific Relations, 1953); Hsin Ying, *The Price Problems of Communist China* (Hong Kong: URI, 1954).

[129] *The Marriage Law of the People's Republic of China* (Peking: FLP, 1950, 1951, 1953). See also W. W. Rostow et al., *The Prospects for Communist China* (Cambridge, Mass. and New York: The Technology Press, M.I.T., Wiley, 1954), p. 159. For a discussion of the newness and legal substance of the measure, see Vermier Y. Chiu, "Marriage Laws of the Ch'ing Dynasty, the Republic of China, and Communist China," in *Contemporary China* (Hong Kong: Hong Kong U. P., 1958), Vol. II, pp. 64-72, and S. L. Fu, "The New Marriage Law of Communist China," *ibid.*, Vol. I, pp. 115-138. Also M. J. Meijer, "Early Communist Marriage Legislation in China" [1931-50], *Contemporary China, 1962-1964, op. cit.*, [1965], pp. 84-102. Cf. the decree on marriage promulgated by the communist government of the Chinese Soviet Republic (Dec. 1, 1931), in Stuart R. Schram, *The Political Thought of Mao Tse-tung* (New York: Praeger, 1963), pp. 228-229.

[130] What the law did not say but what in fact restricted in practice the declared freedom of marriage was that before issuing a marriage certificate, the local government registry demanded recommendations from labor and other organizations at the partners' respective places of work or from residents' associations in the partners' place of residence. Cf. Chapter 9 below.

[131] For an eyewitness account of a divorce trial, see Felix Greene, *The Wall Has Two Sides* (London: Jonathan Cape, 1961), pp. 190-200.

rights for both sexes, prohibited payment of the traditional "body price," bigamy, concubinage, child betrothal, and interference with the remarriage of widows, and spelled out the rights of women, children, and children born out of wedlock. The statutory marriagable age was set at 20 for men and 18 for women (but cf. Chapter 9). Marriages had to be registered with the local government, which was empowered to issue marriage certificates attesting to the legality of the union. Marriage was forbidden in cases of lineal relatives by blood, sexual impotence, venereal disease, mental disorder, leprosy, or any other disease regarded by medical science as rendering a person unfit for marriage.

The measure apparently found slow acceptance in the countryside. For all its positive features, it tended to weaken the cohesion of the traditional family in which marriages were arranged largely on economic grounds. A more extensive adoption of the new procedure had to await the more pervasive change in the kinship structure operated by the introduction of collective farms and rural people's communes (1956-58).[132] Some of the more spectacularly repellent practices which the law set out to abolish, had fallen into desuetude long before the communists took power.

The law was soon to be interpreted in socialist terms. "We workers," wrote *Jen-min Jih-pao* some years later, "get married to promote social development for the benefit of socialist construction. . . . The partners must encourage each other to become builders of socialism. . . . A sincere love does not found itself on high position, or a high salary, or on physical beauty, but rather on a fervent love for socialist enterprise."[133]

EDUCATION

It is often said that one of the more remarkable achievements of communism has been its insistence on universal education, the sending of the whole nation to school, or as the economists like to put it, the formation of human capital on an impressive scale.[134] The statement contains an important truth, but at the same time requires careful hedging. The formation of human capital has two aspects: the training of skills needed by the labor force to raise productivity and promote economic growth, and the infusion of knowledge in order to encourage cultural awareness in the widest sense of that term. The

[132] C. K. Yang, *Chinese Communist Society: The Family and the Village* (Cambridge, Mass.: M.I.T. Press, 1959).

[133] Cited by *FEER* (April 26, 1962), p. 173. On the status of women in Communist China see *URS*, Vol. 40, No. 20 (September 7, 1965), and *ibid.*, Vol. 43, No. 2 (April 5, 1966).

[134] E.g., Isaac Deutscher, *Stalin: A Political Biography* (New York: Vintage, 1960), pp. xii, 337ff.

communists tackled both problems, but their approach to the second differed fundamentally from their attitude toward the first. In technical and scientific education they have as a rule allowed considerable latitude for the exercise of the individual's critical faculties (although here exceptions were not infrequent). On the other hand, in nontechnical, nonhard science areas, they insisted on strict adherence to Party dogma and allowed only a bare minimum of self-expression. One could exercise one's ingenuity in the making of ball bearings but not in political philosophy, history, the arts, and other liberal pursuits. This dual approach to education contains, it would seem, a contradiction which today is causing considerable embarrassment to communist regimes in the Soviet Union and Eastern Europe. The mind once awakened cannot easily be separated into two airtight compartments, one critical, the other passive, uncritical, and submissive. If you train a worker to be discriminating about the product he makes, sooner or later he will be tempted to ask awkward questions about his social, political, and cultural environment.[135] Even Stalin, the greatest practitioner of this type of educational dialectics, shrewdly noted the contradiction, although he believed that it applied only to presocialist regimes. ". . . Nothing could be more dangerous to tyrannical authority," he wrote, "than the people's curiosity."[136] The critical faculty cannot long be confined within artificial barriers: there is a spillover effect here, which the communists have vastly underrated, and the direction of the spill is from free toward chained thought. In time, the shackles of dogma are eroded by the very minds that the dogmatists have been at such pains to cultivate.

On coming to power, the Chinese Communists addressed themselves at once to the task of reforming and restructuring the country's educational system. Two periods may be distinguished: a relatively mild phase from 1949 through 1950, and a harsh one from 1951 through 1952.

In the first period the major task was the political reeducation of teachers, students, technicians, scientists, officials, and the masses. This took three main forms: (a) mass study (*hsueh-hsi*) in which literally everyone had to join in for one or two hours a day, (b) political classes in schools, for teachers, supervisors, students, janitors, cooks, and bottle washers, and (c) "revolutionary universities" the curriculum of which consisted exclusively of ideological and political

---

[135] See Jan S. Prybyla, "Moscow, Mao, and the Cultural Revolution," *International Review of History and Political Science* (February 1968).

[136] J. Stalin, *Sochinenya* (Moscow, 1946), Vol. I, pp. 26-27. But look up Aleksandr I. Solzhenitsyn's account of how this principle was applied, in his novel, *The First Circle* (New York: Harper, 1968).

indoctrination.[137]   The process known collectively as *cheng feng* (ideological remolding plus large-scale purge) was put under the direction of cadres usually working through mass organizations (the Youth League, labor unions, joint faculty-staff committees, the Union of Educational Workers, etc.). The job was done thoroughly. Its objective was to probe the individual's innermost thoughts, to lay bare his soul, leaving no nook or cranny of privacy unexplored,[138] to dredge up past errors and judge them by present rules of Marxist logic, to make a man write a confession, submit it to the group, rewrite it again and again, and then again, incriminate himself before the group, admit his waywardness, be criticized, praised for his application or spurned for his laxity. Party pressure was brought to bear on the group; group pressure was exerted on the individual until he became a whimpering caricature of his former self, indistinguishable from all the other nameless atoms of the mass. Fear and a sense of intellectual guilt played a part in this process of soul-plowing. Many intellectuals had become alienated from the Kuomintang and accepted the communists as the bearers of a promise to restore order, dignity, and prestige to China. At first, no doubt, some of them accepted the communist rectification of their thoughts as something necessary, perhaps even long overdue. Before three years were out, they were in for a rude awakening.

In the second period (1951-52) the squeeze on the intellectuals became tighter, the methods used to make sure of their ideological purity and political allegiance more savage. Confessions were given wide publicity, hysterical struggle meetings became more numerous and frequent, a "reformative study" campaign was launched in 1951 and applied first to university instructors, then to lower-school teachers, village schoolmasters, writers, artists, lawyers, physicians, and research scientists. Many were sent to labor reeducation camps to be

[137] For a good description of the process see Theodore H. E. Chen, *op. cit.*, pp. 12-19. A useful general source is Stewart Fraser (ed.), *Chinese Communist Education: Records of the First Decade* (Nashville, Tenn.: Vanderbilt U. P., 1965). See also Edward Hunter, *Brainwashing in Red China* (New York: Vanguard, 1953), and A. Doak Barnett, *Communist China: The Early Years* (New York: Praeger, 1966), pp. 125-134. The Chinese Communist version can be found in the following: Liu Shih, "China's New Educational System," *People's China*, Vol. IV, No. 11 (December 1951), pp. 5-8; Kuo Mo-jo, *Culture and Education in New China* (Peking: FLP, 1950), and Lu Ting-yi, "Education and Culture in New China," *People's China*, Vol. I, No. 8 (April 16, 1950). Cf. James D. Seymour, *Chinese Communist Policies Toward China's Intellectuals and Professionals*, Ph.D. dissertation, Columbia University, 1967.

[138] The problem should be seen in the perspective of Chinese history. Personal privacy has never been highly prized. Individuality tended to be familial, the family being held accountable for the actions of its individual members, each member's behavior having repercussions on the whole family group. The idea of personal privacy is hardly conveyed by the Chinese language.

reformed by sullying their hands with human and animal excrement. The anti-intellectual strain characteristic of an important segment of the communist regime brutally asserted itself for the first (but not the last) time. The stepped-up remolding campaign could perhaps be traced to three phenomena: the shift in the balance of power within the leadership from moderates to radicals, the national emergency psychosis created by the Korean War (violent anti-Americanism was an important part of the remolding campaign), and a feeling that the initial "mild" phase had broken the spirit of rebellion and that the time had, therefore, come for stronger methods to be used in preparation for the first long-range economic construction plan in which right-thinking intellectuals were to play a crucial part.

On October 1, 1951 the government promulgated a reform of the school system, modelled very largely on Soviet experience. Preference was given to the admission of children of poor peasant and worker origin, and emphasis was put on elementary education and applied industrial arts (technical training). In 1952, 80 percent of primary school pupils were of proletarian extraction, almost 60 percent in secondary schools, and 20.5 percent in universities. In the same year applied industrial arts courses accounted for 34 percent of total enrollment (about 19 percent in 1946 under the Nationalists.)[139] Lectures and discussion groups on Marxism-Leninism, Mao Tse-tung's thought, the Party, and current events as seen from the Party's standpoint, formed an important part of school curricula at all levels.

During 1951 private schools and universities were nationalized and their faculties merged with existing state institutions. With the usual warning about reliability, and bearing in mind that in modern China truth has its class nature, the following communist figures may be of interest. (Note the emphasis on elementary education, applied arts, class origin, and the education of women. See Table 3-16.)

Beneath the deceptively smooth process of educational reform, there was much controversy. When in 1967 Liu Shao-ch'i and others were accused of counterrevolutionary activities, the drama played out in Party couloirs during 1949-52 was brought into public view by

[139] Liao Kai-lung, *op cit.*, pp. 168-169. In secondary schools the percentage was 38. On the Soviet educational system, see Nicholas de Witt, *Education and Professional Manpower in the USSR* (Washington, D.C.: National Science Foundation, 1961); George Z. F. Bereday and Jaan Pennar (eds.), *The Politics of Soviet Education* (New York: Praeger, 1960); William K. Medlin, Clarence B. Lindquist, Marshall L. Schmitt, *Soviet Education Programs* (Washington, D.C.: U.S. Department of Health, Education and Welfare, Government Printing Office, 1962). On the communist-sponsored shift toward technical education, see Elton Atwater, Kent Forster, Jan S. Prybyla, *World Tensions: Conflict and Accommodation* (New York: Appleton, 1967), p. 201.

TABLE 3-16
Educational Measures

	Pre-1949 peak	1949	1952
Number of enrolled students (millions):*			
Primary schools	23.7	24.4	51.1
Middle schools	1.5	1.0	2.5
Technical middle schools	0.4	0.2	0.6
Institutes of higher learning	0.2	0.1	0.2
Number of graduates (millions):*			
Primary schools.	4.6	2.4	5.9
Middle schools	0.3	0.3	0.2
Technical middle schools	0.07	0.07	0.07
Institutes of higher learning.	0.03	0.02	0.03
Number of graduates from institutes of higher learning (thousands)†			
Engineering	4.8	4.8	10.2
Agriculture	2.1	1.7	2.4
Economics and finance	3.0	3.1	7.3
Medicine	1.2	1.3	2.6
Natural sciences	1.7	1.6	2.2
Pedagogy	3.3	1.9	3.1
Liberal arts	2.7	2.5	1.7
Newly literate persons (millions)*		0.7	0.7
Students of worker and peasant origin (percentage of total in each category):			
Middle schools			56.1
Technical middle schools			57.1
Institutes of higher learning.			20.5
Female students (percentage of total in each category):			
Primary schools	25.5		32.9
Middle schools	20.0		23.5
Technical middle schools	21.1		24.9
Institutes of higher learning.	17.8	19.8	23.4
Kindergartens‡			
Number (thousands)	1.3	1.8	6.5
Children in kindergartens (thousands) . . .	130	140	424

*Rounded to the nearest hundred thousand.
†Rounded to the nearest hundred.
‡ The figures in the 1949 column refer to 1950.
Source: Ten Great Years, (Peking: *FLP*, 1960), pp. 192, 194, 196, 198, 200, 201, 202.

the Maoists. Liu and his associates Lu Ting-yi, Lin Feng (then Chairman of the Northeast Administrative Committee), Hsi Chung-hsun (Vice-Director of the State Council's Cultural and Education Committee), and Ch'ien Chun-jui (an official of the Ministry of Education) were accused of having tried to uphold the old system of education, transplant to China the Soviet Union's "revisionist" educational system, and oppose Mao's emphasis on politics in the schools.[140] Instead of wholeheartedly implanting on the "new liberated areas" the educational experience gained in the "old liberated areas," Liu and his group allegedly tried to save what they could of the old, prerevolutionary system. They reportedly advocated "all-out Sovieti-zation" of China's education under the slogan "transplant first, re-form later." At a cadres conference in Tientsin in 1949, Liu was quoted as having said that "for the time being it is important to study culture and technology, while politics will be studied in the future."[141]

The fantastic charges of treason made against Liu and others in 1967-68 must, of course, be seen in perspective and with due allow-ance for the eagerness of the accusers to prove their loyalty to Mao Tse-tung, while taking the opportunity to indulge themselves in per-sonal vendettas. Occasionally, Mao got a backhanded compliment. In saddling Liu with various educational crimes, the accusers compared Liu's ignoble attitude with the purity of Mao's thought on the sub-ject, which was "to use the new educational experience of the old liberated areas, absorb the useful experience of the old educational system, and make use of the experience of the Soviet Union."[142] In fact, anything at all that Liu did before 1966 (or failed to do, for that matter) could be interpreted as anti-Mao in the climate of the Cultural Revolution (see Chapters 11 and 12).

PUBLIC HEALTH AND INSURANCE

A determined effort was made in the first three years to stamp out pests and all kinds of disease carriers from the Chinese mainland. The fight against rats, flies, fleas, and mosquitoes was pressed home with a conviction matched only by the struggle against incorrect thought. The attack was massive (involving more than 120 million people), well organized, led by the cadres, and spearheaded by schoolchildren. Elementary principles of personal and social hygiene were preached to peasants and townspeople with missionary zeal. Spitting, a popular Chinese pastime, went the way of other nui-sances. Beggars, pimps, prostitutes, dope peddlers, deviants, hoboes, thieves, gangsters, highwaymen, drifters, and all the other members

[140] "Chronology of the Two-Road Struggle on the Educational Front in the Past Seventeen Years," *Chia-yu-ko-ming* (Educational Revolution), May 6, 1967, in *Chinese Education* (White Plains, N.Y.: International Arts and Sciences Press, Spring 1968), pp. 3-57.
[141] In 1953 Liu reportedly said that "in building socialism we have not one iota of experience, and must only learn from the Soviet Union." "Outline of Struggle," *URS*, Vol. 53, Nos. 7-8, *op. cit.*, p. 85.
[142] "Chronology," *op. cit.*, p. 4.

of China's thriving underworld, were tracked down, caught, made to register, lectured on man's place in the new society, released, placed under the supervision of the masses, reformed, or sent down to the fertilizer mines if unrepentant and recidivist. The drama was reenacted time and time again, now against this, now against that special target.[143] One result was that by 1952 China was by far the cleanest country in Asia.

Although the communist statistical apparatus was at the time unable to quantify with any degree of precision most of the more bulky socioeconomic variables (total population, for example), it was, we are led to believe, quite at home with the weight and number of flies and fleas fallen victim to the purge. "Available figures show," wrote one authority, "that in 1952, over 120 million rats were killed. By weight, more than two million catties' weight of flies, mosquitoes, and fleas; and by numbers, another 20,000 million of these insects were exterminated. Some 160 million tons of garbage and dirt were cleared away."[144] It is only a guess, but a good one, that much of the weighing and counting and carting away was done by intellectuals undergoing thought reform. Thus the main stress throughout this period was on eliminating the sources and carriers of disease (the "Four Evils"—rats, flies, mosquitoes, grain-eating sparrows), massive inoculations, teaching the population the elements of hygiene (even in 1952 the per capita output of soap was 0.21 kilogram, compared with 2.45 kilograms per head in a not overly clean Russia in 1927-28),[145] and on maternity and child care. Given the high incidence rate in pre-1949 China of smallpox, bubonic plague, cholera, kalazaar, and schistosomiasis, given also the high birth rate, the youthfulness of the country's population and the communists' interest in the young as the continuators of the revolution, the order of

[143] The elimination of rats and other pests has important economic implications. Rats consume a substantial portion of India's grain harvest every year. One hectare feeds 30 men and 275 rats. The Chinese estimated that the antipest campaign saved them 30 billion catties of grain. On the other hand, massive annihilation of particular insects or birds (e.g., the slaughter of Peking's sparrows), tends to upset the delicate ecological balance, and may have unexpected, adverse side effects on agricultural production. Before the war, damage from insects in China was estimated at 12 million tons of cereals per year. See Hughes H. Spurlock, "Communist China's Agriculture," *Foreign Agricultural Economic Report, No. 115* (Washington, D.C.: U.S. Department of Agriculture, Economic Research Service, October 1959). In the United States, more than 100 million rats cause damage estimated at $1 billion a year.

[144] Liao Kai-lung, *op. cit.*, p. 172. Cf. *Culture, Education and Health in China* (Peking: FLP, 1952).

[145] Alexander Eckstein, *Communist China's Economic Growth and Foreign Trade* (New York: McGraw-Hill, 1966), p. 20, Table 2-1. Cf. Chao Kang, *The Rate and Pattern of Industrial Production in Communist China* (Ann Arbor, Mich.: U. of Michigan Press, 1965), Table C-1.

priorities looks plausible. The Chinese Communists assert that after 1949 there has been not a single case of cholera, and that other diseases have been brought under control.[146] In the countryside recourse was made to the half million or so practitioners of traditional medicine, who like everyone else, had first had their thoughts cleansed.[147]

A June 1952 decree brought free medical service to 4 million state employees, out of a total civilian nonagricultural labor force of 36.8 million.[148] Probably because of the continuing shortage of qualified personnel, free medical coverage was extended only very slowly in subsequent years, reaching 6.9 million nonagricultural workers (out of 56.9 million) in 1958. Abuses of the system were reported continuously after 1952, a phenomenon not limited to China.[149] Overspending on medical services by some municipalities was apparently a serious problem traceable to the "comrades' . . . lacking in revolutionary optimism towards illness."[150] At the slightest sign of physical discomfort, persons covered by the scheme would rush to a doctor, call at clinics every day, stock up on medicines, abuse leaves of absence on the pretense of being sick, and generally take the attitude that "after all, the State will pay."[151]

Labor insurance (sickness, accident, disability, maternity, old age, death) was extended from 600,000 workers in 1949 to 3.3 million in 1952. Those covered were mainly employees of state-owned enterprises. Labor insurance schemes were administered by trade unions and financed from enterprise contributions calculated as a fixed percentage of the enterprises' total wages bill.

[146] But see Chapters 8, 11, and 12.

[147] On the meaning of Chinese traditional medicine (acupuncture, moxibustion, and other therapeutic methods) see Ruth Adams (ed.), *Contemporary China* (New York: Vintage, 1966), pp. 113-115 (article by G. L. Willcox, "Contemporary Chinese Health, Medical Practice and Philosophy"); Heinrich Wallnoefer and Anna von Rottauscher, *Chinese Folk Medicine* (New York: Crown, 1965); Ralph C. Croizier (University of Rochester) *Traditional Medicine in Modern China: Science, Nationalism and the Tensions of Cultural Change* (unpublished monograph). China reportedly exports about $1 million's worth of medicinal herbs to Hong Kong every year. *New York Times* (December 15, 1968), p. 28.

[148] *Jen-min Jih-pao*, June 28, 1952. Liu and Yeh, *op. cit.*, p. 69 put total nonagricultural employment in 1952 at 59.39 million, rising to 64.19 million by 1957.

[149] The British went through this after 1945, and so did the French. On the abuse of the French medical insurance scheme, see Prybyla, "The French Economy: Down the Up-Staircase and Into the Market," *Current History* (March 1968), pp. 135-142, 180-181.

[150] *Jen-min Jih-pao* (January 8, 1955) in *URS*, Vol. 38, No. 14 (February 16, 1965), p. 210.

[151] *Ibid.*, p. 210.

TABLE 3-17
Public Health Measures

	Pre–1949	1949	1952
Hospital beds (thousands of units)	66	84	180
Maternity hospitals (units)	81	80	98
Children's hospitals (units)	3	5	6
Health stations for women and children (units)	9	9	2,379
Permanent child care organizations (thousands)	0.1	0.3	2.7
Children under care (thousands)		13	99
Western trained doctors (thousands)* . .		41	52
Nurses (thousands)*		38	61
Midwives (thousands)*		16	22

*The figures in the 1949 column refer to the year 1950. The same source shows that from 1949 through 1952 7,707 students were graduated from medical faculties in China (p. 196). The figures in the above table show an increase of 11,000 "Western trained" doctors (i.e., trained in Western as opposed to traditional Chinese, medicine). The discrepancy (3,293 doctors) could be accounted for by returnees from abroad (this would probably be balanced out by the exodus to Taiwan and Hong Kong), and release of some doctors from the armed forces (questionable in view of the Korean War). The last possibility rests on the premise that the figures in the table refer to civilian doctors only, which is not at all certain.
Source: Ten Great Years (Peking: *FLP*, 1960), pp. 220, 221, 222.

POLITICAL REFORM

CAMPAIGN AGAINST COUNTERREVOLUTIONARIES

China's entry into the Korean War and military reverses suffered by the Chinese in Korea in 1951 led to the intensification of the hunt for spies, saboteurs, and counterrevolutionaries of all kinds in both the fields of action and ideology. On February 20, 1951 the Government Council approved a Statute on Punishment for Counterrevolutionary Activity, Article 18 of which specified that "this Statute is also applicable to counterrevolutionary crimes committed before it came into effect."[152]   Like all Chinese Communist laws, the statute was sweeping and arbitrary. There is little doubt that the outbreak of hostilities in Korea and the various reform measures undertaken by the communists encouraged domestic opposition in many quarters as well as some guerrilla activity by Nationalist groups. The regime's reaction was violent, meant to teach the people and those outside the people an object lesson in the strength and

[152] A. P. Blaustein, *op. cit.*, pp. 215-221. See also "Temporary Regulations for the Surveillance of Counterrevolutionary Elements," *ibid.*, pp. 222-226.

determination of communist power. The campaign against counter-revolutionaries merged with the drive for ideological remolding of the intellectuals and the Three-Anti and Five-Anti campaigns directed against private businessmen.[153]

According to P'eng Chen, Deputy Chairman of the government's political and law committee who presented the decree, in Kwangsi Province over 3,000 communist cadres had been killed by reactionaries organized in "underground armies." Some 40 members of peasants' associations were also allegedly murdered.[154] A gasoline dump at Whampoa containing 3,000 drums of fuel was blown up by Nationalist agents in February.[155]

The reaction was swift and merciless. Details of mass trials and executions were given daily by the Chinese press. At first, suspects (many of them no doubt innocent) were shot in groups of six, fifteen, and nineteen. Until February 15, the largest group executed at one time was officially reported as being 42. About that time, however, reports began to filter out of mass executions, including 300 persons in Swatow.[156] In Peking, 277 persons were shot following a mass trial in July.[157] Nationalist Chinese figures on the number of victims of this particular purge are subject to doubt, but it is likely that the death toll was very high, probably running into the tens of thousands.[158] The slaughter continued unabated throughout the year. In December there were signs that the method of reeducation through forced labor was gaining ground and that the focus had shifted from military to economic saboteurs (the Five-Anti Campaign).

Various estimates have been made of the total number of forced labor camp inmates in the early 1950's. No one, of course, can vouch for their accuracy since this is not the sort of arithmetic which a communist government normally makes public. One guess is 23 mil-

[153] "Since 1952, campaign has succeeded campaign, each one leaving a great wall in its wake, a wall which estranges one man from another. In such circumstances no one dares let off steam even privately in the company of intimate friends, let alone speak his mind in public. Everyone has now learnt the technique of double-talk; what one says is one thing, what one thinks is another." Hsu I-kuan, *Kuang Ming Daily* (June 5, 1957), quoted in Roderick MacFarquhar, *op. cit.*, p. 68.

[154] *New York Times*, February 23, 1951, p. 3.

[155] *Ibid.*, February 25, 1951, p. 17. Five persons were executed in connection with this act of sabotage.

[156] *Ibid.*, February 15, 1951, p. 4, quoting the Hong Kong independent paper *Wah Kiu Yat Pao* of February 14, 1951.

[157] *New York Times*, July 4, 1951, p. 4. In June 208 persons were executed at one time in Shanghai. *Ibid.*, June 5, 1951, p. 4.

[158] The Nationalist Defense Ministry charged on March 8, 1951 that in three southern provinces alone, the death toll exceeded 210,000. *New York Times*, March 9, 1951, p. 3. See also *ibid.*, April 21, 1951, p. 2.

lion people, of whom about 10 million were made to work on water conservancy projects.[159] The figure of 23 millions would represent about 3-4 percent of China's population at the time.

SECURING THE BORDERLANDS

A source of considerable concern for the new regime was the presence in China (especially along the country's borders) of ethnic groups of non-Han ("Chinese") origin. These people have in the past frequently rebelled against Chinese rule, sometimes overruning the country and implanting on it their own rulers (e.g., the Manchus). Many of them were acutely conscious of their ethnic and cultural separateness, and jealous of such autonomy as through the ages they had managed to wrest from the Chinese. Apart from the Hans, comprising about 94 percent of the population, China has some 60 nationalities, totaling about 40 million people. The most numerous among these are the Chuang (about 8 million) inhabiting the south, the Hui and the Uighur (about 4 million each), the Yi (over 3 million), and the Tibetans (under 3 million). Other nationalities ranging in numbers from 2.7 million (Miao) to about 60,000 (Tu), include the Mongols, Puyi, Koreans, Tung, Yao, Pai, Thai, Hani, Li, Lisu, Kazakh, and Kirghiz. Some of them have rich cultural traditions and a written language, others no written language of their own (e.g., the Tu, Hani, Pai, Yao, and Tung), others still, express themselves in newly created languages (e.g., Kirghiz, Lisu, Chung, Yi), while the mother tongue of some (e.g., the Manchus) is no longer used. The minority religions are Buddhism, Taoism, Lamaism, Polytheism, and remnants of Christianity.[160]

The principles of communist policy toward minority nationalities

[159] S. Swianiewicz, *Forced Labour and Economic Development: An Enquiry Into the Experience of Soviet Industrialisation* (New York: Oxford U. P., 1965), p. 285, quoting Yuan-li Wu, *An Economic Survey of Communist China*, p. 323. See also Commission Internationale Contre le Régime Concentrationnaire, *White Book on Forced Labor and Concentration Camps in the People's Republic of China*, 2 vols. (Paris, 1957-58). There is method and consistency to this madness. In October 1967 Mao Tse-tung was quoted by a Red Guard newspaper (*Chukiang Chan Pao*) as having told the Kiangsi Provincial Revolutionary Committee: "We cannot slaughter without teaching . . . We should not punish without teaching those we punish." *URS*, Vol. 50, No. 6 (January 19, 1968), p. 73.

[160] See Chiao-Min Hsieh, *China: Ageless Land and Countless People* (Princeton, N.J.: Van Nostrand, 1967), pp. 64, 74-86, 134-135; W. A. Douglas Jackson, *Russo-Chinese Borderlands* (Princeton, N.J.: Van Nostrand, 1962); C. K. Yang, *Religion in Chinese Society* (Berkeley, Cal.: University of California Press, 1967); Max Weber, *The Religion of China* (New York: Macmillan, 1964); Union Research Institute, *Sourcebook on Buddhism in Mainland China, 1949-1967* (Hong Kong: URI, 1968); Owen Lattimore, *Inner Asian Frontiers of China* (Boston: Beacon Press, 1962).

were laid down in Articles 50 through 53 of the "Common Program of the Chinese People's Political Consultative Conference" adopted in September 1949.[161] They cover such desiderata as equality, regional autonomy, and the freedom to develop dialects and languages, and to "preserve or reform" traditions, customs, and religious beliefs. Rhetoric apart, the communists did appear anxious not to ruffle the minorities too much, too early. Their principal preoccupation was to install in the various minority regions effective instruments of political and economic control and to integrate these areas in the body politic of China. This seems to have been particularly true of Sinkiang, Manchuria, and Inner Mongolia where, in times past, Soviet influence and economic penetration had been marked.[162] An important means to this end was the formation of cadres from among the national minorities. Another was the extension of the communist school system to the various so-called "autonomous regions"[163] and the carrying out of political, social, and economic reforms similar to those of the rest of China. The reforms sometimes met with stiff opposition. This was particularly true of land reform which involved the confiscation of land owned by mosques, temples, and monasteries and the lumping together of spiritual leaders with reactionary elements and superstitious practitioners. The Three-Anti and Five-Anti movements also left deep scars on some religious and national groups, especially the Taoists whose secret societies became the object of communist wrath in 1950 and 1951. The deeply religious and well-organized Moslems (Kirghiz, Kazakhs, Uighur, Hui) inhabiting Sinkiang, Kansu, Ningsia, and Tsinghai, rose in rebellion against the new regime in the spring and summer of 1952. They were savagely put down by the People's Liberation Army.[164] Chinese Christians

[161] A. P. Blaustein, op. cit., pp. 51-52.

[162] Allen S. Whiting, "Sinkiang and Sino-Soviet Relations," The China Quarterly, No. 3, 1958, pp. 32-41; P. H. M. Jones, "Sinkiang Gets to Work," FEER (March 22, 1962), pp. 654-656.

[163] By the end of June 1952, 130 national autonomous regions had been established. These corresponded in administrative status to special regions, counties, districts, and hsiang. The largest was the Chuang Autonomous Region covering about half of Kwangsi Province and one-third of the province's population. The practical meaning of autonomy should not be exaggerated. The autonomous treatment of these regions was a matter of convenience for the central government because of the special linguistic, religious, and other problems in the areas. See Jen Yu-ti, A Concise Geography of China (Peking: FLP, 1964), pp. 5-7, especially the table on pp. 6-7; P. H. M. Jones, "Land of the Kazakhs," [Sinkiang-Uighur Autonomous Region], FEER (February 28, 1963), pp. 422-423.

[164] On the Sinification of Tsinghai see P. H. M. Jones, "China Hustles Tsinghai," FEER (May 11, 1961), pp. 250-254. Also "China's Muslim Region" (with special reference to Ningsia), ibid. (September 14, 1961), pp. 492-494; "Inner Mongolia Sinicized," ibid. (November 9, 1961), pp. 299-303. Cf. Chapters 10 and 11.

and foreign missionaries after being accused of heinous crimes (including ritual murder), were decimated, remolded, or exiled in the course of a vicious campaign unleashed in 1951. In October 1950 the People's Liberation Army invaded Tibet and on September 9, 1951 entered the capital city of Lhasa.[165] The Tibetans appealed to the United Nations for help (November 5, 1950). The request to have the Tibetan question put on the agenda was made, surprisingly enough, by San Salvador. Not a single member of the General Committee of the UN supported the El Salvador proposal. The British delegate, for example, argued that the committee did not know exactly what was going on in Tibet; India expressed the hope that the problem would be solved peacefully (the Tibetan appeal spoke of Chinese attempts to incorporate Tibet "within the fold of Chinese Communism through sheer physical force"); the United States agreed with India; the Soviet Union thought the matter was an internal affair of China. The appeal was put aside. On December 8 the Tibetans called again for help "in agony and despair." The appeal was filed away at the UN. By an agreement concluded with China on May 23, 1951, the Tibetans finally surrendered.[166] The agreement, comprising seventeen points, was signed by a Tibetan goodwill delegation sent to Peking before the Chinese invasion. The emissaries were not authorized by the Dalai Lama and the Tibetan government to conclude any binding agreements, and their action, taken under duress, came as a shock to the Lhasa authorities.

After securing the country's main trade routes and settlements with some 300,000 troops, the Chinese proceeded to implement a new democratic land reform in eastern Tibet, the proximate objective of which was to crush the monasteries as centers of opposition and to eliminate the lamas as a class. Monks and Tibetan lay officials were subjected to ideological remolding by the expedient of incorporating them in press gangs, which, under the supervision of the Liberation Army, widened and improved existing roads and built new ones. Those among the younger Tibetan officials—many of them sons of the aristocracy—who in 1951 welcomed the social and economic innovations introduced by the Chinese, were jolted out of their initial enthusiasm by a massive witch hunt unleashed by the occupiers in 1952-53 as part of the all-China campaign against coun-

[165] Werner Levi, *Modern China's Foreign Policy* (Minneapolis, Minn.: U. of Minnesota Press, 1953), pp. 333-337. The Chinese people, the Peking press reported, danced in the streets with joy on learning these tidings.
[166] Tieh-tseng Li, *The Historical Status of Tibet* (New York: King's Crown Press, Columbia University, 1956), pp. 203-206; *Tibet, 1950-1967*, Rev. ed. (Hong Kong: *URI*, 1968); *Tibetan Sourcebook* (Hong Kong: *URI*, 1964). On the anguished Tibetan appeal to the UN, see Tieh-tseng Li, *Tibet: Today and Yesterday* (New York: Bookman Associates, 1960), pp. 203-206.

terrevolutionaries, and by oppressive taxes levied under the banner of the Three- and Five-Antis and the campaign to aid Korea. A relentless process of Sinification began in the name of class struggle. The Chinese brought with them primary education, health clinics, the "Patriotic Youth League," land reform, and fear. The outside world demurely looked the other way citing present anguish as the necessary price of eventual, perhaps hypothetical, social progress. "The definition of colonialism," said T. B. Kripalani, Leader of the Opposition in India's parliament, "is that one nation by force of arms and fraud occupies the territory of another nation." Such words were rare at the time, common sense having succumbed to convenient rationalizations and the bland intellectualization of aggression.

RELATIONS WITH THE SOVIET UNION

The Soviet Union and its communist allies in Eastern Europe were potentially the main source of external aid for China's rehabilitation and economic modernization. In spite of their insistence on self-reliance, the Chinese needed Soviet help to overcome a handicap of backwardness much greater than that which the Bolsheviks had had to contend with in the Russia of 1917. In February 1950 the two countries concluded a Treaty of Friendship, Alliance, and Mutual Assistance, one of the consequences of which was a Soviet loan to China in the amount of $300 million. Delivery of goods under this loan was to take place between 1950 and 1954. Repayment was scheduled to begin in 1954, and to be completed by 1963. Interest on the loan was 1 percent per year. It should be pointed out that this long-term credit was one of the few that the Soviet Union extended to China. Total Soviet economic loans to Communist China from 1950 through 1969 probably did not exceed $1 billion (including a 1954 long-term loan of $130 million, $320 million credit to cover short-term debts accumulated by China in 1961, and trade credits to cover Soviet deliveries of plant and equipment repayable in Chinese counterdeliveries of food, raw materials, and consumer goods.) There were no economic grants either during the rehabilitation period or at any subsequent time.[167]

The 1950 Treaty is believed to have contained a secret military clause under the provisions of which the Soviets supplied China in 1950-52 with conventional military materiel, sent military advisers to China, and trained large numbers of Chinese officers in Soviet mili-

[167] According to Cheng Chu-yuan, total Soviet loans to China from 1950 through 1959 came to 5,294 million yuan. Of this amount 2,174 million yuan were used before 1952, and 3,120 million yuan during the First Five Year Plan period. For details see, Cheng Chu-yuan, *Economic Relations Between Peking and Moscow, 1949-63* (New York: Praeger, 1964), pp. 76-78.

tary academies. The flow of supplies was stepped up after China's entry into the Korean War. By 1952 the Chinese were in possession of some 2,500 Soviet-made aircraft, few of which were of the latest type. Nothing apparently was done at this stage to help the Chinese establish a modern armaments industry. The amount of military credits extended by the Soviets during 1950-52 is difficult to determine. It may have been as high as $1 billion, probably somewhat less. Whatever the precise figure, the general principle was that the Chinese should, sooner or later, pay for every bit of military assistance—which they did.[168]

Soviet backing for China's reconstruction effort during 1949-52 took mostly the form of trade, much of it on a straight cash or barter basis. The value of this trade may be seen from Table 3-18. China's trade deficits during these years were covered either by part of the $300 million loan already referred to, by trade loans, or by short-term "swing" credits. It is probable that the swing credits carried a 2 percent interest charge unless settled within agreed-on time in each new accounting period.

TABLE 3-18
Sino-Soviet Trade, 1950–52
(Millions of U.S. dollars)

Year	Chinese Exports	Chinese Imports	Chinese Trade Balance
1950	191	388	-197
1951	331	478	-147
1952	414	554	-140

Source: Official Soviet Trade Statistics. Rubles have been converted to dollars at the official exchange rate.

[168] During the brief "Hundred Flowers" liberal interlude (see Chapter 7), criticism was voiced in China of the way in which the Soviets had handled military aid to China during the Korean conflict. One writer said that "it was unreasonable for China to bear all the expenses of the Resist-America, Aid-Korea war." In February 1964 the Central Committee of the Communist Party of China wrote to the Russians that "as for Soviet loans, China used them mostly for the purchase of war materiel from the Soviet Union, the greater part of which was used up in the war to resist U.S. aggression in Korea. For many years we have been paying the principal and interest on these Soviet loans, which account for a considerable part of our yearly exports to the Soviet Union." See Roderick MacFarquhar, *The Hundred Flowers Campaign and the Chinese Intellectuals* (New York: Praeger, and Stevens & Sons Ltd., London. 1960), p. 50, and "Letter of the Central Committee of the Communist Party of the Soviet Union") February 29, 1964), *Peking Review* (May 8, 1964), p. 18. In 1962 Mao reminisced: "Even after the success of the Revolution, Stalin feared that China might degenerate into another Yugoslavia, and that I might become another Tito. I later went to Moscow and concluded the Sino-Soviet Treaty of Alliance. This also was the result of struggles. Stalin did not wish to sign the Treaty; he finally did so after two months of negotiations," *FEER* (October 2, 1969), p. 24.

The importance of this trade for China cannot be overemphasized, even though the Soviets may have charged prices which were somewhat above those obtaining in world markets.[169] The fact is, the Chinese at this stage could not have turned to world markets for supplies of the kind of capital equipment they needed: they had neither the foreign exchange nor the sort of economic and political contacts needed to make trade flow in other than socialist channels.[170] The bulk of Soviet sales to China at this time consisted of producer goods for which the Soviets were willing to accept Chinese consumer goods, mostly of agricultural origin. The distribution of China's total foreign trade among different categories of products may be seen from Table 3-19.

TABLE 3-19
Distribution of Volume of Exports and Import Trade
of China, 1950-1952
(Percentage distribution)

Year	Exports (Total = 100)			Imports (Total = 100)	
	Industrial and Mining Products	Processed Products of Agriculture and Side Occupations	Products of Agriculture and Side Occupations	Capital Goods	Consumer Goods
1950	9.3	33.2	57.5	87.2	12.8
1951	14.0	31.4	54.6	83.1	16.9
1952	17.9	22.8	59.3	90.6	9.4

Source: Ten Great Years, p. 176.

[169] In September 1964 the Chinese reprinted in their press a complaint originally published in the North Korean paper *Rodong Shinmon* regarding alleged Soviet price exploitation of the North Koreans following the end of the Korean conflict. See *Peking Review* (September 18, 1964). On the general problem of price exploitation by the Soviets, see Franklyn D. Holzman, "Soviet Foreign Trade Pricing and the Question of Discrimination," *The Review of Economics and Statistics* (May 1962), and Horst Menderhausen, "Terms of Trade Between the Soviet Union and Smaller Communist Countries, 1955-1957," *ibid.* (May 1959), and his "The Terms of Soviet-Satellite Trade: A Broadened Analysis," *ibid.* (May 1960).

[170] A Western trade embargo was imposed on China during the Korean War. The embargo was of three kinds: (1) cessation of all shipments of armaments, (2) quantitative control list covering certain types of machine tools, precision instruments, equipment, and raw materials, and (3) surveillance list of certain commodities. The enforcement of the embargo was left up to each nation participating in the embargo. In 1950, 25 percent of China's total trade was conducted with communist countries. It was 69 percent in 1953. See *China Association Annual Report, 1963-64* (London), p. 14. Cf. Hsin Ying, *The Foreign Trade of Communist China* (Hong Kong: URI, 1954).

The Soviet Union during this early period was instrumental in the setting up of the Chinese State Statistical Bureau (1952), helped prepare China's First Five Year Plan (1953-57) which followed the Soviet Stalinist blueprint, if only in general outline (Chapter 4), and generally rendered substantial technical and scientific assistance which the Chinese accepted politely but without effusion. Between 1950 and 1952 a total of 370 Chinese students were admitted to Soviet institutes of higher learning; in 1953 the Russians gave about 10,000 books to various Chinese scientific delegations, began sending books and scientific journals to Chinese libraries, and sent (1950-56) about 50 scientists to Peking and other cities.[171]

From the very beginning, however, there were several points of friction between China and the USSR. In the early days of cooperation these were played down by both sides but, as we shall see, they were among the causes of the later open quarrel between the two countries.

First of all there was the question of *joint-stock companies*, three of which were established by an agreement signed in Moscow in March 1950. The activities covered by these companies were the prospecting for and the production and refining of petroleum in Sinkiang, the mining of nonferrous and rare metals and minerals (including uranium) in Sinkiang, and civil aviation (air routes from Peking to Chita, Peking-Irkutsk, and Peking-Alma Ata). A number of other joint-stock arrangements were subsequently made for individual enterprises in the city of Dairen in Manchuria (e.g., a shipbuilding yard, a cement plant, a glass factory, and a plant producing electrical equipment).[172]   The joint-stock company device was primarily a tool of Soviet economic penetration based on a long Tzarist tradition. It was first used by the Soviets in Mongolia, later (1924) in Manchuria (the Chinese Eastern Railway—see below), and after World War II in Eastern Europe. A typical joint-stock company consisted of equal shares of Soviet and a given country's capital (the Soviet share was sometimes quite simply the buildings and machinery already there, left by the Japanese in China or the Germans in Eastern Europe). Expenses, products, and profits were shared equally by the USSR and its partner. Leading managerial positions alternated every three years. In Eastern Europe this arrangement was used to extract repara-

---

[171] Chu-yuan Cheng, *Scientific and Engineering Manpower in Communist China, op. cit.*, pp. 194, 198, 203. To put this in perspective, the following figures are of interest. According to UNESCO's *World of Learning* (1967), The Leningrad Academy of Sciences Library has 14.8 million books, the Leningrad University Library 3.4 million books, and the Liningrad Public Library 15 million books.

[172] Werner Levi, *op. cit.*, pp. 315, 317-320. Cf. Marshall I. Goldman, *Soviet Foreign Aid* (New York: Praeger, 1967), pp. 10-23.

tions from former enemies and allies alike, and to exercise control over strategic sectors of the various countries' economies. Although the Chinese Communists officially approved of this procedure in 1950-52, they were certainly not happy with it. The Soviets themselves later allowed that the joint-stock arrangement had been inequitable. In 1964 they wrote: "We liquidated the economic joint stock companies in China and in other countries. . . . It is not superfluous to note that the Central Committee of the Chinese Communist Party at one time fully approved and set a high value on these steps taken by our Party."[173]   In fact, by 1955, under Chinese prodding, the joint-stock companies had been dissolved. But here again, things were not all that fraternal. Apparently the winding-up agreements stipulated that China was to pay the Soviets with exports for their share of the joint-stock companies, although it is possible that the Soviets gave the Chinese credits to help them pay off these ethically somewhat equivocal debts.

There was also the problem of *Port Arthur and Dairen.* Port Arthur was a naval base, the lease on which was acquired by the Soviets by the Yalta Agreement of February 1945.[174]   By the same agreement, the Soviet Union received Chiang Kai-shek's consent (under American pressure) to the internationalization of the commercial port at Dairen.[175]   The Yalta arrangement was consecrated by Sino-Soviet agreements arising from the 1950 Treaty of Friendship, Alliance, and Mutual Assistance, with the proviso that Soviet troops were to be withdrawn from Port Arthur by the end of 1952, that the naval installations built there by the Russians after 1945 were to be turned over to the Chinese against payment of agreed-on sums, and the question of Dairen was to be taken up upon the conclusion of a peace treaty with Japan. Civilian administration in Dairen was vested in China. Toward the end of the summer of 1952 the Soviet Union granted a Chinese request to stay on indefinitely in Port Arthur. The Soviets also remained in Dairen. It is possible that China's Korean difficulties had something to do with this request, although Soviet pressure cannot be altogether discounted. It was only after the death of Stalin that the Soviet Union agreed to evacuate both places (October 11, 1954), and did so in May 1955. With

[173] Letter of the CC of the CPSU to the CC of the CPC, March 7, 1964 in *Peking Review* (May 8, 1964), p. 7. It is interesting to note that Chiang Kai-shek resisted Soviet attempts to set up joint stock companies and allowed the Soviets only one such concession, the Chinese Eastern Railway.

[174] Russian interest in Port Arthur goes back to Tzarist times (1898).

[175] Chiang Kai-shek gave his consent to the Yalta provisions in a treaty concluded with Moscow in August 1945. This treaty was endorsed by the Chinese Communists. See Klaus Mehnert, *Peking and Moscow* (New York: Mentor, 1964), pp. 267-268, 272-273.

the exception of military stockpiles, Soviet-built naval installations and other assets in Port Arthur were turned over to China free of charge. It is significant that the Russians were the last foreigners to leave Chinese soil, the last ones to renounce special privileges in China. Seven years later, Soviet consulates in China (including the one in Dairen) were ordered closed.

Another source of disagreement, papered over for the time being, was the Soviet interest in the *Chinese Eastern Railway* and its spur system, the Changchun or South Manchurian Railway. The railway was built at the end of the nineteenth century by Russian and Chinese capital and was operated jointly by Russia and China. In August 1945 the Soviets concluded an agreement with the Nationalists regarding the joint ownership of the railway.[176] Previously in 1935 Stalin had sold the railway to Japan's satellite Manchukuo.[177] As a result of an agreement concluded with Mao Tse-tung in 1950, the Soviets agreed to relinquish their rights in the railway, free of charge, not later than 1952, which they did. It is probably not unfair to say the the relinquishment of rights in the Chinese Eastern Railway did not cause much enthusiasm in Moscow. The Soviet Union had always been adamant on this issue, and only accepted to renounce its control of the system when nothing else could be done. As late as 1929 Stalin went to war with the warload Chang Hsueh-liang to preserve Russia's rights to the railway. The Soviets always regarded control over this railroad network as crucial to the defense of the Soviet Union's Pacific provinces.

The *Soviet pillage of Manchurian industry* had already been mentioned (p. 55). Soviet troops, which entered Manchuria in August 1945 as part of their short campaign against Japan, were scheduled to leave the province in November 1945. Actually the departure date was put off again and again, until finally the situation became embarrassing to all concerned, and the Russians withdrew in May 1946.[178]

From 1949 until June 1954, Manchuria was run by Kao Kang, an

[176] D. J. Roads, "The Chinese Eastern Railway," in E. S. Kirby (ed.), *Contemporary China: I, 1955* (Hong Kong: Hong Kong U. P., 1956), pp. 18-31. For an account of the various agreements between the USSR and Nationalist China arising from the Yalta Agreement, see Robert C. North, *Moscow and the Chinese Communists* (Stanford, Calif.: Stanford U. P., 1953, 1963), pp. 217-222. This is also a good juncture at which to gain some background on Sino-Soviet relations in general. See for example Conrad Brandt, *Stalin's Failure in China* (New York: Norton, 1966), and Charles B. McLane, *Soviet Policy and the Chinese Communists, 1931-1946* (New York: Columbia U. P., 1958).

[177] It should be added that under a Sino-Soviet agreement of 1924, the Soviets had no right unilaterally to take this step.

[178] Two good sources on the Manchurian question are Werner Levi, *op. cit.*, Chapter 19 (pp. 248-260), and Klaus Mehnert, *op. cit.*, pp. 271-280.

independent-minded communist revolutionary and "comrade-in-arms" of Mao Tse-tung. In 1954, following the alleged discovery of a plot to make himself the warlord of Manchuria, *Kao Kang* was *purged* and shortly afterward committed suicide. Manchurian autonomy was rescinded and the area integrated more closely with the rest of China. It is possible that Kao Kang's fall after the death of Stalin was not unconnected with his Soviet sympathies. In 1949, for example, Stalin reportedly negotiated directly with Kao Kang the return to China of industries dismantled by the Soviets.[179] It has been suggested that Stalin saw in Kao Kang a possible ally willing to establish in Manchuria a government independent of Peking and closely tied to the Soviet Union, but the evidence remains circumstantial.[180]

The *independence of Outer Mongolia* (in reality its dependency status vis-à-vis the Soviet Union) was recognized by the Nationalists in the August 1945 agreements already referred to. The communists on coming to power acquiesced in this, presumably without too much rejoicing. After relations between China and Russia had deteriorated to the point of open rupture, the Chinese began voicing various claims to Soviet and Soviet-protected territories, including Outer Mongolia.[181]

THE "AID KOREA—RESIST AMERICA" CAMPAIGN

Official adulation of the Soviet Union went hand in hand with an unprecedented campaign of hatred against the United States. Historically, China's relations with the United States had been less strained and humiliating for China than that country's encounters with other Western and Asian powers—France, Britain, and Japan, for ex-

---

[179] See William E. Griffith, *The Sino-Soviet Rift* (Cambridge, Mass.: M.I.T. Press, 1964), p. 231.

[180] Klaus Mehnert, *op. cit.*, p. 276. See also *Documents of the National Conference of the Communist Party of China* (Peking: FLP, 1955), pp. 34-36. "In 1953, all the anti-Party activities carried on by Kao Kang—Jao Shu-shih anti-Party clique had one aim: to cause our great leader Chairman Mao to abdicate, and take over power themselves." *Shanghai Radio* (February 10, 1968) in *URS*, Vol. 50, Nos. 13-14 (February 16, 1968), p. 166.

[181] Dennis J. Doolin, *Territorial Claims in the Sino-Soviet Conflict: Documents and Analysis* (Stanford, Calif.: Hoover Institution Studies Series, No. 7, 1965); Jan S. Prybyla, "Unsettled Issues in the Sino-Soviet Dispute," *Virginia Quarterly Review* (Autumn 1965), pp. 510-524; J. J. Nolde, "Chinese-Russian Relations Since the Seventeenth Century," in *Contemporary China: I, 1955, op. cit.*, pp. 1-17; Hsien-tung Liu, *Border Disputes Between Imperial China and Tsarist Russia*, Ph.D. dissertation, Department of International Relations, Claremont Graduate School, 1967; J. N. Knutson, *Outer Mongolia: A Study in Soviet Colonialism* (Hong Kong: URI, 1959).

ample—although there had been much clumsiness and misunderstanding on both sides. One could even say that there had been fewer head-on collisions between the United States and China than between China and Russia. On the surface, the potential for amicable, or at least reasonably relaxed contacts was there.[182]   But it was not to be. The United States became an obsession with the People's Republic and the feeling of animosity has since 1949 been sustained by a daily dose of vitriolic propaganda for which few parallels can be found in the annals of nation states.

The reasons for this attitude may perhaps be summarized as follows.

1. The Chinese Communists have a fine sense of the world's balance of power realities, in spite of their public pronouncements about "paper tigers"[183]   and their seemingly rash statements on the international situation. They were not slow to grasp the fact that the United States was, in the wake of World War II, the most formidable power not only in the Pacific areas but elsewhere in the world. The philosophy of life, the political, social, and economic system which the United States represented were distasteful to China's Communist leaders. If anyone was capable of stemming or reversing what they considered to be the socialist wave of the future, it was American strength and resolve. In this perspective it was not unreasonable for them to do their best to sap that strength and undermine the resolve.

2. United States support for Chiang Kai-shek, American protection for Formosa which Communist China claims as an integral part of her national territory, the occupation of Japan and the democratization of the country on the American pattern, the advance of American armies toward the Manchurian border, and U.S. opposition

---

[182] See *The China White Paper* (Stanford, Calif.: Stanford U. P., 1967) 2 vols; Wolfgang Franke, *China and the West* (New York: Harper, 1967); U. S. Department of State, *America's Policy Toward the Chinese People* (n.p., n.d. [1958]); A. T. Steele, *The American People and China* (New York: McGraw Hill, 1966); A. M. Halpern (ed.), *Policies Toward China: Views from Six Continents* (New York: McGraw-Hill, 1965); Yuan-li Wu, *As Peking Sees Us* (Stanford, Calif.: Hoover Institution Press, 1969).

[183] The thesis of the "paper tiger" was first made public in an interview granted by Mao Tse-tung to expatriate American Anna Louise Strong in August 1946. See "Talk with the American Correspondent Anna Louise Strong" *SW* (Peking: FLP, 1961), Vol. IV, pp. 97-101. "All reactionaries are paper tigers. In appearance the reactionaries are terrifying, but in reality they are not so powerful. From a long term point of view, it is not the reactionaries but the people who are really powerful." On May 5, 1967, when relations between China and the USSR had got out of hand, an *Izvestia* commentator wrote about the Chinese officials that "there was as much revolutionary spirit in their stereotyped and banal phrases about 'paper tigers' . . . as in the tailoring of their uniforms."

to the admission of China to world councils,[184] strengthened the Chinese leadership's conviction that the United States was out to do them harm, and bent on undoing the revolution. There was probably even at this early stage a suspicion that the world's two nuclear powers (the United States and the Soviet Union) would eventually find a common language and would try and exclude China from the club of great powers. It is interesting to note that as the balance of power in the world shifted in favor of the Soviet Union, so did Chinese hostility. By the end of 1967 the vilification of the USSR yielded nothing to the torrent of abuse poured on the United States.

3. Although it would be rash to formulate it into a law, revolutionary regimes do have a need to find external enemies, foreign threats, and so on, both to distract the people's attention from the social upheavals at home and to serve as an excuse for imposing on society strict discipline and iron rule. Without minimizing the actual extent of tangible provocation by foreigners, it would still be fair to say that appeal to nationalist, even chauvinist emotions in times of revolutionary domestic transformations has been a fairly frequent phenomenon. It may also be suggested that the Chinese Communist leaders really believed in the imminent threat of American intervention and that they reacted accordingly.

4. China's Communist leaders were and remain to this day convinced of the basic instability and inevitable collapse of the American economic system. On this issue their Marxism has been unshakably orthodox. The dialectical explosion of antagonistic contradictions within American society is to them simply a matter of time.

In October 1950, as American forces were swiftly moving toward China's Manchurian border, the Chinese intervened, sending to Korea tens of thousands of so-called "People's Volunteers," i.e., regular

---

[184] The vote in the United Nations on admitting Communist China went as follows:

Year	For Red China	Against	Abstentions
1950	16	32	10
1951	11	37	4
1952	7	42	11

See Franz Schurmann and Orville Schell (eds.), *Communist China: Revolutionary Reconstruction and International Confrontation, 1949 to Present* (New York: Vintage, 1967), p. 647. The heavy vote against seating China in 1951 and 1952 reflected to some extent China's intervention in the Korean conflict. But American pressure was also an important element. By October 1953, in addition to communist countries, the People's Republic of China had been recognized by several noncommunist Asian countries, as well as by Britain, Norway, the Netherlands, Afghanistan, and Israel.

troops,[185] while at the same time unleashing at home a mass movement to aid Korea and resist America. According to a Chinese Communist source, "on a single day, May 1, 1951 . . . the number of people who participated in a demonstration for resistance to U.S. aggression and aid to Korea . . . exceeded 186,430,000, while those who had participated in patriotic demonstrations before this date topped 43,530,000, making a grand total of practically 230 million."[186] The resources of the World Peace Council for a Five Power Peace Pact were mobilized, as were other front organizations throughout the world. Germ warfare and other atrocity charges were leveled against American troops and echoed by a multitude of left-wing intellectuals and groups in the noncommunist world.

* * *

By the end of 1952 China's Communists had transformed the economic, social, and political system at home, repaired much of the damage which years of war and civil conflict had wrought, secured their borderlands, and asserted themselves in the international arena. The time had come for launching a program of socialist construction the long-range aim of which was to usher in an era of modernity as a prelude to the attainment of full communism.

[185] According to a report from General MacArthur dated November 5, 1950, Chinese support for North Korea dated from August 22, 1950. See also Allen S. Whiting, *China Crosses the Yalu* (New York: Macmillan, 1960); Alexander L. George, *The Chinese Communist Army in Action: The Korean War and Its Aftermath* (New York: Columbia U. P., 1967).

[186] Liao Kai-lung, *op. cit.*, p. 139. "Chen Yun together with that old counterrevolutionary P'eng Teh-huai joined in resolutely opposing Chairman Mao's proposal to resist America and aid Korea. They said that to resist America was very 'difficult,' 'arduous,' and that 'whether it is the 37th or the 38th parallel it would be better not to fight . . .' Chen Yun took the view that to fight against the Americans and to continue with economic construction were two incompatible policies." *Red Guard Newspaper*, February 1967. On P'eng Teh-huai, see Chapters 8 and 11.

4 | The First Five Year Plan, 1953-57: Strategy

THEORETICAL AND REAL LIFE-SPAN

Communist China's first long-range economic plan theoretically covers the years 1953 through 1957. For the purpose of this chapter the period 1953-57 will be accepted as a unit.

In fact, however, the plan was not approved until April 1955 and the original draft underwent far-reaching revisions in mid-1956.[1] It could, therefore, be argued that during twenty-seven months (1953-March 1955) the economy was run on the basis of makeshift annual plans, the original version of the First Year Plan was applied over some fourteen months, and during the remainder of the plan period (mid-1956-57) a modified rendering of the original plan was in force. There are indications that this latter version began to be abandoned in the last few months of 1957.

PLAN STRATEGY

SOVIET EXAMPLE

The question that faced the Chinese leaders around 1952-53 was what kind of planning was to be pursued, or to put it differently, what blueprint for modernization was to be followed?

In answering this question the Chinese had recourse to the planning experience of the Soviet Union, for the following reasons.[2]

---

[1] With Soviet assistance, a State Planning Commitee was set up in the autumn of 1952 (headed by Kao Kang), and paralleled by planning bureaus in economic ministries and government offices concerned with economic problems. The Committee was reorganized in 1954 as the State Planning Commission and placed under the direction of a new organ, the State Council. Li Fu-chun was made Chairman of the Commission. Another reorganization took place in May 1956. At that time the State Planning Commission was made responsible for long-term planning. Short-term planning (annual, quarterly) was vested in a State Economic Commission. Capital construction in 1954-57 was under the authority of a State Construction Commission set up in 1954.

[2] See K. C. Yeh, *Soviet and Chinese Communist Industrialization Strategies* (RAND, May 1965); Nicolas Spulber, "Contrasting Economic Patterns: Chinese

1. The Soviet (Stalinist) model of socialist economic development was the only one at once available, ideologically acceptable, and tested in practice. It had shown itself effective insofar as its stated priorities were concerned, in spite of many drawbacks.[3] The drawbacks, incidentally, were most noticeable in the field of political ethics, something that did not overly disturb the Chinese Communists. In fact, long after they had rejected the economic mechanics of Stalinism, the Chinese nurtured the personality cult components of the model (Chapters 8-12 below).

2. The adoption by China of the economics of Stalinism also apparently made sense from the standpoint of expected foreign aid. The Soviets could, and at that time would, send to China equipment for heavy industries, complete plants, and so on. The technical assistance which the Soviet Union was capable of giving was geared to long experience in the ways and manners of the Stalinist model.

3. The Chinese Communists do not appear to have had a workable alternative of their own: their economic theorizing and practice did not go much beyond the stage of new democracy,[4] there was no clear conception of the exact meaning of socialist construction in the special conditions of China, most of their professional economists had been trained abroad (in Western countries), and as it now transpires there was disagreement among the leaders on the question of the pace of transformation and the shape of the future economy.

Although relying on Soviet example and experience, the Chinese did not take over the Soviet-Stalinist model lock, stock, and barrel for at least two reasons.

and Soviet Development Strategies," *Soviet Studies* (July 1963), pp. 1-16; Alexander Eckstein, "The Strategy of Economic Development in Communist China," *American Economic Review*, Papers and Proceedings (May 1961), pp. 508-517.

[3] The Soviet-Stalinist model had been imposed on all Eastern European countries during Stalin's lifetime. In 1948 the Yugoslavs rejected it and shortly thereafter came up with their own substitute, which was repeatedly and sharply condemned by both the Soviets and the Chinese. On the Yugoslav model, see Svetozar Pejovich, *The Market-Planned Economy of Yugoslavia* (Minneapolis: U. of Minnesota Press, 1966). See also Jan S. Prybyla (ed.), *Comparative Economic Systems* (New York: Appleton, 1969), Part IV; Branko Horvat, An Essay on *Yugoslav Society* (White Plains, N.Y.: International Arts and Science Press, 1969); Joseph T. Bombelles, *Economic Development of Communist Yugoslavia* (Stanford, Calif.: Hoover Institution Press, 1968).

[4] A series of meetings under the sponsorship of the Institute of Economics of the Academia Sinica was organized in Peking in December 1954. Their purpose was to analyze and define the "economic laws of the transitional period." The first issue of a bimonthly professional journal, *Economic Research*, appeared on May 12, 1955. See also E. F. Szczepanik, "The Economic Policy of Maoism," in E. S. Kirby (ed.) *Contemporary China: I, 1955, op. cit.*, pp. 50-65, and Werner Handke, "The Law of Proportional Development," *ibid.*, *II, 1956-57*, pp. 100-104.

First, China's factor endowments in the 1950's were very different from Russia's in the late 1920's and early 1930's.

Second, Stalin died in 1953 and the Stalinist economic model began to wither away shortly thereafter. At the very time that the Chinese First Five Year Plan was ready to be put into effect (1955), both the Russians and the Chinese began to have second thoughts about Stalinist economics, each of them for their own special reasons.[5]

Uneasily brought together in Stalinism, the Russians and the Chinese parted ways, until by 1967 one could speak of two very different communist economic systems, each swearing by Marx and Lenin. Economic Stalinism in China was never more than a transplant which produced complications in the mid-1950's. But it was (with the qualifications mentioned in the previous section) the only period of long-term economic planning that China has known so far. It was also the one most clearly marked by solid achievement, and the best documented.

PLAN STRATEGY DEFINED

Objective

The main objective of the strategy of economic development adopted by the Chinese from the Soviets and adapted by them to the special conditions of China was rapid growth of output. Concentration on the increase in the volume of output involved some sacrifice of quality. Workers', peasants' and managers' performance norms ("success indicators") were geared to the physical output criterion expressed in weights and measures.

---

[5] Officially, de-Stalinization in the Soviet Union dates from N. S. Khrushchev's speech to the closed session of the 20th Congress of the Communist Party of the Soviet Union (February 24-25, 1956). However, economic reform was in the air for at least a year prior to that. It was being hinted at even more insistently in Poland. The reader may wish to acquaint himself with the course of Soviet economic reforms since 1956. The literature is enormous and growing daily. An excellent survey is to be found in Eugene Zaleski, *Planning Reforms in the Soviet Union, 1962-1966* (Chapel Hill, N.C.: U. of North Carolina Press, 1967). See also Myron E. Sharpe (ed.), *Planning, Profit and Incentives in the U.S.S.R*, 2 vols. (White Plains, N.Y.: International Arts and Sciences Press, 1969); George R. Feiwel (ed.), *New Currents in Soviet-Type Economies: A Reader* (Scranton, Pa.: International Textbook, 1968). For a comparison of levels of development in the USSR (1928, 1932) and China (1952, 1957), see K. C. Yeh, "Soviet and Communist Chinese Industrialization Strategies," in Donald W. Treadgold (ed.), *Soviet and Chinese Communism: Similarities and Differences* (Seattle, Wash.: U. of Washington Press, 1967), esp. p. 343, Table 2.

Components

The strategy of economic development adopted in spirit by the Chinese from the Soviets and adapted by them to the special conditions of China may be described as selective growth under conditions of austerity.[6]

Selective growth means:

1. Resources are channeled primarily into modern, capital-intensive, heavy industry which is expected to lead to rapid economic growth per unit of invested resources in the long run. The absolute size of the modern industrial sector is seen as the main determinant of national power.

2. Investment in human capital (education) of a particular type, i.e., development of scientific and technical skills.

3. Application of up-to-date technology to certain segments of both the priority and nonpriority sectors, together with intensive use of underemployed labor (technological dualism).

4. Attitude toward agriculture ranging from relative neglect to outright exploitation for the benefit of industry, especially producers' goods industry. Investment in agriculture is made primarily in order to increase the portion of marketable agricultural output going to the state (state procurement). The real costs incidental on this procedure are borne by the peasants, and, to a lesser degree, by urban consumers. In the special circumstances of China this particu-

[6] Anthony M. Tang, "Agriculture in the Industrialization of Communist China and the Soviet Union," *Journal of Farm Economics* (December 1967), p. 118. The Soviet-Stalinist model has been analyzed by Evsey Domar, "A Soviet Model of Growth," in *Essays in the Theory of Economic Growth* (New York: Oxford U. P., 1957); Alexander Erlich, "Stalin's Views on Soviet Economic Development," in E. J. Simmons (ed.), *Continuity and Change in Russian and Soviet Thought* (Cambridge, Mass.: Harvard U. P., 1955); Oleg Hoeffding, "State Planning and Forced Industrialization," *Problems of Communism* (RAND Corporation), Vol. 8 (November-December 1959) pp. 336-346; Gregory Grossman, "Scarce Capital and Soviet Doctrine," *Quarterly Journal of Economics*, Vol. 47, 1953, pp. 311-343, and his "Notes for a Theory of the Command Economy," *Soviet Studies* (October 1963), pp. 101-123; Jan S. Prybyla, "The Economic Problems of Soviet Russia in Transition," *Indian Journal of Economics* (October 1964), pp. 135-151. A dissenting view on the nature of the Soviet economic system may be found in Paul Craig Roberts, "The Polycentric Soviet Economy," *Journal of Law and Economics*, Vol. 12, No. 1 (April 1969), pp. 163-179. An interesting account of the "real" origins of Soviet long-term planning and industrialization may be found in Leon Smolinski, "Grinevitskii and Soviet Industrialization," *Survey* (London, April 1968), pp. 100-115. A basic treatment of Soviet-type economics may be found in Heinz Kohler, *Scarcity Challenged: An Introduction to Economics* (New York: Holt, 1968), Chapters 12-14 and 23, and his *Welfare and Planning: An Analysis of Capitalism Versus Socialism* (New York: Wiley, 1966) Chapters 7-9.

lar component of developmental strategy was—as will be shown be-low—significantly modified.

By Soviet count, from 1928 through 1953 capital goods produc-tion in the Soviet Union increased about thirty times, the production of consumer goods 7.4 times, agricultural output 18 percent. Agricul-tural output actually declined in 1928-40 and 1948-53.[7] According to Chinese Communist data, between 1949 and 1958 the output of the means of production increased 21 times, the output of consumer goods 5.3 times, and agricultural output 2.3 times.[8]

5. Relative neglect of domestic trade and services, and of resi-dential housing construction and maintenance.

6. Reliance on domestic sources of capital formation rather than on foreign trade and assistance.

In sum, selective growth means sectoral disproportions and im-balanced growth. The breakthrough-on-a-narrow-front method re-sults in violations of internal consistency, which have to be set right by continuous ad hoc adjustments. These adjustments may be either official, or informal and illegal.[9]

Conditions of austerity mean two things:

1. The economy starts from low per capita income levels, low productivity, modest educational standards, and a small degree of intersectoral integration.

2. The rate of investment is high. In the setting of an underdevel-oped economy this means that consumption, while regarded as the ultimate goal, is seen during the development process as an inter-mediate activity of secondary significance, except insofar as it affects worker morale and productivity, and thus the fulfillment of the plan. "Steel was a final good to Stalin, and bread an intermediate one."[10]

[7]Soviet data cited by Michael E. Bradley, "New Approaches to an Old Problem: Soviet Agriculture in Transition," in Jan S. Prybyla (ed.), *Communism at the Crossroads* (University Park, Pa.: Pennsylvania State U., 1968), p. 74.

[8]*Ten Great Years*, pp. 81, 112. These official figures must be taken with an average dose of skepticism. See Introduction, p. 5.

[9]For example, in 1959 the Kazakh Gosplan (regional planning authority) changed its planned allocation of rolled steel 538 times. To smooth out the internal inconsistencies of the plan, arising from the breakthrough method of planning and the high value attached to plan overfulfillment in physical terms, Soviet enterprise managers employ large numbers of so-called *tolkachi* or pushers whose contacts enable them to detect surpluses available in different parts of the economy and to transfer them informally where needed. Eight thousand *tolkachi* visited the Dnepropetrovsk sovnarkhoz (regional economic council) in 1959 alone. See Prybyla, "The Soviet Economy: From Libermanism to Liberal-ism?" *Bulletin*, Institute for the Study of the U.S.S.R., July 1966, pp. 19-20.

[10]Attributed to A. Bergson by Peter Wiles in *The Political Economy of Communism* (Cambridge, Mass.: Harvard U.P., and Basil Blackwell Ltd., Ox-ford, 1962), p. 283. Franklyn D. Holzman in his *Soviet Taxation* (Cambridge,

The same attitude could be ascribed to the Chinese Communists in the period 1953-57, with, however, a qualification or two.

Selective growth under conditions of austerity is not the easiest thing in the world to achieve within a framework of political democracy and social pluralism as understood in the West, even on the assumption that democratic and pluralistic precedents existed in the country undergoing the process of austere selective growth. Implicit in the strategy is a bias in favor of totalitarian modes of behavior. [11] The nation, and that means the poor—and that, for all practical purposes, means the peasants—has to be made to save out of meager income, save at high rates, that is trim its already modest consumption standard, or, at the very least, postpone consumption increases and surrender to the state produce where there is hardly enough to cover minimal needs. The resources so extracted are channeled into projects which reflect planners' preferences, or more exactly, the preferences of the top leadership imposed on the planners. The projects, moreover, have to be built quickly in a climate of impatience and hurry. Everyone, from the planners all the way down the line of command, is set high targets which cannot reasonably be reached with the allotted inputs and which, therefore, call for extra effort and ingenuity, if only to circumvent the regulations. This "planners' tension" is a normal feature of the model.

The system is socially stratified, although social mobility through approved channels (the Party, governmental bureaucracy, science, enterpise management) is encouraged. [12] The system blends advancement based on merit (especially technical merit) and allegiance to the

---

Mass.: Harvard U.P., 1955) shows that Stalin imposed a tax of 70-80 percent on the price of bread (p. 153). Naum Jasny in *Soviet Industrialization, 1928-1952* (Chicago: U. of Chicago Press, 1961. © 1961 by the University of Chicago) points out that while there was not enough grain to make bread from, all the grain needed to make vodka was available. "The sale of vodka," he says, "was a big item in financing the building of 'socialism' and in making the Party 'the victors.' " (pp. 102-103). It was a form of material incentives as well as a source of revenue for the state.

[11] For a discussion of this question, see Alec Nove, *The Soviet Economy: An Introduction* (New York: Praeger, 1961), pp. 303-306; Robert Theobald, *The Rich and the Poor: A Study of the Economics of Rising Expectations* (New York: Mentor, 1961), pp. 47-57; Peter T. Bauer and Basil S. Yamey, *The Economics of Under-Developed Countries* (Chicago: U. Chicago Press, 1957), pp. 190-194. Basic to the discussion of this problem is Ragnar Nurkse, *Problems of Capital Formation in Underdeveloped Countries* (New York: Oxford U. P., 1961).

[12] See Milovan Djilas, *The New Class* (New York: Praeger, 1957); Isaac Deutscher, *Stalin: A Political Biography* (New York: Vintage, 1949, 1960), pp. 338-340. Donald W. Klein, "A Question of Leadership: Problems of Mobility, Control, and Policy-Making in China," *Current Scene*, Vol. 5, No. 7 (April 30, 1967).

Party line, the latter being the more important ingredient. Income differentials, while significant, are less decisive than privilege which depends on access to sources of decision-making at the top.[13]

INSTITUTIONAL TOOLS

Selective growth under conditions of austerity has recourse to a set of institutional arrangements fashioned so as to give effect to the stated objective of the strategy. These tools include the Communist Party and governmental machinery, both based on the principle of "democratic centralism" (see above, p. 28), the nationalization of industry, banking, domestic and foreign commerce, and a portion of agriculture (state farms), the collectivization of the rest of agriculture, comprehensive central planning using the material balances method,[14] and an ideological core to which society is expected to adhere. These are examined in Chapters 5 and 6.

GROWTH PERFORMANCE

In this section we shall try and determine whether the objective of rapid growth of output had been achieved during the First Five Year Plan period. Since Chinese statistical concepts and procedures differ from those used in Western countries, two sets of data will be shown wherever possible: the official Chinese, and Western recomputations.

[13] Abram Bergson, *The Economics of Soviet Planning* (New Haven: Yale U. P., 1964), pp. 106-126, 178-200; David Brodersen, *The Soviet Worker: Labor and Government in Soviet Society* (New York: Random House, 1966), pp. 100-117; David Granick, *The Red Executive: A Study of the Organization Man in Russian Industry* (New York: Doubleday Anchor Books, 1961); Raymond A. Bauer, Alex Inkeles, Clyde Kluckhohn, *How the Soviet System Works* (New York: Vintage, 1961), pp. 29-30, 254; John Wilson Lewis, *Leadership in Communist China* (Ithaca, N.Y.: Cornell U. P., 1963). In a developing command economy in which resources are managed by administrative decisions, the telephone is not only a status symbol. Connected with the right people, it may be the very means of social and material advancement. The phenomenon is not absent from other societies. However, where the bulk of economic, political, social, and cultural decisions is made by bureaucrats in pyramid fashion, ready access to influential people, and hence to special favors and dispensations, becomes crucial. See Marshall I. Goldman, *The Soviet Economy: Myth and Reality* (Englewood Cliffs, N.J.: Prentice-Hall, 1968), pp. 71-73.

[14] A good description of the material balances method of planning may be found in Heinz Kohler, *Scarcity Challenged*, *op. cit.*, Chapter 13; Abram Bergson, *The Economics of Soviet Planning*, *op. cit.*, Chapter 7; Edward Ames, *Soviet Economic Processes* (Homewood, Ill.: Irwin, 1965), p. 72ff.

NATIONAL PRODUCT

Communist Data

According to the Chinese Communists, national income (Chinese Communist definition, i.e., net material product), developed as shown in Tables 4-1 and 4-2.

TABLE 4-1
National Income (Net Material Product)
(Billions of Yuan at 1952 prices)

1952	61.1
1957	93.7
Average annual growth rate 1952-57 (percent)	9.0

Sources: Ten Great Years, p. 20. Reprinted from Nai-Ruenn Chen, *Chinese Economic Statistics* (Chicago: Aldine, 1967). Copyright © 1967 by the Social Science Research Council, p. 140, Table 2.3; Liu and Yeh, *The Economy of the Chinese Mainland, op. cit.*, p. 220.

TABLE 4-2
Increases of National Income
(Percentage)

Year	1952 = 100	Preceding Year = 100
1953	114.0	114.0
1954	120.4	105.7
1955	128.3	106.5
1956	146.3	114.0
1957	153.0	104.6

Source: Ten Great Years, p. 20.

Western Data

Western estimates of China's national product performance, during the period under review, vary according to the methodology used. Five such estimates are given in Table 4-3.

The following comments may be of help.

As regards the absolute magnitude of national product in 1952, the discrepancies between the communist figure (61.1 billion yuan) and Western estimates are traceable, for the most part, to the exclusion by the communists in their concept of net material product of the contribution of service sectors and a possible understatement of agricultural output. A figure of about 71 billion yuan in 1952 seems

TABLE 4-3
Western Estimates of Communist China's National Product
(Billions of 1952 yuan)

Year	Hollister (Gross National Product) (1)	Li (net National Product) Reconstructed Communist Estimate (2)	Liu-Yeh (net Domestic Product) Reconstructed Communist Estimate (3)	Liu's Own Estimate (4)	Wu (net National Product) (5)
1952.	67.9	72.9	68.6	71.4	72.4
1957.	102.4	111.8	104.2	95.3	94.8
Average annual growth rate 1953-57 percent	8.6	8.8	8.8	6.0	5.6

Sources: Adapted from Ta-chung Liu, "The Tempo of Economic Development of the Chinese Mainland, 1949–65," in *An Economic Profile of Mainland China, op. cit.,* p. 56, Table 5.

Col. (1): W. W. Hollister, *China's Gross National Product and Social Accounts,* 1950–57 (New York: Free Press, 1958), p. 2.

Col. (2): C. M. Li, *Economic Development of Communist China* (Berkeley and Los Angeles: U. of California Press, 1959), p. 106.

Col. (3): *The Economy of the Chinese Mainland: National Income and Economic Development, 1933–1959,* by Ta-Chung Liu and Kung-Chia Yeh (Copyright © 1965 by The RAND Corporation), published 1965 by Princeton U.P., p. 213. This estimate was reconstructed from basic communist data without corrections for reliability, but was computed on standard Western concept of net domestic product.

Col. (4): Liu and Yeh, *ibid.,* p. 66.

Col. (5): Y. L. Wu, F. P. Hoeber, and M. M. Rockwell, *The Economic Potential of Communist China* (Menlo Park; 1964), p. 241.

to fairly accurately represent the actual level of total product in that year.

As regards differences in the growth rate (ranging from the communist 9 percent for net material product to Wu's 5.6 percent for net national product), the problem is somewhat more complex. In general, the difference between the (high) communist rate and the (lower) Western estimates is due to

(a) Understatement by the communists of data on agricultural production in 1952 and a resulting overstatement of the rate of growth of agricultural output in subsequent years.

(b) Exaggeration by the communists of increases in the output of consumer goods.

(c) Upward bias in the growth rate resulting from the manner in which the value of industrial production was computed.[15]

[15] For a discussion of this point as well as the variations between communist and Western data, see Ta-chung Liu, *op. cit.,* pp. 57-58.

(d) Communist omission from the employment estimate of workers in a number of traditional sectors (handicrafts, trade, native transportation). Since the output of these workers did not increase much during the period, the omission would give an upward bias to the overall growth rate.

(e) Falsification of statistical reporting at the local level.

(f) Exclusion by the communists from net material product of services which probably grew more slowly than the activities covered by the notion of net national product. The Liu-Yeh reconstructed estimate (without corrections for reliability) reflects this omission, Column (3).

The differences between the various Western estimates of the growth rate are traceable to different emphases put by the respective authors on this or that correction for reliability, and to the procedures followed in correcting the Chinese figures.

It is not possible to say with any degree of certainty, which of the various estimates is the most accurate. What can be said, however, is that even the lowest estimate (5.6 percent) reveals a growth rate that is creditable. From this it may be concluded that the objective of rapid growth was achieved during the First Five Year Plan period, in so far as national product was concerned. Although high national product growth rates have also been achieved by other developing Asian countries, the Chinese rate (even on the lowest estimate) is higher than all, except the rates for Japan and the Philippines.[16]

PER CAPITA PRODUCT

Given a relatively high rate of natural population increase (estimated 2.3 percent per annum, which also represents a large absolute increase), it is interesting to find out how the increase in total product fared when set against the rise in population in the period 1952-57.

Official communist data, reconstructed without adjustment for reliability by Professor Liu, indicate an annual rate of growth in per capita gross domestic product of 6.6 percent (6.5 percent net). The

[16] See United Nations, *Economic Survey for Asia and the Far East, 1961.* The average rate of growth in product (percent) was 9.1 for Japan (1950-59), and 6.0 for the Philippines (1950-59). For 1951-55 the annual percentage increase in GNP was 5.9 for Bulgaria, 3.6 for Czechoslovakia, 7.2 for East Germany, 5.5 for Hungary, 4.8 for Poland, and 8.6 for Rumania. The total for Eastern Europe was 5.7 percent (or 5.9 percent unweighted average). The total for Western Europe during this period was 5.9 percent (or 5.3 percent unweighted average). Maurice Ernst, "Postwar Economic Growth in Eastern Europe," in *New Directions in the Soviet Economy* (Washington, D.C.: Government Printing Office, 1966), Part IV, p. 880, Table 4.

Liu-Yeh estimate, adjusted for reliability, gives an annual growth rate in per capita gross domestic product of 3.9 percent (3.6 percent net).[17] This again is very respectable. Moreover, the reconstructed communist estimate would put China above 40 out of 44 noncommunist countries compared in a study by S. Kuznets, and the Liu-Yeh estimate would put China above 32 of those countries.[18] Even the lower Liu-Yeh estimate gives China an edge over the Soviet Union at a comparable period (1928-40).

PERSONAL CONSUMPTION PER CAPITA

According to reconstructed communist estimates for the postwar years and the Liu-Yeh estimate for both prewar and postwar years, per capita consumption was lower in 1952 than in 1933. The respective calculations indicate rates of growth of household consumption between 1952-57 of 5.2 and 1.9 per cent. The reconstructed communist estimate shows that in 1957 per capita consumption was 8 per cent above 1933.[19] The Liu-Yeh estimate suggests that the 1933 level was not reached by 1957.[20]

Wu's calculations (gross domestic product minus estimated values of investment and government consumption divided by midyear population estimate) show a per capita personal consumption of 94.6 yuan in 1952 and 100.3 yuan in 1957,[21] i.e., a very low rate of increase and an absolute level just compatible with the long-run preservation of political viability.[22]

INDUSTRIAL OUTPUT

Communist Data

Communist figures for *gross industrial output* in 1952 and 1957 are given in Table 4-4.

[17] Ta-chung Liu, *op. cit.*, p. 62, Table 6, 1952 prices. Per capita income (net national product) was, according to official sources, 107 yuan in 1952 and 152 yuan in 1957, or (based on the official exchange rate of 2.355 yuan to one U.S. dollar) $45.5 and $64.5 respectively. See Cheng Chu-yuan, *Communist China's Economy,1949-1962, op. cit.*, p. 109, Table XI.

[18] S. Kuznets, "A Comparative Appraisal," in A. Bergson and S. Kuznets (eds.), *Economic Trends in the Soviet Union* (Cambridge, Mass.: Harvard U. P., 1963), Tables VIII.4 and VIII.2.

[19] Ta-chung Liu, *op. cit.*, p. 63.

[20] *Ibid.*, p. 63.

[21] Yuan-li Wu, *The Economy of Communist China: An Introduction, op. cit.*, p. 91, Table V.1. From 1950 to 1964 per capita consumption increased by 20 percent in Czechoslovakia, 47 percent in Hungary, and 39 percent in Poland. These increases were much below those of most Western European countries. See Maurice Ernst in *New Directions in the Soviet Economy, op. cit.*, p. 880.

[22] Yuan-li Wu, *loc. cit.*, p. 90. A useful source is Cheng Chu-yuan, *Income and Standard of Living in Mainland China*, 2d ed. (Hong Kong: URI, 1958).

TABLE 4-4
Gross Value of Industrial Output at Constant (1952) Prices
by Sector
(Billions of yuan)

	1952	1957
Total	34.3	78.4
Modern Factory.	22.1	55.6
Handicraft industry:		
Handicraft factory	5.0	9.4
Other (individual and cooperative)	7.3	13.4

Source: Reprinted from Nai-Ruenn Chen, *Chinese Economic Statistics* (Chicago: Aldine, 1967). Copyright © 1967 by the Social Science Research Council, p. 207, Table 4.37, adapted, rounded. The communist definition of modern industrial output covers modern and handicraft factory.

On the basis of the figures, the average *annual growth rate in the gross-value of output* of all industry is 17.9 percent (1952-57). The average annual growth rate for modern factory output is 20.8 percent, that for handicraft factory output 14.2 percent, and 13.2 percent for other handicrafts. In short, modern factory output registered the most significant rates of growth, or an overall growth of 152.3 percent for the period. These results are impressive.

Western Data

The communist figures are believed to be less than satisfactory. The reasons for doubting them are:

TABLE 4-5
Western Estimates of Annual Average Rate of Growth
of Modern Factory Output, 1952-57
(Percent)

(1) Adjusted Official Estimate (percent)	(2) Kang Chao (percent)	(3) Liu-Yeh (percent)	(4) Communist (percent)
17.7	14.4	19.4	20.8

Sources:
    Col. (1): Yuan-li Wu, *op. cit.*, pp. 112-113.
    Col. (2): Kang Chao, *The Rate and Pattern of Industrial Growth in Communist China* (Ann Arbor, Mich.: U. of Michigan Press, 1965), p. 92, Table 21.
    Col. (3): *The Economy of the Chinese Mainland: National Income and Economic Development, 1933-1959,* by Ta-Chung Liu and Kung-Chia Yeh. Copyright © 1965 by The RAND Corporation, published 1965 by Princeton U.P., p. 66, Table 8.
    Col. (4): See above, p. 121.

1. The communist figures are for gross industrial output. This method of computing industrial output involves double counting.

2. The figures probably conceal changes in output induced by changes in statistical coverage of industrial products.

3. The series is probably inflated because of the addition, after 1952, of a fast-rising volume of new products priced at experimental prices. These tended, on the whole, to be significantly higher than normal production costs.[23] (See Table 4-5.)

TABLE 4-6
Sectoral Origin of National Income:
Communist Data, 1952-56
(Percent based on 1952 prices)

	1952	1956
National income	100.0	100.0
Agriculture	59.2	48.1
Industry	18.0	26.4
Construction	3.0	5.6
Transportation and communications	4.0	4.4
Trade	15.8	15.5

Source: Reprinted from Nai-Ruenn Chen, *Chinese Economic Statistics* (Chicago: Aldine, 1967). Copyright © 1967 by the Social Science Research Council, p. 142, Table 2.5. The national income in 1952 was, according to these sources, 61.1 billion yuan; 88.8 billion yuan (1952 prices) in 1956.

TABLE 4-7
Sectoral Origin of National Product: Western Estimates, 1952-57
(Percent)

	Liu-Yeh Net Domestic Product (percent)		Wu et al. Gross National Product (percent)
	1952	1957	1957
Total	100.0	100.0	100.0
Agriculture	47.9	39.0	39.2
Modern industry	11.5	20.7	20.3
Construction	2.6	4.8	
Handicrafts	6.6	5.6	5.7
Others	31.4	29.9	34.8

Source: Choh-ming Li, "China's Industrial Development, 1958-1963," in Choh-ming Li (ed.), *Industrial Development in Communist China* (New York: Praeger, and *The China Quarterly*, London, 1964), p. 18, Table 5. The original source, *The Economy of the Chinese Mainland: National Income and Economic Development, 1933-1959*, by Ta-Chung Liu and Kung-Chia Yeh. Copyright © 1965 by The RAND Corporation, published 1965 by Princeton U.P.

[23] These reasons are enumerated and analyzed by Yuan-li Wu, *op. cit.*, pp. 110-111. For an explanation of adjusted official estimates, see *ibid.*, p. 111.

It would be quite fair to say that during the period under review, modern industrial production in China grew at an average annual rate of somewhere between 14 and 19 percent—a creditable performance.

The *contribution of industry to national product* developed in the way shown by Table 4-6.

Western estimates are shown in Table 4-7.

OUTPUT OF PRODUCERS' AND CONSUMERS' GOODS

It has been suggested earlier (p. 113) that selective growth was the objective to be maximized, and that selectivity meant the priority promotion of the industrial producers' goods sector. There is no doubt that this target was in fact reached.

Communist Data

Communist figures on the growth of the producers' goods sector of industry are given in Table 4-8.

TABLE 4-8
Priority Development of the Means of Production, 1952-57
(Billions of 1952 yuan)

Year	Gross Output Value of Industry	Output Value of Means of Production	Output Value of Consumer Goods
1952	34.3	12.2	22.1
1957	78.4	37.9	40.5
Average annual percentage increase, 1953–57	18.0	25.4	12.8

Source: Ten Great Years, pp. 87, 89.

The record for individual industries was uneven, reflecting planners' priorities. The fastest expansion was registered by power machinery (average annual rate of output increase 1953-57 = 81.5 percent according to communist data), locomotives (52.9 percent), steel (31.7 percent), merchant vessels (27.5 percent), crude petroleum (27.3 percent), sulfuric acid (27.1 percent), pig iron (25.2 percent), electric power (21.6 percent), and soda ash (21.4 percent).[24]

It should be pointed out that the high growth rates during this period were due in part to the fact that established industries were being rehabilitated and their capacity was used more fully. However, additions to existing plant appear to have been the more important factor after 1953.

[24] *Ten Great Years*, pp. 102-103.

Another way of looking at the problem is to consider the change in the contribution of the producers' and consumers' goods industries to the gross output value of industry (Table 4-9).

TABLE 4-9
Percentage Shares of the Output Value of Producers'
and Consumers' Goods in the Total (Gross)
Output Value of Industry, 1952, 1957

Year	Output Value of Producers' Goods (percent)	Output Value of Consumers' Goods (percent)
1952	35.6	64.4
1957	48.4	51.6

Source: Ten Great Years, p. 90.

AGRICULTURAL OUTPUT

The official data show that the *gross value of agricultural production* (in 1952 prices) rose by 25 percent from 1952 to 1957, implying an average growth rate of 4.5 percent per annum. The communist figures (1) through (3) total are given in Table 4-10. They include

TABLE 4-10
Gross Agricultural Output, 1952-57*
(Billions of yuan at 1952 prices)

Year	(1) Total	(2) Marketed Value	(3) Retained Total	Retained Value Estimate per farmer (yuan)
1952	48.390	12.970	35.420	91.5
1957	60.350	20.280	40.070	94.7

*Gross value output of agriculture in Communist Chinese usage covers the output value of the following:
  1. Food crops (paddy rice, wheat, miscellaneous cereals, potatoes)
  2. Soybeans
  3. Other oil-bearing crops (peanuts, rapeseed, sesame, cottonseed)
  4. Plant fibers (cotton, hemp).
  5. Other industrial crops (sugar cane, sugar beets, tobacco, tea)
  6. Vegetables
  7. Fruits
  8. Animal products (cattle, horses, mules, donkeys, sheep, goats, hogs, poultry)
  9. Forest products (timber, tung nuts, general forest products)
  10. Fishery products
  11. Miscellaneous agricultural products.
Sources: Columns (1) through (3) total, Ten Great Years, pp. 118, 168, Col. (3) total is derived by subtracting col. (2) from col. (1). The per farmer retained value is based on a farm population of 387 millions in 1952, and 423 millions in 1957. For methodology, see Anthony M. Tang, "Agriculture in the Industrialization of Communist China and the Soviet Union," *Journal of Farm Economics* (December 1967), p. 1126, Table 3, note.

the value of farm subsidiary production, which during the period may have accounted for as much as 30 percent of the total gross value of agricultural output.

Fluctuations in the growth rate of gross agricultural output during the First Five Year Plan are shown in Table 4-11.

TABLE 4-11
Growth Rate of Gross Agricultural Output
in Current Year
(Percent)

Year	Rate
1953	3.2
1954	3.3
1955	7.7
1956	4.9
1957	3.5

Source: Derived from *Ten Great Years*, p. 118.

Notice that the accelerated collectivization (described in the next chapter) was carried out after the bumper crop year 1955.

Official Chinese Communist data show an increase in grain crops output of 20 percent between 1952 and 1957, or an average annual rate of increase (1953-57) of 3.7 percent. Table 4-12 presents the official figures. By far the greater part of the increase in grain production during this period was due to multiple cropping.

TABLE 4-12
Production of Grain Crops, 1952-57
(Cereals and potatoes in grain equivalent)

Year	Output, Millions of Metric Tons
1952	154.4
1953	156.9
1954	160.5
1955	174.8
1956	182.5
1957	185.0

Source: Ten Great Years, p. 119.

Professor Chi-ming Hou has listed the indexes and growth rates of output, sown area, and unit yield of 16 crops, which together accounted for 93 to 95 percent of the total crop acreage in

1952-57. [25] The original data were drawn from communist sources
(Table 4-13).

TABLE 4-13
Indexes and Growth Rates of Output, Sown Area, and Unit Yield
of 16 Crops*
1952 = 100

Year	Sown Area	Unit Yield Index (1952 = 100)†	Output
1952	100.00	100.00	100.00
1953	101.52	99.68	101.14
1954	103.76	98.19	101.91
1955	105.39	106.18	111.81
1956	110.65	105.60	116.79
1957	108.37	109.11	117.96

Growth Rates
(Previous Year as Base)

1953	1.52	-0.32	1.14
1954	2.21	-1.49	0.76
1955	1.57	8.14	9.71
1956	4.99	-0.55	4.45
1957	-2.06	3.32	1.00
Mean	1.65	1.82	3.41

*The 16 crops are: rice, corn, miscellaneous grains, potatoes, soybeans,
cotton, flue-cured and sun-dried tobacco, jute, flax, sugar cane, sugar beet,
peanuts, rapeseed, sesame.

†Weights used are the 1952 sown area of the 16 crops. No significant
difference occurs when the 1957 sown area is used as weights.

Sources: Original data are from Ministry of Agriculture, Planning Bureau,
Nung-ch'an t'ung-chi hui-pien (Peking 1959), and *Wei-ta ti shih-nien*, as given in
Richard Y. C. Yin, "Agricultural Reorganization and Crop Production in Mainland China, 1952–1957," paper read at the Inaugural Meeting of Asian Studies
on the Pacific Coast, June 16–18, 1966, San Francisco.

Official Chinese data for food grain production and population
indicate a per capita food grain availability in 1952 of 220 kilograms—that is, less than half the Soviet level in 1928 (i.e., at the
beginning of the Soviet First Five Year Plan). Depending on the
assumption about the rate of net population increase during
1952-57, the food grain availability per capita in 1957 may have
been 256 or 290 kilograms.[26] Even the latter figure represents a

[25] Chi-ming Hou, "Sources of Agricultural Growth in Communist China,"
The Journal of Asian Studies, Vol. 27, No. 4 (August 1968), p. 724, Table 1.

[26] The first figure is from A. M. Tang, *op. cit.*, p. 1123. The second figure is
from Prybyla, "Communist China: The Economy and the Revolution," *Current
History* (September 1968), pp. 137-138. Note that between 14 and 22 percent
of the food grain output during 1952-57 was probably diverted to other than
human consumption uses.

modest level of per capita grain availability by international standards. During the starvation year 1932 in Russia, per capita grain availability on farms (net of forced collections) was about 375 kilograms. Total availability per person, urban and rural, was 415 kilograms.[27]

Cotton output, according to official communist sources, increased during the period by 26 percent over 1952, or an average annual rate of increase of 4.7 percent. There were, however, considerable fluctuations in output from year to year which resulted in sharp variations in the output of light industry. Since profits of light industry were a major source of state investment funds, these variations affected the volume of state investment and the state's financial position. The number of big draught animals was said to have increased by 9.6 percent from 1952 to 1957, that of sheep and goats by 59.6 percent, and that of pigs by 62.5 percent.[28]

The indexes for cultivated area, sown area, and irrigated area are given in Table 4-14.

TABLE 4-14
Cultivated Area, Sown Area, Irrigated Area (Index)

	1952	1953	1954	1955	1956	1957
Cultivated area.	100.0	100.6	101.3	102.1	103.6	103.6
Sown area	100.0	102.0	104.7	107.0	112.7	111.3
Irrigated area.	100.0	103.1	109.4	115.6	150.0	162.5
Irrigated area as percentage of						
total cultivated area	19.8	20.2	21.3	22.4	28.6	31.0

Source: Chi-ming Hou, "Sources of Agricultural Growth in Communist China," Journal of Asian Studies, Vol. 27 (August 1968), p. 727, Table 2. Based on Wei-ta ti shih-nien, pp. 113, 115.

Western Estimates

Western economists believe that the communist data cannot reasonably be accepted at face value. Most agree that the published and implied growth rates have an upward bias, but it is not always easy to pinpoint the origin or quantify the extent of the bias.

[27] A. M. Tang, op. cit., p. 1123. This sheds interesting light on the political reasons for the starvation of millions of Russian "kulaks" (rich peasants) and their families. Official Chinese figures show that per capita consumption of food grains (national) was 227 kilograms in 1953-54, and 262.25 in 1956-57. Rural per capita consumption of food grains in 1953-54 was 218.2 kilograms and 258.9 kilograms in 1956-57. The relevant figures for urban areas were 289.8 kilograms and 282.35 kilograms respectively. Reprinted from Nai-Ruenn Chen, Chinese Economic Statistics (Chicago: Aldine, 1967); copyright © 1967 by the Social Science Research Council. p. 437, Table 9.13.

[28] Ten Great Years, pp. 120,132.

Instead of the 25 percent increase in gross agricultural production during the First Five Year Plan, Liu and Yeh estimate an increase of 8.7 percent.[29] Instead of the 4.5 percent average annual growth rate of gross agricultural production, Tang suggests 3 percent.[30]

Instead of the 20 percent increase in food grain output between 1952 and 1957, claimed by the communists, Liu and Yeh suggest an increase of 5 percent.[31] Wu's adjusted communist estimate shows hardly any advance at all (0.8 million tons or 0.4 percent).[32] Jones and Poleman estimate the increase to have been about 12 percent, and Hollister suggests 14 percent (including animal products).[33] In all probability the increase in food grain output barely kept pace with the rise in population.

The main reasons cited for not accepting the official data at their face value are:

(a) The pre-1956 output figures for crop production appear to be understated on the basis of per capita consumption requirements (Liu-Yeh).

(b) The planted area during 1950-55 was probably underreported (Wu). The Wu estimate of food grain output rests on the assumption that the cumulative underestimate for 1950-55 works out at 181.8 million metric tons. This volume is distributed by him over the individual years in the same proportion as the assumed underreporting of equivalent planted area during the period.[34] Wu advances the hypothesis that the reported increase in cultivable and planted areas between 1950 and 1956 was statistical; due to better reporting coverage.

Given these assumptions, the official communist foodgrains figures compare with Wu's adjusted figures in the way shown in Table 4-15.

(c) Because of the relatively low level of "arithmetical literacy" in the countryside, there were bound to be errors in local statistical

[29]Ta-chung Liu and Kung-chia Yeh, The Economy of the Chinese Mainland: National Income and Economic Development, 1933-1959, op. cit., p. 140.

[30]Anthony M. Tang, "Policy and Performance in Agriculture," in Walter Galenson, Alexander Eckstein, and T. C. Liu (eds.), Economic Trends in Communist China (Chicago: Aldine, 1967).

[31]Liu and Yeh, loc. cit., pp. 45, 132.

[32]Yuan-li Wu, The Economy of Communist China: An Introduction, op. cit., p. 140.

[33]Philip P. Jones and Thomas T. Poleman, "Communes and the Agricultural Crisis in Communist China," Food Research Institute Studies, February 1962 (Food Research Institute, Stanford University), p. 4.

[34]Wu, op. cit., pp. 140, 143-144. This reasoning has been challenged by Chi-ming Hou in his "Sources of Agricultural Growth in Communist China," Journal of Asian Studies (August 1968), pp. 721-723.

TABLE 4-15
Production of Cereals and Potatoes in Grain Equivalent
(Millions of metric tons)

Year	Communist Figures	Yuan-li Wu's Adjusted Estimate
1952	154.4	184.2
1953	156.9	180.0
1954	160.5	177.1
1955	174.8	184.1
1956	182.5	182.5
1957	185.0	185.0

Source: Communist figures are from Ten Great Years, op. cit., p. 119. Yuan-li Wu's adjusted figures from Yuan-li Wu, The Economy of Communist China: An Introduction (New York: Praeger and the Pall Mall Press, London, 1965), p. 140, Table VII-2.

reporting. Extension of statistical coverage in the later years of the Plan contributed to the official upward bias.

(d) Fairly large discrepancies probably existed between "biological yield" and "barn yield."[35]

(e) The 1957 figures for livestock, especially pigs, are probably exaggerated. One reason given for the possibly inflated figures is the shift in the inventory date from June 30 to December 31, which may have led to some confusion and double counting.[36]

Although the official claims to production successes in agriculture have probably to be revised downward, the extent and precise reasons for the presumed overstatement can—as we have just seen— merely be guessed at. The assumption that the rate of growth was inflated by underreporting of the cultivated and sown areas in the early years of the Plan period has been questioned. [37] It has been suggested by one writer that the collectivization drive of late 1955 and 1956 had adverse effects on statistical reliability. [38] If this were true, it would be difficult to accept the official 1956 figures as in fact is done by Wu. The 1957 figures are usually accepted by Western economists. Yet at the very time that the 1957 statistics were being compiled, the radical elements in the Party had gained enough strength to launch a massive water conservation drive which shortly

[35] Yuan-li Wu, op. cit., pp. 136-137.
[36] Marion R. Larsen, "China's Agriculture Under Communism," in An Economic Profile of Mainland China, op. cit., p. 234.
[37] E.g., by Chi-ming Hou; see note 34 above.
[38] Marion R. Larsen, op. cit. While the index of cultivated area (1952=100) was 103.6 in 1957, the index of cultivated area per labor unit (1952=100) dropped to 94.4. In the case of sown area the relevant 1957 indices (1952=100) were: total sown area 111.3; sown area per labor unit 101.4

developed into an all-round leap forward that included statistical reporting (Chapters 7 and 8 below).

In these circumstances it is not unreasonable to conclude that agricultural output increased during the First Five Year Plan period, perhaps quite substantially, if unevenly. An annual average increase of between 2 and 3 percent seems plausible. The increase was due to a more widespread and intensive use of traditional inputs, especially labor (i.e., nonbudgeted investments by the peasants themselves). China's subsequent experience (especially the apparent stagnation of output after the Great Leap Forward) tends to support the contention that during the First Five Year Plan traditional inputs and methods of production were pushed almost, but not quite, to their theoretical limits, and that further output increases had to be sought in the application to farming of modern science and technology, and in a fundamental change in the production function. [39] "During the period of the First Five Year Plan and the 1957-1958 period," said a *Ta Kung-pao* editorial of November 21, 1961, "there has been a development of the productive forces in our country. . . . But generally speaking, during those periods, the productive forces in our countryside have undergone no fundamental change." By 1957 the margin available for experiments with traditional ways of farming was extremely narrow.

RATE OF INVESTMENT

It will be recalled that the strategy of economic development used by China during the First Five Year Plan involved high rates of investment.

The proportion of output channeled into increments in the capital stock (investment) is usually presumed to be determined by the rate of saving. The ratio of saving to national income (rate of saving) is a function of per capita incomes. There is a specific relation between increments to capital and increments to national income. This relation is known as incremental capital-output ratio, or ICOR for short. The rate of growth of national income, therefore, is determined jointly by the rate of saving and ICOR. [40] During the period

[39] The point is made by Chi-ming Hou in "Sources of Agricultural Growth in Communist China," *op. cit.*

[40] See William W. Hollister, "Trends in Capital Formation in Communist China," in *An Economic Profile of Mainland China, op. cit.*, p. 124. The ICOR concept must be used with care. Increases in total output result not only from increments to capital (investment), but also from increases in the labor force, improvements in technology, rising educational levels of the labor force, etc. On this see Stephen Enke, *Economics for Development* (Englewood Cliffs, N.J.: Prentice-Hall, 1963), pp. 172-175. Cf. Clair Wilcox, W. D. Weatherford, Holland Hunter, and Morton S. Baratz, *The Economies of the World Today: Their Organization, Development, and Performance* (New York: Harcourt, 1962, 1966), pp. 15, 18.

under review (1953-57) the implied ICOR for China was relatively low, i.e., small additions to investment resulted in big additions to output.[41]

During the period, the Chinese sustained high rates of investment and directed investments primarily into the producers' goods sector. Deliberate choice and chance circumstances were both responsible for this policy. The chance to import some 156 complete producer goods projects from the USSR, equipped with up-to-date capital was not missed by the Chinese even though it meant introducing labor-saving devices into a labor surplus economy.

Communist Data

Communist figures for fixed investment by the state are given in Table 4-16.

TABLE 4-16
State-Fixed Investment at Current Prices
(Billions of Yuan)

	Total	Index	
		Preceding Year = 100	1952 = 100
Total First Five Year Plan	55.00	—	—
1953	8.00	184	184
1954	9.07	113	208
1955	9.30	103	214
1956	14.80	159	340
1957	13.83	93	317

Source: Ten Great Years, p. 55.

Western Data

To arrive at *gross fixed investment*, Hollister[42] adds to the above figures for state fixed investment, estimated amounts of the following: (a) self-financed agricultural investment, (b) supplementary budget allocations for agriculture, (c) nonagricultural investment by private enterprises and households, and (d) major repairs. The resulting figures for gross fixed investment are given in Table 4-17.

[41] Hollister, *loc. cit.*, p. 126, puts the ICOR for China in 1953-57 at 0.8. The implied ICOR for Japan (1950-59) was 2.4; Burma (1951-59), 3.4; India (1950-59), 4.8, and Pakistan (1950-59), 3.0. Liu's reconstructed communist estimate, however, puts the ICOR for China (computed in 1952 prices) during 1953-57 at 2.7 gross and 2.3 net. The ICOR for fixed capital is put by him at 2.0 gross and 1.6 net. Liu, *op. cit.*, p. 62.

[42] W.W. Hollister, "Trends in Capital Formation in Communist China," *op. cit.*, Appendix, p. 151, Table A-1.

TABLE 4-17

W. W. Hollister's Estimates of Gross Fixed Investment
and Gross Domestic Investment, 1953–57
(Billions of Yuan at Current Prices)

Year	Gross Fixed Investment	Gross Investment*
1953	12.59	18.45
1954	14.12	19.40
1955	13.92	19.14
1956	19.87	19.69
1957	18.77	25.31

*Gross domestic investment takes into account changes in inventories.
  Source: W. W. Hollister, "Trends in Capital Formation in Communist China," in *An Economic Profile of Mainland China, op. cit.*, p. 125, Table 1.

Various estimates of the *average annual ratio of investment to national product* in China (1953-57) have been made in the West. It would not be stretching the point too much to conclude that the average annual rate of gross investment was between 20 and 24 percent of gross national product (using current market prices). Gross investment includes changes in inventories. Adjusting for changes in inventories, the rate of gross fixed investment (i.e., increases in productive facilities, net of inventory changes) would be 15-17 percent of gross national product.[43] These rates are high, both when compared with China's estimated prewar performance, and with investment rates for other developing countries. They approximate the Soviet rates during Russia's industrialization drive of 1928-37. In 1928 gross investment represented 14 percent of Soviet GNP (in 1950 rouble factor cost), and 27 percent in 1937.[44] Using current

---

[43] Hollister, *op. cit.*, p. 125. Cf. Ta-chung Liu, "The Tempo of Economic Development of the Chinese Mainland," *op. cit.*, p. 62, Table 6; Yuan-li Wu, *The Economy of Communist China: An Introduction, op. cit.*, p. 91, Table V-1. These estimates roughly agree with the official Chinese Communist data for "accumulation." See Cheng Chu-yuan, *Communist China's Economy, 1949-1962, op. cit.*, pp. 117-118.

[44] A. Bergson, *The Real National Income of Soviet Russia Since 1928* (Cambridge, Mass.: Harvard U. P. 1961), p. 237. Gross investment was 28 percent of Soviet GNP in 1950, and 27.9 percent in 1955 (in terms of current rouble factor cost). From 1928 to 1955 Soviet gross investment increased at almost twice the rate of gross national product and about three times that of personal consumption. J. P. Hardt, D. M. Gallik, and V. G. Treml, "Institutional Stagnation and Changing Economic Strategy in the Soviet Union," in *New Directions in the Soviet Economy, op. cit.*, Part I, p. 33. It should be pointed out, however, that Chinese producer goods during the period 1953-57 appeared to have been overvalued relative to consumer goods. Revaluation in, say, 1933 prices, would tend to give a substantially lower ratio of gross capital investment to gross domestic expenditure than the 20-24 percent yielded by calculations in current prices.

rouble factor cost, the 1928 rate was 25 percent and the 1937 rate was 25.9 percent.

SOURCES OF INVESTMENT FINANCING

The bulk of investment financing during 1953-57 was generated domestically. Only a negligible portion of China's budgetary revenues came from foreign economic loans, and not all of these loans represented the purchase abroad of investment goods. [45] According to one estimate, foreign economic loans accounted for not more than 1.5 percent of China's capital investment from 1953 through 1957.[46]

Chinese data on domestic sources of investment are given in Table 4-18. State revenues were the major source of investment financing, with the possible exception of agricultural investment (below, p. 138).

It will be seen that the single most important source of state revenue throughout the period had been taxes, followed by revenue from state enterprises. Within taxation, industrial and commercial taxes were important; of these, taxes on state enterprises yielded the most revenue.

However, beginning in 1954, revenue (mainly profits) from state enterprises began to play an increasingly important role in total revenue, exceeding that of industrial and commercial taxes. [47] By 1957 revenue from state enterprises almost equaled tax revenue, reflecting the large-scale nationalization of private enterprises in 1955-56. The absolute and relative increase in revenue from state enterprises as a component of state revenues is a very important phenomenon. It implies that increasingly the high rate of capital formation was indirectly financed by preempting the national product for that pur-

[45] According to "Statistics on State Budgetary Revenue and Expenditure During the First Five Year Plan Period," *Ts'ai-cheng* (August 5, 1957), pp. 32-33, Reprinted from Nai-Ruenn Chen, *Chinese Economic Statistics* (Chicago: Aldine, 1967); copyright © 1967 by the Social Science Research Council, p. 157, Table 3.18A, the situation in 1952-55 was as follows:

Year	State Revenue Including Foreign Loan Proceeds (Millions of Yuan)	State Revenue Excluding Foreign Loan Proceeds (Millions of Yuan)
1952	17,560	17,367
1953	21,762	21,270
1954	26,237	24,443
1955	27,203	24,842

[46] F. H. Mah, "The Financing of Public Investment in Communist China," *Journal of Asian Studies*, Vol. 21, No. 1 (November 1961), pp. 33-48.

[47] "Revenue from state enterprises" covers profits (calculated as a percentage of costs), depreciation charges, income arising from changes in the valuation of fixed assets, and surplus working capital.

TABLE 4-18
Sources of State Revenue, 1953-57
(Millions of current yuan)

	1953	1954	1955	1956	1957
Total	21,760	26,230	27,200	28,740	31,020
Tax Revenue	11,970	13,220	12,750	14,090	15,490
Industrial and commercial					
taxes	8,250	8,972	8,725	10,098	
Private business	3,422	2,872	1,671		
Cooperatives	534	925	1,128		
State-private joint enterprises	265	422	556		
State enterprises	(4,029)	(4,753)	(5,370)		
Agricultural taxes	2,711	3,278	3,054	2,965	2,970
Salt taxes	461	521	481	483	
Customs duties	505	412	466	542	
Revenue from state enterprises . .	7,670	9,960	11,190	13,430	14,420
Revenue from credit and insur-					
ance operations	490	1,790	2,360	724	700
Domestic bonds.	—	836	619	607	650
Foreign loans	438	877	1,654	117	23
Insurance operations	(52)	(77)	(87)	—	27
Other revenue	1,630	1,260	900	500	410

Source: Reprinted from Nai-Ruenn Chen, Chinese Economic Statistics
(Chicago: Aldine, 1967). Copyright © 1967 by the Social Science Research
Council, p. 441, Table 10.1. Figures in parentheses derived as residual. All
figures are drawn from Chinese Communist sources.

pose rather than by taxing private and business earned income. [48]
Agricultural taxes, it will be noticed, remained at a more or less
constant level throughout the period. This must be interpreted carefully. It might suggest a relatively light burden on the peasants in the
matter of capital formation, and hence a significant departure from
the Stalinist model of economic development. Such a conclusion
would be hasty, but there is a grain of truth in it. [49] The subject will
be taken up below.

Another interesting set of figures is given in Table 4-19.

Note the decline of the accumulation contribution of individual
and capitalist sectors—a reflection of changes in the property structure of the economy around 1955. This will be discussed at greater
length in Chapter 5.

[48] Yuan-li Wu, op. cit., pp. 94-95. Forced saving and deficit financing should
be added to the "preemptying" procedure.
[49] Lawrence J. Lau, "Peasant Consumption, Saving and Investment in Mainland China," paper prepared for the Conference on "The Agrarian Question in
the Light of Communist and Noncommunist Experience," University of Washington, Seattle, August 1967, p. 85. On the real burden, see below, pp. 138-140.

TABLE 4-19
Sources of Accumulation by Type of Ownership
1953 and 1956

	Percent	
Source	1953	1956
Total	100.0	100.0
Government administration and state economy	80.0	75.5
Public-private joint economy	1.6	6.0
Cooperative economy, total.	4.8	14.3
Agricultrual producers' cooperatives.	0.05	12.1
Individual economy	9.1	1.1
Capitalist economy.	2.5	0.1
Inhabitants	2.0	3.2

Source: Reprinted from Nai-Ruenn Chen, *Chinese Economic Statistics* (Chicago: Aldine, 1967). Copyright © 1967 by the Social Science Research Council, p. 156, Table 3.17. Based on communist sources.

INVESTMENT BY SECTORS

The Stalinist strategy of economic development is more than high rates of capital formation. It is the formation of a particular type of capital, i.e., modern industrial capital, especially heavy industrial capital. In the period 1928-37, 39 percent of Soviet gross investment was channeled into industry, and 40 percent in 1953-59.[50] In the original Stalinist model this type of investment allocation was made at the expense of agriculture, and to an extent, of trade, services, and residential construction. In the Stalinist model the state's policy toward agriculture is extractive rather than developmental. It has already been suggested that, given China's factor endowment, such a course of action could not have been followed to the letter without seriously endangering the political viability of the regime. This argument will be developed in later pages. First, however, we shall take a look at official Chinese Communist data regarding sectoral distribution of state investment in the period 1953-57. This is done in Tables 4-20 and 4-21.

There seems to be little doubt that the priorities are those of the Stalinist model. The emphasis put on the development of heavy industry is beyond question.[51] In the Soviet Union during 1928-55,

[50] N. Kaplan in A. Bergson (ed.), *Soviet Economic Growth*, p. 52, and S. Cohn in *JEC, Dimensions of Soviet Economic Power* (Washington, D.C.: Government Printing Office, 1962), p. 83. Simple averages.

[51] Additional evidence of this trend is supplied by *Ten Great Years*, p. 90.

TABLE 4-20

State Investment in the Departments of the National Economy and Culture, 1953–57

(Percentage of shares)

Year	Industry	Building	Prospecting	Agriculture*	Transport and Telecommunications	Trade	Culture, Education, Scientific Research	Public Health	Urban Public Utilities
1953	35.4	4.5	2.4	9.7	13.4	3.4	7.8	1.9	3.1
1954	42.3	3.9	3.2	4.6	16.5	4.3	7.5	1.7	2.6
1955	46.2	3.5	2.7	6.7	19.0	3.7	6.3	1.1	2.4
1956	46.1	4.4	2.7	8.0	17.7	5.1	6.7	0.7	2.4
1957	52.3	3.3	2.2	8.6	15.0	2.7	6.7	0.9	2.8
1953–1957	45.5	3.9	2.6	7.6	16.4	3.9	6.9	1.2	2.6

*Including forestry, water conservation, and meteorology.

Percentage share of government administration: 1953, 3.4; 1954, 2.3; 1955, 1.5; 1956, 1.1; 1957, 1.3; 1953–57, 1.8. In 1928–32 the realized gross investment share of Soviet industry was 49 percent of GNP. A. Erlich, op. cit., p. 509.

Source: Ten Great Years, pp. 59–60.

TABLE 4-21
Investment in Heavy and Light Industry, 1953-57
(Percentage distribution)

Year	Industry Total	Light Industry	Heavy Industry	Ratio of Light to Heavy Industry
1953	100	17.6	82.4	1 : 4.7
1954	100	17.6	82.4	1 : 4.7
1955	100	12.3	87.7	1 : 7.1
1956	100	13.8	86.2	1 : 6.2
1957	100	15.2	84.8	1 : 5.6
1953-1957	100	15.0	85.0	1 : 5.7

Source: Ten Great Years, p. 61.

over 90 percent of industrial investment typically went to producer goods industries.[52]

Many Western analysts have taken the 7.6 percent investment rate in agriculture as an indication that the Stalinist blueprint was also followed in this sector. In fact, were the communist figures to be accepted at face value, the Chinese would appear to have out-Stalined Stalin in their neglect of agriculture during this period.[53] Such conclusion would be unwarranted.

AGRICULTURE

The investment rate of 7.6 percent tells only part of the agricultural story. The 7.6 percent of total realized *state* investment de-

___

Relative Shares of Means of Production and Consumer Goods in the Total Value of Industrial Output of Communist China, Percent

Year	Output Value of Means of Production	Output Value of Consumer Goods
1953	37.3	62.7
1954	38.5	61.5
1955	41.7	58.3
1956	45.5	54.5
1957	48.4	51.6

In 1928 producers' goods accounted for 40 percent of Soviet gross industrial output, and 58 percent in 1937. *Narodnoie khoziaistvo SSSR v 1962 godu* (Moscow, 1963), p. 120.

[52] *Narodnoie khoziaistvo SSSR v 1959 godu* (Moscow, 1960), pp. 60, 550-551.

[53] In Eastern Europe at the height of Stalinism (1950-54) the percentage shares of agriculture in total investment were as follows: Bulgaria 17, Czechoslovakia 10, East Germany 12, Hungary 14, and Poland 10. Maurice Ernst, *op. cit.*, p. 890, Table 13.

voted to agriculture represents a figure of 4.19 billion yuan. In order to arrive at total realized investment one should add to the 4.19 billion yuan the following, not included in that amount:

(i) self-financed investment by peasants;

(ii) allocations to the army to reclaim wasteland;

(iii) relief funds for rural areas;

(iv) state agricultural loans;

(v) investment in agriculture, water conservation, and forestry by industrial departments.

From the total, one must subtract investment in the lumber industry by the Ministry of Forestry.

Figures for planned investment are given in Table 4-22.

TABLE 4-22
Planned Investment Allocations to Agriculture, 1953–1957

		Billions of Yuan	Percent of Total State Investment*
Total state investment in agricultural, water conservancy, and forestry departments ..		6.10	8.0
Fixed investment	3.26		
Miscellaneous	2.84		
ADD: Allocations to army to reclaim wasteland		0.30	
Relief funds for rural areas		1.06	
State agricultural loans		1.52	
Investment by industrial departments.		0.22	
		9.20	
SUBTRACT: Investment in lumber industry by the Ministry of Forestry		0.80	
		8.40	
ADD: Estimated investment by peasants. .		10.00	
Fixed investment	6.00		
Circulating capital	4.00		
Total investment by state and industrial departments, and self-financed investment by peasants.		18.40	

*"State investment" includes here direct state appropriations and investments by economic departments under the central authorities, provincial and municipal administrations.

Source: Calculated from *First Five Year Plan for the Development of the National Economy of the People's Republic of China in 1953–1957* (Peking: FLP, 1956), pp. 27–33.

What Table 4-22 shows is that total investment in agriculture, by the agencies of the state and by the peasants themselves, was to have been considerably higher than the state investment figures (6.1 billion yuan or 8 percent of total state investment) indicate. If realized investment was anything like the plan, the direct state investment figure of 4.19 billion yuan and the rate of 7.6 percent (see Table 4-20) should similarly be revised upward. In that event it would be more appropriate to say that the share of agriculture in total investment was more than 20 percent during the period, which represents a satisfactory level in China's conditions.[54] This relatively high level of investment in agriculture should not, however, blind one to the fact that it was very largely to be achieved through the financial exertions of the peasants themselves and that this type of peasant investment was mostly of the traditional (labor-intensive) type. Notice, for instance, that while state fixed investment in agriculture was scheduled to be 3.26 billion yuan, the peasants were expected to increase fixed capital by 6 billion yuan. While total state investment in agriculture (all departments) was to have been 8.4 billion yuan, the peasants were asked to contribute 10 billion yuan. It is difficult to say whether these expectations regarding peasant self-financed investment actually materialized, and if so, to what extent.[55] But the burden of investment was squarely placed on the peasants. The bulk

[54] Cf. William W. Hollister, "Trends in Capital Formation in Communist China," *op. cit.*, pp. 128–129. Chi-ming Hou in his "Sources of Agricultural Growth in Communist China," *Journal of Asian Studies* (August 1968), p. 737, puts investment in agriculture during 1952–57 at "no less than 18 percent of total investment." The data were supplied by K. C. Yeh of the RAND Corporation. Hollister's estimated sector shares of gross fixed investment are given below (current prices).

Sector*	1953	1954	1955	1956	1957
Agriculture†	20.7	22.4	24.5	22.8	23.0
Industry, construction, public utilities.	33.0	34.4	34.3	37.8	41.3
Heavy industry	(17.1)	(20.2)	(24.6)	(26.2)	(29.2)
Light industry	(10.2)	(8.2)	(4.0)	(4.6)	(5.7)
Transport and communications	9.4	11.0	13.8	13.8	12.6
Residential construction . .	10.2	9.5	10.5	8.4	9.7
Service and trade	26.5	22.8	16.8	17.0	13.4
Total fixed investment‡ . .	100.0	100.0	100.0	100.0	100.0

*Sector investments are based on estimates of investment for nonproductive purposes that are subtracted from the sector allocations for state investment. All private investment other than industrial investment, handicrafts, and native transportation have been included under investment in trade although small amounts of this investment may properly have fallen under other sectors.

†One-third of self-financed agricultural investment is estimated to be construction, and half of this is assumed to be for housing.

‡Subtotals do not necessarily add to the total because of rounding.

Hollister, *op. cit.*, p. 128, Table 4.

[55] According to Hollister, *op. cit.*, p. 151, self-financed investment by peasants amounted to 12.1 billion yuan during 1953-57. If, as he assumes, one-sixth of this was for housing, the resulting figure would roughly agree with the planned expenditure of 10 billion yuan in 1953-57.

of direct state investment in agriculture went into water conservancy projects intended to raise per acre yields.

The burden on the peasants was made heavier by the disparity between prices of agricultural crops and the prices of products purchased by the peasants. The seriousness of this "scissors" movement is subject to some question. While conceding the price disparity, Professor S. H. Chou argues that the scissors gap was "far less serious than what was experienced in Soviet Russia" at a comparable period of development. [56] Relatively low prices of agricultural products, price concessions to users of producers' goods, and the use of high consumer prices to curtail consumption were, according to Chou, less important in China than in the Soviet Union at a roughly similar developmental stage. The Chinese seem to have resorted more to direct controls (such as the rationing of daily necessities, state measures to expand the cultivable area, and so on) to increase food production and restrict consumption than to price differentials.

Hollister, who agrees that agriculture was not starved in order to support heavy industry, holds that the troubles which beset Chinese agriculture were due more to the allocations of heavy industry investment within heavy industry itself (i.e., import of machinery and equipment instead of chemical fertilizer) than to insufficient allocations to agriculture. [57] This view needs qualification. The output of chemical products rose from 3.2 percent of the gross value of industrial products in 1953 to 6.6 percent in 1957. Thirty-three out of the 694 "large projects" were in the chemical industry, seven of these being ferilizer plants. The range of chemical products was expanded to include not only ammonium sulfate but also ammonium nitrate and some superphosphate. [58] It remains probably true, however, that the chemical industry was promoted as part of the heavy industry push rather than because of any conscious intent to support agriculture. Certainly there was in China during this time less reliance on heavy agricultural equipment than in the Soviet Union at a corresponding period (see Chapter 5).

The safest conclusion would be that during the First Five Year Plan the Chinese Communists tried to combine an extractive and developmental policy toward agriculture, much of the latter being devolved onto the peasants themselves. The degree of forced extraction may be seen from the fact that during the entire 1953-57

[56] S. H. Chou, "Prices in Communist China," *Journal of Asian Studies*, Vol. 25 (August 1966), p. 654.

[57] Hollister, *op. cit.*, p. 129.

[58] See Jung-chao Liu, "Fertilizer Supply and Grain Production in Communist China," *Journal of Farm Economics* (November 1965), pp. 917-918, and his "Fertilizer Application in Communist China," *China Quarterly* (October-December 1965), pp. 28-52.

period, the retained value of agricultural output per peasant remained at about 92 yuans, while total marketed value rose from 12.97 billion yuan in 1952 to 20.28 billion yuan in 1957, or by 56.4 percent.[59]

RESIDENTIAL HOUSING

Sharp disagreement exists among Western economists regarding the residential housing situation in China during the Five Year Plan period.

Professor Kang Chao[60] argues that (a) only 8.6 percent of total fixed investment was given to housing construction during the period; (b) the government was reluctant to mobilize private funds for house building to alleviate the housing shortage, and in any event (c) the general income level of workers was too low for them to buy or build new houses; (d) the low rental level for public housing (2-3 percent of a family's income on the average) set a conventional ceiling for private rentals, which meant that private rental income was too low to induce owners to make investments in new housing; (e) difficulties in obtaining building materials and construction workers obstructed the construction of private housing; (f) there was a lack of proper maintenance and repairs as a result of which large numbers of private dwellings collapsed every year (on August 9, 1954, for example, more than 3,000 houses in Peking fell to the ground after a heavy rain); (g) many residential houses were demolished in order to widen streets and make room for new industrial construction; (h) there was a rapid influx of people into the cities. As a result of all these factors, and assuming a very modest depreciation rate (2 percent per annum), replacement needs in the period 1953-57 were just barely met, the total stock of urban residential housing reaching the 1949 level in 1957. Even in 1960 the total stock of urban housing was, according to Chao, only 10 percent higher than in 1949, while the urban population had more than doubled over the period. By 1957 per capita housing declined by one-third from the

[59] Anthony M. Tang, "Agriculture in the Industrialization of Communist China," op. cit., p. 1129. Ten Great Years, p. 168.

Rate of Marketable Output in Total Output of Food Grains, percent

1952	1953	1954	1955
23.4	25.2	30.8	26.7

Reprinted from Nai-Ruenn Chen, Chinese Economic Statistics (Chicago: Aldine, 1967). Copyright © 1967 by the Social Science Research Council, p. 405, Table 7.35.

[60] Kang Chao, "Industrialization and Urban Housing in Communist China," China," Journal of Asian Studies (May 1966), pp. 381–396.

1949 level (i.e., 6.3 square meters in 1949, to 4.0 square meters in 1957).

Professor Hollister [61] while agreeing that investment in housing by all socialist enterprises was below 10 percent of fixed investment, maintains that a substantial amount of residential construction was undertaken by the private sector. From 1950 through 1955 private investment in urban housing was, according to this argument, about 70 percent of the official figures for investment by socialist enterprises. Hollister also holds that major repairs were sufficient to keep the existing stock of urban housing habitable and inhabited during 1950-59, but that the rise in urban housing was barely sufficient to maintain a low living standard in urban areas for housing, in view of the rapid increase in the urban population. [62] Hollister believes that if Chao's estimate of the deterioration in the per capita housing situation were to be accurate, "such a trend would involve massive efforts in rationing housing space in urban areas and tensions that do not seem to have occurred. . . ." [63] Moreover, the alleged difficulty experienced by the private sector in obtaining building materials and construction workers is countered by the fact that much urban residential housing uses dirt to be packed into walls and other materials not subject to state controls, and that most of the labor involved can be furnished by the residents themselves and by craftsmen available outside the state apparatus. [64] Dick Wilson ("Portrait of Peking," FEER, July 16, 1964, p. 118) reported that from 1949 through 1963, 156 million square feet of new housing space were built in Peking, in addition to 8 million square feet of hospitals and sanitoria.

TRADE AND SERVICES

It would seem that the brunt of the heavy industry push was taken by allocations for trade and nonagricultural services. According to Western estimates, the share of fixed investment in this sector declined during the 1953-57 period from 26.5 percent in 1953 to 13.4 percent in 1957. [65]

[61] Hollister, "Trends in Capital Formation in Communist China," op. cit., pp. 129-131.

[62] Ibid., p. 130.

[63] Ibid., p. 130. There was, however, informal rationing, of urban housing in the sense that many of those who migrated to the cities had relatives there and were forced to live with them because of the difficulty of finding living quarters elsewhere.

[64] Other sources on housing: Christopher Howe, "The Supply and Administration of Urban Housing in Mainland China: The Case of Shanghai," China Quarterly (January-March 1968), pp. 73-97; Wang Pi, "Urban Housing in New China," Peking Review (November 20, 1960), pp. 23-24.

[65] Hollister, op. cit., p. 128, Table 4. Cf. p. 139 footnote 54 above.

The figures for this sector probably include allocations for military construction. It is unlikely that this component of allocations to the sector decreased markedly during the period. Thus, the decline in actual trade and civilian nonagricultural services was probably sharper than the estimates indicate.

DEFENSE OUTLAYS

This is a thorny subject because meaningful information on miltary expenditures is not normally published. Eckstein[66] cites various estimates suggesting that in 1952 defense absorbed about 6 percent of GNP at market prices, 7 percent in 1955, and 6 percent in 1957. The estimates are the result of a breakdown of government consumption figures, but it is difficult to say how reliable they are.

Presumably, in view of the Korean conflict and the important role assigned to the military in early political and economic reform, China had at this time a large standing army, possibly 6 million men. Over a longer period (1957-67) the size of the army may have fluctuated between 2.5 and 3 million men.[67]

Such a large defense establishment would suggest a relatively heavy burden on the economy.[68] It has been mentioned earlier (Chapter 3) that Soviet military credits during 1950-52 may have been as high as $1 billion, and that all of this aid had to be paid back. It should also be added that in 1955 China and the Soviet Union concluded an agreement on what was described as the peaceful uses of atomic energy, but which, in time, seemed to have veered mainly toward military applications. Chinese scientists (about a thousand) were sent to the Soviet atomic research institute at Dubna. Twenty percent of the cost of this venture was apparently covered by the Chinese. By the end of 1957 preparations were being made for the installation in China of a Soviet experimental nuclear reactor and a gaseous diffusion plant. An Institute of Atomic Energy was set up in Peking in May 1957. In October of that year a top-level Chinese military delegation visited the USSR and, according to the Chinese, got Soviet promises of aid in the development of China's

[66] Alexander Eckstein, *Communist China's Economic Growth and Foreign Trade: Implications for U.S. Policy* (New York: McGraw-Hill, 1966), p. 42, Table 3-1.

[67] J. G. Godaire, "Communist China's Defense Establishment: Some Economic Implications," in *An Economic Profile of Mainland China, op. cit.*, Vol. 1, p. 161.

[68] Defense accounted for 21.11 percent of total state budgeted expenditures in 1954 and 33.8 percent in 1950. *China News Analysis*, No. 44 (July 19, 1954), and Po I-po, "The Draft Budget for 1950," in *New China's Economic Achievements, 1949-1952* (Peking: FLP, 1952), pp. 34-44. *Ten Great Years* cites higher figures. See also Chapter 6, Table 6-3.

military nuclear capability—a promise on which the Soviets allegedly went back a year later. [69] Although not all the expenditures on the development of nuclear capacity can be ascribed to military uses, there is no doubt that a substantial portion of them went into such channels.

It has been argued, on the other hand, that the operating costs of the Chinese military establishment have had a relatively small economic impact over the long run, or as one writer put it, "the net cost of this force has been roughly equal to zero." [70] The reasons given for this contention are: (a) the army does not represent an important percentage of the labor force of the country, so that the addition of soldiers to the civilian labor force would represent a small increment to national income; (b) since the group is not, on the average, equipped with critical skills, its productivity in civilian employment would be low; (c) the army, as we have seen in Chapter 2, is not only a fighting force but a labor force as well. It is probable that to an important degree the army is self-sufficient in food. Moreover, at harvest time it is used in field work, and participates in such capital construction projects as road and railroad building, construction of dikes and irrigation ditches, the establishment of state farms in inhospitable regions, and so on. Over the long run this argument may be valid. It appears less convincing for the period 1953-57 when debts had to be incurred to equip the army with expensive modern weapons and to set up modern armaments industries. It could also be argued that the hypothesis of low skills is tenuous. The modern army is in a sense a vocational education extension institution.

CONCLUSION ON STRATEGY

In general it can be said that during 1953-57 the Chinese followed the broad outlines of the (Stalinist) strategy of selective growth under conditions of austerity with three important qualifications.

[69] "The Origin and Development of the Differences Between the Leadership of the CPSU and Ourselves," Comment on the Open Letter of the Central Committee of the CPSU by the Editorial Departments of Jen-min Jih-pao and Hung-ch'i, Sept. 6, 1963, in The Polemic on the General Line of the International Communist Movement (Peking: FLP, 1965), p. 77. This document said, among others, that "the Soviet Government unilaterally tore up the agreement on new technology for national defense concluded between China and the Soviet Union in October 1957, and refused to provide China with a sample of an atomic bomb and technical data concerning its manufacture" (p. 77). Cf. Chapters 8 and 9 below.

[70] J. G. Godaire, op. cit.

First, the exploitation of agriculture for the benefit of heavy industry was less glaring than that practiced during a comparable period in the Soviet Union.

Second, investment in agriculture was largely extrabudgetary, i.e., self-financed by peasants—hence traditional and labor-intensive. This represented a departure from the Soviet Stalinist model which relied on the early application to farming of large amounts of heavy agricultural machinery.

Third, profits from state enterprises played an increasingly more important part in state budgetary revenues, and hence in state investment expenditures than they did in the Soviet Union at a comparable period of time.

The Soviet model could not be transplanted to China in its entirety because of (a) China's different factor endowments as compared with the USSR; (b) the gradual loss of confidence in Stalinism in general and Stalinist economics in particular; (c) the increasingly strained relations between China and the Soviet Union; and (d) the corresponding Chinese desire to find a native solution to the problem of development, and to force the rate of modernization.

*   *   *

The strategy of selective growth under conditions of austerity made use of a number of institutional tools, to the consideration of which we now turn.

5 | The First Five Year Plan, 1953–57: Institutional Reform in Agriculture and Industry

In this chapter we again take up the theme of Chapter 3: the reform of economic, social, and political institutions in the direction of socialism as the Chinese envisaged it. The basic purpose of the reforms was to put the leadership in a position to effectively implement the strategy of selective growth under conditions of austerity. It meant the quasi-total nationalization or collectivization of the private sector in agriculture, industry, and trade, and a corresponding strengthening of governmental and Party machinery. Reconstruction and reform (which had been examined in Chapter 3)—Mao's "new democracy"—was merely a phase to be gone through before the inauguration of socialist modes of production and distribution. As has been mentioned before, the timing of the transition from new democracy to socialism had been the subject of dispute among policy makers. We shall see in this and the following chapters that the modalities of socialist reform were also seen differently by different members of Mao Tse-tung's entourage.

COLLECTIVIZATION OF AGRICULTURE

THE SOVIET PRECEDENT

Stalin's collectivization drive and the accompanying "dekulakization" (elimination of the so-called "rich" peasants) meant in practice the forcible removal from their farms of some 10 million people in four years. Deaths among the deportees may have been as high as 3-4 millions, and this is probably a conservative estimate. Stalin himself admitted to Winston Churchill that the collectivization process was "fearful," that it was "a terrible struggle," and that he had to cope with 10 million people.[1] In its original form, the First Soviet

[1] Winston Churchill, *The Second World War: The Hinge of Fate* (Boston, Mass.: Houghton, 1950), Vol. IV, pp. 447, 498–499.

Five Year Plan foresaw the collectivization of a maximum of 20 percent of the farms by 1933. In the spring of 1929 Stalin still asserted that private farms would continue in the future to play a most significant role in Russia's agriculture. By the end of the year the drive to collectivize the peasants and destroy the kulaks was in full swing, class struggle was fanned in the countryside, forced labor camps were bursting at the seams. Within a few years Russia's agriculture had been collectivized at an appalling price in human life. Literally doomed to death, the richer and middle peasants resisted by burning houses and crops, and by slaughtering their own livestock. According to Stalin, these peasants destroyed 17,400,000 horses, 30,000,000 head of cattle, and 100,000,000 sheep and goats.[2] Land was left untilled and famine stalked the land.

The story of man's brutality to man, of the incredible suffering and degradation imposed on millions of human beings by a dictator's whim, has not been fully told to this day. Stalin confided in Churchill that "it was absolutely necessary for Russia."[3] It was not. Professor Karcz's hypothesis that it was all a terrible mistake due to Stalin's erroneous and inconsistent use of marketing figures, makes the tragedy all the more stark and senseless.[4] Yet one cannot escape the impression that it was due as much to Stalin's twisted personality as to the doctrine which he held.[5]

To the Chinese Communists, Stalin's way of dealing with the peasant problem was both an inspiration and a warning. It is safe to say that all factions within the top leadership believed collectivization to be necessary in order to eventually make the communist dream come true, but some were more wary about how collectivization was to be carried out, more fearful of the possible immediate consequences than others. There was no telling how the freshmen owners of land might react, how much violence and destruction cooperativization might bring in its train.

[2] J. Stalin, *Problems of Leninism* (Moscow, 1947), p. 480. According to Naum Jasny, *The Socialized Agriculture of the U.S.S.R.: Plans and Performance* (Stanford, Calif.: Stanford U. P., 1949), p. 324, Table 25, between 1928 and 1933, 18.5 million horses were lost, 36.7 million cattle, 17 million hogs, and 104.1 million sheep and goats.

[3] Winston Churchill, *op. cit.*, p. 447.

[4] Jerzy F. Karcz, "Thoughts on the Grain Problem," *Soviet Studies* (April 1967), p. 339.

[5] See Prybyla, "Moscow, Mao, and the Cultural Revolution," *International Review of History and Political Science* (February 1968), pp. 84, 86, and Prybyla, "Communism: Its Growing Diversity," *Journal of General Education* (October 1966), pp. 207–218.

SOVIET AND CHINESE COLLECTIVIZATION[6]

There are a number of striking *similarities* between Stalin's and Mao's ways of handling the institutional problem in agriculture. On closer analysis, some of these turn out to be rather superficial.

1. Both the Soviets and the Chinese started with a reform which gave land to individual peasant households. In the Soviet Union this type of small peasant agriculture was stabilized for seven years.

2. Both embarked on collectivization via lower-level, transitional cooperative arrangements in which for a time voluntary participation by peasants played a dominant role.[7]

The transitional arrangement in the Soviet Union from 1918 to 1927 was the TOZ ("Cooperative for the Working of the Land"), a flexible producers' association in which all productive livestock and most of the workstock were privately owned, while the working of the soil and farm machinery were partly collectivized. The product was shared in accordance with labor, land, and capital contributed.[8] The arrangement, which served as the prototype for the later fully fledged collective, was the artel in which field work was almost totally collectivized as was most of the productive livestock. Artel households were allowed to cultivate for themselves small plots of land (vegetable gardens) and to own some livestock.

The transitional arrangements in China consisted of (a) mutual aid teams, and (b) lower-level agricultural producers' cooperatives. These arrangements lasted from about 1950 to 1955.

Mutual aid teams were of two kinds: seasonal and year-round. "Peasants joining mutual aid teams worked together, while their land, draught animals, farm tools and other means of farm production remained their own private property; the farm produce of each piece of land went to the family that owned it. . . . At the very beginning the organization of such mutual aid teams was temporary and seasonal; they were later developed into round-the-year mutual aid teams in which there was, on the basis of working together, a certain degree of division of labor and line, and a small amount of collectively owned property."[9]

---

[6] On the general problem of agricultural cooperation and collectivization, see Louis P. F. Smith, *The Evolution of Agricultural Co-Operation* (Oxford: Oxford U. P., 1961); K. R. Walker, *Planning in Chinese Agriculture: Socialization and the Private Sector, 1959-1962* (London: Frank Cass, 1965).

[7] Remember that in a totalitarian state the notion of voluntary participation is somewhat elusive and ambiguous.

[8] Naum Jasny, *The Socialized Agriculture of the USSR, op. cit.*, pp. 49 and 299-300; Lazar Volin, *Survey of Soviet Russian Agriculture*, Agriculture Monograph No. 5 (Washington, D.C.: U.S. Department of Agriculture, 1951), p. 21.

[9] Liao Lu-yen, "Agricultural Collectivization in China," in *Socialist Industrialization and Agricultural Collectivization in China* (Peking: FLP, 1964), p. 28.

The lower-level (or elementary) agricultural producers' cooperatives "pooled land and practised unified management and distribution of income. The principle followed in their distribution was that a smaller part of the income was distributed as land payment proportionate to the amount of land pooled by the members, which was an expression of the continued private ownership of land [the land payment share varied from 30 to 60 percent of the crops harvested]; while the greater part of the income was distributed as work payment according to the quantity and quality of the work done by the co-op members taking part in collective labor. . . . This was the main organizational form . . . put in practice in China's countryside from 1953 to 1955."[10] Each household was allowed a "retained plot" of arable land for private use. These plots were located in the pooled fields, the plot area per head being fixed at a maximum of 5 percent of the average arable area per head in the village.

The final step was the advanced agricultural producers' cooperative or fully fledged collective farm (kolkhoz) in which land payment was abolished. "The co-op members' privately owned draught animals, farm tools, and other major means of production were pooled and their money value turned into the collective property of the co-ops. After setting a part of the value of the draught animals, farm tools, etc., against the cost of shares necessary for membership, the rest of their value was repaid by the co-ops in installments. After deducting the costs of production and management, reserve funds, public welfare funds, and agricultural tax, all income of the co-ops was distributed among the members according to the socialist principle 'to each according to his work, and more income for those who work more.' "[11] Private plots were allocated to members of the collective according to the 5 percent rule (see above).

The rapid transition from TOZ to artel in the Soviet Union in 1930-33 and the equally spectacular transition from elementary (lower level) to advanced cooperatives in China in 1956-57 may be seen from Table 5-1.

See also John Wong, "Mutual Aid Co-Operation in China's Agricultural Collectivization," *The China Mainland Review* (Hong Kong), June 1967, pp. 369-389; Tung Ta-lin, *Agricultural Co-Operation in China* (Peking: *FLP*, 1959); the *Draft Decision on Mutual Aid Co-Operatives* (drawn up in December 1951) in *New China Monthly*, Vol. 42, No. 4 (1953), pp. 118-121; "Agricultural Collectivization," *China News Analysis* (June 13, 1969).

[10] Liao Lu-yen, *op. cit.*, pp. 28-29. The organizational principles of lower level collectives were set out in *Model Regulations for an Agricultural Producers' Co-Operative*, adopted by the Standing Committee of the National People's Congress on March 17, 1956, at its 33rd meeting (Peking: *FLP*, 1956). The dividend for land pooled was slowly reduced, so that in the end payments were to be for labor input exclusively.

[11] Liao Lu-yen, *op. cit.*, pp. 29-30. See also, *Decisions on Agricultural Co-operation* (Peking: *FLP*, 1956).

TABLE 5-1

The Disappearance of the TOZ (Soviet Union) and the Elementary Agricultural
Producers' Cooperative (China)

Soviet Union			China		
Year	Number of TOZ (thousands)	Number of Arteli (thousands)	Year	Number of Elementary Cooperatives (thousands)	Number of Advanced Cooperatives (thousands)
1927	6.4	7.1	1950	0.018	0.001
1928	19.9	11.6	1952	3.6	0.010
1929	34.3	19.2	1953	15.1	0.015
1929[a]	42.0	20.8	1954	114.2	0.201
1930	14.9	63.5	1955	633.2	0.529
1931	9.9	193.6	1956[b]	700.9	302.800
1932	4.5	202.4	1956	681.7	311.900
1933	4.3	216.2	1957[c]	84.0	668.000
			1957	—	700.000
			1958[d]	—	740.000

[a]October 1.   [b]End of May 1956.
[c]March 1957.   [d]July 1958.
Sources: Soviet Union—Naum Jasny, *The Socialized Agriculture of the
U.S.S.R., op. cit.,* p. 320, Table 24. China—1950–May 1956, State Statistical
Bureau, *Report on Fulfilment of the National Plan of the People's Republic of
China in 1955* (Peking: FLP, 1965), p. 38; 1957, H. Yin and Yi-chang Yin,
Economic Statistics of Mainland China (Cambridge, Mass.: Harvard U. P., 1960),
p. 38; 1958, Henry J. Lethbridge, *The Peasant and the Communes* (Hong Kong:
Green Pagoda Press, 1960), p. 189.

Table 5-2 shows how the drive to (a) establish mutual aid teams
and lower level agricultural cooperatives, and (b) transform the transitional arrangements into advanced agricultural producers' cooperatives, fared in China in terms of member peasant households.[12]

3. Both the Soviets and the Chinese unleashed a campaign to
eliminate landlords and rich peasants as a class. The drive, it might be
added, also tended to eliminate physically many landlords and some
rich peasants.[13]

4. Both, up the the last moment, assured the peasants that advanced collectivization was reserved for a fairly distant future, that
for the time being individual agriculture would remain dominant, and
that joining the kolkhozy would always be a question of the individ-

[12]"Under the First Five Year Plan we must further develop and improve
agricultural mutual aid organizations in their various forms. . . ." *First Five Year
Plan for Development of the National Economy of the People's Republic of
China in 1953-57* (Peking: FLP, 1956), p. 120. Compare this statement with the
figures in Table 5-2.
[13]For the contrasting experience of the Soviet Union and China on this
score, see p. 157 below.

TABLE 5-2

Development of Mutual Aid Teams and Agricultural Producers'
Cooperatives in China

	Percentages of Peasant Households Belonging to Mutual Aid Teams and Cooperative Organizations						
	1950	1952	1953	1954	1955	1956	1957*
Total of peasant households . . .	100.0	100.0	100.0	100.0	100.0	100.0	100.0
Belonging to mutual aid teams and cooperative organizations (elementary and advanced). . . .	10.7	40.0	39.5	60.3	64.9	96.3	97.0
Agricultural producers' cooperatives.		0.1	0.2	2.0	14.2	96.3	97.0
Advanced . .						87.8	
Elementary .		0.1	0.2	2.0	14.2	8.5	
Mutual aid teams	10.7†	39.9	39.3‡	58.3	50.7	—	—
All-year round	—	10.1	11.5	26.2	27.6	—	—
Seasonal . . .	—	29.8	27.8	32.1	23.1	—	—

*End of May 1957. Almost all the agricultural producers' cooperatives were
of the advanced type by this time.
†Most of these were concentrated in north and northeast China.
‡There were considerable regional variations.
Sources: State Statistical Bureau, *Report on the Fulfilment of the National
Economic Plan of the People's Republic of China in 1955* (Peking: FLP, 1956),
p. 37; *Ten Great Years*, p. 35; H. Yin and Yi-chang Yin, *Economic Statistics of
Mainland China* (Cambridge, Mass.: Harvard U. P., 1960), p. 38.

ual household's voluntary and unconstrained decision. Both reneged
on the promise.

The First Soviet Five Year Plan (October 1928-September 1933)
foresaw in its original version (prepared in 1928) the collectivization
of 12.9 million peasants by 1932-33, leaving 121 million peasants
outside the collectives. By 1933-34, 18.6 million peasants were to
have been collectivized, with about 117 million peasants left outside
the kolkhozy. In actual fact, over 100 million peasants were whipped
into some 250,000 collectives in the brief span of four years. The
Gosplan kept revising its collectivization targets upward, but could
not keep up with Stalin's fury.

A somewhat similar development took place in China. The Draft
First Five Year Plan stated that "by 1957, about one-third of all the
peasant households in the country will have joined the present agricultural producers' cooperatives of elementary form. . . . The individ-

ual peasant economy still possesses a certain amount of latent productive power which should in suitable ways be brought into play as
fully as possible to raise the yield per unit area." [14] As early as March
1953, and again in the spring of 1955, the moderate segments of the
Party openly opposed hasty collectivization. In the first half of 1953
they actually succeeded in reducing the number of mutual aid teams
in the name of consolidating the new democratic system.[15] The
left-wing elements, however, counterattacked in June. In November
they consolidated their position in the course of the Third National
Conference on Mutual Aid and Cooperativization. The Central Committee "Decisions on the Development of Agricultural Producers'
Cooperatives" adopted in December 1953 said that "it is absolutely
impermissible to try and carry out the socialist transformation of
small peasant economy merely by issuing a call from above. . . . Compulsion, commandism, and expropriation of the peasants' means of
production are criminal acts." [16] This was to be interpreted in a
Machiavellian dialectical manner two years later. After all, it was
argued, (a) collectivization is not expropriation but merely a change
from individual to group ownership, and since each individual is part
of the group, he is also part owner, and (b) by definition, "collective
ownership is established voluntarily by the peasants and handicraftsmen under the leadership, and with the assistance of the Party and
the state power of the proletariat." [17] Those who reject that leadership and assistance and balk at proletarian power, are enemies of the
people, bourgeois elements, freaks and monsters who do not count in
the reckoning.

In a decision adopted on March 3, 1955, the State Council spoke
of insufficient experience and preparation in the matter of running
collective farms, restiveness of the peasants, and loss of livestock and
forest land resulting from both. [18] Mao countered with a speech on

[14] First Five Year Plan, op. cit., pp. 119-120.

[15] The "gust of right opportunism" was fanned by a March 26, 1953 Jen-
min Jih-pao editorial entitled "Wherein Lies the Leadership of Agricultural Production."

[16] Hsiao Shu, "The Peasant Question in the Socialist Revolution," Hung-
ch'i, No. 6, 1961 in Peking Review (May 26, 1961), p. 15.

[17] Ibid., p. 15.

[18] Four years later Liu Shao-ch'i gave more details of the controversy.
"There were at one time controversies between different viewpoints within our
Party on the question of agricultural cooperation. One viewpoint was that the
level of our industrialization was still very low and that we were not yet in a
position to effect the mechanization of agriculture, so it was impossible and
improper to introduce agricultural cooperation too soon. . . . Another viewpoint
was that the rapid realization of cooperation would inevitably lower agricultural
production. . . . Still another viewpoint was that the realization of agricultural
cooperation at such high speed would impair the unity of the peasants, or, in
other words, that in addition to the rich peasants, the well-to-do middle peasants
would also feel dissatisfied with us or even oppose us while only those peasants

July 31, 1955, which in many respects, is reminiscent of Stalin's article in *Pravda* of November 7, 1929.[19] In the speech Mao referred to those who wanted to slow down the collectivization process as "tottering along like a woman with bound feet, always complaining that others are going too fast." Even then, however, the Maoist program scheduled the absorption of half the peasant households in lower level cooperatives by 1958. The rest were to be absorbed between 1958 and 1960. As late as December 1955 Mao reiterated his conviction that collectivization would come in three or four years, i.e., by 1959 or 1960.[20]

5. The tempo of collectivization was, at its peak, broadly similar in both countries. This is shown in Table 5-3.

Notice the sudden burst of collectivization in Russia around 1929-30 and in China in 1955-56. What took the Soviets eight years to accomplish, was done in China in just one year (Table 5-4). After the second winter of the collectivization drive, Stalin was forced to back down for a while: in March 1930 he blamed the officials in charge of the process for having become "dizzy with success" and for misunderstanding his order.[21] As a matter of fact, everybody had

---

who were relatively worse off would support us." Liu Shao-ch'i, "The Victory of Marxism-Leninism in China" (September 14, 1959), in *Collected Works of Liu Shao-ch'i, 1958-1967* (Hong Kong: URI, 1968), p. 55. Also available in pamphlet form from Peking, FLP, 1959. See also "An Outline of the Struggle Between the Two Lines on the Front of Agricultural Mechanization," by the Mass Criticism Group of the Revolutionary Great Alliance Committee of the Administrative Bureau of Agricultural Mechanization, Eighth Ministry of Machine Building, *Agricultural Machinery and Technique* (Peking), No. 9 (September 8, 1968), pp. 8-21. Special issue on Revolutionary Mass Criticism in *URS*, Vol. 53, Nos. 5-6 (October 15-18, 1968), pp. 50-76, and Vol. 53, Nos. 7-8 (October 22-25, 1968), pp. 77-99. Referred to throughout as "Outline of Struggle." See particularly pp. 54-55.

[19] Mao Tse-tung, "On the Question of Agricultural Co-Operatives," *People's China* (November 1, 1955), pp. 3-17. Joseph Stalin, "A Year of Great Change," *Problems of Leninism* (Moscow: Foreign Languages Publishing House, 1954), pp. 389-413. Mao's speech was addressed to provincial Party secretaries, bypassing the Rural Work Department. It is also available in *Communist China 1955-1959: Policy Documents with Analysis* (Cambridge, Mass.: Harvard U. P., 1965), and in *Selected Readings from the Works of Mao Tse-tung* (Peking: FLP, 1967). For an analysis of the speeded-up collectivization process in China, see Kenneth R. Walker, "Collectivization in Retrospect: The 'Socialist High Tide' of Autumn 1955-Spring 1956," *China Quarterly* (April-June 1966), pp. 1-43.

[20] Mao's Preface to *Socialist Upsurge in China's Countryside* (Peking: FLP, 1957), p. 8. In his alleged third confession (1967), Liu Shao-ch'i had reportedly admitted his hesitations about agricultural collectivization in 1951. He did not refute Ten Tzu-hui's "mistaken views" on collectives. As an indirect result of this, 20,000 cooperatives were eliminated. Wall poster in Peking, July 1967 in *Chinese Law and Government* (White Plains, N.Y.: IASP), Vol. I, No. 1 (Spring 1968), p. 77.

[21] J. Stalin, "Dizzy with Success," *Problems of Leninism, op. cit.*, pp. 419-425.

TABLE 5-3
Comparison of Collectivization in the Soviet Union and China

Soviet Union*		China	
Year	Peasant Households, Percent	Year	Peasant Households,† Percent
1918	0.1	1950	—
1927	0.8	1951	—
1928	1.7	1952	0.1
1929	3.9	1953	0.2
1930	23.6	1954	2.0
1931	52.7	1955	14.2
1932	61.5	1956	96.3
1937	93.0	1957‡	97.0
1940	99.0		

*1939 territory.
†In agricultural producers' cooperatives (elementary and advanced).
‡End of May 1957.
Sources: Soviet Union—Tsentraln'oe statisticheskoe upravlenie, Narodnoie khoziaistvo SSSR v 1958 godu: statisticheskii sbornik (Moscow: Gosstatizdat, 1959), p. 346. China—Ten Great Years, p. 35; H. Yin and Yi-chang Yin, Economic Statistics of Mainland China (Cambridge, Mass.: Harvard U. P., 1960), p. 38.

perfectly understood his orders. From 1931 to 1933 only about 10 percent of what was left of peasant individual holdings were collectivized. There was a somewhat similar episode in China in 1957 when the government moved to reduce the size of collective farms, increase the size of the kolkhozniki's private plots, and ease controls on rural markets. As early as June 1956 the Party's right wing tried to slow down the pace of collectivization (see Table 5-4). The Party's Central Propaganda Department published an editorial in Jen-min Jih-pao titled "To Oppose Also Rashness While Opposing Conservatism" (June 20, 1956) which was allegedly approved by Liu Shaoch'i in person. Taking their cue from the double-wheel, double-share plow fiasco (see below, p. 163), the moderates attacked "impetuosity and rash advance." The article signaled the right wing's counterattack, which developed in the autumn and winter of 1956. During the winter of 1956 thousands of peasants withdrew from the newly formed collectives. In the Soviet Union's Russian Republic at a comparable time (i.e., following Stalin's "Dizzy with Success" article) the proportion of households in collectives fell (in a two months' period) from 60 percent to 23.4 percent.[22] As in Russia, so also in China the interlude was brief. In China the short halt was called after advanced

[22] Naum Jasny, op. cit., p. 308. According to Chu-yuan Cheng (Communist China's Economy, 1949-1962, op. cit., p. 36), in Kwangtung Province during the winter of 1956, about 160,000 peasant households applied for withdrawal from advanced collectives and 80,000 succeeded.

collectivization had been substantially completed; in Russia, after the first massive outburst. In Russia the brief and relative liberalization was imposed by Stalin on his bureaucrats; in China the reverse seems to have taken place—the bureaucrats briefly forced Mao to rest on his oars.

TABLE 5-4

Collectivization in China: December 1955 to December 1956

	Households in	
	Advanced Agricultural Producers' Cooperatives	Elementary Agricultural Producers' Cooperatives
	As Percentage of Total Households	
1955		
December	—a	14.2
1956		
January	30.7	49.6
February	51.0	36.0
March	54.9	34.0
April	58.2	32.1
May	61.9	29.3
June	63.2	28.7
July	63.4	29.0
August	66.1	26.8
September	72.7	21.8
October	78.0	17.6
November	83.0	13.1
December	87.8	8.5

aNegligible.

Source: State Statistical Bureau, Agricultural Cooperation and Statistical Materials on Income Distribution of Agricultural Producers' Cooperatives in 1955 (Peking, 1957) in John Wong, "Mutual Aid Co-Operation in China's Agricultural Collectivization," The China Mainland Review (June 1967), p. 370, Table I.

6. Both the Soviet Union and China followed during the period of collectivization a policy of self-sufficiency in food. Even during the worst famine years, the Soviets exported grain, sometimes at dumping prices. Imports of grain were ruled out because, it was argued, Russia did not have the necessary foreign exchange to pay for such purchases. The Chinese adopted the same attitude. Grain imports were eliminated, and exports of grain were used to pay for the purchase abroad (mainly in the USSR) of capital equipment for the producers' goods industry. This trend was not reversed until 1961.[23]

[23] Exports of agricultural products typically accounted for three-fourths of China's total exports under the communists. Exports of foodstuffs declined from one-half of total exports in 1953 to one-fourth of the total in 1960. See Robert F. Dernberger, "Factors Influencing China's Trade," Communist Affairs (May-June 1967), p. 6.

7. The Chinese adopted from the Soviets the idea of Machine Tractor Stations (MTS). In the Soviet Union the MTS served the twin purpose of concentrating, and thus husbanding, scarce agricultural machinery and technical manpower, and politically supervising the peasants. By 1955 about 140 such centers were in operation in China's countryside; by 1962, after their suppression during the Great Leap Forward (1958-60—see Chapter 8), there were more than 2,000 of them.[24]

The outward similarities tend to conceal far-reaching *differences* in the collectivization processes in the two countries.

1. The Soviet drive to herd the peasants into collectives met with bitter resistance and led to huge loss of life and serious disruptions of agricultural production. Apparently the Chinese process did not—or at least led to nothing like the Soviet slaughter, famine, and fall in output.

This should be qualified in at least five ways.

(i) There was loss of livestock in China during the winter of 1956 and the spring of 1957, due in part to peasant lassitude and indifference. In Kiangsu Province, according to one survey, 60,000 draught animals perished. In Shantung Province, 30 percent of draught animals were found to have been undernourished.[25]

(ii) Traditional peasant subsidiary occupations (sideline production) suffered as a result of the peasants' incorporation in the collectives. Pig raising was the activity most affected: between the end of 1954 and June 1956, China's pig population declined by an estimated 17 million animals.[26]

(iii) The loss of draught animals and pigs consequent on collectivization, led to a decline in the supply of manure and created a shortage of motive power in the countryside. In the north China plain, for example, human labor had to take the place of animals in pulling plows.[27]

(iv) Collectivization gave an impetus to the migration of peasants townward. This gave rise to employment difficulties in the cities, since urban job opportunities did not rise enough to absorb the migrants whose skills, incidentally, were low. The urban housing situation also suffered.

[24] 390 tractor stations were set up during 1953-57. The tractor stations operated by the state, were a favorite of the right-inclined, bureaucratic Party faction. The left wing of the Party was inclined toward transferring the stations' machinery to the collective farms and, after 1958, to the communes (see Chapter 8).

[25] Cheng Chu-yuan, *Communist China's Economy, 1949-1962, op. cit.,* p. 35, citing *Jen-min Jih-pao* of April 19, 1957.

[26] *Ibid.*, pp. 35-36.

[27] Audrey Donnithorne, *China's Economic System, op. cit.*, p. 41.

(v) According to the Maoists, "when the cooperatives were established, [the class enemies] attacked the activists, destroyed public property, killed the livestock of the cooperatives or tried to sneak into the cooperatives to seize leadership. Some even tried to undermine the cooperatives by committing murders, setting fires, and poisoning people." The better-off middle peasants "on joining the cooperatives, sold their means of production, withdrew their capital funds, felled trees, and so forth."[28]

2. In Russia collectivization went hand in hand with the drive to wipe out the rich and middle peasants. In China the rich peasants and many middle peasants as well, had been attacked during reconstruction and reform, though official fear of them remained. Put another way, the collectivization drive in Russia came hard on the heels of a relatively liberal period: the New Economic Policy (NEP). In China, collectivization followed a period of acute class warfare and repression. Although there had been some resurgence of "private property mentality" in the Chinese countryside during the Korean conflict (see p. 50 above), the fact remains that the bulk of the peasants to be collectivized in China were poor and hard put to scratch out a living from the tiny farms which they got from land reform. These peasants were more likely to join collective farms without fuss than other groups. Their experience in farming their own land was brief and not encouraging, and their "private property mentality" may well have been an acquired rather than a natural trait. There was, therefore, in China a *prima facie* case for less compulsion and violence during collectivization than there had been in the Russia of the Soviets.

The earnings position of the various social strata before and after collectivization may be seen from Table 5-5.

It will be seen that collectivization reduced the earnings of rich peasants and former landlords below those of poor peasants in line with the left wing's philosophy of eliminating social stratification in the countryside and relying on the poor peasantry as the mainstay of rural revolution. The relative improvement in the position of rich peasants and former landlords in 1957 is discussed in Chapter 7.

The fall in livestock numbers and the decline in sideline production, mentioned earlier, may at first appear to contradict the thesis of a relative lack of resistance to collectivization. But this need not be so. Advanced collective farms were put together hastily; there was a lack of forethought and an acute shortage of qualified administra-

---

[28]"How the Attack on the Cooperatives Stopped," *Chung-kuo Ching-nien Pao*, April 11, 1963, in *URS*, Vol. 32, No. 8 (July 26, 1963), pp. 139-140 and 142.

TABLE 5-5
Per Capita Earnings of Peasant Households*
(Yuan per year)

Class (Communist Definition)	1954[1]		1956[2]		1957[2]	
	Gross Earnings (yuan)	Index	Net Earnings (yuan)	Index	Net Earnings (yuan)	Index
Poor peasant	116.4	1.000	61.3	1.000	60.2	1.000
Lower-middle peasant ⎱	154.8	1.330	67.6	1.103	69.9	1.161
Upper-middle peasant ⎰			77.2	1.259	79.0	1.312
Rich peasant	209.2	1.797	55.3	0.902	58.7	0.975
Former landlord.	118.4	1.017	59.0	0.962	66.2	1.100

*Figures for 1954 show average per capita earnings of 16,000 peasant households classified by stratum; figures for 1956 and 1957 provide the same data for 4,321 cooperative households. Derived from the excellent unpublished thesis by P. Shran, "The Structure of Income in Communist China," University of California, Berkeley, 1961, p. 204.

[1] See *T'ung-chi Kung-tso (Statistical Work)* (May 29, 1957), pp. 31-32.
[2] See *T'ung-chi Kung-tso*, August 23, 1958, pp. 11-12.
Source: Victor C. Funnell, "Social Stratification," *Problems of Communism* (March–April 1968), p. 19, Table 2.

tors and agronomists. The poor peasants' hopes were raised only to be shattered on first contact with communal life. What individual initiative and technical knowledge there was, seems to have been squandered and stifled by red tape. The shortage of pork in 1956 and 1957 was due in large part to the very low prices paid by the state for live hogs. The decline in sideline production was probably the result of a combination of collective control over the peasants' working schedule (which left little time for subsidiary occupations) and the low prices offered by the state for the products of sideline industry. For example, the state's price for dried sunflowers in Fengchien County (Szechwan) in 1955 was about one-third of prewar. The total value of sunflowers sold by the peasants in 1955 declined to 60 percent of the 1954 figure.[29]

It was the recognition of such problems that led the ascendant moderate communist faction in September 1956 to decentralize authority on the collective farms, limit the size of kolkhozes, raise the price for live hogs, and ease controls over sideline production.

3. In the discussion of transitional arrangements it was suggested that there was a certain similarity between the early Soviet collective institutions and those used in China. The Chinese mutual aid teams

[29] Chao Kuo-chun, "Agricultural Production in Mainland China," in E. S. Kirby (ed.), *Contemporary China: II, 1956-57* (Hong Kong: Hong Kong U. P., 1958), pp. 16-17. The 1955 target for pig production was not reached. See *ibid.*, p. 205.

and lower-level collectives represented, however, more subtle gradations in the movement toward fully fledged collective farms than did the Soviet TOZ and arteli. Moreover, mutual aid teams had a long history in China, responding as they did to a need for cooperation in the tilling of land and the use of scarce capital. The first communist mutual aid teams were introduced in the Kiangsi Soviet in 1933, and again in north and northwest China during the war with Japan. [30] While incorporating communist ideals, they owed their creation to economic necessity.

It should also be recalled that a laboratory experiment in agricultural producers' cooperatives (both elementary and advanced) had been carried out in communist controlled "new democratic" areas of north, northeast, and northwest China. As likely as not, these experiments fed the communists misleading data about the effectiveness of cooperative farming, and this for three reasons. (i) The membership of the early collectives was made up of highly motivated cadres, (ii) the climatic and soil conditions in north, northeast, and northwest China were quite different from those of the center-south and south (i.e., in the latter regions cultivation was more intensive than elsewhere), and (iii) the early experimental collectives were nursed with subsidies and given other delicate attentions. Such aid was not feasible when the prototype became a mass movement.

There was also another difference between the Soviet and Chinese experience with transitional collective arrangements in agriculture. Very early in the Bolshevik revolution, rural communes were set up in Russia in response to radical demands. The commune was at first regarded as the highest form of communist agricultural organization: everything in it was held in common. The distributive principle was "from each according to his ability, to each according to his needs." A model statute for the commune was drafted and approved in 1919. The communes were staffed for the most part with city workers. Most of them were Party members. The means of production were supplied by the state. At their height (1931) the communes numbered 7,600 and represented (in 1930) 8.8 percent of all collectives. [31] After 1931 they were rapidly liquidated. The Chinese, on the other hand, launched their commune movement in 1958, after collectivization of the countryside had been completed. Moreover, the Chinese communes (see Chapter 8) differed quite markedly from their Soviet ancestors of the 1920's and early 1930's.

4. One of the reasons given by the communists for the establish-

[30] See Mao Tse-tung, "Get Organized" (November 1943), *SW* (Peking: *FLP*, 1965), Vol. III, pp. 153-161.
[31] Naum Jasny, *op. cit.*, p. 320, Table 24.

ment of collective farms is that they allow more productive cultivation through the use of machinery. Some large Chinese state farms have reported that a changeover from the use of traditional farm tools to semimechanization raised labor productivity by 70 percent, and that a changeover from semimechanization to mechanization raised labor productivity another 150 percent. [32] There was a striking difference between the Soviet and Chinese situations on this score at the beginning, during, and at the end of their respective collectivization drives. Table 5-6 shows the respective tractor outputs of the two countries.

By 1932 (when 61.5 percent of peasant households had been collectivized), roughly 50 percent of the collectives in Russia were

TABLE 5-6
Output of Tractors in the Soviet Union and China
(Thousands of 15-hp units)

Soviet Union		China	
Year	Thousands of 15-hp Units	Year	Thousands of 15-hp Units
Beginning of Collectivization			
1928–29	3.6	1953	0
1929–30	9.1	1954	0
During Collectivization			
1931	35.1	1955	0
1932	50.8	1956	0
1933	79.9	1957	0
1934	118.1		
1935	155.5		
1936	173.2		
1937	66.5		
After Collectivization			
1938	93.4	1958	0.957
		1960 (Planned)	20.0
		1960–61 (Claimed output)	40.0

Sources: Soviet Union—G. Warren Nutter, The Growth of Industrial Production in the Soviet Union. A Study by the National Bureau of Economic Research (Princeton, N.J.: Princeton U. P., 1962), p. 434, Table B-2. China—Ten Great Years, p. 98; Yang Ling, "Agriculture: Foundation of the National Economy," Peking Review (October 18, 1960), p. 17; NCNA (February 18, 1962). The Soviet data in 1,000 hp have been translated into 15-hp units in which the Chinese data are presumably given.

[32] Yuan-li Wu, The Economy of Communist China: An Introduction, op. cit., pp. 154-155.

plowed by the Machine Tractor Stations; by 1937 (when 93 percent of peasant households had been collectivized) about 90 percent of the collectives were ploughed by the MTS. The area cultivated by tractors in China in 1959 (when farm communization was complete) was roughly 5 percent of total cultivated land.

In terms of tractor stock the difference between the Soviet Union and China was sharp. There were only 8,094 tractors (15-hp units) in China at the beginning of collectivization (1955), and 19,367 when collectivization had been completed in 1956. In 1925-26 the Soviets planned to import 17,500 tractors. By the end of the twenties annual tractors imports were running at 23,000 units in addition to an annual domestic production of some 9,000 (15-hp) units. [33] At the beginning of 1953 the Soviet tractor stock was 650,000 (including 108,000 row-crop tractors). [34] At that time China had about 2,000 tractors (15-hp units). In 1955 the Soviet tractor stock was 1,439,000 standard (15-hp) units or about 844,000 physical units. In that year China had 8,094 standard units or 957 physical units. [35] The per capita comparison was, of course, much more unfavorable for China. The Chinese tractor stock and import figures are shown in Table 5-7.

The sudden increase in tractor output in China between 1958 and 1961 was due to the completion of the Soviet-designed tractor plant near Loyang. Construction began in 1955, and in 1958 the plant trial produced some 54-hp "East is Red" (*Tung Fang Chung*) diesel caterpillar tractors—modified version of a Soviet model. Serial production of these started on October 1, 1959. The annual capacity of the plant was said to have been about 15,000 "East is Red" 54-hp units. In Tientsin another factory began operations in 1959. It produced the "Iron Ox-40" diesel-engine, wheeled tractors. Both plants were expanded in 1962. A plant in Chungchun began production in 1960. A number of smaller plants were completed around 1961-62 in Kiangsi, Shenyang, Anshan, and Shanghai. They turned out the 35-hp "Harvest" and 25-hp tractors, as well as a small 7-hp "walking tractor." [36]

In 1956 it was thought that by 1967 China would need 750,000 tractors (in 15-hp units), and more than 200,000 combine harvesters. [37] Even with large imports of tractors from socialist countries,

[33] Maurice Dobb, *Soviet Economic Development Since 1917* (New York: International Publishers, 1948), p. 213.

[34] Naum Jasny, *Soviet Industrialization, 1928-1952* (Chicago: U. of Chicago Press, 1961), p. 313.

[35] Henry Lethbridge, "Tractors in China," *FEER* (March 21, 1963), p. 617.

[36] Cf. Chapter 9 below.

[37] Chao Kuo-chun, *op. cit.*, p. 21. A minimum requirement of 800,000 tractors to be used to work 80 million hectares of arable land suitable for the use of tractors has been mentioned in *Jen-min Jih-pao* of June 20, 1963.

TABLE 5-7

China: Tractor Stock and Imports of Tractors from the USSR

Year	Tractor Stock (in 15-hp units)	Number of Tractors Imported from the USSR (Physical Units)	Imports of Agricultural Tractors from the USSR (Millions of Old Roubles)
1949	401		
1950	1,286		
1951	1,410		
1952	2,006		
1953	2,719		
1954	5,061		
1955	8,094	ca. 22,000[a]	28.9
1956	19,367		23.7
1957	24,629		1.8
1958	45,330	2,656	43.1
1959	59,000	941	10.6
1960	81,000	1,579	
1961	67,000*	33	
1962	100,000†		

[a]Imports from USSR, Bulgaria, Czechoslovakia, Hungary, Rumania in standard (15-hp) units. In Shensi Province tractors imported a decade earlier were still in storage because of shortages of spare parts.

See Henry Lethbridge, "Tractors in China," *FEER* (March 21, 1963), pp. 616–619, and "China: Collectivization and Mechanization," *ibid*. (February 14, 1963), pp. 309–312. Also, Tang Tsung-lieh, "China's Fast Growing Tractor Industry," *Peking Review* (May 5, 1961), pp. 18–19.

*The drop in tractor stock in 1961 may perhaps be explained by (a) changes in statistical categories, (b) depreciation outstripping production and imports. In mid-1960, over 20 percent of China's tractors were said to have been out of action.

†The big increase from the preceding year may have been due to the putting into service of reconditioned tractors. About 20,000 tractors were concentrated in Heilungkiang Province. Another 1,000 were to be found on farms around Peking.

Sources: Ten Great Years, p. 135; *Hung-ch'i*, No. 4 (February 16, 1960); *Jen-min Jih-pao* (November 22, 1960); *Ta Kung Pao*, Hong Kong (October 1, 1961); *Ching-chi Yen-chiu* (December 17, 1962); Yang Ling, "Agriculture: Foundation of the National Economy," *Peking Review* (October 18, 1960) puts number of tractors in 1960 at 100,000 and planned output in 1960 at 20,000; Soviet official trade statistics; Feng-hwa Mah, "The Terms of Sino-Soviet Trade," in Choh-ming Li (ed.), *Industrial Development in Communist China* (New York: Praeger, and *The China Quarterly*, London, 1964), p. 180, Table 1.

which incidentally fell sharply after 1958, the attainment of that objective was improbable.

The very low level of China's agriculture got China's communist leaders into an unseemly dispute. One of the accusations made against Liu Shao-ch'i and his group during the Cultural Revolution of the late 1960's (Chapters 11-12) was that they opposed the collectivization of agriculture, arguing that mechanization should precede rather than follow the establishment of collective farms. [38] Liu was also alleged to have held that agricultural machinery should be manufactured in series, in large, specialized, modern plants. Mao's position was that less complex equipment should be produced in local factories (artisan workshops), using what material there was, and turning out small and medium-size farm tools and sets of equipment. [39] After 1957, and throughout the Great Leap Forward (Chapter 8), Mao's thesis had the upper hand. In April 1959, all provinces, autonomous regions, and municipalities were ordered to set up farm tool institutes directly under the control and supervision of the central authority. [40] The institutes were to give thought to methods of improving and developing various types of small implements and mechanized tools, and relay the results of their reflections to local manufactories. Seven hundred such institutes were immediately set up and, according to the Maoists, made concrete use of the "unparalleled revolutionary enthusiasm and boundless wisdom" of the masses. [41] Liu, according to the same source, refused to give the institutes the necessary governmental support. His hesitation was linked by his opponents to his preference for machines from foreign countries, for which he allegedly paid high prices in order to copy the imported samples. [42] One result of the implementation of Mao's philosophy on agricultural technology was a large increase in the production of double-wheel, double-blade plows: from 60,000 units in 1954 to 1.8 million units in 1956. Actually, only a fraction of those plows was sold in 1956. P'eng Chen, a member of the Party's

[38] Liu Shao-ch'i "threw out a set of fallacies on 'mechanization preceding cooperativization' in a vain attempt to seek a 'theoretical' basis for [the 'rightists'] objection to agricultural cooperativization." In January 1950 Liu reportedly said: "A collective without machinery can never be consolidated." In May 1951, at the National Conference on Propaganda Work, he was quoted as saying that nationalization of land and collectivization of agriculture had to await the nationalization of industry capable of supplying the peasants with large quantities of farm machinery. Po I-po argued at the time that "without a powerful state chemical engineering industry, it is not possible to have agricultural collectivization on a full scale." This was broadly a Stalin-type argument. See "Outline of Struggle," *URS*, Vol. 53, Nos. 5-6, *op. cit.*, pp. 60-61. For the economically rational grounds of the controversy, see Chen and Galenson, *op. cit.*, pp. 120-122.

[39] *Agricultural Machinery and Technique*, No. 5 (August 8, 1967), in *URS* Vol. 49, No. 4 (October 13, 1967), p. 56ff. Cf. "Struggle Between the Two Roads in China's Countryside," *China Pictorial*, No. 3 (1968), pp. 2-7, and the rest of that issue.

[40] The trouble was that a good part of the "central authority" was in the hands of the relative moderates, i.e., Liu's men.

[41] *Agricultural Machinery and Technique*, *op. cit.*, in *URS*, *op. cit.*, p. 61. The order was contained in the "Party's Internal Bulletin" approved by Mao.

[42] In 1953 Liu was credited with saying: "first copy, then transform." See "Outline of Struggle," *URS*, Vol. 53, Nos. 7-8, *op. cit.*, pp. 85-86.

Secretariat, allegedly referred to the popularization of the plow (which was too heavy) as "doing a stupid thing." Po I-po, Chairman of the State Economic Commission, called it "making a mess."[43]

It can hardly be denied that had China waited for adequate mechanization before proceeding with collectivization, the ideological imperative of a collective economy in agriculture would have remained very remote indeed. As in other decisions of like kind, the moderates lost out. The spirit of the revolution militated against their empiricism, relative as this was. Their counsel of prudence could acquire meaning only if the militant course which they opposed, produced economic disaster. Even then, rational calculation was relegated to the dust heap of history as soon as the first shock wave had been absorbed and the worst damage had been made good.

The bureaucratic moderates saw mechanization of agriculture (and hence collectivization) as a long drawn out process. They were not opposed to mechanization, as their adversaries later maintained, but they were not disposed to rush into it, and were certainly hesitant about collectivization preceding mechanization. In this they were nearer to the original Stalinist blueprint than were the Maoist ideologues.[44] Among their arguments in support of caution and selectivity on this score was that "seen from the conditions of any country, the development of agricultural mechanization has always been due to shortage of manpower. The important role of agricultural mechanization is to raise labor productivity, while its role in raising per unit area output is not very great. . . . Therefore, under the conditions of rich resources of labor power in our country, the technical policy of agricultural mechanization deserves further consideration."[45] This line of reasoning was embodied in a memorandum submitted to the Central Committee and Mao Tse-tung on March 12, 1957.

The moderates' hesitations reveal a grappling with some complex points of theory. As Davies has pointed out, large-scale technical changes—in agriculture as elsewhere—"tend in the long run to render

[43]Ibid., Nos. 5-6, p. 57. On this and related subjects see Leslie T. C. Kuo, "Agricultural Mechanization in Communist China," in Choh-ming Li (ed.),Industrial Development in Communist China (New York: Praeger, 1964), pp. 134-150. A later report put the number of "double-single-share plows popularized" in 1954 at 22,566 and 1.086 million in 1956. See below Table 7-2.

[44]Stalin stepped-up collectivization arguing that the Soviet Union had "the most mechanized agriculture in the world," which was simply not true. Even in 1953 farm mechanization was spotty and not integrated.

[45]"Outline of Struggle," URS, Vol. 53, Nos. 5-6, p. 63. Po I-po argued in 1956 that "mechanization means that we have no way to solve the problem of surplus labor in the rural areas." Ibid., p. 62. Cf. W. A. Lewis, "Economic Development with Unlimited Supplies of Labour," Manchester School of Economic and Social Studies (May 1951).

present cost equations (including the capital-labor cost ratio) irrelevant. To get to the new set of equations you cannot start at once from what is cheapest, given present parameters, but must introduce modern technology in lumps into the existing situation."[46] Even though the newly introduced capital intensive sectors may for a time be used in a labor-intensive way, they will tend to act as leaders to the rest of the economy, and they will train personnel in the up-to-date skills.

5. *State farms.* In the ascending order of communist ideological liking, state farms are above collective farms. State farms are directly owned by the Party-State (i.e., by "the whole people" in communist parlance) and are thus more amenable to central control than the kolkhozy; the method of remuneration approximates that of nationalized industrial enterprises; they are generally larger and more mechanized than the collectives. The first state farms were set up in the Soviet Union in 1918-19, and up to 1927 were formed out of former large private and Tzarist estates. As has been mentioned earlier, there were no such latifundia in pre-1949 China. The Soviet collectivization campaign of 1929-37 was flanked by a drive to establish gigantic state farms (sovkhozy). Between 1928 and 1932 their number trebled and their sown area increased eight times. According to Jasny, the experiment was "nothing short of a catastrophe."[47] The farms were too large, too cumbersome and unwieldy, overcentralized, staffed by inexperienced, lax, semiliterate, dishonest, or simply harried officials, poorly organized, and generally backward. Between 1932 and 1935 the size of many state farms was reduced and the most obviously unprofitable ones were done away with.

Notice (Table 5-8) that in the Soviet Union the development of state farms went hand in hand with collectivization. In China the big state farm push came only after collectivization had been completed, and especially after the Great Leap Forward of 1958-60 (Chapter 8).

The first Chinese state farms were set up in 1948 in the counties of Tungpei and Ning-an located in communist-controlled areas of the northeast. A major function of state farms in China was the opening up of waste lands and the political consolidation of borderlands. Great emphasis was put on the formation of such farms in Sinkiang, Inner Mongolia, Hainan Island, Heilungkiang (Manchuria), and Yunnan. To the army was assigned an important role in setting up state farms in these frontier regions. In Inner Mongolia the number of state farms rose from 8 in 1952 to 21 in 1958, and their produc-

---

[46] R. W. Davies, "Planning for Rapid Growth in the U.S.S.R.," *Economics of Planning*, Vol. 5, Nos. 1-2, 1965, in Jan S. Prybyla (ed.), *Comparative Economic Systems* (New York: Appleton, 1969), p. 240.

[47] Naum Jasny, *The Socialized Agriculture of the U.S.S.R.*, *op. cit.*, p. 246.

TABLE 5-8
State Farms in the Soviet Union and China

Soviet Union	1928	1932	1938	China*	1953	1954	1955
Number of farms . .	1,400	4,337	3,992	Number of farms . .	2,376	2,415	2,242
Sown area (millions of				Cultivated area (millions of			
hectares)	1.7	13.4	12.4	hectares)	0.251	0.295	0.395
				Employees and			
Thousands of				workers, thou-			
workers	316.8	1,891	1,319.7	sands	111	137	134
				Workers.	78	103	105
Thousands of				Thousands of			
tractors	6.7	64.0	85.0	tractors.	1.6	2.2	2.8
Thousands of harvester com-				Thousands of harvester com-			
bines.	—	12.3	26.0	bines.	0.35	0.43	0.66

State farms and ranches under the Ministry of State Farms and Reclamation (including penal farms, military reclamation farms, and army production-construction corps in the Greater Northern Wilderness—see Chapter 3)

	1957	1958	1960
Number of farms . .	710	1,442	2,490
Cultivated land (millions of			
hectares)	1.0	2.3	5.2
Employees and workers, thou-			
sands	500	990	2,800
Number of tractors, thousands 15 hp			
units.	10.2	16.96	28.0†
Thousands of harvester com-			
bines.	1.5	1.98	3.3†

*The first set of figures refers to both mechanized and nonmechanized farms operated by central and local governments. At the end of 1952, for example, there were 52 large mechanized farms and 2,336 local state farms. In May 1956 a Ministry of State Farms and Land Reclamation was established to control state farms throughout the country. The second set of figures (1957, 1958, 1960) relates to farms supervised by this Ministry, and excludes state farms under the supervision of local authorities.

†March 1961.

Sources: Soviet Union—Alexander Baykov, *The Development of the Soviet Economic System: An Essay on the Experience of Planning in the U.S.S.R.* (Cambridge: Cambridge University Press, 1950), p. 333. China-Reprinted from Nai-Ruenn Chen, *Chinese Economic Statistics* (Chicago: Aldine, 1967). Copyright © 1967 by the Social Science Research Council, p. 367, Tables 5.95, 5.97; Cheng Chu-yuan, *Communist China's Economy 1949-1962, op. cit.*, p. 102.

tive area from 48.2 thousand *mou* to 2.49 million *mou*.[48] State livestock farms in the autonomous region increased from 16 in 1952 to 55 in 1958, and their total area from 8 million *mou* to 27.8 million *mou*. [49] Since many of them were staffed by ethnic Chinese, state farms in the border areas were, in a significant respect, the vehicles of cultural and political penetration by the Hans.

The basic economic purpose of state farms was to supply the state with marketable grain, cotton, and meat. To enable them to do this, they received a significant portion of available tractors and other mechanized farm machinery. According to one report, in 1961 machinery handled about 50 percent of the state farms' reaping and 80 percent of their threshing operations. [50] In 1956, average grain yields on state farms were said to have exceeded those of agricultural cooperatives by 4 percent, and cotton yields were 66 percent higher.[51]

CONCLUSION

As with the adoption by the Chinese of the broad outlines of the Soviet Stalinist strategy of economic development, so also with the institutional changes in agriculture: the Chinese took over the general framework, but adapted the details to their own special circumstances. In China the margin between food and mouths to feed was narrower than in Russia at a similar stage of development, the rate of population increase was faster (perhaps as much as double that of the Soviet Union), the amount of cultivable land per head much smaller (Table 5-9). The narrowness of the hunger margin in China is a fundamental datum which at all times has to be taken into account in policy formulation. That is why no foreign model can ever quite be right, no matter how ideologically alluring it may be. Yet the changes which the Chinese made in the Stalinist-Soviet blueprint went deeper than this. Mao had long before Sinfied Marxism-

[48] Reprinted from Nai-Ruenn Chen, *Chinese Economic Statistics* (Chicago: Aldine, 1967), copyright ©1967 by the Social Science Research Council, p. 368, Table 5.98. 1 *mou* = 1/6 acre.

[49] Reprinted from Nai-Ruenn Chen, *Chinese Economic Statistics* (Chicago: Aldine, 1967), copyright ©1967 by the Social Science Research Council, p. 368, Table 5.99. In Sinkiang more than 180 state farms were established north and south of the Tienshan Mountains. By 1959 their cultivated acreage was 8.03 million *mou*. In 1960 they reportedly opened up another 3.57 million *mou*. Wang Chen (Minister of State Farms and Land Reclamation), "China's State Farms—Production Bases of Farm and Animal Products," *Hung-ch'i* (April 1, 1961) in *Peking Review* (April 28, 1961), p. 16.

[50] "State Farms Expand Acreage," *Peking Review* (July 28, 1961), p. 4. The size of state farms was said to have varied from 30,000 to 1,500,000 *mou*.

[51] Wang Chen, *op. cit.*, p. 16.

Leninism, imbued it with Chinese manners, and articulated it in ways more in tune with China's history. In his better days, Mao was something of a poet and a self-taught classical scholar. He was, above all, a soldier. In his hands Marxist propositions were sometimes gently, sometimes violently reshaped, and Leninist policies met with a similar fate. Stalinism, too, was deeply changed. But Stalin did not take kindly to revisions of Marxist doctrines as he understood them, and his successors watched with growing apprehension the metamorphosis in China of their leader's teachings and of their own neo-Stalinist beliefs into something not only alien but unabashedly anti-Soviet.

TABLE 5-9

Cultivated Land per Capita in the Soviet Union and China at the Beginning of Their Respective First Five Year Industrialization Plans, and in 1938–39 (USSR) and 1956 (China)

(Hectares)

	Soviet Union		China	
	1926–28	1938–39	1953	1956
Total population	.738	.720	.187	.180
Rural population	.936	1.195	.216	.209

Source: Alexander Eckstein, "The Strategy of Economic Development in Communist China," American Economic Review, Papers and Proceedings, Vol. LI, No. 2 (May 1961), Table 2, p. 510.

THE FULLY FLEDGED COLLECTIVE FARM IN 1957

The organizational principles of an advanced agricultural producers' cooperative in China at the end of the First Five Year Plan may be summarized as follows.[52]

Membership. All working peasants who had reached the age of 16 and other working people able to take part in the work of the cooperative were eligible for membership. The following could be admitted to membership or candidate membership only after thorough screening by the township people's council:

(a) Counterrevolutionaries in the countryside who had committed only minor crimes and had since repented.

(b) Counterrevolutionaries in the countryside guilty of serious crimes but who had since atoned for their trespasses by rendering

[52]The relevant theoretical document is Model Regulations for Advanced Agricultural Producers' Co-operatives adopted by the First National People's Congress of the People's Republic of China at its Third Session on June 30, 1956 (Peking: FLP, 1956). Actually these regulations were in force for only about one year. The advanced collective was replaced by the rural people's commune in April-August 1958.

outstanding services during the suppression of counterrevolutionaries (i.e., informers and the like), and those who behaved well after serving their sentences in prisons, labor camps, and other places of intellectual reform.

(c) Former landlords, rich peasants, and counterrevolutionaries could be admitted to work on the collective in order to reform themselves into new men. If they behaved well, they could be admitted as members or candidate members.

However, former landlords, rich peasants, and counterrevolutionaries did not have the right to stand for elections (i.e., be appointed) to offices in the collective after becoming working members. Semantics aside, the principle was: once a class enemy, always a class enemy.

Ownership. The following were owned collectively.

(a) Land.

(b) Important means of production, e.g., draught animals, livestock, large farm tools.

(c) Irrigation works on land formerly owned by members.

(d) Saplings and seedlings.

(e) Large groves (orchards, tea, mulberry, and bamboo groves, tung oil trees, lacquer trees).

(f) Large timber producing forests.

The following were owned privately by the members.

(a) Household goods

(b) Small holdings of trees, poultry, and domestic animals (mostly pigs and milk cows).

(c) Small farm tools and tools needed for subsidiary cottage occupations.

(d) Small household plots for growing vegetables and other products. The size of the household plot was determined by the number of persons in the household who were cooperative members. However, the amount of land so used by each person was not to exceed 5 percent of the average arable land holding in the village in question, but in practice the 5 percent criterion was apparently rarely reached.

(e) Graveyards and building sites owned by members.

Payment for land shares was abolished. Payment for draught animals, livestock, and farm tools was to be made to members according to normal local prices, spread over three to five years, after deductions for membership shares.

Funds. Members were required to contribute to the collective share funds (payable in means of production) according to the amount of land they pooled.

Organization. Members were organized into:

(a) Production brigades (*sheng-ch'antui*).

(b) Production teams (a subdivision of (a), where necessary).

The production brigade, which comprised about 200 households, was to have been the basic, permanent unit of collective organization. Two kinds of brigades were distinguished: field production brigades and subsidiary occupations brigades. In September 1957 a directive was issued abolishing lower levels of management (e.g., production teams), where these existed, and specifying that no further changes in managerial organization should thereafter be made for a period of ten years.

In fact, largely because of the shortage of trained personnel, many instances occurred of collective farms' merging with the lowest units of rural administration, the *hsiang*, or with credit cooperatives. [53] This meant that some agricultural cooperatives were much larger than planned, comprising several thousand people. The relative size of advanced agricultural co-ops is shown in Table 5-10.

TABLE 5-10

Size of Advanced Agricultural Producers' Cooperatives Compared
with Elementary Cooperatives and Mutual Aid Teams

	Average Number of Households				
	1952	1953	1954	1955	1956
Advanced Agricultural Producers' Cooperatives (kolkhozy)	184.0	137.0	58.6	75.8	246.4
Elementary Agricultural Producers' Cooperatives	15.7	18.1	20.0	26.7	51.1
Mutual aid teams					
Seasonal	5.4	5.7	6.2	6.9	—
All-year round	6.5	7.3	8.1	10.4	—

Source: State Statistical Bureau, *Agricultural Cooperation and Statistical Materials on Income Distribution of Agricultural Producers' Cooperatives in 1955* (Peking, 1957), p. 10, in John Wong, *op. cit.*, p. 372, Table II.

Payment for Work. [54] The cooperative fixed norms for various jobs. The norm for each job was supposed to have been based on the quantity and quality of work which an average member working dilligently under normal conditions could do in one day on that particular job. With a disarming lack of precision, the model regulations laid down that the norms "should not be set too high or too low." [55] Participation in collective work was obligatory for all members.

[53] Audrey Donnithorne, *China's Economic System, op. cit.*, p. 43.

[54] The description of income distribution, which follows, applied also to the post-1960 period. See Chapter 9.

[55] *Model Regulations, op. cit.*, p. 19.

The system of reward (*p'ing-kung chi-fen*) drew its inspiration from the Soviet method of computing *trudodni* (work days). A standard "work day" or production norm was established for each job, depending on skill and labor intensity involved in the job.[56] This work day norm was expressed in work points. As a rule, ten work points equaled one work day—that is, a reasonably assiduous and responsible worker could earn ten work points on the average for a day's work. The system represented, in effect, an approach to piece-work payments. When the peasant accomplished the work norm for his particular job, he was credited with the given number of work points assigned to that norm. If he overfulfilled the norm, he was credited with work points in excess of the standard amount. Under-fulfillment of the norm was punished by fewer work points than the standard being credited to the individual involved. Innovations, improvements, "political consciousness" applied to the job, similarly received rewards in terms of above-norm work points. A rough attempt was made to introduce quality standards into the work-point system. As a rule, if a given job was done 80 percent or better up to the standard, the worker got the full number of work points established as norm for that job.

Here are a few typical examples of work-point fixing.[57]

Example 1. Cutting stalks of ripe grain in the field and bringing the stalks to the threshing machine earned 3 work points per 100 catties (ca., 110 lbs.). Threshing earned 1.2 work points per 100 catties.

Example 2. Keeping a bullock (including housing and feeding): 10 points per day (i.e., a time rate was used in this instance since no convenient piece rate existed for measuring livestock tending). The keeping of two bullocks doubled the number of work points earned.

Example 3. Mending river dikes with clay: 15 points per 100 cubic feet of clay delivered at the dike.

Example 4. Serving as team leader: 12 points per day (in one farm); 70 points per day (in another). Since the team leader usually calculated and assigned work points for his team and its members,

[56] It was estimated that there were in China more than 100 varieties of crops and several thousand types of farm jobs. Many jobs were performed by groups (e.g., production teams). This necessitated the splitting up of the group work points among the individual members according to some set of logical rules. The cadres—to save time—were tempted to divide the group work points equally among the individual participants. Since this tended to have disincentive effects on the individual's productivity, it was opposed by higher-up authorities.

[57] The examples are borrowed from an excellent article by Andrew Nathan, "Paying the Chinese Farmer," *FEER* (February 27, 1964), pp. 457-458. See also, Andrew Nathan, "China's Work-Point System: A Study in Agricultural 'Splittism,' " *Current Scene* (April 15, 1964), pp. 1-13.

trouble at times developed regarding the leader's integrity in assigning work points to himself (See Chapter 9).[58]

Example 5. Work points for planting and cultivating vegetables, sugar cane, and rice, as well as for collecting and spreading mulch and night soil were usually calculated on an area (per *mou*) basis. Work points for the harvesting of crops, fishing, gathering of grass and leaves were usually based on weight (i.e., per so many catties).

Example 6. In addition to livestock tending, time rates were frequently used for such subsidiary occupations as carpentry, ditch digging, and maintenance work in general.

Within each major job category, a very large number of subprocesses and stages were distinguished. Each of these was assigned its value in work points.

The system looks terribly complicated as in fact it is. However, in practice what seems to have happened was this: "In most places it has been established that if Lao Pai-hsing gets ten points on Tuesday ploughing for 12 points per *mou*, he'll get about ten points on Wednesday planting sugar cane at 15 points per *mou*, and next month will get ten points per day as a member of the second labor brigade when the production team delegates men to fix the roads or dykes."[59] That is not quite what Marx had in mind, but it saves a lot of time and bother. Lao Pai-hsing, of course, may have his own views about the equity of the assessment, but what he can actually do about it depends on a large number of variables: who his team leader is, how vocal the other members of the team are, what political year it is, what Lao's class genealogy is, and so on.

After deducting the agricultural tax (paid by the collective farm to the state), costs of production for the current year, sums for the reserve fund, and a sum for the welfare fund, the year's net income was divided by the total number of work days (or work points) accumulated by the members. In this way, the value of a work point or work day for the current year was arrived at. Each member then (i.e., usually after the second harvest) received payment in kind and cash according to the total value of work points (or work days) accumulated by him during the year. As in the Soviet Union, the farmer was a residual claimant on the farm's income.

[58] The job of work-point calculation and assignment was sometimes done by an accountant (*hui-chi*), or by the team leader with the help of an assistant. Team leaders, assistant team leaders, and accountants were elected officials who, at least in theory, could be fired by disgruntled co-op members.

[59] Andrew Nathan, *op. cit.*, p. 458. Nathan's account of work point calculation shortcuts may not tell the whole story. There is some evidence to suggest that not infrequently much time was spent and wasted in the evenings to determine work points.

Provision was made for advances to members out of farm produce harvested in the spring and summer. Sometimes such advances were made monthly. The final settlement was made when the year's harvest was in. A similar provision was made regarding advance cash payments. In practice there were instances of grain distribution to member households according to criteria unrelated to labor input (e.g., number of people in a household, status). In other cases the collectives failed to count work on capital construction projects as work days.[60]

A feature of the income distribution system was also the rationing of rice. A monthly basic ration was normally set for the various types of workers and each worker was given a ration booklet. The worker could obtain his monthly rice ration at an "official price" (i.e., a price lower than that prevailing on the free market) and the cost of the ration was deducted from his work-point income (paid either after the second harvest, after each harvest, or monthly, depending on the condition of the collective). The rice ration could be kept at home or in the collective storehouse. In the latter case the peasant could withdraw the amounts he needed at regular intervals on the basis of his ration booklet. The monthly rice ration was constant for each worker in a given category, irrespective of age. Apart from rice, rationed goods varied in different localities and at different times. They frequently included sugar, salt, oil, cloth, matches, tobacco, and kerosene.

An example will illustrate the whole procedure.[61] Lao Pai-hsing (a bachelor) earned, say, 3,200 work points during the year. In July he got 20 yuan net, plus a ration of 132 catties of rice which represented a six months' portion of a monthly ration of 22 catties given to laborers in his class. In December the value of the work point was determined for that particular year. He then got another 132 catties of rice and 50 yuan. Since a bicycle might cost 150 yuan, Lao's net annual cash income of 70 yuan would not leave him much to splurge with on modest comforts. To supplement his cash income, he could sell the produce of his private plot activity (e.g., pigs, eggs, chicken) on the open market. To supplement his income in kind, he could

[60] Charles Hoffmann, "Work Incentive Policy in Communist China," in Choh-ming Li (ed.), Industrial Development in Communist China, op. cit., p. 98.

[61] Nathan, op. cit., p. 458. Audrey Donnithorne, op. cit., pp. 77-78, cites figures for average annual incomes per worker in some communes and data regarding the fluctuations in the value of a work day. In one Heilungkiang commune, average annual per worker income was 200 yuan. In 1964 cash receipts per worker ranged from 10 yuan to 200 yuan in above average prosperity communes. On the subject of rationing in urban areas, see Ralph W. Huenemann, "Urban Rationing in Communist China," China Quarterly (April-June 1966), pp. 44-57.

consume part of the produce grown on the household plot. Apparently he was not above selling his ration coupons when circumstances warranted.

Management. The administrative structure of the cooperative was as follows.

(a) The general meeting of members or of members' delegates (highest body).

(b) Management committee headed by a chairman and one or several vice-chairmen. All were to be elected by the members' general meeting, and were to be responsible for the day-to-day management of the collective's affairs.

(c) Supervisory committee elected by (a).

The members' general meeting was supposed to have been convened by the management committee at least twice a year.

The various organizational principles of the advanced collective were copied from the Soviets. As in the Soviet Union, there were in actual practice important departures from the model. For one thing, the general meeting of members certainly did not, in fact, exercise the powers vested in it by theory. Ultimate authority was, in practice, exercised by the management and supervisory cadres who were Party members answerable for Party goals, but who were at the same time uncomfortably subject to pressures from their fellow-villagers.

NATIONALIZATION OF INDUSTRY AND COMMERCE AND THE COLLECTIVIZATION OF HANDICRAFTS

At this point a little exercise in comparison will be of interest. In Chapter 3 we have seen that during the period of reconstruction and reform (1949-52) certain transitional arrangements were made in China's industry, commerce, and handicrafts. The intent was to move industry, trade, and crafts in the direction of socialism. In the preceding section it was shown that a broadly similar development took place in agriculture both before and during the First Five Year Plan. Table 5-11 sets out the three groups of transitional arrangements side by side.

The rate of transformation of private industry, transport, commerce, and handicrafts in the course of the First Five Year Plan may be seen from Tables 5-12, 5-13, 5-14, and 5-15.

A study of Tables 5-11 through 5-15 reveals a strange and at first sight puzzling phenomenon. The Chinese Communists went to great pains to evolve transitional forms of industrial, commercial, and handicraft organization, institutions which would gently ease the workers into socialized enterprises. The implication of this complex

TABLE 5-11
Transitional Institutional Arrangements in Agriculture, Industry, Commerce, and Handicrafts, 1949–57

Form of Ownership	Agriculture	Industry and Commerce	Handicrafts
Private	1. Individual peasant holdings	1. Private industrial and commercial establishments (national capitalism)	1. Private individual craftsmen
Collective-Private	2. Mutual aid teams: (a) seasonal (b) all-year-round	2. Part of output produced and/or marketed by private enterprises themselves (free sale)	2. Supply and marketing: (a) groups (b) cooperatives
	3. Elementary agricultural producers' cooperatives	3. Elementary state capitalism (In small-scale trade: cooperative groups)	3. Lower level handicraft producers' cooperatives
Collective	4. Advanced agricultural producers' cooperatives	4. Advanced state capitalism, i.e., joint state-private enterprises (In small-scale trade: cooperative stores)	4. Handicraft producers' cooperatives
State	5. State farms	5. State enterprises	5. State handicraft enterprises and factories

TABLE 5-12
Socialist Transformation of Private Industry, 1953-57
(Percentage distribution of gross output value, handicrafts excluded)

Year	Socialist Industry (State Enterprises)	Advanced State Capitalism (Joint State-Private Enterprises)	Elementary State Capitalism (Private enterprises executing orders and processing goods for the State)	Private Industry (i.e., that part produced and marketed by private industry on its own)
1953	57.5	5.7	22.8	14.0
1954	62.8	12.3	19.6	5.3
1955	67.7	16.1	13.2	3.0
1956	67.5	32.5	—	—
1957	n.a.	n.a.	—	—

n.a.—Not available.
Source: Ten Great Years, p. 38. "In 1956 the capitalist enterprises came under joint state-private operation by whole trades. These enterprises actually were not very different from socialist enterprises except that the capitalists still drew a fixed rate of interest." [See p. 180 below.]

TABLE 5-13

Socialist Transformation of Private Transport Enterprises

(Percentage Distribution of Freight Turnover)

Year	State Enterprises	Advanced State Capitalism (Joint State-Private Enterprises)	Private Enterprises
1950	95.3	—	4.7
1953	95.8	1.3	2.9
1954	95.3	3.1	1.6
1955	94.8	4.6	0.6
1956	99.3	0.7	—
1957	99.7	0.3	—

Source: Ten Great Years, p. 41. Freight turnover of wooden junks, animal-drawn carts, wheelbarrows, and other nonmechanical vehicles excluded.

TABLE 5-14

Socialist Transformation of Private Commerce

(Percentage distribution of retail and wholesale sales)

Year	Retail Commerce			Wholesale Commerce	
	State	State-Capitalist and Cooperative	Private	State and Cooperative	Private
1950	14.9	0.1	85.0	23.9	76.1
1953	49.7	0.4	49.9	69.7	30.3
1954	69.0	5.4	25.6	89.8	10.2
1955	67.6	14.6	17.8	95.6	4.4
1956	68.3	27.5	4.2	100.0	—
1957	65.7	31.6	2.7	100.0	—

Sources: Ten Great Years, p. 40; Kuan Ta-tung, The Socialist Transformation of Capitalist Industry and Commerce in China (Peking: FLP, 1960), p. 66.

structure was that the Party and state were anxious to avoid sharp and brutal transitions from private to public ownership, from market orientation to central, administrative planning. There is enough evidence to show that some influential leaders were in fact thinking along those lines; hence the delicate gradations and carefully prepared schemes. Yet if one looks at the years 1955-56 it becomes immediately apparent that this elaborate structure was swept aside in an outburst of collective zeal. Almost overnight the whole industry, commerce, and handicrafts were socialized or collectivized. Not only that, but (as we have seen in Chapter 3) workers, peasants, and national capitalists were made to celebrate the event with pipes, drums, fireworks, and joyous songs.

TABLE 5-15

Development of Handicraft Cooperation

	1949	1950	1951	1952	1953	1954	1955	1956
Number of cooperatives and teams ..	311	1,321	1,066	3,658	5,778	41,619	64,591	99,322
Number of persons joining handicraft cooperatives	88,941	260,000	139,613	227,786	301,487	1,139,009	1,874,590	5,095,186
Producer cooperatives.				218,018	271,297	521,209	849,485	3,697,834
Supply and marketing cooperatives				4,288	15,851	227,216	507,343	674,578
Production teams				5,480	14,339	390,584	517,762	332,774

Reprinted from Nai-Ruenn Chen, *Chinese Economic Statistics* (Chicago: Aldine Publishing Company, 1967). Copyright © 1967 by the Social Science Research Council, p. 185, Table 4.5A.

According to *Ten Great Years*, p. 36, the number of persons engaged in cooperative handicrafts represented the following percentages of the total number of persons engaged in cooperative and individual handicrafts: 1952—3.1; 1953—3.9; 1954— 13.6; 1955—26.9; 1956—91.7.

The sudden burst of collectivization and nationalization ignored the relationship between the size of the units and the requirements of production. This was especially evident in handicrafts. The movement, reflected one official later, "was basically healthy, but because of its rapid pace, there were some shortcomings," which in Party language means large-scale errors. "One was the premature or hasty centralization of production, the pooling of profit and sharing of loss in some trades which were more successful when scattered and better able to cope with ever changing market conditions and meet the needs of consumers. Another was the merger or expansion of cooperatives blindly, without considering the objective conditions. Centralization of production and management did not fit all handicraft trades which were complicated and numerous. There were many repair trades and personal services as well as manufacture. Some could serve their customers better if they were not centralized; they could make widely varied products. Others could adopt different forms with greater flexibility so as to provide direct service to their customers and to make it easier for members of handicraftsmen's families to take part in production as assistants. Blind concentration on production and aimless large-scale management after these trades were organized into producers' cooperatives, sometimes brought about a reduction in the variety of products, a lowering of their quality, imbalance of supply and demand, disruption of coordination, and caused great inconvenience to the customers. So some of the advantages of separate production and management as described above were lost. The members themselves would also suffer from reduction in income."[62]

Whatever one chooses to call it, the contradiction between elaborate theoretical blueprints and rash action illustrates the way the Chinese economy has been managed since 1949—by fits and starts and sudden changes of course. Over and over again guerrilla politics took charge of economic policy, frontal mass attacks were followed by brief retreats and shady goings-on behind the scenes.[63]

---

[62] Hsueh Mu-Ch'iao et al., op. cit., pp. 154-155. See also Chen Yun's speech to the 8th National Party Congress, September 1956 (Vol. II, p. 163).

[63] According to Mao "political work is the life blood of all economic work: the lack of a correct political point of view is like having no soul." "Mass movement is indispensable for any work. Nothing can be achieved without mass movement." "Insist on putting politics in command." See "Two Diametrically Opposed Lines in Building the Economy," Jen-min Jih-pao (August 25, 1967) in Chinese Economic Studies (White Plains, N.Y.: IASP), Vol. 1, No. 2 (Winter 1967-68), pp. 3-10. To the opposition, the primacy of politics was at worst "mere bluffing, and quick medicine." At best, "good politics must mean good professional affairs. Good professional affairs must mean good politics." "Outline of Struggle," op. cit., URS, Vol. 53, Nos. 7-8, p. 91.

More of the same was to come in 1958 and 1966. That the economy withstood these erratic thrusts, witnesses to the ruggedness and patience of the Chinese people.

The abortive attempts by some leaders to stem the mass revolutionary tide and to instill into the movement some sense and order, will be discussed in Chapter 6. Here we need simply note that in 1956 Liu Shao-ch'i tried to argue for an end to the class struggle unleashed by the Maoists: "The question of who will defeat whom in China, between socialism and capitalism has already been resolved now," he reportedly said in September."[64] The task of proletarian dictatorship was becoming smaller, the job or organizing social life bigger. As early as December 1954, Liu called for a strengthening of the legal system and the establishment of order, which would enable the leaders to control rather than be controlled by events. In place of direct action by the organized masses and the "turbulence of revolution," he wanted to see the smooth development of productive forces and strict adherence to the law (September 1956). In answer to the assertion that the laws were there but had not been properly carried out, he observed that "in recent years . . . there was not even Party law" (May 1962).[65] In his *How To Be A Good Communist* (1962 ed. p. 71) he lashed out against the "left opportunists," those "near-lunatics" who wallowed in intra-Party struggle and shunned all

[64] In 1959 Liu Shao-ch'i reminisced: "There were also some controversies between different viewpoints within our Party on the socialist transformation of capitalist industry and commerce. One view held that capitalist industry and commerce should only be utilized but should not be restricted and transformed, or that we had placed too many restrictions and had carried out the transformation too hastily. . . . Another view contended that we had 'compromised too much' since we not only had carried out the transformation of capitalist industry and commerce in a step-by-step process, but had also practised redemption, given the bourgeoisie the right to vote, and given a definite political status to the representatives of the bourgeoisie." Liu Shao-ch'i, *The Victory of Marxism-Leninism in China* (September 14, 1959), *op. cit.*, p. 56. The enumeration of the contending positions on the socialization of industry and commerce (as well as agriculture, above p. 152 footnote 18) by Liu, was an oblique way of defending what seems to have been Liu's own moderate stance. On April 1, 1967 *Jen-min Jih-pao* published eight questions addressed to Liu by Ch'i Pen-yu. Question 3 asked: "Why, after Liberation, did you make every effort to oppose the socialist transformation of capitalist industry and commerce? Why did you oppose agricultural cooperatives and cut them back?" Question 4: "Why, after the completion of the three great socialist transformations, did you do your best to propagate the theory of the extinction of the class struggle, actively promote a class cooperation and do away with class struggle?" See *Collected Works of Liu Shao-ch'i, 1958-1967, op. cit.*, p. 368.

[65] "Thoroughly Expose Liu Shao-chi'i's Counterrevolutionary Revisionist Crimes in Political and Legal Work," *Cheng-fa kung-she*, Peking, April 16, 1967 in *Chinese Law and Government* (White Plains, N.Y.: *IASP*), Vol. 1, No. 1 (Spring 1968), pp. 67-75.

consensus.[66] Repeatedly, this kind of appeal for moderation, Party consensus, a measure of stability, law and order on communist terms, strict Party-bureaucratic control, gradualness, and experimentation in social policy was drowned by the sound and fury of Party fanatics running amock in the country.

We have seen in Chapter 3 that during the period of reconstruction and reform (1949-52) the private "national" sector of industry, trade, and handicrafts was first used in the task of rebuilding, while so used it was restricted, and finally (beginning with the 1951-52 terror campaigns) it was liquidated. Here we are concerned with the *coup de grâce* dealt the national capitalists late in 1955 and early in 1956 which was reminiscent of the overnight collectivization of agriculture.

A communist writer sums up the process: "At the end of 1955, an upsurge of socialist transformation occurred throughout the country. It first appeared in agricultural cooperation. . . . Under such an impact, a movement for joint state-private operation of capitalist industry and commerce *by whole trades* was soon in full swing. The capitalists paraded in the streets, beating cymbals and drums, while sending in their petitions for the changeover of their enterprises to state-private operation. In a few months, all capitalist enterprises were virtually changed over, *trade by trade*. . . . That the capitalists paraded, with the beating of cymbals and drums, while sending in their petitions for the changeover might appear rather strange, yet it was precisely a vivid manifestation of the great success achieved in transforming capitalist enterprises in the interim years since the establishment of the People's Republic."[67] [Emphases added]. Whereas under the regime of advanced state capitalism (joint state-private enterprises) before 1956, the private partner received share dividends on net income from the jointly managed business, after that date the dividend was replaced by a fixed interest payment of 5 percent per year on the private shares. Payment of interest was to end in 1962, but it seems to have continued into 1966, although the effective interest rate had been lowered to 3.5 percent in 1957.[68] While before

[66] "Thoroughly Smash Liu Shao-chi'i's Counterrevolutionary Conspiracy: A Brief Comment on the 1956 Revised and Expanded Edition of *How To Be A Good Communist*," by the Editors of *Ching-kang-shan* (Tsinghua University), February 8, 1967 in *Chinese Law and Government, ibid.*, p. 65.

[67] Kuan Ta-tung, *The Socialist Transformation of Capitalist Industry and Commerce in China* (Peking: FLP, 1960), pp. 83-84. See also Chi Chao-ting, "Capitalists Cross Over," *China Reconstructs*, No. 3, 1956, pp. 2-5; Pan Ching-yuan, "How to Deal with the Capitalists After the State-Private Joint Operation," *Shih-shih Shou-tse (Current Events Handbook)*, December 25, 1956, in *EFCMM*, No. 72 (March 4, 1957), pp. 23-25.

[68] See I. Gavrilov, "Hung Weiping and Capitalists," *Izvestia* (February 9, 1967), p. 2. The author claims that these former capitalists, "elderly, corpulent men," were receiving 5 percent interest a year on the estimated value of their

1956 the nationalization of industrial and commercial undertakings was carried out firm by firm, after that date it was done by branches of industry and whole trades, usually around a specialized state-private enterprise the main function of which was to promote this transformation. Moreover, the elementary state capitalist stage was, after 1955, skipped in the nationalization process: private businesses were either nationalized outright (i.e., turned into state enterprises) or became advanced state capitalist enterprises managed "jointly" by the state and their former owners.

A STATE-PRIVATE (ADVANCED STATE CAPITALIST) JOINT ENTERPRISE IN 1957

Earlier in this chapter we showed what a fully fledged collective farm was like in 1957. To complete the picture let us take a look at the operational mechanics of a joint state-private enterprise.

Ownership and Payment. Two types of joint state-private ownership were distinguished:

(a) Ownership by individual enterprise—this form was common before 1956.

(b) Ownership by whole industrial branches and trades—a form that became dominant after 1955.

As regards (a), the assets of the capitalists became private shares following inventory taking and state-sponsored revaluation of assets. Dividends were thenceforth paid to the private individuals concerned on these shares, out of the net income of the jointly owned enter-

---

assets (the estimated value of these assets, it should be added, was probably lowered in 1957, giving an effective interest rate below 5 percent), and that they had all kinds of civil and political privileges—a slight exaggeration, no doubt. "Their children live expensively, frequent the best restaurants, buy records from Hong Kong, and dress according to the latest fashion. Several hotels with restaurants in Peking, Shanghai, and other cities are for the exclusive use of the Chinese bourgeoisie. Working people come there only in one capacity: as servants of these parasites." It is true that in 1966 there were Red Guard demands for the abolition of interest payments to former capitalists. Circumstantial evidence that some members of Chinese society lived in relative material ease, though under great psychological stress, is provided by Ma Sitson's account of his escape from China in "Cruelty and Insanity Made Me a Fugitive," *Life*, June 2, 1967, pp. 25-29, 63-66. Se also Liu Shao-ch'i's alleged statement in Shanghai on September 27, 1958 that to isolate the capitalist "the idea . . . is to let him eat and dress better; the more he does so, the more isolated he becomes, and the less political capital he will have. . . . China's bourgeoisie, though limited in number, has great political influence." To remove this influence, according to Liu, it was necessary to give the bourgeois "the right to vote, political status, high wages, fixed interest. When he is permitted to do this, his influence among the people of China will diminish steadily." "Thoroughly Expose Liu Shao-ch'i's Counterrevolutionary Revisionist Crimes in Political and Legal Work," *Cheng-fa kung-she* (Politics and Law Commune), Peking, April 16, 1967 in *Chinese Law and Government* (White Plains, N.Y.: *IASP*), Vol. 1, No. 1 (Spring 1968), p. 69.

prise. State investments (which in some cases may simply have consisted of the state's claim to a certain portion of the revalued private assets) became the state share, and the state became entitled to the portion of the net income represented by its shares.

As regards (b), the individual jointly owned businesses were amalgamated by trades or branches of industry in various localities and grouped under specialized corporations or trusts. The private dividend was replaced by the payment to the private partner of a fixed interest rate on his share of the business. The individual businessman's ownership status was thus changed from that of a stockholder to that of a bondholder. He had no longer even a nominal ownership claim to any assets. After 1955 this type of "three-quarter socialism" became typical of advanced state .capitalism in industry and commerce.[69]

Management. In type (a) joint enterprise, the former owners were usually retained as managers working alongside state appointed managers. Although having little say in the final decisions, they did exert a teaching influence on their state partners insofar as technique and other detailed operations of the business were concerned. It should be recalled that at this stage (i.e., before 1956) state control over the market was still incomplete, and the joint business acted to some extent in response to and in a setting of market forces. The knowledge and experience of the former owners were indispensable to the state during that time. However, important decisions were not for them to make.

In type (b) joint enterprise, the former private owner became a state appointee pure and simple. The amalgamated enterprise was a cog in the state economic plan, and no longer functioned as an individual decision-making unit within a partial market setting.

The branch and trade groupings of joint state-private enterprises were under the control of the Central Administration of Industry and Commerce, an organ directly under the State Council. The ex-capitalists were grouped in the All-China Federation of Industry and Commerce, a mass organization the purpose of which was to relay orders to its members and keep an eye on the execution of those orders. The work of supervision over the joint enterprises was also parcelled out among a number of central government ministries. All in all, by 1956, the joint enterprises became assimilated in fact, if not yet quite in theory, with state industry and commerce. Because of this, the following description of the financial and other features of a

[69] As late as September 1966 (and probably to this day), most medium-sized and small stores and factories were joint state-private enterprises, and were identified as such on their signboards and letterheads. At that time the Red Guards demanded the removal of the character "private" from all signboards.

state enterprise can be applied with only minor modifications to joint state-private firms.

ANATOMY OF A STATE INDUSTRIAL ENTERPRISE AROUND 1957[70]

Ownership. A state enterprise was a legal person exercising ownership of assets on behalf of "the whole people" (i.e., the state), but it was given a certain latitude in using these assets. Enterprise assets were of two kinds:

(i) Fixed, i.e., worth over 500 yuan (before 1956) and over 200 yuan after that date, with a working life of more than one year, and covering such things as plant buildings, residential houses, machinery, vehicles, and roads. No interest was paid on fixed assets.

(ii) Working capital. This was either self-owned (portion of retained profits) or derived from the state budget and the People's Bank. It consisted of raw materials, work in process, fuel, spare parts, supplies, etc.[71]

Economic Accounting System. The state enterprise was subject to the state plan. The system under which the plan was worked out and implemented was known as *ching-chi ho-suan* or "economic accounting" modeled on the Soviet *khozraschet.* The term meant that an individual enterprise was responsible for the management of its work and that the results of enterprise activity were appraised by higher authorities on an enterprise basis. In other words, the enterprise operated as an autonomous unit with its own capital, state-made production and other plans, an account with the People's Bank, and the right to enter into purchase and sales contracts within the plan. The enterprise was accountable to higher authority for the portion of the state plan specifically assigned to it. This higher authority could be any state administration right down to the *hsien.*

The economic accounting, or perhaps better, accountability system was supplemented by the system of "responsibility" (*pao-kan*

[70] The analysis which follows applies, with minor variations, to state enterprises from 1957 through 1965 and, in spite of all the shouting, possibly to this day.

[71] Some relevant sources: Government of the People's Republic of China, Ministry of Finance, *Collection of Laws Relating to Financial Administration in 1955* (Peking: Financial and Economic Publishing House, 1957). Ma Wen-kuei, "China's State Owned Industrial Enterprises—Their Nature and Tasks," *Peking Review* (June 26, 1964), pp. 23-26; Vincent King, "Industrial Enterprise Planning Process in China," *The Mainland China Review* (March 1967), pp. 241-256; Ching-wen Kwang, "The Economic Accounting System of a State Enterprise in Mainland China," *The International Journal of Accounting* (Spring 1966), pp. 61-99; Audrey Donnithorne, *China's Economic System* (New York: Praeger, 1967), pp. 25-28, 157-168. On the general subject of communist state enterprises see George R. Feiwel, *The Economics of a Socialist Enterprise* (New York: Praeger, 1965).

chih-tu) which was a Chinese version of the Soviet principle of *edinochalie* (unity of authority), under which each unit of the enterprise (individual or work group) was responsible for its assigned task, guaranteed its performance, and was judged accordingly.

Management. The state enterprise was managed by state appointees. A typical industrial enterprise usually had, in addition to a director, a deputy manager and chief engineer, a planning and statistical department, a personnel division, and a labor-wages division. Subordinate departments included finance and accounting, supply and sales, administration, and transportation and storage. The productive operations were organized in workshops and, below them, production teams and shifts. To prevent the emergence of a rift between management and the workers, the enterprise usually had a "workers' representative council" which was supposed to act in an advisory capacity to the manager and chief engineer. Meetings of this council were to be held regularly, once or twice a month.

Targets. Each state enterprise had to fulfill certain production and financial plans communicated to it by the state planners (see p. 188 below). These plans were annual, quarterly, or monthly, the latter two being operationally the most common.

Plans were expressed in mandatory targets to be reached. These included (after November 1957) total quantity of major products, total number of workers, total wages fund, and profit. Before November 1957 there were, in addition, targets for the total value of output, trial manufacture of new products, technical-economic norms, rate and amount of cost reduction, average wage, labor productivity, and number of workers at the end of the year. After November 1957 these became nonmandatory.

Even with only four major targets, the focus of attention tended to be gross physical output. The preoccupation with quantity affected the quality of production and was criticized by a number of Chinese economists in 1956-57 and later years. Sun Yeh-fang, for example, pointed out in 1957 that the index of gross output led to faulty statistical computations through double and triple counting; it could not indicate the optimum scale of enterprise production, and encouraged waste of materials. Being computed in constant prices, it could not realistically be used to evaluate the financial performance of enterprises whose transactions were based on current prices. It made difficult, not to say impossible, the proper valuation of fixed capital, and rendered depreciation policies arbitrary. The system "induces everyone to emphasize the fulfillment of the 'gross output' plan and results in many incorrect phenomena and false reporting." [72] Sun advanced the substitution of profit (calculated according to the "law of value") for gross output (in constant prices).

The mandatory targets (norms) could be changed only with the permission of the State Council. However, as with other laws and regulations in China, the importance of any target at any given moment hinged more on the political climate of the time and the precise alignment of forces within the Party and government rather than on a strict reading of the written instructions.

Profits. Profits, calculated as a percentage of costs and on sales, as well as basic depreciation charges were state property and had to be remitted to the relevant controlling agency of government. If the profit target was overfulfilled, certain sums were paid into the enterprise's bonus fund (see below, Remuneration), and a portion of the above-target profit (net of the bonus fund deductions) was transferred to the particular level of government controlling the enterprise. After November 1957 steps were taken to enlarge the enterprise's freedom of action: thereafter, a portion of the realized profit norm was left to the enterprise.

Financial Control. All the enterprise's financial transactions involved in the carrying out of the state plan were to be made through branches of the People's Bank. Enterprises were not permitted to extend credit directly to each other or to make interenterprise financial settlements. The Bank was the sole source of short-term credit for the enterprise and supervised (through special agencies) all allocations for capital construction.

Remuneration and Personnel. Wage and salary payments during the First Five Year Plan period (and again from 1961 through 1966) tried to combine the following characteristics.

(i) The total wages bill was to be such as to enable the state to sustain a high rate of capital formation (cf. Chapter 4).

(ii) Wage differentials were to reflect differences in productivity.

(iii) Increases in wages were not to exceed one-half of the increases in labor productivity. The annual money wage rate during 1952-56 increased 14 percent, and the real wage rate 13 percent.

---

[72] Sun Yeh-fang, "Starting from the Value of Total Output," *Tung-chi Kung-tso* (Statistical Work), No. 13 (1957), pp. 8-14. Sun developed his argument in favor of basing planning on the application of the Marxist law of value in "Put Planning and Statistics on the Basis of the Law of Value," *Ching-chi Yen-chiu* (Economic Research), No. 6 (1956), pp. 30-38, and in "On Value," *Ching-chi Yen-chiu*, No. 9 (1959), pp. 42-68. He was attacked for his views during the Cultural Revolution in *Hung-ch'i*, No. 10 (1966). The attack is reproduced in English in two articles in the *Peking Review* of October 21 and 28, 1966. Cf. Chapter 6 below.

Labor productivity in the material goods sector of the economy increased by 22 percent during this period.[73]

(iv) Income differentials between agricultural and industrial workers and between wage-earners and salaried employees (including professional workers and bureaucrats) were to be narrow. During the period 1953-57 the ratio of per capita annual consumption (communal consumption included) of wage earners' families to peasant families was said to have been 2.3:1, a rather wide discrepancy.[74]

(v) The real incomes of unskilled industrial workers and peasants were to be roughly equal. This, apparently, was not achieved in practice, mainly because of the difficulty of increasing real incomes of the large number of peasants, a step that would have involved substantial increases in consumption, and thus contradict desideratum (i).

These five guidelines articulated a philosophy of low wages and egalitarianism, as much of it, at any rate, as would be compatible with raising output and productivity. The egalitarian streak was especially noticeable among the Maoists.

The Chinese Communists never quite made up their minds about what kind of incentives were most likely to stimulate production and productivity. During the First Five Year Plan period the main stress was on material incentives rather than on politico-psychological boosts, although not all factions within the leadership were happy with this approach. Basically, the system of wage payments was copied from the Soviets, but nonmaterial incentives tended, at all times, to play a more significant role in China than they did in the USSR.[75]

Basic wages of industrial workers were normally graded in eight categories, from the least to the most skilled in that particular branch of activity, the pay ratio of the most to the least skilled being 3:1. Absolute wage amounts in each skill category would be higher in

---

[73] Yuan-li Wu, *The Economy of Communist China: An Introduction, op. cit.*, p. 80. Cf. Yuan Feng, "The Ratio of Increase Between Labor Productivity and Wages," *Hsin Chien-she* (December 3, 1956) in *ECMM*, No. 71, pp. 10-18.

[74] Wu, p. 85.

[75] The main sources are Charles Hoffmann, "Work Incentives in Chinese Industry and Agriculture," in *An Economic Profile of Mainland China, op. cit.*, Vol. 2, pp. 471-498; his *Work Incentive Practices and Policies in the People's Republic of China, 1953-1965* (Albany, N.Y.: State University of New York Press, 1968), and his "Work Incentive Policy in Communist China," *The China Quarterly* (January-March 1964), pp. 92-110; Report by Ma Wen-jui (Minister of Labor), *SCMP*, No. 405 (July 26, 1956). Cf. *Income and Standard of Living in Mainland China*, 2 vols., by Cheng Chu-yuan (Hong Kong: Union Research Institute, 1957).

priority industries than in industries of a lower official priority.[76] In 1956 the top priority industries (in descending order of importance) were oil, timber, coal, electric power, chemicals, machine tools. Different departments of a given industry were also classified in the order of importance attached to them. In some cases each skill category was divided into three quality grades: A, B, and C. Achievement of the quantity norm (target) plus an A for quality would earn the standard pay for that job category. Grade B work would earn, say, 93 percent of the basic pay, and grade C output would be returned and no wages paid for it until the quality specifications reached A or B standards. The basic wage grade scale applied to all types of payment mechanisms: piece rate, time rate, and time plus bonus.

The most common wage payment mechanism in an industrial enterprise consisted of straight piece rates, unlike the practice in the Soviet Union where progressive piece rates were more widespread.[77] Thus a worker in, say, skill category 4 (medium skill) would receive the basic wage applicable to that category for fulfilling his output norm (and, in some cases, his grade A quality norm as well), plus additional payments for exceeding the norm (and the reverse for underfulfilling the norm). The bonus payment could be limited to a given percentage of the basic wage or it could be unlimited if the worker or his team consistently exceeded the assigned output (and in some cases quality) norm. For China as a whole, above-norm bonus payments normally did not exceed 20 percent of the total wages bill.[78] This was substantially lower than in the Soviet Union. Additional pay was given to piece workers who were temporarily transferred to jobs the remuneration for which was below the average pay for their permanent employment, and to pieceworkers who suffered

[76] In 1964, according to a London *Times* report (March 3, 1964, p. 19), the highest grade (8) worker in a Peking steam turbine plant earned 127 yuan per month, while the highest grade (7) worker in the Wusih rubber factory earned 68 yuan per month. A grade 1 worker would earn 30-35 yuan per month. A research scientist might earn as much as 300 yuan a month. Mao Tse-tung's monthly salary was officially put at 400 yuan in 1966. In August 1965 the State Council announced a list of standard salaries of technical personnel (engineers, technicians, assistant technicians, and apprentices). For the purpose of remunerating technical personnel, industry was divided into five categories (top to lowest priority) and each category into several grades. Similar scales existed for administrative and other personnel. Wage scales were also differentiated according to regions. The August 1965 wage regulations listed 11 wage regions for state employees, the differential between the highest and lowest paid regions being about 30 percent.

[77] A progressive piece rate means that the rate of pay rises more rapidly than above-norm output.

[78] Charles Hoffmann, "Work Incentives in Chinese Industry and Agriculture," *op. cit.*, p. 475.

loss of earnings for reasons beyond their control (e.g., lack of adequate supplies or equipment on the job).

Where piece rates could not conveniently be used, time rate payments with bonuses for cost reductions, safety, above-norm quality, etc., were applied. In this instance, overfulfillment of the norm was evaluated by the workers' supervisors. Time rate above-norm bonuses were usually limited to 15 percent of the basic monthly wage in the given skill category.

Basic wages and above-norm bonuses were often supplemented by various allowances (overtime, night, holiday, or dangerous work), rewards for inventions and innovations, regional cost of living allowances, and social security benefits, the last being graded according to wages (see Chapter 6).

Material incentives (wages, allowances, benefits) went hand in hand with nonmaterial incentives ranging from "socialist emulation" campaigns sponsored by mass organizations, through "mass cooperation," to the threat of forced labor.

ANATOMY OF A STATE HANDICRAFTS ENTERPRISE AROUND 1957

A state handicrafts enterprise in 1957 (and again after 1961 until 1965) resembled the state industrial enterprise in all major respects. Members of an advanced handicraft producers' cooperative who "voluntarily" elected to be nationalized, were supposed to receive a refund on what they had invested as shares in the cooperative. They became wage employees with a right to enjoy the benefits stipulated by the state labor regulations. Only the most technically and ideologically advanced cooperatives were nationalized before 1965.

THE PLANNING PROCESS

The Chinese adopted from the Soviets the method of formulating state economic plans which involved the principle of "from top down and from bottom up." The agencies involved in the preparation of plans included the Party leadership, the State Planning Commission (for long-range plans), the State Economic Commission (annual and quarterly plans), the State Construction Commission (capital construction), the central economic ministries, regional and provincial departments, supervisory bodies, the managements of individual enterprises, and the enterprise workshops. The idea was to involve everyone in the drafting of the plan, but only to the extent compatible with democratic centralism. In theory, this involved two-way vertical movements from the top planning organs down to the enterprise shops and vice versa.

The steps in the planning process may be summarized as follows.

1. "Control figures" reflecting leadership priorities and goals were issued by the State Planning Commission (SPC) and communicated to the State Economic Commission (SEC) for' translation into short-term plans. On the basis of these instructions, the SEC formulated annual control figures and transmitted them to central economic ministries and regional or provincial economic departments. The latter thereupon issued control figures to their subordinate "supervisory agencies," which communicated these to the planning departments of individual enterprises.

2. Based on the control figures received from above, the enterprises then prepared draft plans for the coming year, based on production performance of the preceding six months. The plans were to be ready in the third quarter of each year. The enterprise draft plans included (a) a production plan, (b) a labor and wages plan, (c) a material-technical supply plan (materials, inventory, power, transport), (d) a plan for costs, (e) a plan for technique and organization, and (f) a financial plan (physical plans translated into monetary terms). The enterprises' draft plans were then sent upward through the various hierarchical levels, and were adjusted and revised on the way so as to dovetail into each other. On reaching the SEC, the various synthesized enterprise plans were reevaluated in the light of the material balance (inputs-outputs) for the economy as a whole.

3. The revised plan was then sent back through the ministries, regional and provincial departments, and so on until it nestled back in the enterprises. Here it was revised and adjusted accordingly, and up it went again to the SEC.

4. Finally the plan was approved by the SEC, submitted by the SEC to the relevant government organ (State Council), and by the State Council to the National People's Congress for adoption. The adopted plan then traveled back all the way down the chain of command until it reached the enterprise, where it became the operational plan for the year.

That is the ideal outline. Of course, there was considerable shuttling back and forth, some bargaining between the various planning levels, and certainly much less smoothness than appears on the surface. During the period of relatively free cricticism in 1957, the Minister of the Timber Industry, Lo Lung-chi, complained that "in the drawing up of plans, the practice was not to have the plans prepared at the lower levels and submitted to the higher levels, and then returned to the lower levels. The higher levels simply decided on the plans, and assigned tasks to the lower levels." [79] The whole pro-

[79] *NCNA*, May 22, 1957.

cedure, at least as outlined in the blueprint, presupposes a widely disseminated mathematical and economic knowledge, which in China's circumstances was probably imperfectly realized. It also assumes that the planners be left in peace to do their job, which clearly they were not. Although the centrally formulated targets (i.e., at the SEC level) covered at most 200 industrial products, the state plan supplemented by local and other plans covered at least 70 percent of the commodities and services produced by the economy. That was a big job—one, moreover, that certain segments of the leadership never quite understood. "Being basically not versed in construction," Mao later admitted, "I knew nothing about industrial planning."[80]

[80] Speech on the failure of the Great Leap Forward, July 23, 1959. *New York Times*, March 15, 1970, p. 8.

6 | The First Five Year Plan, 1953-57: Social, Fiscal, Monetary, Foreign Trade, and Political Measures

SOCIAL REFORMS

EDUCATION

The leadership dispute about the nature and directions of Chinese education mentioned in Chapter 3 (pp. 90-92) continued into the period 1953-57. The Maoists pressed for universal schooling with strong political content, emphasized the class composition of the student and teacher body, promoted five-year primary schools and special (vocational) local schools for poor and lower-middle peasants, and argued for the fusion of study with physical labor. Mao's "Three-Good" (san-hao) for education announced in June 1953 were good health, (shenti-hao), good study, (hauesi-hao), and good (physical) labor, (kungtsu-hao), in that order. "Our educational work," wrote Lu Ting-yi (later to be branded as a counterrevolutionary revisionist), "is like a hundred flowers in bloom, like 'ten thousand horses galloping ahead.'. . . All the social sciences must be guided by politics, and education is no exception. People require education to wage the class struggle and the struggle for production."[1]

The same Lu Ting-yi, together with Liu Shao-ch'i and others, were later (1967) accused of having sabotaged the Maoist line on learning. Instead of promoting universal schooling with a strong political content, they worked, it was alleged, for elitist education with minimal political content. In June 1956, Liu apparently said that "universal education is still not too urgent now; the question now is still higher education and the need for specialists."[2] The

[1] Lu Ting-yi was at that time an alternate member of the Politbureau of the Chinese Communist Party. These words were written in the midst of the Great Leap, when everyone, including those who harbored reservations about Maoism, jumped on the bandwagon. The quotation is from his Education Must Be Combined with Productive Labour (Peking: FLP, 1958), pp. 2, 5.

[2] "Chronology of the Two-Road Struggle on the Educational Front in the Past Seventeen Years," Chia-yu-ko-ming (May 6, 1967) in Chinese Education (White Plains, N.Y.: IASP), Spring 1968, p. 18. Consult, Chao Chung and Yang I-fan, Students in Mainland China (Hong Kong: URI, 1956).

Maoists later interpreted this as a call for pure expertise rather than redness. In 1953, according to the same sources, Liu and his group abolished political classes for the first year of junior middle schools; in 1954 political classes of the second year went overboard; in 1955 the same fate befell indoctrination courses in the first and second years of senior high schools; finally, by 1956, with the exception of the third-year senior middle schools, political classes for all other years were jettisoned. The anti-Maoist opposition was also charged with coddling bourgeois teachers and dragging their feet on Mao's plan to create rapid courses for children of poor and middle peasants. In fact, in 1955 these courses were apparently suspended. Instead stress was put on academic degrees, professional competence divorced from the correct revolutionary spirit, and on introduction of Soviet "revisionist" models. In 1956 the Ministry of Education introduced the Soviet system of language and geography teaching in middle schools and adopted various Soviet-type rules and regulations pertaining to degrees, fellowships, curricula, and so on. This was merely the continuation of a trend which started, according to the Maoists, as far back as 1949 and which was formalized in July 1953. Beginning in 1954 all college students had to study Russian, while the teaching of English was discontinued. In 1955 most higher educational institutions went from a four to a five-year curriculum, and medical schools to eight years. In some middle schools the period of study was extended to six years.[3] There was also opposition to Mao's preoccupation with group physical fitness and the combination of manual work and study. Study per se, Mao's adversaries argued, was labor. If the opposition really did all this, it must have been extremely powerful, a majority of the Party and government, no less, and not "a handful" as the Maoists contend. In fact, if the accusations are to be believed, the whole state was subverted from top to bottom. The Maoists were particularly concerned about the elitist character of secondary and higher education, about the "blue-blood" schools which—like Peking and Tsinghua Universities—perpetuated the tradition of concentrating on academic excellence, thus favoring students of middle-class family background. Special ire was reserved for the system of college entrance examinations, which, it was argued, discriminated against the culturally disadvantaged but politically reliable sons and daughters of poor and lower-middle peasants. The academically oriented college entrance examinations produced, in turn, elitist middle schools which were the main suppliers of elite universities.

---

[3] "In China," explains Lu Ting-yi in the pamphlet already cited, "the primary schools cover the first six years of schooling. Middle schools account for the years after primary school, up to college." *op. cit.*, p. 31, note 1.

A Party school, copied from the Soviets and named the Chinese People's University, was set up in Peking in 1953. It offered courses in economics, history, philosophy, and law. It was criticized by its own faculty during the Hundred Flowers campaign, as a "beehive of doctrinairism."

For the record, Table 6-1 presents the official data on education for the period 1953-57.[4]

During the blooming of the hundred flowers in April-May 1957 (see Chapter 7) many other criticisms of the educational system came to the surface. There was, for example, impatience in some educational quarters with the blind acceptance of Soviet models, as much a manifestation of "dogmatism" as of "empiricism." Professor Chueh-min of Nankai University, for example, complained at a forum organized by the *People's Daily* (April 14, 1957), that he was "forced to accept all things from the Soviet Union, lock, stock, and barrel, despite the fact that some of the things were not convincing enough [to him]."[5] Many curricula were abolished simply because no such curricula existed in the Soviet Union. A Reuter dispatch of April 13, 1957 noted that in spite of the progress in education, about four million school children leaving primary school in 1957 (or 32.5 percent of the graduating class) would be unable to get into junior middle schools, and some 800,000 students leaving junior middle schools would not be able to go on to senior grades. About 90,000 senior school graduates would not find places in institutions of higher learning. The schools and universities were overcrowded, many worked on two shifts. There was a growing frustration among school and university graduates because frequently they had to work in jobs for which they had not been trained or were sent down to the country, a direction not particularly appealing to them. Too much time was taken up with mass rallies and meetings, while political study intruded on what should have been the core of the curriculum. Impatience and frustration among the young often turned into idleness and nihilism, and disillusionment with the system.

REFORM OF THE CHINESE WRITTEN LANGUAGE

The Chinese written language has played a unifying function in China's diverse society, but it has also been an obstacle to the progress of general literacy, and more recently to scientific research. A Soviet scientist who had spent some time in China as an adviser

---

[4] Cf. Chapters 3 and 10.

[5] *Jen-min Jih-pao*, April 21 and 22, 1957, reported in R. MacFarquhar, *The Hundred Flowers Campaign and the Chinese Intellectuals* (New York: Praeger, and Stevens & Sons, Ltd., London, 1960), p. 27.

TABLE 6-1
Educational Measures, 1953–57

	1953	1954	1955	1956	1957
Number of enrolled students (millions)*					
Primary schools.	51.7	51.2	53.1	63.5	64.3
Middle schools	2.9	3.6	3.9	5.2	6.3
Technical middle schools. . .	0.7	0.6	0.5	0.8	0.8
Institutes of higher learning .	0.2	0.3	0.3	0.4	0.4
Number of graduates (millions)*					
Primary schools.	9.9	10.1	10.3	12.3	12.3
Middle schools	0.5	0.6	1.0	0.9	1.3
Technical middle schools. . .	0.1	0.2	0.2	0.2	0.1
Institutes of higher learning†.	0.05	0.05	0.06	0.06	0.06
Number of graduates from institutes of higher learning (thousands)‡					
Engineering	14.6	15.6	18.6	22.0	17.2
Agriculture.	2.6	3.5	2.6	3.5	3.1
Economics and finance	10.5	6.0	4.7	4.5	3.7
Medicine	2.9	4.5	6.8	5.4	6.2
Natural sciences.	1.8	0.8	2.0	4.0	3.5
Pedagogy	9.7	10.6	12.1	17.2	15.9
Liberal arts.	3.3	2.7	4.7	4.0	4.3
Newly literate persons (millions)*	3.0	2.6	3.7	7.4	7.2
Students of worker and peasant origin, percentage of total in each category					
Middle schools	57.7	60.7	62.2	66.0	69.1
Technical middle schools. . .	55.9	58.8	62.0	64.1	66.6
Institutes of higher learning .	21.9	—	29.0	34.1	36.3
Female students (percentage of total in each category)§					
Primary schools.	32.9	—	—	—	34.5
Middle schools	23.5	—	—	—	30.8
Technical middle schools. . .	24.9	—	—	—	26.5
Institutes of higher learning .	23.4	—	—	—	23.3
Kindergartens§					
Number (thousands).	6.5	—	—	—	16.4
Children in kindergartens (thousands)	424	—	—	—	1,088
Number of people attending spare-time schools (millions)*.					
Primary schools.	1.5	2.0	4.5	5.2	6.3
Middle schools	0.4	0.8	1.2	2.2	2.7
Middle technical schools . . .	0.001‖	0.2	0.2	0.6	0.6
Institutes of higher learning†	0.01	0.01	0.02	0.06	0.08

*Rounded to the nearest hundred thousand.
†Rounded to the nearest ten thousand.
‡ Rounded to the nearest hundred.
§ Figures in 1953 column refer to 1952.
‖Rounded to the nearest thousand.
Source: Ten Great Years (Peking: *FLP*, 1960), pp. 192, 194, 196, 198, 200, 201, 202.

noted some of the difficulties: for 90 percent of the chemical elements the Chinese have invented names which have no connection with those in international use—"imagine," he writes, "the problem of representing tungsten or plutonium by means of an ideogram."[6] The secretariat of the Physics Institute of the Chinese Academy of Sciences in Peking had in 1958 one Chinese typewriter, an ancient model with 1,200 characters.

The Chinese communists were alert to the difficulty. Research on *simplifying Chinese characters* began soon after 1949. In January 1955 a special committee drew up a draft scheme for simplifying the written language; a year later the State Council published it. In all, 544 characters and 54 radicals were simplified. "The 544 characters which are simplified . . . have in their original forms a total of 8,745 strokes or an average of 16.08 strokes a character. After being simplified, they are reduced to 515 characters with a total of 4,206 strokes, each character taking only 8.16 strokes on the average. . . . Before the simplification there were [among the 544 characters] only 34 characters with less than ten strokes and after the simplification the number rises to 409. . . . The popularization of simplified characters greatly facilitates children's education, elimination of illiteracy, and writing in general."[7] By 1965 the number of simplified characters had increased to 2,238 and a "Complete Table of Simplified Characters" had been published.[8]

The reform apparently did not go down well with everyone. Wu Yu-chang darkly hinted at "a number of rightists" who "launched vicious attacks against the reform," alleging that it was a failure. The authors of the reform themselves admitted that there were many imperfections and difficulties, ambiguity of the simplified characters being among the more serious. As Chou En-lai put it: "There are some who freely coin simplified characters which nobody except themselves can make out."[9]

The next step in the language reform movement was *popularization of the common speech (putonghua)*. "Among the Han people, a great diversity of dialects exists—the diversity being mainly in pro-

[6] Mikhail A. Klochko, *Soviet Scientist in Red China* (New York: Praeger, and The Bodley Head, London, 1964), pp. 27-28.

[7] Wu Yu-chang, "Report on the Current Tasks of Reforming the Written Chinese Language and the Draft Scheme for a Chinese Phonetic Alphabet," in *Reform of the Chinese Written Language* (Peking: FLP 1965), p. 27. See also, Wei Chueh, "Making Chinese Easier to Learn," *Peking Review* (March 11, 1958), pp. 14-16; "Simplifying Chinese Characters," *FEER* (October 18, 1962), pp. 139-142.

[8] *URS*, Vol. 40, No. 8 (July 27, 1965).

[9] Chou En-lai, "Current Tasks of Reforming the Written Language" (January 10, 1958), in *Reform of the Chinese Written Language, op. cit.*, p. 6.

nunciation. People in different areas, each speaking their own dialect, can hardly understand one another . . . Without a common speech we shall, to greater or less extent, meet with difficulties in our national construction. It often happens that the listener fails to understand an important report or an important class lecture due to the dialectal barrier." [10] To solve this problem, the communists have promoted the use of the phonetics of a common speech with Peking pronunciation. At the end of 1957 there were among the language teachers of primary, secondary, and pedagogic schools, 721,000 who had been trained in the phonetics of the common speech. The People's Liberation Army was used to teach recruits the elements of the common speech. [11]

The third step in the language reform consisted in the *development of a Chinese phonetic alphabet*, which involved annotating the existing characters phonetically and popularizing the common speech. In the future, the intention was to adopt the Latin alphabet for the Chinese phonetic alphabet. Moreover, non-Han nationalities were to be urged to follow suit. A preliminary scheme for a Chinese phonetic alphabet was passed by the National People's Congress in February 1958. [12] With its issue of November 1, 1961 the Peking, *Jen-min Jih-pao* began giving Chinese phonetic alphabet equivalents for the more difficult characters. In 1964-65 nationwide efforts were made to popularize phonetic words. On the basis of Chinese language phonetization, steps were taken to introduce (a) an alphabet for the deaf and dumb, (b) new Uighur and Kazakh written languages, (c) a flag signal code, and (d) a light signal code. [13]

LABOR PROTECTION AND SOCIAL SECURITY [14]

Total civilian nonagricultural employment in China in 1957 was roughly 40 million. Of these workers, just over 16 million belonged

[10] *Ibid.*, pp. 8-9. The dialectal barrier may sometimes be subtly dialectical when the listener elects not to understand an important report or an important class lecture.

[11] "Common Speech for All," *Peking Review* (September 14, 1960), p. 5.

[12] For a sample of professional criticism of the written language reform made during the Hundred Flowers interlude, see Roderick MacFarquhar, *The Hundred Flowers Campaign, op. cit.*, pp. 80-81. See also Li Hui, "Phonetic Alphabet—Short Cut to Literacy," *Peking Review* (July 12, 1960), pp. 17-19; and P. H. M. Jones, "Scripts for Minorities," *FEER* (April 12, 1962), pp. 62-64.

[13] "New Trends in the Reform of the Chinese Written Language," *URS*, Vol. 40, No. 8 (July 27, 1965).

[14] The principal Chinese communist sources are *Labour Insurance in New China* (Peking: FLP, 1953); *Labour Protection in New China*, (Peking: FLP, 1960); *Important Labour Laws and Regulations of the People's Republic of*

to trade unions, 11.5 million were covered by labor insurance, and 6.6 million by free medical care. It is probable that labor insurance was limited to workers in modern factories and mines, modern transport and communications, and large construction projects. Collective farmers' welfare was supposed to have been taken care of by the collective farms out of their welfare funds. In 1957 agricultural cooperatives set aside about 10 percent of their gross income for this purpose. Hospitals and clinics in the countryside were administered by the *hsien* authorities, although some collective farms had simple dispensaries and clinics of their own. Industrial social insurance benefits were financed out of deductions from enterprise total monthly payrolls, the rate being about 3 percent, but possibly higher in actual practice. A part of the sum resulting from these deductions was turned over to the All-China Federation of Trade Unions which administered the collective labor insurance system on behalf of the state (clinics, sanatoria, rest homes, libraries).[15] The remaining part was retained by the enterprise and expended on welfare schemes under its control (current pension and relief payments, plant clinics, hospitals, dispensaries). Trade union members were theoretically entitled to free medical care, insurance against sickness, accident and old age, but actual application seemingly remained spotty especially as regards free medical care. Actual operation of the system was somewhat erratic, depending on locality, type of enterprise, and so on. There were just not enough trained people to go around and not enough facilities. Welfare payments were geared to wage scales and performed a nonmaterial incentive function insofar as they were made to leading workers, labor heroes, and others displaying an uncommon measure of socialist consciousness.

Injury or disablement sustained while at work. Workers and staff members injured while at work were to be treated at the hospital or clinic of the enterprise concerned or at a hospital designated by the enterprise. Total expenses for treatment, medicines, hospitalization, and travel involved, were to be borne by the management. The injured worker was entitled to full wages throughout the period of treatment. A disabled worker was entitled to a monthly invalid pension from the labor insurance fund. The pension was to be 75 per-

---

China (enlarged ed.) (Peking: *FLP*, 1961); Lu Kuang, "Labour Protection in China," *Peking Review* (May 3, 1960), pp. 33-35. A good Western source is Charles Hoffmann, *op. cit.* Also, J. P. Emerson, *Non-Agricultural Employment in Mainland China, 1949-58* (Washington, D.C.: U.S. Bureau of Census, 1965). With minor changes, the discussion of the labor protection and social security system is applicable to the post-1957 period.

[15] Paul F. Harper, *Trade Unions in Communist China*. Ph.D. dissertation, Cornell University, 1968.

cent of the worker's former wages for permanent disability, payable for the rest of his life; in cases where a totally disabled person was "not in need of other people to take care of him," the pension was to be 60 percent of his wages; partial disability qualified for an allowance of between 10 and 30 percent of the worker's wages, but this sum together with his wages after resuming work was not to exceed his wages prior to being disabled.

Sickness, injury or disablement sustained while not at work. The patient was to be treated at the enterprise's hospital or clinic or by designated doctors of traditional Chinese or Western schools. All expenses for treatment, operations, hospitalization, and ordinary medicines were to be borne by the enterprise. Total cost of expensive medicines, meals at the hospital and travel was to be paid by the patient. Absence from work for purposes of treating injuries sustained while not working entitled the patient to 60-100 percent of his original wages, provided the period of absence did not exceed six consecutive months. After six months, his monthly benefits dropped to 40-60 percent of his original wages, until he resumed work, or was classified as disabled, or until death. If classified as totally disabled he was entitled to monthly benefits at the rate of 50 percent of his former wages if unable to take care of himself, or 40 percent if he did not need other people to take care of him. A lineal dependent of an insured worker was entitled to treatment at the enterprise's hospital or clinic or from designated doctors. Fees for operation or ordinary medicine were borne to the extent of 50 percent by the management of the enterprise, while expensive medicines, travel, meals, etc., were to be paid by the patient.

Death benefits for workers, staff members, and their lineal dependents. (a) If the worker died while at work, funeral expenses were borne by the enterprise, the amount being three months' wages based on the average wages of workers and staff members in the enterprise. A monthly pension, based on the number of lineal dependents, was to be paid to these dependents. The pension was to be 25-50 percent of the wages of the deceased. (b) Death from sickness or injury not sustained at work qualified the worker's dependents for a funeral allowance equivalent to the deceased worker's two months' wages and a relief benefit equivalent to 6-12 months' wages, according to the number of dependents. (c) Death of a worker after retirement because of complete disability resulting from injury sustained at work entitled his lineal dependents to benefits as specified under (a), while death after retirement due to sickness or injury sustained while not at work entitled the dependents to benefits as specified under (b). A funeral allowance was to be paid in the case of the death of a lineal dependent of a worker or staff member. The amount was to be equivalent to 50 percent of the monthly average wages of workers and staff employees in the enterprise if the deceased was ten years of age or more. If the deceased was 1-10 years old, the amount was one-third of the average wages, and no allowance was paid for death of a dependent whose age was less than one year.

Old-age pensions. Male workers were entitled to monthly old-age pensions from the enterprise on reaching the age of sixty and provided they had worked for 25 years, including five years in the enterprise concerned. The pension was payable until the retiree's death. The amount was to be calculated according to the number of years of work in the enterprise concerned, and was to range from 50-70 percent of the retiree's former wages. If the interest of the enterprise called for the worker's staying on at his job after he was qualified for old-age retirement, he was to receive in addition to his original wages, a monthly old-age work pension according to the number of years he has worked in the enterprise concerned. This pension was to be the equivalent of 10-20 percent of his wages. Female workers or staff members were qualified for retirement at 50 after 20 years of work, including five years in the enterprise concerned. Their pensions were to be paid on the same principles as those for men. Men workers who worked in mines or in places which were constantly at temperatures below 32°F or at or above 100°F were entitled to retire at 55 and women workers in these employments at 45. Benefit payments were to be as for other workers, except that under such employment conditions one year's work was to be counted as one year and three months. Where the work was directly detrimental to health (lead, mercury, arsenic, phosphorus, acids, etc., industries) the insured were eligible for retirement at the ages specified for mining workers, except that in calculating the number of years of employment, including those in the enterprise concerned, one year's work was to count as one year and six months.

It should be added that business and industrial enterprises each received a quota of new workers from the annual list of school graduates. Many of these replaced overage workers and employees qualifying for pension. In such cases the enterprise enjoyed a margin of savings on its payroll, since the pensioner received from 50-60 percent of his latest pay, while the new worker normally received less than half of that amount.[16] On the other hand, the enterprise had usually to train the recruit on the job and possibly absorb some broken cutlery in the process. To balance this, however, was the fact

---

[16] "Changing Face," *FEER* (February 18, 1965), p. 277. Cf. Chapter 9 on the "Worker-Peasant" System.

that the educational level of new workers was higher than that of the old timers, and probably their adaptability greater.

Maternity benefits. Women workers and staff members were entitled to a total of 56 days' leave of absence from work before and after confinement. Wages were to be paid in full during maternity leave. In cases of miscarriage, the leave of absence with full wages was up to 30 days during the first seven months of pregnancy. In cases of difficult delivery or the birth of twins, an additional leave of 14 days with full pay was allowed. The enterprise was to pay for prenatal examinations and child delivery at the enterprise's hospital or clinic. Other expenses were to be paid by the patient. If at the end of maternity the woman worker was certified as unfit to resume work, she was entitled to the same benefits as those for the sick. In the case of childbirth, a worker, staff member or wife of a male worker or staff member were respectively to receive a maternity benefit of 40,000 yuan (old currency) or 4 yuan (new currency).[17]

Collective labor insurance undertakings. All workers and employees working in enterprises which provided insurance benefits were entitled to benefits from the collective labor insurance undertakings administered by the All-China Federation of Trade Unions. The primary trade union committee of an enterprise together with the management were to run collective labor insurance undertakings such as sanatoria and nurseries according to the financial conditions of the enterprise and the needs of the workers. The All-China Federation of Trade Unions was to run or entrust local trade union organizations or industrial unions with the management of sanatoria, rest homes, homes for the aged, orphanages, homes for the disabled, and other institutions of like kind.

Workers and employees who worked in enterprises which provided labor insurance but who were not trade union members, were to receive benefits in cases of injury, disablement, or death sustained while at work, as well as childbirth, medical care for sickness or injury not sustained at work, and medical care for their lineal dependents. However, they were entitled to only half the amount prescribed of wages and relief benefit.

Preferential labor insurance benefits. Model workers and staff members and demobilized army combat heroes were entitled to special benefits on the recommendation of the primary trade union committees and with the approval of the provincial or municipal trade union organizations or the national committees of the industrial unions concerned. These benefits included the cost of expensive

[17]The new yuan was introduced on March 1, 1955. The rate of exchange was 1 new yuan to 10,000 old yuan.

medicines, travel, meals at the hospital during treatment for sickness or injury sustained at work. Moreover, during the first six months of treatment wages were to be paid in full. Sickness, injury, or disability sustained not at work entitled these beneficiaries to 60 percent of the wages. Invalid pensions for disablement sustained at work were to be equivalent to the full amount of wages of the person concerned. Allowances for disability sustained at work were to be equivalent to the difference between wages received before disability and wages received after resuming work. Death incurred while at work entitled the lineal dependents of the deceased to a pension equivalent to 30-60 percent of the wages of the deceased. Old-age pensions upon retirement were to be 60-80 percent of the wages of the person concerned. Old-age pensions for persons continuing to work beyond the retirement limit were to be 20-30 percent of the wages of the person concerned. Model workers, employees, and army combat heroes were also entitled to priority in receiving benefits from collective labor insurance undertakings. Disabled ex-servicemen were to be paid full wages during the first six months of their absence from work, to receive medical treatment for sickness or injury not sustained at work, regardless of the length of time they worked in the enterprise concerned. After six months the benefits would be dealt with in the same manner as for other workers.

According to a survey carried out between 1954 and 1956 there were about 1.7 million blind and 3 million deaf-mute people in China. In September 1959 there were 32 schools for blind children, 120 schools for the blind, deaf, and mute, and another 145 for the deaf-mute. At the end of 1959, 35,000 blind, deaf-mute, and blind-deaf-mute were employed. In 1964 there existed 178 spare-time study classes for these people. Almost 80,000 copies of books in Braille had been published by the end of 1964.[18]

A word of warning once again. The scheduled social security benefits read well, are modern and progressive. The social security legislation of some Latin American countries also reads well and is more progressive than that of many more developed countries. The question, however, is not so much how the rules read, but how they are implemented. It has already been mentioned that the actual coverage was quite limited and that the enforcement was spotty. This is not to say that the whole system is a fraud. A much more reasonable explanation is that the intent of the legislation outruns China's means. Also, in a country such as China the state's concern with the welfare of the ill and the disabled is something relatively new. The psychological impact of the intent on the workers should not, there-

[18]*URS*, Vol. 44, No. 24 (September 20, 1966), pp. 358-359.

fore, be dismissed lightly. Where the system has been applied, it has contributed substantially to per capita consumption in a form ideologically acceptable to the communists. The system just described re-

TABLE 6-2
Public Health Measures*

	1952	1953	1957
Hospital beds (thousands of units)	180	215	364
Maternity hospitals (units)	98		96
Children's hospital (units).	6		16
Health stations for women and children (units). .	2,379		4,599
Permanent child care organizations (thousands). .	2.7		17.7
Children under care (thousands).	99		488
Western trained doctors (thousands)	52		74
Nurses (thousands)	61		128
Midwives (thousands)	22		36

*Refer to Table 3-17, p. 95.
Source: Ten Great Years (Peking: FLP, 1960), pp. 220, 221, 222.

mained in force, with minor modifications, until the outbreak of the Cultural Revolution in 1966. Possibly, below the turbulent surface of the Cultural Revolution events, it has continued to function.

FISCAL AND MONETARY POLICY

FISCAL POLICY

In Chapter 3 we have discussed some of the measures taken by the communists in 1949-52 to establish fiscal and monetary order in the economy and to lay the groundwork for future planning.

In the period 1953-57 this work was pushed forward. The government budget and the state banking system became the main instruments for financial control over the Five Year Plan, especially after the liquidation of the private sectors in industry, trade, and agriculture. Farm investment excluded, 88.5 percent of capital formation during the Plan was carried out through the central government budget, the rest by enterprises from their own resources, local governments from funds outside the consolidated state budget, and by private businesses.

GOVERNMENT BUDGET[19]

Table 6-3 presents the official data for state budgetary revenues

[19] A good reference source is George N. Ecklund, Financing The Chinese Government Budget: Mainland China 1950-1959 (Chicago: Aldine, 1966).

TABLE 6-3
State Budget, 1953-57*
(Millions of yuan)

Year	Revenue								
	Taxes		Income from State Enterprises		Credits and Insurance		Other		Total
	(1)	Percent	(2)	Percent	(3)	Percent	(4)	Percent	
1953	11,970	55.0	7,670	35.2	490	2.3	1,630	7.5	21,760
1954	13,220	50.4	9,960	38.0	1,790	6.8	1,260	4.8	26,230
1955	12,750	46.9	11,190	41.1	2,360	8.7	900	3.3	27,200
1956	14,090	49.0	13,430	46.7	720	2.5	500	1.8	28,740
1957	15,490	49.9	14,420	46.5	700	2.3	410	1.3	31,020

Year	Expenditure										
	Economic construction		Social, Cultural, Educational		National Defense		Government Administration		Other		Total
	(1)	Percent	(2)	Percent	(3)	Percent	(4)	Percent	(5)	Percent	
1953	8,650	40.2	3,360	15.7	5,680	26.4	2,120	9.9	1,680	7.8	21,490
1954	12,360	50.2	3,460	14.1	5,810	23.6	2,160	8.7	840	3.4	24,630
1955	13,760	51.1	3,190	11.9	6,500	24.1	2,150	8.0	1,320	4.9	26,920
1956	15,910	52.1	4,600	15.0	6,120	20.0	2,660	8.7	1,290	4.2	30,580
1957	14,910	51.4	4,640	16.0	5,510	19.0	2,270	7.8	1,690	5.8	29,020

Total Revenue and Expenditure

Year	Revenue	Expenditure	Balance
1953	21,760	21,490	+ 270
1954	26,230	24,630	+1,600
1955	27,200	26,920	+ 280
1956	28,740	30,580	-1,840
1957	31,020	29,020	+2,000

*Refer to Table 3-13, p. 82.
Source: Ten Great Years (Peking: FLP, 1960), pp. 21, 22, 24.

and expenditure during the First Five Year Plan period.

General comments. In 1953 taxes contributed 55 percent of state revenues and revenue from state enterprises 35.2 percent. By 1957 the respective shares were: taxes, 49.9 percent, revenue from state enterprises 46.5 percent.

In 1953 state expenditures on economic construction represented 40.2 percent of total state expenditures. In 1957 the proportion had risen to 51.4 percent (52.1 percent in 1956).

Local budgets are thought to have accounted for about 50 percent of the annual totals.[20]

[20]Francois J. Durand, Le Financement du Budget en Chine Populaire (Paris: Editions Sirey, 1965).

Revenues –

1. Taxes

The Chinese relied less on taxes to finance their budgetary expenditures than the Soviet Union. During the period 1955-58 taxes
represented about 47 percent of China's state budgetary revenues,
and 73 percent in the USSR. [21] Commodity taxes and direct taxes on
income and wealth were also substantially less important in China's
state revenue than in that of the Soviet Union. During the same
period, loans from abroad were only 1.4 percent of state revenues.

The relatively heavy reliance on revenues from state enterprises
may be explained by the fact that much of the peasants' income was
in kind and the monetary tax base was, therefore, limited compared
with the state's desired expenditure levels. The absolute increase in
tax revenues between 1953 and 1957 (3.5 billion yuan) reflects the
widening of the tax base, especially in the urban areas.

The elimination of the private sector by 1956 meant a decrease
in the administrative cost and in complications attendant on tax
collections.

Taxation has been retained in China because it guarantees a certain minimum of revenue to the state, whereas enterprise profits
fluctuate, and because it gives the state considerable leverage on
enterprise managements. The following were the major types of
taxes:

Agricultural taxes

Taxes on industry and commerce

Customs duties

Agricultural taxes were levied on the "set yield" of the land, not
on actual yield in a given year. The set yield was determined by
governmental authorities for each locality on the basis of such
factors as soil and rainfall conditions, irrigation, amount of fertilizer
used, etc. The set yield, in other words, was the expected normal
yield. Once determined, the set yield was supposed to remain in
force for a number of years. In this way it was hoped that it would
provide an incentive for peasants to raise actual output without fear
of upward revisions in the tax base. During the Great Proletarian
Cultural Revolution (Chapters 11,12) Teng Hsiao-p'ing, the Party's
General Secretary, was criticized for his adherence to the "set yield"
incentive. At an industrial conference of the Party's Shanghai Municipal Committee on February 20, 1958, he was alleged to have said

---

[21] *Ten Great Years, op. cit.*, pp. 21, 22; Tsentral'noye Statisticheskoye
Upravleniye, *Narodnoye khozyaystvo SSSR v 1958 godu* (Moscow: 1959),
p. 899.

that "the production assignment target of the commune is about 20 percent lower than the actual target. Thus the members of the commune obtain the benefit from the excess and the masses' interest is aroused." [22] In cases of grain losses through natural calamities, a tax reduction expressed as a percentage of the set yield was allowed. After completion of land reform proportional rather than progressive tax rates were applied to the set yield. The agricultural tax was used during the period 1953-57 to encourage the cultivation of certain industrial crops (e.g., cotton). This was done by means of tax exemptions and preferential tax rates. Out of total tax revenues collected by the state in 1957 in the amount of 15.5 billion yuan, the agricultural tax yielded almost 3 billion yuan. In 1952 agricultural taxes represented 7.5 percent of the gross value of agricultural output and output of sideline occupations. In 1956 the relevent figure was 6.04 percent.[23]

Taxes on industry and commerce consisted of (a) business taxes, (b) commodity tax, (c) salt tax, and (d) stamp tax.

(a) Business taxes were levied on gross receipts of industrial and commercial enterprises, whatever the form of their ownership. Exceptions included state monopoly enterprises, poor artisan workshops, and subsidiary occupations. Tax rates were higher on service sales than on commodity sales, and on nonpriority industries than on such heavy industries as iron and steel, coal, and machine building. The tax rate on commodity sales varied from 1 to 3 percent, and could be as much as five times as high on nonessential service receipts.

(b) Commodity taxes were based on the wholesale prices of goods and were payable by manufacturers or wholesale buyers at widely differing rates, according to the planners' set of priorities.

(c) The traditional salt tax was taken over by the communists and collected at the production level. Out of total tax revenues of 15.5 billion yuan in 1957, the salt tax yielded about 620 million yuan. While this was not much, the tax was reliable and easy to collect. Its real burden was borne entirely by the consumer. Industrial salt was exempt from the tax.

[22] From PLA semimonthly *Literature and Arts* (March 1968) in *URS*, Vol. 51, No. 3 (April 9, 1968), p. 44.

[23] Nai-Ruenn Chen, *op. cit.*, pp. 441, 443. According to novelist Han Suyin, the agricultural tax was 12 percent during the First Five-Year Plan, declining to 7 percent in 1966. There was also a tax on the slaughter of pigs. Miss Han Suyin is inclined to view China's experiment in Maoist socialism with admiration. See Derek Davies, "Interview with Han Suyin," *FEER* (November 24, 1966), p. 430. See also Hsiao Ku, "A Preliminary Study of the Agricultural Tax in the Next Couple of Years," *Ts'ai-cheng* (December 5, 1956) in *ECMM* No. 66, pp. 27-36.

(d) Stamp taxes on commercial and legal transactions were applied throughout the period. The duty was either a given amount or a percentage of the value of the business transacted by the document. Industrial and commercial taxes (including salt tax) contributed 11.9 billion yuan out of total tax receipts of 15.5 billion yuan in 1957. Taxes on state enterprises represented that year about 6 billion yuan, taxes on joint state-private enterprises 2.9 billion yuan, while cooperatives paid about 2.2 billion yuan. Surviving private businesses contributed the remainder.[24]

Customs duties. Ad valorem tariffs on c.i.f. (cost, insurance, and freight) value of imports ranged from 5-100 percent, depending on the place which any given commodity held in the planners' preference scale. There were also tariffs on a very small number of export commodities. During the period customs duties accounted for about 3 percent of the state's budgetary revenues.

Local authorities during the period 1953-57 levied a number of taxes the purpose of which was to funnel additional revenue into local governments. The most important of these was a flat tax of 5 percent on income from interest on bank deposits, bonds, and loans to employees.

2. Revenue from State Enterprises[25]

Revenue from state enterprises grew at a fast pace during the period. It consisted of (a) profits, (b) depreciation reserves for fixed assets, (c) return of surplus working capital, and (d) income from the sale or revaluation of fixed assets.

(a) *Profits.* In Chinese communist usage and practice "profit" means the difference between sales at state-determined (or approved) prices and "costs." [26] Costs include "constant capital" (Marx's *c*) and

---

[24] Han Suyin reported that house rents were taxed (1966) at the rate of 25 percent.

[25] This covers joint state-private enterprises. With minor modifications, the following discussion applies also to the post-1957 period.

[26] Profits per unit of product may be determined in relation to cost of production, total capital, or labor cost.

The distribution of total profit (surplus product) in proportion to cost of production may be represented by the formula

$$p = c + v + (c + v)\frac{S}{C + V}$$

p is the price of a product, *c* is constant capital (branch average cost of material inputs—including depreciation of plant and equipment—per unit of the product), *v* is variable capital (branch average wage cost per unit of the product), *S* is the total value of the surplus product in the economy (that portion of the total value of net domestic material product which is not paid out as rewards for labor), *C* is the total cost of material inputs, and *V* is the economy's total wages bill.

"variable capital" (Marx's v) and cover interest on borrowed variable capital, but exclude all other interest and rent on land. Constant capital means material cost plus depreciation embodied in materials used in production; variable capital means the wages bill. Note that the exclusion of land rent and interest from the concept of cost makes cost unusable for comparisons of the efficiency in the use of land and capital where these factors are important components of the production process.

State-determined (or approved) prices are of three kinds: ex-factory prices of manufactured products, agricultural procurement prices, and retail prices.

Ex-factory prices are transfer prices at which enterprises sell their products to other enterprises or to wholesale distributors. There are three elements in ex-factory prices: factory costs (labor, administrative expenses, basic and subsidiary raw materials, depreciation), taxes, and profits. The factory cost for a given enterprise is arrived at by taking the average cost of the various enterprises in the same production branch weighted by the planned outputs of the enterprises. Another method is to take only a few model firms (a sort of Marshall's "representative firm" procedure) producing a given commodity and compute their average cost of production, which is then used to price the products of all enterprises in the branch. Sometimes retail prices are taken as the starting point. Distribution costs and trade profits are then deducted from these prices and the result is labeled ex-factory price. Planned profit margins are determined according to the planners' scale of priorities regarding the development of this or that product or industrial branch. The same principle applies to tax margins.

In other words, state-determined or approved "value" of a product (ex-factory transfer price) means $c + v + s$ where c and v are as

---

The distribution of profit in proportion to total (fixed and working) capital may be represented by the formula

$$p = c + v + k\frac{S}{K}$$

where p, c, v, and S are as described above, k represents the average amount of fixed and working capital per unit of the product, and K is the total amount of fixed and working capital in the economy as a whole.

Distribution of total surplus product proportionately to labor cost (i.e. wages bill) is represented by the formula

$$p = c + v + v\frac{S}{V}$$

See, Nai-Ruenn Chen, "The Theory of Price Formation in Communist China," *The China Quarterly*, July-September 1966, pp. 41-42.

defined above, and s is "surplus value" or "product for society" or
"profit." Theoretically this leaves unanswered the question of how s
(for each product separately) is to be determined "rationally" in an
opportunity cost sense, since s does not automatically identify itself,
as it does in a market economy.[27] The whole procedure is based on
an average cost plus pricing formula inherited from the Soviets with
all its inconveniences. The Soviets, in turn, got their trouble from
Marx, who got it from a Hegelian preconception that had little to do
with allocative rationality. In short, "profit" in China is not a criterion for resource allocation because the cost component of profit
excludes the relative scarcity measurement of the factors land and
capital (land rent and interest), and because prices are not as a rule
allowed to adjust to excess supply or demand. Even where they are
allowed so to move, the performance of the enterprises tends still to
be judged, among others, by planned profits and prices rather than
the actual (i.e., changed) prices and profits. This point was brought
out by Sun Yeh-fang in one of his discussions concerning the socialist
law of value. "The [central] planning and statistical indicator accounts and those of industrial management [i.e., of the enterprises]
should be integrated rather than being mutually restrictive. . . ."[28]
The indicator should be expressed in current prices, correctly estimated according to the law of value. For purposes of long-term plan
evaluation, constant prices should be used as a sort of shadow index.

In 1953-57 the Chinese communists departed from the Soviet
practice of fixing relatively low prices on heavy industrial products
and priced these products at relatively high levels, thus extracting
substantial profit margins from this sector. This procedure was reasonable in the setting of capital scarcity and provided the Chinese
with at least an approximate picture of relative scarcities in their
economy, besides furnishing the state with revenue which it would
have found difficult to obtain from agriculture.

Another departure from Soviet precedent consisted in the almost
total absorption of enterprise profits by the state. Whereas in the
USSR enterprises were permitted to retain a portion of net profits
for fixed and working capital uses, and welfare and bonus disbursements, in China the quasi-totality of profits went to the state. The
exception was a small (about 3 percent) deduction for the enter-

[27]Cf. Chapter 9 below.

[28]Sun Yeh-fang, "Starting from the Value of Total Output," *Tung-chi
Kung-tso*, (Statistical Work), No. 13, 1957, pp. 8-14. The whole concept of
pricing was discussed and severely criticised in 1956-57 and again in 1961-65.
Apparently nothing much was done about it. See, G. W. Lee, "Current Debate
on Profits and Value in Mainland China," *Australian Economic Papers* (December
1965), pp. 72-78.

prise's bonus fund. In 1957 an additional deduction was made: a portion of above-norm enterprise profits transmitted to local government units or central government offices in charge of industrial enterprises for capital construction and capital reserve purposes. Still, even with that extra quasi-retention, over 90 percent of enterprise profits were sent in monthly installments to the central government. Thus the Chinese enterprise was almost wholly dependent for its working and fixed capital funds on the central government budget.

(b) *Depreciation reserves.* Depreciation charges were made only on actually used productive equipment. They were remitted in toto to the state treasury. Budgetary expenditures on fixed capital replacements were generally well below the depreciation remittances to the state. The idea was to use existing, somewhat outdated equipment, a procedure criticized by some economists. Sun Yeh-fang, for example, complained that "our depreciation policy covers only physical wear and tear, but excludes invisible depreciation, i.e., fails to take account of world-wide technological improvements and innovations, and, in fact, obstructs such improvements and innovations in China."[29]

(c) *Return of surplus working capital.* This was done through local government units. The local unit used any surplus working capital returned to it from an enterprise under its control to make up working capital deficiencies in any other enterprises controlled by it. The balance was remitted to the state treasury.

(d) *Income from sale and revaluation of fixed assets.* This consisted of proceeds from the sale of fully depreciated assets not needed by an enterprise, or income resulting from an upward revaluation of given enterprise fixed assets by the appropriate authority.

Of the four subcategories of revenue from state enterprises, profits were by far the most significant.

3. Credits and Insurance

This category covers (a) domestic bonds, (b) foreign loans, and (c) income from insurance activities.

(a) *Domestic bonds.* The "People's Victory Real Unit Bonds" issued in 1950 have been discussed in Chapter 3. There were no reported bond issues from 1951 through 1953. From 1954 through 1957 the government floated each year so-called "National Economic Construction Bonds," the planned annual amount of which was 600 million yuan. The issues were reportedly oversubscribed each time. The maturity period of the National Construction bonds was ten years except for the 1954 issue (eight years), and the interest

[29] Sun Yeh-fang, *op. cit.*

TABLE 6-4
Distribution of Domestic Bonds 1950, and 1954-57
(Thousands of yuan)

Year	Total	Workers and Employees	Peasants	Private Industry and Commerce	All Others
1950	260,120	30,170	17,950	183,650	28,350
1954	836,130	273,190	140,460	394,020	28,460
1955	619,310	217,080	135,170	244,420	22,640
1956	606,535				
1957	650,000		290,000		

Source: Reprinted from Nai-Ruenn Chen, Chinese Economic Statistics (Chicago: Aldine, 1967). Copyright © 1967 by the Social Science Research Council, p. 445, Table 10.6.

rate was 4 percent. Table 6-4 shows the distribution of domestic bonds in 1950 and 1954-57.

(b) *Foreign loans.* Loans from the USSR from 1953 through 1957 totaled 3.1 billion yuan. They represented 2 percent of budgetary revenue in 1953, 3.3 percent in 1954, 6.1 percent in 1955, 0.4 percent in 1956, and 0.1 percent in 1957. After that date the Chinese budget shows no further receipts from this source. In addition to an economic loan of $300 million in 1950 (see Chapter 3, p. 100) the Soviets extended a further $130 million in 1954. Other receipts of credits from the USSR were reported merely as budgetary receipts and expressed in yuan without detailed analysis of their terms, conditions, and purposes. Thus in 1955 a Soviet loan was received, apparently for the purchase of the Soviet shares in the four Sino-Soviet joint stock companies referred to earlier (Chapter 3, pp. 103-104). A military loan was also received that year.

(c) *Income from insurance activities.* This covers compulsory insurance of state enterprises, cooperatives, and transport and communications, as well as various schemes of voluntary insurance. The insurance system was administered by the National People's Insurance Corporation. Exactly what the budgetary insurance receipts represented is not clear, but the sums paid into the state budget were probably excess reserves, i.e., amounts over and above those needed for payments by the Insurance Corporation according to actuarial schedules.

4. Other Budgetary Revenues

This consisted of various items such as fines, fees for miscellaneous administrative services, extra income from state-financed projects, and so on. Fines were probably a major item, especially fines on private enterprises. Receipts from this source were substantial in 1953 and 1954 and sharply declined thereafter.

Expenditure

The expenditure side of the state budget has been discussed in a roundabout way in Chapter 4. Only a few additional comments need be made here.

It will be noticed (Table 6-3) that expenditure on economic construction, national defense, and government administration together exceeded by very substantial margins the disbursements on social, cultural, and educational projects. This meant that during the period 1953-57 the relatively high tax burden on the Chinese consumer was not lightened very much by communal additions to consumption. The problem, however, must be kept in perspective. The tax burden on the Chinese citizen has at all times been heavy. Before the communists came to power taxes were not only high but arbitrary, and the benefits to the consumer not immediately apparent. Even though modest, the social services introduced by the communists were there for all to see, and their positive impact on taxpayer attitudes should not be underestimated.

During the period there was a sharp increase in indirect taxes. By 1957 indirect taxes represented about 80 percent of total money taxes paid by consumers as compared with about 70 percent in 1953. About 30 percent of a consumer's personal money income went in taxes in 1957, that is about the same proportion as in the United States. It should, however, be remembered that in the United States per capita money income in 1957 was almost 60 times that in China.

Repayment of principal and interest on Soviet loans was made each year from 1954 through 1957.

THE BANKING SYSTEM

Some aspects of Communist China's banking system and credit policy have been discussed Chapter 3. A few additional remarks are made here for clarification.

As has been pointed out earlier, the People's Bank is the central bank, a savings and deposit institution, and commercial bank rolled into one. It is directly under the control of the State Council. In the period 1953-57 the People's Bank exercised control over the following.

(a) Two specialized banks—the Bank of China and the Joint State-Private Bank. From 1955 through 1957 the People's Bank also exercised authority over the Agricultural Bank of China, which, however, was abolished in 1957, only to be revived at the end of 1963 and placed under the State Council.[30] (It may be added that the Construction Bank of China and the People's Insurance Corporation were subordinated not to the People's Bank but to the Ministry of Finance, and through it to the State Council. A Bank of Communications which at one time was controlled by the People's Bank has probably ceased to exist).

(b) Branches of the People's Bank in large cities, subsidiary offices in small towns and large rural settlements, temporary subsidiary offices in rural areas. (There were about 34,000 such branches in 1965.)

(c) Credit cooperatives numbering some 130,000.

The functions of the People's Bank were:

1. To issue notes and coin which were the only legal tender.

2. To keep accounts for all government organs, enterprises, cooperatives, army units, and savings deposits of individuals. Every government organization or enterprise was required to deposit its cash receipts with the Bank on the day the cash was received except for petty cash balances not exceeding three days' requirements. All transactions between government organizations, state enterprises, cooperatives, and so on, had to be made by transfer of book entries in the People's Bank. In this way the Bank was cash controller in the economy and had a comprehensive view of financial dealings in the country. The Bank thus exercised financial control over the physical plan applicable to the economy during any given period.

3. The Bank was charged with gold and silver transactions.

4. It was also charged with foreign currency receipts and payments, and settlements of China's international accounts. (This was done mainly through the Bank of China, and included the handling of remittances from overseas Chinese.)

5. The Bank received appropriations from the state budget and distributed these among the various sectors and enterprises of the economy.

6. It made loans to industries, state enterprises, and agricultural producers' cooperatives.

The main function of the Joint State-Private Bank was to handle savings deposits for the People's Bank.[31]

During 1955-57 the Agricultural Bank of China was responsible for the management of budgetary funds allotted to agriculture and

---

[30] See Chapter 9.

[31] In 1966-67 the annual interest rate on fixed deposits by individuals was given as 3.96 percent. Ordinary deposits earned 2.16 percent per year. Robert Trumbull (ed.), *This Is Communist China, op. cit.*, p. 171.

fisheries, forestry, water conservation, and related activities, and extended loans to agricultural cooperatives, state farms, individual peasants, and rural credit cooperatives, and accepted savings in the countryside.[32]

Credit cooperatives accepted rural deposits and extended short-term loans to individual peasants.

The Construction Bank of China, set up in 1954, and subordinated to the Ministry of Finance was the principal channel through which investment funds from the state budget were directed to enterprises. It also made investment grants for capital projects.

In managing currency and credit, the People's Bank adhered to a cash plan and a credit plan prepared by the planning authorities. The credit plan specified the sources and uses of funds received and disbursed by the People's Bank during a given plan period. The cash plan defined the cash circuit between the Bank and government enterprises, cooperatives, etc. Both plans translated the material economic plans into monetary terms. Their consistency ultimately hinged on the internal consistency of the physical plan. Where inconsistencies arose, e.g., an excessive outflow of cash into the economy giving rise to inflationary pressure on nonpegged prices, the problem was more often than not dealt with by direct measures (rationing, tax increases, forced savings), mostly of a fiscal character.[33]

The division of powers between the Ministry of Finance and the People's Bank did not always work smoothly. In fact, there appears to have been a continual conflict between the hierarchies of these two sources of liquidity in the country. In the setting of fiscal conservatism, each of these institutions tried to avoid being accused of creating excessive liquidity. Thus the people in Finance kept budgetary appropriations low and shifted responsibility for supplying sufficient funds to the Bank. The Bank for its part did its best to keep its loans down, arguing that the various agencies and enterprises should go to Finance for the needed funds. Credit cooperatives were inclined to lend to the richer peasants because these were the most credit worthy, while ignoring the poorer peasants whom the state favored for ideological and political reasons. Conflict at the top was accompanied by deviousness at the bottom of the economic pyramid. As in other communist countries, the rule of thumb for lower echelon agencies and enterprises was to inflate their initial budget requests as

---

[32] For the extended functions of this bank after its revival in 1963, see Chapter 9.

[33] On the general problem of finance in China, see Norman M. Linke, *Finance in Communist China*. Ph.D. dissertation, Department of Economics, Stanford University (1968).

a hedge against sudden and announced budgetary cuts during the plan period. Since budgetary appropriations to state organs were allocated quarterly, the method was to request a large grant in the first quarter and decreasing appropriations thereafter. [34] When added to dissimulation of enterprise and branch capacity and reserves in the course of plan formulation, these procedures certainly did not contribute toward an efficient running of the economy.

FOREIGN ECONOMIC RELATIONS

During the First Five Year Plan period China's foreign trade policy rested on the following general principles:

1. "Lean to one side," i.e., foreign trade was oriented toward communist countries, particularly the USSR. Trade with Western countries was confined to items which could not be obtained in the communist world.

2. Imports were composed primarily of raw materials for industry and modern capital goods, and among these, equipment for heavy industry (including complete plants) was the most important. [35] Secondarily, imports were used to ease domestic shortages of other than capital goods. Technical and scientific know-how imports were accorded a high ranking.

3. Exports were promoted primarily to pay for the required imports, and included agricultural and mineral products, especially those with relatively high per unit values. Exports were to be the principal source of foreign exchange earnings, to be supplemented by remittances from overseas Chinese.

4. Remittances from overseas Chinese. In order to encourage such remittances, certain investment facilities for overseas Chinese were made on the Chinese mainland.

5. Trade with noncommunist developing countries was developed so as to further Chinese political and ideological objectives in these areas. Modest amounts of aid were given to both communist and noncommunist developing countries.

A few comments on each of these general principles are in order.

"LEANING TO ONE SIDE"

This trend already observed in the period of reconstruction and reform (1949-52) was continued during 1953-57, with some qualifications.

[34] Michael C. Oksenberg, "Aspects of Local Government and Politics in China: 1955-58," *Journal of Development Studies* (October 1967), pp. 39-40. This section is heavily indebted to this study.

[35] Imports of military hardware were also important.

TABLE 6-5
Direction of Chinese Communist Trade, 1950-57
(Millions of U.S. dollars)

Year	Total Trade	Trade with Noncommunist Countries	Trade with Communist Countries			
			Total*	USSR	East Europe†	Far East
1950	1,210	860	350	320	20	5
1951	1,895	920	975	750	205	20
1952	1,890	575	1,315	965	320	30
1953	2,295	740	1,555	1,165	340	50
1954	2,350	615	1,735	1,270	370	95
1955	3,035	785	2,250	1,700	435	115
1956	3,120	1,065	2,055	1,460	465	120
1957	3,025	1,090	1,935	1,295	500	130

*Including Yugoslavia.
†Excluding Yugoslavia.
Sources: Robert L. Price, "International Trade of Communist China," in An Economic Profile of Mainland China (Washington, D.C.: Government Printing Office, 1967), Vol. 2, p. 584, Table 1, and "Communist China's Balance of Payments, 1950-65," ibid., p. 644, Table 10. Figures rounded to nearest $5 million. Cf. Table 8-6.

The situation can be seen from Tables 6-5 and 6-6; the qualifications are noted below. Figures for 1950-52 are added for comparison.

A certain number of qualifications should be appended to the statement that during the 1953-57 period the Chinese applied the prescription of "leaning to one side."

It will be seen that Chinese trade with noncommunist countries reached a low in 1952, during the Korean War and the embargo

TABLE 6-6
Direction of Chinese Communist Trade, 1950-57
(Percentage distribution)

Year	Total Trade	Trade with Non-communist Countries	Trade with Communist Countries	
			Total*	USSR
1950	100	71.0	29.0	26.4
1951	100	48.5	51.5	39.5
1952	100	30.4	69.6	51.1
1953	100	32.2	67.8	50.8
1954	100	26.2	73.8	54.0
1955	100	25.9	74.1	56.0
1956	100	34.1	65.9	46.8
1957	100	36.0	64.0	42.8

*Including Yugoslavia, Albania, North Korea, North Vietnam, and Outer Mongolia.
Source: Derived from Table 6-5.

placed by Western countries on trade with Communist China. After 1952 trade with the West began to expand in absolute terms, very slowly at first. As the restrictions on trade with China began to be relaxed, the expansion was accelerated. By 1956 the volume of China's trade with noncommunist countries exceeded the pre-1956 high of $920 million (1951). However, until 1954 the rate of expansion of trade with noncommunist countries was slower than that of total Chinese foreign trade, so that one could say that during this period the "lean to one side" prescription continued to be implemented. The importance of the Soviet Union in China's international dealings began to decline both absolutely and relatively after 1955. The main reason for the absolute decline was a sharp fall in Chinese imports from the Soviet Union (from about $1 billion in 1955 to $715 million in 1956, and $545 million in 1957). The major reason for the drop in Chinese imports from the USSR between 1955 and 1957 was the Chinese effort to begin repaying earlier loans obtained from the Soviets, which implied a limitation of imports and a rise in exports. Chinese exports to the USSR rose from $645 million in 1955 to $745 million in 1956, and $750 million in 1957. Put another way, Chinese purchases from the Soviet Union in the period 1950-54 were helped along by the $300 million Soviet loan extended in 1950. This loan was exhausted in 1954.

In fact, from 1950 through 1955 China was a net capital importer. From 1956 to 1957 it was a net capital exporter. It may be added that except for a small net import of capital in 1960, the net capital export trend continued through 1964.

COMPOSITION OF IMPORTS

The principle of selectivity noted in Chapter 4 in connection with Communist China's strategy of economic development during the period of the First Five-Year Plan was fully applied to imports.

Machinery and equipment (including transportation equipment) accounted for about one-third of Chinese imports during the period. The bulk of these came from the Soviet Union. Within this general category, complete plants constituted a major item. In 1957, for example, imports of complete plants represented about 20 percent of total imports. During the period almost three out of four complete installations exported by the Soviets went to China, and almost one-sixth of Soviet machinery exports were purchased by the Chinese. Chemical products, petroleum and petroleum products, metals, and rubber and rubber products together accounted for another third of Chinese total imports. To ease domestic shortages and bottlenecks, smaller quantities of foodstuffs, manufactured consumer goods, drugs, textile fibers, and building materials were purchased abroad.

From 1950 through April 1956 agreements for the construction of 211 industrial and transportation projects were concluded between China and the Soviet Union. As a result of mergers, this number was eventually reduced to 166. Complete sets of equipment supplied by the Soviet Union during this period were valued at about $2 billion.[36]

The import of complete sets of equipment was accompanied by the import of Soviet and East European technicians and other specialists. An average of 20 such experts were assigned to each complete plant. In many instances their numbers ran into the hundreds.[37] Between 1950 and 1960 an estimated 11,000 Soviet scientists and specialists worked in China for various periods, 5,400 of them in industrial enterprises, 2,000 in transport and communications, 1,000 in agriculture, water conservation and forestry, 700 in education, 300 in public health, 850 in scientific research, and 750 in other branches (mainly in government administration, planning, etc.).[38] The Soviets later claimed that from 1954 to 1963 they gave China more than 24,000 sets of scientific and technical documentation.[39] Between 1950 and 1960 almost 38,000 Chinese students, scientists, and others were trained in the Soviet Union. This included some 20,000 workers. From 1953 through 1957, about 6,000 students were sent to the USSR.[40]

Later, when relations between China and the Soviet Union had deteriorated to the point of unalloyed rudeness, the Chinese answered Soviet complaints about ingratitude with a backhanded compliment. "We have always had a proper appreciation of the friendly Soviet aid," they wrote, "which began under Stalin's leadership."[41] The Soviets had claimed, probably with justice, that enter-

[36] Robert L. Price, op. cit., p. 591, Table 6. See also "On the Struggle of the CPSU for the Solidarity of the International Communist Movement," Report by M. A. Suslov on February 14, 1964 at the Plenary Session of the Central Committee of the CPSU, Pravda, April 3, 1964, pp. 1-8. English translation in New Times (Moscow), April 15, 1964 and Peking Review, May 1, 1964, the latter with comments by the Chinese.

[37] Alexander Eckstein, Communist China's Economic Growth and Foreign Trade (New York: McGraw-Hill, 1966), p. 169.

[38] Chu-yuan Cheng, Scientific and Engineering Manpower in Communist China (Washington, D.C.: National Science Foundation, Government Printing Office, 1965), p. 194, Table 39.

[39] M. Kuranin, "14th Anniversary of Soviet-Chinese Treaty," Pravda (February 14, 1964), p. 5.

[40] Chu-yuan Cheng, op. cit., pp. 196, 198.

[41] Letter of the Central Committee of the CPC of February 29, 1964 to the Central Committee of the CPSU, Peking Review (May 8, 1964), p. 13.

prises created with Soviet assistance accounted for 70 percent of China's output of tin, 100 percent of the output of synthetic rubber, 25-30 percent of electric power production, and 80 percent of the output of trucks and tractors. [42] The Soviets had a hand in the construction of the Wuhan and Paotow steel complexes, the high quality steel mill in Tsitsihar, the Chungchun automotive plant, the chemical plant in Kirin, the Finman hydroelectric power station, the thermal plants at Fushan and Kirin, the development of the Sinkiang oil fields, the reconstruction and modernization of the Anshan steel works, the boiler and turbine plants in Harbin, and the building of China's atomic reactor and cyclotron. [43] To all this the Chinese replied that "so far from being *gratis*, Soviet aid to China was rendered mainly in the form of trade and that it was certainly not a one-way affair. China has paid and is paying the Soviet Union in goods, gold, or convertible foreign exchange for all Soviet-supplied complete sets of equipment and other goods, including those made available on credit plus interest. It is necessary to add that the prices of many of the goods we imported from the Soviet Union were much higher than those on the world market."[44]

CHINESE EXPORTS

"Up to the end of 1962," the Chinese went on, "China has furnished the Soviet Union with 2,100 million new roubles' worth of grain, edible oils, and other foodstuffs. Among the most important items were 5,760,000 tons of soya beans, 2,940,000 tons of rice, 1,090,000 tons of edible oils, and 900,000 tons of meat. . . . Over the same period China furnished the Soviet Union with more than 1,400 million new roubles' worth of mineral products and metals."[45]

During the whole period 1950-57 China's merchandise exports more than doubled. During the First Five Year Plan period, exports were the main source of China's international receipts, accounting for almost four-fifths of total receipts. From 1950 through 1957 export earnings amounted to some $1.1 billion on the average per

---

[42] M. A. Suslov, *op. cit.*, Professor Galenson believes that machinery exports to China during 1956-59 cost the Russians about 5 percent of their industrial growth annually, more if the rest of the export trade were taken into account. See Walter Galenson, "Economic Relations Between the Soviet Union and Communist China," in Nicolas Spulber (ed.) *Study of the Soviet Economy* (Bloomington, Ind.: Indiana University Publications, 1961), p. 47.

[43] A. Smirnov, "Soviet Technical Assistance in the Construction of Plants Abroad," *Problems of Economics* (January 1960). Cf. Chapters 8 and 9.

[44] Letter of the CC of the CPS (February 29, 1964), *op. cit.*, p. 13.

[45] *Ibid.*, p. 13.

year, while the annual average drawings on credits received were about $176 million (this compares with annual average import payments of $1.2 billion and debt repayments of $51 million).

Exports of metals, metal ores, and concentrates accounted for about 20 percent of China's total exports to the USSR during 1953-57, soya beans and oilseeds for some 15 percent, and livestock products for about 10 percent.

REMITTANCES FROM OVERSEAS CHINESE

Communist China's balance of payments from 1950 through 1957 may be summarized in the way shown in Table 6-7.

TABLE 6-7
Summary of China's Balance of Payments 1950-57
(Millions of U.S. dollars)*

	Noncommunist Countries		Communist Countries	
	Credit	*Debit*	*Credit*	*Debit*
Current account (net)	415	—	—	630
Merchandise trade balance	—	215	—	405
Freight and insurance	—	225	—	75
Overseas remittances	855	—	—	—
Other transactions (net)	—	—	—	150
Capital and monetary gold (net)	195	—	270	—
Credits and grants extended:				
Net drawings	—	25	—	445
Credits received:				
Drawings	—	—	1,405	—
Repayments	—	—	—	405
Transfer of Soviet-owned assets†	—	—	—	330
Expropriation of convertible currencies. . .	250	—	—	—
Other transactions (net)	—	30	45	—
Errors and omissions (net)‡	—	610	360	—

*Data are rounded to the nearest $5 million.
†This transfer was financed by Soviet credits.
‡Assumed to be changes in foreign currency balances (free world) and clearing balances (communist countries).
Source: Central Intelligence Agency, "Communist China's Balance of Payments, 1950-65," in *An Economic Profile of Mainland China, op. cit.,* Vol. 2, p. 628, Table 2.

In spite of heavy merchandise imports and the concomitant freight and insurance charges, China's balance of payments position was strengthened during the period 1950-57. The year-end balances in 1957 were as shown in Table 6-8.

It should be pointed out that foreign exchange reserves were negligible in 1950. Notice that in spite of a great merchandise export

TABLE 6-8
China's International Financial Resources at the end of 1957
(Millions of U.S. dollars)*

Foreign exchange reserves	645
Foreign currency balances†	610
Monetary gold holdings‡	35
Clearing account balances (with communist countries)§	360
Net international financial resources	285

*Data are rounded to nearest $5 million.

†Net balance of errors and omissions (from China's balance of payments with noncommunist countries), which are assumed to be almost entirely changes in foreign currency balances arising from transactions with noncommunist countries.

‡Net balance of changes in holdings of monetary gold.

§Net balance of errors and omissions (from China's balance of payments with communist countries) which are assumed to be almost entirely clearing account balances arising from transactions with communist countries.

Source: As in Table 6-7; p. 629, Table 3.

effort, the net balance on merchandise trade during this period was a debit of $620 million. Together with freight and insurance charges, the negative balance rises to $920 million (Table 6-7). This is partly covered by remittances from overseas Chinese amounting during the period to $855 million.

Overseas Chinese remittances are foreign currencies sent by Chinese residing in noncommunist countries to their families in China. Realizing the importance of this income, the communists have made overseas remittances into a fine art. There are various ways in which hard currency balances may be accumulated by means of remittances.[46]

(a) *Food parcels.* Overseas Chinese send important quantities of food to their families in China (some 7.5 million pounds from Hong Kong in 1961 alone). Until 1963 the communists allowed the foreign exchange potential of this traffic to slip through their fingers. In that year they set up four syndicates under the supervision of the China Travel Service to accept food parcel orders plus a substantial postage charge. In 1962 the postage charge was estimated to have brought the Chinese about $27 million in foreign exchange.

(b) *Fertilizer for rice coupons.* This method became popular after 1960, and consisted of an arrangement whereby overseas Chinese could purchase (in foreign currencies through Chinese gov-

[46] Jan S. Prybyla, "Communist China's Foreign Exchange," *Queen's Quarterly* (Winter 1965), pp. 519-527. The discussion below applies to the years after 1960, when many of these arrangements were developed. However, some of the methods described here were already in existence during 1953-57. On the subject of overseas remittances see the instructive study by Chun-hsi Wu, *Dollars, Dependents and Dogma* (Stanford, Calif.: Hoover Institution Press, 1967).

ernment agencies) coupons representing a given amount of fertilizer to be shipped to an agricultural administration in China. In exchange for this, the buyer's designate in China received either an equivalent sum in Chinese currency, or extra food (rice, pork, vegetables, fish), or he could have the amount of his claim deposited in a savings account earning interest at official rates and repayable after three years. The amount of fertilizer which a single overseas Chinese was permitted to order was from one to twenty tons per year. It was estimated that daily purchases in Hong Kong in 1961 were from 300 to 500 tons. [47] In 1966 it was reported that for every HK $50 remitted, the beneficiary on the mainland received 30 extra catties of rice, 3 yards of cotton cloth, 2 catties of vegetable oil, 2½ catties of sugar plus varying amounts of soya beans, flour, sugar, and cigarettes. [48] The red and green purchasing cards issued to mainland designates entitled the latter to buy otherwise unavailable goods in special Overseas Chinese Department Stores. The goods included nylon and silk stockings, fine cotton fabrics, bamboo sleeping mats, rayon and silk (red purchasing cards) and high-quality clothing materials (green cards).

(c) *Import duties on gifts* sent by exile Chinese to friends and relatives in China.

(d) *Emigrant remittances.* These are accepted by Chinese communist banks overseas at artificially high exchange rates. In 1962 this source amounted to an estimated $112 million.

(e) *Chinese overseas corporations.* These are corporations set up for the express purpose of attracting investments by emigrant and exile Chinese. Bonds in these corporations are sold to the overseas Chinese who designate within China the recipients of the 8 percent per annum interest based on a 12-year investment. At the end of the 12 years the principal can be collected by the overseas investor in a lump sum (Chinese currency). Alternatively, it can be deposited in a bank for six years, earning 7 percent annual interest (one-quarter payable in commodity coupons). [49] The mainland residents designated, receive half of the 8 percent per annum interest amount in Chinese currency (which could be transferred abroad by special permission) and the other half in "commodity supply coupons" which can be used locally to purchase food. The proceeds of the bonds are used to build fertilizer and farm tool plants, sugar and paper mills, rubber processing plans, and small hydroelectric power stations in

[47] Ng Wing Bo, "Fertiliser Bonds," *FEER* (December 7, 1961), p. 446.
[48] Robert Tung, "The Sins of the Capitalists," *FEER* (September 8, 1966), p. 442.
[49] Colina MacDougall, "Good Dividends," *FEER* (July 4, 1963), pp. 6-7.

China. In 1964 there were about 100 enterprises of this type, most of them in Kwangtung.

Overseas Chinese remittances fluctuate with the internal political situation in China. The average annual remittances appear to be around $150 million, although during periods of particular political stress in China, they probably drop to half that figure.

TRADE WITH AND AID TO NONCOMMUNIST DEVELOPING COUNTRIES[50]

During 1953-57 Communist China began developing trade and aid relations with a number of noncommunist developing countries in Asia and Africa. The movement gathered momentum after 1955. Total grants and loans from 1956 through 1957 may have been as high as $72 million, the main beneficiaries being Cambodia, Indonesia, Nepal, Ceylon, and Egypt. At the height of the Suez crisis in November 1956, the Chinese gave Egypt a grant of 200 million Swiss francs (about $5 million) for military purposes. As far as is known this was the only foreign currency transaction, the other aid projects being tied to purchases of Chinese goods.

In 1957 China's trade with southeast Asia represented about 8 percent of China's total exports, and about 9 percent of her imports. Trade with sub-Saharan Africa was small, amounting to about $14 million in 1957. At that time, China's most important trading partner in Africa was Egypt.

China also provided aid to communist Asian countries and to Hungary and Albania. The total of these economic loans and grants was roughly $500 million during 1953-57. The beneficiaries, besides Albania, included North Korea, North Vietnam, and Mongolia. Hungary was given a loan equivalent to $40 to help her rebuild the economy disrupted by the revolution of 1956.

POLITICAL REFORMS

Some of the more important political developments in 1956-57 will be dealt with in Chapter 7. It will be recalled that in Chapter 2 a brief outline was given of Communist China's governmental structure as it was informally in place during the period of reconstruction and reform. The Constitution of 1954 transformed the Chinese People's Political Consultative Conference into the *National People's Con-*

---

[50] See Milton Kovner, "Communist China's Foreign Aid to Less-Developed Countries," in *An Economic Profile of Mainland China, op. cit.*, Vol. 2, pp. 611-620; Alexander Eckstein, *op. cit.*, Chapter 6, pp. 183-241.

gress, nominally the highest state organ, but in fact, like its predecessor, a consultative body which was expected merely to approve what the Party and governmental leadership have decided. The Constitution provided that the Congress should elect the *Chairman of the People's Republic* (up till 1959, Mao Tse-tung). The Congress was supposed to meet every year. The People's Government Council became in 1954 the *State Council*—the highest administrative organ and, on paper, the executive organ of the Congress.[51] The State Council was composed of a premier, vice-premiers, ministers, heads of commissions, and a secretary general. The Council had *six offices*, and controlled a number of commissions, bureaus, and the central ministries. The offices included internal affairs, agriculture and forestry, industry and communications, finance and trade, culture and education, and foreign affairs. Each office exercised control over several *ministries* within its sphere of interest. The *commissions and bureaus* subordinated directly to the State Council ranged from the State Planning Commission and the State Economic Commission to the People's Bank of China, and more than twenty other bodies. The six Great Regional Administrative Councils (see Figure p. 27) were abolished. The number of provincial authorities was reduced. After 1955 there were 21 provinces (not counting Taiwan, regarded as a province of Communist China), 5 autonomous regions, and two great cities (Peking and Shanghai).[52]

[51] The March 9, 1955 meeting of the State Council was attended by the Dalai and Panchen Lamas who were forced to agree to a decision concerning the establishment of a Preparatory Committee for the Autonomous Region of Tibet. It took the Committee ten years to complete its preparations.

[52] See Audrey Donnithorne, *China's Economic System, op. cit.*, pp. 20-22. The full text of the 1954 constitution may be found in *The Constitution of The People's Republic of China (September 1954)* (Peking: FLP, 1961). See also J. Gray, "The Communist Party and the System of Government," *Political Quarterly* (July-September 1964), pp. 270-284.

7 | The Liberal Interlude, October 1956 to June 1957

The years 1956 and 1957 represent an important watershed in Communist China's domestic and external policies. It was about this time that a heated debate must have taken place within the Party's leadership regarding the nature and pace of socialist construction and the future of China's relations with the Soviet Union and the rest of the communist bloc. In this Chapter we shall be concerned with domestic issues, leaving the problem of external policies to a later section.

Sometime between April and September 1956 the disagreements between the proponents of a hard and those of a relatively moderate line in economic construction came to a head.[1] The year began, as we have seen, with a leap forward in the socialization of agriculture and the elimination of the private sector in industry, trade, and handicrafts. The victory of the radicals was not without attendant production problems, later described by Liu Shao-ch'i as "individual defects in our work during the leap forward in [early] 1956."[2] These individual defects were sufficiently grave for the moderates to gather enough strength for a counteroffensive aimed at slackening the pace of the reforms and introducing into economic policy a measure of rational calculation. In place of the original Maoist plan, which envisaged a broadening of the 1956 leap into a general great leap forward on all fronts, the moderates succeeded in pushing through a series of proposals the main concern of which was to minimize the damage to production and productivity caused by the sudden flurry of institutional reforms. It is possible that the showdown came during the enlarged meeting of the Political Bureau of the Party's Central Committee held in April 1956. In any event, by the time of the first session of the Party's Eighth National Congress (September 1956), the moderates had temporarily carried the day and the leapers were in retreat.

[1] Recall the opposition's article "To Oppose Also Rashness While Opposing Conservatism" published in Jen-min Jih-pao on June 20, 1956. Above, p. 154. In 1968 this article was called by the Maoists a "big poisonous weed."
[2] Liu Shao-ch'i, "Report on the Work of the Central Committee of the Communist Party of China to the Second Session of the Eighth National Congress" (May 5, 1958) in Second Session of the Eighth National Congress of the Communist Party of China (Peking: FLP, 1958), p. 38.

The major document which emerged from that first session is known as the *Proposals of the Eighth National Congress of the Communist Party of China for the Second Five Year Plan for the Development of the National Economy (1958-1962)*.[3] The report on the *Proposals* was delivered by Chou En-lai on September 16, and the document itself was adopted on September 27. Although in a quite formal way the *Proposals* pay heed to Mao Tse-tung's report on "Ten Sets of Relationships" delivered at the April meeting of the Politbureau and to his January 1956 "Draft National Program for Agricultural Development, 1956 to 1967," the net effect was to soften both the Relationships and the Draft in such a way as to come out with a relatively moderate plan of action. The Draft and the Relationships were, in effect, the programmatic statements of the radicals. Their intent was to immediately follow up the socialization leap with an all-round leap in production, science, technology, and culture, to prevent the pace of reform from slackening, and forge ahead regardless of consequences.[4] The first session of the Eighth National Party Congress put a temporary halt to this course.

The struggle, however, went right on through the moderately liberal interlude. The apogee of the liberal drive was reached between March and early June 1957. Thereafter the radicals renewed their pressure sealing their victory with the reports and resolutions of the second session of the Eighth National Party Congress in May 1958.

[3] Peking: *FLP*, 1956.

[4] In December 1955, Mao Tse-tung wrote in the preface to the book *Socialist Upsurge in China's Countryside* (Peking: *FLP*, 1957), pp. 9-10: "The Problem facing the entire Party and the nation is no longer one of combating rightist conservative ideas about the speed of the socialist transformation of agriculture. That problem has already been solved. Nor is it a problem of the speed of transformation of capitalist industry and commerce, by entire trades, into state-private enterprises. That problem too has been solved. In the first half of 1956 we must discuss the speed of the socialist transformation of handicrafts. But that problem will easily be solved too. The problem today is none of these, but concerns other fields. It affects agricultural production (including state, joint state-private and cooperative industries); handicraft production; the scale and speed of capital construction in industry, communications and transport; the coordination of commerce with other branches of the economy; and the coordination of activities in science, culture, education, public health and so on, with various economic undertakings. In all these fields there is an underestimation of the situation which must be criticised and corrected if these activities are to keep pace with the development of the situation as a whole. People's thinking must adapt itself to changed conditions. . . . The problem today is that rightist conservatism is still causing trouble in many fields and preventing work in these fields from keeping pace with the development of the objective situation. The present problem is that many people consider impossible things which could be done if they exerted themselves. It is absolutely necessary, therefore, to keep criticising rightist conservative ideas which actually exist." Mao's "Ten Sets of Relationships" (April 1956) are to be found in *Second Session, op. cit.*, pp. 36-37.

While in retreat on the ideological front (antirightist campaign), the moderates managed to salvage some of their economic measures until the final unleashing by their adversaries of the Great Leap Forward in the spring of 1958. Already in September 1957, however, it was clear that they were losing ground. At that time the third plenary session of the Central Committee of the Party reaffirmed the need to adhere to Mao's call of January 1956 (contained in the "Draft National Program for Agricultural Development") to achieve greater, faster, better, and more economical results in building socialism, and shortly thereafter released a revised version of the Draft. The revised version was even more radical than the original, reflecting as it did the supremacy of those who held that economic construction depended on political inspiration and mass enthusiasm, brought into being, controlled, and guided by those in the Party whose political consciousness was correctly Maoist. The new general line for building socialism was sanctioned by the second Session of the Party's Eighth National Congress in May 1958 (see Chapter 8 below).

THE MODERATE BLUEPRINT

The *Proposals* is a compromise document, the Party moderates calling the tune but not without challenges and dissonances. The leading theme is the need for caution in economic construction, with an if and a but always tucked on at the end. Often the result is woolly: an enumeration of all desirable goals to be reached simultaneously. While all this simultaneous activity went on, priority was to be given, as of old, to the development of heavy industry. "The central task of our Second Five Year Plan [1958-62] is still to give priority to the development of heavy industry. . . . While giving priority to the development of heavy industry, we should suitably speed up the growth of light industry on the basis of a higher level of agricultural development. . . . The output of grain should be ensured. . . . At the same time increased production of major industrial crops . . . should be ensured. . . . In carrying on large-scale industrial construction in the interior, we must, however, at the same time, make vigorous efforts to make full use of, and suitably develop the existing industries in the coastal areas."[5] All this was to be done gradually: the Second Five Year Plan could make a dent in the problem, but a comprehensive industrial system and the transformation of backward agriculture would take "approximately three five-year plans."[6]

[5] *Proposals, op. cit.*, pp. 15, 16, 17.
[6] *Ibid.*, p. 10.

In 1958 the radicals took over many of the ideas of the moderates and simply speeded up the implementation, thus distorting the basic assumption on which the moderates' balanced development plan rested. The original caution and relative moderation contained in the *Proposals* can be quantified in the light of subsequent developments, when measured advance suddenly became frenetic leap (Table 7-1).

TABLE 7-1

Targets for 1962 Laid Down in the *Proposals* and Claimed Output
Allegedly Achieved in 1958 and 1959

	1962 *Proposals* Target	Claimed Actual Output	
		1958	1959
Coal (millions of tons) .	190–210	270	347.8
Steel (millions of tons).	10.5–12	11.08 (8.0)	13.35
Electricity (millions of kwh)	40,000–43,000	27,530	41,500
Metal-cutting machine tools (million units) .	0.06–0.065	0.05	0.07
Power generating equipment (millions of kw)	1.4–1.5	0.8	2.15
Chemical fertilizers (millions of tons)	3–3.2	0.81	1.33
Timber (millions of cubic meters)	31–34	35.0	41.20
Cement (millions of tons)	12.5–14.5	9.3	12.27
Cotton yarn (millions of bales)	8–9	6.1	8.25
Cotton cloth (millions of meters)	7,290–8,060	5,700	7,500
Edible vegetable oils (millions of tons) . . .	3.1–3.2	1.25	1.47
Grain (millions of tons)	250	375–250	270
Cotton (millions of tons)	2.4	2.1	2.41
Soya beans (millions of tons)	12.5	10.5	11.5

Sources: *Proposals, op. cit.*, pp. 14, 15, 18; *Ten Great Years, op. cit.*, pp. 119, 124, 95-100; *Jen-min Jih-pao* (December 19, 1958); Li Fu-chun, "Report on 1960 Economic Plan." Cf. Table 8-11 below.

The figures for 1958 and 1959 are unreliable and probably say more about the psychological tensions under which the statisticians worked than about the economy's actual performance. It should be pointed out that the 1962 *Proposals* targets were revised *downward* in December 1957 when the overall picture of achievements under the First Five Year Plan became available to the planners. Among the targets lowered, were those for petroleum, metal-cutting machine tools, food grains, ginned cotton, and pigs. The target for cement was fixed at the *Proposals'* lower figure (12.5 million tons). The target for chemical fertilizer was more than doubled (compared with the higher *Proposals'* figure), that for coal was raised to 230 million tons and that for steel fixed at the *Proposals'* upper limit of 12 million tons.

With all its leftist qualifying clauses, the *Proposals* are still a fairly mild document emphasizing a "forward looking and completely sound basis."[7] The compromise is most clearly expressed in the following conclusions:

"[The central and local authorities] must, on the one hand, take full account of all favorable conditions and combat the rightist, conservative tendency to ignore the latent forces and underestimate the socialist enthusiasm of the masses. On the other hand, they must take full account of all unfavorable conditions and difficulties that are liable to occur, and combat the impetuous and adventurist tendency to depart from actual realities, give no consideration to possibilities, and overlook the planned and well-proportioned development of the various branches of the national economy."[8]

REASONS FOR LIBERALIZATION

A study of the *Proposals* gives a clue to the specific reasons which had prompted the leadership to embark on a carefully hedged and limited liberal course in the latter part of 1956. They may be summarized as follows:

1. "Leftist deviation," meaning reckless rushing around in economic work. This recklessness had two aspects:

(a) There was a tendency toward overconfidence and a lack of economic calculation at the center, which the *Proposals* criticized in veiled language. ". . . When conditions are favorable, we must discern the unfavorable factors confronting and ahead of us, and guard against impatience and rashness."[9]

(b) There was wrong-headed zeal in plan implementation: "Some departments and localities, impatient for success, attempted to accomplish within three or five years, or even two years, tasks that required seven or twelve years to complete." [10]

---

[7] *Ibid.*, p. 36.

[8] *Ibid.*, p. 36.

[9] *Ibid.*, pp. 51–52.

[10] *Ibid.*, p. 52. In December 1956, at the Standing Committee Conference of the National People's Congress, Liu Shao-ch'i reportedly said that "the whole problem is that we have taken too quick steps. Next year [1957] we should slow down a little. Greater speed will give rise to many problems." "Outline of Struggle," *URS*, Vol. 53, Nos. 5-6, *op. cit.*, p. 57.

This tendency toward overconfidence and rashness typical of the Maoist left and its almost exclusively political approach to economic construction is cautioned against in such phrases as: "we should ... set a reasonable rate for the growth of the national economy," "place the Plan on a ... completely sound basis," "ensure a fairly balanced development of the national economy," proceed "step by step," "so far as conditions permit," "in accordance with local needs and resources," "when conditions ... are ripe," "commensurate with our strength in technical personnel, financial and natural resources, and labor power," "proceed gradually and with proper emphasis where needed," "in a planned and well-prepared way," bring about change "by degrees," and "gradually build," "take practical measures," and so on.

The difficulty under which the pragmatists labored was that there was not in Chinese economic theory any concept of what "reasonable," "practical," "ripe," "balanced," and so on meant. The highly politicized Chinese economic science failed to supply independently rational criteria of decision making, so that on analytical grounds alone, economic decision makers (the planners) had to fall back on politics.[11] And when they did, they found themselves in worse disarray than before, since "reasonable," "practical," "ripe," and "balanced" meant one thing to the romantic, guerrilla-oriented, ultraleftists, and another to the conservative wing. Whenever Chinese economists showed signs of coming up with a definition of economic rationality in other than purely institutional Marxist terms, they were squelched by the political powerholders of the left as well as of the right and center. This alliance of bureaucrats of all economic persuasions remains a major obstacle to the advancement of allocative rationality in the communist world in general and in China in particular. The moderately inclined Chou En-lai is perhaps the most conspicuous personification of this united political establishment front paradox. The bureaucrats may, and do in fact, disagree among themselves, but in general they unite against reform proposals inspired by other than Marxian sources, and they are suspicious of experts who try to be more expert than red.

The leftist deviation was quite remarkable in the latter part of 1955 and the first half of 1956—the period of accelerated collectivization of agriculture and nationalization of industry and commerce.

---

[11] The reason why Chinese economic science failed to supply rationality criteria for decision making was that, it was (and remains) hamstrung by Marxist dogma. Now, Marxian economic theory, for all its metaphysical interest, ignores marginal magnitudes and utility, and hence finds it difficult to arrive at general welfare functions. This was true of China as of the Soviet Union and Eastern Europe. See Prybyla, "Patterns of Economic Reform in Eastern Europe," *East Europe* (November 1968).

The wave of institutional changes was merely the concrete manifestation of the communist radicals' impatience with what they considered to have been a too relaxed pace of socialist transformation
and construction, especially during the first half of 1955. This impatience came to the surface in other ways.

2. One of them was the lack of balance in economic development
or, as it came later to be known, the policy of "leaning to one side."
This meant:

(a) Overinvestment in certain intermediate goods industries (e.g.,
steel) resulting in 1956 in serious shortages of raw materials (e.g., pig
iron, building materials, especially timber), and underutilization of
the rashly created industrial capacity. In 1956 capital investment
within the State plan increased 62 percent over the previous year's
level. These sectoral and subsectoral disproportions are a built-in
feature of communist central-command planning, and this sort of
shortage-now, surplus-tomorrow problem is not limited to China. But
in China, as in Stalin's Russia, the problem was made more acute by
the politically induced degree of imbalance—the dogmatic preoccupation with the rapid development of this or that sector and industry,
to the neglect of others which supply the favored industries and
sectors or consume their products. In 1956 Chou En-lai admitted
that "we failed to strike a proper balance between capital construction and the capacity for supplying materials. . . . As a result, not
only were our national finances somewhat strained, but there occurred a serious shortage of building materials such as steel products,
cement, and timber." [12] In other words, there were serious strains in
the already tense commodity markets and growing inflationary pressures.

(b) A similar imbalance occurred with regard to the relationship
between the planning center and local authorities, with too much
authority (and detailed busywork) being vested in the former. The
concentration of power at the center led to "subjectivism and bureaucracy among the leadership" and "commandism" (i.e., blind execution of orders to curry favor) at lower levels—in short, to rigidity
and inability to respond quickly and appropriately to changing circumstances. [13]

---

[12] Proposals, op. cit., p. 51. ". . . Certain industrial enterprises advanced too
rapidly so that the raw materials needed were not all available. The result was
that it was impossible for those enterprises to give full play to their productive
capacity." Ibid., p. 53.

[13] Proposals, op cit., p. 57. "Subjectivism" is used in communist jargon to
denote two types of deviation: "dogmatism" and "empiricism." Dogmatism
means the blind application of Marxist theory without reference to actual conditions. Empiricism consists in a tendency to ignore theory altogether and proceed
only according to the conditions of the moment. "Bureaucracy" means red tape
in which Party and government functionaries tie themselves up.

The complaint against bureaucracy, commandism, "self-compla-
cency and conceit"[14] was in effect a reflection on central administrative planning and indirectly a suggestion to devolve some planning
and management tasks on markets and other spontaneous but supervised manifestations of the masses. "We still lack experience in
planning and our plans are often incomplete and inaccurate."[15] "In
certain parts of our annual plans for 1955 and 1956, we erred on the
side of setting targets too high or too low, which gave rise to certain
difficulties in our work."[16]

(c) There was also an imbalance between construction work
undertaken by the central authorities (mostly large-scale works) and
that allotted to local organs. This meant that big projects were frequently hampered in their operations by lack of ancillary facilities.

(d) An imbalance also occurred with respect to the development
of interior and coastal areas: "we laid emphasis on construction work
in the interior, but paid inadequate attention to that in the coastal
areas."

3. A special instance of imbalance, which became particularly
serious around mid-1956, was the retarded condition of agriculture, a
difficulty rendered more agonizing by widespread damage caused by
floods and drought. "In 1956 many areas have suffered severely from
floods, water-logging, typhoons, and drought, resulting in a measure
of damage to certain crops, especially cotton."[17] It has been estimated that the area damaged by floods in that year was 164.8 million *mou* and that drought affected another 65 million *mou*.[18] These
figures were the highest since the communist takeover in 1949.
Typically, the *Proposals* did not prescribe a vast campaign to remedy
the situation overnight, but rather suggested that one must "strive to
reduce damage caused by heavy floods and drought, and step by step
end damage caused by less serious floods and drought."[19] The effort
to promote water conservancy and flood control should not be just
"vigorous" but "well-planned." Agricultural difficulties, however,
were not all due to natural calamities; man had a hand in them too.

[14] *Ibid.*, p. 57.
[15] *Ibid.*, p. 54. According to a *New China News Agency* report of May 16,
1957, one complaint voiced during this period was that "the first five-year plan
was about to be fulfilled, and yet the country still had not enacted regulations
governing weights and measures."
[16] *Ibid.*, p. 50. A suggestion to abandon direct planning in agriculture was
made during the Congress by Teng Tse-hui. See *Eighth National Congress of the
Communist Party of China*, (Peking: FLP, 1956), Vol. II, pp. 192-193.
[17] *Proposals, op. cit.*, p. 44. Cotton output fell from 30.4 million *tan* in
1955 to 28.9 million *tan* in 1956.
[18] Cheng Chu-yuan, *Communist China's Economy, 1949-1962, op. cit.*,
p. 144.
[19] *Proposals, op. cit.*, p. 21.

The second priority accorded to agricultural development in the First Five Year Plan was endangering the whole industrialization effort: "To retard the development of agriculture would not only have a direct adverse effect on the development of light industry and the betterment of the people's livelihood, but greatly affect the development of heavy industry, as well as of the national economy as a whole; it would also adversely affect the consolidation of the worker-peasant alliance. Therefore, in the Second Five Year Plan period we should continue [sic] to make great efforts to develop agriculture so that its development may be coordinated with that of industry." [20] Already in 1954 "discontent arose among a section of the peasants," [21] and now that collectivization had been forced, there was surely need for a breathing spell. Following a poor harvest in 1956 restlessness manifested itself among peasants in desertions from the newly created collective farms. [22] "In 1957 . . . a gust of foul wind swept across the countryside; people attacked the cooperatives and withdrew from the cooperatives. Some people took back their livestock and farm tools; others reaped the crops of the cooperatives and secretly distributed the cooperatives' grain; still others sowed crops on the small plots of land that once belonged to them; some people even beat and cursed the cadres. Some localities were in great confusion for some time." [23] The moderates seemed to hope that this time for reflection and consolidation would become a more or less permanent feature of China's planning and management. The radicals saw in it exactly what it said: a spell. [24]

THE COMPONENTS OF LIBERALIZATION

The relaxation from above, made public in September 1956 and abruptly brought to an end in early 1958, consisted in the following

[20] *Ibid.*, p. 61.
[21] *Ibid.*, p. 42.
[22] *New China News Agency*, Canton, May 14, 1957.
[23] "How the Attack on the Cooperatives Stopped," *Chung kuo Ching-nien Pao* (April 11, 1963) in *URS*, Vol. 32, No. 8 (July 26, 1963), p. 139.
[24] The radicals' *credo* rejecting the moderates' contention that the problems of mid-1956 were caused by the rash policies of 1955-early 1956 was summed up in an editorial of the *People's Daily* (*Jen-min Jih-pao*) published on February 28, 1958, after the leftists had again managed to have the upper hand in policy making. ". . . Some people were stunned by the disequilibrium in the development of the national economy caused by these leaps [i.e., the leaps in nationalization and collectivization of latter 1955-early 1956]. These people saw only the unavoidable and temporary difficulties in the course of progress brought about by such disequilibrium, thought that there were difficulties everywhere and were terrified. . . . They erroneously raised the slogan: 'Oppose too hasty progress' which threw cold water on the enthusiasm of the masses at that time."

measures:

1. Free markets for some commodities were reopened. The free market had been eliminated in 1955 not by any specific decree, but through the quasitotal socialization of commerce. [25] There was clearly no intention in 1956 to introduce a market economy, but only to relieve pressure on the planners and the state sector, allow the forces of supply and demand to smooth out some inconsistencies of the plan as regards consumer goods supply, and improve the distribution of commodities. [26]

In agriculture, free-market trading was to apply to those goods "which the peasants retain after planned purchases by the state and those which are not covered by the plan." [27] This included an important portion of the products of peasant subsidiary occupations (including rural handicrafts), with the notable exception of hog production by individual peasants. [28] The commodities produced by subsidiary occupations accounted in 1955 for about 30 percent of gross agricultural production. Apparently, soon after the new course was inaugurated, peasants began to sell on the free market produce that should have been earmarked for compulsory deliveries to the state, as well as commodities fully covered by the plan. In August 1957 a decree was, therefore, issued specifying which particular goods could, and which could not be sold on the free market.

In addition to free markets per se, the state in 1956 and 1957 used its own controlled prices more flexibly in line with its intent to use price and income incentives as supplements to administrative control in raising production of desired agricultural commodities. In this, however, the authorities were less successful. Collective farm cadres responded less readily than individual peasants to price differentials since income maximization was still not the collectives' main success indicator. The result was that in 1957 the production of every crop whose price was raised, fell, in some instances very sharply, thus reinforcing the skepticism of the radicals about the whole concept of indirect (price) control and the effectiveness of

---

[25] As early as 1953 free agricultural markets were severely restricted by the introduction of centrally determined compulsory delivery quotas for a number of major products.

[26] "This will expedite commodity circulation and satisfy the people's needs." *Proposals, op. cit.*, p. 24.

[27] *Ibid.*, p. 24. Chen Yun, Minister of Commerce, was in charge of the reintroduction of free markets in subsidiary foodstuffs. His removal from that office in September 1958 may have been connected with the black-marketeering which accompanied the reopening of free markets in 1956.

[28] However, hog prices were raised by the state in 1956 and in 1957 in a sort of simulated market move. This resulted in a substantial increase in the supply of live hogs by peasants who responded to the price incentive.

material incentives in raising production. Where, as in the case of subsidiary occupations, output responded to price changes, it was interpreted by the radicals as an ideologically dangerous premium on "spontaneous capitalist forces" in the countryside. As we shall see in the next Chapter, failure of flexible price controls to stimulate collective production in agriculture[29] (while price changes spurred initiative on the peasants' private plots), was one of the reasons for the reversal of policy in early 1958 and one of the motive forces behind the Great Leap adventure.

In residential areas of towns and villages, "small traders and pedlars" were allowed to operate.[30] More important, the prices of nonrationed perishable goods and some other commodities were permitted to fluctuate in response to market conditions, and so find clearing levels. Administratively determined retail prices of commodities in fairly steady supply were changed periodically, supplanting to some extent the allocation of goods by the queue. In this way the distribution of consumer goods through the price system was given more importance than in 1955, but the bias in favor of price freezing and direct controls was by no means eliminated.

2. The maximum size of private plots was raised from 5 percent to 10 percent of the average arable land per head in the collective.

3. Greater powers were given to local government organs and to individual enterprises.[31] The centralized distribution of a number of important commodities was ended, the number of centrally set targets was reduced, and industrial as well as commercial enterprises were given more latitude to choose the goods they needed. This decentralization was, however, circumscribed by an increase in Party control within enterprises, so that often the new authority granted to enterprises was nominal. In agriculture, the central plans, once they reached the *hsien* level, were to be regarded as general guidelines, although they were not to be totally ignored. To see to this, *hsien* Party and government organs' authority over the cadres was strengthened.

The decentralization measures were contained in a November 1957 decree on the reform of the industrial management system. In industry they affected principally enterprises making consumer goods: by June 1958 virtually all manufacture of consumer commodities was under the control of major local authorities supervised

[29] The actual flexibility of state prices during this period was certainly less than that of prices on the free markets. Controlled prices were changed periodically on the basis of partial, and often erroneous information.

[30] *Proposals, op. cit.*, p. 25.

[31] *Ibid.*, p. 30 and 87-90.

by a number of central ministries, rather than directly (as before) by the Ministry of Light Industries. The number of mandatory targets for industrial enterprises was reduced from twelve to four (total quantity of output of major products, total number of employees, total wage bill, and profit). Earlier, during the 1956 Eighth Congress discussions, a suggestion was made to let plants manufacturing articles of daily use set their own production plans in accordance with market conditions, and to allow the amount of profits to be handed over to the state treasury to be determined by the enterprises' actual receipts at year's end. These "revisionist" suggestions were probably never widely implemented. The November 1957 decree stipulated that in the case of decentralized enterprises 20 percent of enterprise profits were to be handed over to the local authorities concerned with the enterprises, and 80 percent to the central government. This ratio was to hold good for an experimental period of three years. For commercial establishments the centrally set targets comprised the purchase plan, sales plan, number of employees, and profit, the last target being communicated to the supervisory local authority but not to the enterprise. With the exception of the grain trade, the distribution of profits as between local and central authorities was to be the same as for decentralized industrial enterprises. The decree stipulated that most producer goods enterprises were to remain under central control. The same was true of the main railway system and major civil aviation lines.

4. A parallel development was the reaction against Stalinist-type gigantism in industry, commerce, and agriculture. [32] The motive was to increase flexibility, the smaller enterprises and shops being "operationally fairly flexible and . . . easily . . . adapted to serve the many-sided needs of society." Existing small industrial firms and agricultural producers' cooperatives, provided they were "properly operated," were not to be "recklessly merged into larger units." [33]

[32] "Some hold that we should establish more large enterprises and fewer small or medium enterprises because to set up large enterprises is more rational economically and technically. Some other people, however, think we should set up more small and medium enterprises and fewer large enterprises, because to set up the former requires less time, and the investments yield a quicker return. We think that neither is true in all cases." Ibid., pp. 69-70.

[33] "Regarding the scale of the agricultural producers' cooperatives in Honan, there was a zigzag process of change between 1956 and 1958. There were also heated arguments among Party and non-Party comrades over the question: Which is superior, a large co-op or a small one? . . . Some comrades did not believe in the truth of what Comrade Mao Tse-tung had said [about the superiority of large cooperatives in his editorial comments on the book Socialist Upsurge in China's Countryside, 1957]. . . . Closing their eyes to [the superiority of large co-ops] and yielding to the demand of a small number of well-to-do middle peasants, a few rightist-opportunists within the Honan provincial Communist

Future creation of enterprises and cooperatives was to be balanced between large, medium, and small firms.

In all this there was, of course, a lack of precise economic guidelines to what proper operation, correct balance, large, medium, and small meant. Depending on which political faction within the leadership held sway at any given moment, the definition was likely to change. What was large enterprise to one group, may have been small to another. So long as economics remains the political economy of the ascendant faction, and as long as it is shackled by dubious and ambiguous doctrines, it cannot be expected to hand down independent judgment on such issues.

The antigigantism drive was realistic in that Chinese agriculture demands management by relatively small units consistent with natural socioeconomic systems shaped by rural trade, but the drive had also more subtle implications. Institutionally, small and medium enterprises meant state-public undertakings. In saying that it was imprudent to promote large enterprises and those only, the *Proposals*, in effect, made a plea for slowing down the rate of socialization. In this they were in tune with the trend toward limited free markets and, more generally, toward stimulating grass-roots initiative.

5. Grass-roots initiative required material incentive or, as the radicals chose to call it, a degree of "economism." Increases in workers' incomes were given a hearing in the *Proposals* and were sanctioned so long as "a correct proportion [was] maintained between the rise in labor productivity and the increase in wages." [34] Increases in personal consumption were to be "correctly" correlated with improvements in communal consumption: "the scope of labor insurance should be extended, and the system of labor insurance should be improved." [35]

6. Grass-roots initiative (within the confines of the Party's will) could be stimulated not only by material rewards commensurate with productivity, but by greater freedom to think problems out for oneself. This was more efficacious than direct bureaucratic appeal to socialist consciousness. "We should continue to adhere to the principle of 'letting flowers of many kinds blossom,' " [36] provided the blossoming took place in the Party's ideological hothouse. Intellec-

---

Party committee . . . indiscriminately tried to compel all the large co-ops to split up. As a result the number of co-ops in Honan increased to 54,000, each averaging 180 households, with the smallest containing less than 30. But thanks to the persistent effort of the Party committees at various levels, 495 large co-ops were retained." Wu Chih-Pu, "From Agricultural Producers' Cooperatives to People's Communes" *Hung-ch'i*, No. 8, Sept. 15, 1958.

34 *Proposals, op. cit.*, p. 32.
35 *Ibid.*, p. 33.
36 *Ibid.*, p. 29.

tual like economic freedom, was functional: it was desirable to the extent that it produced more and better goods, and turned them out at a saving to the Party. The Party defined its limits, sanctioned it, and took it away. The Party broadened its scope when needed, and restricted it when necessary. And what was needed and what was necessary was likewise laid down by the Party, or more accurately, by the Party's dominant faction.

7. As a matter of expediency the bureaucratic moderates advanced the thesis of the attenuation of class struggle under socialism. "Attention should . . . be paid to forging unity with and educating those who represent the interests of private capital of [state-private] enterprises. We should make full use of their knowledge of production techniques and useful experience in management and help them turn into working people in the full sense of the term." [37] The theory of the attenuation of class struggle under socialism was not, as the Maoists later maintained, a brazen opposition to the basics of Marxism-Leninism. Insofar as it rested on the assumption that dying out came about through using out, that the opposition had to be absorbed, and that it would be absorbed because there was no alternative course for it to follow, it was orthodox though not quite Stalinist. It was allegedly because Liu Shao-ch'i advocated "peaceful economic competition to determine who can run enterprises better under much the same conditions," rather than deciding the question in advance in favor of state appointees, that he was later branded a "clown who vainly tried to turn back the wheel of history." [38] Loss of administrative power implied *ipso facto* a condemnation and distortion of the ideas of the losers. In the last analysis the disagreement between the proponents of administrative centralization and administrative decentralization was about tools and tactics. Those who favored the employment of material incentives and a greater diffu-

---

[37] *Ibid.*, pp. 24-25. "We should not assume a discriminatory attitude towards them. By so doing, we shall do good to the enterprises as well as to the state and the working class. . . . We must make full use of their production skill and what is useful in their management experience." *Ibid.*, pp. 86-87. In the accepted communist manner of explaining and defending one's defeated position by tracing its lineage to true Marxism-Leninism, Liu Shao-ch'i in 1959 explained the 1956-57 moderation in the matter of class struggle in the following terms: "Have we adopted a policy of 'class collaboration' in handling the contradiction between the proletariat and the bourgeoisie? Certainly not! Such doubts represent a misunderstanding or distortion resulting from complete ignorance of Marxism-Leninism. As a matter of fact, the policy of uniting with the national bourgeoisie and struggling with it, which we adopted to resolve this contradiction, is a very firm proletarian class policy which has nothing in common with the policy of class collaboration." Liu Shao-ch'i, *The Victory of Marxism-Leninism in China, op. cit.*, p. 57.

[38] "Struggle Between Two Lines in Transforming Capitalist Industry and Commerce," *Peking Review* (July 19, 1968), pp. 23, 28.

sion of executive authority (including limited resort to markets), differed from the radicals (who championed the use of administrative repression), in degree only. The quarrel was about the precise mix of the carrot and the stick in promoting socialist construction and transformation. But the carrot, even in the hands of the moderates, often turned into a club.

8. The quality of output was given emphasis as against an earlier overwhelming preoccupation with quantity.[39] The moderates proposed to fix industrial prices according to the quality of goods. Commercial organs were to gradually introduce a system of selective purchase of certain commodities, and producing enterprises were urged to pay greater attention to quality targets. The intent does not seem to have had much practical impact since the whole system of success indicators continued to be heavily weighted in favor of physical output, and in the absence of a thorough reform of the price system in the direction of opportunity cost-efficiency pricing, the fixing of this or that price according to the quality of products remained a vague and impractical ideal. As we shall see in Chapter 9, the problem was taken up again in 1962, and at that time, if only for a while, it was attacked in the right way. The right way was to first air the theoretical issues involved. In 1956 action was taken in a near analytical vacuum. In 1962, theory got a brief hearing. But analytical arguments, and those who made them, were suppressed three years later by yet another wave of ideological fervor.

9. The Maoist penchant for relying on the inventive ingenuity of the masses and for rushing from the drawing board to the factory and farm with only half-developed and untried prototypes, was challenged: "In order to prevent loss from indiscriminate popularization, the latest experience gained in increasing production should first be tried out experimentally and then, after the method has been mastered, popularized step by step in areas with more or less the same conditions."[40]

The misbegotten, rashly popularized double-share plows, a "white elephant" as Liao Lu-yen called them, were to be "hung on the wall" or quite simply scrapped. According to a later account by the Maoists, 230,000 of them were destroyed.[41] The same report,

---

[39]". . . Some construction units concerned themselves only with speed, and overlooked quality and safety, thus resulting in poor quality, many accidents, and waste in construction work. This should be a lesson to us." *Proposals, op. cit.*, p. 43.

[40]*Ibid.*, pp. 20-21.

[41]The relevant document was "Opinions Concerning the Problem of Disassembling and Destroying Some Double-Share Ploughs" published in May 1957. "Outline of Struggle," *URS*, Vol. 53, Nos. 5-6, *op. cit.*, p. 58. The plow was personally rehabilitated by Mao in early 1958.

accusing the Party rightists of sabotaging agricultural mechanization and rapid popularization of inventions spawned by the masses, argued that there was a correlation between the ups and downs in farm-tool popularization and the "wavy development of mutual aid and agricultural cooperativization." Whenever "the adverse current of right opportunism" prevailed (e.g., first half of 1953 and in 1957), the development of the national economy took on a "saddle shape."[42]

TABLE 7-2

Principal New Type Farm Tools Popularized In the Country
(Number of sets)

	1950	1951	1952	1953	1954	1955	1956	1957
Double-single share plows . . .	166	582	1,499	15,136	22,566	425,907	1,086,009	733,135
Walking plows . .	594	5,717	237,368	178,033	224,242	304,757	1,022,464	96,945
Sprayers	—	—	164,074	197,988	309,973	429,215	1,179,952	540,526
Water wheels . . .	67,270	95,095	222,718	174,562	117,816	164,444	619,436	247,222

Source: "Outline of Struggle," URS, Vol. 53, Nos. 5-6, op. cit., p. 58.

"In the past few years, we have put undue emphasis on numbers and neglected quality. . . . The number of students [should] not be recklessly increased to the detriment of quality."[43] Learning from foreigners was not to be regarded as a blow to the nation's prestige. On the contrary, because of the "shortage of teachers and the low quality of students," efforts were to be made to send faculty members and students abroad to study subjects absent from Chinese curricula. The radicals' hobby-horse—spare-time and mass short-course education—was "also" to be developed, but "those who attend these schools must do so of their own free will,"[44] an elusive concept, even when held by the moderates. In scientific research, the Hundred Schools of Thought rule was to be applied, and "free discussion of academic questions encouraged." International contacts and cooperation were likewise to be promoted.

[42] The "saddle shape" or "U-shaped development" thesis was used in 1958 and later to beat the moderates with. See below, Chapter 8.

[43] Proposals, op. cit., p. 91.

[44] Ibid., p. 92. Compare this with "Chairman Mao's Latest Directive" published in the Peking Review on August 2, 1968, p. 3: "It is still necessary to have universities; here I refer mainly to colleges of science and engineering. However, it is essential to shorten the length of schooling, revolutionize education, put proletarian politics in command, and take the road of the Shanghai Machine Tools Plant in training technicians from among the workers. Students should be selected from among workers and peasants with practical experience, and they should return to production after a few years of study." On the Shanghai Machine Tools Plant's road, see Ibid., pp. 9-14.

10. The *Proposals* are relatively internationalist in tone, and see "unity and cooperation among the socialist countries . . . growing ever closer."[45] "At present [one month before Suez and the Polish and Hungarian uprisings] the international situation has definitely tended towards relaxation."[46] The Second Five Year Plan was posited on massive Soviet aid both in the construction of large industrial plants and in the supply of technical and scientific know-how. "In the future, we will go on earnestly learning from them [the Soviets]."[47]

11. The *Proposals* urged moderation in the rate of growth. "Because our national economy is still very backward, with agriculture still occupying a relatively large part, and because the standard of living of our people is still relatively low, the portion of national income going to accumulation cannot and should not be increased too much and too fast, but may be slightly bigger than that in the first five-year period."[48] Capital investment in 1957 was trimmed to a level 92.6 percent of 1956, agricultural output targets were reduced and modern industrial production rose by only 6.9 percent, the slowest rate of the whole First Five Year Plan.[49] The retrenchment was short-lived however. Total investments in capital construction in 1958 were almost double the 1957 figure. The *Proposals* thought that it was necessary and possible to cut down in the state budget the proportion of expenditure going to national defense and administration and to raise that going to economic, cultural and educational undertakings. This was interpreted in 1958 in the leap way shown in Table 7-3.

"We deem it necessary to suitably increase the percentage of investments in light industry."[50] In 1957 light industry received 15.2 percent of total industrial investments; in 1958 it got 12.6 percent.

The economic liberalization of 1956-57 rested on the largely erroneous assumption that all that needed to be done to remedy the disproportions, rigidities, inconsistencies, and shortages in the econ-

---

[45] *Proposals*, p. 9.
[46] *Ibid.*, p. 9.
[47] *Ibid.*, p. 102.
[48] *Ibid.*, p. 64.
[49] "They [the rightists] started to chop off and retrench capital construction and restrict development. Consequently in 1957 the development of the national economy formed the shape of a saddle, that is the total value of industry and agriculture of the country slowed down in its rate of increase from 16.5 percent in 1956 to 7.8 percent, and that of industry slowed down from 31 percent in 1956 to 10.9 percent." "Outline of Struggle" *URS*, Vol. 53, Nos. 5-6, *op. cit.*, p. 57.
[50] *Proposals*, p. 65.

TABLE 7-3
Percentage of State Budgetary Expenditures Going to
Economic Construction, Social, Cultural, and
Educational Projects, National Defense,
and Government Administration

Year	Economic Construction	Social, Cultural, Educational Projects	National Defense	Government Administration
1957	51.4	16.0	19.0	7.8
1958	64.1	10.6	12.2	5.6

Source: Ten Great Years, op. cit., p. 24.

omy was to rectify the Party's and government organs' style of work, that "you could make a totalitarian regime acceptable simply by rectifying the conduct of those who held power."[51] The decentralization measures, the limited use of markets, the calls for gradualness and caution really did not get down to the substance of the problem. They were administrative cures imposed from above, ad hoc substitutes for real remedies. Being overwhelmingly bureaucratic, they never touched the foundations of the system and erred in assuming that the contradictions between the government and the governed were due exclusively to administrative distortions. The reforms underestimated, because the reformers had no sure means of finding out, the reservoir of bitterness and resentment that had built up against the system and its use and abuse of total power. By shifting some authority from the center to local levels, the reforms created many small bureaucrats where formerly there were only a few. The retrenchment measures combined with the disproportions, inconsistencies, and imbalances inherited from the previous period resulted in a rise in urban and rural unemployment and led to the application of stringent measures to stem the flow of rural migrants into the cities. Like the partial reforms of Khrushchev and his successors, the reforms of 1956-57 courted failure, and failure meant one of two things: a reversal to the old, hard line, or a disintegration of the Party's monopoly of power. In the event, the outcome was a return to leaping and storming and using the naked force of the totalitarian machine. "A hundred schools have to contend; but as a result of contention, there is only one truth under a fixed set of circumstances."[52] The set of circumstances was fixed by the communists

[51] Roderick MacFarquhar, The Hundred Flowers Campaign and the Chinese Intellectuals (New York: Praeger, and Stevens & Sons, Ltd., London, 1960), p. 13.

[52] Kuang Ming-pao, April 21, 1957, quoted in R. MacFarquhar, op. cit., p. 29.

beforehand, and the contention became a symbolic dance with pure motion lording it over reason.

THE HUNDRED FLOWERS AND THE ANTIRIGHTIST CAMPAIGNS

CHRONOLOGY

While the relative and very largely bureaucratic liberalization of the economy was going on, there took place in China a curious incident, which came to be known as the Campaign of the Hundred Flowers. It was a brief affair lasting not more than six weeks— roughly from the end of April to early June 1957. The Hundred Flowers was in a rough and rather superficial sense the equivalent of the Soviet post-Stalin "thaw." [53] It began as part of the campaign to rectify the Party's style of work, which it will be recalled, was directed against the "three evils" of bureaucratism, subjectivism, and sectarianism. The theoretical blessing for the Hundred Flowers was given by Mao Tse-tung in a speech made to a closed session of the Supreme State Conference in Peking on February 27, 1957, entitled "On the Correct Handling of Contradictions Among the People." [54] The text of this speech was not published until June 18 when the Hundred Flowers had already been trampled underfoot by the Anti-Rightist Campaign. The published text had been amended, so that to this day the original version is not known. [55] The speech was fol-

[53] The Soviet liberalization or "thaw" began in May 1954. The name derives from the title of a novel published by Ilya Ehrenburg, a leading Soviet writer. The first installment of the novel appeared in the May 1954 issue of the magazine *Znamya*. There were many differences between the Soviet thaw and the Chinese flowers. See S. H. Chen, "Artificial 'Flowers' During a Natural 'Thaw,' " in Donald W. Treadgold (ed.), *Soviet and Chinese Communism: Similarities and Differences* (Seattle: U. of Washington Press, 1967), pp. 220-254. On the relationship of the Hundred Flowers in China to the 1956 events in Hungary, see Edward Friedman, "The Revolution in Hungary and the Hundred Flowers Period in China, *Journal of Asian Studies*, Vol. 25, No. 1 (November 1965), pp. 119-122.

[54] The date of the speech is also given as May 2, 1956. The Supreme State Conference was a body convened by the Head of State and comprising top Party and non-Party functionaries. It usually met in national emergencies (at least seventeen times prior to March 1962). The proceedings were normally kept secret, at least for a time. Cf. Chapter 9. Cf. also Chou En-lai, *Report on the Question of the Intellectuals* (January 1956), (Peking: *FLP*, 1956).

[55] Since the publication of Mao's February speech coincided with the unleashing of the campaign of repression, it may be surmised that the amended published version of the speech emphasized those original passages that related to the permissible limits of discussion and criticism. This was probably done by the simple process of suppressing some of the more liberal original paragraphs and adding a few authoritarian ones. The question is discussed more fully below.

lowed by the usual discussions in the Party's inner circles, and then on April 30 a directive of the Party's Central Committee appeared in the *People's Daily* instructing the cadres to launch a campaign of criticism and discussion concerning the problem of how to correctly handle contradictions among the people, particularly as these concerned the Party's style of work (i.e., the Party's relations with the people).[56] On June 8, 1957 the *People's Daily* published an editorial, which for all intents and purposes, put a stop to the outpouring of criticism and unleashed a repressive campaign against those who, in response to earlier instructions, had "bloomed and contended." The Hundred Flowers had overnight been designated as a thousand weeds to be ruthlessly uprooted.

CONTRADICTIONS AND THE HUNDRED FLOWERS

The Hundred Flowers Campaign ordered Party and non-Party people (the latter drawn from the academic, scientific, and national bourgeois communities and from the ranks of the united front non-communist parties) to publicly say what was on their minds and in their hearts regarding the Party's style of work. Criticism was to have been carried out like "a gentle breeze and mild rain," everyone was to take part except counterrevolutionaries and other enemies of the people.[57] The general guidelines for the "blooming and contending" of the Hundred Flowers and the Hundred Schools of Thought were laid down in Mao's "Contradictions" speech, then still unpublished, and only commented on and explained in newspaper editorials.

The central idea of the speech was that contradictions existed in all things, these contradictions being the motive force of progress. In class societies contradictions between classes were antagonistic and had to be resolved by force. In People's China contradictions still existed and were of two kinds. First, there were still some antagonistic contradictions "between ourselves and our enemies." Secondly, there existed contradictions among the people. "At this stage of building socialism, all classes, strata, and social groups that approve, support, and work for the cause of socialist construction belong to

---

[56] Note that in economic administration this campaign was already in force. It began as early as October of the previous year. For earlier Party rectification campaigns, see *Selected Works of Mao Tse-tung* (Peking: FLP, 1964) Vol. I, pp. 105-116 ("On Correcting Mistaken Ideas in the Party," December 1929), and *ibid.*, Vol. III, pp. 35-51 ("Rectify the Party's Style of Work," February 1, 1942).

[57] "As far as unregenerate counterrevolutionaries and wreckers of the socialist cause are concerned the matter is easy: We simply deprive them of their freedom of speech." Mao Tse-tung, *On the Correct Handling of Contradictions Among the People* (Peking: FLP, 1957). Cf. Lu Ting-yi, *Let Flowers of Many Kinds Blossom, Diverse Schools of Thought Contend!* (Peking: FLP, 1957).

the category of the people, while those social forces and groups that resist the socialist revolution and are hostile to and try to wreck socialist construction are enemies of the people."[58] Given this definition, contradictions among the people are of two kinds: those among the working people (nonantagonistic) and those between the exploited classes and the exploiters (i.e., those between the working class and other sections of the working people on the one hand, and the national bourgeoisie on the other). This last type of contradiction has "a nonantagonistic aspect as well as an antagonistic one."

Contradictions among the people include those within the working class, within the peasantry, within the intelligentsia, between the working class and the peasantry, between the working class and other sections of the working people on the one hand, and the national bourgeoisie on the other, within the national bourgeoisie, "and so forth." Significantly, even though the communist government was said to be one that "truly represented the interests of the people and served the people," certain contradictions apparently did exist between it and the masses. The nonantagonistic contradictions among the working people and the contradictions between the working people and the national bourgeoisie (antagonistic but with a nonantagonistic aspect to them) could be resolved in a peaceful way, provided they were properly handled.

This is the crux of the message. It is as far as the philosophy of the Chinese thaw was prepared to go in the Khrushchevian direction of peaceful coexistence and peaceful transition. It was, even on the most liberal interpretation, not very far. The whole concept is so riddled with qualifications, so permeated by the dialectical spirit that the idea of the peaceful handling of contradictions among the people is almost suffocated by the *caveats*. Nonantagonistic contradictions among those who are willing to work for the communist cause could be, but had not necessarily to be resolved without recourse to force; it was only one possibility. With regard to the treatment of the national bourgeoisie, the possibility of a forceful resolution of contradictions was very real. And, of course, there were always those

[58] Mao-Tse-tung, *On the Correct Handling of Contradictions Among the People, op. cit.* One could infer from a previous passage that by then there were only "people" in China, and hence that contradictions were only of the "among the people" kind. "Led by the working class and the Communist Party, and united as one, our 600 million people are engaged in the great work of building socialism" (*Ibid.*). Such inconsistencies, however, can be explained away dialectically as "the same but opposite." "Are the landlords, rich peasants, counterrevolutionaries, bad elements and rightists considered as men?" cried the besieged and harassed Liu Shao-ch'i in 1966. "(Audience interrupted: 'As men but not as people')." Which Liu countered with: "They are mankind; not animals," Liu Shao-ch'i, "Talk to Cultural Revolution Corps," *op. cit.*, p. 338.

who were outside the people: "In China . . . remnants of the over-thrown landlord and comprador classes still exist, the bourgeoisie still exists, and the petty bourgeoisie has only just begun to remold itself. The class struggle is not yet finished. . . . In this respect, the question whether socialism or capitalism will win is still not really settled."[59]

The question is how much of this theorizing was added later and how much of it was there from the beginning. One can only specu-late, since, as we have said before, the original text of Mao's speech is not available, and the published text we have has been doctored. It seems reasonable to assume that the original version contained some qualifications, but possibly not as many and as strong as the ones found in the later edition. It is also plausible to assume that the general tone and thrust of the original speech was somewhat more liberal than the published text. Probably also, the speech at the time it was made was intended to give a blessing to the relative liberaliza-tion movement, and one cannot discount the possibility that it was made under pressure from the Party moderates.[60] Even if all this is accepted, there were apparently in the original speech enough loop-holes and dialectical twists and turns for the message to be used in any way any faction chose to use it. One witness to the February meeting noted the following qualification: "Not only a hundred schools, there could be a thousand schools," the Chairman said. And in the next breath: "fundamentally, however, there are only two schools."[61] In other words, there was the "correct" and revolution-ary school of Marxism-Leninism as interpreted at any moment by the Chair, and the "incorrect" and counterrevolutionary schools (all 999 of them).

The peaceful resolution of conflicts among the people was to take the form of "discussion," "criticism," and "persuasion." A hun-dred flowers were to bloom unhindered, and a hundred schools of thought were to contend in professing. There was to be a general airing of views, a confrontation of opinions sponsored by an appar-ently broad-minded and benign Party. It all looked like a democracy of the spirit imposed from above. "Democracy sometimes seems to be an end, but it is in fact only a means," Mao (revised) said. ". . . This freedom," he continued, "is freedom with leadership and this democracy is democracy under centralized guidance, not

---

[59] On the Correct Handling of Contradictions Among the People, op. cit.
[60] But see the alternative explanations for the campaign, below, p. 248.
[61] Yu P'ing-po, "Casual Remarks on the Hundred Schools," Wen Yi Pao, No. 1, April 14, 1957, p. 9, quoted in S. H. Chen, "Artificial 'Flowers' During a Natural 'Thaw,' " op. cit., p. 227.

anarchy."[62] The whole speech with its almost unreal vision of reality, the rhetoric with mercurial overtones, illustrate the communist compulsion to cast into and interpret in terms of Marxian dialectical and historical materialism every policy move from the gravest to the most insignificant. Everything has to be sanctioned by the *ex cathedra* authority of theory. The actual formulation of the theory, as we have seen, is such as to leave the door wide open for later interpretations and reinterpretations and all sorts of action by the guardians of correctness. By overstressing the nonantagonistic aspect of contradictions between the working people and the national bourgeoisie, for example, one could be accused of the heresy of the "dying out of the class struggle" in a society building socialism (as Liu Shao-ch'i was later said by his detractors to have done). By overemphasizing antagonism, one could fall into the trap of dogmatism and doctrinairism, and be bludgeoned out of office the moment the first interpretation gained ground. Heads I win, tails you lose. Keeping quiet was no solution either, since the authorities demanded open discussion as a national and proletarian duty. Keeping silent might make one suspect and liable to being branded an enemy of the people.

MAIN CHARACTERISTICS OF THE HUNDRED FLOWERS CAMPAIGN

The campaign let loose a flood of increasingly bitter criticism of the way the Party ran the country. As the weeks progressed the critique became more strident and biting, more and more directed against the very concept of a monocratic system and a monopoly Party. For all its unprecedented virulence and the courage of the critics, the Hundred Flowers interlude still gives the impression of the cadres' never really having lost control of the movement. The best available account of the various forums organized by Party and non-Party newspapers, educational institutions, and so on, at which the critics spoke out is to be found in Roderick MacFarquhar's collection, *The Hundred Flowers Campaign and the Chinese Intellectuals* (New York: Praeger, and Stevens & Sons, Ltd., London, 1960). The reader is referred to this book for a survey of what went on during this brief period of relatively free speech. Here we need only note some of the more general characteristics of the Hundred Flowers interlude.

1. The "thaw" in thought and speech was not a spontaneous movement from below, but rather the obedient response to instruc-

---

[62] Mao Tse-tung, *On the Correct Handling of Contradictions Among the People, op. cit.*

tions from above. It was imposed by an authoritarian bureaucracy, which at that particular moment perhaps saw in it a useful means of supplementing its various economic decentralization measures. "Marxism teaches us," Mao said, "that democracy is part of the superstructure and belongs to the realm of politics. That is to say, in the last analysis, it serves the economic base. The same is true of freedom. Both democracy and freedom are relative, not absolute, and they come into being and develop under specific historical circumstances." [63] Toward the end of May and the first days of June 1957, it looked as if the cadres were losing their hold on the wide ranging discussion and criticism, but on the whole the Hundred Flowers bloomed and the Hundred Schools contended to order.

2. The criticism voiced during the campaign showed little theoretical sophistication and not much intellectual depth. The complaints were mostly of a personal and material nature, often verging on the trivial. The campaign released long pent-up emotions and grudges, violently and bitterly phrased, but produced no intellectually satisfying theoretical alternative to the communist system. One reason for this lackluster performance was certainly the mental anguish to which the communists had subjected the intellectuals in earlier years: the best and most independent thinkers had been weeded out, remolded, or rendered harmless in labor camps. There was no possibility for those who survived to work out theoretical social schemes and test them in the fire of rational criticism and debate. For years only collective thoughts, officially approved and prepared in advance, were allowed to have an airing, and even here one had to be careful lest one be accused of ideological deviation. Long controlled and manipulated by intellectual primitives, thought released from its trammels floundered and found expression in cries of anger at personal and professional slights and hardships. "Even the calendars placed in different offices vary; the Principal has the largest ones, next come the Directors, next come the Departmental heads, and the heads of Pedagogic Rooms have the smallest ones." [64] The main theme of businessmen's (national capitalists') contending was whether the government should pay 35 percent or 100 percent compensation for the private businesses it took over, and whether the 5 percent per annum fixed interest paid to former (reformed) capitalists should be extended to twenty years. Artists complained that Chinese traditional paintings had been consigned to lavatories, leaving traditional-style painters "without hope and in spiritual agony."

[63] *Ibid.*

[64] Roderick MacFarquhar, *op. cit.*, p. 97. Part of statement by Professor Lu Ya-heng of the Central China Engineering Institute in Wuhan.

A few critics warned the Communist Party that unless it thoroughly reformed itself, the masses would turn against it: "China belongs to 600 million people including the counterrevolutionaries. It does not belong to the Communist Party alone. . . . For the past few years the Party has been increasingly estranged from the masses. Most of the people absorbed by the Party have been flatterers, sycophants, and yes-men. . . . The government must not be in the hands of one Party, the Communist Party."[65]

The absence of an alternative program, the total lack of a blueprint for the reformation of Chinese society, and the superficiality of many of the criticisms can also be explained by the campaign's shortness.[66] There was no time to work anything out, just enough respite to unburden oneself of the things that hurt most. In spite of the personal bravery verging on recklessness that marked some of the comments, there was always the nagging disbelief that such things could happen, the suspicion that it was all another plot to weed out the dissidents, that the files of the secret police were rapidly being filled for future reference, and that the day of punishment would inevitably come.

3. The Hundred Flowers Campaign was strongly nationalistic and inward looking. As contrasted with the *Proposals*, there were in it pointed criticisms of the wholesale copying of Soviet models in various areas of life and a reassertion of the qualities of Chinese scholarship and culture. Chauvinism, which was to be one of the major themes of the later Cultural Revolution (1966-69), was kept in check, but already there were signs of an impatient chafing at the foreign bit, a willingness to liberate China of what to many seemed an excessive dependence on Soviet example and Soviet advice. The official policy of "leaning to one side" (i.e., the Soviet side) was not openly questioned, but it was indirectly challenged in the name of national self-consciousness. Already at this time, in fact ever since Khrushchev denounced Stalin in February 1956 without consulting the Chinese, relations between the USSR and China were becoming strained, although the mounting disagreement was still papered over. Soviet economic commitments to an increasing number of noncommunist underdeveloped countries, including India, and Khrushchev's many revisions of Stalinist ideological positions must have slowly but surely convinced the Chinese leadership that the expected massive

---

[65] The quotations are from various blooming and contending forums, cited in MacFarquhar, *op. cit.*, pp. 87, 74, and 57 respectively.

[66] Professor Cheng Chu-yuan calls my attention to a number of alternative programs suggested by leaders of the right-bureaucratic wing, notably Chang Po-chun (Minister of Communications) and Lo Lung-chi (Minister of Timber Industry). They advocated a bicameral system.

aid for China's Second Five Year Plan was becoming elusive and problematical, and perhaps even not all that desirable. The Hundred Flowers' occasional anti-Soviet blooming thus in a way foreshadows later events. The disillusionment with the Soviet Union voiced by some of the critics was not yet officially condoned, but it was possibly shared by many persons in positions of authority.

THE ANTIRIGHTIST CAMPAIGN

Ominous signs that the tidal wave of criticism was about to turn against the critics, appeared as early as May 25, when blooming and contending was only one month old. On that day, Mao Tse-tung warned delegates to a youth congress that all words and actions which deviated from socialism were completely wrong. On June 8, the campaign was stopped short by an editorial in *People's Daily* which noted that some incidents during the campaign showed that class struggle in China had not died out and that "rightists" were plotting to push China along a capitalist and Western-style democratic path. The blooming and contending instantly turned into criticism of rightists instead of the Party, as before. On June 18, Mao's February "Contradictions" speech was released by the New China News Agency in an appropriately amended form. In addition to a shift in emphasis, already mentioned, the text contained an obvious addition, which took the form of the so-called "six criteria of correct criticism." These tests can be regarded as the frame of the ideological hothouse within which the blooming of artificial flowers was thenceforth to take place. As reported by *NCNA*, "words and actions can be judged right if they

"1. Help to unite the people of [China's] various nationalities, and do not divide them.

2. Are beneficial, not harmful, to socialist transformation and socialist construction.

3. Help to consolidate, not undermine or weaken, the people's democratic dictatorship [i.e., the dictatorship of the Communist Party].

4. Help to consolidate, not undermine or weaken, democratic centralism.

5. Tend to strengthen, not to cast off or weaken, the leadership of the Communist Party.

6. Are beneficial, not harmful, to international socialist solidarity and the solidarity of the peace-loving peoples of the world."[67]

[67]*NCNA*, June 18, 1957. Text of Mao Tse-tung's February 27, 1957 speech "On the Correct Handling of Contradictions Among the People."

Mao's retouched panorama of the Hundred Flowers in *chiaro-scuro* was careful to bring out one crucial feature: that "of these six criteria, the most important are the socialist path and the leadership of the Party."[68] In radical communist perspective, the criteria were of a nature to "foster, and not hinder, the free discussion of various questions among the people." In every other perspective, the criteria dealt a death blow to what little freedom of discussion there had been.

The Antirightist Campaign to uproot the Hundred Flowers (poisonous weeds, as they were now called), bore all the marks of the resurgent influence in Party councils of hard-line leftists.[69] It was a summer and autumn cleaning-up job in preparation for more radical things to come (the Great Leap Forward). The economic liberalization measures, not yet nine months old, were imperiled by the ideological and political deep freeze; their demise was not far off. For a while—until early spring of 1958—the hard line in ideology and politics coexisted with a relatively moderate course in economics. But this contradiction could not survive very long. Ever since late May, the trend was toward yet another radicalization of the country and the sort of recklessness against which the *Proposals* had come out in September of the previous year.

The Antirightist Campaign systematically dragged out those who had heeded the Party's call to bloom and contend. They were made to go through the by then familiar ordeal of public confessions and self-incrimination, apology, and promise to reform. Denunciation meetings followed one another in rapid succession, the main attacks being made, at the Party's behest, by friends and associates of the victims. The number of those accused of rightist deviation is not known with any degree of precision; one source (basing itself on a figure officially cited in connection with a later amnesty) mentions 26,000.[70] This probably refers only to the very top rightists.

Confessions, public recantations, and all the other trappings of the chilling drama, were exhibited for all to see and take warning.

---

[68] *Ibid.*

[69] Liu Shao-ch'i said, or was made to say, in September 1959 that "in our garden, the hundred flowers of socialism should be in full bloom and . . . the antisocialist poisonous weeds should be weeded out." Liu Shao-ch'i, *"The Victory of Marxism-Leninism in China"* (September 14, 1959) (Peking: *FLP*, 1959) in *Collected Works of Liu Shao-ch'i 1968-1967* (Hong Kong: *URI*, 1968), p. 62. Cf. Fu-sheng Mu, *The Wilting of the Hundred Flowers: The Chinese Intelligentsia Under Mao* (New York: Praeger, 1963).

[70] Roderick MacFarquhar, *op. cit.*, p. 265. The amnesty was made public as "Resolution of the Party Central Committee and the State Council on the Rehabilitation of Rightists (September 16, 1959)," *Jen-min Jih-pao*, September 18, 1959.

But the awing of the masses by the force of negative example was only one act of the tragedy. The bawling and whimpering of those sacrificed on the altars of revolutionary fervor was matched by a new drive to indoctrinate the whole nation, and so stamp out any vestiges of ideological infection which the rightists might have left in the minds of the people. A vast program of political education, and of education combined with physical labor was launched, brains were washed in the sweat of endless meetings and toil on farms and construction sites. Students who during the Hundred Flowers Campaign were particularly critical, vociferous, and restless were ordered to sober up in menial jobs in the countryside. Thus the Antirightist Campaign combined the weapons of public denunciation and self-criticism with political indoctrination and a "downward transfer" (hsia fang) of students, intellectuals, and recalcitrant cadres. The flowers bowed their heads and admitted their guilt. Unreservedly, they accused themselves and each other of improbable crimes against socialism, the Party, and the state, and cried out that they were worse than the worst poisonous weeds. "It is not a bad thing," said Liu wistfully, "to let poisonous weeds come out in their true colors."[71]

Alleged transgressions against the Party, socialism, and the unity of the nation were classified in the order of their gravity. "Leading rightists within the Party" were expelled, a step which in any communist country is of the utmost seriousness, depriving as it does the accused of the protection which Party membership brings with it. Expulsion from the Party's ranks amounts to driving the victim into the wilderness where former friends ignore and shun him. "Localists" and "nationalists," as well as those who committed "right-opportunist mistakes" or "opposed the Party line, carrying out anti-Party activities" were publicly exposed. Their punishment consisted in the writing and rewriting of statements of self-examination which were analyzed and criticized in endless struggle sessions.

THE U-SHAPED DEVELOPMENT

From what has been said it is clear that between the first session of the Eighth National Party Congress (September 1956), which inaugurated the moderate economic course and the second session

[71] Liu Shao-ch'i, "The Victory of Marxism-Leninism in China" (September 14, 1959) (Peking: FLP, 1959) in Collected Works of Liu Shao-ch'i, 1958–1967, (Hong Kong: URI, 1968), p. 63. See also Chalmers A. Johnson, Communist Policies Toward the Intellectual Class (Hong Kong: URI, 1959), and Teng Hsiao-p'ing, Report on the Rectification Campaign, September 23, 1957, (Peking: FLP, 1957).

(May 1958) which sealed its fate and sanctioned the Great Leap
Forward, there took place a sharp shift within the leadership toward
the radical left. The shift crystallized at the Third Plenary Session of
the Party's Eighth Central Committee in autumn 1957 and at the
Nanning and Chengtu Conferences held early the following year. The
reports and resolutions of the second session of the Eighth National
Party Congress differ in tone and substance from the *Proposals*, at
times to the point of open disavowal of the *Proposals'* message and
denunciation of the *Proposals'* authors. Ironically, the task of disavowal and condemnation fell to Liu Shao-ch'i who, it may be presumed, had been behind the *Proposals*. [72] "The [second] Session
reflected the victory of the rectification campaign and the struggle
against the rightists, and the big forward leap in socialist construction. It was itself a session for rectifying style of work, opposing
international revisionism and the rightists and localist and nationalist
elements who had infiltrated into the Party, a session which itself
signified a big leap forward." [73] Taking Marx's words literally, the
basic thesis of the second session was that twenty years should be
concentrated in a day. Impatience and rashness, cautioned against in
the *Proposals*, were hailed as supreme socialist virtues in the second
session's reports and resolutions. The authors and proponents of the
moderate course were made to perform a hardly disguised public
self-examination and self-criticism by hailing the new radical course.
All in all, it was a return to the socialist upsurge tenets that had
marked the accelerated socialization of 1955 and early 1956
(summed up in Mao Tse-tung's introduction to *Socialist Upsurge in
China's Countryside*, published in December 1955) and a continuation of Mao's revised philosophy *On the Correct Handling of Contradictions Among the People*. The moderate interlude of late 1956 and
1957 was dismissed as the product of incorrect thinking by "some
comrades [who] still clung to such outmoded ideas as 'keeping to the
right is better than keeping to the left,' 'it's better to go slower than
faster,' or 'it's better to take small steps than to go striding forward.'
The struggle between the two methods in dealing with this question
was not fully decided until the launching of the rectification campaign and the antirightist struggle." [74] The leap philosophy of 1955
and June 1957 was updated and, if possible, speeded up in a series of
documents to which reference will be made in the next Chapter. The

[72] In his report to the Second Session, Liu mentioned Mao's name over
twenty times; at the first (*Proposals*) session only four times.
[73] *Second Session of the Eighth National Congress of the Communist Party
of China* (Peking: FLP, 1958), p. 5.
[74] *Ibid.*, p. 34.

economic performance of the liberal interlude was subjected to severe criticism within the framework of a "U-shaped theory of development."[75]

"The development," said Liu Shao-ch'i, "is U-shaped, that is, high at the beginning and the end, but low in the middle. Didn't we see very clearly how things developed on the production front in 1956-1957-1958 in the form of an upsurge, then an ebb, and then an even bigger upsurge or, in other words, a leap forward, then a conservative phase, and then another big leap forward? The Party and the masses have learned from this U-shaped development."[76] The lesson which the Party, including Liu, had ostensibly learned was that the upsurge phases of the U were correct, while the trough was incorrect, that reliance on the spontaneous forces and genius of the masses, with all the storming that this implied, was right, and that economic calculation and the careful weighing of alternatives were wrong. But there were indications that all doubts about the wisdom and practicability of the radical, guerrilla approach to economic construction were not dispelled and that the strength of the relatively moderate opposition was still formidable. "Many of those comrades," Liu continued, "who expressed misgivings about the principle of building socialism by achieving 'greater, faster, better, and more economical results,' have learned a lesson from all this. But some of them have not yet learned anything. They say: 'We'll settle accounts with you after the autumn harvest.' Well, let them wait to settle accounts. They will lose out in the end!"[77] Hindsight suggests that Liu himself was among those who "have not yet learned anything," and that his formal denunciation of the moderate line and his praise of the leap method were more a ritualistic exercise in surface leadership unity than an honest statement of his convictions. While about it, Liu denounced what in effect was the *Proposals'* major thesis: that reckless advance was not the way to build socialism and that it, rather than a step-by-step progress, dampened the enthusiasm of the

[75] For a Western evaluation of Communist China's economic cycles, see Cheng Chu-yuan, *Communist China's Economy 1949-1962, op. cit.*, pp. 160-165.
[76] Liu Shao-ch'i, "Report on the Work of the Central Committee of the CPC. to the Second Session of the Eighth National Congress (May 5, 1958), in *Second Session of the Eighth National Congress, op. cit.*, p. 39. See also Wyndham Newton, "China's 'Saddle-Shaped' Economic Construction," *Far Eastern Economic Review*, October 30, 1958, pp. 545-546. Compare this with the politically induced Soviet business cycles under Stalin (discussed by Jasny in his *Soviet Industrialization 1928-1953*) and with the more recent Soviet experience with production cycles—Marshall I. Goldman, "The Reluctant Consumer and Economic Fluctuations in the Soviet Union," *Journal of Political Economy* (August 1965), pp. 366-380.
[77] *Second Session*, p. 39.

masses, as much of it at any rate as the masses could whip up after almost ten years of alternating tension and relaxation. "Through this he showed the necessity of firmly maintaining the policy of achieving greater, faster, better, and more economical results and the mistake of 'opposing reckless advance.' " [78] ". . . The Party soon corrected this error."[79]

The call now was for "a technical and cultural revolution," a tremendous mobilization of the masses, unprecedented in China's history, a leap forward in agriculture, industry, handicrafts, communication, transport, commerce, science, technology, and culture. The emphasis was on speed, "the most important question confronting [China] since the victory of the socialist revolution."[80]

Liu managed in his report to adroitly insert the objections to the program of total mobilization and total haste, which he himself was made to sponsor. The objections presented as the aberrations of "some people" were the following: [81]

1. "Some say that speeding up construction makes people feel 'tense,' and so it's better to slow down the tempo."

2. "Some people wonder whether the implementation of the policy of consistently achieving greater, faster, better, and more economical results won't lead to waste. Of course, if this policy is followed out piecemeal and if we merely go in for quantity and speed and neglect quality and economy, or vice versa, then of course there will be waste. 'Greater' and 'faster' results are concerned with quantity and speed; 'better' and 'more economical' with quality and cost. They supplement and condition each other."

3. "Others are worried that implementation of this policy will throw the various branches of production off balance as well as financial revenue and expenditure." [82]

4. "Some comrades are worried that, though the development of agriculture can accumulate funds for industrialization, it will for the present at least divert some funds which could be used by the state for industrialization."

5. "Some people doubted whether agricultural production could expand very rapidly. They quoted authoritative works, chapter and

[78] *Ibid.*, p. 9.
[79] Liu Shao-ch'i, *op. cit.*, p. 38.
[80] *Ibid.*, p. 43.
[81] *Ibid.*, pp. 44, 45, 47, 48. On the Party rightists' political and economic plank, see also Chapter 8.
[82] "There is no absolute balance. Of course, in order to conform to the objective law of the proportionate development of socialist economy, a balance should be maintained between the various branches of our national economy over a certain period of time and to a certain extent. This is precisely the purpose of planning in a socialist state." *Ibid.*, pp. 45-46.

verse, to prove that agriculture could only advance slowly and that, what is more, its growth could in no way be guaranteed. Some scholars even asserted that the rate of agricultural growth could not keep pace with the growth of population. They argued that as the population grows, consumption will increase and there won't be much of an increase in accumulation."

6. "Some people say that ideological and political work can produce neither grain nor coal nor iron."

Each objection was rejected as unfounded. Temporarily the forces of relative moderation had lost and the race was on.

The Party's new general line of "going all out, aiming high and achieving greater, quicker, better, and more economical results in building socialism," which was to become the charter of the Great Leap Forward, contained five basic points:

1. To mobilize all positive factors and correctly handle contradictions among the people.

2. To consolidate and develop socialist ownership by the whole people and collective ownership and consolidate the proletarian dictatorship and proletarian international solidarity.

3. To gradually carry out the technical and cultural revolutions, while completing the socialist revolution on the economic, political and ideological fronts.

4. To develop industry and agriculture simultaneously while giving priority to heavy industry.

5. To develop, under centralized leadership, and with overall planning, proper division of labor and coordination, national industries simultaneously with local industries, and large enterprises simultaneously with medium-size and small enterprises.

The simultaneous development of everything was, as we have seen (p. 226) a feature of the 1956 *Proposals*, but at that time the moderates made sure that it was a purely formal desideratum. It was inserted, one may presume, to mollify the minority faction of the time, but still the major emphasis was on planning and gradualness, on heavy industry, central control, and initiative from above. By May 1958—the odds having shifted in favor of the radicals—the *Proposals'* formal simultaneousness was taken quite literally: China thenceforth was to "walk on two legs"—or more exactly, in the manner of a centipede. Everything was to be done at once, mostly by the peasant masses whose revolutionary energy and scientific inventiveness were counted on to subdue nature and bring about Marx's dream within the actuarial life of Mao Tse-tung—hopefully sooner.

8 | The Great Leap Forward, 1958–60

"The countryside was in convulsion. Marching in columns and working in dense crowds, immense peasant masses were spending their over-spilling energy. As in some fabulous pantomime, innumerable men, women and adolescents were on the move, perpetually purposeful and with apparently precise missions. Enormous crowds were carrying sand to swell embankments along rivers. Innumerable little figures were swinging their shovels to dig new canals. Marchers in formation were following coloured flags on bamboo poles, on their way to replace teams laying railway tracks. Monumental ant-heaps were busy on the sites of future reservoirs. Endless lines of blue-clad men and women were filling up mountain-sides like some unnatural stream changing course. In the background, scattered all over the fields, multitudes of people were moving around with two buckets hanging from their shoulder poles. All together, they recalled the rhythmic breathing of some mythological colossus, suddenly awakened and flexing its milliard muscles in a supreme effort to change the face of the earth. . . . Literally millions of [backyard furnaces] were built around villages, along railway lines or even in the gardens of schools and houses in the towns. Like innumerable glow-worms they shone in China's night. Seeing them all over the country one had the haunting impression of fanatical alchemists feeding the flames in desperation to turn into gold the rocks they had carted from the mountains. . . . By the spring of 1959 the movement was left to peter out. The millions of abandoned mud structures stood like silent witnesses to yet another demoniac expenditure of human energy."[1]

COMPONENTS OF THE LEAP

Mende's eyewitness account of the awesome dimensions of the Great Leap Forward is corroborated, if in more exalted terms, by the official Chinese themselves.

[1] Tibor Mende, *China and Her Shadow* (New York: Coward-McCann, and Thames and Hudson, Ltd., London 1962), pp. 70-71, 93. Copyright © 1960 by Tibor Mende.

256

"All the peasants—men and women, old and young—are busy at work. They dig canals and repair dams; they level mountains to bring them under the plough; they change the nights into days, the moon into the sun, and the slack season into busy season. On the work sites are red flags everywhere in the daytime, and lights everywhere at night. In work all vie with one another in fortitude and courage."[2]

"Everywhere in the country one heard the saying: 'If the mind does not freeze, neither will the earth'. . . . Everywhere the land was a surging wave of people in the daytime and a sea of light at night."[3]

"The peasants created devices as they worked. At a steep cliff the peasants worked in mid-air, being suspended with a rope let down from the top of the precipice. Picks were so worn that only 4 or 5 inches of their 2-foot heads was left. When the workers had no more tools they went home for more. At night they would light torches so as to enable them to continue their work. This made the construction site look like the business centre of a city."[4]

Dante's Inferno had come to pass. Economic planning and the use of relatively crude but effective analytical tools evolved by the Soviets during two decades of Stalinist construction were discarded and replaced by inspirational slogans. The magic of collective wisdom and group strength was to usher in the millenium almost overnight. "They gave them neither money nor materials. They gave them, however, a magic formula: 'Whenever there are difficulties, go to the masses for help.' "[5] The Leap did not mean that the tasks earlier set out in the draft Second Five Year Plan were to be neglected. On the contrary, they were to be increased and carried out more rapidly— within two or three instead of five years—while at the same time the untapped reservoir of muscle was to be put to work on other, labor-intensive projects. The approach was labeled as one of "walking on two legs": the old, capital intensive one, and the other—allegedly not fully used till then—of massive labor power and peasant inventiveness; the old stressing heavy industry, and the new promoting industry and agriculture equally, with industry being the more equal of the two.[6] Centralization of powers was to be combined with decen-

---

[2] *China's Big Leap in Water Conservancy* (Peking: *FLP*, 1958), p. i.

[3] *Ibid.*, pp. 3-4. "Vice plus drive" was another name given to the mind's overcoming all obstacles. "Although a vice was their sole equipment, they worked hard day and night . . . [and] moved from making wooden weighbeams to the manufacture of metal scales." Chin Yu-huang, "A Paupers' 'Plant,' " *Peking Review* (March 15, 1960), p. 19.

[4] *China's Big Leap in Water Conservancy, loc. cit.*

[5] Yu Kuang-yuan, "The Simultaneous Use of Modern and Indigenous Production Methods," *Peking Review* (June 9, 1959), pp. 6-8.

[6] "By 'two legs' was meant simultaneous development in industry and agriculture; in heavy and light industries; in centrally and locally managed enter-

tralization. In short, the essence of the Leap was the massive mobilization of hidden rural savings.

The Great Leap Forward comprised four mass campaigns, four overlapping phases.[7]

1. A drive for *water conservancy* unprecedented in scope and intensity.
2. A drive for *tool improvement* based on peasant innovations.
3. A drive to build *local, small-scale, do-it-yourself industries* throughout the length and breadth of the country (paralleled by state investment in capital-intensive, modern industries).
4. The establishment of *people's communes.*

While these major campaigns were going on, the antirightist and rectification movements continued unabated, supplemented by a drive against waste and conservative practices in economic construction. These three campaigns had a number of tributaries, as for instance, the "Give Your Heart to the Party" drive launched in March 1958, the campaign against the "Five Bad Airs" (bureaucratic airs, extravagant airs, arrogant airs, and finicky airs), the "Multi-Million Poem Movement,[8] and the continuing health drive against the "Four

---

prises; in large, medium, and small enterprises; in modern and native technologies; in centralized leadership and mass participation. Simultaneous development did not mean development at the same rate, however, for industry was still given priority over agriculture, heavy over light industries, large over medium and small enterprises, modern over native techniques, central over local enterprises. Simultaneous development was deemed feasible despite scarcity of capital. The scarce capital was to be used, as previously, primarily for the development of heavy industry, while labor was to be the main input for other development." Chi-ming Hou, "Communist China's Economic Development Since the Great Leap," in Jan S. Prybyla (ed.), *The Triangle of Power, Conflict and Accommodation: The United States, the Soviet Union, Communist China* (University Park, Pa.: Pennsylvania State, 1967), p. 75.

[7] In 1961 [Liu Shao-ch'i] viciously cried: 'In these years [1958-60] so many movements had been launched. These movements were mostly like a gust of wind. . . . Every time a mass movement was over, the masses were like frost bitten crops, having suffered some loss and damage, and having been frustrated in their enthusiasm." "Outline of Struggle," *URS*, Vol. 53, Nos. 5-6, *op. cit.*, p. 78.

[8] Here are some examples taken from *China's Big Leap in Water Conservancy* and *People's Communes in China:*

> Thousand threads were used
> In mending my clothes.
> But my grandmother's concern for me
> Means much more than all this:
> I won't go home
> Until the reservoir is completed
> So as to repay my grandmother's kindness.

> Of their ability, men of the No. 2 team have pride.
> In making the "big leap forward" they took a rocket ride.

Evils"[9] (Chapter 3). There was also an explosion of *tatze-pao* or newspapers of large ideograms, each paper usually consisting of two or three sheets displayed on walls of buildings, in corridors, vestibules, and wherever space could be found. [10] These wall newspapers contained the current slogans, denounced laggards, and listed various items of mutual, often very personal, recrimination. Everyone was expected, that is, ordered to edit his or her own *tatze-pao* and display it prominently for all to see, comment upon, and criticize in another *tatze-pao*. Besides the usual call to aim high and produce better, faster, and more economical results, the *tatze-pao* recounted stories drawn from their authors' personal experience in revolutionary endeavor, and accused others of revolutionary malpractises. A second wave of *tazte-pao* was to hit China nine years later during the Great Proletarian Cultural Revolution (Chapter 11).

Externally, the Great Leap Forward expressed itself in a more militant foreign policy and a worsening of relations with the Soviet Union. This aspect of the Leap will be discussed in the concluding sections of this chapter.

WATER CONSERVATION

Water conservation and flood control have been at all times the most important and sensitive issues in China's economic life and a standard by which the fitness of a dynasty to rule was judged. [11] One

---

Under the brilliant light of the General Line
Communism has blossomed in full glory.
Spring waters murmur in the distance,
To the accompaniment of the hissing electric planers
And the humming of flour mills.
We've bought our tractors and disc harrows,
And installed electric lamps and telephones.
And now we can speak before a microphone!

For other samples of this street-corner poetry see S. H. Chen, "Multiplicity in Uniformity: Poetry and the Great Leap Forward," *The China Quarterly*, No. 3, 1960. See also Wyndham Newton, "China Turns Inward for Cultural Inspiration," *FEER* (November 20, 1958), pp. 669-670; "Poetry for the Man in the Street," *Peking Review* (April 29, 1958), p. 5; Wu Pin, "Folk Songs of Today," *Peking Review* (May 13, 1958), pp. 15-16.

[9] In Chungking, 1,080,000 rats were killed in a seven-day battle. Eighty-five year-old Chang Teh of Peking trapped 30,000 sparrows in one winter and passed on his skill to many eager learners. *Peking Review* (March 25, 1958), pp. 16-17; "Peking's Anti-Pest Drive," *Peking Review* (April 22, 1958), p. 5.

[10] They were "also stuck upon improvised frames made of stalks, out in the fields for everyone to see and read." *Peking Review* (April 1, 1958), p. 5.

[11] In 3,000 years the Yellow River had flooded its banks or breached its man-made dikes 1,500 times. During this time it had shifted its course 26 times, destroying towns and villages and drowning millions of people. In 1936 Nationalist troops cut the river's bank in an attempt to stem a Japanese advance. An estimated 900,000 people lost their lives in the ensuing flood and the lives of another 12 million were disrupted. *New York Times* (May 1, 1966), p. 13.

of the accusations made by Deputy Premier T'an Chen-lin at the Second Session of the Eighth National Party Congress against "certain persons" who in 1957 had opposed the allegedly reckless advance, was that as a result of such conservative thinking the "labor enthusiasm of the masses was dampened" and that in the period from the winter of 1956 to the spring of 1957, the irrigated area was increased by only a little over 36 million *mou*.[12]

The Second Session of the Eighth National Party Congress, which repudiated the go-slow policies of later 1956—mid 1957 was followed, as we have seen in Chapter 7, by a militant Third Plenary Session of the Party's Central Committee in September 1957, and the publication of a revised version of the 1955 National Program for Agricultural Development. All three, but especially the last two, gave the green light to a new massive drive on all fronts, beginning with agriculture.[13]

After the autumn harvest of 1957, the gigantic mobilization of peasants for an enormous water conservation assault was in full swing. The emphasis was on making use of peasant labor power during the slack season, on small rather than large projects, on storage rather than drainage of water, and on local instead of central financing and technical know-how.[14] Above all, what mattered—at

[12] *Ten Great Years* shows an increase of over 43 million *mou* in 1957.

[13] The National Program for Agricultural Development, a twelve year projection (or better, listing of desirable goals) was the subject of much controversy. Originally formulated at the end of 1955, it underwent no less than eight revisions before being approved, but only "in principle" by the Second Session of the Eighth National Party Congress in May 1958. The text of the revised program may be found in *National Program of Agricultural Development, 1956-1967* (Peking: FLP, 1960). See also "Twelve Year Plan for Agriculture," *Peking Review* (March 11, 1958), pp. 11-13. The Program called for the wiping out of illiteracy in five to seven years, control of the "Four Evils," within twelve years, the construction of a comprehensive network of local roads and radio stations in twelve years (the radio station construction program was revived in June 1969), and large scale planting of trees. Six million two-wheeled, double-shared plows were to be introduced in the countryside within three to five years as a first step toward agricultural mechanization. The plows, as we have seen earlier, were a failure. Not only were they unsuitable over much of the country and too heavy, but their mass production caused a shortage of steel. See Roderick MacFarquhar, "Communist China's Intra-Party Dispute," *Pacific Affairs*, December 1958, p. 325ff., and Parris H. Chang, *Patterns and Processes of Policy-Making in Communist China 1955-1962: Three Case Studies* (Unpublished Ph.D. dissertation, Columbia University, 1969). The latter examines in detail the troubles and tribulations of the National Program for Agricultural Development.

[14] On the economic rationale for the intensive use of unskilled labor, see below, pp. 335-340. After the establishment of people's communes late in 1958, stress was again put on the construction of large projects, including large reservoirs. This trend continued through 1959. In 1959 emphasis shifted from water

least in the campaign's early stages—was quantity: the more ponds, pools, and reservoirs to store water, the better. [15] The promoters of the Leap claimed that "an unprecedented advance has been made in agricultural capital construction since the advocates of the capitalist road were fundamentally defeated economically, politically, and ideologically."[16]

From October 1957 to the end of April 1958 about 100 million peasants supplemented by army personnel, office workers, teachers, students, and prisoners were thrown into the feverish task of transforming in the space of a few years the ageless face of China's countryside. [17] The irrigated area during this period was said by Liu to have increased by 350 million *mou*, or 23.31 million hectares (compared with slightly more than 43 million *mou* in the whole of 1957), or 80 million *mou* more than the total added during the eight years since the communist seizure of power, and 110 million *mou* more than the total acreage brought under irrigation in the thousands of years before October 1949. Liu also claimed in his Second Session (May 1958) report that simultaneously, more than 200 million *mou* (13.32 million hectares) of low lying and easily waterlogged farmland

---

storage facilities to canal building. Even before the Great Leap, small water conservation projects were, as a rule, financed and executed by the peasants themselves. During the Leap, however, the peasants were asked to do the same for medium-sized projects and to volunteer money, materials, and labor for large projects. For example, 75 percent of the man-days expended on the construction of the Ming Tombs reservoir were reportedly furnished by organized volunteers. *JPRS*, No. 3,446 (June 29, 1960), p. 3. Small-scale projects in Chinese Communist parlance refer to reservoirs of less than 1,000 cubic meters capacity; medium-sized projects are those of between 100,000 and 1,000,000 cubic meters capacity. Large reservoirs have a capacity of 100 million cubic meters and up.

[15] Quality began to be emphasized in 1959. The Minister of Water Conservation was supposed to supervise the planning and execution of each and every project, no matter how small. In practice, given the very large number of such projects in 1957-59, this proved impractical. Such central control over quality as there was, boiled down to the hope that local architects (i.e., the unskilled peasants) would be guided by a few sample projects designed by the center.

[16] "Resolution of the Central Committee of the Chinese Communist Party on the Establishment of People's Communes in Rural Areas," in *People's Communes in China* (Peking: *FLP*, 1958), p. 1.

[17] By the first week of February 1958, 1.3 million office workers "had begun a new life on the farms, in factories, or in local administrations." *Peking Review* (March 4, 1958), p. 4. The army allegedly contributed 15 million man-days in the first four months of 1958. In 1959, 77 million people were drafted for water conservancy work (of whom about 30 million were women). *NCNA* (April 9, 1960 and February 28, 1960). In 1960 the number of people engaged on water conservancy projects dropped to 70 million. *NCNA* (April 9, 1960). All this compares with a total of 20 million people engaged on this task between 1949 and 1952. *JPRS*, No. 350 (November 4, 1958), p. 2.

were transformed, and irrigation facilities were improved on another 140 million *mou* of land. [18]

Other data concerning the water conservation front during the Great Leap Forward, based on communist sources, are given in Table 8-1.[19]

Considerable doubt attaches to the statistical claims for the Great Leap years, especially for 1958. The figures are inflated, but they cannot be dismissed outright. In the course of 1958 and early 1959, the statisticians (like everyone else) succumbed to the headiness of the Great Leap and produced their own bigger and more economical results—certainly bigger; more economical by virtue of the fact that the statistical apparatus together with planning had all but broken down. There was little time or possibility to check the accuracy of the data, and there was even less political profit in it. After a while local cadres began feeding the central authorities with incredible figures, which shed more light on the cadres' inventive ingenuity than on the factual situation in the field. "If I should pick the big mistake from which grew many others," wrote Anna Louise Strong in 1963, "I would take those grain statistics of 1958 which had to be changed next year. . . . Peasants who had formerly measured by buckets with an eye to taxes were guessing in a new dimension without scales or measures, with no danger of increased taxation and with desire to make a record. . . . [They] 'estimated' [the] harvest and then went off and left part of it in the fields. The statistical office in Peking couldn't believe the figures so they cut them according to their best judgment. Later the higher authorities had to cut them again. The trouble with this was not that China 'lost face' by confused statistics. . . . The real trouble was that the Chinese believed their figures and acted on them for a year, at all levels."[20] The total mobilization

[18] The *Peking Review* (March 4, 1958), p. 4, claimed that in a matter of months, the peasants had "built enough water conservancy projects to put 165 million *mou* of land under irrigation." The total irrigated area in precommunist China was given by the same source as 240 million *mou*. According to the Communiqué on the Development of the National Economy in 1958, issued by the State Statistical Bureau on April 14, 1959 (*Peking Review*, April 21, 1959, p. 35), from October 1957 to September 1958 (irrigation year) the irrigated area was extended by 480 million *mou*. This involved moving 58,000,000 cubic meters of stone and earth.

[19] See also Li Chiang, "New Trend in Water Conservancy," *Peking Review* (June 10, 1958), pp. 11-12.

[20] Anna Louise Strong, *China's Fight for Grain* (Peking: FLP, 1963), p. 4. This problem is dealt with in the present Chapter, below, p. 302. Strong's discussion concerns grain output statistics, but the problem was more general. Cf. "At present the central authorities are compiling targets for the Second Five Year Plan, but have not been able to catch up with the swift changes in practical conditions that require upward revision of the targets almost every day." *T'sai-cheng* (Finance), No. 8 (August 5, 1958), cited by Choh-ming Li, "China's Industrial Development 1958-63," in Choh-ming Li (ed.), *Industrial Development in Communist China, op. cit.*, pp. 8-9.

TABLE 8-1
The Great Leap Forward in Water Conservation
(Official claims)

I. Number of New Irrigation Projects

Period	Large Reservoirs	Large Projects Drawing Water from Rivers	Small and Medium-Sized Projects (thousand)		
			All Types Other than Wells	Wells	Total
1949–52	0	230	1,000	668	2,000
1953–57	9	770	9,000	5,332	14,000
1958	16	1,800	8,000*	3,000	11,000
1959	31	1,200	1,000	1,000	2,000

II. Earthwork and Man-Days Spent in Water Conservation

Period	Earthwork (billions of cubic meters)	Man-Days (billions)
1949–52	1.7	1.7
1953–57	6.3	4.2
1958	58.3	29.2
1959	13.0	5.4
1960	27.0 (through April)	9.0

III. Increase in Irrigated Area Annually and Total Irrigated Area

Year	Claimed Increase (millions of hectares)	Total Area Claimed (millions of hectares)
1949	N.A.	16.0
1950	0.80	16.8
1951	1.86	18.6
1952	2.68	21.3
1953	1.20	22.5
1954	1.07	23.5
1955	1.48	25.0
1956	7.91	32.0
1957	2.87	34.6
1958	32.03	66.7
1959	4.67	71.3
1960†	9.00	80.3

IV. Extent of Improved Irrigated Area

Period	Improved Irrigated Area (millions of hectares)
1949–55	24.0
1956	4.8
1957	4.7
1958	14.0
1959	N.A.
1960 (through April)	19.3

Explanatory footnotes have been omitted. Data in II based on irrigation year ending September 30 of the year stated.

*Not considering medium-sized projects.

†NCNA, Hong Kong, February 21, 1960. Projection.

Source: Central Intelligence Agency, The Program for Water Conservancy in Communist China, 1949–61 (May 1962), Appendix A.

of manpower and the round-the-clock activity attested to by Chinese officialdom, refugees, and foreign visitors alike, must surely have produced impressive quantitative results, perhaps not as impressive as even the corrected published figures claim, but monumental all the same. While one can legitimately quibble over the physical amount of work actually accomplished, the quality of the work and its economic meaningfulness are subject to much less controversy. Insofar as the cost of alternatives foregone was concerned, the Leap was blind.

That much of the feverish effort was wasted can be gathered from the following.

(a) On June 3, 1959 T'an Chen-lin, a deputy premier, who at the Second Session of the Eighth National Party Congress ridiculed those who in the past had opposed reckless advance, wrote in the *People's Daily* that of the claimed 71.3 million hectares under irrigation in 1959, only 46.7 million hectares met the requirements stipulated in the revised National Program for Agricultural Development of withstanding a drought ranging from 30 to 70 days.[21]

(b) Chou En-lai reporting to the Standing Committee of the Second National People's Congress on August 16, 1959 stated that only 33.3 million hectares of farmland could be properly irrigated (as against the 1959 claim of 71.3 million hectares). Another 13.32 million hectares could benefit from irrigation if adequate leveling of fields and digging of ditches were carried out. This statement corroborated the one made by T'an Chen-lin, but introduced an additional qualification. T'an's 46.7 million hectares had to be reduced by the 13.32 million hectares of *potentially* irrigated land.[22]

(c) Apparently much of the reservoir construction work was destructive of the soil, the regular functioning of rivers, and of existing irrigation systems. The reason was that the upsurge in water conservation lacked adequate geological surveying, technical backup, and consistent planning. The hasty, uninformed, and haphazard building of dams, pools, ponds, reservoirs, and canals, the absence of forethought and integration resulted in alkalization of the soil over a wide area. In the rush to build reservoirs, the question of whether it was possible to fill them with water was often ignored. Hence a second rush (in 1959) to construct canals, many of which leaked. According to Hsu K'ai, a deputy to the 1960 National People's Congress, loss of water through leakages in drainage works was 40 to 60 percent, and more than 60 percent in a number of serious

---

[21] T'an Chen-lin was purged as a rightist capitalist-roader during the Cultural Revolution of 1966-69 (Chapter 11).

[22] Marion R. Larsen, "China's Agriculture Under Communism," in *An Economic Profile of Mainland China, op. cit.*, Vol. 1, p. 242.

cases. [23] An editorial in the *People's Daily* of November 23, 1961 noted that in north China "most of the water reservoirs completed only their main body without building channels, control gates, and ditches. This is not only useless in agricultural production but it has also raised the underground water level and turned much good soil into alkaline or swampy soil."[24]

The "natural" disasters which ravaged China from 1959 through 1961 may be attributed in large part to man-made mistakes, the mindlessness of the Great Leap effort at water conservation, and the propensity to equate raw peasant muscle with scientific and engineering expertise. While from 1949 to 1956 the area of China's farmland affected by flood and drought rarely exceeded 30 million acres in a single year, it reached 78 million acres in 1958, 108 million acres in 1959, and 150 million acres in 1960.[25]

It has been argued that "in years of normal weather conditions the new water projects have proved beneficial in regulating water flow and in extending the irrigated acreage." [26] In view of the poor quality of much of the work done during 1958-59, the incidental damage done to the soil, and the encroachment on farmland—see point (d) below—the assertion may be questioned. Assuming, however, that the argument is substantially correct, it still remains true that the major objective of the massive water conservation effort was to protect China from abnormal weather conditions, to win at one fell swoop and once and for all the age-long battle against the elements. From this standpoint the campaign was a failure. It could, in fact, be contended that the campaign made abnormality more abnormal by raising the underground water level in many parts of the country, alkalizing, salinizing, and waterlogging the soil, and upsetting the existing pattern of irrigation. The construction of millions of small reservoirs tended to lower the potential of large and medium-sized projects and even halt the flow of numerous streams and rivers. [27] In many instances basic irrigation projects were completed, while the necessary system of irrigation channels was left unfinished or was not begun at all. There were cases where irrigation channels were completed without provision for drainage. Dry paddy fields were transformed into water fields, and the volume of water flowing

[23] *Jen-min Jih-pao* (April 10, 1960), p. 14.
[24] Cited by Cheng Chu-yuan, *Communist China's Economy, 1949-1962, op. cit.*, p. 143.
[25] Cheng Chu-yuan, *loc. cit.*, p. 143. See also E. S. Kirby, "Bad Weather or Bad System? The Agricultural Crisis in Mainland China," *Current Scene* (June 29, 1961), pp. 1-8.
[26] Marion R. Larsen, *loc. cit.*, p. 242.
[27] *JPRS*, No. 854D (August 1, 1959), p. 75, and No. 922D (September 18, 1959), p. 16. *NCNA* (June 7, 1960).

into the rivers was decreased.[28] The northeastern provinces were hit
hardest by the drought of 1959-61. Yet it was precisely there that
the Great Leap irrigation effort had been the most strenuous and
widespread. Professor Cheng Chu-yuan has shown that there exists a
positive correlation between the claimed expansion of irrigation and
conservation of water and soil in China during the Great Leap and
areas suffering from flood and drought during 1959-60.[29]

The total area affected by drought and flood in 1959 was, according to the New China News Agency, 43.4 million hectares or 107.24
million acres (of which 33.3 million hectares suffered from drought).
Of the 43.3 million hectares, 26.6 million hectares were said to have
been seriously damaged.[30] By early August 1959, 82 percent of the
small and medium-sized reservoirs in Hupeh Province had dried up.[31]
In Kiangsu Province half the reservoirs dried up. Similar reports came
in from other parts of the country. Of 4.3 million hectares of farmland
in Hupeh, no less than 3.6 million were reportedly affected by
drought.[32] The drought spread to twenty provinces and autonomous
regions.[33] An "antidrought army" composed of men, women, children, students, soldiers, disabled veterans, the blind, and the ailing
was quickly organized. Water was carried in buckets to irrigate the
fields and urine was liberally dispensed to irrigate some rice fields.[34]
By mid-1959 it became fairly clear that the majority of small and
medium-sized reservoirs thrown together in 1958 and 1959 were
unable to supply water to the parched fields. On the other hand,
severe floods occurred in Kwangtung in June-July 1959. The
calamity continued into 1960. Spring and summer droughts affected
some 40 million hectares of land. In Hopei, Honan, Shantung, and
Shansi over 60 percent of cultivated land suffered from drought
lasting six to seven months. At the peak of the disaster, eight of the
twelve major rivers in Shantung Province dried up. Three provinces
(Kwangtung, Fukien, and Liaoning) were hit by typhoons and
floods. As a consequence of the floods and drought, vast areas of
farmland became infested with insects. "In old times," wrote the
Peking Review before the disaster hit, "the Chinese peasants were at
the mercy of nature's whims. Now . . . they are telling one another

[28] Kung Mien-jen, "Natural Calamities on the Chinese Mainland in 1960," in
Communist China 1960 (Hong Kong: URI, 1962), Vol. I, p. 50. Cf. Robert
Carin, *River Control in Communist China* and his *Irrigation Scheme in Com-
munist China* (Hong Kong: URI, 1962, 1963).

[29] Cheng Chu-yuan, *op. cit.*, p. 144, Tables XXXIV and XXXV.

[30] *NCNA* (January 22, 1960; December 22, 1959).

[31] *NCNA* (November 22, 1959).

[32] *Jen-min Jih-pao* (September 9, 1959). *NCNA* (November 22, 1959).

[33] *Jen-min-Jih-pao* (December 23, 1959).

[34] *NCNA* (January 10, 1960).

that the days when 'man proposes and God disposes' are definitely coming to an end."[35]

(d) The construction of ponds, reservoirs, and canals took out of cultivation a significant amount of farmland. Had this shrinkage been compensated for by an important expansion of irrigated land, the problem would not be worth mentioning. Apparently it was not so. In the plains of Honan, the Great Leap irrigation facilities reduced the cultivated area from 80 hectares per square kilometer to 53-67 hectares per square kilometer. [36] Thus much of the Great Leap effort in water conservation was probably nil or negative. By 1967 grain output was perhaps only about 2 million metric tons above the 1957 figure of 185 million metric tons with, presumably, a significantly higher labor input.

It is interesting to note that in 1958 the cultivated and sown areas were below the 1957 level. [37] The cultivated area was the smallest since 1951 and the sown area since 1955. A further reduction in area sown to food crops apparently took place in 1959. The phenomenon may be explained in various ways, including the one just given. It is possible, for example, that the peasants distracted by water conservation work and the industrial effort demanded of them (see below) were unable to devote their attention to farm work proper. Another explanation may be found in the leadership's confidence about the grain output and yield situation, a self-assurance abetted by faulty information from the production front. In December 1958 the Central Committee, elated by reports of phenomenal production successes, proposed a "Three-Three System of Cultivation." "In a number of years to come, local conditions permitting, we should try to reduce the area sown to crops each year, say, to about one-third of what it is at present. Part of the land so saved can lie fallow by rotation or be used for pasturage and the growing of green manure; the rest can be used for afforestation, reservoirs, and the extensive cultivation of flowers, shrubs, and trees to turn our whole land with its plains, hills, and waters into a garden."[38]

The scheme was quietly dropped in the summer of 1959. It is,

[35] *Peking Review* (March 4, 1958).

[36] *JPRS*, No. 845D (August 1, 1959).

[37] The cultivated area in 1957 was 1,677,450 thousand *mou*. It dropped to 1,616,800 thousand *mou* in 1958. The sown area in 1957 was 2,358,660 thousand *mou*, and 2,344,020 thousand *mou* in 1958.

[38] "Resolution on Some Questions Concerning the People's Communes" (Adopted by the Eighth Central Committee of the Communist Party of China at its Sixth Plenary Session on December 10, 1958) in *Sixth Plenary Session of the Central Committee of the Communist Party of China* (Peking: FLP, 1958), p. 28. Cf. these arguments with the reasons for the reduction in the sown area in 1957 as compared with 1956, below, p. 335.

TABLE 8-2

Great Leap in Water Conservation (Fluctuations in Official Claims and Targets)

Increase in Irrigated Area

Source of Claim and Date	Period Covered	Area (millions of hectares)
Liu Shao-ch'i, *Report* to the 2nd Session, 8th National Party Congress (May 5, 1958)	October 1957– end April 1958	23.31
State Statistical Bureau, *Economic and Cultural Statistics on Communist China* (Sept. 1, 1959) p. 121	1958	32.03
NCNA, Apr. 6, 1960	1959	4.67
NCNA (Hong Kong), Feb. 21, 1960, projection	1960	9.00
9th Plenary Session, 8th Central Committee, *Communiqué* (Jan. 20, 1960): "effectively irrigated."	1958-60	20.00

Planned Increase in Irrigated Area

Source of Projection and Date	Plan Period	Area (millions of hectares)
People's China (Dec. 16, 1957)	Second Five Year Plan 1958–62	13.4
NCNA, Feb. 4, 1958	1958–62	33.3
NCNA, Aug. 28, 1957 (original plan for 1958)	1958	2.3
Peking Radio, Feb. 6, 1958	1958	6.0
Po I-po, *Peking Review*, March 4, 1958, p. 4	1958	17.7
NCNA, Oct. 13, 1958 (original plan for 1959)	1959	33.3
NCNA (Hong Kong) May 26, 1959	1959	6.5

however, reasonable to suppose that it had some connection with the reduction of sown area in 1958 and 1959.[39] In June 1959 the *People's Daily* published an editorial reversing the drive and calling for a policy of "planting more and reaping more."[40] The new drive

[39] See Kung Mien-jen, *op. cit.*, pp. 49-50.

[40] In 1960 Li Fu-chun said that "the fundamental solution for China's agriculture in the future lies in actively promoting its technical transformation, so as both to continuously extend the area of land cultivated by each unit of labor power and steadily to raise the yield per *mou*." Li Fu-chun, *Raise High the Red Flag*, p. 20.

was pushed vigorously until the end of 1960 under the "Ten Sides" slogan. This urged the masses to cultivate land on the sides of rice fields, slopes, roads, streams, rivers, hills, ponds, houses, aqueducts, and reservoirs.

The fluctuations in official claims regarding the results of and plans for the water conservation drive are summarized in Table 8-2.

The campaign for water conservation was paralleled by a drive for afforestation. During the First Five Year Plan (1953-57) a total of 169.35 million *mou* of land was reportedly afforested. In 1958 the target was 300 million *mou*. In the first quarter of that year, 221.74 million *mou* were said to have been planted with trees. Encouraged by this, one may presume, statistical success, the promoters of the Leap decided that in the following ten years China's forest area was to be doubled, i.e., from 10 percent to 20 percent of the country's surface.[41]

DRIVE FOR TOOL IMPROVEMENT

" 'Every rural township with its inventions, every cooperative with its improvements.' This is the current slogan; in many places it has become a fact."[42]

For all its proclaimed intention to technologically "walk on two legs," the Great Leap Forward in agriculture relied primarily on the intensive use of labor in close planting, deep plowing, the application of natural fertilizer, construction of simple irrigation facilities, and technological improvement.[43] The technological base remained traditional, but it was exploited more intensively, with local materials and financing, and in the last analysis, with more waste motion than before. Technological innovation was to spring from the practical experience and the inventive genius of the masses rather than from laboratories, academies, universities, and other centers of research and learning. "By breaking through the bonds of superstition and the veil of 'mystery' surrounding science and technology, the people's wisdom and skill will be unleashed in inexhaustible profusion."[44]

[41] Hu Ku-yueh, "Turning the Whole Country Green," *Peking Review* (April 22, 1958), pp. 14-16.

[42] Yang Min, "Revolution in Farm Tools," *Peking Review* (May 13, 1958), pp. 10-12. Cf. Yang Min, "New Farm Implements," *ibid.* (May 27, 1958), pp. 10-12; Hsu Lu, "A Boost to Rural Electrification," *ibid.* (May 27, 1958), p. 15; Yang Min, "Peasant Inventions for Irrigation," *ibid.* (June 10, 1958), pp. 13-14.

[43] 957 tractors and 545 combine harvesters were produced in 1958. China's first big tractor plant at Loyang (Honan Province) went into full production in November 1959.

[44] Hsu Lu, "The People Invent," *Peking Review* (June 3, 1958), p. 15. "Bourgeois science," wrote *Hung-ch'i* in March 1958, was "a pile of garbage."

The process of mass invention and innovation was to be accompanied by a vast emulation drive in which the backward were to learn from, catch up with, and outdistance the advanced. As has been pointed out before, the mass line was infused with an anti-intellectual sentiment, a distrust and fear of the pure expert whose fervor was interpreted by those in power as ideological immaturity verging on subversion. After April 1959 mass farm research institutes were set up in special districts and counties.

The campaign for improved tools was launched at the end of 1957.[45] The sort of improvement involved in the drive consisted, for example, in the substitution of carts for shoulder poles and baskets, or the introduction of foot-pedaled earth pounders and brick and earthenware gas generators.[46] "Two lads—one fourteen years old and the other only twelve—are in the spotlight as inventors of farm tools. The fourteen-year-old, Chang Yu-fu of Kansu Province, has invented three ingenious tools in rapid succession, although he has had no more than a primary school education. The twelve-year-old, Chang Kou-tiu, is the son of a peasant family in a farm co-op in Honan Province. The new type water wheel he invented has attracted attention far and wide. The publicity given to the inventions has made others feel that what is known as science is not that mysterious after all."[47]

"The greatest achievement of the Great Leap," wrote Anna Louise Strong, an expatriate American in the service of Peking, had been "that it awoke to life a new type of peasant, conscious of his power to bend nature to his will." "The process," she added, "proved more complex than at first [had been] thought. . . . Everyone you ask will say: 'The greatest thing we learned was the power that lies in the Chinese people. We also learned the need for clearer plans.' "[48] "Many difficulties, of course, arose in the course of the movement, but they were overcome one after another," wrote another observer. "The peasants, for instance, had no technical knowledge."[49] It was precisely those peasants with no technical knowledge

---

[45] It was probably discussed at the Third Plenary Session of the Party's Eighth Central Committee (Autumn 1957) and at the Nanning and Chengtu Conferences (early Spring 1958). It was elaborated on in the Chengtu Conference's "Opinions Concerning the Problem of Agricultural Mechanization" (March 1958) and the "Party's Internal Bulletin" (April 1959).

[46] "Science No Mystery," *Peking Review* (June 3, 1958), p. 4.

[47] Hsu Lun, "The People Invent," *Peking Review* (June 3, 1958), p. 15. Cf. Li Ching-yu, "From Better Tools to Modern Farming," *ibid.* (March 10, 1959), pp. 12-13. Peasant scientific research organizations often bore colorful names such as the "Hundred Flowers Youth Team," "Five Old Shepherds," "Ten Lady Researchers," *Peking Review* (January 13, 1961), p. 4.

[48] Anna Louise Strong, *China's Fight for Grain, op. cit.,* pp. 12-13.

[49] Sun Li, "Building a New World," in *China's Big Leap in Water Conservancy, op. cit.,* p. 4.

and without clear plans who were expected to "bring about an up-surge in the technical and cultural revolutions . . . unfolding in China."[50]

The campaign for tool improvement based on mass research was soon declared an unprecedented smash. The proof, it was said, lay in labor efficiency improvements, many examples of which were cited, in the rise of yields per hectare, in the record time within which the various projects were completed, and in the number of inventions.

As regards labor efficiency, the figures in Table 8-3 are of interest.

Together with allegedly better methods of cultivation (deep plowing, soil improvement, close planting, field management) the campaign for tool improvement was credited with raising yields per hectare, as shown in Table 8-4.[51]

Since, as has been noted earlier, the entire agricultural output series relating to the Great Leap years is subject to legitimate doubt,

[50] Hsu Lun, *op. cit.*, p. 15.

[51] A few more examples of tool improvement and improvements in methods of cultivation: "Chang-ho, formerly a poor peasant in Sanho County, took off the rear wheel of his much treasured bicycle and used it in the construction of a big barrow." *China's Big Leap in Water Conservancy, op. cit.*, p. 114. "Chu Yung-chen, who had been a swineherd for a landlord since his childhood, hit upon a new idea and made himself a giant-sized cart with an old motor wheel he bought himself. He could transport a cartload of nearly 1,000 catties of earth over a three-*li* distance 24 times a day." *Ibid.*, p. 115. "Ho-lu, of the young men's shock brigade from Chihsien . . . [together with six others, bought] some wooden boards and nails . . . to renovate their carts and rigged up a movable board in the front part so as to load more earth. Inspired by the selfless spirit . . . all the peasants from his county launched a drive for reforming their tools." *Ibid.* A "young scientist . . . Wang Pao-ching, 27 years old, chairman of the Beacon Farming Co-op in Shensi . . . saw that an improved strain of wheat, Pima No. 1, could yield 20 percent more than ordinary varieties. He wanted to know how it could be more widely produced. Told that it was obtained by special hybridization, which had to be done by experts and which common peasants could not learn, he refused to accept this limitation. He was confirmed in his ideas when he found later that the initial experiments in the Northwest Agricultural College were actually carried out by peasants guided by academic people. Now he has not only learned how to conduct sexual and vegetative hybridization, but helped 25 other members of his co-op to learn. By collective effort they have produced eight new high-yielding strains of wheat, maize, and cotton suitable for local conditions. His co-op today is experimenting with no less than 112 strains of wheat, and Wang has become a research associate of the Shensi Provincial Institute of Agricultural Science." Hsu Lun, "The People Invent," *Peking Review* (June 3, 1958), p. 15. Tool improvement (*kung*) was part of Mao Tse-tung's "Eight Character Charter for Agriculture," a condensed version of the National Program of Agricultural Development. The eight characters were *shui* (water conservation), *fei* (fertilization), *t'u* (soil conservation), *chung* (seed selection), *mi* (close planting), *pao* (plant protection), *kung* (tool improvement), and *kuan* (field management). See Wu Yi-cheng, "Eight Measures for Higher Yields," *Peking Review* (June 23, 1959), pp. 11-13. In 1958, over 800 million *mou* were allegedly plowed to a depth of 33 centimeters and 1.7 billion *mou* of farm crops used improved strains. *Ibid.*, pp. 11-13.

TABLE 8-3
Labor Efficiency in Water Conservation: Official Claims*

Period	Work Efficiency per Man-Day (cubic meters per man per day)
1949-52	1.0
1953-57†	1.5
1958	2.0
1959	2.4
1960‡	3.0

*Based on the irrigation year ending September 30 of the year stated.
†Estimated.
‡Claim as of December 1959.

Source: Central Intelligence Agency, The Program for Water Conservancy in Communist China, 1949-61 (May 1962).

TABLE 8-4
Per Mou Yields of Grain Crops and Cotton: Official Claims
(Catties)

Year	Grain Crops (including potatoes)*	Cotton
1949	142	22
1952	183	31
1957	204	38
1958	275	49

*Potatoes are converted into grain equivalent at the ratio of four catties to one.

Source: Ten Great Years, p. 121. The per mou yield is calculated on the basis of sown areas.

the per hectare yield figures must be taken with extreme caution and skepticism.[52]

The speed with which work was performed thanks to the wave of peasant innovations was cited as one great achievement of research by the untutored but inventive masses. "A reservoir with a capacity of 250,000 cubic meters was built in a matter of a few days. Under the guidance of some male members, 400 women members of four cooperatives of Hsinglungchuang built the 'Women's Reservoir' in three days. It can irrigate more than 300 mou of land. The 'Red Scarf Reservoir' was built by 780 teachers and students in one day. It can irrigate more than 200 mou of land."[53] It is possible that the

[52] Early rice yields in Anhwei in 1958 were said to have reached 83.28 tons per hectare. In Honan, winter wheat yields that year were put at 54.9 tons per hectare.
[53] China's Big Leap in Water Conservancy, op. cit., p. 4.

jobs were, in fact, completed within the time limits stated. Whether the reservoirs could irrigate the areas cited to the full or at all, is questionable. That the rapid construction may have been of poor quality while causing damage to the soil and existing irrigation systems, was not mentioned. In Honan and elsewhere, many water conservancy projects were built with "native cement"—a mixture of lime and clay—invented by the masses as a substitute for cement.[54] The effectiveness and durability of the invention have not been discussed.

The number of improvements, innovations, and inventions which the masses came up with was said to have been staggering. For example, between 1949 and 1957, more than 2.5 million new-type steel plows and disc harrows had been introduced on 13.3 percent of the cultivated area. Between October 1957 and April 1958, in thirteen provinces alone, 6.9 million new or improved farm tools were put into use; by the end of 1959 the total number of these in the country as a whole was said to have risen by 520 million units.[55] While in 1957 Chinese industry produced 265 thousand horsepower of diesel, gasoline, and wind-operated engines for drainage and pumping, in 1958, the peasants and industry were said to have produced 1.8 million horsepower of these instruments, and the plan for 1960 was 2.5 million horsepower. In 1958 alone, 40,000 farm tool plants and workshops were set up.[56]

When the mass line in the advancement of science and technology was rejected in 1961-62, Liu Hsien-chou, first Deputy President of Tsinghua University, summed up the Great Leap experience in a gentle understatement: "When the mass line was implemented, there was evidence of oversimplification."[57]

To try and raise agricultural (as well as industrial) output and productivity through small improvements in traditional tools and methods of production and through appeal to the latent talents of workers and peasants is not in itself erroneous in capital-deficient underdeveloped countries. The Great Leap, however, distorted the idea by making it compulsory, claiming too much for it, and introducing into it an element of haste. Instead of subjecting each improvement or innovation to expert scrutiny and trying it out in pilot projects, the rule was to popularize it immediately on a vast scale, irrespective of its possible side effects or purely local applicability

---

[54] *Peking Review* (May 6, 1958), p. 5.
[55] Li Fu-chun, *Raise High the Red Flag of the General Line and Continue to March Forward* (Peking: FLP, 1960), p. 7.
[56] Wu Yi-cheng, "Eight Measures for Higher Yields," *op. cit.*, p. 13.
[57] Cited by Cheng Chu-yuan in: *Scientific and Engineering Manpower in Communist China, 1949-1963, op. cit.*, p. 33. Compare this with Chen Feng-tung, "The Great Victory of the Party's Mass Line on the Agricultural Scientific Front," *Jen-min Jih-pao* (April 11, 1960), in *JPRS* 2908 (August 1960).

and relevance. The test of whether any given improvement scheme was worthwhile or not was quite simply its class character: so long as it was thought up by the masses, it was all right and worthy of instant emulation. Class politics was in complete command of economics, physics, engineering, and all other branches of knowledge.[58]

It should be added that the mass campaign for popular innovations was not limited to agriculture but spread through industry, the crafts, commerce, and China's technical-scientific community and educational system. In 1958, for instance, Chinese doctors made a solemn pledge to Mao Tse-tung to conquer cancer in three years.[59] In response to the center's "Directive Concerning Educational Reform," issued in 1958 and calling for a great leap forward in education, local authorities introduced a wide variety of school systems which claimed to turn out greater numbers of graduates with greater speed and economy.[60] For example, a primary school in Liaoning Province reported that a mathematics course which used to take six months was, under the new dispensation, completed in four weeks.[61] After Vice-Premier Chen Yi's call for a "cultural atomic blast" to obliterate illiteracy in China in five to seven years, 60 million people were thrown into a campaign against *wen-mang* (letter blindness).[62] Within a few weeks, Heilungkiang Province reported that it had wiped out letter blindness and was launching a mass campaign to "Read a Hundred Books and Write Ten Thousand Characters."[63] According to Yang Hsiu-feng, the Minister of Education, in 1958 alone, 100 million adults became literate. Between January and April 1960, another 30 million adults were taught to read.[64] The movement to expand spare-time education resulted in the establishment of numerous labor academies in which theoretical studies were combined with work at the lathe or in the fields. Some of these spare-time educational establishments were run by factories and communes.[65]

---

[58] "Only 23 this year, Hsu Jung-ching was a cowherd in 1956, but today he regularly lectures at the Nanking Chemical Engineering Institute. His first lecture was on the assessment of free calcium oxide and problems related to the formation of asbestos and cement. It is a big leap from cows to chemicals, but in this society this is neither unexpected nor extraordinary." *Peking Review* (July 19, 1960), p. 30.

[59] Mikhail A. Klochko, *Soviet Scientist in Red China, op. cit.*, p. 108.

[60] Cf. the discussion of education during the Great Leap, below, Chapter 10.

[61] I Wo-sheng "Education in Communist China in 1960," in *Communist China 1960, op. cit.*, Vol. I, p. 62. Cf. *Communist China 1958, Communist China 1949-1959*, 3 vols., *Communist China 1961* (Hong Kong: URI)

[62] *Peking Review* (March 11, 1958), p. 5.

[63] *Peking Review* (May 6, 1958), p. 5.

[64] *NCNA* (August 3, 1960).

[65] "Spare-Time Studies," *FEER* (September 17, 1964), pp. 505-506. Cf. Chapters 10 and 12 below.

DRIVE TO BUILD LOCAL, SMALL-SCALE, LABOR-INTENSIVE INDUSTRIES

"In the period of the First Five Year Plan," reported Liu Shao-ch'i to the May 1958 Second Session of the Party's Eighth National Congress, "we paid attention first of all to the development of industries run by the Central Government, to giant enterprises; this was absolutely necessary. But not enough attention was paid to the development of local industries and small and medium-sized industries; this was a shortcoming . . . [which] must be remedied. . . . In quite a short space of time, industrial plants will dot every part of the country like stars in the sky provided the twenty-odd provinces, municipalities under the central authority and autonomous regions, over 180 special administrative regions and autonomous *chou*, over 2,000 counties and autonomous counties, over 80,000 towns and townships, over 100,000 handicrafts cooperatives, and over 700,000 agricultural cooperatives in the country display full initiative in a proper way in developing industry. In that case, industrial development in our country will naturally be much faster than if it depended solely on a number of big enterprises run by the Central Government."[66]

The vision of industries dotting the countryside like stars in the sky was, however, qualified in the next paragraph. "A big development of local industries, and of small and medium-sized enterprises, will give rise to many new problems which it is difficult for us to foresee at the moment. But here it must be especially emphasized that this growth of local industries and small and medium-sized enterprises which we encourage must be placed under centralized leadership and overall planning, with a proper division of labor and coordination of efforts; there must be no blind development, nor development through free competition."[67] The arguments advanced in favor of the creation of local labor-intensive industries were (a) that these industries would produce a wide range of small commodities for local consumption, thus making many areas self-suffi-

---

[66] *Second Session, op. cit.*, p. 50. Is one being oversensitive in detecting a note of irony in this enumeration of large numbers?

[67] *Ibid.*, p. 50. Since there was no question of "free competition" in a market sense, this could only refer to "mass socialist emulation." " 'Emulate, learn from, and overtake the advanced!'—this is a resonant slogan inspiring 600 million people in their march toward socialism. An emulation drive has been launched among individuals, factories, cooperatives, localities, and other units. Emulate whoever is advanced—this is the rule of the day. Not a single individual, unit or locality is left out of the upsurge in socialist construction. . . . Such an emulation drive knows no end. In this way, the revolutionary cause of the Chinese people will develop by leaps and bounds." Niu Chung-huang, *China Will Overtake Britain* (Peking: *FLP*, 1958), pp. 63-64.

cient in at least some consumer goods, (b) that they would put to use China's plentiful labor and save on scarce capital, and (c) that they would relieve pressure on the transportation system.

The signal once given, the warnings were quickly forgotten. Soon a mass movement was on foot to build local, small-scale, and medium-sized "industries" everywhere at the same time, using what materials were on hand and applying more labor where equipment was lacking.[68] Many of the new industries were primitive clay and brick structures hastily thrown together. Their raw materials consisted quite frequently of scrap iron, ore, coal, pots and pans, and other household utensils "voluntarily contributed by the masses" or otherwise secured locally. Reports from Chinese cities at that time indicated that iron and steel utensils and fixtures had almost entirely disappeared from every household. They were fed into the hundreds of thousands of backyard furnaces which mushroomed in the countryside and in the towns as if by magic, engaging the labor of some 60 million people.[69] In one area of Shansi, 30,000 blast furnaces were put up within a few months, that is, roughly one to every five hundred inhabitants.[70] One report put the number of locally built furnaces at 30,000 in July 1958 and over 170,000 in August.[71] "In August 1958, iron smelting furnaces employing indigenous methods began to spread like a prairie fire throughout the country. . . . They were followed two months later by numerous home-made steel mak-

[68] Some of the reported numerical increase in local industries during the Great Leap was due to the operation of workshops in individual factories as independent "micro factories," the merging of handicraft producer cooperatives with local or state-private enterprises, or with subsidiary employment groups in collective farms, and the transformation of service trades into "service factories." By 1958, according to Hsueh Mu-chiao et al., (op. cit., p. 157), 37 percent of the handicraftsmen worked in workshops "owned by the whole people," and 28 percent retained their collective ownership as cooperative factories or handicraft cooperatives in cities. The remaining 35 percent were handicraft cooperatives in rural areas which were under the direction of the people's communes. By May 1959, 13.3 percent of the more than five million handicraft cooperative members of 1956 were reportedly in cooperatives of the old type (mainly handicraft producers' cooperatives); 13.6 percent were in amalgamated units called handicraft cooperative factories; 37.8 percent were in locally controlled industry, and 35.3 percent in commune factories. Audrey Donnithorne, China's Economic System, op. cit., p. 224. The product mix of these newly constituted units changed in favor of producer goods.

[69] FEER (November 20, 1958), p. 648. Miss Donnithorne (China's Economic System, op. cit., p. 225) calls attention to the disappearance of a multitude of small trades and services as a by-product of the small industry drive. This added to China's already striking drabness.

[70] NCNA (November 26, 1958). Four years later there was not a single furnace in this area. Peasants had to go to nearby towns to have their tools made. Audrey Donnithorne, op. cit., p. 225.

[71] FEER (September 18, 1958), p. 360. In August 1959 Chou En-lai gave the capacity of small blast furnaces as between 6.5 and 100 cubic meters each.

ing furnaces to turn the iron produced into steel." By June 1959 it was planned to have small and medium-sized blast furnaces produce 20 million tons of pig iron per year.[72] In fact, in August 1959, Chou En-lai reported that these furnaces were able to produce 10 million tons of pig iron that year, of which 4 to 5 million tons "were not suitable for steel making, but good for the manufacture of simple farm implements and tools."[73] It is possible that the product was too brittle even for that.

The slogan which inspired the movement was launched by the Politbureau in August 1958: "Taking steel production as the core and achieving a comprehensive leap forward." It echoed an earlier Central Committee call to overtake Britain within fifteen years "or in less time" in the production of iron, steel, and other major industrial products. "The Soviet Union has outlined its program to surpass the United States within fifteen years in major industrial and agricultural products. China, likewise, has mapped out its plan to surpass Britain within fifteen years in the output of iron and other main industrial products."[74] Steel output was said to have risen from 5.35 million tons in 1957 to 11.08 million tons in 1958, of which 3.08 million tons consisted of "native" steel. Even in 1964, China's per capita steel production was about 2.5 percent of the British level. 1959 output was said to have been 13.35 million tons (later scaled down to 8.63 million tons), rising to 18.45 million tons in 1960. The 2.65 million tons increase in industrially usable steel (1957-58) was mainly due to the expansion of the large steel works at Anshan and Shanghai and the putting into production of new blast and open hearth furnaces at Wuhan and Paotow (Inner Mongolia).[75]

Already in June 1958 it was confidently predicted by Chang Lin-chih, Minister of the Coal Industry, that in 1959 rather than in 1972 China would overtake Britain in coal production. By early 1959 it was announced that this particular race had been won. "Millions of people with picks, shovels, and any digging equipment available, went to the mountains to dig coal. In three months the number

[72] *Peking Review* (June 17, 1958), p. 4. Cf. Daniel Wolfstone, "China's Steel Story," *FEER* (January 8, 1959), p. 49.
[73] Chou En-lai, *Report on Adjusting the Major Targets of the 1959 National Economic Plan and Further Developing the Campaign for Increasing Production and Practising Economy*, delivered at the Fifth Meeting of the Standing Committee of the Second National People's Congress on August 26, 1959 (Peking: FLP, 1959), pp. 5-6.
[74] Niu Chung-huang, *China Will Overtake Britain* (Peking: FLP, 1958), p. 5. This particular imitation of the Soviet catching-up drive probably resulted from the November 1957 meeting between Khrushchev and Mao Tse-tung in Moscow.
[75] See Cheng Chu-yuan, *Anshan Steel Factory in Communist China* (Hong Kong: URI, 1955)

of small coal pits jumped from 20,000 to over 100,000 and their monthly output soared from 2 million tons in September to 40 million tons in October."[76] In most of these mines coal was lifted by hand from the pit bottom. Total coal output was said to have jumped from 130 million tons in 1957 to 270.3 million tons in 1958, an increase of 108 percent.

Refuting the moderates' contention that bigger and faster was incompatible with better and more economical, Chou En-lai argued that "the cost of building large blast furnaces formerly averaged 25,000 yuan per cubic meter of furnace volume. Now it averaged only 14,000 to 18,000 yuan, a drop of 28 to 44 percent. The cost of constructing big coal mines formerly averaged 33 yuan per ton of production capacity. Now it averages only 22-yuan, a drop of 33 percent."[77] That, of course, was missing the moderates' point. As it transpired later, an important portion of the coal and steel output produced by indigenous methods in locally designed enterprises was unusable.[78] By late 1959, the prairie fire was being hastily extinguished, or as the Party put it, "raised to a new stage." By then the major virtue of the campaign was said to have been that it had "served to 'temper people': it has enabled the masses to acquire technical skill and knowledge and large number of cadres to gain experience."[79] It could, however, be argued that more than that, the iron and steel campaign, and the coal campaign too, had disrupted the pattern of local skills (artisans were diverted from their trades and made to produce iron, steel, and coal), that it had been a huge waste of labor and raw materials, and that the little teaching it did do, was in old-fashioned and often quite obsolete techniques.

As with coal and steel, so also with electricity. When in August

[76] Ting Shu-yi, "China Ahead of Britain in Coal," *Peking Review* (January 13, 1959), p. 16.

[77] Chou En-lai, *A Great Decade* (Peking: FLP, 1959), p. 31. "Some people hold that during last year's mass campaign to make iron and steel, much manpower was used, much money was spent, and part of the total products was made by indigenous methods. As a result, it was 'more loss than gain' or at most 'loss and gain was a 50-50 affair.' We consider this view utterly wrong." Chou En-lai, *Report on Adjusting . . .*, op. cit., p. 5. See also "Coal Mines," *China News Analysis*, No. 266, (February 27, 1959), pp. 1-7.

[78] Mikhail A. Klochko, a Soviet scientist who spent two tours of duty in China, including one during the Great Leap, argues that coal extracted from small local mines could perhaps be used in kitchen stoves. He estimates that of the 4 million tons of iron processed by indigenous methods, hardly more than 1 percent was usable, the rest being slag, unwashed ore, or a pure invention of the statisticians. *Soviet Scientist in Red China*, op. cit., p. 81. In 1961 the *Peking Review* (October 27, p. 4) admitted that small coal mines were subject to flooding in the rainy season.

[79] Chou En-lai, *Reporting on Adjusting . . .*, op. cit., p. 7.

1958 a power shortage arose in Lushun-Talien, a mass campaign was launched to remedy the situation. "Factories, mines, shops, government offices, schools, and nurseries—even housewives, cooks, and barbers—all began to produce electricity for their own use. By means of ingenious popular inventions, more than twenty new ways of getting electricity from various sources have been found. 'Homemade' devices got power from water, wind, methane gas, coal gas, steam and oil. In three months thousands of small power generating units with a total capacity of 130,000 kw arose, using old lorry, tank, and aeroplane engines, repaired steam engines, and improvised turbines. . . . In the single county of Yung-chun (Fukien Province), over 1,000 small hydroelectric power and hydraulic stations have been set up."[80] While in 1957 China's output of turbines was (in capacity terms of) 216,000 kw, in 1958 this was said to have risen to 600,000 kw, and 740,000 kw in 1959. Electric power output which in 1957 was 19,340 million kwh, apparently jumped to 27,530 million kwh in 1958 and was to soar to 39,000 million kw in 1959.[81]

The same happened in the production of chemical fertilizers. Thousands of do-it-yourself fertilizer plants sprang up overnight, while millions of people dug manure and made fertilizer all over the country. In response to a Central Committee and State Council Directive of January 28, 1959, four million people in Anhwei Province took part in the movement to collect manure, one million in Yunnan, three million in Fukien, one million (or one-fourth of the rural labor force) in Heilungkiang.[82] Over 10 billion tons of farmyard and natural manure were collected in 1958.[83] The quality of chemical fertilizer produced by small plants with indigenous methods was, no doubt, inferior. The quantitative overall performance was—if it can be believed—impressive. From a total of 871,000 metric tons

[80] Liang Kuang, "Electric Power Shoots Ahead," *Peking Review* (January 20, 1959), p. 10. See also Lin Tien, "Road to Rural Electrification," *ibid.* (September 6, 1960), pp. 14-16.

[81] Chou En-lai, *A Great Decade, op. cit.*, p. 3; *Ten Great Years*, p. 95. It will be recalled that the 1956 *Proposals* target for 1962 was 40,000-43,000 million kwh (Table 7-1 above).

[82] "Warming Up for a New Leap," *Peking Review* (March 3, 1959), pp. 14-15. Cf. Wang Jun-tung, "China's Expanding Chemical Industry," *ibid.* (March 3, 1959), pp. 10-11, and Ku Wei-lin, "Small Plants Boost Chemical Output," *ibid.* (February 3, 1961), pp. 15-17. The *Peking Review* of June 23, 1959 (p. 12) spoke of "huge numbers of workshops to produce fertilizer by indigenous methods" as having been set up. Their total output, according to the same source, "ran to tens of millions of tons." Cf. *NCNA* news releases of November 18, 1959, December 20, 1959, July 9, 1960, September 24, 1960, in *SCMP* Nos. 2142 (1959), 2164 (1959), 2296 (1960) and 2349 (1960).

[83] *Contemporary China* (Hong Kong: Hong Kong U. P., 1961), p. 196.

in 1957, output rose to 1.5 million metric tons in 1958, and 1.8 million metric tons in 1959.[84]

There was a big leap in cement, too. In 1958, 41,000 native-style kilns were put into production in thirteen provinces and municipalities, employing over 80,000 novices.[85] Cement production which stood at 6.86 million tons in 1957, had reportedly reached 9.3 million tons in 1958, an increase of almost 36 percent.

Everything else was also reportedly soaring to unparalleled heights, with the exception of cotton cloth (an increase of only 12.9 percent in 1958 over 1957). There was, for example, a mass movement to search for ore deposits, to establish meteorological organizations, to load, haul, and unload better, faster, and more economically, and to organize native transportation in support of local iron and steel production. To put some order into the proceedings, "Dragon Chain" systems of transport cooperation between railway administrations and industrial enterprises were popularized (unified train schedules and use of equipment) and "Networks Intertwined With Dragons" were introduced. This "resulted in a situation in which the 'bigger dragons' [were] comprised of 'smaller dragons', 'smaller dragons' helped 'bigger dragons', main lines promoted sublines, sublines helped main lines ... etc."[86] At the China People's University (an institution specializing in Marxism-Leninism) 180 "factories," a farm, and two department stores were set up within the school grounds. All of them were built by teachers and students. Not content with this achievement, the students and faculty immediately proceeded to put up an iron and steel plant, a coke oven, a heat-resistant materials enterprise, a workshop for the production of chemical fertilizers, an agricultural implements plant, and a radio repair workshop.[87]

A big leap forward was also claimed in the area of public health. In addition to a 21 percent increase in the number of regular hospital beds in 1958 as compared with the preceding year, 922,000 second

[84] Jung-chao Liu, "Fertilizer Supply and Grain Production in Communist China," *Journal of Farm Economics* (November 1965), p. 918, Table I. Chemical fertilizer production (excluding ammonium nitrate) was given as 631,000 tons in 1957 and 811,000 tons in 1958—an increase of 29 percent. *Communiqué on the Development of the National Economic Plan in 1958* (Peking: State Statistical Bureau, April 14, 1959) in *Peking Review* (April 21, 1959), p. 33. See also Kao Kuang-chien, "China's Chemical Fertilizer Industry Leaps Forward," *ibid.* (October 25, 1960), pp. 13-15.

[85] Su Chi-kuang, "The Big Leap in Cement," *Peking Review* (January 27, 1959), pp. 13-15.

[86] Chu Chi-lin " 'Dragon Chain' Transport" *ibid.*, September 6, 1960, pp. 16-18.

[87] *FEER* (September 4, 1958), p. 307.

grade beds (or ten times the number in 1957) were made available. [88]
The campaign to promote traditional Chinese medicine (Chapter 3)
was revived as part of the "walking on two legs" drive. There was
probably a punitive character to the campaign during the Great Leap
years: it was a way of getting rid of finicky medical airs. Hand-picked
young doctors trained in Western medicine were to undergo a two-
year training in traditional medical practices. The 2,000-odd candidates for this type of education were all to be under thirty years of
age, Party or Youth League members, and leftist in sympathies. They
were to work side by side with both native medical practitioners and
regular medical doctors, wielding influence by reason of their political affiliations, ideological astuteness, and two-leg professional training. [89] In 1960 the area sown to medicinal herbs increased by 60 percent over 1959.[90] In addition to state-financed maternity hospitals
(the number of which jumped from 96 in 1957 to 230 a year later),
some 134,000 maternity clinics were established locally, totaling
416,000 beds. The number of permanent child care organizations
(both regular and "indigenous") was said to have increased from
17,700 in 1957 to 3,186,300 in 1958. On the other hand, the number of people covered by free medical care rose by only 4.6 percent
(or about 300,000 people) in 1958 as compared with 1957, and the
number covered by labor insurance by 19.8 percent.[91]

It should be added that the mass campaign to promote local
small-scale industries went hand in hand (at least during the early
months) with a far-reaching decentralization of administrative control
over industry, agriculture, and other activities. By mid-1958 about
80 percent of the factories under the Ministries of the State Council
had been transferred to local authorities in the provinces, municipalities, and autonomous regions. By mid-June of that year, 880 such
units had been taken over by these authorities. Local authorities also

[88] *Ten Great Years*, p. 220.

Cultural Great Leap Forward

	1950 '	1957	1960 (first half)
Workers' cultural palaces and clubs (units)	700	19,000	32,000
Trade union libraries (units) .	300	26,000	70,500

Source: "China's Workers in 1960," *Peking Review* (May 5, 1961), p. 17.

[89] Wyndham Newton, "Peking and Traditional Medicine," *FEER* (December 18, 1958), pp. 807-808; "The Combination of Chinese Traditional Medicine
and Western Medicine," *URS*, Vol. 24, No. 18 (September 1, 1961).

[90] Ho Shan, "More Medicinal Herbs to Protect Health," *Peking Review*
(May 12, 1961), p. 17.

[91] *Ten Great Years*, pp. 218-221.

controlled about 74 percent of higher educational institutions. The devolution of authority onto local government organs was, however, accompanied by a strengthening of the authority of local and plant Party committees. These soon overshadowed the regular governmental and managerial lines of authority. Party secretaries exercised their power through mass organizations (labor unions, youth league, etc.) bypassing the administrative hierarchy within a plant, bank, or locality. Insofar as they paid heed to central directives, they tended to interpret them in an ultraleftist sense. The breakdown of management in 1958 was hastened by two other reforms instituted that year: the revision of the many enterprise rules and regulations (evolved during the First Five Year Plan period) "in the interest of the masses of workers," and the forcing of managerial personnel to regularly take part in physical labor while workers were encouraged to participate in managerial decisions. [92] Local economic units soon began to promote their own self-sufficiency without regard to the needs of other localities and the flow of goods between localities. In a sense, China reverted to its traditional localism. This trend was to have been countered by the fact that local control was vested in the hands of Party men who were expected to be responsive to the central Party directives. Since, however, the central leadership was at odds with itself, decentralization soon produced the old phenomenon of "localism," and "base-ism" with each economic unit, right down to a factory workshop, looking out after itself.

Some Other Leaps

1. The trains ran faster too. "All trains in China now run to faster timetables. This is one of the benefits passengers have derived from the campaign against waste and conservative ideas and practices launched by the railwaymen."[93]
2. "A hen laid four eggs in a single day. The eggs weighed 207 grammes in all."[94]
3. On May 25, 1960, a Chinese mountaineering expedition "for the first time in human history reached the summit of Mount

[92] Cf. a similar development during the later stages of the Cultural Revolution of 1966-69 (Chapter 12). A good reference source for the study of the decentralization movement is Audrey Donnithorne, "Background to the People's Communes: Changes in China's Economic Organization in 1958," *Pacific Affairs*, Vol. 32, No. 4 (December 1959).

[93] "Trains Run Faster Too," *Peking Review* (June 10, 1958), p. 4. A Western visitor to China in 1964 reported that because of ancient rolling stock, most Chinese trains did not exceed 30 miles per hour. The 1,500-mile Canton-Peking trip took 50 hours. Some new, double-decker trains introduced in 1963-64 and theoretically capable of speeds of up to 90 miles an hour, also ran at not more than 30 mph.

[94] "Champion Hen," *Peking Review* (January 20, 1959), p. 17.

Jolmo Lungma from the north face. The victory is precisely the result of scorning difficulties strategically and taking full account of them tactically."[95]

4. From the inauguration of the Great Leap Forward to September 1, 1960, Chinese swimmers improved five times on the 100-meter breast stroke world record.[96]

5. "Young aeroplane model makers chalked up new records with piston engine helicopters flying 137.5 kilometers in distance, 4,760 meters in altitude, and 2 hours 16 minutes 30 seconds in duration."[97]

6. "Young record holder, Tien Chao-chung, with a brilliant effort, covered 16.35 meters in the hop, step, and jump."[98]

7. A big leap forward into paleontology. "Preliminary research on stone tools and weapons found during [1958-59] excavations at a site in the southwestern tip of Shansi Province, north China, shows that they may belong to an earlier period of human life than that of Peking man (*sinathropus pekinensis*) who lived more than half a million years ago."[99]

8. Eleven large buildings were built in Peking, each in less than 12 months. These included the Great Hall of the People and the building housing the museums of Chinese history and the museum of Chinese revolution. The cost of the 11 buildings was 300 million yuan.

PEOPLE'S COMMUNES[100]

"Between the summer and autumn of 1958 the more than 740,000 cooperatives throughout the country, each averaging about 160 households, were merged and reorganized into more than 26,000 communes, averaging about 4,600 households each; later, after check-up, they were further reorganized into more than 24,000 communes averaging more than 5,000 households each, in other words, more than 30 times as large as the original agricultural cooperatives.

[95] Li Fu-chun, *Raise High the Red Flag . . . , op. cit.*, p. 37.
[96] *Peking Review* (September 6, 1960), p. 5.
[97] *Peking Review* (January 13, 1961), p. 24.
[98] *Peking Review* (January 13, 1961), p. 24.
[99] *Loc. cit.*, (October 6, 1961), p. 20.
[100] On the people's communes see Edgar Snow, *The Other Side of the River: Red China Today* (New York: 1962), Chapter LVI; Joan Robinson, "The Chinese Communes," *The Political Quarterly* (July-September 1964), pp. 285-297; Gargi Dutt, *Rural Communes of China* (Bombay: Asia Publishing House, 1967); C. S. Chen, *Rural People's Communes in Lien-chiang* (Stanford, Calif.: Hoover Institution Press, 1969); *People's Communes in Pictures* (Peking: FLP, 1960); *Women in the People's Communes* (Peking: FLP, 1960); Tao Chu, *The People's Communes Forge Ahead* (Peking: FLP, 1964). For a description by two Swiss students of a Canton suburban commune, see R. Gut and A. Aebi, "A Commune," *FEER* (June 29, 1961), pp. 632-634.

Big in scale and strong, the people's communes are not only able to develop production and construction rapidly in agriculture, forestry, animal husbandry, side occupations, and fishery, but also achieve unified leadership over the work of industry, agriculture, trade, education, and military affairs in the rural areas, realizing the integration of economic organizations and basic organs of state power. Rural people's communes are still economic organizations with collective ownership of the means of production. While the principal means of production still belong to the production brigades, which correspond roughly to the former agricultural producers' cooperatives, the commune level already owns part of the means of production and may draw every year certain sums from the various production brigades for its accumulation fund. A certain amount of free supplies is included as part of the system of distribution in the income of commune members."[101]

Having distributed land to the peasants, formed mutual aid teams, lower level cooperatives, and advanced cooperatives, which took the land away from the peasants, the leadership now took what was organizationally and ideologically another great leap forward. In April 1958 the first rural people's communes (still referred to as cooperatives) were organized in Honan by merging several small advanced producers' cooperatives into one, the average ratio being 10 to 1. Among the earliest was the Weihsing (Sputnik) Commune in Suiping County of Honan Province, the regulations of which were given wide publicity, possibly with a view to serving as a model charter for all communes. The Sputnik commune was formed on April 27 out of 27 small cooperatives. It comprised 9,300 households, with a total of 43,000 people.[102] In July 1958 the Party's theoretical organ *Hung-ch'i* issued Mao's call to combine industry, agriculture, commerce, education, and the militia into a big commune which would form the basic unit of society.[103] On August 29 the Central Committee adopted a resolution "On the Establishment of People's Communes in Rural Areas," thus formalizing the movement.[104] That there was strong opposition to the commune concept within the leadership is evidenced by the fact that the Honan experiment was not mentioned in the Party's resolution on agriculture adopted at the Second Session of the Eighth Party Congress in May 1958. "This [the Honan experiment] was, in essence, already the start of the movement for people's communes. But people were not yet aware of the real nature of this development. Only after Comrade

[101] Chou En-lai, *A Great Decade, op. cit.*, p. 23.
[102] "Tentative Regulations (Draft) of the Weihsing (Sputnik) People's Commune" (August 7, 1958) in: *People's Communes in China* (Peking: FLP, 1958), pp. 61-80.
[103] *Hung-ch'i*, July 16, 1958.
[104] *People's Communes in China, op. cit.*, pp. 1-8.

Mao Tse-tung gave his directive regarding the people's communes did they begin to see things clearly, realize the meaning of this new form of organization that has appeared in the vast rural and urban areas, and feel more confident and determined to take this path."[105]

Individual peasant holdings had been collectivized in twelve months; the collectives were communized in just five months. Table 8-5 reveals the process.

TABLE 8-5
Development of the People's Communes in the Countryside (1958)*

	End of August	Early September	Mid September	Late September	End of December
Number of people's communes	8,730	12,824	16,989	26,425	26,578
Number of peasant households in people's communes (thousands)	37,780	59,790	81,220	121,940	123,250
Percentage of peasant households in people's communes to total number of peasant households	30.4	48.1	65.3	98.0	99.1
Average number of households in each commune	4,328	4,662	4,781	4,614	4,637

*In October 1964 China's Minister of Agriculture, Liao Lu-yen, writing in the Cuban periodical *Cuba Socialista*, put the number of communes in 1958 at 74,000. See Liao Lu-yen, "Collectivization of Agriculture in China," *Peking Review* (November 1, 1963), pp. 7–14. By 1966 the national average was 1,620 households per commune. The number of communes at that time was put at 70,000–80,000 ranging in size from a few hundred to about 10,000 hectares. *NCNA* (March 22, 1966). In 1959 the number of communes reportedly fell to a little more than 24,000 with an average of 5,000 households per commune, a total of 500,000 brigades, and over 3 million production teams. Henry J. Lethbridge, *op. cit.*, p. 74.

Source: Ten Great Years, p. 43. "As to the establishment of communes of more than 10,000 or even more than 20,000 households, we need not oppose them, but for the present we should not take the initiative to encourage them." Resolution of the CC of the CPC on the Establishment of People's Communes in the Rural Areas, *op. cit.*, p. 3.

"When the leading organs of certain counties did not have a sufficient estimate of the development of the situation, the co-ops of themselves formed up communes, and, beating gongs and drums, went to them to report the good news."[106]

[105] Wu Chih-pu, "From Agricultural Producers' Cooperatives to People's Communes," *Hung-ch'i*, No. 8 (September 16, 1958).

[106] Lin Tieh, "The People's Commune Movement in Hopei," *Hung-ch'i*, No. 9 (October 1, 1958).

By the end of June 1959 the people's communes were said to have established about 700,000 industrial production units. The output value of commune industries represented 10 percent of the gross output value of China's industry in the first half of 1959. The communes also reportedly set up 3.4 million community dining rooms, over 3.4 million nurseries and kindergartens, 150,000 "homes of respect for the aged," 60,000 cultural halls and stations, 500,000 clubs, and over 180,000 amateur dramatic groups.[107]

Urban people's communes began to be formed at about this time by neighborhood committees, factories, schools, government offices, and mass organizations, but the movement does not seem to have really taken root, in spite of some fantastic claims to the contrary.[108]

The people's commune was intended by its creators to be something much more than just a very big collective farm.

Ideologically the commune was regarded in the Party's extremist circles as a distinct advance toward communism,[109] and this for five reasons:

1. Some of the commune's assets were owned "by the whole people" rather than collectively by the members. This was so because "the rural people's communes and the basic organizations of state power [township or the *hsiang*] have been combined into one; because the banks, stores, and some other enterprises owned by the whole people, originally existing in the countryside, have been placed under the management of the communes; because the communes have taken part in establishing certain undertakings in industrial and

[107] *Ten Great Years*, p. 44. On July 21, 1960 Peking Radio reported that 50 million children were being brought up in commune nurseries and kindergartens. Cf. Chuan Nung-tiao, "How Commune Dining Rooms Serve the Peasants," *Peking Review* (January 12, 1960), pp. 16-17; Kung Mai, "Collective Welfare Services in a Commune," *ibid.* (May 17, 1960), pp. 45-47.

[108] See Wu Chih-pu, "From Agricultural Producers' Cooperatives to People's Communes," *Hung-ch'i*, No. 8 (September 16, 1958); Henry Lethbridge, "Time for the Test," *FEER* (March 23, 1961), pp. 522-524; Audrey Donnithorne, *China's Economic System, op. cit.*, pp. 226-231; Shih Ch'eng-chih, *Urban Commune Experiments in Communist China* (Hong Kong: URI, 1962); Chao Kuo-chun, "Urban Communes: A First Hand Report," *FEER* (September 29, 1960), pp. 715-720; H. J. Lethbridge, *China's Urban Communes* (Hong Kong: Dragonfly Books, 1961); Janet Salaf, "The Urban Communes and Anti-City Experiment in Communist China," *China Quarterly* (January-March 1967), pp. 82-110.

[109] "It [the commune] will become the basic unit in the future communist society, as thinkers—from *many outstanding utopian socialists* to Marx, Engels, and Lenin—had predicted on many occasions." "Hold High the Red Flag of People's Communes and March On," *Jen-min Jih-pao* editorial, September 3, 1958 [emphasis added]. The utopian element in left-wing Chinese Marxism is further brought out in the following aim of the Chinese radicals: "The function of the state will [in at most six plus "a few years"] be limited to protecting the country from external aggression; it will play no role in domestic affairs." *Ibid.*

other construction which are by nature owned by the whole people; because in many counties the county federations of communes, exercising unified leadership over all the people's communes in these counties, have been formed and have the power to deploy a certain portion of the manpower, material and financial resources of the communes to undertake construction on a county level or even bigger scale."[110]

2. The establishment of the rural people's communes involved a sharp reduction in private ownership by the peasants. The peasants' private plots were abolished after having been allowed to expand the year before.[111] A good part of the livestock, farm implements, machinery formerly owned by the state tractor stations, and even household goods (that is those which had not found their way into the backyard furnaces) were communized. Many household activities (e.g., preparation and taking of meals, rearing of children, the making and repairing of family clothing) were taken over by the communes so as to liberate women for other, more productive and properly socialist tasks, such as the digging of irrigation ditches, manure collection, and so on. In Honan alone during 1958 about 7 million women were reportedly liberated from household chores by community canteens.

3. Part of the income of commune members was distributed free of charge (e.g., meals) or "according to need." ". . . The free supply system adopted by the people's communes contains the first shoots of the communist principle of 'to each according to his needs.' "[112]

---

110 "Resolution on Some Questions Concerning the People's Communes," adopted by the Eighth Central Committee of the CPC, at its Sixth Plenary Session on December 10, 1958, in *Sixth Plenary Session, op. cit.*, p. 19. In fact, the federations of communes within a *hsien* turned out in the end to have been the old *hsien* authority with a new name. The original idea was to have one commune per *hsien*. "Both collective ownership and ownership by the whole people are socialist ownership; but the latter is more advanced than the former because the state, representing the whole people, can directly make a unified and rational distribution of the means of production and the products of enterprises owned by the whole people according to the requirements of the national economy as a whole, while this cannot be done with regard to enterprises run under collective ownership, including the existing rural people's communes." *Ibid.*, p. 20. This does not square too well with *Jen-min Jih-pao's* state playing "no role in domestic affairs." Cf. footnote 109 above.

111 Choh-ming Li argues that private plots did not disappear during the Leap. In 1958, he argues, they constituted about 9 percent of the total cultivated area. Some of the communes may have been simply formed on paper by renaming the former agricultural producers' cooperatives and leaving it at that. See his "Comment on China's Descending Spiral," *China Quarterly* (October–December 1962), p. 35.

112 *Sixth Plenary Session, op. cit.*, p. 21. Cf. "We consider erroneous and incorrect the statements of leftists in the international Communist movement to the effect that since we have taken power into our hands we can at once introduce Communism, by-passing certain historical stages in its development." N. Matsovsky, *Pravda* (June 12, 1960).

However, "even after the transition from collective ownership to ownership by the whole people, the people's communes will, during a necessary period of time, retain the system of 'to each according to his work,' owing to the fact that there is not as yet an abundant enough supply of social products to realize communism. Any premature attempt to negate the principle of 'to each according to his work' and replace it with the principle of 'to each according to his needs,' that is, any attempt to enter communism by over-reaching ourselves when conditions are not mature—is undoubtedly a Utopian concept that cannot possibly succeed."[113]

4. The policy of the communes of running industry and agriculture simultaneously and combining them had, according to the radicals, "opened up the way to reduce the differences between town and countryside, and between worker and peasant."[114] By the end of 1959, more than 200,000 industrial production units were being run by the communes. A little more than half their gross output value served agricultural production.[115]

5. The communes were expected to facilitate the eradication of differences between mental and physical labor through commune-run "red and expert" schools in which the working people could "attain an adequate amount of general knowledge and master science, technology, and culture. Meanwhile the intellectuals and cadres are required to take part in manual labor, and thus identify themselves with the workers and peasants."[116]

These five ideological merits claimed for the people's communes expressed the communist left's view of the historical process: comprehensive ownership by the state "of the whole people," moral incentives to production, vast mobilization of the creative energies of the masses, and the policy of walking on two legs. However, even in the Resolution on Some Questions Concerning the People's Communes (December 1958), the earlier apocalyptic exuberance was moderated by the realization that the transition to communism might be tougher and more drawn out than had been expected.[117]

[113] *Sixth Plenary Session*, op. cit., p. 23. The qualification was inserted during the commune "checkup" period and bears the marks of the opposition's viewpoint. It may, however, have been necessitated simply by the resource constraints of the time, and the threat which a widespread adoption of the free supply system represented for the fledgling communes.

[114] *Ibid.*, pp. 21-22.

[115] Li Fu-chun, *Raise High the Red Flag . . . op. cit.*, p. 7. Compare this figure with the 700,000 units counted by *Ten Great Years*, p. 44, and above, p. 286.

[116] Wu Chih-pu, op. cit. Cf. Chapter 12.

[117] "We should not groundlessly make declarations that the people's communes in the countryside will 'realize ownership by the whole people immediately,' or even 'enter communism immediately,' and so on. To do such

The first to be jettisoned was free supply. In time the attempt to communize family life was also abandoned. Later, as we shall see, a version of the free market in the guise of trade fairs was reintroduced (September 1959), private plots were restored (summer 1960), the size of the communes was reduced, and many of the communes' functions were once again devolved on either the *hsien* or on production brigades and teams.

Functionally, the rural people's communes were a labor-capital mobilization and income rationing device. The magnitude and broad sweep of the tasks demanded of the masses by the General Line and the Great Leap Forward were soon found to be beyond the capacity and ability of existing administrative units and collective farms to handle.[118] The order to walk on two legs (which in reality meant walking on a thousand legs) required the total mobilization of manpower throughout the country for the simultaneous performance and coordination of a variety of jobs. It called for multipurpose units of management which could combine agricultural, industrial, commercial, fiscal, political, cultural, and military affairs, mobilize labor reserves, employ them as inputs where needed, and exercise strong local control over all activities, or "get organized along military lines," as the August 29, 1958 resolution put it. The commune was thought to be the answer to this problem of synchronized mobilization. It was vested with authority over the implementation of central economic guidelines, compulsory education at all levels, militia and public security affairs, banking, taxation, commerce, and a variety of other tasks formerly carried out by collective farms and various levels of governmental administration. Thus for example 70 percent of the country's farm machinery was transferred from the state machine tractor stations to the communes. The area within which the writ of the people's commune was to run differed, but in general the idea was to equate it with the *hsiang*. In fact, however, the practice seems

---

things is not only an expression of rashness, it will greatly lower the standards of communism in the minds of the people, distort the great ideal of communism and vulgarize it, strengthen the petty-bourgeois trend towards equalitarianism and adversely affect the development of socialist construction." *Sixth Plenary Session, op. cit.*, p. 24. The hand of the moderates seems to be behind this statement. The accusation of rashness was anathema to the radicals. Cf. the leftist attack on those who "oppose the building of socialism by way of mass movements, which, they say, is no more than 'petty-bourgeois fanaticism'," See also Tetsuya Kataoka, "Political Theory of the Great Leap Forward," *Social Research* (March 1969), pp. 93-122.

118 ". . . The agricultural cooperatives, which are small in size, meager in items of production, and low in the degree of collectivization, are becoming handicaps to the further development of the productive forces." "Hold High the Red Flag of People's Communes and March On," *Jen-min Jih-pao* editorial, September 3, 1958.

to have been several *hsiangs* per commune.[119] The communes were also supposed to mobilize capital more effectively than the collective farms and the former local levels of government. Professor Cheng Chu-yuan has pointed out that while in 1956, 70 percent of total agricultural income was distributed among the peasants (and 53.2 percent in 1957), after communization, the part of total income distributed to the peasants fell to 30 percent, while 70 percent went to investment.[120]

The enormous and varied activities stipulated by the Great Leap Forward called for a careful rationing of income. The establishment of communal kitchens, mess halls, kindergartens, and sewing groups, and the vesting in the communes of authority over the handling of the communes' enterprise profits, were designed toward that end.[121] However, the objective of a careful husbanding of resources came in conflict with the communist distributive ideal of egalitarianism and free supply ("to each according to his need"—provided he is politically reliable) which bore little relation to the peasants' productivity. The pooling of production brigades' profits and losses at the commune level implied that all production brigades—rich and poor alike—were treated equally for income distribution purposes. Under the "Seven Guarantees" members of "better situated" communes, "when the economic situation allowed," were to have been guaranteed basic amounts of food, clothing, medical care, and housing, as well as expenses of childbirth, marriage, and burial. Where the "Ten Guarantees" were in operation, fuel for winter, haircuts, and theatre attendance were added to the list. At one time the total of these free food and welfare services was said to have constituted one half of the peasants' income.[122] Following a tidying-up campaign launched in

[119] In 1958 there were approximately 80,000 *hsiangs* (townships) with 120 million peasant households in all. By the end of December 1958 there were about 26,600 people's communes. In 1958 there were 1,750 *hsien* (counties), or 14 communes (3 to 4 *hsiangs*) per county. During the rush to form people's communes there was some talk of amalgamating the counties with the communes, i.e., one commune per county, but this project was apparently dropped. See, "How To Run a People's Commune," *Jen-min Jih-pao* editorial, Sept. 4, 1958 in: *People's Communes in China, op. cit.*, p. 85. Cf. footnote 110 above.

[120] Cheng Chu-yuan, *Communist China's Economy, 1949-1962, op. cit.*, p. 42.

[121] Marion R. Larsen, "China's Agriculture Under Communism," *op. cit.*, p. 219. The advantages of communal feeding were said to have been the following: (a) it freed women for collective work, (b) made rationing easier, (c) made it more difficult for peasants to hoard grain, (d) saved fuel, (e) provided good opportunities for political education and control. Some of the alleged advantages are disputed by Audrey Donnithorne, *op. cit.*, p. 63.

[122] "Community dining rooms should be managed democratically. Their administrative staffs and cooks should be chosen from among those who are politically reliable." *Sixth Plenary Session, op. cit.*, pp. 36-37. The semisupply, semiwage system was not, however, completely divorced from productive effort.

December 1958 the free supply aspect of income distribution was deemphasized, and payments to commune members (including meal tickets) tended increasingly to be tied to the individual's productive performance.[123] By September 1959, free supply accounted for 20-30 percent of members' total income and its purpose was "to ensure that provision is made for the livelihood of those who are not able-bodied and of children."[124] It thus became a form of social insurance in new ideological garb. The wage part of a commune member's income (calculated on the income of the whole commune) was paid monthly to each individual member rather than through the head of the family. It was determined to some extent by the member's contribution to output, but also (especially before December 1958) by his attitude toward labor, physical prowess, technical skill, and political maturity. The payment of wages to individual recipients was, according to the Maoists, "warmly welcomed by the young people and women who now receive direct what has been earned by themselves. The patriarchal system carried over from the old society is thus effectively shattered."[125] Together with communal discipline, loyalty, dining rooms, creches, laundries, and sewing teams, the new wage payment system was thus intended to bring about the disappearance of the family unit with its allegedly spontaneous capitalist and rightist opportunist tendencies. Monthly wage payments were to be supplemented by bonuses and awards not to exceed one-fourth of the total annual basic wages. Deductions from wages were made when a member absented himself from work and for slovenly work. The fact that wages were calculated on the basis of the income of the whole commune rather than of the production brigade or team, meant the removal of the last link between reward and the amount

---

"By semisupply is meant that grain is supplied gratis to members according to the standard stipulated by the state, or, a step further, that members can eat in the community canteen free of charge. Of course, the principle 'if any would not work, neither should he eat,' is still applied while this supply system—either supply of grain or supply of meals—is being carried out. By semiwage is meant that, apart from grain or meals, other living expenses are paid to the members in the form of money according to the principle 'he who does more work shall receive more pay.' " Lin Tieh, "The People's Commune Movement in Hopei," *Hung-ch'i* (October 1, 1958).

[123] "Some people, attempting to 'enter communism' prematurely, have tried to abolish the production and exchange of commodities too early, and to negate at too early a stage the positive roles of commodities, value, money, and prices. This line of thinking is harmful to the development of socialist construction and is, therefore, incorrect. . . . As stated above, this distribution system includes the first shoots of communism but in essence is still socialist—based on the principle of 'from each according to his ability and to each according to his work.' " *Sixth Plenary Session, op. cit.*, pp. 31, 32.

[124] Liu Shao-ch'i, *Victory of Marxism-Leninism in China, op. cit.*, p. 69.

[125] Wu Chih-pu, *op. cit.*

of work performed by the recipient, and thus accentuated the disincentive, egalitarian trend already present in the cooperatives.

Organizationally, as we have seen, the people's communes were intended to be coequal with the *hsiang*, the *hsiang* People's Congress and People's Council being transformed into the Commune People's Congress and the Commune Administrative Committee. "The administrative setup of the commune may in general be divided into three levels, namely the commune administrative committee, the administrative district (or production brigade), and the production teams. The administrative district (or production brigade) is in general the unit which manages industry, agriculture, trade, education, and military affairs in a given area and forms a business accounting unit, with its gains and losses pooled in the commune as a whole. The production team is the basic unit of labor organization. Under the unified leadership of the commune administrative committee, necessary powers should be given to the administrative district (or production brigade) and the production team over such matters as the organization of production work and capital construction, finances and welfare, in order to bring their initiative into full play. . . . What we describe as getting organized along military lines means getting organized on the pattern of a factory. . . . Militia organizations should be set up at corresponding levels of the production organizations in the people's commune. The leading bodies of the militia and production organizations should be separate."[126] As early as August 1959 the production brigade was also designated as the basic unit of ownership. It is difficult to make any meaningful generalizations about the communes' lower levels, i.e., the production brigades and production teams. Their size and functions varied from place to place and over time, and even the nomenclature was changed several times.[127] Assuming a "standard" commune to be equated with the *hsiang* (township), a production brigade would roughly correspond to an advanced agricultural producers' cooperative (kolkhoz, comprising on the average some 200 to 300 households), while the production team would correspond to an elementary agricultural producers' cooperative (lower level collective farm) with some 20-30 households

[126] "Resolution on Some Questions Concerning the People's Communes," in *Sixth Plenary Session, op. cit.*, pp. 40-42. Cf. Articles 11 and 12 of the Weihsing Regulations, *op. cit.*, pp. 68-69.

[127] See Audrey Donnithorne, *op. cit.*, p. 51. Also Chao kuo-chun, *Economic Planning and Organization in Mainland China* (Cambridge, Mass.: Center for East Asian Studies, Harvard University, 1963), and T. A. Hsia, *The Commune In Retreat As Evidenced in Terminology and Semantics* (Berkeley, Calif.: U. of California Press, 1964).

on the average.[128] The comparison must, however, be interpreted carefully since wide variations existed both in theory and application. The interesting fact is that as early as December 1958, the production brigade rather than the commune seems to have been the effective unit of organization, and that by late summer 1959, the brigade became also the basic unit of ownership. Under this dispensation, members of production brigades were to receive income differentiated according to each brigade's resources and productivity. Later, as we shall see, the production team (or even in some cases a smaller unit, the job group roughly corresponding in terms of peasant households—about 10—to the defunct mutual aid teams) became the basic accounting unit and to a degree a unit of ownership, although the continued existence and merits of communes were repeatedly stressed.[129]

RETREAT FROM THE GREAT LEAP

By mid-1960 there were unmistakable signs that the Great Leap Forward and the more radical tenets of the General Line were being abandoned. By the end of the year the Leap was for all practical purposes dead—only the symbols and the semantics remained. The radicals were in retreat once again, disgruntled, bitter, shifting positions, and waiting for the next opportunity to stage a comeback. In fact, evidence could already be found in the winter of 1958 that the four major mass campaigns described earlier were meeting with serious difficulties and had therefore to be revised, adjusted, and trimmed. Still, the day of final reckoning had to await the results of a succession of bad harvests.

[128] ". . . The production brigades . . . are equivalent in size to the former advanced agricultural co-ops." Tao Chu (Member of the Central Committee of the CPC and First Secretary of the Secretariat of the Central-South Bureau of the CC of the CPC), *The People's Communes Forge Ahead* (Peking: *FLP*, 1964), p. 22.

[129] "The production team under the production brigade is still another level of ownership and constitutes the basic accounting unit of the commune." *Ibid.*, p. 22. "As we have only just started to mechanize agriculture, most farm work is still done by men and draught animals; the production team is still the unit that directly organizes production. Under these circumstances, with the production team functioning as the basic accounting unit, the unit directly organizing production and the basic accounting unit are one and the same. . . . Over the past few years, the overwhelming majority of people's communes have made the production teams their basic accounting units; this gives freer scope to the great enthusiasm and initiative of the teams in developing collective production and strengthening the collective economy. . . . In most cases, only part of the ownership of the means of production is vested in the production brigade and the commune." *Ibid.*, pp. 25, 26-27. Note that this was written in 1964 (the original article appeared in *Hung-ch'i*, No. 4, 1964).

The reasons for the abandonment of the Great Leap may, for purposes of discussion, be divided into objective and subjective, the first relating to the havoc in production, the second to opposition by some Party and government leaders and cadres, as well as peasants.

Objective Reasons

1. Food Shortages

Food shortages appeared in 1959 and were accentuated in 1960. In his Report on the 1959 Economic Plan, Chou En-lai pointed out that in the spring grain shortages occurred in areas equivalent to about 5 percent of the country's territory.[130] In late summer 1959 rations were cut from 15 to 12 catties of grain per month in Peking, Tientsin, Tsinan, and other northern towns, as well as in Shanghai. In south China grain rations varied from a high of 14 ounces per day to a low of 3.5 ounces.[131] Refugees in Macao reported that on January 1, 1961 the rice ration in their areas had been cut from about 7 ounces per meal to about one-third of that amount.[132] Travelers to Shanghai in the sping of 1961 said that the grain ration in the city had been cut from 13 to 10 catties per month (17 to 13.3 lb) composed of 40 percent rice and 60 percent wheat. The already very modest sugar and oil rations were to be halved.[133]

"The natural calamities in 1959 were the worst we suffered in many decades. They struck some 650 million *mou* of land in the countryside [108.3 million acres], affecting as much as 30 percent of the total sown area."[134] In 1960 calamity struck again with even greater force. Some reports indicated that in mid-1960 areas suffering from natural disasters totalled over 900 million *mou* [150 million acres] or about half the country's cultivable area.[135]

In the winter of 1960-61 malnutrition became widespread and disease ravaged many parts of the country. There was an outbreak of cholera in Kwangtung, reportedly claiming many lives. For a while (especially in April and May 1962) masses of refugees descended on Hong Kong from neighboring Kwangtung Province. The sudden influx of refugees into Hong Kong in late April and early May 1962

---

[130] *Peking Review* (September 1, 1959).

[131] T. C. Lee, "The Food Problem," in: *Contemporary China* (Hong Kong: Hong Kong U. P., 1961, p. 1).

[132] A. R. McGuire, "China's Food Shortage and Its Repercussions," *FEER* (February 9, 1961), p. 233.

[133] Colina MacDougall, "Refugee Riddle," *FEER* (May 17, 1962), p. 312.

[134] *Press Communiqué on the Growth of China's National Economy in 1959* (Peking: FLP, 1960), p. 20. Cf. W. K., "Communist China's Agricultural Calamities," *China Quarterly* (April-June 1961), pp. 64-75.

[135] *Communist China in 1960* (Hong Kong: URI, 1962), p. 6. On man's contribution to these "natural" calamities, see above, p. 265.

remains, however, something of a puzzle. Most of the refugees had exit permits issued by local authorities in Kwangtung, and it was even rumored that before departure they were fed bowls of congee to give them sustenance on their trip. When caught and returned to China by Hong Kong police, they were said to have been again fed and either given a train ticket back to their homes or allowed to stay near the border and try again. In the first two weeks of May, 25,000 were sent back by the Hong Kong authorities who for a time suspected that the unarmed invasion of the colony was organized by the Chinese to embarrass the Hong Kong government then grappling with a business recession. The suspicion proved unfounded. Following official British representations in Peking, border control on the Chinese side was strengthened and the flow reduced (by May 25) to its normal proportions of 100 or so a day, including 50 legal quota entries. Although food shortages were one of the motives for the exodus, other reasons seem to have played a more important part.[136]

Beginning in 1961, for the first time since the communists' accession to power, China became a net importer of food, buying that year 5.6 million tons of grain, almost all of it from capitalist countries. The claim to a 1958 output of 375 million tons of grain and potatoes in grain equivalent (which was probably one of the reasons for the establishment of the partial free supply system) turned out to have been false. The amount was later officially reduced to 250 million tons, but even this figure is subject to doubt. Professor Yuan-li Wu places the 1958 output of grain (including potatoes in grain equivalent) at 175.4 million tons, that is a decline of 9.6 million tons from the 1957 level. In 1959, according to official figures, grain production was said to have reached 270 million tons, but Wu's recomputations point to not more than 154.4 million tons, a decrease of 30.6 million tons from the 1957 level. By 1960, according to Wu, grain production dropped to 130 million tons, or to a level 55 million tons below 1957.[137] Given the abandonment of earlier

---

[136] See Chapter 9 below. On the refugee problem see Colina MacDougall, "Refugee Riddle," *FEER* (May 17, 1962), pp. 311-312; "Exodus," *ibid.* (May 24, 1962), p. 359; "Spring in Kwangtung," *ibid.* (May 31, 1962), p. 455. Communist China considers Hong Kong and Macao to be Chinese national territory. Chinese nationals going to these places are, from China's viewpoint, not refugees, and require only travel permits issued by local authorities in China.

[137] The official figures are from *Jen-min Jih-pao*, December 19, 1958 (grain figure of 375 million tons in 1958), *Ten Great Years* (250 million tons), Li Fu-chun, "Report on the Draft 1960 National Economic Plan" (presented to the National People's Congress, March 30, 1960), *Jen-min Jih-pao*, April 1, 1960. The Western figures are from Yuan-li Wu, *The Economy of Communist China*, *op. cit.*, p. 140, Table VII-2. Following his interview with Mao Tse-tung and Chou En-lai, Lord Montgomery cited 150 million tons of grain in 1960 (see Chapter 9).

(1956-57) birth control campaigns, the per capita food situation must have been extremely precarious by 1961, so dangerous, in fact, as to make a reversal of policies almost inevitable. Alexander Eckstein estimates that assuming an annual population growth rate of 1.5 percent, the index of per capita availability of domestically produced food crop was 82.4 in 1960 (1957 = 100). If a 2 percent annual population growth rate is assumed, the 1960 index of per capita availability of domestically produced food crop would be 81.2, and 80.0 if a 2.5 percent rate is assumed.[138] Since livestock production probably declined more sharply than grain production, the qualitative deterioration in the available food supply must have been serious. Given the low-caloric intake at the outset (estimated at 2,000-2,200 calories per day), a reduction in the quantity and quality of food supplies during 1958-61 was bound to have grave effects on mass enthusiasm, which the Maoists relied on as the driving force of the Great Leap Forward. Food parcels sent by Hong Kong Chinese to their relatives in China rose from 870,000 units of two pounds each in 1959, to 3,700,000 in 1960, and 13,600,000 in 1961, and this in spite of a consolidated tax of 20-50 percent *ad valorem* placed by the Chinese authorities in May 1959.[139] A directive issued in October 1959 mobilized the population to collect wild plants. Canned meat was rationed, and the allocation of vegetables was limited to one pound per day per family. In August 1960 an editorial in *Jen-min Jih-pao* admitted that "the past three years witnessed an increase of some 20 million in population in the cities and industrial and mining areas. . . . There has . . . been a very large number of people engaged in agricultural capital construction, with the peak figure exceeding 70 million involved in water conservancy construction during last winter and spring; they consumed more grain than other peasants. All this has greatly expanded the volume of grain consumption. The demand for cotton creates a similar situa-

[138] Alexander Eckstein, *Communist China's Economic Growth and Foreign Trade, op. cit.*, p. 65, Table 3-8.

[139] Chun-hsi Wu, *Dollars, Dependents and Dogma: Overseas Chinese Remittances to Communist China* (Stanford, Calif.: Hoover Institution Press, 1967), p. 69, Table 8. The imposition of the tax in a time of food shortages may be explained in the context of deteriorating relations between the overseas Chinese and the communist regime during the Leap Forward. Overseas dependents on the mainland were forcibly integrated in the people's communes, and the former moderation toward them was gone. The authorities were also anxious to transform commodity aid from abroad into hard currency remittances. Cf. Lu Yu-sun, *Programs of Communist China for Overseas Chinese* (Hong Kong: URI, 1956), and Tull Chu, *Political Attitudes of the Overseas Chinese in Japan*, Report of a study conducted by the Institute for Oriental Studies during August and September 1965 (Hong Kong: URI, 1967).

tion."[140] The October 1, 1961 editorial in *Jen-min Jih-pao* was more explicit and frank: "The reduction in the output of grain, industrial crops, and subsidiary products," it said, "has affected production in both light and heavy industries, commodity supplies, and the people's livelihood."

It would seem that one explanation of the disappointing performance of agriculture was that by the end of 1958, whatever slack there had been in production carried on by labor-intensive methods, had been taken up, and that any further increases in production had to be sought in technical changes in production methods and the introduction of new inputs. In other words, between 1949 and 1958 the production possibility curve had probably been shifted outward as far as it could go and the marginal productivity of farm labor had approached zero. To raise output above the 1957 level (i.e., above 185 million tons in the case of grain) and to sustain the rise over time, called for large injections of chemical fertilizer, massive and properly integrated water and drought control works, selected seeds, discriminate mechanization, and so on. Without raising the technological ceiling, output was likely to stagnate at the limits permitted by traditional production methods. And it was not mass peasant innovation and haphazard earthwork that would raise the technological ceiling.

2. Managerial Problems Caused by Excessive Bigness

(a) *Social ownership.* Already in December 1958, in the very resolution which rectified some questions concerning the commune movement, warnings were issued against excessive haste and utopian expectations regarding the transition from socialism to communism. While in August 1958 the transition from collective ownership to ownership by the whole people was expected to take from three to six years, by December it was expected to occur in twenty years or more. While in August the commune was the basic functional and ownership unit, by December the production brigade was designated the basic functional unit (i.e., the main organizer of production) and, some months later, the unit of ownership.[141] The Eighth Plenary Session of the Eighth Central Committee formalized the so-called "Three Levels of Ownership" (commune, brigade, team). In April 1960 the Second Session of the National People's Congress laid down

---

[140] "Let the Whole Party and the Whole People Go in for Agriculture and Grain Production in a Big Way," *Peking Review* (August 30, 1960), p. 13.

[141] The nomenclature is far from clear. In the early period (August 1958-December 1958 and possibly into April 1959) the "production brigade" may have meant "production great brigade" (or "production contingent") a unit larger than the former advanced agricultural producers' cooperative.

the "Four Conditions" for transition from basic ownership by the production brigades to basic ownership by the people's communes. These stipulated that the shift in the level of ownership could take place only when (1) the average annual income of commune members reached 150-200 yuan per head (in 1960 the national average was estimated at about 85 yuan per head), (2) commune ownership had reached a preponderant position in the overall commune economy, (3) the poorer production brigades had caught up with the richer ones, and (4) mechanization had become more widespread in the countryside.[142]

Finally, on January 1, 1962 an editorial in *Jen-min Jih-pao* acknowledged that the production team was the basic functional unit within the commune's theoretical three level system of ownership. In fact, that is in actual practice and in the setting of first rate confusion, agricultural decision making seems to have been exercised (at least since mid-1961) by work groups of ten households or so.

The retreat from hugeness of local organization[143] was not as smooth as this progression would suggest: the tidying-up campaign of December 1958-August 1959 was followed by another leap (this time under the leadership of production brigades), and then another retreat. Many mess halls which had been closed down in the spring of 1959 were reopened in the fall, only to be liquidated again in 1961. In general, however, the trend was toward smaller units of management, in the direction—that is, of the former advanced (and later elementary) collectives, with the commune increasingly playing the part of a rather nominal federation of collective farms.

(b) *Private ownership.* The same was true of the regime's attitude toward the peasants' private plots. From August to December 1958 no private plots were allowed; in the spring of 1959 and until the harvest, "limited freedom and small private ownership" were tolerated again; then in the fall, the plots were recollectivized (while private plots for hog raising were tolerated), only to be reintroduced in the summer of 1960, and encouraged in 1961. The general idea was for each commune to allocate about 5 percent of its cultivable land to its members for private use.

(c) *Use of labor.* In September 1959 the Eighth Plenary Session

[142] These conditions were contained in a report presented on April 6, 1960 to the Second Session of the Second National People's Congress by T'an Chen-lin and published in *Jen-min Jih-pao* the following day. See Ronald Ye-lin Cheng, "Changes in the Rural People's Communes," *Contemporary China, 1961-1962* (Hong Kong: Hong Kong U. P., 1963), p. 92.

[143] "A bigger size and a more socialist nature—this suffices to prove the superiority of the people's communes." Wu Chih-pu, "From Agricultural Producers' Cooperatives to People's Communes," *Hung-ch'i*, No. 8 (September 16, 1958).

of the Eighth Central Committee decided that, given the shortage of labor in the rural areas, backyard steel production was to be determined in the future by local authorities in accordance with local conditions and needs. This type of activity would thenceforth no longer be included in the state plan. This amounted to calling off the backyard furnaces drive and dealing a death blow to the whole idea of local, do-it-yourself industry. The impetus earlier given to the local industry drive was, however, such that it took another year before the whole venture was—for the time being—buried. In the summer of 1960 limits were placed on the amount of labor time which communes could demand of their members for nonfield work. These limits became increasingly stringent. In mid-1961 it was laid down that the do-it-yourself commune industry should not absorb more than 2 percent of the labor of production brigades, and production brigade industry not more than 5 percent of the laborers in production teams.

(d) *Free markets.* Rural fairs were reintroduced in September 1959 ostensibly as "an interesting facet of present-day prosperity in the countryside," but, in fact, to soften the impact of the breakdown in the socialized distribution network, and to market the products of peasant subsidiary activities (after state purchase quota fulfillment).[144] The degree of freedom in these markets was restricted by exchange offices (also called "service departments") which promulgated so-called "price references" (i.e., set limits on price fluctuations). Peasants were encouraged to deposit their "spare money" from sales on the markets in banks established at the fairs. "Dining room" markets were introduced in community canteens in some areas. These were swap arrangements institutionalized to control small transactions carried out by peasants at meal times. Although nominally the open market was eliminated during the Great Leap, it may have survived in an illicit form because of diminished central control over commodities. There can be little doubt, however, that Party organs at the local level interfered with the working of the illegal market mechanism. A case could thus be made out for the contention that the post-1959 restoration of markets in some sectors

[144] "At Village Fairs," *Peking Review* (November 22, 1960), p. 4. The fairs were described as a "happy supplement to the state stores which handle the lion's share of trade in the countryside." The document authorizing the reopening of supervised village fairs is the Central Committee and State Council "Directive on Organizing Rural Fairs" (September 23, 1959), *NCNA* (Peking, September 24, 1959). A move in this direction was already noticeable in the first half of 1959. In November 1959 the Central Committee called for simultaneous public and private rearing of domestic animals, with emphasis on public. By August 1961 private raising of such animals (especially hogs) was stressed. *Jenmin Jih-pao* editorial, August 4, 1961.

of the economy amounted to the granting of official recognition and legality to what was already there.

This erratic course skirting chaos, reflects a leadership torn by strife, knowing where it wants to go but not how, and reacting to events by *ad hoc* measures, themselves a product of bickering. The Great Leap was, in effect, a succession of leaps interspersed with hard falls, an exercise in collective neurosis on a majestic scale.

The retreat from organizational bigness was necessitated by the following facts.

(i) Chinese agriculture seems to call for management by relatively small units, i.e., when the bulk of field work is done by hand, large production units appear not to be suitable.

(ii) The commune ignored the natural socioeconomic systems shaped by rural trade.[145]

(iii) Where large units of organization might have been expected to be most effective (e.g., water conservancy, rural industries), the failures were most noticeable.

(iv) Coordination of decision making at different levels of the commune proved difficult. The Party commune leadership, under pressure to show spectacular results in capital construction and industrial projects, usually won over the demands of production brigades concerned with field work.

Thus not only was the quality of the product poor, but the diversion of between 30 and 50 percent of the available peasant labor power to these tasks contributed to the failure to bring in much of the 1958, 1959, and 1960 harvests. Partly as a result of the diversion of labor away from field work, partly due to peasant lassitude and passive resistance (abetted by hastily conceived and badly executed water conservancy works), weeds ran riot on more than 300 million *mou* of agricultural land in 1960. In Shantung alone, one-third of the farmland (some 48 million *mou*) was covered with weeds.[146] To remedy this situation, a series of ad hoc measures were taken. Cadres were transferred from their desks to the fields where they were required to follow the "Three-Seven" system (take part in manual labor on seven out of every ten days) or the "Two-Five" system (participate in labor five days a week).[147] Young people from the

---

[145] The point is made by G. W. Skinner in "Marketing and Social Structure in Rural China" (Part 3), *Journal of Asian Studies* (May 1965), p. 394. Cf. Audrey Donnithorne, "The Organization of Rural Trade in China Since 1958," *China Quarterly* (October-December 1961), pp. 77-91.

[146] *Jen-min Jih-pao*, August 14, 1960.

[147] Tao Li-wen, "Cadres to the Front Line of Production," *Peking Review* (August 2, 1960), pp. 14-17. The remaining two days under the "Two-Five" were to be spent in holding meetings, inspecting work, and studying political theory and Party policies. The policy of sending cadres to the countryside or

towns began to be sent in large numbers to the production front in the countryside, a policy which was continued through 1965 and revived in 1968-69. In October 1960, for example, over a million young people left the cities to work in rural areas.[148]

The overt and hidden rural unemployment and underemployment existing in 1957 was in the course of a few months transformed into a labor shortage. Everyone seemed to be doing everything at the same time, and there were not enough hands to go around. There was no planning, no forethought, no coordination—merely appeals to an undernourished *esprit de corps* which was expected to make the economy surge ahead, irrespective of imbalances and fluctuations. In 1958 the shortage of labor was estimated at 100,000 million days, half of which was made up by continuous day and night work. The shortage was aggravated by the campaign for intensive cultivation and the collection of manure. Because of the shortage of draught animals, manpower was substituted for animal draught power in many areas. In Liaoning in 1958, 75 percent of animal draught power was replaced by manpower.[149] By 1960 the Leap was organized anarchy eluding the organizers. In September 1959, as we have seen, word spread that labor in the communes was to be readjusted: limits were set on the number of peasants detached to commune-run and state-run industries, the rule of thumb being that not more than 5 percent of the available labor power in any given commune was to be diverted to industrial occupations and that 80 percent of the remainder was to be directed to field work during the busy season. "At the present time," Li Fu-chun lectured the masses a year later, "the key to the growth of agricultural production lies in economizing on the use of labor power in all fields so as to reinforce the agricultural front. . . . In allocating rural labor power, consideration should be given both to capital construction and to current productive work, with priority given to current production; farming, forestry, animal husbandry, side occupations, fishery, and rural industries, commerce, and cultural, educational and health undertakings must all be taken into account, but the main attention should be given to farming. In agricultural production, attention should be given to grain and to industrial and other crops, but with the main attention to grain."[150] The revisionist policy of agriculture as the foundation and industry as the leading factor was, not surprisingly, attributed to Mao

xiafang was continued through 1965, and stepped up in 1968-69 (Chapters 11, 12). See, "*Xiafang* Cadres Do Their Stuff," *Peking Review* (December 20, 1960), p. 3.

[148] *Jen-min Jih-pao* (November 22, 1960).
[149] T. C. Lee, "The Food Problem," *op. cit.*, pp. 20-21.
[150] Li Fu-chun, *Raise High the Red Flag . . . op. cit.*, pp. 21-22.

Tse-tung, yet it was, in fact, the end—for the time being—of Mao's
dream of walking on many legs. The new emphasis on agriculture
(especially grain production) as the very essence of socialist construction, was first contained in Li Fu-chun's report to the National
People's Congress in March 1960, and repeated by P'eng Chen in his
report to the Third Session of the Third Peking Municipal People's
Congress (June 24-30, 1960).[151] As will be shown in Chapter 9, it
was to become the main feature of the relatively moderate and pragmatic economic program of the period between the collapse of the
Great Leap Forward and the launching of the Great Proletarian Cultural Revolution (1961—end 1965).

The problems just discussed were made more intractable by the
statistical confusion in which the Leap Forward took place. In 1958
and 1959 the power of the State Statistical Bureau to collect agricultural statistics was decentralized down to the commune level with
deleterious effects on the reliability of the figures communicated by
the communes to the central authorities in an atmosphere of target
leaping. In 1959 crop production figures ceased to be published,
except for grain, cotton, and soya beans. As the statistical emulation
proceeded, the center lost all knowledge of what was really going on
at the production front and failed to see ominous signs of crisis all
around. For a time (until late 1958) it seems that the central authorities took the inflated field reports at face value and did nothing to
stem the tide of the cadres' leftist inclination to go one better than
the next commune, at least in statistical reporting.

3. Overinvestment (i.e., Misallocation of Investment Resources)
and Other Disproportionalities

Walking on two legs meant large investments by both the central
and local authorities with progressively less coordination. State investments both within and outside the state plan rose from 13.8 bil-

---

[151] *Jen-min Jih-pao*, March 31, 1960 and *ibid.*, July 2, 1960. P'eng Chen, a
member of the CPC Central Committee and Politbureau and mayor of Peking,
was among the first top leaders to be purged during the Great Proletarian Cultural Revolution. Out of public view since March 1966, he was removed from
office in June. The shift in strategy (examined in detail in Chapter 9) was explained in the following way: "Two years ago, the Communist Party formulated
the General Line for Building Socialism which incorporated the policy of making
agriculture the foundation and industry the dominant factor, and the simultaneous development of industry and agriculture, while giving priority to heavy
industry. . . . In August 1959 at the Eighth Plenary Session of the Communist
Party's Eighth Central Committee and afterwards, Chairman Mao Tse-tung repeatedly elaborated the theses of making agriculture the foundation for the
growth of the national economy and placing it foremost in drawing up the
national economic plan. At the same time, he issued a great call to the nation for
'universal support to agriculture.' " "Industry Supports Agriculture," *Peking Review* (August 9, 1960), p. 19.

lion yuan in 1957 to 26.7 billion yuan in 1958, or by 93.5 percent. Investment in industry went up from 7.24 billion yuan in 1957 to 17.3 billion yuan in 1958. Investment in agriculture rose from 1.19 billion yuan in 1957 to 2.63 billion yuan in 1958 (of which water conservation took 730 million yuan in 1957 and 1.96 billion yuan in 1958).[152] Large increases were also registered in investments directed to transport and communications. Much of the Leap Forward in industrial production claimed for 1958 could simply be accounted for by the completion in that year of large projects initiated earlier. Some 700 such projects were completed in 1958 and immediately went into production. Sectors which registered a decrease in state investments between 1957 and 1958 included building, culture, education and scientific research (these were to be taken care of by spontaneous mass research and local effort) as well as public health and welfare (supposedly taken care of for the most part by the communes on their own initiative and at their expense). Industry, which in 1957 received 52.3 percent of total state investments, got 64.8 percent a year later, while agriculture's share rose from 8.6 percent in 1957 to 9.9 percent in 1958 (of which water conservation accounted for 5.3 percent in 1957 and 7.3 percent in 1958).[153] If note is taken of peasant self-investment and other items discussed earlier (Chapter 4), agriculture's share of gross fixed investment may be put at 24 percent in 1958, and 23.2 percent in 1959 (compared with about 23 percent in 1957).[154] According to Hollister,[155] gross investment, which was 22.6 percent of gross national product in 1957, jumped to an unprecedented 32.3 percent in 1958, and 33.2 percent in 1959. These large investments resulted in the production of capital goods which could not easily find employment because of shortages of complementary factors. The GNP growth during 1958 and 1959 was thus largely illusory. There was in Keynesian terms, a "sudden collapse in the marginal efficiency of capital" leading almost inevitably to retrenchment.

[152] *Ten Great Years*, pp. 55-57. "So long as we know how to rely on this great force of our 500 million peasants, we can greatly expand the scope of agricultural construction even if there is no increase in state investments in agriculture." Liu Shao-ch'i, "Report to the Second Session of the Eighth National Party Congress," *op. cit.*

[153] *Ten Great Years*, pp. 55-60.

[154] William W. Hollister, "Trends in Capital Formation in Communist China," in: *op. cit.*, p. 128, Table 4. On this calculation, the share of heavy industry in 1958 was 41.1 percent (29.2 percent in 1957), and that of light industry 5.9 percent (5.7 percent in 1957).

[155] William W. Hollister, *op. cit.*, p. 125, Table 1. According to Wu et al., *The Economic Potential of Communist China, op. cit.*, p. 340, the investment rate (gross investment to gross national product) was 28.8 percent in 1958, 35.9 percent in 1959, and 43.7 percent in 1960.

The Great Leap Forward was characterized by an easy money policy of staggering proportions. Agricultural loans made by Party apparatchik-controlled banks in 1958, were reportedly equal to the total amount of bank credit made available during the period 1953-57, or about 9 billion yuan.[156] The flood of loans, supplementary budget allocations, and extrabudgetary financing removed whatever pressure there had been on the communes to give attention to profit and income targets (i.e., to paying their way as the cooperatives were earlier expected to do), and encouraged commune leaderships to focus their efforts on achieving and surpassing physical output goals, which were more often than not set by neighboring communes in the course of frenetic mass emulation. In spite of the statistical difficulties involved, there is evidence that repressed inflation was very much in evidence in 1960-62.[157] There appears to have been no attempt, and in due course no possibility, to dovetail and coordinate the various lavish investment expenditures with the result that bottlenecks and disproportions, and hence a monumental waste of resources appeared. One of the major bottlenecks seems to have arisen through the relatively insufficient development and absolutely reckless exploitation of the country's raw materials base: newly constructed factories and processing plants began to stand idle or operate below capacity due to raw materials supply shortages. Because of the disappointing performance of agriculture, industries relying on raw materials supplied by that sector were especially affected. The 1961 New Year's editorial of *Jen-min Jih-pao* admitted that "the 1960 production plans for agriculture and light industry which relies on agriculture for its raw materials, have not been fulfilled." In 1960 a campaign was launched to collect wild plants for use as raw materials and to save sesame stalks, rice bran, bean chaff and peanut peel as sources of oil. Greasy refuse from restaurants, hotels, and offices was carefully collected.[158] In 1962 a campaign was initiated in Shanghai to grow castor oil plants on empty city lots. Some of the larger industrial projects were badly hurt in mid-1960 by the sudden withdrawal of Soviet experts and the

[156] *China News Analysis*, No. 258 (January 2, 1959), p. 5. In 1942 in his *Economic and Financial Questions During the Period of the Anti-Japanese War*, Mao wrote: "Financial difficulties can be overcome only by down-to-earth and effective economic development. To neglect economic development and the opening up of sources of finance, and instead to hope for the solution of financial difficulties by curtailing indispensable expenditures, is a conservative notion which cannot solve any problem." *SW, op. cit.*, pp. 111-112.

[157] Yuan-li Wu, *The Economy of Communist China, op. cit.*, p. 96, note 20. An interesting contribution is Dwight H. Perkins, "Price Stability and Development in Mainland China (1951-63)," *Journal of Political Economy* (August 1964), pp. 360-375.

[158] *FEER* (October 19, 1961), p. 147.

concurrent cutback in Soviet capital deliveries (see below, p. 316). Existing machinery, like the men who serviced it, was used thoughtlessly, without proper arrangements for rest, repair, and proper maintenance. The deterioration of steel producing machinery (especially large precision finishing equipment) was particularly serious. Quality problems with special steels (sheets, plates, tubes, fittings) became acute. Trouble was also experienced in the copper, aluminum and electricity industries.

The durability of equipment in the tens of thousands of local, do-it-yourself industries was very low, maintenance costs high. Great pressure was put on local transport to ship the products of native industries to their destinations. The problem was made worse by the habit of evaluating the success of transport enterprises in terms of volume of freight shipments, a manner of proceeding which led naturally to emulation in making unnecessary trips.[159]

Already in 1960 Li Fu-chun referred to the "mutually restricting contradictions" between production and capital construction, and advised that "We ought gradually to enlarge the scale of capital construction, provided that an upsurge in production is first assured. We should not undertake too many projects at a time and extend our frontline, ignoring the order of importance and urgency. To do so would be incompatible with the requirement of getting greater, quicker, better, and more economical results. . . . All nonproductive construction projects which are at present unnecessary or can be postponed, should be canceled or postponed. As for productive construction projects, they should be built as simply as possible, and more things should be done at less cost."[160]

As had been noted earlier, the expansion of producer goods output during the Leap generated much purchasing power which could not find an outlet in a larger quantity of consumer goods. The official retail price index does not reveal this presumed inflationary situation, partly because of the index's downward bias. It has been suggested that inflation was to a degree kept in check by sizable peasant hoarding and peasant purchases of agricultural capital through commune-controlled channels. It was also suppressed by rationing of cotton and some industrial consumer goods. Urban purchasing power spilled into the black market in 1960-61, and was responsible for the upward pressure on prices in the rural fairs (Chapter 9). On the whole, the suspicion that inflationary pressures existed rests on the assumption of an unintended relaxation of physical controls accompanied by increased money flows in the later phases of the Great Leap.

159 Yuan-li Wu, *The Economy of Communist China, op. cit.*, p. 101.
160 Li Fu-chun, *Raise High the Red Flag . . . , op. cit.*, pp. 33-35.

In his "The Victory of Marxism-Leninism in China" written in September 1959 overtly in defense of the Great Leap Forward, but covertly in partial explanation and justification of the dissenters' viewpoint, Liu Shao-ch'i lashed out against "certain people" who asserted that the Big Leap was "an abnormal phenomenon, that organizing mass movements in economic construction can only cause dislocation in production and that even though a temporary leap forward may be effected it will inevitably result in such disproportions in the national economy that it will be impossible to keep the leap forward going."[161] He admitted that "when a mass movement is in full swing, some production regimes will be upset," but he rejected the contention of "some people" (at least 50 percent of the Central Committee, one is inclined to think) "that the adoption of a leap forward rate of advance goes against objective economic laws and will give rise to disproportions in the various branches of the national economy."[162] What China wanted, he asserted, was "both a high speed and overall balance. This is not easy to achieve; in high-speed development it is more likely that certain imbalances will occur."[163] Those who "described our great cause as being in an awful mess" were characterized by Liu as "hostile forces."[164] Now by September 1959 everybody in China knew that when a mass movement was in full swing, some production regimes would be upset, that high speed and overall balance were not easy to achieve simultaneously, and that the great cause was in an awful mess. Liu's tongue-in-cheek justification of the Big Leap policies and of their underlying philosophy, could not but make the leap look even worse than it was. "Coal and iron will not walk by themselves and had to be transported by rolling stock," Mao mused at Lushan in July 1959. "I did not anticipate this point."

There is a voluminous literature from Schumpeter to Wiles about this very subject of growth versus choice, or the question of balanced versus imbalanced growth. It is legitimate to argue, as did Schumpeter, that "a system—any system, economic or other—that at every given point of time utilizes its possibilities to the best advantage, may yet in the long run be inferior to a system that does so at *no* point, because the latter's failure to do so may be a condition for the level

---

[161] Liu Shao-ch'i, *op. cit.*, p. 63. Cf. ". . . The Machians imagined that through reliance on the role of the psychological factor they could do whatever they pleased, but the result was that they ran their heads against a brick wall of reality and went bankrupt in the end." Teng T'o, "Two Foreign Fables," Evening Chats at Yenshan, Vol. V, pp. 91-93. First published in *Peking Evening News* (November 26, 1961). See Chapter 11.

[162] Liu Shao-ch'i, *loc. cit.*, pp. 64-65.

[163] *Ibid.*, p. 66.

[164] *Ibid.*, p. 70.

or speed of long-run performance."[165] Rapid growth, Wiles has argued, tends to float off many allocation errors (even permanent ones), eases the problem of forecasting, and in the long run reduces the seriousness of violating consumers' sovereignty.[166] Or as Liu put it, there is no need to give way to "fear of the wolf in front and the tiger behind, vainly hoping for a haven of peace by adopting the method of reducing speed unjustifiably to achieve balance."[167] Provided, of course, there is growth, and growth sustained over time. The degree of imbalance is crucial. Where imbalance is such as to stunt growth, where it becomes a mere psychological underpinning of mass drives and campaigns and an intellectual shorthand, it defeats what rationale can be mustered in its defense. Wiles has put it more forcefully. "There are," he says, "good arguments as well as bad for deliberately unbalanced growth, and there are arguments for not worrying too much about imbalance if it is the by-product of a greater good. But the whole matter must be looked at soberly. While it is absurd to die in the last ditch of 'choice' it is still foolish to go a-whoring after the new bitch-goddess, growth. In particular, poverty does not excuse such a shift of affections. For if poverty makes growth more necessary it also makes waste more intolerable."[168] There is such a thing as waste growth—the end result of erratic waste motion. Much of the product of the Great Leap was just such waste growth.

4. The Soviet Exodus[169]

Trouble between the Russians and the Chinese had been brewing ever since the early spring of 1956. Khrushchev's de-Stalinization speech at the closed session of the Soviet Party's 20th Congress caught the Chinese by surprise. For a time they tried to make the best of it by going through the motions of a new look in politics and

[165] Joseph Schumpeter, *Capitalism, Socialism and Democracy* (New York: Harper, 1947), p. 83.

[166] Peter Wiles, "Growth versus Choice," *The Economic Journal* (June 1956), pp. 244-255, and "Scarcity, Marxism, and Gosplan," *Oxford Economic Papers* (October 1953), pp. 288-316.

[167] Liu Shao-ch'i *op. cit.*, pp. 66-67. On the Party's contribution to the bad years, see Alexander Eckstein, "On the Economic Crisis in Communist China," *Foreign Affairs*, Vol. 42, No. 4 (July 1964), pp. 655-668, and Kang Chao, "Economic Aftermath of the Great Leap in Communist China," *Asian Survey* (May 1964), pp. 851-858.

[168] Peter Wiles, *The Political Economy of Communism* (Cambridge, Mass.: Harvard U. P., and Basil Blackwell, Ltd., Oxford, 1962), p. 218.

[169] For an interesting interpretation of the genesis of the Sino-Soviet conflict, see Adam B. Ulam, *Expansion and Coexistence: The History of Soviet Foreign Policy, 1917-1967* (New York: Praeger, 1969). For the post-Stalin development of Sino-Soviet relations, see Peter Mayer, *Sino-Soviet Relations Since the Death of Stalin* (Hong Kong: URI, 1962).

economics, but there was deep unease within the Chinese Party's leadership about how wise it was to follow the Soviets along what looked like an increasingly revisionist path.

Khrushchev's emphasis on the peaceful transition to socialism and on peaceful coexistence of states with different social systems as a long-term strategy rather than a tactical slogan, ran counter to the Maoist dialectical view of the world as a continuous clash of class opposites. Mao's 1957 essay on contradictions was intended to theoretically elucidate this question. Although primarily addressing itself to China's domestic situation, it contained an implied international message.[170] It was meant to stem the tide of revisionism and subtly give notice that there were still true Marxist-Leninists in the socialist camp who intended to keep the revolutionary pot boiling.

Among some sections of the Chinese leadership (the Maoist radicals) there had developed a disappointment with the scale of Soviet economic aid, irritation with Soviet lack of tact, a contempt for the ideological mediocrity and intellectual crudeness of Khrushchev, and a deepening suspicion that the Soviet model of economic development was not applicable to China, except in its broadest and most general outline. With the death of Stalin, Mao Tse-tung emerged as the logical *doyen* of Marxist-Leninist theoreticians by reason of his intellectual output, his command over communism's most populous nation, his understanding of the problems of developing non-European areas (at least insofar as the toppling of the old regimes

[170] The Chinese had their own "Five Principles of Peaceful Coexistence" which, much more than the Soviet coexistence thesis, were compatible with brush wars in support of local "national liberation" movements. The Five Principles were first formulated in an agreement which China signed with India in April 1954. The agreement acknowledged China's sovereignty over Tibet and contained provisions for trade between Tibet and India. In June 1954, Jawaharlal Nehru and Chou En-lai issued a joint communique in New Delhi in which they reiterated the Five Principles, or as they were often referred to, the *Panch Sheela*. The Principles are general and platitudinous, but tactically astute. They had, at the time, a strong appeal to Asian neutralist opinion. They covered: (1) mutual respect for each other's national territory, (2) nonaggression, (3) noninterference in each other's internal affairs, (4) equality and mutual benefit, (5) peaceful coexistence. From June 1954 to mid-1957 the Five Principles became the *leitmotiv* of Communist China's diplomacy. They were incorporated, with only minor modifications, in the Bandung Declaration of Asian and African Powers (1955), and in nearly all treaties and agreements concluded by Asian countries in the years immediately following the Bandung Conference. The text of the original Five Principles may be found in *NCNA* release of Apr. 29, 1954. Liu Shao-ch'i referred to them and to the "Bandung Spirit" in his official pronouncements as late as May 1963. See also A. M. Halperin, "Communist China and Peaceful Coexistence," *The China Quarterly*, No. 3, 1960, pp. 16-31. It had been rumored in Indian government circles that Prime Minister Nehru had hoped to insert into the April 1954 agreement a delimitation of the ill-defined and disputed Sino-Indian boundary. This was not, however, included in the document.

was concerned), and his longevity. The creative aspects of Mao's Marxism in both theory and practice began to be stressed with growing frequency: what mattered was the creative fusion of the universal truths of Marxism-Leninism with the "concrete conditions of China." Since China was poor and blank, such a combination of truth and the concrete circumstances of the poor and the oppressed, contained in it lessons of universal validity for Asian, African, and Latin American countries striving, as the Chinese put it, to overthrow the yoke of capitalist imperialism. The Russians had grown fat and indolent, flabby as revolutionaries go, more concerned with filling their larder than helping others rid themselves of hunger and colonial oppression. The reforms which they initiated in their own country and passed off as orthodox Marxism-Leninism, were in reality (so argued the Chinese radicals) revisionist refinements, poor imitations of capitalist marginal balancing, more concerned with rationalizing a semiopulent status quo than with forging ahead in the true tradition of communist revolutionaries. In their obsessive concern with refrigerators and printed dresses, the Soviets had lost their communist vision and hence their right to speak for the world's rural proletariat. "Khrushchev's 'communism,' " the Chinese remonstrated, "is indeed 'goulash communism,' the 'communism of the American way of life,' and 'communism seeking credits from the devil.' "[171] The great nuclear and industrial power at the disposal of the Soviets was being misused and squandered in futile material pursuits, in talking up to the great of this world, and talking down to the poor. Even without ideological refinements, the Soviet economic model had, in the eyes of the Maoists, become irrelevant for China because it was a model of a relatively industrialized, semideveloped country calling itself socialist, and not a blueprint for breaking out of destitution. It had too much to do with consumption and too little with revolution in production. It was becoming too cost-oriented, too complex and delicate an instrument, and too refined in its tools to serve as a plan for revolutionary transformation in the world's underdeveloped regions. It lacked *élan*. In these circumstances the revolutionary peoples of the world—including first and foremost the Chinese people—would be well advised to strike out independently, to rely on their own resources, and bear in mind the experience of China immortalized in the theoretical writings and creative thoughts of Mao Tse-tung. The moderates within the Chinese Party, those old-line bureaucrats and Party bosses, were wary of such arguments not because of any par-

171 "On Khrushchev's Phoney Communism and Its Historical Lessons for the World," Ninth Comment on the Open Letter of the Central Committee of the Communist Party of the USSR by the Editorial Departments of *Jen-min Jih-pao* and *Hung-ch'i* (July 14, 1964) in *The Polemic, op. cit.*, p. 465.

ticular admiration of and love for the Soviet Union, but because they were apprehensive of the staggering magnitude of going it alone in economic construction and because they sensed the importance of scientific and technological borrowing in a world of rapid change.[172] They were suspicious of charisma applied to economic development, of inspirational slogans allegedly materializing in millions of bare arms, unsupported by modern machinery and the reasoned calculation of the odds. They feared a break with the Soviet Union—that is, with the only significant foreign supplier of both commodities: capital and brain power. They were willing to accept a measure of revisionism (adapted to the "concrete conditions of China") as the necessary price for China's orderly emergence from the grips of poverty. In this they miscalculated the tactical virtuosity of the radicals and imperfectly appraised the precise nature and mobilizing potential of nationalist sentiment in China.[173] The apparat-men were temperamentally predisposed to take Marxism at its word, that is, "scientifically"; they tried to understand its laws, economics, and logic. The Maoists, more in tune with China's psychological makeup, sought out the symbolic meaning of Marxism: its vision, promise, ritual, and its subjective impact on the mass of practitioners faced with occult forces.[174]

China's—or more precisely, the Chinese Communist left's— disillusionment with the scope of Soviet economic assistance, the Soviet developmental model (especially with the revisions operated on that model after the death of Stalin), and the quality and purpose of the Soviet Union's international socialist leadership was enhanced by the events of October-November 1956 in Eastern Europe. The Chinese left interpreted the Polish and Hungarian revolts (the first contained within a communist framework, the second almost breaking out of that framework) as the inevitable result of Soviet revisionist policies. China adopted a dialectical attitude toward these events, supporting the Poles and urging armed Soviet intervention to stem what it considered to be a counterrevolutionary tide in

[172] In his Introduction to the *Collected Works of Liu Shao-ch'i, 1958-1967* published by the Union Research Institute, Hong Kong, in 1968, Chang Kuo-tao, a cofounder of the Communist Party of China, has this to say: "Some people consider Liu Shao-ch'i pro-Russian; this view is unreliable. In the Chinese Communist Party it is Chen Shao-yu and his followers who are pro-Russia. Liu Shao-ch'i's discontent for Soviet Russia should at least equal that of Mao Tse-tung, but Liu probably does not approve of the extent of the present split with Soviet Russia. And he would never approve of a foreign policy which antagonized the whole world." (p. ix.)

[173] For a summary of the moderate position on various issues, see below, pp. 324-332.

[174] See Amaury de Riencourt, *The Soul of China* (New York: Coward-McCann, 1958), pp. 267-271, and Thome H. Fang, *The Chinese View of Life* (Hong Kong: URI, 1957).

Hungary. Such an attitude seems to reflect the position of what has been described as the moderate elements within the Chinese Party, preoccupied as these were and continue to be with the retention and protection of the monopoly power of the Communist Party. At the same time, however, the policy accommodated the leftists, concerned with "big power chauvinism" and what they viewed as the Soviet Union's propensity to meddle in the internal affairs of fraternal countries. Overall, the Polish and Hungarian events of 1956 constituted a considerable embarrassment to the Soviets and provided China with the first opportunity to make its voice heard in matters of European policy. Ever so discreetly, the events also weakened the position of China's moderates who, in spite of many qualifications, saw in the continued leadership of the Soviet Union a not undesirable phenomenon from the standpoint of China's socialist construction.

Khrushchev's Party difficulties after the Polish revolt and the Hungarian revolution (the "anti-Party" struggle of mid-1957) and his domestic economic problems, tended to strengthen the hand of the Chinese leftists who, for all their dialectical acrobatics, were consistent in viewing revisionist experiments as detrimental internally and externally to the cause of socialism. In the late summer and early autumn of 1957, at the very time that the wave of radicalism was once again rising in China, the Soviet Union successfully launched its first intercontinental ballistic missile and orbited its Sputnik. The interpretation put on these achievements by the ascendant radical faction in China was that thenceforth strategic superiority had passed from the United States to the USSR and that, therefore, the time had come for a more aggressive communist policy in support of national wars of liberation, even at the risk of a wider, possibly nuclear, conflict. Mao's thesis that the atomic bomb was a "paper tiger" was resurrected.[175] The bluff of the imperialists had to be called, whatever the risk. Now was the time to settle accounts with the capitalist camp once and for all. The Soviets were unimpressed. A close look at the awesome might of modern weapons did not allay, but on the contrary, sharpened Soviet apprehensions. "The atomic

---

[175] "The atom bomb is a paper tiger which the U.S. reactionaries use to scare people. It looks terrible, but in fact it isn't. Of course, the atom bomb is a weapon of mass slaughter, but the outcome of a war is decided by the people, not by one or two new types of weapons." Mao Tse-tung, "Talk with the American Correspondent Anna Louise Strong" (August 1946), *SW*, Vol. IV, p. 100. See also Anna Louise Strong, "Reminiscences on Interview with Chairman Mao Tse-tung on the Paper Tiger," *Peking Review* (November 29, 1960), pp. 13-17. "The atom bomb can scare only cowards who have lost their revolutionary will; it cannot scare revolutionary people." Lo Jui-ching (Chief of the General Staff of the PLA) in *Peking Review* (September 3, 1965), p. 33.

bomb," the Soviets later lectured the Chinese, "does not draw class distinctions—it destroys everybody within the range of its destructive power."[176] The corollary to this line of reasoning, one, moreover, that catered to the Soviet Union's leading socialist-power ambitions and her fears of a rocket-armed, unpredictable, and wayward neighbor, was to do everything possible to keep too many inexperienced hands from fingering the nuclear trigger.

In the meantime the Chinese kept up the pressure. On October 15, 1957 a high level Chinese military delegation reportedly obtained from the Soviets assurances of help in the development of China's nuclear military capacity. The Soviet promise was probably designed to improve the climate for the impending meeting in Moscow of sixty-four communist parties. But the meeting (November 1957) went rather badly for the Soviets. The Declaration of the Moscow meeting (not subscribed to by the Yugoslav delegates) bears the marks of Soviet authorship and Chinese influence, the latter especially with regard to internal problems of the international communist movement. It contains references to "intensified struggle against opportunist trends" within the movement and to "the main danger ... [of] revisionism or, in other words, right-wing opportunism, which as a manifestation of bourgeois ideology paralyzes the revolutionary energy of the working class and demands the preservation or restoration of capitalism."[177] Mao Tse-tung who attended the meeting, demanded equality of treatment for China at the pinnacle of international communism.

"The East wind," he lectured the assembled delegates, "prevails over the West wind," meaning (as the Chinese press explained) that "the superiority of the forces of socialism over those of imperialism, the forces of national liberation movement over those of colonialism, the revolutionary forces over the reactionary forces, the forces of peace over those of war, has become ever more marked." "In the struggle between the truth of Marxism and the fallacies of the bourgeoisie and all other exploiting classes, either the East wind prevails over the West wind or the West wind prevails over the East

[176]"Open Letter of the Central Committee of the CPSU, to All Party Organizations, to All Communists of the Soviet Union" (July 14, 1963), in *The Polemic, op. cit.,* p. 542. For years after the meeting the Soviets kept referring to the "fundamentals" of the Moscow Declaration; the Chinese to the "revolutionary principles" of that document. See for example, "Give Full Play to the Revolutionary Spirit of the 1957 Moscow Declaration," *Jen-min Jih-pao* editorial, November 21, 1960, in *Peking Review* (November 29, 1960), pp. 6-8.

[177] The text of the Moscow Declaration may be found in G. F. Hudson, Richard Lowenthal, Roderick MacFarquhar, *The Sino-Soviet Dispute* (New York: Praeger, 1961), pp. 46ff.

wind, and there is absolutely no such thing as equality [before the truth]." [178]

"Some people," wrote Teng T'o (see Chapter 11), "have the gift of the gab. They can talk endlessly on any occasion, like water flowing from an undammed river. After listening to them, however, when you try to recall what they have said, you can remember nothing. . . . As chance would have it, my neighbor's child has recently often imitated the style of some great poet and put into writing a lot of 'great empty talk.' . . . . Not long ago he wrote a poem entitled 'Ode to Wild Grass' which is nothing but empty talk. The poem reads as follows:

> The Venerable Heaven is our father,
> The Great Earth is our mother,
> And the Sun is our nanny;
> The East Wind is our benefactor,
> And the West Wind is our enemy.

Although such words as heaven, earth, father, mother, sun, nanny, the East wind, the West wind, benefactor, and enemy catch our eye, they are used to no purpose here and have become mere clichés. Recourse to even the first words and phrases is futile, or rather, the more such clichés are uttered, the worse the situation will become." [179]

The November 1957 Moscow experience gave the Soviets a jolt from which they never quite recovered. In 1958 they apparently reneged on their nuclear promise to China and "put forward unreasonable demands designed to bring China under Soviet military control." [180] What these unreasonable demands were, may only be guessed at. On second thoughts the Soviets probably suggested to the Chinese that the best solution was to have Soviet nuclear armed units stationed on Chinese territory. The suggestion was, according to the Chinese, "rightly and firmly rejected by the Chinese government." By June 1959 there was no further question of Sino-Soviet nuclear cooperation. At that time (June 20, 1959), the Chinese say, "the Soviet Government unilaterally tore up the agreement on new technology for national defense concluded between China and the Soviet

[178] "Circular of the Central Committee of the Communist Party of China," May 16, 1966 (published May 18, 1967).

[179] "Great Empty Talk," *Frontline* (Peking) No. 21, 1961, in *The Great Socialist Cultural Revolution*, No. 2 (Peking: FLP, 1966), pp. 13-14.

[180] "The Origin and Development of the Differences Between the Leadership of the CPSU and Ourselves," Comment on the Open Letter of the Central Committee of the CPSU by the Editorial Departments of *Jen-min Jih-pao* and *Hung-ch'i*, September 6, 1963, in *The Polemic, op. cit.*, p. 77. Note also that in August-September, 1958, Khrushchev failed to support China in the offshore islands crisis.

Union in October 1957, and refused to provide China with a sample of an atomic bomb and technical data concerning its manufacture."[181] About that time (August 1959) Defense Minister P'eng Teh-huai who pinned his hopes for the modernization of China's armed forces on Soviet help and opposed the army's involvement in economic construction, was fired. (See Chapter 11.) With him went a whole "anti-Party" group, including the army's Chief of Staff, Huang Ko-cheng.[182] In conformity with the stress on self-reliance, the Chinese set up their own Institute of Atomic Energy and launched a program of nuclear weapons development. In an ungentlemanly outburst of proletarian levity, Nikita Khrushchev opined that the development of nuclear capacity cost so much money that the Chinese might have no money left to make trousers with. Foreign Minister Chen Yi assured a group of Japanese visitors in October 1963 that China would make nuclear weapons, with or without pants.[183] The initial cost of a nuclear development program has been estimated at about $130 million a year, and to reach a French-type (1968) strike capacity might cost about $1 billion per year, or about 25 percent of China's estimated defense outlays. Such magnitudes are not beyond the reach of *sans-culottes*, provided, as Mao would phrase it, the spirit is willing and the priorities are right. In her development of nuclear capability China profited from the services of American-trained H. S. Tsien and some eighty other scientists educated at American universities. Tsien returned to China from the United States in 1955 and was soon thereafter named director of the Institute of Mechanics of the Academy of Sciences.[184]

In October 1964, a year after Soviet scientist Klochko predicted that "it will be a long time before China joins the nuclear club,"[185] the Chinese exploded a uranium atomic device. The event was hailed by the Chinese press as "a major contribution made by the Chinese

181 *Ibid.*

182 See "The Reactionary History of P'eng Teh-huai," Collected Materials on P'eng Teh-huai published by the Peking Red Guard Congress, Tsinghua University Chingkangshan Corps, November 1967, in *URS*, Vol. 50, No. 15 (February 20, 1968); No. 16 (February 23, 1968); No. 17 (February 27, 1968). *SCMP*, No. 4032 (1968), pp. 1-5. "Central Committee of the CPC: Resolution Concerning the Anti-Party Clique Headed by P'eng Teh-huai (August 1959), first published in *Peking Review*, August 18, 1967, pp. 8-10.

183 Japanese News Agency *Kyodo* news dispatch (October 28, 1963) reported by *The New York Times* (October 29, 1963), pp. 1, 14. © 1963 by The New York Times Company. Reprinted by permission. See also Alexandra Close, "Bombs or Trousers?" *FEER* (October 29, 1964), p. 237.

184 For the Tsien story see William L. Ryan and Sam Summerlin, *The China Cloud: America's Tragic Blunder and China's Rise to Nuclear Power* (Boston: Little, Brown, 1969).

185 Mikhail A. Klochko, *Soviet Scientist in Red China*, *op. cit.*, p. 208.

people to the cause of the defense of world peace," and an example of what could be done by "relying on [one's] own efforts."[186]

As the ideological and practical wrangling went on behind the scenes, occasionally bursting into the open, the Chinese leadership launched the Great Leap Forward, in one respect a declaration of economic independence from the Soviet Union. At first the Soviets were taken aback. They were shortly to be dumbfounded by the rural people's communes and the ideological rider attached to them. By late 1959 they had sorted out the evidence, gathered their wits about them, and drawn pessimistic conclusions regarding the Leap's meaning and future. The Soviet soul-searching and initial disarray are clearly revealed by the trade figures (Table 8-6).

TABLE 8-6
Sino-Soviet Trade, 1957-61
(Millions of U.S. dollars)

Year	Soviet Exports	Soviet Imports	Total	Soviet Balance
1957	545.0	750.0	1295.0	-205.0
1958	634.0	881.2	1515.2	-247.2
1959	954.5	1100.0	2054.5	-145.5
1960	817.1	848.1	1665.2	- 31.0
1961	367.3	551.4	918.7	-184.1

Sources: Official Soviet foreign trade statistics; M. Sladkovskii, "The Development of Trade Between the Soviet Union and the People's Republic of China," *Vneshniaia torgovlia* (Moscow, October 1959); "Communist China's Balance of Payments 1950-65," in *An Economic Profile of Mainland China, op. cit.*, p. 645, Table 12, and R. L. Price, *ibid.*, pp. 592-593. Cf. Tables 6-5 and 9-7.

Caught by surprise, the Soviets stepped up their exports of industrial raw materials and capital equipment, especially complete plants in 1958-60 (Table 8-7). Complete plants which in 1957 accounted for about 20 percent of Chinese imports from the USSR, rose to 26 percent in 1958, 42 percent in 1959, and 46 percent in 1960, then dropped to 21.5 percent in 1961, and a mere 3.8 percent in 1962.[187] According to the Soviets, deliveries to China of metal-cutting lathes

[186] *NCNA*, Peking (October 16, 1964). Cf. Chapter 9 below. "China is manufacturing atom bombs in order to liquidate them. . . ." Ch'en Yi, *Important Remarks at a Press Conference Attended by Chinese and Foreign Correspondents* (Peking: FLP, 1966).

[187] USSR Ministry of Foreign Trade, *Vneshniaia torgovlia SSSR za 1955-1959 godi: Statisticheskii Sbornik; ibid.*, 1961. Foreign trade statistics of China's trading partners. Soviet aid for 47 additional large projects was agreed on—at short notice—in August 1958. Another 78 projects (worth $1.25 billion) were added to the list in February 1959. Cf. Table 9-8 below.

rose from 280 units in 1957 to 738 in 1958; drilling machines from 129 to 296; tractors from 68 to 2,656; trucks from 284 to 20,595. Exports of machinery and equipment to China in 1958 constituted 40 percent of total Soviet exports of those goods, and 50.2 percent of Soviet exports to China. There was also an increase in Soviet sales to China of iron and steel rolled products, pipe, and aluminum. In return the Soviet accepted meat and meat products, rice, ores and concentrates, nonferrous metals, fruit, and manufactured consumer goods.[188]

TABLE 8-7

Commodity Composition of Soviet Exports to China, 1958–1961
(Millions of U. S. dollars)

	1958	1959	1960	1961
Machinery and equipment.	318.0	597.5	503.9	108.1
Complete plants	(166.2)	(399.8)	(373.8)	(78.9)
Industrial raw materials . .	173.4	176.3	188.7	166.9
Petroleum and products.	(92.4)	(117.7)	(113.1)	(120.7)
Ferrous metals	(60.8)	(48.0)	(59.3)	(34.7)
Nonferrous metals.	(15.8)	(6.4)	(10.5)	(6.5)
Consumer goods	9.2	6.6	4.4	67.2
Foods.	(1.1)	(0.5)	(negl.)	(63.8)
Other merchandise	17.0	12.3	13.1	6.1
Other unspecified	116.4	161.4	107.0	19.1
Total	634.0	954.5	817.1	367.3

Sources: Exports f.o.b. as in Table 8-6. Components may not add up to total because of rounding.

As the Leap progressed and regressed bouncingly and apparently without rhyme or reason, the Chinese at very short notice asked Moscow for stepped-up deliveries of all kinds of equipment which the Soviets had not earmarked for export in their long-range plans. Not only that, but Peking with fraternal insouciance and a disregard for the rules of the planning game, kept changing its orders and specifications and demanded now this, now that alteration in previously concluded agreements and protocols on economic, scientific, and technical assistance.[189] Centrally planned economies of the Soviet species are not geared to that kind of elasticity; they typically suffer from supply rigidities when it comes to sudden and unforeseen

[188] "The Foreign Trade of the USSR in 1958—A Survey," Problems of Economics (January 1960), p. 52. "In 1959, Soviet-Chinese economic contacts were nearly double those of 1953, while deliveries for China's building projects increased eightfold in that period." M. A. Suslov, op. cit.

[189] In addition to deliveries scheduled by the trade protocol for 1958, the Soviets claimed that they had supplied China in 1958 with a "considerable amount" of machinery and equipment. "The Foreign Trade of the USSR in 1958—A Survey," op. cit., p. 52. Cf. Table 8-7 above.

changes in demand, and not infrequently when it is simply a question of planned and foreseen demands. Such economies are not well prepared to respond to foreign demand shifts, as seen in the constant grumbling by domestic firms and consumers that unwanted goods are being forced on them, and by foreign customers that revision of long-term contracts in response to changed circumstances is almost impossible.

Thus even though the Soviets may not have been overly enthusiastic about China's new ventures into independent neoplanning, their reticence about revising scheduled supplies and technical cooperation contracts was, to a considerable extent, a function of the very nature of their centralized command economy. But there was, of course, in addition to such objective irritants, the subjective annoyance with having to feed China's declaration of economic independence, and growing reluctance to aid and abet irrational socialist behavior. The Soviets later argued that they "became upset by a turn that had become apparent in the development of the Chinese national economy in 1958,"[190] and which in essence consisted in the disregard by the Chinese of Soviet advice on how to be a good communist. As the figures in Tables 8-6 and 8-7 show, by mid-1960 they had worked themselves up to a level of exasperation at which the only course open to them was to stop the whole thing—which they proceeded to do. They had, no doubt, hoped that a drastic reduction in Soviet supplies and other measures to be discussed presently, would teach the Chinese a lesson in the meaning and nature of socialist planning and in the modalities of fraternal cooperation. The decline in Soviet economic assistance did, indeed, hurt the Chinese badly, but the psychological lesson which the Soviets' draconian measures were meant to convey to the Chinese romantics apparently did not sink in. On the contrary, it merely supplied the radicals in Peking with a persuasive explanation for the three years of hardship: the foreigner, fraternal or not, could not be trusted. The lesson which the Chinese leadership drew from the incident was that the Soviets had violated the principle of mutual assistance between socialist countries and had used their experts as "an instrument for exerting pressure on fraternal countries, butting into their internal affairs, and impeding and sabotaging their socialist construction."[191]

[190] *Izvestia*, September 21, 1963, p. 2. Cf. Prybyla, "Sino-Soviet Economics," *The Quarterly Review* (London, July 1965), pp. 283-292, and "The Economics of the Sino-Soviet Dispute," *Bulletin*, Institute for the Study of the USSR (Munich, December 1963), pp. 17-24.

[191] "Letter of the Central Committee of the Communist Party of China to the Central Committee of the Communist Party of the Soviet Union," February 29, 1964, *Peking Review* (May 8, 1964), p. 14. It may be noted here that in his official speeches and writings, Liu Shao-ch'i carefully avoided a head-on attack on the Soviet Union right up to his fall.

The Soviet Union's allies in Eastern Europe followed the example set by the USSR, if somewhat grudgingly, and with a lag.[192]

In mid-1960 the Soviets abruptly withdrew their scientific, economic, and military experts from China, blueprints, technical specifications, and all. According to the Soviets, for some time prior to this withdrawal, the Chinese refused to listen to the experts' advice, tried to indoctrinate the experts with the ideas of Mao Tse-tung, and placed them "in conditions excluding the possibility of normal work and humiliating for their human dignity."[193] "The last years of our specialists' stay in the CPR," Suslov told his listeners in February 1964, "coincided with the 'big leap' policy, which unbalanced economic development and led to violation of accepted technical standards. The Soviet specialists could not help seeing the dangerous implications of this policy. They warned the Chinese organizations against violating technical standards. But their advice fell on deaf ears. Due to the fact that the recommendations of the Soviet specialists were ignored and that the Chinese officials grossly violated technical standards, large breakdowns occurred, some of them involving loss of life. This happened on the building site of the Hsinan-tsien Hydropower Station, where thousands of tons of rock crashed down because technical requirements were disregarded and work on the project was considerably delayed. At the Hsinfung-tsien hydropower project the dikes burst and the pit was flooded for the same reason. In both cases there was loss of life. . . . Furthermore, beginning in 1960 the Chinese authorities began 'indoctrinating' the Soviet specialists, trying to incite them against the Central Committee of the CPSU and the Government of the USSR. . . . Soviet specialists were placed under stricter surveillance, searches of personal belongings became more frequent, and so on."

According to the Chinese, 1,390 experts were involved in the exodus. This step, which was to bedevil Sino-Soviet verbal exchanges for years to come, resulted in the scrapping by the Soviets of 343 contracts and 257 projects of scientific and technical cooperation.[194] The Soviet withdrawal had, according to the Chinese, "inflicted incalculable difficulties and losses on China's economy, national defense, and scientific research."[195] On the other hand, following the collapse of the Great Leap adventure, the Soviets agreed to fund over

[192] See Jan S. Prybyla, "The China Trade," *East Europe* (March 1967), pp. 15-20, and "Albania's Economic Vassalage," *ibid.* (January 1967), pp. 9-14.

[193] *Izvestia* (September 21, 1963), p. 2.

[194] *Jen-min Jih-pao* editorial, December 4, 1963 and Chou En-lai, "Report on the Work of the Government to the First Session, Third National People's Congress," December 21-22, 1964 in *Peking Review* (January 1, 1965), p. 9.

[195] Fan Chung, "All-Round Improvement in China's Economy," *Peking Review* (August 23, 1963).

a five-year period $320 million of outstanding Chinese short-term debts and offered China $46 million to still hunger by importing 500,000 tons of Cuban sugar.

Subjective Reasons for Withdrawal from the Great leap

1. Opposition Within the Party

Throughout the Great Leap Forward, the forces of opposition to reckless advance were not dormant. "The wind would not let the trees remain quiet. . . . In the revolutionary torment of the Great Leap Forward, the handful of capitalist-roaders in the Party also jumped out, and from the side of the rightists or from that of the extreme 'Leftists,' opposed Chairman Mao's proletarian revolutionary line."[196] While unable to directly influence the course of events, the opposition argued its case in Party councils, possibly had a hand in Mao Tse-tung's "proposal that he would not stand as candidate for Chairman of the People's Republic of China for the next term of office,"[197] (i.e., in his removal from the headship of government), and generally bided their time rightly estimating that the logic of things would eventually prove them right. As Liu Shao-ch'i put it mildly in September 1959, "there have been controversies between different views within our Party on the questions of distinguishing between the two types of contradictions, the big leap forward, and the people's communes."[198]

The "dizzy with success" communiqué of the Sixth Plenary Session of the Eighth Central Committee of the Communist Party of China (December 10, 1958) is a most interesting document. Read carefully with due allowance for the communist manner of voicing reservations and qualifications in Aesopian terms, "pointing at the mulberry bush and reviling the locust tree," the communiqué suggests a deep malaise within the top leadership, a continuing muted struggle between the two philosophies of socialist construction. Although, unlike the earlier *Proposals* (Chapter 7) the communiqué's

---

[196] "Outline of Struggle," *URS*, Vol. 53, Nos. 5-6, *op. cit.*, p. 70. "In 1959, with the support of China's Khrushchev [Liu Shao-ch'i], P'eng Te-huai's anti-Party clique jumped out, frantically opposed the Three Red Banners [the General Line, the Great Leap Forward, and the People's Communes]. P'eng Te-huai viciously vilified the Party's general line of socialist construction as 'Left adventurism,' slandered the great leap forward as 'being out of proportion,' and 'bringing about losses which cannot be made up by the gains,' disparaged the people's commune as 'making a mess,' and 'going to collapse,' and calumniated the revolutionary mass movement as 'getting feverish in heads,' and 'petty-bourgeois madness.' " *Ibid.*, p. 70.

[197] *Sixth Plenary Session of the Eighth Central Committee of the Communist Party of China* (Peking: FLP, 1958), pp. 1-11.

[198] Liu Shao-ch'i, *The Victory of Marxism-Leninism in China, op. cit.*, p. 59.

chief authors are radicals and the whole tenor of the document is that of elation and the promise of great things to come, there creeps into the text a sour note, a reminder of the need for balance, careful planning, and effective central control, and a warning against the dangers of fanaticism in economics.[199] Here are some examples. What appear to be the moderates' qualifications have been underscored.

". . . It is necessary in carrying on socialist construction in 1959 to continue to oppose conservatism, *do away with blind faith*, strictly carry out the Party's general line for socialist construction, continue to carry out the policies of simultaneously developing industry and agriculture, heavy and light industries, national and local industries, and large enterprises and medium-sized and small enterprises, of simultaneously employing modern and indigenous methods of production; to continue to carry out in industry the policy of achieving an all-round forward leap with steel as the key link and the policy of combining centralized leadership with a full-scale mass movement. At the same time, *it is necessary to endeavor to put economic planning on a completely reliable basis, and to maintain suitable proportions between the various targets in accordance with the objective law of the proportions of development of the various branches of the national economy.* . . . To bring the 1959 national economic plan to realization, we must continue to oppose conservatism, *get rid of blind faith*, and advocate boldness in thinking, speech, and action; go all out, aim high, and defy difficulties strategically. . . . In the meantime, *we must pay full attention to difficulties* tactically and pursue a good, solid, style of work that displays energy, perseverance, and ingenuity, fix targets in a forward-looking way, and take measures that will more than guarantee their fulfillment, *insist on careful calculation of the facts, proper arrangements and practical inspection, guard against exaggeration and oppose concealment of shortcomings.* Economic work must be done in an ever more thoroughgoing way and *made to conform completely or as nearly as possible to reality.* The Plenary Session also pointed out that to carry out the plan for 1959, it is necessary to persist in putting politics in command, to rely on the masses, and to continue to follow the mass line and organize mass movements in construction. . . . The economic plan for 1959 worked out in the light of the above main targets will be a great leap forward plan."[200]

199 An early analysis of China's Party problems is Roderick MacFarquhar's "Communist China's Intra-Party Struggle," *Pacific Affairs* (December 1958), pp. 323-335. In the light of subsequent events, MacFarquhar's implicit classification of Liu Shao-ch'i with the radicals (or as he calls them, "sloganeers") appears erroneous.
200 *Sixth Plenary Session, op. cit.,* pp. 6-8.

Superficially, this is orthodox Maoism: boldness verging on recklessness in strategy, caution and careful calculation in tactics. Yet
there is enough incompatibility and contradiction here, too many
qualifying clauses, for it to be the product of unanimity. One may
presume that the drafters of the communiqué had had an unenviable
job.[201] Also it would not be the first nor the last time in the annals
of communist prose that dissent and passive resistance were couched
in terms of implied agreement with the leader's philosophy.

On January 4, 1967 Mao reportedly admitted that the December
1958 "dizzy with success" Central Committee meeting was anything
but a dizzily successful event. He had found himself in a minority
and had been compelled to give up the presidency of the republic.
The following April Liu Shao-ch'i was elected President of the National People's Congress. For some years afterwards Mao, in his own
words, was treated by his opponents (especially Liu and Teng Hsiao-
p'ing) like "one of their parents whose funeral was taking place."[202]
Passive resistance by the opposition in whose hands, after all, rested
the implementation of many Leap policies, seems to have been quite
important. Deputy Premier T'an Chen-lin, for example, was later
(1968) accused of having during the Leap years given orders blindly
and of fanning "the wind of pompous prolixity to interfere with
Chairman Mao's proletarian revolutionary line." In September 1958
(after earlier opposing the wholesale popularization of the deep
plow) T'an allegedly ordered that the plow (Mao's favorite) be
adopted in the whole country within one month, "otherwise you'll
have to answer for it!" In 1960 he ordered that two million paddy
transplanters invented by the masses be produced right away. Since
these had not yet been extensively tested or properly designed, "they
brought about great losses."[203]

"The imperialists and bourgeois elements said that [the radical
general line] was impossible. They asserted that 'greater and faster'
could not go together with 'better and more economical,' as this
would amount to 'keeping a horse running while giving it no feed.'
The right opportunists within our ranks, echoing them, also said that
it was impossible. But we firmly replied that it was possible, because

---

[201] Interestingly enough, the Soviets in one of their polemical letters to the
Chinese, referred to statements by Liu Shao-ch'i and Teng Hsiao-p'ing made at
the Eighth Congress as showing the Chinese Party's basic agreement with the
Soviet line on certain issues. The quotation from Mao also given in the letter is
more general and equivocal. See, "Open Letter of the CC of the CPSU to All
Party Organizations, to All Communists of the Soviet Union," July 14, 1963,
Pravda (July 14, 1963); *Soviet News* (July 17, 1963), pp. 29-43.

[202] *The Cultural Revolution in China*, Keesing's Research Report (New
York: Scribner's, 1967), p. 6.

[203] "Outline of Struggle," *URS*, Vol. 53, Nos. 5-6, *op. cit.*, pp. 70-71. Some
of the transplanters were later given away as goodwill gifts to foreign governments (e.g., Ceylon, May 1961).

we place our reliance first and foremost on the creators of history—
the mass of the people. . . . One of the fundamental reasons why
some people in our Party have fallen into the bog of right opportunism is that they do not recognize the active role of the mass of the
people in construction. . . . They oppose the building of socialism by
way of mass movements which, they say, is no more than 'petty-
bourgeois fanaticism,' which would 'only bring greater, faster, but
not better or more economical results,' and would cause 'more loss
than gain.' The right opportunists seized on individual, temporary
defects in the work and, without making any analysis, exaggerated
them freely in order to achieve their goal of negating the big leap
forward and opposing the general line."[204]

"A handful of dissatisfied right opportunists in the Party reflected the resistance of a section of bourgeois elements and a small
number of well-off middle peasants to the victory of the socialist
cause. They frantically attacked the Party by taking advantage and
exaggerating shortcomings which were hardly avoidable and had already been overcome. They carried on factional activities to oppose
the correct leadership of the Party's Central Committee and Comrade
Mao Tse-tung. They dubbed the vigorous mass movements 'petty-
bourgeois fanaticism,' and the big leap forward 'left adventurism.'
They claimed that the people's communes were 'founded too early'
and were 'in a mess,' that the making of iron and steel in a big way
had resulted in 'more loss than gain'; panic-stricken and nonplussed
in face of certain local and temporary imbalances which could hardly
be avoided in the big leap forward, they labeled such imbalances
'disproportions' in the national economy as a whole. The Eighth
Plenary Session of the Eighth Central Committee held in Lushan in
August 1959 utterly smashed the attacks of the right opportunists
inside the Party and forcefully repudiated all their absurd arguments."[205]

[204] Chou En-lai, A Great Decade (Peking: FLP, 1959), pp. 27-30. Chou
En-lai generally considered a moderate, has at all times been extremely sensitive
to the twists and turns and changes in the Party line. A Great Decade represents
one of his many rapid adjustments to the dominant left trend of the moment.
Chou has for years been a skillful practitioner of what the Chinese call "sailing
the seas under a false flag." See Kai-yu Hsu, Chou En-lai: China's Gray Eminence
(Garden City, N.Y.: Doubleday, 1968).

[205] Li Fu-chun, Raise High the Red Flag, op. cit., p. 4. Li Fu-chun, Chairman of the State Planning Commission, was himself branded a right opportunist
during the Cultural Revolution, but survived the storm (Chapters 11, 12). Raise
High the Red Flag of the General Line and Continue to March Forward (Peking:
FLP, 1960) was first published in Hung-ch'i, August 16, 1960. Another criticism
of the people's communes mentioned by Liu Shao-ch'i was that they "outstep
the level of social development and the level of the people's political consciousness," and that they were "merely a utopian measure divorced from reality." See
"The Victory of Marxism-Leninism in China," op. cit., pp. 67, 69.

In the April 1, 1967 issue of *Jen-min Jih-pao*, Liu Shao-ch'i was ordered to answer publicly eight questions put to him by the leftists. Question 5 read: "Why, in the period of the three years of hardship [i.e., 1959-61] did you join the chorus with freaks and monsters within the country and poisonously attack the Three Red Banners [General Line, Great Leap Forward, People's Communes], and promote the revisionist line of the Three Freedoms and One Contract and the Three Reconciliations and One Reduction [Chapter 9 below]?" Liu denied having opposed the Three Red Banners and shifted responsibility for the Three Reconciliations and One Reduction onto "an individual comrade." In his self-criticism of October 23, 1966, Liu allegedly admitted that the Three Reconciliations and One Reduction ran counter to the General Line and were "formed on the basis of a wrong estimate of the domestic and international situations."[206]

It has been suggested that the opposition, never quite out of the picture, pressed its case at a Central Committee meeting in Lushan in July 1959 before the opening of the Eighth Plenary Session of the Eighth Central Committee (August 1959). It was in the course of that meeting that Defense Minister P'eng Teh-huai criticized the Great Leap Forward and the People's communes, arguing that the suffering they caused brought the country to the verge of a Hungarian (1956) type revolt. In his confession extracted from him in the course of an interrogation in custody from December 28, 1966 to January 5, 1967 (during which he tried to commit suicide) P'eng said that in an open letter addressed to Mao on July 13, 1959 (shortly after the Lushan meeting) he had written that "the Great Leap Forward of 1958 had its losses and gains; mainly losses." "In reality the increases were somewhat lower than what had been announced," he added in the confession. He also criticized the sending of tens of millions of people to make steel as "a frenzy," which Mao—who immediately called P'eng on the carpet—interpreted as meaning "petty-bourgeois frenzy."[207]

The major points at issue between the Party's sloganeers (Maoists) and the bureaucratic pragmatists (established bosses) are summarized in Table 8-8. The pragmatists' case takes longer to recount

---

[206] *Collected Works of Liu Shao-ch'i, 1958-1967*, op. cit., p. 361. Cf. Chapter 9 below.
[207] *URS*, Vol. 50, No. 17 (February 27, 1968), p. 206. Cf. "A Condensation of P'eng Teh-huai's Talks at the Lushan Conference in 1959," *Chinese Communist Affairs: Facts and Figures*, Vol. II, No. 9 (February 19, 1969), pp. 27-29; "P'eng Teh-huai's So-Called Letter of Opinion to Chairman Mao at the 1959 Lushan Conference," *Ko-ming Ch'uan-lien (Revolutionary Liaison)*, Peking, in *SCMP*, No. 4032 (1967), pp. 2-3.

TABLE 8-8

Factional Struggle Within the Communist Party of China: The Radical
and Moderate Positions on Major Issues—A Tentative Outline

Radicals (The Power of the Idea)	Moderates (The Power of the Apparat)
1. Politics must be in command of economics and all other work. Economic construction relies on "calls which grip the imagination of hundreds of millions of working people [and who are thus] transformed into an immense material force."[a]	1. Politics, while important, cannot be substituted for economic calculation based on a knowledge of "objective" (Marxist) economic laws and on a keen appreciation of technological and resource constraints. "Leaders . . . must combine revolutionary enthusiasm with business-like sense. They must be able not only to put forward advanced targets, but to ensure the realization of the targets. They must not indulge in empty talk and bluff. The targets we put forward must be those that can be reached with hard work. Do not lightly publicize as plan that which is not really attainable, lest failure dampen the enthusiasm of the masses and delight the conservatives."[b] "We should talk about political truths, but they must be affirmed by science."[c]
2. Economic construction calls for the mobilization of the masses on a gigantic scale and reliance on the creative enthusiasm and inventiveness of the broad masses of peasants and workers, especially the poorest among them. It is more important to be Red than expert. Science is not a mystery which the peasants and workers cannot grasp quickly. Aided by the beacon of Mao Tse-tung's thought, the masses can learn rapidly.	2. The primary task of a developing country is to form experts who are loyally Red. Mass movements, while ideologically and psychologically necessary to break down the barriers of tradition, must be handled with circumspection lest they get out of hand and turn into anarchy. The reservoir of mass enthusiasm is limited and must not be squandered. Inventions and innovations should come primarily from experts and should first be tried on a limited scale. There is much to be said for pure research. There is danger in mass

aLiu Shao-ch'i "Report to the Second Session of the Eighth National
Party Congress," *op. cit.*

bIbid.

cAttributed to T'an Chen-lin in "Outline of Struggle," *URS,* Vol. 53,
Nos. 7–8 *op. cit.,* p. 92.

TABLE 8-8 (Continued)

Radicals (The Power of the Idea)	Moderates (The Power of the Apparat)
	research applied rashly and indiscriminately. Given the shortage of educated men capable of producing inventions and innovations, the less than perfect Redness of some experts should be tolerated while efforts are made to correctly remold the needed brains. The techniques of ideological remolding are there for the asking, but their effective use requires time, patience, and a subtle application of reward, praise, and fear.
3. Class struggle continues through the socialist stage and should be used to push society forward. The revolution is permanent. It must constantly renew and purify itself	3. Class struggle while not completely dead, and undesirable class sentiments even though potentially dangerous in the superstructure of society, are not the distinguishing characteristic of the socialist stage. Spontaneous capitalist tendencies are checkmated by the socialist ownership of the means of production and distribution, and the power of the Communist Party and State. Left and Right deviations can be handled through reeducation of the deviants. The socialist state is sufficiently strong and well established to tolerate within itself politically and economically powerless dissenters who may be useful to the communist cause. They should be won over to communism, "united with" wherever possible, remolded rather than beaten down. "They should be fed, should do farming, and reform themselves through labor so that they will be made to change their thinking . . . Those who have not been executed should be considered as mankind."[d] The

[d]Liu Shao-ch'i, "Talk to the August 1 Combat Corps" (August 3, 1966) in *Collected Works of Liu Shao-ch'i, 1958-1967, op. cit.*, pp. 341-342, On the Trotskyist overtones of the thesis of permanent revolution as expounded by Mao and his group, see *China News Analysis*, No. 768 (August 8, 1969), pp. 2-4.

TABLE 8-8 (Continued)

Radicals (The Power of the Idea)	Moderates (The Power of the Apparat)
	definition of a correctly thinking socialist must be flexible: "Some statements have been changed back and forth for scores of years, yet they still present problems."[e]
4. Poverty equally shared is a source of strength and a virtue in a country like China building a communist future. Poverty and blankness are dynamic qualities. On an empty page beautiful things can be written.	4. China's poverty is a source of her weakness domestically and internationally. While recognizing the revolutionary potential of destitution, poverty should not be idealized during socialist construction. The aim is to eliminate this drag on the achievement of a happy and prosperous communist future; not to glorify it and confuse it with the goal of socialist construction. Asceticism is a painful necessity, not the aim of socialism and communism. It should be alleviated to the extent possible and practicable during the long march toward communism.
5. Moral incentives to production are ideologically superior to and economically more effective than material incentives. Material incentives carry with them the danger of capitalist restoration.	5. Even socialist men respond to material incentives, which should become the main prods to production and productivity. Moral incentives—exhortations, praise, medals, citations, honors, and the like—and moral disincentives—public denunciations, self-criticism, struggle sessions, forced labor—should be combined with, but not replace increases in real wages.[f] It is not incorrect for the socialist man to try and better himself materially, so long as he does this within a general rise in living standards shared by all and approved by the Party and State.

[e]Liu Shao-ch'i, "Talk to Peking College's Work Team," (August 4, 1966) in *ibid.*, p. 349.

[f]Professor Ota Šik, the author of Czechoslovakia's short-lived New Economic (socialist market) Model (suppressed by the Soviets in mid-1968) argued that "a society which has only a sort of superstructural, political, moral, etc., stimulus for performing socially necessary labor. . . while the direct, immediate economic incentives are lacking . . . must perish sooner or later." Ota Šik, *Plan and Market Under Socialism* (Prague: Academic Publishing House of the Czechoslovak Academy of Sciences, 1967; U.S. distributor, *IASP*), p. 162.

TABLE 8-8 (Continued)

Radicals (The Power of the Idea)	Moderates (The Power of the Apparat)
	Communism is not a lot of hungry men sitting around an empty table in perfect equality.
6. The mighty surge toward a communist society is "U-shaped." Disproportionalities and an occasional absence of internal consistency and balance in economic construction are the necessary ingredients of the dialectical movement forward and upward. Ideologically, periods of tension alternate with periods of relative relaxation. The building of socialism and communism proceeds by twists and turns. This is normal and necessary.[g]	6. Progress toward a communist society is not a surge willed by subjective thought, but rather a long-term and unspectacular daily solving of intricate practical and theoretical problems. It must take full account of objective economic laws, especially of the "Law of Value" (things should not be sold below cost and, by implication, cost should be carefully calculated), and the "Law of Planned, Proportional Development of the National Economy." One should distinguish between revolutionary upheaval in overthrowing the old society and the need for a measure of stability in socialist construction: the one is primarily political, psychological, and military (in a guerrilla sense), the other reflective, calculating, and scientific. A major claim of Marxian socialism is to have abolished capitalist business cycles and the anarchy of the market. It is a disservice to the cause of socialism and communism to replace bourgeois business cycles with politically induced economic ups and downs, and capitalist spontaneity with the anarchy of political thought parading as Marxism-Leninism. The destruction of feudalism, capitalism, and capitalist colonialism and imperialism calls for strength of will and the barrel of the gun; socialist

[g]The economist Sun Yeh-fang who during the Cultural Revolution (Chapter 11) was denounced as a rightist, bourgeois, revisionist "bad egg," reportedly put it this way: "As soon as the Party lays its hands on the economy, the economy dies, the Party worries; when it worries, it relaxes its hold, the economy is in disorder; when the economy is in disorder, the Party takes a firm hold of it . . . now one thing, now another." L. F. Goodstadt, "The Great Divide," *FEER* (February 2, 1967), p. 162.

TABLE 8-8 (Continued)

Radicals (The Power of the Idea)	Moderates (The Power of the Apparat)
	construction demands other qualities and means—scientific thought combined with strength of will and perseverance in the attainment of attainable objectives.
7. Changes in the relations of production should as a rule precede and not follow changes in the material productive forces. Communes, for example, can be established even though agriculture has not yet been mechanized. "In the course of the socialist transformation of agriculture, every change in the relations of production inevitably promoted further growth in the productive forces."[h]	7. Changes in the relations of production must take careful account of changes in the material productive forces. Collectivization and communization of agriculture, for example, should not be introduced rashly on an insufficiently developed productive base. To do so is to discredit socialist and communist institutional arrangements and hamper rather than promote the development of the material productive forces.[i]
8. Speed and quantity are of the essence of economic construction. So is organizational bigness at the local level.	8. Socialist construction is a long-drawn-out process. There exist objective limits to the pace of advance, and these limits should not be rashly violated, lest the result be disruption of production. Excessive preoccupation with quantity at the cost of quality and consistency must be shunned. Organizational bigness is not an absolute virtue. Size of enterprises, farms, etc., should be determined on the basis of eco-

[h]T'an Chen-lin, "Speeding Up Mechanization of China's Agriculture," *Peking Review* (September 27, 1960), p. 6. Cf. "We are believers in dialectical materialism. We definitely recognize that the relations of production [i.e., system of ownership of the means of production, distribution, and exchange] must suit the nature of the forces of production [i.e., land, labor, capital, state of technology, etc.], and we are against hasty advance which outruns the stage of historical development." Lo Keng-mo in *Ta Kung-pao*, Peking, November 27, 1961. Cf. Hung Hsueh-ping, "The Essence of 'Theory of Productive Forces' Is To Oppose Proletarian Revolution," *Peking Review* (September 19, 1969), pp. 5–8.

[i]"They [the rightist capitalist-roaders in the Party] thought that social development was only the natural result of the development of productivity, particularly of the development of the tools of production and productive techniques. They said that as long as productivity developed, society would undergo spontaneous revolution in a natural way." "Outline of Struggle," *URS*, Vol. 53, Nos. 5–6, *op. cit.*, pp. 60–61.

TABLE 8-8 (Continued)

Radicals (The Power of the Idea)	Moderates (The Power of the Apparat)
	nomic calculation and related to the opportunities which it provides for effective central control and supervision.
9. Reliance on one's own resources (especially raw muscle), national genius, ability, and energy are primary; foreign aid and the importation of advanced capital equipment and models of economic development are secondary.[j]	9. Self-reliance is important but insufficient to break out of underdevelopment. Measures should be taken to learn from advanced, fraternal, socialist countries in such matters as technology, science, and planning methodology. While one should not give in to erroneous foreign ideological models of either Left or Right, one should strive to preserve the unity of the socialist camp.
10. If a section of the Party's leadership shows revisionist, rightopportunist, and rightist inclinations, and if it is impossible to dislodge the rightist villains, it becomes correct and legitimate to take power away from these people by, for example, administrative decentralization, or if this fails, by making recourse to extraParty forces, i.e., popular movements organized and directed by the left leadership. A revisionist Communist Party must be destroyed.[k]	10. The Party is absolute and sacred and must not be rebelled against. Disagreements within the leadership must be settled behind closed doors, resolved on the basis of democratic centralism, and not carried beyond the Party's ranks.[l]

[j]This position represents a bias against what Wallich calls "derived development," i.e., development derived from innovations made abroad. Henry C. Wallich, "Some Notes Toward A Theory of Derived Development," in Agarwala and Singh (eds.), *The Economics of Underdevelopment* (London: Oxford U. P., 1958). On Soviet technological borrowing from the West during the period 1917–1930, see Antony C. Sutton, *Western Technology and Soviet Economic Development, 1917–1930* (Stanford, Calif.: Hoover Institution Press, 1969).

[k]"Comrade Mao Tse-tung has often said to comrades from fraternal Parties that if China's leadership is usurped by revisionists in the future, the Marxist-Leninists of all countries should . . . resolutely expose and fight them, and help the working class and the masses of China to combat such revisionism." "Refutation of the New Leaders of the CPSU on 'United Action,' " *Jen-min Jih-pao* and *Hung-ch'i* editorials in *Peking Review* (November 12, 1965), p. 20.

[l]"Anything that hinders the Party's centralization and unity through separatist behavior, or impairs the Party's organization and discipline, makes the Party disoriented and weak, and impairs the task of socialist construction." *Hung-ch'i* (February 10, 1962).

TABLE 8-8 (Continued)

Radicals (The Power of the Idea)	Moderates (The Power of the Apparat)
11. Problems of war and revolution, socialist economic construction in the concrete conditions of China, and all other problems have been dealt with and solved by the invincible thought of Mao Tse-tung. Reference to Mao Tse-tung's thought should be made at all times.	11. Problems of war and revolution, socialist economic construction in the concrete conditions of China, and all other problems have been dealt with and solved by the invincible thought of Mao Tse-tung. Reference to Mao Tse-tung's thought should be made at all times. It is also useful to study Liu Shao-ch'is *How To Be A Good Communist.* A subtle distinction should be made between Mao Tse-tung's pre-1949 writings which creatively developed Marxism-Leninism, and his later pronouncements, which amounted to *ex-post* justification of certain policies in terms of ideology ("legitimizing phase"). "In order to smash the attacks of modern revisionism, we should first of all seek instructions from Marx, Engels, Lenin, and Stalin, conscientiously study their works, and grasp this incisive weapon, Marxism-Leninism. We should also make a serious study of lessons provided by teachers by negative example, including writings of modern revisionists, those of Bernstein, Kautsky, Plekhanov, and other old-line revisionists, as well as imperialist evaluations of modern revisionism. We should also, of course, read the writings of modern revolutionary Marxist-Leninists. In this way we should be able to make a comparative study and see on each question now under controversy . . . This is, I think, a method of study which links theory with practice; this is the Leninist method of study."[m] The common char-

---

[m] Liu's *How To Be A Good Communist,* first published in 1939, and required reading for Party personnel during the rectification campaign of 1942, was republished in 1962 with "slight changes in phraseology and some additions to its content" made by the author. The quotation is from Liu Shao-ch'i

TABLE 8-8 (Continued)

Radicals (The Power of the Idea)	Moderates (The Power of the Apparat)
	acteristic of Left and Right error is "the belief that the Chinese revolution could be directed by relying on subjective imagination of the moment, or merely adducing isolated quotations from certain books."[n]
12. Populationism. People are China's greatest asset—the more of them, the better. Population control is a bourgeois fallacy, a Malthusian error that should be rejected. A socialist system is capable of accommodating any rate of population increase. "The more people we have, the better, faster, greater, and more economical will be the results of our socialist construction," said *Hung-ch'i* in the midst of the Great Leap Forward. In 1961 Mao Tse-tung wrote: "It is a very good thing that China has a big population. Even if China's population multiples many times, she is fully capable of finding a solution; the solution is production. . . . Of all things in the world, people are the most precious. Under the leadership of the Communist Party, as long as there are people, every kind of miracle can be performed."[o]	12. Birth control. The rate of population increase should be tailored to China's food producing ability. A rate of population increase which substantially outstrips the capacity of agriculture to supply increasing amounts of food will cancel out any apparent gains in production and productivity. "Promotion of planned childbirth is the established policy of our country during the socialist construction period."[p]
13. In national defense man is primary and weapons secondary. The relations between officers and men, the army and civilians	13. A modern army is first and foremost a professional body. Modern equipment is of the utmost importance. There is little room for

"Speech at the Nguyen Ai Quoc Party School" (May 15, 1963), *NCNA* News Release No. 051571 (May 16, 1963).

[n] Liu Shao-ch'i, *Address at the Meeting in Celebration of the 40th Anniversary of the Founding of the Communist Party of China* (Peking: FLP, 1961), p. 18.

[o] Cited by Dick Wilson, "Counting the Heads," *FEER* (January 6, 1966), p. 22. On the evolution of the Soviet attitude to population problems see Harry G. Shaffer and Jan S. Prybyla (eds.), *From Underdevelopment to Affluence: Western, Soviet, and Chinese Views* (New York: Appleton, 1968).

[p] *Nan-fang Jih-pao* (Canton), reporting on a family planning conference, April 14, 1965.

TABLE 8-8 (Continued)

Radicals (The Power of the Idea)	Moderates (The Power of the Apparat)
must be "democratic" (i.e., collective); politics must be in control of the army and pure professionalism must be curbed. Army personnel should take part in economic construction. The army is a form of mass organization of the people. It should be supplemented by a mass people's militia. The army's strategy and tatics should draw on the rich experience of China's guerrilla and mobile warfare (i.e., protracted war waged by the people).[q]	egalitarianism and the guerrilla type informality between officers and men (unity of command). For purposes of training and discipline, ranks, titles, honors, conscription, and special rules and regulations for entry into the officer corps are needed. The army's direct participation in labor should be held to a minimum. The usefulness of mass militia should be carefully reexamined in the light of changing conditions of warfare. In the nuclear age, the first blow is decisive; it throws considerable doubt on the theory of protracted war.

[q]See Ellis Joffe, "Moscow and the Chinese Army," *FEER* (April 2, 1964), pp. 13–15.

because it is more shaded, subtle, and qualified than the battle cry of the radicals.[208]

From the standpoint of economic theory the debate between the Right and the Left may be seen as one between the proponents of the view that economic development should be an orderly process promoted by efficient allocation of existing resources, which are assumed to be steadily expanding, the efficient allocation being implemented through proper management of domestic savings and investment, attention to internal consistency, and the like, and the view that economic development can be brought about only by disorderly changes—social revolution and technological innovation by the masses. "Development planning," Professor Myint has pointed out, "is by definition an orderly approach: on the other hand, genuinely far-reaching and disruptive social changes cannot be turned on and turned off in a predictable way and incorporated into the planning framework. Thus one may advocate social revolution now and planning later, but one may not advocate social revolution and planning at the same time without getting into serious contradictions."[209] Chinese experience appears to corroborate this.

[208] Cf. H. Hellbeck, "The 'Rightist' Movement in 1959," in *Contemporary China* (Hong Kong: Hong Kong U. P., 1961), pp. 48-53.
[209] H. Myint, "Economic Theory and Development Policy," *Economica* (May 1967), p. 126.

In 1958-60 the opposition probably counted among its numbers Liu Shao-ch'i (Chairman of the People's Republic of China since April 1959, Vice-Chairman of the Central Committee of the CPC, member of the Party's Politbureau), Chou En-lai (Premier and member of the Politbureau), Ch'en-yun (Deputy Premier, Minister of Commerce during the liberal interlude, Chairman of the National Construction Commission, and member of the Politbureau), Li Fu-chun (Chairman of the State Planning Commission), Li Hsien-nien (Minister of Finance and member of the Politbureau), Po I-po (Chairman of the State Economic Commission and alternate member of the Politbureau), Teng Tzu-hui (Deputy Premier), Teng Hsiao-p'ing (the Party's General Secretary), Hsueh Mu-ch'iao (Director of the State Statistical Bureau), P'eng Te-huai (Minister of Defense relieved of his duties in 1959 and replaced by the leftist Lin Piao), Chang Wen-tien (Deputy Minister of Foreign Affairs), Huang Ko-cheng (Army Chief of Staff), Lu Ting-yi (Director of the Propaganda Department of the Party since 1948 and alternate member of the Politbureau), P'eng Chen (member of the Party's secretariat and Mayor of Peking), Liao Lu-yen (Minister of Agriculture) and Ma Yin-ch'u (President of Peking University, relieved of his duties in April 1960). Of these, the most adroit were Chou En-lai, Li Fu-chun, and Li Hsien-nien. They not only managed to adapt themselves to the rapid shifts in line, but (as of 1969) survived the traumatic experience of the Great Proletarian Cultural Revolution (Chapter 11).[210]

2. Opposition Within the Country

Economic development through great leaps is for those who like excitement, but the excitement wears off and apathy sets in. It is fairly obvious, yet it can stand repetition that one cannot ask for night and day toil from even the most ideologically fired-up masses without at some point meeting the payroll. The Great Leap did not meet the payroll, and the predictable result was widespread resentment and passive resistance. In some instances passive resistance turned into open rebellion by the masses.

The tragic case of Tibet merits at least passing notice. Trouble

[210] A Japanese team sent to China in 1966-67 by the newspaper *Yomiuri Shimbun* suggested that the pro-Liu faction comprised many former resistance fighters who during the Sino-Japanese war operated in Japanese occupied areas. They allegedly harbored resentment against those around Mao who from the relative safety of faraway Yenan had called on those under Japanese occupation to resist and make revolution. Thus, in addition to other differences between the two broad factions (social level was one), there was the exiles-versus-underground fighters division common also in some Eastern European countries after World War II. See Robert Trumbull (ed.), *This Is Communist China* (New York: McKay, 1968), p. 43. Cf. Shih Ch'eng-chih, *People's Resistance in Mainland China 1950-1955* (Hong Kong: URI, 1956).

had been brewing in Tibet ever since the little big leap of 1956. In February of that year major uprisings occurred in the eastern part of the country. They were dealt with savagely, so cruelly, in fact, that the outside world—still reeling from the horrors of national socialism—refused to believe that Marxian socialism could be capable of similar conduct, Stalin's bloody record notwithstanding. Leaders of the revolt were put to the torture, they had boiling water poured over their heads, they were dragged to their death behind horses, they were stabbed and mutilated. The threat of genocide only helped to stiffen Tibetan (especially Kham) resistance. Beginning in September 1956 and for some months thereafter (the "liberal interlude" in China proper) the Chinese authorities relented a bit and agreed to postpone the great march toward socialism for six years. But the interlude was brief. Another wave of terror coincided with the inauguration of the Great Leap Forward. The Tibetans once again found themselves fighting for their very existence.[211]

The Chinese military command in Lhasa invited the Dalai Lama to attend a "cultural show" at its headquarters on March 10, 1959. Suspecting a kidnapping attempt, about 10,000 Tibetans surrounded the Dalai Lama's summer residence in Norbulinka to prevent their leader from attending the function. Two days later fierce fighting broke out in Lhasa in the course of which an estimated one thousand Tibetans were killed and thousands more were deported to forced labor camps. The monasteries of Sera, Drepung, and Ganden were shelled by Chinese artillery and the first two destroyed beyond repair. On March 15 the Dalai Lama escaped from his palace and after a perilous journey arrived in India on April 18 where he was granted political asylum. Two hundred members of the Dalai Lama's bodyguard who had been left behind in Lhasa, were disarmed by the Chinese and publicly machine gunned. Chinese troops conducted a house-to-house search in the capital city; where arms were found, the whole family would be taken out and shot on the spot. At the very time that these events were taking place, Prime Minister Nehru went on record as saying that in his view what was taking place in Tibet was a clash of minds, not a clash of arms.

---

[211] See George N. Patterson, *Tibet in Revolt* (London: Faber, 1960); and his "New Crisis in Tibet," *FEER* (January 28, 1965), pp. 130-132; Chanakya Sen (ed.), *Tibet Disappears: A Documentary History of Tibet's International Status, The Great Rebellion, and its Aftermath* (London: Asia Publishing House, 1960); W. D. Shakabpa, *Tibet: A Political History* (New Haven: Yale U. P., 1967). Also the literature on Tibet given in Chapter 3, note 166. The Chinese Communist version may be found in Anna Louise Strong, *Tibetan Interviews* (Peking: New World Press, 1959), and *Concerning the Question of Tibet* (Peking: *FLP*, 1959).

RATIONALE BEHIND THE LEAP

Retrenchment and Recession

When the radicals looked at the record of 1957 and compared it with that of the previous year[212] they had reason to be fretful. The retrenchers, liberalizers, and opponents of reckless advance were indeed in the process of righting the disproportions, distortions, and inflationary pressures generated by the socialization push of 1955-56, but while doing this they neglected speed—that "most important question confronting China since the victory of the socialist revolution." What the radical saw is shown in Table 8-9.

A slowing down in the rate of advance was, of course, implicit in the task of correcting the various imbalances (reviewed in Chapter 7) and in cooling down the economy overheated by the leap of 1956. The trimming of investment was, for example, a measure consciously taken by those at that time responsible for the conduct of economic policy.[213] The increase of 62 percent in state capital investment in 1956 occurred at the very time that for incentive reasons it was necessary to raise worker and peasant incomes. The result was inflationary pressure and shortages of construction materials. The inflationary pressure was aggravated by the financing of agricultural investments by bank loans. The increase of over 88 million *mou* in area sown to grain crops and cotton in the single year 1956 together with a rush irrigation job meant that much of the sown area was not properly taken care of. The per *mou* yield of grain and cotton declined that year. In 1957, therefore, the sown area was reduced and per *mou* yields of grain crops and cotton rose substantially. The sharp drop in two-wheeled double-share plows supplied to agriculture reflected the belated correction of a mistake made earlier. Large stocks of these plows were lying around unused in the countryside and the peasants could not be persuaded to use them.

It could, therefore, be argued that the retrenchment and recession of 1957 were the result of earlier policies conducted under the

---

[212]The first nine months of 1956 were dominated by left-wing policies. The brakes were not put on until October.

[213]In his implicit self-examination or leftist-opportunist speech to the Second Session of the Eighth National Party Congress, Liu Shao-ch'i noted that "as a matter of fact, in the winter of 1955 when it was apparent that a decisive victory of the socialist revolution was to be won very shortly and when a mass upsurge in production and construction was beginning to take place, the 'norms' set in the First Five Year Plan should have been revised upward. Comrade Mao Tse-tung issued a timely call for a speedier tempo than that envisaged in the First Five Year Plan." *Second Session, op. cit.*, p. 35. The responsibility for the 1956 leap was thus squarely placed where it belonged.

TABLE 8-9

Economic Performance in 1957 Compared with that in 1956

	1957	1956
Percentage growth in national income over preceding year	4.6	14.0
Combined gross output value of industry and agriculture (index numbers, preceding year = 100)	107.8	116.5
Gross output value of industry (including handicrafts) (index numbers, preceding year = 100)	111.4	128.2
Gross output value of agriculture (index numbers, preceding year = 100)	103.5	104.9
State revenue from agricultural tax collections (millions of current yuan)	2,970	2,965
State expenditures on economic construction (millions of yuan)	14,910	15,910
Increase in total investment in capital construction (index numbers, preceding year = 100)	93	159
Increase in investment within the State plan (index numbers, preceding year = 100)	90	162
Investment in agriculture, forestry, water conservation and meteorology (millions of yuan)	1,190	1,190
Investment in building (millions of yuan)	460	650
Investment in prospecting for natural resources (millions of yuan)	300	400
Investment in transport and communications (millions of yuan)	2,070	2,610
Investment in trade (millions of yuan)	340	760
Investment in heavy and light industry (index numbers, preceding year = 100)		
Light industry	117	179
Heavy industry	104	156
Investment in capital construction in national minority areas (index numbers, preceding year = 100)	99.1	175.5
New productive fixed assets (index numbers, preceding year = 100)	117	143
Output of wheat (million catties)	47,300	49,600
Output of coarse grains (million catties)	105,300	106,800
Output of tea (thousand tan)	2,230	2,410
Output of cocoons of cultivated silkworms (thousands of tan)	1,360	1,450
Cultivated area (thousands of mou)	1,677,450	1,677,370
Sown area (thousands of mou)	2,358,660	2,387,590
Increase in irrigated area (thousands of mou)	43,090	118,700
Area of transformed water-logged, low-lying land (thousands of mou)	51,730	84,640
Area under preliminary water and soil conservation (square kilometers)	51,543	73,650
Afforested area (thousands of mou)	65,330	85,850
Output of cotton yarn (thousands of bales)	4,650	5,250
Output of cotton cloth (millions of meters)	5,050	5,770

TABLE 8-9 (Continued)

	1957	1956
Increase in volume of retail sales (index numbers, preceding year - 100)	102.9	117.5
Increase in total amount of means of production supplied to agriculture (index numbers, preceding year = 100)	88.1	131.2
Water wheels supplied to agriculture (thousands of units)	247	619
Two-wheeled share plows supplied to agriculture (thousands of units)	733	1,086
Walking plows supplied to agriculture (thousands of units)	97	1,022
Sprayers supplied to agriculture (thousands of units)	541	1,180
Commodity price index numbers (nationwide, average prices of the preceding year = 100)		
Wholesale prices	100.9	99.5
Retail prices	102.2	100.0
Purchasing prices paid for agricultural products	105.0	103.0
Retail prices of industrial products in the countryside	101.2	99.0
Total volume of import and export trade (millions of yuan)	10,450	10,870
Increase in number of workers and employees over preceding year (thousands of persons)	276	5,154
Increase in engineering and technical personnel (index numbers, preceding year = 100)	110.5	130.5
Index of net earnings of rich peasants and former landlords (net income of poor peasants = 1.000)		
Rich peasants	0.975	0.902
Former landlords	1.100	0.962

Sources: Ten Great Years, various pages. Reprinted from Nai-Ruenn Chen, *Chinese Economic Statistics* (Chicago: Aldine, 1967). Copyright © 1967 by the Social Science Research Council, p. 441, Table 10.1; Victor C. Funnell, "Social Stratification," *Problems of Communism* (March–April 1968), p. 19, Chart 2 (index of peasant net earnings based on a sample survey of 4,321 cooperative households); *Agricultural Machinery and Technique*, Peking, No. 9 (September 8, 1968) in *URS*, Vol. 53, Nos. 5–6 (October 15 and 18, 1968), p. 58.

banner of politics first. The radical elements within the leadership did not, however, see it that way. They blamed the 1957 situation on rightist and right-opportunist thinking and cited the quantitatively modest performance as one reason for the reversal of policy which, they argued, had to come at once. Although the relatively liberal interlude was too short-lived to produce the healing results expected of it by its sponsors, it is reasonable to argue that behind the quantitative performance there was some qualitative progress.[214] To argue thus is, however, to meet with incomprehension on the part of those to whom the most important indicator of economic progress is rapid increase in quantity irrespective of internal inconsistencies, quality considerations, and optimal plan variants. The notion of optimality, consistency, and balance was not part of the Maoist economic lexicon. Speed, quantity, and the ability to solve intricate resource allocation problems by resort to political slogans and mass mobilization were the core of the radical faction's economic philosophy.

It may be presumed that one of the reasons behind the launching of the Great Leap Forward was therefore the left wing's dissatisfaction with the pace of economic advance during a period when the radicals' influence on economic policy was on the wane. The sins of the radicals were visited on the moderates: they were accused of slowing down the rate of economic growth through their excessive caution and lack of revolutionary pep, whereas it would, in fact, have been more correct to ascribe the relative sluggishness of the economy during the liberal interlude to earlier economic excesses.

Reemergence of Social Stratification in the Countryside

The Party's left wing has at all times feared that the former oppressor classes would try and stage a comeback and that too great an emphasis on differential material incentives would lead to the emergence of new social strata and of a new bourgeois-bureaucrat mentality, especially among the intellecturals (scientists, technicians, cultural workers). The rural liberalization measures of 1956-57 (private plots, free markets) gave the ideologues scant reason for rejoicing. According to sample surveys carried out in 1956 and 1957 (see Table 8-9 and Chapters 3 and 5), the net earnings position of former landlords and rich peasants relative to poor peasants improved in 1957 compared with 1956. The per capita net earnings of former landlords, rich, and middle peasants rose (in the case of former landlords quite substantially), while those of poor peasants declined (from 61.3 to 60.2 yuan). The spread between the highest and lowest paid state employees (bureaucrats and technicians) was said to have been 28:1 in 1956. In 1958 it was apparently reduced to 20:1.

It is sometimes said in defense of the Great Leap Forward that it

---

[214] Besides righting a few of the disproportions mentioned earlier, the policy of retrenchment and greater attention to quality was in part responsible for increases in per acre yields of grain crops and cotton (although relatively good weather had something to do with it too), and for an important increase in 1975 in the area sown to improved seeds and staple crops.

did stimulate the production of certain key commodities. Output was increased, it is argued, in some cases very substantially.

In 1956 the planners had set a number of targets for 1962, which they considered realistic in the light of the resources that China could supply from domestic sources during the period of the Second Five Year Plan. They were maximal targets. After the figures for the First Five Year Plan were in, some of the 1962 targets were raised, others were lowered. It would seem that the planners were approximately right. After all the fuss and furor of the Great Leap and two years of readjustment (needed to bring a semblance of order into the economy), production of key commodities in 1962 was roughly where the planners had originally said it would be (Table 8-10).

TABLE 8-10

Output Targets for Selected Products Set for 1962 Before the Great Leap Forward During the Leap, and Estimated 1962 Output of These Products

Product	Unit	1962 Target Set by the *Proposals*, September 1956	Revised 1962 Target Set in December 1957	Revised 1962 Target Set in August 1959— A Great Leap Revision	Estimated 1962 Output Minimum	Maximum Estimate
Coal	millions of tons	190-210	230	335	180	250
Crude oil	millions of tons	5-6	"Less"	—	5.3	6.8
Electric power	billions of kwh	40-43	—	—	30	31
Steel	millions of tons	10.5-12.0	12.0	12.0	7	10
Aluminum ingot	thousands of tons	100-120	—	—	100	
Chemical fertilizer	millions of tons	3-3.2	7	—	2.05	2.17
Cement	millions of tons	12.5-14.5	12.5	—	6	8
Timber	millions of cubic meters	31-34	—	—	29	34
Cotton cloth	billions of linear meters	7.29-8.06	—	—	3	3.3
Sugar	millions of tons	2.4-2.5	—	—	0.5	1.3
Paper	millions of tons	1.5-1.6	—	—	1	2.7
Food grains	millions of tons	250	240	275	160	180
Ginned cotton	millions of tons	2.4	2.15	2.31	0.97	

Sources: 1962 target of September 1956, *Proposals, op. cit.*, pp. 14, 15, 18. Revised 1962 target of December 1957, Choh-ming Li, "China's Industrial Development, 1958-63," in *Industrial Development in Communist China, op. cit.*, p. 7, Table 1; Estimates of 1962 output, K. P. Wang, "The Mineral Resource Base of Communist China," in *An Economic Profile of Mainland China op. cit.*, p. 174; R. M. Field, "Chinese Communist Industrial Production," *ibid.*, pp. 293-294; J. Ashton, "Development of Electric Energy Resources in Communist China," *ibid.*, p. 307; E. F. Jones, "The Emerging Pattern of China's Economic Revolution," *ibid.*, p. 93. Table 7-1 and accompanying pages.

Unemployment and Underemployment

Unemployment, estimated by some Western economists at about 32 million male nonagricultural workers in 1957, was certainly an important motivating factor in the decision to launch the labor-intensive Great Leap. Unemployment is thought to have increased between 1952 and 1957. In addition, underemployment in 1957 could have been as high as 35 millions.[215] One of the objectives of the Leap, was no doubt, to reduce existing unemployment and underemployment and to provide jobs for new entrants into the labor force.

[215] Nai-Ruenn Chen and Walter Galenson, *The Chinese Economy Under Communism, op. cit.,* pp. 45-46. Chen and Galenson seem to ascribe the decision to launch the Great Leap almost exclusively to that consideration.

9 | 1961–65: The Policy of Readjustment, Consolidation, Filling-out, and Raising Standards

In 1961 "China's Khrushchev [Liu Shao-ch'i] openly clamored: "Our economy is approaching the brink of collapse. I propose to call the present a period of emergency."[1]

Unable to cope with the bouncing forces they had unleashed, the Party's leftists began to bow to the inevitable in the summer of 1960, and discreetly retreated behind a smokescreen of face-saving semantics. The people's communes were still being declared Chinese socialism's greatest contribution to the transition from socialism to communism, but they were, in fact, changed beyond recognition. Confronted with the threat of famine, it was neither the production brigade nor the production team, nor even the work group, but the individual peasant household which became the mainstay of China's agriculture. In 1961 the fixing of production quotas on the basis of households was not only openly discussed in theoretical terms, but seems to have been the common practice in at least one Kwangtung *hsien*. In some localities the practice survived well into 1965.[2] The mass movement of peasant technical and scientific innovation (popular mechanics) was still said to be surging ahead. In fact, it was being controlled, trimmed, and supervised by experts. The local industry explosion of 1959 was contained, and water conservation was put on a different, less rash, more rational basis.

The period 1961-65 is one of caution and moderation in socialist construction. There is much solid achievement, not very spectacular, but real. However, the relatively moderate "walk slow" policy implemented during that time was constantly being challenged by the forces of the left, first in the realm of ideology ("socialist education"—Chapter 10), later in the fields of government and economics. The period ends with yet another apocalyptic upheaval—the Great Proletarian Cultural Revolution, the apotheosis of the political will, the humiliation, rout, and temporary destruction of the bureaucratic moderates.

[1] "Outline of Struggle," *URS*, Vol. 53, Nos. 5-6, *op. cit.*, p. 72.
[2] Audrey Donnithorne, *China's Economic System*, *op. cit.*, pp. 53-54.

THE PROLOGUE

It has been noted in the preceeding chapter that the disorganization, mass exhaustion, food problems, and strains generated by the Great Leap Forward led to a rethinking of the whole Leap concept, a strengthening of the moderates' hand, and finally a reversal of policy. The process of change was gradual, beginning—as we have seen—with the commune checkup of 1958-59, gathering momentum with every drought, flood, and bad harvest, and culminating in Li Fu-chun's March 1960 report on the draft economic plan for 1960 and P'eng Chen's call in June 1960 to "grasp agriculture" and make of it priority number one.[3] In July 1960 a campaign to help the countryside was launched in Liaoning, Kirin, and Heilungkiang. It soon spread to the whole country. A spate of articles extolling the new line of agriculture as foundation and industry as the leading factor in socialist construction, followed.[4] At the Ninth Plenary Session of the Eighth Central Committee (January 14-18, 1961), the forces of opposition to reckless advance seem finally to have carried the day. The communiqué issued at the conclusion of that meeting said that a rectification campaign would be launched among Party personnel who "lacked sufficient understanding of the distinction between socialist ownership by the collective and socialist ownership by the whole people, of the three levels of ownership in the people's communes, and of the socialist society's principles of exchange of equal values 'to each according to his work' and more income to those who work more—all of which the Party had repeatedly publicized."[5] It was now the turn of leftist cadres and leftist opportunists to be rectified. Although the communiqué also promised a rectification drive against landlords and bourgeois elements who engaged in sabotage of the economy during those difficult times, it hastened to add that their numbers were "exceedingly small." In fact, a process of removing rightist labels was already in progress. In November 1960, 260 leading rightists had been declassified and relieved of that brand.

---

[3] The idea of agriculture as foundation of the national economy is embodied in the National Program for Agricultural Development adopted by the Second Session of the National People's Congress in April 1960. However, it is there still interpreted primarily in Great Leap terms.

[4] E.g., "Let the Whole Party and the Whole People Go in for Agriculture and Grain Production in a Big Way," *Jen-min Jih-pao* editorial, August 25, 1960 in *Peking Review* (August 30, 1960) pp. 11-13; Liao Lu-yen (Minister of Agriculture), "The Whole Party and the Whole People Go In for Agriculture in a Big Way," *Hung-ch'i*, No. 17, 1960, in *Peking Review* (September 14, 1960), pp. 32-36; Yang Ling, "Agriculture: Foundation of the National Economy," *Peking Review* (October 18, 1960), p. 17.

[5] *Jen-min Jih-pao* (January 21, 1961), in *Peking Review* (January 27, 1961), pp. 5-7 (the quotation is on p. 6). Cf. Stalin's contention (March 1930) that his cadres had "misunderstood" his orders, Chapter 5, p. 153 above.

In September 1961, 1,100 rightists in Shanghai and 317 rightists and "local nationalists" in the Sinkiang-Uighur Autonomous Region were declassified, and 370 more were rehabilitated in December.[6] This "reversal of judgments" continued through the greater part of the period 1961-62.[7] The Ninth Central Committee Session formalized what had already been aired for some time. A new economic policy was officially announced.

It was given the rather cumbersome name of "Readjustment, Consolidation, Filling-Out, and Raising Standards": readjustment of the pace of socialist construction, consolidation of existing agricultural and industrial enterprises, filling out (or reinforcement) of weak links in the production process, and the raising of quality standards. Although everyone present at the meeting officially subscribed to the new course in a display of unshakable unity, the leftists were later to accuse their adversaries of having altered the content of the slogan to "Retrenchment, Closing-Down, Suspension, Amalgamation, and Transfer of Enterprises (see below).

Beginning in December 1960 a series of secret documents began to be issued for the guidance of the Party's cadres in the field.[8] Together, these documents constitute the charter of the new economic course. Some of them were later (1968) denounced by the Maoists as revisionist "black goods for the restoration of capitalism." The most important of these were

• 35 Articles of Handicraft Policy (issued by the State Council in December 1960)

---

[6] The delabeling was carried out in pursuance of a Central Committee and State Council Decision "On Measures Regarding Rightist Elements Who Have Reformed," dated September 16, 1959.

[7] The rehabilitation drive was supported by a series of articles in *Ch'ien Hsien* (Frontline), *Pei-ching Jih-pao* (Peking Daily), and *Pei-ching Wan-pao* (Peking Evening News) authored by the historian Wu Han with the approval of Teng T'o, (editor-in-chief of *Frontline*) and of the Peking Municipal Committee. The articles, appearing in the column "Evening Chats at Yenshan" and "Three Family Village," came under attack during the Cultural Revolution's early stages in 1966 (see Chapter 11 below).

[8] The first three and the sixth of these documents are discussed by Choh-ming Li in his "China's Industrial Development, 1958-63," *op. cit.*, pp. 10-11. They had been smuggled out of China and are available at the Union Research Institute in Hong Kong. The fourth and fifth documents are referred to in "Outline of Struggle," *URS*, Vol. 53, Nos. 7-8, *op. cit.*, pp. 89ff. The 70 Articles (or Points) of Industrial Policy are discussed by Audrey Donnithorne, *op. cit.*, pp. 190, 282, 308. See also *Draft Articles on Rural Communes* (Peking: 1961), (Taiwan edition in Chinese); "12 Emergency Regulations and Draft of 60 Articles of Rural People's Communes," *URS*, Vol. 28, No. 12 (August 10, 1962). Teng's 10-Point (Draft) Directive was discussed in *Liberation Army Daily* and *Hung-ch'i* editorials, November 23, 1967 under the heading "The Struggle in China's Countryside Between the Two Roads." The "early" 10 Points were dated May 1963. The "later" 10 Points date from September of that year. The document was again revised in September 1964.

●60 Articles of the By-Laws (Draft) for Rural People's Communes (issued by the Party's top authorities around May 1961)

●70 Articles of Cultural and Educational Policy (issued by the Party probably in May 1961)

●80 Articles on the Management of the Agricultural Machinery Industry (July 1961)

●60 Articles on the Management of Enterprises of Agricultural Mechanization (July 1961)

●70 Articles of Industrial Policy (issued by the Party's high command in December 1961)

●10-Point Directive (Draft) for the Party's Policy in the Countryside allegedly prepared by the Party's Secretary General Teng Hsiao-p'ing "in opposition to" a 10-Point Directive on the same subject authored by the Party's left over the signature of Mao Tse-tung

●29 Articles on the Status of Accounting Personnel (adopted by the State Council in November 1962)

The substance of the various Articles emerges from the discussion of the new course which follows. A short version of the Articles was given by Chou En-lai on March 27, 1962 in his "Ten Tasks" for the national economy.[9] These included retrenchment of basic construction, the sending of urban workers to the countryside, and the development of the economy in the order of agriculture, light industry, and heavy industry. The Articles (except those on Accounting personnel) were probably thrashed out at a closed door session of the Supreme State Conference held shortly before the March 1962 meeting of the National People's Congress. By the Tenth Plenum of the Eighth Central Committee (September 1962) the new policy appears to have been firmly in place. However, it was precisely at this time that the left launched its counteroffensive. "In 1962, at the Tenth Plenary Session of the Eighth CCP Central Committee, the great leader, Chairman Mao creatively developed the Marxist-Leninist theory of class struggle, made the great call 'Never Forget Class Struggle,' and sounded the bugle for an all out counteroffensive of the proletariat against the bourgeoisie."[10] The counterattack took the form of (1) a socialist education campaign with Chairman Mao's thought as core and Chairman Mao's "good soldiers" as model, (2) "industry should learn from Taching," (3) "agriculture should

[9] *Jen-min Jih-pao*, April 17, 1962. The full text of the Ten Tasks may be found in *FEER*, Special Supplement (September 27, 1962), p. 586.

[10] "Outline of Struggle," *URS*, Vol. 53, Nos. 7-8, *op. cit.*, p. 94. The communiqué of the Tenth Plenary Session may be found in *Peking Review* (September 28, 1962), pp. 5-8.

learn from Tachai," (4) "the whole nation should learn from the People's Liberation Army," its spirit, its regulations, its history, and its Spartan way of life. The economy was more or less in shape again, and it was time to experiment with emotional political economy once more.[11]

OUTLINE OF THE NEW ECONOMIC POLICY

As explained by the New Year's editorial of the Party's theoretical journal *Hung-ch'i*, the new policy of readjustment, consolidation, filling out, and raising standards meant that "it is necessary, at this time, to make suitable adjustments in the altered relations between the various branches, consolidate the great gains scored by the productive forces and production relations in the course of these developments and changes, enrich the content of newly developed undertakings, and raise the quality of those new things that need further improvement."[12] In short, it was necessary to clean up the mess.

Two interesting features of the new approach to economic development were: a reversal of the accepted communist sectoral priorities (i.e., heavy industry, light industry, agriculture) adopted by China from 1953 through 1957 and implicit in the Great Leap in spite of all the furor about agriculture,[13] deemphasis of the hitherto overwhelming concern with quantity and speed (except during the liberal interlude, 1956-57), and a concern with the quality of output and the market-orientation of production. This was made clear in Chou En-lai's statement in December 1964 that "the plan for national economic development should be arranged in the order of priority of agriculture, light industry, and heavy industry. The scale of industrial development should correspond to the volume of marketable grain and the industrial raw materials made available by

---

[11] The Tenth Plenary Session operated several changes in the membership of the Central Committee's Secretariat. Huang Ko-cheng and Tan Cheng who had been associated with P'eng Teh-huai were dismissed. Among the new appointees was Kang Sheng, a theoretician who was to play an important role in the Cultural Revolution after 1965 and was probably the leading spirit behind the many open letters which the Central Committee sent to their Soviet counterpart in the years 1963-65.

[12] "Forward Under the Banner of the General Line," *Hung-ch'i* editorial, No. 1, 1961, in *Peking Review* (January 6, 1961), p. 10.

[13] "Taking steel production as the core and achieving a comprehensive leap forward." See Chapter 8, p. 277.

agriculture."[14] Chou's summing-up of the new economic policy contains, it will be noticed, one other point which loomed prominently
after 1962: the importance of the national economic plan (with
emphasis on control through economic accounting) and hence of the
professional planner and expert. Comprehensive central planning had
become impossible during the Great Leap Forward and had to be
rebuilt piece by piece.[15] Only after 1962 was it possible again to
think in terms of a centrally conceived, centrally enforced, national
economic plan.

The methodological guidelines for the new course were, thus,
gradualness, a modicum of intersectoral balance (the rate of industrial growth was to be determined by and coordinated with the
growth of marketable grain and industrial raw materials made available by agriculture), an appreciation of the overwhelming rural
realities of China's society, and a new understanding of quality as an
important dimension of economic growth.[16] However, as had been
mentioned earlier, hand in hand with the policy of prudence, moderation, realism, and restraint went a renewed assault from the left on
the citizens' political consciousness under the name of "Socialist
Education" (Chapter 10). Launched in 1962, at the very time that
the new economics was beginning to bear fruit, the socialist education campaign, with its emphasis on rebirth through correct (Maoist)
political faith, was aimed at preventing the essentially revisionist economic policies from seeping through into the realms of culture and
politics and turning into the much-feared Soviet-type revisionism
after the disappearance of the present generation of Chinese leaders.
Both in its intensity and the shrillness with which it was pursued,
contrasting sharply with the concurrent matter-of-fact economic
policy, the socialist education campaign revealed the anxiety with
which China's aging leftist leaders viewed the possible future course
of events in the country, and the continued suspicion in which they

[14] Chou En-lai, "Report on the Work of the Government to the First Session, Third National People's Congress," December 21-22, 1964 in *Peking Review* (January 1, 1965), p. 10. The theoretical justification for the application of
the policy is to be found in an article by Lin Hung, "Actively Develop Diversified Operations, Promote Overall Soaring of Agriculture," *Ching-chi Yen-chiu*
(Economic Research), No. 10 (October 20, 1965) in *SCMM*, No. 503
(December 20, 1965), pp. 1-20. The strategy presumably included an absolute
and relative increase in investment in agriculture. In 1963 it was reported that
bank investments in agriculture were 26 percent higher than in 1962. *NCNA*
(May 23, 1963).

[15] If the claim that the Second Five Year Plan (1958-62) had been fulfilled
in three years were true, the Third Five Year Plan should have started in 1961.
In fact, it was not announced until January 1, 1966, and then only in the most
general and vague terms.

[16] For a summary of the new economic policy see Prybyla, "Communist
China's Strategy of Economic Development: 1961-1966," *Asian Survey* (October
1966), pp. 589-603. Also available in Jan S. Prybyla (ed.), *Comparative Economic Systems* (New York: Appleton, 1969), pp. 368-383.

held the rising generations of technocrats, engineers, and other experts.[17]

The main guideposts of the new economic policy may be summarized as follows:

I. Agriculture is the foundation of economic construction.

II. Industry is the leading factor in that construction.

III. Economic construction must be guided by a central plan.

IV. Quality is an important dimension of economic growth.

V. Scientific and technical education is crucial to economic development and socialist construction.

VI. Self-reliance is the cornerstone of economic development and socialist construction, but does not exclude learning from foreigners, especially in the fields of science and technology.

VII. In foreign trade the policy is one of "leaning to all sides," i.e., diversification of trade partners.

VIII. The rate of population increase should be slowed down.

IX. Class struggle should be attenuated (a much disputed objective).

I. AGRICULTURE: THE FOUNDATION

In proclaiming agriculture to be the foundation of economic construction, the aim was to make sure that the rapidly growing population be adequately fed, that industry receive the needed raw materials of agricultural origin, that the export trade be supported, and that the recurrence of the "three bad years" be prevented.[18]

PRIORITIES

While trying to achieve a balance among the various subsectors of agriculture, dovetailing them into one another, the following priorities were to be respected:

1. First place was to be accorded to grain output. "Grain is the foundation of foundations."[19]

[17] For a clear expression of this anxiety see Edgar Snow's interview with Mao Tse-tung, *The Sunday Times* (London), February 14, 1965, p. 11; and "Mao Tse-tung: A Worried Man at 72?" *China Report* (New Delhi), June 1965, pp. 1-3. Cf. Mao Tse-tung's disappointment with the young generation, below, Chapters 11 and 12.

[18] The "agriculture as foundation" policy was also sometimes summed up in the slogan of the "Four Changes": (1) mechanization, (2) electrification, (3) irrigation, and (4) application of chemical fertilizer—that is, modernization.

[19] Yang Ling, "Agriculture: Foundation of the National Economy," *Peking Review* (October 18, 1960), p. 17. The slogan also read: "Diversified agriculture with grain as the key link." A good general source is Yuan-li Wu and J. L. Buck, *Food and Agriculture in Communist China* (Stanford, Calif.: Hoover Institution Press, 1966); also Kenneth R. Walker *Planning in Chinese Agriculture: Socialization and the Private Sector, 1956-1962* (Chicago: Aldine, 1966).

2. Grain output was to be geared to livestock raising (especially pigs). This was expected to yield quick returns in the form of meat (material incentive to farmers and urban workers), and manure—both helping to increase grain yields.

    3. Raw materials for industry (especially cotton).

    4. Export crops (rice, oil seeds).

    5. Sideline production on private household plots (especially

TABLE 9-1

Output of Food Grains

(Millions of metric tons)

	1957	1958	1959	1960	1961	1962	1963	1964	1965
Official Data									
Official first target		196	525	297		250			
Revised target			275			240⎰ 275⎱			
Official first claim.....	185	375	270						
Revised claim.		250							
Miscellaneous official estimates ..				150	+160	+170	183	200	200
Western Estimates									
Wu	185	175.4	154.4	130	140	160			
E. F. Jones ..	185				162				200
Werner Klatt .				160				182.7	179.9
Economist Intelligence Unit	185				166-7	±175	179-80	185-90	
O. L. Dawson	185	204	170	160	170	180	185	195	193-200
Hong Kong ..	185	193	168	159	166	179	179	183	181

Sources: Official Data: *Jen-min Jih-pao* (December 19, 1958); *Ten Great Years*; Li Fu-chun, "Report on the Draft 1960 National Economic Plan" (March 30, 1960), *Jen-min Jih-pao* (April 1, 1960). Miscellaneous official estimates come from various interviews granted by Chinese top officials to Western visitors. Western Estimates: Yuan-li Wu, *The Economy of Communist China*, op. cit., p. 140, Table VII-2; Edwin F. Jones, "The Emerging Pattern of China's Economic Revolution," in *An Economic Profile of Mainland China*, op. cit., Vol. I, p. 94, Table III; Werner Klatt, "China's New Leap Forward," *FEER* (July 21, 1966), p. 107; "Communist China's Agricultural Calamities," *China Quarterly*, No. 6 (April-June 1961), pp. 74–75; "Comment on 'Economic Growth in China and the Cultural Revolution,' " *ibid.* (July–September 1967), p. 154; The Economist Intelligence Unit, *Quarterly Economic Review: China Hong Kong, North Korea* (August 1965), p. 5; O. L. Dawson in E. F. Jones, *loc. cit.*, p. 93, Table II; Hong Kong diplomatic estimates cited in *Current Scene* (January 15, 1964), and *FEER* (March 12, 1964), p. 556. Cf. Robert M. Field, "How Much Grain Does Communist China Produce?" *China Quarterly*, No. 33 (January-March 1968), pp. 98–107; S. Swamy and S. J. Burki, "Foodgrains Output in the People's Republic of China, 1958-1965," *ibid.*, No. 41 (January-March 1970), pp. 58–63. Cf. Table 8-10 above.

fruit, vegetables, poultry, oxen, pigs, tung trees, silkworms, essential oils, bamboo, native paper, fisheries, wooden farm implements).

In short, the farm sector was expected to furnish both a larger quantity than hitherto and a greater variety of commodities for domestic consumption and for export, and in this way secure funds which could be plowed back into grain production.

Since (as we have repeatedly pointed out) the Chinese communists have refrained from publishing output data after 1959 (scattered, local, percentage reports aside), the figures in Tables 9-1 and 9-2 have to be taken with a liberal dose of skepticism.

It will be seen that in spite of rather wide variations in the post-1960 estimates, there seems to be general agreement that food grain output from 1957 through 1965 stagnated at or near the "traditional plateau" of 180-200 million tons. All estimates agree that output in 1959 through 1962 was below the 1957 level.

A breakdown of the estimates is given in Table 9-2.

TABLE 9-2
Estimates of Food Grain Production
(Millions of metric tons)

	Rice		Wheat		Misc. Grains		Potatoes*		Total	
	Offi-cial	Esti-mated	Offi-cial	Esti-mated	Offi-cial	Esti-mated	Offi-cial	Esti-mated	Offi-cial	Esti-mated
1957	87	—	24	—	53	—	21	—	185	—
1958	114	90	29	24	62	50	45	29	250	193
1959	—	80	—	24	—	42	—	22	270	168
1960	—	77	—	22	—	38	—	22	—	159
1961	—	80	—	16	—	45	—	25	—	166
1962	—	81	—	20	—	54	—	24	—	179
1963	—	78	—	22	—	55	—	24	—	179
1964	—	82	—	24	—	55	—	22	—	183
1965	—	85	—	22	—	54	—	20	—	181

*Grain equivalent at a ratio of 4:1.

Sources: Based on diplomatic estimates in Hong Kong, in P. H. M. Jones, "China's Grain Harvest," *FEER* (March 12, 1964), p. 556; Dick Wilson, "China's Farming Prospects," *ibid.* (August 6, 1964), p. 235; *ibid.* (October 1, 1964), p. 25; Harald Munthe-Kaas, "China's Fields and Factories," *ibid.* (February 3, 1966), p. 153. Cf. *FEER* (December 5, 1963), p. 494. Compare totals with Table 9-1 above.

MODALITIES

In order to reach the objective of diversified agriculture with grain as the leading link, i.e., increase the quantity and variety of marketable agricultural products, the following policies were implemented during the period 1961-65.

1. Consolidation, i.e., De Facto Dissolution of the Rural People's Communes

The mystique of the communes was, however, preserved. This has already been discussed in Chapter 8. To recall:

(a) The communes were sharply reduced in size. In 1958 the number of rural people's communes was given as 26,578, the number of communized households as 123,250,000, and the number of households per commune as 4,637 (cf. Table 8-5). In October 1964 the number of communes was given as 74,000 with an average of 1,620 households per commune.[20] The reduction in the size of communes was not uniform throughout the country. It would appear that commune size was reduced mainly in mountaineous and national minority areas. In Kwangtung, for example, the number of communes remained the same, while in Kwangsi it jumped from 1,000 in 1958 to 20,000 after 1961.[21]

(b) Efforts to federate all communes within a county were abandoned.

(c) Most communal mess halls were closed. Where these were retained, membership in them was made voluntary.

(d) Encouragement of communal small-scale industry was dropped.

(e) Private plots of commune members were reintroduced, and household sideline production was encouraged. The plots were not to exceed 7 percent of a production team's land. Commune members were permitted to reclaim small plots of wasteland, provided they adhered to state regulations and obtained clearance from commune authorities. The produce of private plots was to be exempted from compulsory sales, and crops produced on the plots were not to be counted in estimating the peasants' grain retention standards before liability for compulsory sales was calculated.[22] In practice, however, this was usually violated. Private plots of commune members were to be exempted from the agricultural tax. However, in May 1962 the produce sold on rural trade fairs, (f) below, began to be taxed on entering the market, on sale, or on entering a warehouse. Since much of this produce came from private plots,[23] the tax exemption was inoperative in practice. As state pressure on private plots mounted

[20] According to information obtained by *FEER* editor Dick Wilson, a model commune near Peking which he visited in 1964, had 50,000 members (roughly 10,000 households). Another commune (near Shanghai) had 25,000 members (roughly 5,000 households) divided into 14 production brigades, and 148 production teams.

[21] Dick Wilson, "China's Farming Prospects," *FEER* (August 6, 1964), p. 235.

[22] Audrey Donnithorne, *op. cit.*, p. 352.

[23] *Ta Kung-pao* (November 20, 1961). According to data obtained by Wilson in two model communes in 1964, private plots were 66 square meters per member in one commune (near Peking) and $1/10$ *mou* per member in the second

toward 1964-65 and the spare time available to adult commune members for private plot activities shrank, more and more work on the plots tended to be done by children under sixteen. Subsidiary production of livestock (especially pigs and poultry), fruit, vegetables, wood oil (*tung yu*), other oils, silk, sugar and tea accounted in 1965 for about one-third of the total value of commune output and contributed importantly to China's export trade. More than half of China's hard currency sales to Hong Kong and West Germany, and about one-third of the country's exports to Britain consisted of raw or processed products of subsidiary activity. Much of this activity was "private" in the sense of originating in the team members' household plots. For example, 80 percent of the pigs and almost all the poultry raised in China came from private plots. However, most piglets were bought from communes and sold live or as pork to rural supply and marketing cooperatives or other procurement agencies of the state at state-fixed prices. During the Cultural Revolution (1968) it was alleged that in 1962 the private grain harvest in Yunan was bigger than the collective, that in 1961-62 more than 20 percent of communal land was given over to the private sector in southwestern China, that some peasants earned more than 1,000 yuan out of private cultivation, and that even in 1964 there was more private than communal cultivation in Kweichow and Szechuan. During the "bad years" (1959-61) private plots in Yunan allegedly represented 20-50 percent of cultivated land. In the Huahsing commune near Shanghai, experiments with family production quotas has apparently been authorized by Liu Shao-ch'i, while Tao Chu experimented in Kwangtung with land distribution to individual families according to their labor capacity (the so-called "Production Responsibility System").[24] Private intercropping on communal land was said to have been encouraged in Kweichow by Party Secretary Chia Chi-yuan.

By 1963 emphasis shifted to collective (team, brigade, and commune level) sideline activities and warnings were once again being issued about capitalist tendencies inherent in private sideline occupations.[25]

(near Shanghai). In the latter case, private plots represented about 7 percent of total commune land. See also "The Nature of Private Plots," *Ta Kung-pao*, March 15, 1961, in: *SCMP*, No. 2478 (April 18, 1961), and Chu Tai-hsien, "Proper Relationship Between Group Production and Family Side-Line Enterprises," *Ta Kung-pao*, June 25, 1961, in *JPRS* No. 10563 (1961).

[24] Dick Wilson, "The China After Next," *FEER* (February 1, 1968), p. 193.

[25] See "Contradiction Between Collective Economy and Peasants' Individual Incomes and Living," *URS*, Vol. 31, No. 11 (May 7, 1963), and "The Development of Collective Sideline Production in Agriculture," *ibid.*, Vol. 32, No. 24 (September 20, 1963).

(f) Primary markets in rural areas were revived in the fall of 1960, although the state attempted to exercise control over transactions in these markets by fixing the upper limits of price fluctuations and establishing on-the-spot supervision over market activities.[26] Grain, cotton seed and other oil seeds were not to be bought and sold on these markets. By the spring of 1963 further restrictions were imposed on the rural trade fairs to curb undesirable manifestations of spontaneous capitalism. What seems to have happened was that the more abundant supply of vegetables, eggs, poultry, fruit, and other products of private plot activity had induced some peasant households and not a few people in the towns to turn to full-time trading and hawking, the rural fairs providing them with convenient and legitimate places of business. The 1963 regulations tried to stamp out this trend and prevent people from deserting farm work for full-time trading. Aside from ideological hostility to the rebirth of market mentality, there was a practical motive behind the move: to supply the rural fairs, commune members gave more attention to their private plots than to the growing of wheat and rice which the state wanted for export and industrial development, and which it bought from the communes at low prices. There wasn't too much living to be made out of socialism, quite a bit, and then some, out of peddling. Since to supplement their income, production teams and brigades were also allowed to sell the products of their sideline activity on these markets, they tended to neglect production for the state in favor of subsidiary production for the market. The uneasy coexistence between collective and private economies was sharply felt by the local cadres harried from above and pressed from below, often yielding to corruption, and closing their eyes to gross violations of socialist morality on the farms.

(g) The "Three Level of Ownership" system was consolidated. Originally ownership of assets was vested primarily in the production brigade (corresponding roughly to the former advanced agricultural producers' cooperative). In time the tendency was to vest ownership increasingly in the production team (roughly equivalent in terms of size to the former elementary agricultural producers' cooperative).

(h) Tractors, other agricultural machinery, and large tools, the ownership of which was vested in the communes during the Leap, were taken away from the communes and returned to the newly revived state machine tractor stations. By the end of 1962, according to the Maoists, 88 percent of such commune owned assets had been

---

26 The former Party Secretary of Kweichow, Chia Chi-yuan, was accused in 1967 of having said: "To oppose the opening up of a free market for fear of speculation and profiteering is to give up eating for fear of choking." *Kweiyang Radio* (June 16, 1967). See also "Development of Rural Markets," *Ta-kung Pao* (Peking), January 13, 1961, in *JPRS*, 8414 (June 1961).

so transferred. The November 1962 Central Committee "Opinion on Readjusting and Improving the Work of Tractor Stations" (inspired, according to the Maoists, by the "capitalist-roader" T'an Chen-lin "and his minions"), stated that "when many tractor stations were changed to commune-owned and commune-run regime, the original set of rules and regulations was abolished, the utility of machines was decreased, and damage was serious."[27] The problem had become more intractable with the transfer of accounting functions to production teams. "At present," Liu was alleged to have said, "the peasants can't do it—the state has to do it. In the initial stage it is up to the state to run tractor stations."[28]

(i) Rural supply and marketing cooperatives, which in the fall of 1958 had been transformed into supply and marketing departments of the rural people's communes, were after mid-July 1961 reestablished as independent entities subject to state supervision.

(j) The production team (20-30 households) became typically the planning and accounting unit within the commune (i.e., it planned output within the general directives laid down by the state, and dealt with income and expenditure distribution).[29] The production brigade ran enterprises jointly owned by the production teams, and organized team cooperation. The commune, through its executive committee (nominally) elected by the whole commune membership, organized interbrigade cooperation, ran major water and soil conservancy works, operated some repair workshops and livestock farms, and was the lowest unit of government in the countryside. The communes financed themselves from brigade contributions and from state grants and loans. Frequently the planning of output quotas was devolved by the team onto work groups or *tso-yeh-tsu* (roughly corresponding in terms of membership to the former mutual aid teams), "small teams" (*hsiao-tui*), or even onto individual households.

The devolution of effective grassroots authority over production

[27] "Outline of Struggle," in *URS*, Vol. 53, Nos. 7-8, *op. cit.*, pp. 81-82.

[28] *Ibid.*, p. 83. It was estimated that in 1961 China had 1 tractor for every 10 production brigades. Colina MacDougall, "Industry to the Rescue," *FEER* (July 27, 1961), p. 167.

[29] The policy was clearly spelled out in a *Jen-min Jih-pao* editorial of January 1, 1962. Cf. "To run well the production teams and strengthen the core of leadership in the production teams is the decisive key to consolidating the collective economy of the people's communes and to developing agricultural production." "Strengthen the Core of Leadership in Production Teams," *Jen-min Jih-pao* editorial, January 11, 1963 in *SCMP*, No. 2905, *Extracts from China Mainland Publications*, No. 105 (August 19, 1964), p. 1. "The production team should be the main force for developing sideline production in the countryside since it is the basic accounting unit of the people's commune and the basic unit directly in charge of organizing production and distribution of grain." "Actively Develop Sideline Production in the Countryside," *Jen-min Jih-pao* editorial, January 30, 1963, in *SCMP, ECMP*, No. 105 (August 19, 1964), p. 2.

and finance onto the production team did not go unnoticed or unopposed by the Party's left wing. In an article entitled "Questions and Answers on Class Struggle," published in the Canton *Nan-fang Jih-pao* of August 24, 1963, the proponents of permanent revolution, sharp class struggle, and bigness of local organization argued that "facts of real life prove that in a production team where the leadership is held by the upper middle peasants, influences of spontaneous capitalism will raise their heads, the Party's policies and measures cannot be carried out fruitfully, and abandonment of agriculture in favor of commerce, speculation, and manipulation are grave. In those teams where the upper middle peasants hold the upper hand, the leadership is likely to be usurped by the landlords and rich peasants, who would then stage a counterrevolutionary comeback. This is what we must especially guard against."[30] From 1963 onward, production teams were required to show they were "Five-Good," that is, good at (1) executing the Party's policies, (2) promoting political education, (3) carrying out the tasks of collective agriculture and collective sideline production, (4) operating thriftily and industriously, and (5) fulfilling the tasks assigned to them by the state.[31]

The architects of the Great Leap Forward were even more disturbed by the growing tendency to assign output quotas to work groups of about 10 households each, or even to individual households. Believing as they did that "more progressive property relations" evoked higher output and greater productivity (cf. Chapter 8), they saw in the assignment of production quotas to ideologically "lower" organizational units a retreat to the presocialist years 1949-52 and a betrayal of the revolution. Those in charge of the new economic policy, on the contrary, held that in China's conditions, the proper care and management of the soil called for small basic units of organization, at least in the premechanization, prechemicalization era. Socialism in such a context would mean not much more than the setting of feasible output targets, which via material incentives, the center would then try and induce the small units to reach.[32]

---

[30] *SCMP*, No. 3106, *ECMP*, No. 105 (August 19, 1964), p. 6. The statement reflects the left wing's irritation with the dismissal of many Party cadres at the commune and lower levels in the early years of the new course. Cf. John Wilson Lewis, "The Leadership Doctrine of the Chinese Communist Party: The Lesson of the People's Commune," *Asian Survey*, Vol. 3, No. 10 (October 1963), pp. 457-464.

[31] *URS*, Vol. 34, No. 1 (January 3, 1964), p. 1.

[32] E.g., in July 1962, long-term, interest-free People's Bank loans (repayable within two to five years in a lump sum or by installments) were initiated. By September, 300 million yuan were loaned, mostly to production teams in the major grain producing areas. *Peking Review* (November 30, 1962), p. 3.

The radicals' *bête noire* was the "Three Assignments and One Reward," which they considered to have been particularly revisionist and capitalist-roading.[33] The "three assignments" were (1) physical output, (2) production cost, and (3) consumption of manpower by production teams or lower units. The reward was for any achievement over and above the centrally assigned quotas for output, cost, and manpower utilization. In the eyes of the radicals the revisionism of the Three Assignments and One Reward rested in the heavy reliance on material rewards for such allegedly capitalist-roading pursuits as cost reduction and manpower economy. There was, they thought, too much crass calculation of profit and loss in it, too much fussing over abstract economic laws and the propensity of men to respond to real income gains, too little attention to the creative possibilities of correct political faith and the mountain-moving strength of inspired peasant masses.

Another "poisonous weed," according to the leftists, was the "Three Self and One Assignment" allegedly promoted from 1960 through 1962 by right opportunists, revisionists, and other top persons in the Party taking the capitalist road. The policy consisted of (1) giving up commune land to individual households, (2) setting up free markets, (3) giving more responsibility to enterprises in the handling of their own profits and losses, and the assignment of production quotas to households.[34]

(k) The abortive attempt to introduce the free supply-type system of income distribution was abandoned.[35] Piecework wages based on assessment of work points for given tasks (*p'ing-kung chi-feng*) were reintroduced, and in general, the emphasis was once again on material incentives to production.[36] "To reduce the income of commune members," cautioned an editorial in *Nan-fang Jih-pao* (Dec. 3, 1963), "would dampen their production enthusiasm." As a matter of fact, at that time the commune members' production en-

[33] Also sometimes translated as the "Three Guarantees and One Reward" and advocated in a *Jen-min Jih-pao* editorial of December 29, 1960. See Feng Tien-fu, "On the 'Three Guarantees and One Reward' System," *Ching-chi Yen-chiu* (Economic Research), No. 2 (1961), in *JPRS* 15776 (October 18, 1962), pp. 1-30.

[34] This has also been rendered as "Three Freedoms and One Contract"—the contract referring to a household's contractual obligation to produce a fixed quantity of grain assigned by the state.

[35] The production teams were, however, supposed to make provision for a sort of social security system known as the "Five-Protection Households." This prescribed "good treatment" of families of servicemen, martyrs, cadres, model workers, and the care of households in difficulties.

[36] On the piecework system of remuneration, see Chapter 5. Dick Wilson, editor of the *FEER* who visited two above-average (model) communes near Peking and Shanghai in early 1964 was given the following figures for average annual cash income of the communes' members.

thusiasm must have been quite damp already. The mood soon spread to the rural cadres whose discouragement expressed itself in the so-called "Three Opinions," namely that production on high yield farms had reached a plateau; in "ordinary places there was little room left for output increases; and in calamity-stricken areas it was next to impossible to raise production."[37]

The calculation of work points and work days by semiliterate and arithmetically disadvantaged cadres was difficult at the best of times. It became extremely elusive in the years following the Great Leap when peasant pressure was brought to bear on the cadres while various rectification campaigns left the cadres fearful and confused. Their position in the village was unenviable, trapped as they were between democratic centralism and spontaneous democracy. There must have been much abuse of socialist legality, a good deal of corruption and dissimulation. "With peasant cupidity sharpened by concessions, the urge to engross, to corrupt officials and for officials to be corrupted, and the urge to pay less attention to the collective economy must all be growing in strength," wrote one observer in 1961. "The shrewd peasant, for example, knows that it was his attitude to work in the past three years, his refusal to be hurried into a collectivized world, which helped to produce these pleasant concessions [private plots, rural fairs, team accounting, etc.]. It is extraordinarily difficult in any case to turn peasants with a long tradition of family unit farming (either as owners or tenants) into socialist farm laborers. The institutional and organizational changes are not difficult to effect: the difficulty lies in getting the correct response to the change, so that production does not decrease too drastically and morale slump."[38]

Peking		Shanghai	
1964	320 yuan for a strong man, excluding side earnings	1964	241 yuan for an average member; 400 yuan for a strong man
1958	170 yuan	1958	130 yuan for an average member

Dick Wilson, "In the Chinese Communes," *FEER* (May 7, 1964), p. 292. Average annual income of peasants in Hua *hsien* commune, Kwangtung, was reported as follows: 1957, 65 yuan; 1963, 188 yuan; 1964 (anticipated), 200 yuan. Presumably this was cash income. Derek Davies, "A Kwangtung Commune," *FEER* (December 17, 1964), pp. 564-567.

[37] See "Lethargy of Peasants in Agricultural Production," *URS*, Vol. 34, No. 18 (March 3, 1964), and "Organizing for a New Peak in Agricultural Production," *ibid*. (February 18, 1964). Cf. Chapter 8 above.

[38] Henry Lethbridge, "Contradictions in Communes," *FEER* (November 9, 1961), pp. 305, 307. Put somewhat differently, the age-old problem is that, as a rule, to perform socially useful tasks, men have to be personally motivated. Exclusively communal incentives normally tend to make individuals engage in tasks which promise mainly personal gains.

Around 1964 the central planning and judiciary organs finally got around to checking up on the financial deals and target reporting of the production teams and the investigation apparently disclosed numerous irregularities in which the rural cadres were implicated. The tightening up of central control over the teams actually began in early 1963 when thumb-twiddling brigade level cadres were transferred *en masse* to the team level, there to live with the toilers and do some useful work for the state. By mid-1964 the Socialist Education Campaign (Chapter 10), inaugurated in 1962 as an antidote to the alleged economic revisionism of the new course, suddenly veered toward the rural technical, administrative, and supervisory cadres who were accused of corruption, extravagance, and negligence. The practical cause of the rural cadres rectification campaign launched in earnest in September 1964 seems to have been the state's failure to supply the countryside with cheap goods (especially textiles) with which to mop up the peasants' increased purchasing power derived from free-market sales and rising state procurements.[39] Although the main problem was that there were not enough consumer goods to go around, there is ample evidence that the commercial network was caught by surprise when confronted with a sudden increase in peasant purchasing power. *Hsien* level state wholesale bureaus, and the basic level supply and marketing cooperatives and state trading corporation outlets got bogged down in bureaucratic red tape, stocked up on producer goods rather than on small consumer items which they thought bothersome and unprofitable to handle, failed to communicate, and shifted blame from one level and form of organization to another.

A subsidiary cause of the rectification drive was the ancient problem of communication between the center and the provinces, the rural cadres siding with and abetting economic localism, an exercise rendered all the easier by the rough correspondence of the basic rural decision-making unit (the team) with the old Chinese village. A major point of conflict mentioned by *Nan-fang Jih-pao* on December 26, 1964 was the inaccurate allocation of work points to the peasants by production team officials and falsification of team production accounts which underrated the teams' production performance and resulted in produce hoarding at the team level. This was perhaps inevitable in view of the policy of devolving local capital construc-

[39] In 1964 state procurements of agricultural products increased 10 percent over the previous year. Harvest yields did not rise by that much. Cotton output rose from 1.02 million tons in 1963 to 1.25 million tons in 1964. Most of the increase was used in the manufacture of cotton cloth for export. Cotton goods supplied to the countryside in 1964 absorbed about 30 percent of peasant income, while sales of cotton to the state generated 11-15 percent of peasant income.

tion responsibility on the teams, brigades, and communes. Team leaders were also accused of competing in the construction of offices and other bureaucratic prestige amenities for themselves. According to secret Chinese military papers captured by Khamba guerrillas in Tibet in late summer 1961, many local cadres were charged with murder, rape, extreme cruelty, and serious misuse of mass line techniques.[40]

In pursuance of the "Four Withs," judicial cadres (including high officials from central judiciary organs) were sent down to the countryside and instructed to investigate[41] abuses of socialist morality by (1) eating, (2) living, (3) working, and (4) discussing together with poor and lower-middle peasants. In this way, by encouraging the rural proletariat to pour out its woes into the ears of representatives of state power in the course of door-to-door "comradely chats" with poor and lower-middle peasants, lax and corrupt cadres could be rooted out and all manifestations of spontaneous capitalism nipped in the bud.[42] The "Four Clearance" movement was intended simultaneously to (1) correct cadre corruption in respect of financial affairs, (2) work points, (3) accounts, and (4) storage of produce.[43] The "Three Fixes and One Substitution" involved the assignment of rural cadres to (1) fixed labor bases, (2) at which they had to report at fixed hours, (3) work for a fixed length of time each day, and—as for the substitution—learn the jobs of regular workers so as to be ready to replace the regular workers whenever necessary. The whole "Fixes and Substitution" program was to be administered and supervised by officials of high rank directly answerable to the center. In 1965 government organs at all levels reportedly had sent between

[40] See *China Quarterly* (April-June 1964).

[41] The "Three Investigations" which the investigating teams were to carry out included (1) one's family and personal history, (2) one's thought (class stand), and (3) one's work.

[42] The "Four Withs" were to be applied with special vigor during a "Love the People" month following the Spring Festival. See Chapter 10.

[43] The "Four Clearance" movement was the offshoot of a wider "Four Clean-Ups" (*si-ching*) campaign launched during the December 1964 Fourth Session of the National People's Congress, but decided on at a Central Committee work conference in June. The object of the campaign was to clean up political, economic, ideological, and organizational work as well as to clear the channels of information between the basic units of organization and the state planning agencies. The guiding principles of the Four Clean-Ups were spelled out in Mao Tse-tung's "23-Point Directive," which apparently Liu and his people tried to sabotage by making it "Left in form, but Right in essence." According to this Directive, the Four Clean-Ups were to last seven years, and were to be conducted district by district. Once it became clear to the Party's leftists that the essentially rural campaign was not going their way, they turned to the cities (Great Proletarian Cultural Revolution—Chapters 11 and 12 below). The rural Four Clean-Ups campaign dissolved in the Cultural Revolution in mid-1966. In a sense, the Cultural Revolution was an enormous urban Clean-Up movement. See Harald Munthe-Kaas, "China's 'Four Clean-Ups,' " *FEER* (June 9, 1966), pp. 479-484.

one-third and one-half of their personnel to "squat at a point" in the countryside and take part in field labor.[44] Poor and lower-middle peasant associations, dormant since new democracy days, were re-activated for the express purpose of helping central organs supervise and report on local rural cadres. The associations which comprised financial supervision groups, usually operated through production brigade Party branches. Team members were encouraged to report their grievances directly to those organs, bypassing team-level author-ities. Throughout 1964 and 1965 congresses of poor and lower-middle peasants' representatives were held all over China. More and more often they called for a new great leap forward in agricultural production and a new upsurge of socialist consciousness.[45]

In the spring of 1964 a movement of "Comparing, Learning, Overtaking, and Helping," originally applied in industry, was ex-tended to the agricultural front. The objective was to break down local barriers to the flow of technical and innovational information, a problem besetting all command-type economies.

One ominous result of the 1964 rectification drives was the dis-missal in December of that year of Vice Premier Teng Tzu-hui who from 1953 to 1959 headed the Party's Rural Work Department and up till October 1962 was Director of the State Council's Office of Agriculture and Forestry. Teng was a staunch advocate of a cautious and pragmatic approach to economic development and is believed to have opposed the Leap policies of 1955-56 and 1958-60.

(l) Stress was put on local conditions and feasibility rather than on grandiose schemes divorced from reality.

(m) The communes and their constituent units were instructed to "correctly handle" the relationship between themselves and the State in conformity with the slogan of "linking one's family with Tien-An Men." In the new political context this meant that the communes, brigades, teams, work groups, and households were to pay attention to and strictly obey central directives. To link one's family with Tien-An Men was to integrate cultivation according to local conditions with the fulfillment of state plans for grain, cotton, and other key commodities, and the sale to the state of the stated portions of the products of subsidiary occupations.

2. Emphasis on Maximizing the Area of High and Stable Yields in Respect to Staple Crops

During the period 1961-65 "diversification of agriculture with grain as the leading link" was interpreted primarily as concentration

---

[44] *URS*, Vol. 45, No. 3 (October 11, 1966). Cf. "Farm and Factory Work for Cadres," *Peking Review* (March 25, 1965), pp. 28-29.
[45] *URS*, Vol. 43, No. 14 (May 17, 1966).

on existing high yield areas (especially on state farms) rather than on ambitious land reclamation. While there was plenty of reclaimable wasteland (estimated at over 1 million square kilometers), the decision was taken to consolidate what was already under the plow, leaving major land reclamation projects to a later date.

State investments in large water conservation projects, electric power plant, soil improvement, local transportation, and state agricultural loans were to be directed into areas where highest returns could be expected.[46] Elsewhere the communes and their constituent units were to rely on their own resources.

The areas of high and stable yields were to benefit from the development of *electrically powered irrigation schemes*. The favored areas included the grain and cotton growing districts of Hopei, Hupeh, Anhwei, Honan, Shansi, and Shensi, the rice districts of Kwangtung (especially the Pearl River delta), Kiangsu, and Chekiang, and the vegetable farms in the neighborhood of large cities. Electrically powered irrigation areas in 1962 comprised some 3.4 million hectares out of a total cultivated area of 106.7 million hectares. The total capacity of pumping stations in that year was said to have been twenty times the 1957 capacity. The Pearl River delta project reportedly had 200 irrigation stations and 300,000 kw of power. About 40 percent of the vegetable farms near Peking were said to have been irrigated by electric power in 1962, and about one-third of the wheat and cotton land in Hopei. Rather than build new power stations, the policy appears to have been to construct transmission lines from the cities using existing power sources. The projects were financed mainly by central and local state authorities with communes paying for small equipment and purely local power generating stations. The area of farmland irrigated by mechanical pumps was said to have doubled between 1961 and 1965. There seems to have been some trouble with equipment maintenance and repairs.[47] Part of the trouble was due to the overintensive use of pumps and shortage of lubricants and to the absence of product standardization. Too many different types of pumps were being produced, many factories set up during the Great Leap were closed down (leaving users of their products without replacement parts), and in general producers did not turn out spare parts in sufficient quantities—a phenomenon shared by most command economies and traceable to defects in enterprise success indicators.

[46] State agricultural loans: 1950-58, 12.6 billion yuan (1.4 billion yuan per year); 1959, 3.5 billion yuan; 1963, 1 billion yuan.

[47] See, for example, *Peking Review* (December 29, 1961), p. 4. Beginning in the winter of 1960-61, annual winter inspections of tractors, mechanical pumps, and other farm machinery were ordered.

In the areas of high yields and on experimental farms attention was given to the *development of new plant strains* adapted to local soil and climatic conditions. Among the reported innovations were a typhoon-resistant rice plant, strong-rooted, tough-stemmed, and high yielding; an early ripening rice plant, which reportedly ripened before the onset of the summer monsoons in the south; a tall-stemmed rice plant, the ears of which could be kept above the water level during flooding; and disease-resistant cotton strains. In this as in other matters there was a new willingness to learn from abroad, especially, it would seem, from Japan.[48] Most of the rice plants used around Wuhan, Nanking, and Shanghai, for example, were imported from Japan.[49]

The areas of high and stable yields were also to benefit from the *development of light transport* suited to local conditions.

The big success story of the period 1961-65 was in the area of *chemical fertilizers, pesticides, and insecticides.*[50] The new course placed agricultural chemicals high on the list of priorities. After 1960 the chemical industry became one of China's fastest-growing industrial sectors; for one thing, the bulk of industrial imports was in support of the chemical industry, especially of its agricultural component. Two fertilizer plants each with a capacity of 300,000 tons per year were purchased in Italy, and other installations were bought in Japan, Britain, and the Netherlands. New chemical fertilizer plants were commissioned at Wuching (at a cost of $25 million) and Canton. China's preoccupation with agricultural chemicals is understandable in view of the following data (Table 9-3).

A number of qualifications should be mentioned.[51] First, the high level of chemical fertilizer application in Japan and the Netherlands is in part attributable to the high per hectare population density—the intensive use of chemicals compensating for lack of arable land. Second, China uses more manure, manure crops, and livestock fertilizer per hectare than chemical fertilizer. The use of these is limited in Japan by the small size of farms and the high proportion of land used for planting. Third, the lack of fertilizer is compensated for to some degree in China by the use of rotation systems, which is much less the case in Japan. Even so, the level of

---

[48] The scientific and technological open-mindedness is exemplified by T'an Chen-lin's speech to the February-March 1963 Conference on Agricultural Science and Technology sponsored by the State Council and the Party's Central Committee. T'an Chen-lin was later denounced as a capitalist-roader.

[49] Robert Trumbull (ed.), *This Is Communist China, op. cit.*, p. 141. For example, the "domestically developed" Nung No. 58 variety was actually the Japanese Norin No. 58.

[50] On the chemical and petrochemical industry, see below, pp. 381-383.

[51] Jung-Chao Liu, *op. cit.*, pp. 39-40.

TABLE 9-3

Consumption of Chemical Fertilizer

Country	N + $P_2 O_5$ + $K_2 O$ (kilograms per hectare of arable land)	Population Density on Arable Land (persons per hectare)
Netherlands	356.1	11.0
Japan	303.7	15.3
Formosa	203.8	12.2
Korea	134.5	11.8
United States	38.4	1.0
Soviet Union	10.3	0.9
China	6.7	6.0
India	2.3	2.7

Source: Jung-Chao Liu, "Fertiliser Application in Communist China," The China Quarterly, No. 24 (October–December 1965), p. 39, Table 4.

For Communist China, 1962 consumption is divided by 1957 arable land. Population is an estimated figure for 1960 by extrapolating the 1953 census population of 583 million with assumed rate of growth, 2 percent per annum. Other countries are from FAO, Fertilisers: An Annual Review of World Production, Consumption, and Trade, 1962, p. 18. Consumption data are those of the 1960-61 fertilizer year (July 1-June 30). Population data are those of 1960.

The Economist Intelligence Unit's Quarterly Economic Review: China, North Korea, Hong Kong (December 1963), p. 3 gives somewhat different figures for supplies of fertilizer per hectare (1962). Japan, 228 kg; Taiwan, 110 kg; China, 5 kg. Dick Wilson, "Chemicals in the Communes," FEER (June 11, 1964), pp. 533-535, cites the figure of 535 kilograms per hectare in Japan (1963) and 62 kilograms per hectare in China (1963).

fertilizer use in China is low, given the known deficiency of Chinese soil in nitrogen, phosphate, and potash. The Chinese themselves estimate that they need a minimum of 250 kilograms per hectare or some 20 million tons of chemical fertilizer per year. This compares with an estimated 1966 domestic production of about 6 million tons plus imports of between 2.3-3 million tons (most of them from Western Europe and Japan). Increased application of chemical fertilizers cannot be carried out in vacuuo. For example, more intensive per hectare use of chemicals in rice cultivation calls for the prior development of rice strains capable of absorbing and withstanding high rates of fertilizer input.[52]

3. Agricultural Extension and Experimental Farms

The popularization of modern farming practices was to be based on persuasion through example rather than on force and mass emula-

[52] Ibid., p. 39.

tion. A nationwide network of agrotechnical stations was established, the purpose of which was to evaluate the economic viability of existing farming practices in given areas, the development of modern techniques of field management, rational close planting,[53] plant protection and seed selection, and the training of agrotechnicians. The results were tested on experimental plots set up within the area of a production team and compared with the results obtained from nearby control plots farmed like the rest of the fields. The stations were under the direction of agronomists and work on the experimental plots was done by veteran farmers under the direction of the specialists. Production team members were invited to visit the plots and compare the results. It was hoped that seeing being believing, the farmers would voluntarily adopt the new methods and plant strains. It is difficult to say how far this expectation materialized in practice. Truly voluntary adoption of modern methods of cultivation by tradition-bound farmers (especially where traditional methods of cultivation had for years been officially encouraged) is unfortunately not a matter of merely seeing and believing. It hinges on whether the adoption of modern farming practices benefits the farmers in personal terms—that is, in terms of increases in their real income. This in turn depends on whether the state is willing to allow peasant money incomes to rise with the adoption of modern farming methods, whether the inputs are available, and whether the rising peasant money incomes can be translated into consumer goods. There is implicit in the process some conflict between the state's accumulation needs and the peasants' desire for a higher standard of living now, and there is also a danger of potential income, hence class, differentiation in the countryside.[54] The experiment is Bukharinistic in conception and vulnerable to attack by those who hold socialist planning to be imperative rather than indicative.

4. Agricultural Mechanization

Agricultural mechanization, as we have seen (Chapters 3, 5, and 8), had been the subject of bitter controversy in the Party's *couloirs* ever since the time of new democracy. Marxist dogma about which comes first, the development of the material productive forces (broadly, technique) or higher relations of production (organizational structure) was combined with scraps of economic theorizing about the desirability of changing existing labor/capital cost para-

[53] Close planting of cotton common during the Great Leap years was rejected because it tended to suffocate the cotton plants.

[54] See Henry Lethbridge, "Trend in Chinese Agriculture," *FEER* (May 30, 1963), pp. 499-500.

meters by introducing new technology in bulk, and the contribution of tractors to raising per acre output. There was uncertainty about the relative merits of mechanization and semimechanization and about the advantages of technical borrowing (derived development) from abroad.

On the whole, the bureaucratic moderates opted for widespread, but controlled, semimechanization and supervised, quality-controlled tool improvement, with mechanization (large and medium-sized machines) being pushed in established grain producing areas. Out of a total tractor stock of 100,000 (15-hp units) in 1962, the wheat and cotton growing areas of Hopei had 10,000 tractors, the wheat, corn, cotton, and potatoes growing area north of the Huai about 800, the northeast 28,000 (Heilungkiang 20,000), the farms around Peking 1,000, and the Pearl River delta 1,000. Most of the tractors in the north and northeast were concentrated on state farms where between 60 and 70 percent of all farm work was reportedly mechanized. In 1964 China was said to have had 2,000 large mechanized farms, some of them over 20,000 hectares in area; 36 of these farms were in Heilungkiang.[55]

"Mass research" of the kind practised during the Great Leap was opposed after 1960; expertise, careful testing, and prudent popularization of mechanized farm tools were insisted upon. In line with this, the bureaucratic moderates liquidated one by one Mao's county and special district "mass research institutes." Out of several hundred of these institutes set up during the Great Leap, only 92 were left by 1961.[56] Instead of spreading scarce tractors, combines, and other machinery thinly over the whole country, they proposed setting up 100 key mechanized counties—most of them in proven grain-producing areas. To assure machine maintenance and proper servicing of existing machinery, they sent out work teams to the countryside to train and educate the peasants and established a trust—the Chinese Agricultural Machinery Corporation.[57] In 1964 the China Tractor Internal Combustion Engine Spare Parts Corporation was set up and a year later the China Tractor Internal Combustion Engine Industrial

[55] P. H. M. Jones, "Machines on the Farm," *FEER* (September 10, 1964), pp. 479-480; "Creeping Mechanisation," *ibid.* (November 12, 1964), pp. 350-352. In 1964 state farms cultivated an estimated 4 million hectares of land.

[56] According to the Maoists, investment in local agricultural machinery industries was 83 percent of total investment in agricultural machine-making in 1960. By 1963 this had been reduced to 23 percent, and to 19 percent by 1966. "Outline of Struggle," *URS*, Vol. 53, Nos. 7-8 (1968), p. 84. Cf. Ku Fu-sheng, "Rationally Arrange Agricultural Science Research," *Hung-ch'i*, No. 20, 1962, in *JPRS*, 16602 (December 10, 1962), pp. 36-53.

[57] In 1965, 80 percent of tractor drivers and of those who tended to drainage and irrigation pumps and engines were educated young people. *Peking Review* (July 16, 1965).

Corporation. These took over more than 100 agricultural machinery enterprises from the localities and operated under central direction through eight regional branch corporations. Given the Soviet unwillingness to supply China with agricultural equipment, the bureaucratic moderates proposed to look elsewhere for prototypes which could be copied at home. Until 1964 they bought patents of liquid pressure equipment and portable gasoline engines from France and Japan. U-650 tractors and spare parts were purchased from Rumania, as well as 25-hp and 50-hp "Zetor" tractors from Czechoslovakia. Liu Shao-ch'i was alleged to have said in 1960 that "now that the Soviet Union won't give us the techniques, we can import some techniques from capitalist countries. . . . The northeast should copy the Soviet Union, north China should copy West Germany, and south China should copy Japan."[58]

It has been shown in Chapter 5 that the overintensive use of agricultural machinery during the Great Leap, the shortage of spare parts after 1960, and the neglect of maintenance resulted in a substantial drop in China's tractor stock in 1961. In 1962 the number of tractors (15-hp units) was in the region of 100,000. Assuming an annual domestic production of 40,000 standard units, and ignoring depreciation, the tractor stock in 1965 may have reached and possibly exceeded 220,000 standard units—still a drop in the ocean. One of the limiting factors was steel. The production of one tractor calls for about 2.5-5 tons of steel of some 400 different varieties. The production of one truck requires about 600 different specifications of steel. Even in 1965 steel output was probably not much more than 11 million tons, and problems with special steels were still being encountered. These problems were traceable to continuing shortages of such raw materials as nickel and the absence of sufficient quantities of precision finishing equipment.[59] Varying amounts of ordinary steel were imported from Japan, rolled, pressed, and galvanized steels were bought in Germany, Britain, and France, and some steel products in Eastern Europe. Most of the imported steels apparently did not go to the agricultural machinery industry, but rather to the chemical industry.

The 1961-65 policy makers interpreted mechanization and semimechanization flexibly and in a broad sense. They were not obsessed with ambitious ideas about tractors dotting the countryside, nor

---

[58] "Outline of Struggle," *URS*, Vol. 53, Nos. 7-8, *op. cit.*, p. 86.

[59] Visitors in China in mid-1964 remarked that even the country's main iron and steel complexes (e.g., Anshan, Wuhan, Shanghai) were still working at only 50-60 percent of capacity. Alexandra Close, "China Streamlines Her Steel," *FEER* (March 4, 1965), p. 365. In 1965 the steel industry was said to have turned out 500 new varieties of steel. Cf. Yuan-li Wu, *The Steel Industry of Communist China* (Stanford, Calif.: Hoover Institution Press, 1965).

were their ideas riveted to unreachable time schedules. Insofar as tractor production was concerned, they stressed variety geared to local topographical conditions and the requirements of the particular job to be done. During this period at least six types of light, heavy, medium, and small tractors were trial-produced, ranging from the 100-hp "Red Flag" used in land reclamation to the 7-hp ("Worker-Peasant") tractor suitable for use on small plots, vegetable gardens, orchards, and in hilly areas. But mechanization meant to the policy makers much more than this. It implied the introduction of mechanized power to drainage and irrigation projects in watered paddy fields and to well irrigation schemes in key pastoral areas; it involved the provision of light transportation in the main producing regions; and above all it meant the replacement of human power with grindstones, flails, simple threshers, huskers, tillers, harrows, multishare plows, sowers, and so on, i.e., semimechanization.[60] To help the farms in this task some 25,000 farm tool workshops (employing more than 800,000 people) were established under the Second Ministry of Light Industry. These workshops were in addition to the 1,500-odd machine tractor stations servicing the more mechanized farms in the north, northeast, and near the larger urban centers. In 1965 alone the tool workshops were said to have turned out 1.3 million tools of more than 100 different varieties.

All in all, under the heading of mechanization the difference between the Great Leap and the 1961-65 Consolidation and Filling-Out periods consisted in (a) a shift of stress from social to technical reform, and (b) a shift in control over mechanization and semimechanization from the local to the central level with an emphasis on quality. The bureaucratic moderates brought the relations of production "down" to China's existing level of agricultural technology, that is to the team level. They then proceeded to gradually raise the level of technique through incremental improvements in tools and methods of production.

II. INDUSTRY: THE LEADING FACTOR

PRIORITIES

Under the new economic policy the role of industry (and of transportation and commerce too) was envisaged primarily as aid to agriculture. "The growth of the national economy must be based on

---

[60] In the first half of 1962, 40,000 semimechanized implements and 20 million small farm tools were reportedly produced. In 1965 a billion small and medium-sized agricultural tools was said to have been turned out, using 1 million tons of steel.

agriculture. . . . Only when agriculture has been restored and developed, will it be possible to harmonize relations between industry and agriculture, gradually improve the people's livelihood and promote further industrial growth."[61] "All departments and trades should orientate themselves to serve agriculture and the countryside. The department of heavy industry should, in the first place, provide increasing amounts of machinery, chemical fertilizer, insecticides, fuel, electric power, irrigation equipment, and building materials to agriculture and at the same time provide more and more raw and other materials to light industry. To meet these demands it is essential to speed up the development of heavy industry, and first and foremost of the basic industries still further."[62]

Notice that just as in agriculture, the priorities set down for industry were coordinated with the growth pattern of the economy as a whole. They reflected a renewed preoccupation with internal consistency, balance, and feasibility.[63] They did not soar in the realm of the daring and the fanciful and did not grip the imagination. But neither did they offend reason. Briefly, the scale of priorities within the industrial sector was to be as follows.

1. First place was to be accorded to the development of light industry and handicrafts. These supplied the countryside with articles of daily use (i.e., concrete material incentives to production), small farm tools and implements, and building materials. Light industry was also an important foreign-exchange earner. By 1963 a gradual shift from light to heavy industry, transportation, and communications could be detected, probably linked to the renewed stress on defense.

2. With regard to heavy industry, a demand-oriented policy was adopted. The placing of heavy industry at the bottom of the list of priorities did not imply a neglect of that sector. It merely related heavy industry's investment requirements to the needs of agriculture and light industry. The demands of heavy industry were no longer to

[61] Fang Chung, "An Economic Policy That Wins: A Survey of the Policy of 'Readjustment, Consolidation, Filling-Out, and Raising Standards'," *Peking Review* (March 13, 1964), p. 7.

[62] Chou En-lai, "Report on the Work of the Government" to the First Session, Third National People's Congress, December 21-22, 1964 in *Peking Review* (January 1, 1965), p. 10. This guideline was repeated during the formal launching of the Third Five Year Plan in January 1966.

[63] "All departments, localities, and economic concerns must, when drawing up and implementing their plans, be true to the spirit of regarding the entire economy as a single, coordinated 'chess game.' That is to say, they should consider their work within the framework of the unified state plan." Po I-po, "For New Victories in China's Industrial Production and Construction," *Hung-ch'i*, Nos. 3-4, 1961, in *Peking Review* (February 24, 1961), p. 7. The "whole economy as a chess game" slogan was already advanced in January 1959. It was repeated at regular intervals thereafter.

be absolute—as they had tended to be for a while under the First Five Year plan. Marx, it was recalled, had said that "constant capital is never produced for its own sake, but solely because more of it is needed in spheres of production whose products go into individual consumption."[64] Or as Po I-po put it, "heavy industry itself needs continuous expanded reproduction, but the aim of such expanded reproduction is to promote expanded reproduction in other branches of the economy and the expanded reproduction of means of consumption."[65] The policy objective of industry aiding agriculture presupposed the development of such heavy industry branches as chemicals, special steels, agricultural machinery, irrigation equipment, electric power, and so on, all of which, in turn, presupposed the development of steel production, and particularly special steels.

The following guidelines were to be observed:

(i) Overinvestment in certain manufacturing branches of heavy industry (e.g., steel) was to be corrected through the application of a number of measures (described under *Modalities* below).

(ii) New investments in heavy industry were to be primarily directed toward the extractive industry, but even here the investment was to be selective. Among the branches picked for priority treatment were coal, petroleum, iron ore, certain nonferrous metals, raw materials for the chemical industry (other than petroleum, e.g., sulfur, phosphates), and timber. The idea was to correct the imbalance between processing and extractive branches of heavy industry. Geological surveys and prospecting were to be pushed ahead, with special emphasis on the search for phosphoritic rocks, pyrites, and kainite (for the chemical fertilizer industry), arsenic, limestone, and fluorspar (for the insecticides industry).

(iii) Those departments of heavy industry directly serving agriculture (e.g., chemicals, agricultural machinery) were to be next in line.

(iv) Next came those departments serving light industry (e.g., rolled steel for farm implements, tubes, angle and flat bars for drainage and irrigation machinery, high-quality and special steels). Investment in steel began to rise modestly in 1963 and the upward trend continued since that time. In 1963 the Anshan steel works completed a dozen new construction projects, but most of them seem to have been designed to help increase the production of raw materials (iron, limestone, magnesite). However, even in 1964 the imbalance

---

[64] *Capital* (Moscow: Foreign Languages Publishing House, 1959), Vol. III, pp. 299-300.

[65] Po I-po, "For New Victories in China's Industrial Production and Construction," *op. cit.*, p. 6.

between steel capacity and raw materials supply (especially iron ore), which was at the root of the 1961-62 retrenchment, was still worrying the industry.

(v) Defense industries (including nuclear development) appear to have been accorded a relatively high priority, at least since 1964. By the end of 1968 China had successfully exploded seven nuclear devices.[66]

Table 9-4 summarizes the estimated performance of Chinese industry during the period 1961-65. Figures for 1957-60 have been added for comparison.

MODALITIES

The way in which industrial priorities were interpreted in the course of the new economic policy may be summed up in the following way.

1. A moratorium was declared on "the front of capital construction" especially in certain manufacturing branches of heavy industry (1961-62).

This seems to have been particularly true of steel in the years 1961 and 1962. The "70 Articles of Industrial Policy" (above, p. 344) ordered a halt to basic construction except for specifically authorized projects.[67] The retrenchment was justified by supply bottlenecks created by insufficient development, reckless exploitation and low quality output of China's raw materials base, the deterioration of the country's steel-producing machinery, especially of large precision equipment, the decline of supplies of machinery and replacements from the USSR, and the shortage of technical personnel consequent on the withdrawal of Soviet experts. During the Great Leap years equipment had been used mercilessly with little heed given to repairs and maintenance. The drastic reduction in Soviet supplies of spare parts lent additional urgency to the problem. As late as 1964, the imbalance between steel manufacturing capacity and raw materials supply was, as we have mentioned earlier, still besetting the industry.

According to one Western estimate, the rate of investment (gross investment as proportion of gross national product) declined from 43.7 percent in 1960 to 21.6 percent in 1961, and 21.3 percent in

[66] First test of an atom bomb: October 1964; second test, May 1965; third test, May 1966; fourth, October 1966 (missile with a range of up to 600 miles, armed with a nuclear warhead equivalent to 20,000 tons of TNT); fifth test, Christmas Eve 1966; sixth, June 1967 (hydrogen bomb); unsuccessful test in January 1968; eighth test (hydrogen blast) December 1968.

[67] Choh-ming Li (ed.), *Industrial Development in Communist China, op. cit.*, p. 11.

TABLE 9-4
Production of Selected Industrial Commodities*

	1957	1958	1959	1960	1961	1962	1963	1964	1965
Crude steel (millions of metric tons)									
Large mills	5.35	8	8.63-13.35	15.2-18.45	9.5-12	7-10	7-12	8-14	10-11
Native		3.08							
Coal (millions of metric tons)									
Large mines	130-130.7	226.4–	292.4–	325–	180-250	180-250	190-270	200-290	210-230
Indigenous and small mines		167.7 / 102.6	205.2 / 142.6	138.8 / 261.2					
Crude oil (millions of metric tons)	1.46	2.26	3.7	4.5-5.5	4.5-6.2	5.3-6.8	5.9-7.5	7-8.5	8
Electric power (billions of kwh)	19.34	27.53	41.5	47	31	30-31	31-37.5	32-36	40
Chemical fertilizer (millions of metric tons)	0.63-0.87	0.81-1.46	1.33-2	1.68-2.48	1.43-1.45	2.05-2.17	2.6-3	3.4-3.6	4.6
Cement (millions of metric tons)	6.86	9.30	12.27-12.7	13.5	6-8	6-8	7-10	8-11.5	9
Timber (millions of cubic meters)	27.87-28	35	40-41.2	33-39	27-34	29	32	34	36
Cotton cloth (billions of linear meters)	5.05	5.7	7.5	6-7.6	3	3-3.3	3.3-3.6	3.6-4.5	3.9
Paper (millions of metric tons)	1.22	1.63	2.13	2.13-2.8	1-2.6	1-2.7	1.1-2.85	1.5	1.5†
Sugar (millions of metric tons)	0.86	0.9	1.13-1.26	0.92-1.26	0.7-1.2	0.48-1.3	0.54-1.3	1.05-1.84	1.5

*Figures for 1957-60 include, insofar as available, official Chinese data for some commodities (e.g., coal). Figures for 1961 and later years are low and high Western estimates drawn from a variety of sources.

†According to FAO, paper production in 1959 was 1.63 million tons; the 1963 target was 2.75 million tons; and estimated 1964 output, 3 million tons.

1962, the latter being roughly comparable to the investment rate in 1953 and below that of 1957.[68] The drop in the investment rate, according to Wu, was 67 percent in 1960-61 with a recovery in 1961-62.[69] Another estimate points to a 1961 drop in fixed investment demand of between 46 and 54 percent as compared with 1959 for agriculture, small-scale heavy industry, light industry, Soviet-aid heavy industry, heavy industry producing goods for heavy industry itself, and modern transport and communications.[70]

Residential housing construction was also cut down, especially in 1960-63. One Western observer commented in 1964 on the many abandoned construction sites he saw in Peking and other Chinese cities, with expensive construction equipment rusting on the sites.[71]

From 1949 through 1958 about 1,000 kilometers of railroad track were added every year (22,000 kilometers of track in 1949; over 31,000 kilometers in 1958). Between 1960 and 1962 annual additions did not exceed 800 kilometers, rising to about 1,300 kilometers a year after the latter date. In 1964 China's total railway network was about half that of India. The most important railroad project completed between 1958 and 1963 was the line to Urumchi, the capital of Sinkiang. The original plan was to extend the line to the Soviet border where it was to link up with the Soviet line to Alma Ata.[72] The plan never materialized. Between 1959 and 1965 about 100,000 kilometers of highways were built, mostly for military purposes in Sinkiang, Tibet, and Inner Mongolia.

2. The moratorium on capital construction was to be accompanied by appropriate "filling-out" of existing capacity.

This involved completing essential projects and establishing a proper balance among the various types of equipment within an enterprise, equipment maintenance and repairs (neglected during the Great Leap years), economy in the use of raw materials and fuel, multipurpose utilization of materials, development of efficient busi-

---

[68] Y.L. Wu et al., *op. cit.*, p. 340.

[69] Yuan-li Wu, *The Economy of Communist China, op. cit.*, p. 103. Wu compares this drop with the decline of gross investment in the United States at the time of the Great Depression, which was at the rate of 33 percent in 1929-30, 33 percent in 1930-31, 73 percent in 1931-32, and 33 percent in 1932-33.

[70] William W. Hollister, "Capital Formation in Communist China," in Chohming Li (ed.), *Industrial Development in Communist China, op. cit.*, p. 51, Table 4.

[71] Dick Wilson, "Portrait of Peking," *FEER* (July 16, 1964), p. 118.

[72] Jan S. Prybyla, "Transportation in Communist China," *Land Economics* (August 1966), pp. 268-281; Harald Munthe-Kaas, "Roads and Rails in China," *FEER* (February 17, 1966), pp. 275-276, 325; Holland Hunter, "Transport in Soviet and Chinese Development," *Economic Development and Cultural Change* (October 1965), pp. 71-84. The total highway length in 1958 was 400,000 kilometers.

ness accounting procedures, and more rational use of labor and management. These as well as the careful testing ("scientific appraisal") of innovations and advanced experiences and their coordination with the production requirements of individual enterprises were part not only of the filling-out drive, but of the new appreciation of quality as a significant dimension of economic growth. "Proceeding from the productive capacity of the existing equipment of the various industrial departments and the various links in the production process . . . [the present task is to] fill up the gaps and achieve a proper balance."[73]

For example, filling-out in the coal industry (which supplied 95 percent of China's fuel consumption), meant strengthening the formerly weak links in the production process such as tunneling, coal dressing, safety, and transport (local transport during the Leap having been overcharged, coal was apparently piled up at the mine heads).[74] The machine industries were urged to supply the major coal centers such as Fushun and Tatung with pneumatic shovels, rock drills, high pressure water pumps, crushers, vibration screens, hoists, belt and scraper chain conveyors, shuttle cars, drainage pumps, lamps, and ventilators which had not been delivered in sufficient quantities and qualities in the past. The timber industry was directed to increase its supply of pit props to the mines. In the meantime concrete supports were introduced as a substitute.

To ease the strain on the railroad transportation network, some factories were moved near to raw materials sources. The raw materials factor was also taken into account in the location of new enterprises. However, the policy was interpreted empirically and frequent warnings were issued to the effect that it should not be overdone. As

[73] Po I-po, "For New Victories in China's Industrial Production and Construction," *Hung-ch'i*, Nos. 3-4, 1961, in *Peking Review* (February 24, 1961), p. 6. About this time the Soviets had their filling-out problems too. "We have not yet overcome the incorrect, anti-state practice of dispersing capital investments over many projects. . . . It often happens that new projects are started before those already under construction are completed. This leads to the freezing of enormous funds over many years. . . . Some projects have been under construction for 10 or 12 years, that with rational management could have been built in 3 or 4 years or even less. . . . Projects that cannot be supplied with material resources must under no circumstances be begun; we must not repeat the erroneous practice that has existed up to now." N. S. Khrushchev, Speech to the Plenary Session of the Central Committee of the CPSU, June 21, 1963, *Pravda* (June 29, 1963), pp. 1-4.

[74] Between 1949 and 1964 railways carried more than half the value of all goods transported by modern means. In spite of the policy of streamlining the railroad organization and an annual (1965) production of some 25,000 motor vehicles, transportation was still at the end of the period one of the economy's major bottlenecks. In 1965 China had an estimated 300,000 trucks, 10,000 buses, and 50,000 passenger cars. Harald Munthe-Kaas, *op. cit.*

with agriculture, the major emphasis was on consolidating areas in which advanced enterprises were already located.

3. Appropriate "filling-out" of existing capacity was to be accompanied by the closing down of plants which suffered losses under the economic accounting system (*khozraschet*).

Most of the Great Leap's backyard furnaces were axed out of existence. Numerous small coal mines, fertilizer plants, homemade power generating stations and other "baby plants" were dealt with in the same way. Where profitability under the economic accounting system could be achieved through amalgamation of individual plants, this was done. The trend throughout the period was to concentrate on the technical improvement and (after 1963) expansion of the larger enterprises and mines, and wherever possible to substitute medium-sized local industries endowed with some mechanical power for the labor-intensive, small-scale creations of the Leap. During the Great Leap years coal production from large and indigenous coal mines was said to have been as shown in Table 9-5.

TABLE 9-5
Coal Production from Large (Modern) and Indigenous Mines, 1958–60
(Millions of metric tons)

	Large Mines	Indigenous and Small Mines	Total	Indigenous and Small Mines' Output as Percentage of Total
1958	167.7	102.6	270.3	38
1959	205.2	142.6	347.8	41
1960	138.8	261.2	400.0	65

Sources: 1959, *China Reconstructs* (June 1960); 1958 and 1960, Li Fuchun's Report in *China News Analysis* (June 2, 1961). Cf. Table 9–4 above for lower official figures.

No official figures for coal output have been released since 1960. Notice the officially admitted drop in the output of large (i.e., modern) mines between 1959 and 1960, due no doubt to tunneling, transport and equipment problems (also flooding), that is precisely to those problems which the post-1960 filling-out policy set out to remedy.[75] As was mentioned in Chapter 8, much of the coal produced in indigenous and small mines was probably unusable for industrial purposes. The post-1960 estimated decline in coal production (Table 9-4) may thus be attributed to (a) the difficulties plaguing the

[75] At the end of 1963, 120 shafts were reportedly being extended and improved at the existing large coalmines, and 134 shafts were under construction.

large mines, and (b) the closing down of most indigenous and small
mines (including many do-it-yourself strip mines). Already in 1959-60
the number of local pits and workers had been reduced by 80 percent and 70 percent respectively. After that date indigenous and
small mines were ruthlessly weeded out. Where technically possible,
these mines were subjected to a process of amalgamation and technical transformation. In Kwangtung, for example, only 280 "technically transformed" small mines remained in 1963 out of some
3,000 created in 1958.[76]

4. To help agriculture, industry was to practice the so-called
"Three Don'ts" and "Four Musts."

The "Three Don'ts" referred to industrial construction in the
countryside and reflected the need to conserve arable land and scarce
peasant housing. Good fields were not to be used for industrial purposes, nor were private homes to be demolished or families evicted.
The "Four Musts" instructed industrial planners to support such
projects as increased the availability of water for agricultural use,
extended agricultural electrification, the supply of manure and pig-
wash. "The fight for every inch of land is in essence a question of
attitude toward the guideline of taking agriculture as the foundation
and industry as the leading factor."[77] In Tientsin, for example
(1962), all land which had earlier been taken from the local production teams for industrial construction was returned to them. The
Shichingshan Iron and Steel Plant was instructed to return 2,000 out
of the 3,000 mou of farmland requisitioned by it in 1958 in the
Ch'ien-an hsien, Hopei Province. A similar transfer was reported in
the case of the Liangshan iron mine in Kiangsi.

5. Workers were not to be recruited from the countryside for a
period of three years. This applied both to urban industrial units and
local governments. A movement to transfer large numbers of re-
dundant workers from the cities to the countryside was launched.[78]

76 Andrew Nathan, "China's Lagging Coal Industry," FEER (November 14,
1963), pp. 354-356. This reference applies to the post-1960 coal output estimates as well.

77 Wang Pin, Tsai Tso-hua, Liu Hing-shu, "Concretely Handle the Relationship Between Capital, Industry, and Agriculture in Capital Construction," Hsin
Chien-she, No. 4 (April 20, 1965) in SCMM, No. 485 (August 16, 1965), p. 31.
Illustration: "When the factory [Pu-ling Machine Works] was constructed, it was
decided to install latrines instead of water closets to enable the peasants to
procure manure locally." Ibid., p. 31. There was a political advantage to this: it
went by the name of "nondivorcement of the workers from the living standards
of the masses." Ibid., p. 34. Ideologically it could be rationalized in terms of the
imperative of reducing the difference between town and country.

78 "Countryside" means "rural area" or less. The 1953 census defined a
rural area as (a) a locality with a population of 2,000 or less, (b) a locality with
a population of more than 2,000 but where 50 percent of the total population
were peasants or people otherwise employed in agriculture.

The massive exodus from the land during the First Five Year Plan and the Great Leap was to be contained. By 1960-61 industry was evidencing an inability to absorb the masses of unskilled workers flocking to the cities, while the countryside suffered from a lack of technicians and more generally from the unwillingness of educated youth to stay on or return to the farm.[79] Between 1961 and 1965 about 40 million young people were said to have returned to the countryside, not without considerable prodding. Of these, 20 million were sent back in the winter of 1960-61.[80]

While some leaders saw the massive population transfers primarily in economic terms, others (the leftists) saw it almost entirely in a political light. The Maoist ideologues were becoming increasingly concerned about the revolutionary stamina of the successors to the revolution, believing that life in the cities, the modest worldly comforts furnished by the workers' state, and the absence of revolutionary tempering of the young in bitter class struggle conspired to render the new generation less fit than had been the old to take over the reigns of leadership. The expert knowledge which had to be given the young for economic reasons, if nothing else, was suspect. It tended to fill the youngsters' heads with all manner of ideas that had little to do with the people's cause, it made them put on airs, imitate their teachers (many of whom had been educated in the West and never quite remolded), and it gave rise to widespread revolutionary flabbiness—the first manifestation of revisionism. In spite of heavy doses of Marxism-Leninism injected into the curriculum, the young showed signs of caring more about their own personal careers and comforts than about the long-term lot of Humanity and the fate of revolutionary transformation. By sending them in large numbers to the countryside, especially to the more remote, pioneer regions of Sinkiang, Inner Mongolia, and Hainan Island, one could kill two birds with one stone: help agriculture and help the youngsters' socialist consciousness.[81] If a high school graduate refused to accept the job assigned to him in the countryside, he would not be offered another, and, in addition, would lose his residence status and with it his ration

[79] According to reports reaching London, the Wuhan Iron and Steel Works laid off 30,000 construction workers in 1961-62. For an exception to the rule of not recruiting unskilled workers from the countryside, see below, p. 377 (the "Worker-Peasant System").

[80] Colin Garratt, "After the Deluge," *FEER* (April 27, 1961), pp. 161-165. A second massive exodus of urban dwellers was ordered in the fall and winter of 1968-69 (Chapter 12).

[81] "Communist China Urges Frontier Life on Youth," *New York Times* (September 12, 1965), p. 9. Service with the Sinkiang Production and Construction Corps was normally to last three years, after which the young volunteers were expected to settle permanently in the land of their involuntary adoption.

card. How much the more or less forcible transfer of young people from towns to country helped agriculture is an open question. Indications are that the youngsters were often despised and harshly treated by the peasants and, in turn, gave back as much as they received. At the first opportunity, they filtered back into the cities, a trickle that became a flood during the Cultural Revolution (especially from 1966 through 1968).[82] According to one source, the youth "find it difficult to grasp the complex revolutionary process, and are all too prone to relax into ease and comfortable living. It is therefore necessary to strengthen their revolutionary education, temper them in class struggles and in the struggle for production, and teach them how to rough it in simple living conditions. One of the best places to give them this needed education and tempering is in the countryside."[83] There education could be combined with manual labor, and some of the physical discomforts of the prerevolutionary era duplicated for the simple reason that they had not yet been removed. In Shanghai and other large cities, recruitment stations for so-called "social youths" (school dropouts, restless, and unemployed school graduates, high school graduates unable to enter college) were set up in 1963-64.

According to Jen-min Jih-pao of March 20, 1966, evasion of the "educated youth to the countryside" order was rampant. "Some intellectual youths sent to villages to do farm work have been found to have entered rural farm-labor schools for selfish motives. They hoped that with education they could have opportunities of getting assigned to work in government organs or enterprises and become cadres. Their hopes were dashed on the first day they entered Kiangsu Labor University. They were told that they would have to return to the communes where they had come from after completing the prescribed terms of study." Opposition to the movement apparently also came from parents reluctant to see their children sent for

[82] Once back in the city, the young intellectual could live off his family for a while, helping for a change in policy. The political approach to population transfers is examined in more detail in Chapter 10. Here we merely note its existence and uneasy coexistence with the pragmatic, economically oriented policies of the period 1961-65.

[83] Ching Yun, "Millions of Educated Youth Go to the Countryside," Peking Review (July 16, 1965) in SCMM, No. 488 (1965), pp. 20-21. "Many [young people] could have continued their studies or worked in the cities and towns, but for the cause of the revolution they made up their minds to become peasants of a new type." Ibid., p. 20. In a speech made to the June 1964 Youth League Congress (the first such meeting since May 1957), Hu Yau-pang, First Secretary of the League's Central Committee, said that "broad sections of young people are being corrupted by capitalism to a grave extent." The Congress heard speeches denouncing "the absurdity of class cooperation." (Cf. below, pp. 419-422.) Cf. URS, Vol. 42, No. 25 (March 29, 1966).

long periods of time into the wilderness of Sinkiang and Inner Mongolia.

Thus the objective of preventing the reemergence of China's age-old problem of social alienation of the intellectuals from the laboring masses was to be attained by making the educated young "engage in the 'dirty work' of shifting muck and manure."[84]

One explanation for the sudden increase in illegal entries into Hong Kong in late April and May 1962 is that it was engineered with the connivance of local authorities in Kwangtung Province.[85] Caught between food shortages and new urban dwellers who dragged their feet about returning to their villages, or who once back on the farms made a nuisance of themselves, the authorities took the easy way out. They made it possible for people to leave China for Hong Kong, thus at one and the same time solving the problem of preference for city life and shifting some of the burden of feeding their citizens onto the colonialists. The colonialists, however, refused to cooperate: they put up extra fences on the border, caught about 80 percent of the refugees, sent them back to China, and informed Peking of their displeasure. By May 24 the center seems to have rectified the local cadres: returned refugees were jailed (for five to ten days) and the illegal crossings of Hong Kong's land frontier were stopped. That, however, was not the end of Hong Kong's refugee troubles. With the closing of the land border, there sprang up a lucrative business of transporting Chinese refugees who had earlier entered Macao (some 60,000 in 1962 alone) in junks to Hong Kong. The Hong Kong authorities estimated that instead of the normal yearly inflow of about 40,000 people from China (half of them legal entrants), arrivals in 1962 would total about 120,000. Together with Hong Kong's natural population increase of about 100,000 per year, this additional burden was bound to put great pressure on the colony's resource balance. (Cf. Chapter 8.)

In order to keep down its wages and benefits expenditures, the government began in 1962 to relax and make controlled exceptions to its rule of not recruiting unskilled labor from the countryside for three years. A system was introduced under which peasants were recruited on a temporary or contract basis to perform unskilled jobs in industry at rates of pay below those of unskilled urban workers, while industrial workers formerly employed in such jobs as coal min-

---

[84] Ching Yun, *op. cit.*, p. 23. The scriptural justification for the movement was found in Mao Tse-tung's essay "The May 4 Movement": ". . . the intellectuals will accomplish nothing if they fail to integrate themselves with the workers and peasants." *SW*, Vol. II (Peking: *FLP*, 1965), p. 238.

[85] On October 19, 1967 the Chinese press accused former propaganda chief Tao Chu of having been responsible for the 1962 flight of refugees to Hong Kong.

ing, loading and unloading at ports and on railroads, lumbering, and so on, were sent to the countryside. The policy known as the "Worker-Peasant System" was unpopular with both categories of workers, especially the urban laborers sent down to the rural people's communes. Frequently the transfer was made just before the laborer qualified for pension benefits. By leaving his regular job in state industry, he automatically lost his state pension and medical benefits rights, and found his wages substantially reduced. On the other hand, farm workers sent to industry under temporary contracts did not qualify for benefits. They also felt discriminated against since they were receiving lower pay than the regular industrial workers for the same job. Tension between regular workers and worker-peasants mounted. The worker-peasants were resented by the unskilled and semiskilled urban laborers since they represented a threat to the latter's continued urban employment and living standards. The system originally instituted as a retrenchment and anti-inflationary measure was extended in 1964 and 1965 increasingly for ideological reasons, i.e., as a way of "eliminating differences between town and country," practising economy while grasping revolution, and training workers in the ethic of left-communist asceticism. It was quite simply a policy of exploitation. There is little doubt that it contributed to widespread worker unrest and "economism" in 1967-68 (Chapters 11 and 12). The Maoists at that time blamed the Liuists for the policy, but themselves showed no inclination to change it.[86]

6. Enterprise managements were forbidden to transfer skilled workers without central approval. Shop foremen had to be notified whenever skilled workers were to be transferred.

An instruction to that effect was issued in 1963 perhaps to prevent overenthusiastic left-leaning local cadres from exerting pressure on plant managements to make wholesale transfers of workers to the countryside. In fact, after 1963 the politically minded left-wing cadres were in the saddle again, and the old red-versus-expert controversy was fanned once again. The increased influence of the left cadres was countered more or less successfully by placing many factories under ministries, the idea being that technical and administrative experts at higher levels could check or undo some of the damage wrought at the plant level by overly ardent militants.

7. Modern light industry (with textiles as the leading factor) was to be promoted as a source of domestic state revenue and a major earner of foreign exchange.[87]

[86] See Colina MacDougall, "Second Class Workers," FEER (May 9, 1968), pp. 306-308. In certain mining areas, worker-peasants constituted from one-half to two-thirds of the mines' working force.

[87] For a survey of the progress made by light industry during this period, see URS, Vol. 40, No. 6 (July 1965); Charles Brennan, "China: 'King' Cotton," FEER (December 22, 1966), pp. 648-649.

Just as China's steel industry was hampered by shortages of coal, iron ore, limestone, and timber, so the country's main source of material incentives and major earner of foreign currencies—the light industry, especially cotton textiles—was, at least until 1964, beset by cotton production problems. Given the limited area of land suitable for agricultural use (especially irrigated area) the question of how to allocate land and other inputs between food crops and cotton faced the policy makers early in their attempt to readjust, consolidate, and fill out. As with food crops, the difficulty was partially resolved by recourse to imports. Raw cotton was imported from Uganda, Tanzania, the United Arab Republic, Sudan, Pakistan, and Mexico. It was processed in Shanghai and other centers, and reexported in the form of cotton fabrics to Hong Kong and southeast Asia. The imported cotton was (except in the case of Mexico) in part payment of Chinese credits. A beginning was also made in developing artificial and synthetic fabrics, but by 1965 this branch of industry was still extremely modest. In 1964 about 20 million meters of synthetic fabrics were produced. The first synthetic fiber plant was built by the East Germans; the first polyvinyl alcohol plant was imported from Japan in 1963. In that year also woolen textiles began to be stressed—a measure intended to relieve pressure on the cotton textiles industry. An upsurge in the construction of new cotton and wool textile mills took place after 1964: in 1965 over 1.4 million spindles were reportedly added, the trend continuing into 1966, when over 2 million people were employed in cotton textile production.

8. Development of selected industrial branches.

Following an initial period of consolidation, attention turned to the development of a number of relatively new industrial branches, particularly nuclear energy, chemicals, and petroleum.

Nuclear Industry

In September 1958 China's Soviet-designed 10,000-kilowatt experimental heavy-water reactor and cyclotron went into operation. It reportedly produced 2.5 kilograms of plutonium per year. By 1960 the plutonium producing industry comprised, in addition to the Peking plant, two other reactors located near Paotow (Inner Mongolia), both equipped with Chinese-made, up-to-date electronic equipment. A gaseous diffusion plant built with Soviet assistance near Lanchow produced uranium-235 needed for the development of H-bomb capacity. The cost of the Lanchow installation may have been as high as $1 billion. The plant was powered by a large hydroelectric station on the Yellow River and probably consumed a very substantial portion of the country's total electric power supply. By

1966 China was believed to have had about 40 nuclear reactors, including one of 2,000 kilowatts at Peking's Tsinghua University. Most of them were built entirely by the Chinese themselves, without foreign assistance. Components for elaborate machinery of the nuclear industry were manufactured domestically by small workshops—some of them reportedly family-sized—on a sort of putting-out system.[88] The money cost to China of exploding the first atomic device in 1964 was in the region of $200 million; by the time of the second test (May 1965) the cost may have exceeded $1 billion.[89] On October 27, 1966 China fired a guided missile with a nuclear warhead at least equal in size to the atomic bomb dropped on Hiroshima in 1945. The missile is believed to have had a range of at least 1,000 kilometers. The nuclear industry absorbed the best of China's scientific brains, may of them—as we have shown earlier—foreign trained.[90] The Chinese Communists considered this sort of brain drain away from economic development well worthwhile. Nuclear development was placed under the Central Committee's Military Affairs Commission, since 1959 presided over by Lin Piao. Atomic scientists were spared the worst excesses of the "politics first" approach to research, but were not altogether immune to Mao-think sessions and other therapeutic seminars in proletarian consciousness. With a per head annual income of less than $70, China in 1965 was well on the way to acquiring the destructive capacity of nations whose per capita income was in the $3,000 range.[91]

[88] Alexandro Casella, "China's Atomic Tiger," FEER (November 10, 1966), pp. 353-354.

[89] Cheng Chu-yuan's interview with U.S. News and World Report, December 28, 1964. China's atomic testing site is believed to be located at Lop Nor, southeastern Sinkiang. According to Casella (loc. cit., p. 353) expenditures on scientific research (including atomic research) were (in U.S. dollars): 16 million in 1955; 133 million in 1958; 340 million in 1959; 459 million in 1960; and $2 billion from 1962 through 1964. Of the last amount, about three-quarters went for research on nuclear weapons and missiles.

[90] In 1966 there were in China about 5,000 U.S.-trained scientists. These included the Head of the country's jet propulsion program, Chien Hsueh-shen, and his chief assistants Chien Wei-chang (formerly of Cal. Tech.) and Wei Chuang-hua (formerly of MIT); the Head of nuclear research, Wang Kan-chang; the developer of China's atomic bomb, Chien San-chiang (trained by Joliot Curie); W. Y. Chang (formerly of Princeton), and C. W. Li (Cal. Tech.).

[91] Instructive references on the subject are Dick Wilson's "China's Nuclear Development," FEER (August 19, 1965), pp. 328 ff; URS, Vol. 42, No. 8 (January 28, 1966); Walter C. Clemens, Jr., "Chinese Nuclear Tests: Trends and Portents," China Quarterly (October-December 1967), pp. 111-131; Communist China and Arms Control: A Contingency Study 1967-1976 by Hoover Institution Researchers (Stanford, Calif.: Hoover Institution Press, 1968); Geoffrey Hudson, "Paper Tigers and Nuclear Teeth," China Quarterly (July-September 1969), pp. 64-75.

Chemicals

Because of the shortage of raw materials, production of chemicals (including agricultural chemicals) tended during the period to be concentrated primarily in a relatively small number of large industrial centers where industrial waste products such as natural gas could be readily utilized. The Great Leap policy of erecting labor-intensive, "native" plants all over the country, gave way to one favoring large, mechanized, integrated factories which were frequently used in a labor-intensive way.[92] The new policy of stressing "high-yield" chemical plants was not rigidly dogmatic: medium-sized plants located in high-yield farm areas were tolerated so long as they passed the muster of economic accounting. Some native plants were combined into medium-size installations and equipped with machinery.

Until 1965 agricultural chemicals were accorded priority over other subsectors of the industry.[93] Next in line came synthetic fibers and chemicals serving as replacements for raw materials normally furnished to light industry by agriculture. By 1965 a gradual shift of investment resources toward chemicals serving the steel, machine tools, and other branches of heavy industry could be detected.

China's main chemical fertilizer producing plants are located at Nanking (ammonium sulphate, annual capacity over 400,000 tons), Kirin (nitrogenous fertilizer), a new plant at Wuching near Shanghai (first stage capacity 100,000 tons per year of ammonium sulphate), Canton and Kaifeng (ammonium sulphate and synthetic ammonia), Lanchow, Chintang, and Fushun. There are also many medium-size plants with capacities of several tens of thousands of tons per year each, including about 100 phosphate fertilizer factories with a total capacity of about 2 million tons (1965), and many small nitrogenous fertilizer plants. In 1961 these nitrogenous fertilizer factories pro-

---

[92] A parallel may be drawn with the steel industry. J. Ashdown reported in 1965 that "one steel plant . . . was very proud of having increased its production from 1,500 tons per year in 1948 to 2,000 tons per day today, but was reluctant to admit that the labor force in 1948 was 300, whereas it is now 13,000, and refused to give even a rough idea of the amount of capital invested in the intervening period." John Ashdown, "China's Proletarian Problems," *FEER* (March 12, 1965), p. 439.

[93] In 1961 about 40 percent of the funds allocated for capital construction in the chemical industry were earmarked for chemical fertilizers. Domestically produced equipment for the agricultural chemicals industry seems to have been manufactured in a large number of small enterprises. Thus, for example, equipment for making urea (produced experimentally for the first time in 1964) was made by 100 Shanghai machine tool factories for the order of Shanghai's Wuching Chemical Works. *Peking Review* (March 26, 1965), p. 28.

duced only 2 percent of the total output of the fertilizer; in 1965, 12.4 percent, expected to reach 18 percent in 1966.[94]

Petroleum

The petroleum industry—important both for agriculture and defense—began to be stressed after mid-1962.[95] The problem was made more urgent by the decline in Soviet sales of petroleum products to China after 1961, and the leverage which the USSR could exercise on China's defense posture by varying the amounts of highly refined fuels supplied to China in times of national emergency. This is shown in Table 9-6.

TABLE 9-6
Soviet Exports of Crude Oil, Gasoline, and Diesel Fuel To China
(Millions of metric tons)

	1960	1961	1962	1963	1964	1965
Crude oil	0.6	—	—	—	—	—
Gasoline	1.0	1.3	0.8	0.5	0.3	0.03
Diesel fuel . . .	0.7	0.8	0.4	0.3	0.08	0.004

Sources: Soviet foreign trade statistics. Note that 1962—63 was a time of Sino-Indian conflict.

After 1962 China began stepping up her petroleum products purchases from Rumania.[96] By 1965 imports of petroleum products may have amounted to some 2 million metric tons, probably about half of this amount being purchased from the Rumanians who also supplied China with drilling rigs and refinery equipment.[97] Small quantities of petroleum products were supplied by Albania during this period. Refinery equipment has also been bought in Western Europe.

In spite of continued products imports, the Chinese announced in 1963 that they were basically self-sufficient in oil. The statement

[94] *Jen-min Jih-pao*, June 15, 1966, p. 2. The annual capacity of a small nitrogenous fertilizer factory ranged from 2,000 to 5,000 tons. See also Alexandra Close, "Down to Earth," *FEER* (December 8, 1966), pp. 517-522; Tseng Yi, "Chemical Fertilizer Industry in Communist China," *Studies on Chinese Communism*, Vol. 9, No. 5 (May 31, 1966), pp. 53-70.

[95] See Jan S. Prybyla, "Petroleum and Communist China," *Military Review* (February 1965), pp. 19-22, and "Communist China and Petroleum," *ibid.* (February 1967), pp. 48-53. Cf. *URS*, Vol. 45, No. 1 (October 4, 1966).

[96] Petroleum products purchases from Rumania (millions of metric tons): 1960, 0.4; 1961, 0.7; 1962, 1.0; 1963, 1.3.

[97] Imports of drilling equipment from the Soviet Union (millions of roubles): 1960, 5.59; 1963, 0.102.

(reported at the end of 1965) does not mean very much by itself, given the rather elastic notion of self-sufficiency and the relatively low consumption of petroleum by China. There is enough evidence, however, pointing to a keen interest in increasing the domestic production of petroleum and enlarging domestic refining capacity. The major producing areas are located at Karamai (Sinkiang), Yumen, Tsaidam, Nanchung, and Taching (Heilungkiang).[98] The Taching oilfield was discovered during the Great Leap Forward and production from the field was first reported in early 1964. The field's exact location has not been revealed, although Taching was to become one of the symbols of the socialist spirit during the Socialist Education Campaign of 1963-65 (Chapter 10). After 1965 the proportion of China's total output of crude oil accounted for by Taching was believed to have progressively declined with the discovery of new fields at Shengli (on the eastern coast) and of another field on the Kwangsi-Kwangtung border. Crude oil production in 1966 was estimated at about 11 million metric tons, to which Taching contributed an estimated 3 million tons.

Refineries are located at Lanchow (annual capacity about 3 million tons), Nanking, Shanghai (capacity of about 1 million tons per year each), at Karamai, in the northeast (two refineries including one at Taching), and at Tushauntzu in Sinkiang (capacity about 500,000 tons per year). There are also several smaller regional facilities with refining capacities ranging from 300 to 300,000 tons per year each.

Pharmaceutical Industry

The pharmaceutical industry, which had known rapid development during the First Five Year Plan, was expanded after 1960 to produce a wide range of antibiotics, including aureomycin and penicillin. In 1965 China independently developed a drug for treating certain forms of schistosomiasis ("snail fever").[99] Keith Buchanan reported that infant mortality in China was said to have fallen from 200 per thousand before the advent of communism to less than 40 "in some areas" around 1965. Although Buchanan's figures may be

[98] The Karamai field, which in 1965 produced an estimated one-third of China's domestic crude oil production, suffered from extensive damage in 1960, following the departure of Soviet experts. The damage was caused by well flooding attributed to erroneously executed injection of water into the oil formations. With regard to the claim of self-sufficiency in oil, note the following: "China's Petroleum Industry Advances with Big Strides on the Road of Self-Reliance," *Peking Review* (September 26, 1969), pp. 17-19.

[99] A similar drug had shortly before been developed by the Swiss firm CIBA.

regarded as somewhat questionable, the trend he describes is probably right.[100]

9. Return to handicraft producers' cooperatives and more elementary cooperative arrangements.

It will be recalled (Chapter 8) that during the Great Leap Forward there was a rush to transform handicraft producers' cooperatives and the still remaining handicraft supply and marketing groups and cooperatives into ideologically higher organizations. In practice this meant that the cooperatives were amalgamated into larger units (factories) run by local state authorities or into commune-run workshops. Within the local state and commune control organs, Party cadres had the most say in policy making. The cooperatives' former supervisory organ at the central level—the Central Handicrafts Administrative Bureau established in 1954 directly under the State Council—was in March 1958 placed under the Ministry of Light Industry and shortly thereafter seems to have lost control over handicraft development at the local level. In 1958 and early 1959 local handicraft administrative organs responsible to the center were disrupted, sometimes discontinued, at times merged with commune Party organs. By May 1959 only 13.3 percent of the more than five million members of the former handicraft cooperatives (mostly producers' cooperatives) were reportedly still working under the old institutional setup. The remainder were mostly employed in newly established handicraft factories under local state administrations (where these managed to survive) or under commune authorities. The new units were urged to turn out capital rather than consumer goods, thus further worsening the consumer goods supply situation in the countryside and contributing to the economic crisis of 1960-61. In October 1961 the Central Handicrafts Bureau (renamed Central General Bureau of Handicraft Industry) was revived and again placed under the State Council in an attempt to give handicraft development some sense of direction and to strengthen central control. The Bureau was once again abolished in 1965 and replaced by the Second Ministry of Light Industry.

Central economic control, however, was not made into a fetish: the guiding principle was to be empiricism. Already in 1960, Hsueh Mu-Ch'iao in explaining the 1958-59 rush toward ownership by the whole people without a fully developed technical base sounded a note of caution, which was to become the basis for the new eco-

[100] Keith Buchanan, *The Chinese People and the Chinese Earth* (London: Bell, 1966). See also "China Builds Up Self-Sufficient Pharmaceutical Industry," *NCNA* release, Peking (April 27, 1963) in *SCMP*, 2971 (May 3, 1963), p. 20; "Rapid Development of the Pharmaceutical Industry in Our Country," *Kuangming Jih-pao* (Peking), December 24, 1962, in *JPRS* 12524 (1962), pp. 43-44.

nomic policy. The passage is worth quoting at length not only as an instance of the new empiricism, but as an example of dialectical exercise. "That some of the handicraft cooperatives quickly changed over from collective ownership to ownership by the whole people was a natural trend, and was beneficial to the development of the national economy. But it did not necessarily follow that all handicraft cooperatives in China should be transformed at once. Handicrafts in China, with their long history and rich variety, are an indispensable and component part of the national economy. . . . With regard to ownership, various forms will need to exist for a fairly long period of time. With the exception of those large mechanized or semimechanized cooperatives, which with the consent of their members were turned into state factories, the rest were allowed to remain under collective ownership as cooperative factories or cooperatives, and, under the direction of the state sector of the economy, continued to expand all the advantages of collective ownership. In the meantime, under the direction of the state sector, individual operation of certain handicrafts was allowed to remain as the situation demanded. All this was favorable to the development of production and the improvement of the people's living conditions. Although it is a natural tendency for certain handicrafts to adapt themselves to mechanization or semimechanization step by step, there will still be many things which will remain handmade for many years. Therefore, a long-range view must be taken in formulating policies for handicrafts. The principle of making overall plans and comprehensive arrangements with due regard being given to all parties concerned should be applied. Energetic measures for expansion should be taken on the basis of preserving the original variety, quantity, and quality of products, so that the constantly rising needs of the whole society may be satisfied to the maximum."[101] This involved piece of dialectical jargon was simply intended to say that the Great Leap changes in the handicraft sector were a big mistake stemming from errors inherent in one of the Party's red banners (the General Line for Socialist Construction).[102] The basic error consisted in the leftists' belief that a change in ownership structure (property relations) would automatically bring about an upsurge in technique, production, and productivity, and that a high tide of cadre-inspired enthusiasm was the only precondition for the change in ownership structure.

[101] Hsueh Mu-ch'iao, et al., *The Socialist Transformation of the National Economy in China, op. cit.*, pp. 158-159.
[102] "In 1958 when the big leap took place, the state needed some of the handicraft cooperatives to be reconstructed and expanded to form the bases of local industries for the purpose of implementing the Party's general line for socialist construction." *Ibid.*, p. 156.

Many handicraftsmen absorbed during the Leap into factories were now urged to take up their old occupations and hire apprentices.[103] The supply of some key raw materials (e.g., steel, pig iron, timber) to the handicrafts was to be included in the state plan so as to ease the raw materials supply situation in the handicraft sector, but on the whole, the revived cooperatives were expected to buy their materials directly from the peasants. Private individual handicrafts were praised and promised that they could continue to exist side by side with state and cooperative handicraft workshops for a long time to come. In fact, it would appear that after 1960 and until 1965 the function of cooperatives in urban areas may have been reduced quite simply to supplying individual craftsmen with capital, distributing materials, and maintaining reserve and welfare funds, with family units being responsible for production, accounting, and marketing. In the rural areas peasant craftsmen seem to have been absorbed into the production teams' system of income distribution. Individual handicraftsmen who carried on their work at home and sold their output for cash were obliged to pay the team a fixed amount of cash for each working day. In return, they were credited by the team with an equivalent number of work days. The amount of cash payments made by the artisans to the production teams was normally 50 to 100 percent greater than the value of the work days with which they were credited in exchange, because the value of a work day was, in the case of those not engaged in crafts, a net payment (i.e., net of taxes, deductions for accumulation, welfare funds, etc.), while artisans' earnings from the sale of their output represented free-market prices.[104]

Particular attention was given during this period to traditional arts and crafts which had a long history of excellent reputation abroad. In 1965-66 two hundred different lines of arts and crafts products were exported, including porcelain, pottery, articles of straw, rattan, bamboo, and willow splits, carvings, furniture, drawn threadwork, lacquerware, cloisonné, and jewelry. About 180,000 full-time workers and 1,700,000 part-time workers were engaged in making these products in 1965.[105]

In 1958 the number of handicraft workers (presumably excluding peasant part-time craftsmen) was given as 1,456,000 (compared with 6,560,000 in 1957). The decline was probably due in large part to a change in definition concurrent on the merging of handicraft cooperatives with local state enterprises and commune industry, but also to migration and lack of replacements. In 1962 full-time crafts-

---

[103] *Jen-min Jih-pao* (July 15, 1961).
[104] Audrey Donnithorne, *op. cit.*, p. 81.
[105] *URS*, Vol. 44, No. 14 (August 16, 1966).

men were said to number nearly 6 million (20 million if part-time peasant craftsmen are included). The 6 millions figure was repeated in 1964.[106] About 60 percent of full-time craftsmen were said to have plied their trade in urban areas in 1961.

III. REASSERTION OF CENTRAL PLANNING AND CONTROL

The decentralization measures put into effect during the Great Leap, the breakdown of the central statistical apparatus, the disappearance of such remnants of market control as still existed in 1956-57, and the excitement that seized local authorities from 1958 through early 1960 meant a diminution in the ability of the center to control the course of events or even to know exactly what was happening on the economic front.[107] One of the objectives of the new economic policy was to bring back central planning and reassert effective central control over the economy.

According to official Chinese Communist sources, in 1957 (1952 price basis) 46 percent of the gross output of all industry emanated in enterprises subject to central control, and 54 percent in locally controlled enterprises. In 1959, centrally controlled enterprises produced only 26 percent of total industrial output in value terms (1952 price basis), and locally controlled enterprises 74 percent. The center retained formal control of about half the heavy industrial output in the latter year, but in view of the breakdown in communications between the center and the production front, this control was probably less effective than the figures suggest.[108]

The reassertion of central control over industry and agriculture after 1960 was not intended to be a return to the bureaucratic cen-

[106] Cited by Audrey Donnithorne, *op. cit.*, p. 222.

[107] "Agricultural crisis and the Soviet withdrawal of assistance aside, the collapse of marginal efficiency of capital in 1960 could have been avoided if there were sound or reasonable planning." Choh-ming Li, "China's Industrial Development, 1958-63," *op. cit.*, p. 21. The difficulty with this formulation is that both the agricultural crisis and the Soviet withdrawal of assistance were due in part to the lack of sound or reasonable planning. For an interesting study of the comparative experience of centralization and decentralization in China and the USSR, see Dwight H. Perkins, "Centralization versus Decentralization in Mainland China and the Soviet Union," *Annals* of the American Academy of Political and Social Science, Vol. 349 (September 1963), pp. 70-80.

[108] In the column "Evening Chats" (*Pei-ching Wan-pao*, June 22, 1961) the editor of *Frontline*, Teng T'o, using a historical simile, wrote: "By the reign of Empress Dowager Ming Su, the Sung government was growing daily more corrupt. There was no intelligent and capable prime minister at the top with responsible assistants to take charge of personnel and administration, while the local officials lower down did exactly as they pleased." This was later (1966) condemned as "a malevolent denigration of the Central Committee of the Party . . . [and] a malicious denunciation of Party cadres at various levels."

tral control of the First Five Year Plan period, but rather to the decentralization principles of November 1957. These principles, it will be recalled (Chapter 7), attempted to combine central supervision through economic accounting with relatively wide freedom of action at the enterprise level. It involved first and foremost the reduction in local Party control over economic activities and the vesting of financial, administrative, and other functions in banks, enterprise financial officers, managers, professional administrators, and technicians. The local Party men of the Great Leap years were to give way to Red technocrats. The Agricultural Bank of China, for example, revived on November 12, 1963 as a means of central financial control over agriculture, was placed directly under the State Council. In a "takeover experiment" launched in February 1965 the Bank was instructed to take charge of the financial and accounting work (including assistance in income distribution and preparation of statistical reports) of communes and production teams, and thus become in effect the principal instrument of state control over the countryside. Already in 1964 the Bank supervised state allocations to state agricultural enterprises, rural capital construction units, communes and teams, in addition to its normal function of extending interest-bearing loans and advancing funds for procurement (the latter repayable without interest).[109] The takeover experiment added to this list credit extended to state farms' processing plants and land reclamation organs, tractor repair and assembly plants, and improved-strain cotton ginning plants. Simultaneously, reflecting perhaps pressures from the Party's left, Bank officials were to go down to the farms, immerse themselves in poor peasant culture, and develop political organs at the *hsien* level and above. In this way, the organizationally oriented method of asserting central control in preparation for the Third Five Year Plan (due to begin in 1966) was wedded to the ideologically oriented policies pervading the Four Clearance Movement. Every move of the bureaucratic-technocratic right was matched by a parallel move of the extreme left.

In March 1965 the State Council resurrected the State Capital Construction Commission (reportedly abolished in 1958) to oversee, on behalf of the central planning authorities, capital construction projects throughout the country.

---

[109] State financial allocations to communes and teams comprised (1) grants to poor teams, (2) subsidies for small water conservancy projects, (3) afforestation, and (4) production expenses in calamity-stricken areas, (5) sums for anti-drought measures, (6) for housing workers transferred by teams to reservoir construction, (7) funds for housing urban youths doing their stint in production teams, and (8) relief funds for demobilized servicemen, dependents of servicemen, and "martyrs." See P. H. M. Jones, "Rural Octopus," *FEER* (August 5, 1965), pp. 241-242.

Earlier the Party's six regional bureaus, which had been abolished in 1954, were reconstituted under the Central Committee "to strengthen leadership" over regional affairs. The regional bureaus, it would appear, were until 1965 the strongholds of anti-Maoists.[110] Their strength derived from their close links to the Central Committee (about 60 percent of whose members were purged in 1966-67), their influence over regional military affairs, and the persistent parochialism of rural China's outlook, with the resulting tendency to seek guidance from leaders recruited locally. As long as the Central Committee and regional Party secretaries were operating on the same wavelength, the center could exercise far-reaching influence over local affairs. When the balance of power at the center shifted in favor of the faction unacceptable to local Party officials, the center found itself temporarily checkmated at the regional level. During periods of strife within the Peking leadership the Party's regional *apparat* was able—at least for a time—to isolate itself from the center and to continue operating in defiance of central instructions, but with reassuring protestations of loyalty. Between 1964 and mid-1966 the muted tug-of-war between the left and right wings of the Party central was translated at the regional Party level into a struggle to take over the key regional bureau positions (usually those of the First Secretary). The left wing's candidates for positions of regional authority were army men loyal to the Mao-Lin Piao line; the right wing's candidates were Party professionals sympathetic to the bureaucrat line of Liu Shao-ch'i and his followers. In early 1966, for example, nine out of the thirteen military district commissarships were held by First Provincial Secretaries considered sympathetic to the authoritarian-moderate-Liu line. The First Political Comissars of the Chengtu and Shenyang Military Regions, for example, were held respectively by Li Ching-chuan (First Secretary of the Party's Southwestern Bureau) and Sun Jen-chiung (First Secretary of the Northwestern Bureau). On the other hand, between 1964 and mid-1966 some commanders of China's thirteen military districts (generally considered sympathetic to the Mao-Lin line) were appointed to regional Party bureaus secretaryships and hundreds of thousands of Mao-Lin army men infiltrated the middle and lower echelons of the Party bureaucracy. Factional sympathies at the regional level were, however, difficult to determine over time, since both military men and Party professionals tended to change positions swiftly in response to their evaluation of the shifts in the power balance at the

---

[110]The regional Party bureaus reconstituted in 1961-62 were those for North, Northeast, Northwest, East, South-Central, and Southwest China. The most bothersome for the Mao-Lin Piao faction was the Northwest China Bureau (covering Sinkiang) and the Southwest Bureau (covering Tibet). See Robert Trumbull (ed.), *This Is Communist China, op. cit.,* pp. 51-55.

center, the prospects of this or that faction, and judgments regarding the political sentiments prevalent in the region. At the center the Mao-Lin people could—after July 18, 1966—count on the army's central leadership; at the regional level reliance on military commanders was somewhat more problematical. At the center, the Liu bureaucrats could—until July 20, 1966—count on most professional Party men; at the regional level one could never be quite sure. At the center the Party's Left commanded the gun. At the regional level the Party's Right frequently commanded the gun. At both levels the Party and the gun had the uncomfortable quality of being of two minds, ready to switch sides whenever the wind changed.

While all this was going on, the state of the economy demanded unified leadership. "The unfolding of mass movements for production increase and economy in implementation of the mass line must be combined with the increase of centralized, unified leadership. . . . All comrades on the industrial front must . . . conceive of the nation as an integral body consisting of many coordinated parts, subordinate the special interests of these individual parts to the common interest of the integral body, and always consider the interest of the integral body first."[111]

A Note on Internal Security

Whatever the differences between the Party's Left and Right conceptions of central economic control, there was at all times agreement on policing the citizenry—that is, on keeping individual citizens under effective and permanent group surveillance. The question was never one of the utility of the police, but rather one of who was to control the police at the center.[112]

Chinese citizens were not required to carry identity cards. However, each person had to be registered with the local public security office or police substation (pai-chu-so) as part of a household on a register of persons (hu-kou-pu). The register carried the household's current and past addresses, as well as the name, age, sex, profession, education, and current place of employment or study of each member of the household. The register took the form of a booklet, one copy of which was kept by the security organs, the other copy being issued to the household. The copy retained by the security organs

111 Po I-po in Kuang-jen Jih-pao, December 31, 1961. Full text in FEER (February 1, 1962), pp. 293-296.
112 The following account draws on Robert Tung, "People's Policemen," FEER (August 8, 1966), pp. 319-321. Cf. "Trial by the Masses," ibid. (August 7, 1969), p. 312.

was supplemented from time to time by other information obtained by the police regarding individual members of the household. Such information was not disclosed to the individuals concerned. The household's booklet served as the basis for the issuance of food rations and purchasing cards, and was also used to keep track of the citizens' movements (i.e., it served as a form of the Soviet-type internal passport). Any citizen setting out on a trip likely to take him away from his permanent place of residence for more than two days was required to notify the local public security office of the date of his departure, his destination, the reason for his trip, and the date of arrival at his destination. Visitors to the household were not allowed to stay in the household for more than three days without reporting to the local security office in order that their names could be added to the host household's register. The visitors were required to explain the reason for their visit, give the intended length of stay, and other relevant information. At least before the upheaval of the Cultural Revolution (Chapters 11 and 12), evasion of these regulations was difficult. Street committees as well as individual informers kept the security office informed of households' activities, movements, visits, and so on.

Minor crimes were dealt with swiftly, the punishment ranging from admonishment to imprisonment or forced labor. Fines were a rare occurrence. Serious crimes (theft, robbery, murder) were punishable by heavy prison or forced labor sentences, frequently by death. Death sentences were often passed at mass rallies, immediately followed by execution. There has been no Ministry of Justice in China since 1959, and few political cases were referred to the courts, except where court trials would serve educational-propaganda purposes. Political crimes and ideological deviations were considered the most serious type of transgression. Punishment ranged from forced labor to death. Persons who had committed minor crimes or were crime-prone were placed under surveillance by street committees, neighborhood, and local police organs, their record being communicated to their employers. Voluntary confessions and recantations by those who had erred were encouraged and frequently cited as examples of patriotism and enlightened class consciousness.

In 1960 the public security organs comprised about 1.7 million men, not counting street committees and other groups engaged in part-time security work. The local urban police substations (*pai-chu-so*) usually consisted of 10-15 men, their jurisdiction extending over ten streets. The substation was responsible to the *fen-chu* or divisional headquarters, which controlled a number of substations, and was in turn controlled by a higher organ, the *kung-an-chu*.

IV. ATTENTION TO QUALITY

The renewed emphasis on quality as an important dimension of economic growth took on various forms. It was not limited merely to the quality of physical output, but covered the manner in which planning was carried out, the way of managing enterprises, economic accounting, and so on.

REEVALUATION OF TECHNICAL INNOVATIONS INTRODUCED DURING THE GREAT LEAP FORWARD

Many of the technical innovations produced during the Great Leap were rigorously tested, scrapped, or rationalized. The testing probably included some type of cost-benefit analysis, certainly a more stringent control over scarce raw materials inputs. Thus, for example, the Shanghai Generator Works which had been a Stakhanovite during the mass innovation movement of 1958-60 found upon checking up on its inventions that the new mechanized and automated production lines introduced in 1959-60 suffered from over 100 quality problems.[113] New rules on inventions and innovations (supplanting the provisional 1954 regulations) were promulgated in October 1963. They reflected the new spirit of strict testing, relevance, and quality. In time, however, the movement for quality control came in for sharp criticism from the Party's factory cadres who objected that the experts who strictly enforced technical and other standards were "irresponsible," "extravagant," and "dogmatic."[114] By 1965 the pressure for mass innovations was on again. Even in 1963, at the very time that the new rules were being prepared, Chen Yung-kang, a peasant with no formal education but a gift for inventing yield-raising techniques for rice, was being lionized in Peking. After spending some time at various research institutes where he lectured the professional agronomists, Chen was rewarded with a demonstration plot near Soochow, which in 1963 alone was visited by over 90,000 peasants.

INFORMATION FLOW

During the Leap's mass emulation drives ("learn from, catch up with, and outdistance the advanced") stress was put on competition

---

[113] *Peking Review* (December 29, 1961), p. 16. "New techniques should be developed and created under proper leadership and in a planned way. . . . Scientific appraisals must be made of all innovations and advanced experiences. They must be popularized in a way that suits the specific conditions of the enterprise concerned. All innovation activities must be closely coordinated with production." Po I-po, *Peking Review* (February 24, 1961), p. 7.

[114] *Workers' Daily*, Peking, March 15, 1966.

among workers' teams, workshops, mines, enterprises, and communes, with little regard to quality or cost, or how the catching up and outdistancing fitted into the general pattern of the economy. In other words, the important thing about emulation was its dialectic. What was important was to catch up with and surpass those with the highest reported output (quantity in the abstract), in spite of much talk about more economical results. After 1960, even though the vocabulary remained more or less the same as before, emphasis shifted to the cooperative aspect of emulation: to learning from the advanced and, more importantly, to the advanced sharing their success story with the backward. Catching up came to mean not only increase in the quantity of output (although that was important enough), but good quality in both goods and working style and attention to cost reductions.[115] Enterprises were urged to work out in concert administrative and technical measures which would "ensure both mass initiative and strict regulatión of work coupled with unified interlocking control."[116]

Pressured into coming up with spectacular quantitative results, state enterprises in almost all communist countries are, as a rule, shy about sharing their technical and managerial secrets with other state enterprises, "ownership by the whole people" or not. This poses acute problems of technical and other information flow in the economy, more formidable, in fact, than those experienced by imperfectly competitive market economies.[117] The post-1960 drive for "Communist Cooperation Pacts" (that is, formal exchange of technical and other information among state enterprises) was intended to stimulate the flow of information within the economy while strengthening the center's control over industrial activity and promoting quality and cost consciousness on the part of managements.[118]

The Communist Cooperation Pacts were supplemented by so-called "Hook-Up" arrangements whereby advanced factories, mines, trade and transport enterprises, as well as schools and research institutes lent support to their laggard colleagues in agriculture and industry under the slogan: "Like two melons on the same vine, workers

[115] The notion of a charge on capital was probably not included in the concept of production cost.

[116] *Peking Review* (January 13, 1961), pp. 3-4. See also "The Emulating, Overtaking, and Assisting Movement in Industrial Enterprises," *URS*, Vol. 34, No. 11 (February 7, 1964), pp. 169-186; Niu Huang, "China's Industries—New Stage in Labor Emulation," *China Reconstructs* (December 1964), pp. 9-11.

[117] Similarly, the secrecy imposed by the Party and state on scientific work obstructed the flow of information among individual scientists. The situation was more relaxed during the 1961-65 period.

[118] See Chu Chi-lin, "Emulation in Shanghai Steel Plants," *Peking Review* (January 27, 1961), pp. 17-18.

and peasants are brothers."[119] Although drawing on a practice which
dated back to the Great Leap and beyond, the hookup was intended
to serve the objective of modernization and rationalization of small
and medium-size enterprises rather than, as used to be the case,
merely assuring the advanced enterprise the needed raw materials
flows through hardly disguised vertical integration. The idea now was
for the advanced plants to train badly needed skilled workers in the
less advanced factories (and farms), carry out time-and-motion
studies (or at any rate something resembling such studies), and to
help decide whether on balance the less advanced enterprise was
worth saving. Teams from provincial factories were sent to work with
shifts and sections in Shanghai and other urban enterprises, and the
same was true of repair teams from the rural people's communes.[120]

The movement was launched in Liaoning Province in early 1960
and by midyear "enthusiasm for providing aid to agriculture
[through the hookup] . . . gripped workers throughout the country."[121] Three variants were known to exist: (1) a single advanced
industrial plant set out to aid one or more rural people's communes
or industrial enterprises; (2) several advanced plants were organized
into a group which "adopted" one or more communes or enterprises;
(3) going beyond municipal boundaries, groups of plants and mines
hooked up with communes or enterprises in other municipalities
where industry was not so well developed.[122] In Shanghai more than
1,000 factories reportedly established links with 172 rural people's
communes in 11 suburban counties and sent 2,000 workers to give
regular help to the communes. Chungking sent 36,000 technicians
and 80,000 workers to its protegées in the countryside.[123] Trade
departments in towns, transport enterprises, and schools followed
suit.[124] For commercial enterprises the hookup implied exerting oneself in "prompt purchase, active sale, brisk business, and liveliness
without chaos."[125] Whether the hookup movement was, in actual
practice, as widespread and voluminous as the official reports made it

[119]"Industry Supports Agriculture," Peking Review (August 9, 1960),
p. 19.
[120]An "Emulate Shanghai" movement spread through the country in 1963.
[121]Peking Review (August 9, 1960), p. 19.
[122]Hua Chu-ching, "Industrial Aid to the Rural People's Communes: A
New Way," Peking Review (July 19, 1960), p. 21.
[123]Peking Review (August 16, 1960), p. 4. Shanghai light industry enterprises supplied the rural people's communes under their care with "a portable
alarm clock that has a ring like a fire alarm. . . . and can be hung on a tree." Ibid.
(November 3, 1961), p. 4.
[124]Yang Chu-chun, "Transport Aids the Farm Front," Peking Review
(November 15, 1960), pp. 19-21; "Aiding Agriculture—The Students' Way,"
ibid. (September 20, 1960), p. 5.
[125]Ibid.

out to have been is not clear. One Western visitor to China noted in 1964 that few of the factories he visited had sent workers to the countryside in spite of the barrage of official propaganda on the subject.[126]

In the absence of foreign scientific and technical assistance, information flows and correct Redness were to be promoted by a vigorous "Combining of the Three." Like the movement of youth to the countryside, the three-in-one combinations represented an effort to raise the technological level of the masses and prevent the emergence of a meritocratic class structure. The combining was to be achieved in several ways. One variety consisted in closely associating workers, political cadres, and scientific-technical personnel in any given task. The fusion of revolutionary muscle and intellect, of "theory" and "practice," could also be achieved through combining the efforts of college teachers, scientific and research personnel, and workers. Alternatively, the three-in-one combination could comprise intellectuals, workers, and members of the People's Liberation Army. The Combining of the Three also meant, in some cases, the combined efforts of specialized enterprises: medium-sized plants, each specializing in its own line, were urged to work in planned harmony so as to adequately supply more than one major assembly plant.[127]

Whatever the sociological merits of the movement, it seemed to have hampered rather than promoted production. In the last analysis, the political participant in the "Three" tended to be more equal than the other two, and not always the best informed. In practice, what it all boiled down to was the shifting of scarce engineering and other qualified personnel in response to ideological criteria, and the remolding of obstreperous intellectuals through contact with the harsh realities of proletarian earthiness, in spite of governmental injunctions to the contrary. In fact, the three-in-one movement looks very much like the brainchild of the Party's left, a way of getting in on what the experts were up to, and it foreshadowed the three-way alliances of later Great Proletarian Cultural Revolution fame (Chapter 12).

MARKET RESEARCH

In the absence of prices responsive to changes in consumer preferences and of producers responsive to price changes, an attempt was

---

[126] John Ashdown, "China's Proletarian Problems," *FEER* (March 12, 1965), p. 440.
[127] See Economist Intelligence Unit, *Quarterly Economic Review: China, Hong Kong, North Korea* (September 1965), p. 7; Shih Ming, "Technical Cooperation," *Peking Review* (March 19, 1965).

made to find out what consumers wanted and did not want by organizing enterprise visiting teams composed of leading cadres, technicians, and workers. These teams called on department stores and individual consumers "to get their views at first hand." In 1960 Shanghai light industry enterprises organized 2,000 such public opinion polls and held 500 exhibitions, quality contests, concerts (presumably to test the quality of musical instruments on the public's ear drums) "for the express purpose of giving the public an opportunity to pass judgment on the quality of the products." Trade organizations, too, initiated "customer's delegates conferences" to find out how to improve their work.[128] Handicraft cooperatives sent investigating teams to the communes and came back with voluminous information about defective farm implements.[129] Given the continued real (as distinct from formal) importance of quantity of output indicators in enterprise plans, such ad hoc and essentially bureaucratic excursions into market research may not have had as much effect as had been anticipated.

TRADEMARKS

In 1962 factories in some of China's major cities (e.g., Shanghai) were instructed to identify their products by trademarks and other imprints, a measure intended to encourage the production of better quality goods. The trademarks were to bear the name of the factory and of the factory's sales agent (state commercial undertaking or the state network's joint state-private agent), and covered a wide range of consumer goods. In the case of perishable items (e.g., canned goods, photographic materials) the date of manufacture was also to be displayed. Where the goods did not lend themselves to trademark stamping, their places of manufacture and sale were to be identified on the packaging. Trademarks on such goods as sewing machines, bicycles, and radio sets were in existence before 1962. The 1962 instruction appears to have been intended to revive their use after a

[128] Chu Chi-lin, "Better Goods, Bigger Choice," *Peking Review* (May 19, 1961), p. 17; "Help from the Customers," *ibid.* (September 1, 1961), p. 3. For the Soviet experience with market research, advertising, etc., see Marshall I. Goldman, *Soviet Marketing: Distribution in a Controlled Economy* (New York: Free Press, 1963).

[129] In the first six months of 1963 handicraft cooperatives in Liaoning Province made such investigations in 123 communes and 570 production teams. See, "Liaoning Province Improves the Quality of Handicraft Products Step by Step," *Ta-kung Pao* (Peking), November 8, 1963 in *URS*, Vol. 34, No. 19 (March 6, 1964), p. 319. In the first half of 1965 light industries in Szechwan sent 400 men who took with them 30,000 products, made 150 visits to 170 production teams under 66 people's communes in 53 counties. *Ta-kung Pao* (November 28, 1965), p. 1, in *URS*, Vol. 44, No. 4 (July 12, 1966). This kind of statistics abounded after 1960.

lapse of some years and to broaden the range of goods bearing such marks.

ADVERTISING

Commercial advertising was introduced after 1960 in the form of hand-painted billboards, ads in magazines and newspapers, and movie projections shown before each show. Greater care was given to the aesthetics of store window displays and the appearance of retail stores. State advertising companies were set up to handle this activity.

ECONOMIC ANALYSIS

Economic theory in the conditions of socialism had been the subject of a wide-ranging discussion during 1956 and 1957. For a time during the Great Leap, economic analysis was swamped by sloganeering, but it was not totally eliminated.[130] The discussion picked up again in 1961 and continued until 1966 when it was stifled completely by the ritualistic repetition of Maoist slogans.

The revived debate was part of a general (although hotly contested) loosening up of control over thought. Symptomatic of this very relative intellectual liberalization was the flowering of learned symposia ("meetings of immortals") and forums sponsored by the so-called democratic parties (Chapter 2), much talk of "carrying forward the policy of letting all flowers bloom and all schools of thought contend," and the reappearance on the intellectual scene of such venerable figures as Ma Yin-chú, former President of Peking University, who in April 1960 had been dismissed as a rightist. Truth was thenceforth, once more, to be arrived at through open if controlled discussion.[131]

The main figures in the 1961-65 debate on economic theory were—on the reformist side—the economist Yang Chien-pai, Ho Chieng-chang, Chang Ling, and Sun Yeh-fang.[132] The main expo-

---

[130] For example Sun Yeh-fang's "revisionist" essay "On Value: A Critique of the Position of Value in Both Socialist and Communist Economy," *Ching-chi Yen-chiu* (Economic Research), No. 9 (1959), pp. 42-68.

[131] See *Hung-ch'i* editorial, No. 5, 1961. The Philosophy and Social Science Section of the Chinese Academy of Sciences which had not met since 1957, held its third plenary session early in 1961. Ma Yin-chú attended. The years 1960-62 also witnessed a flowering of classical Chinese opera, painting, and calligraphy.

[132] The key article is Yang Chien-pai, "The Problems of Balancing the National Economy and Production Prices," *Ching-chi Yen-chiu* (December 1963). Yang's thesis was supported by Ho and Chang in "Production Prices Under the Socialist Economy," *ibid.* (May 1964). Sun Yeh-fang's post-1960 work is not available in the West. During the attack on him in 1966, however, reference was

nents of the opposing viewpoint were Dai Yuan-shen and Chai Chien-hua, but the number of economists opposing Yang Chien-pei and the other reformists rose rapidly with the years.

The economic discussion of 1961-65 while conducted on a theoretical level and within the Marxist analytical framework, had important policy implications. Its major preoccupation was with finding an objective scientific standard for the efficient conduct of enterprises (industrial as well as agricultural) and for rational central planning. While mainly concerned with the microproblem of enterprise efficiency and enterprise pricing policy for individual goods, it touched also on the macroproblem of the rules for social investment which central planning authorities should observe.[133] From a political standpoint the search for objective rules of economic conduct challenged the position of politics as the guide of economic action, that is the voluntarism of the Great Leap Forward and other experiments in pure Maoism.

V. SCIENTIFIC AND TECHNICAL EDUCATION

This subject is discussed in Chapter 10. Here it need only be mentioned that in addition to a new stress on the quality rather than the quantity of educational input and output, the Chinese during this period used foreign economic exhibitions held in China as sources of technical and scientific knowledge. To selectively learn from the

made to "research reports for internal circulation" which he had prepared probably in October-November 1961, and to a draft of a book on the socialist economy. It is probable that the "research reports for internal circulation" contained the substance of three lectures delivered by Sun to the Shanghai Economic Society (October 1961), the Nanking Economic Society (October 21-22, 1961), and the Department of Economics, Shanghai Futan University (November 4, 1961). Two drafts of the proposed book are known to have circulated before August 1961. It is possible that these drafts were closely related to the "research reports." Speculations on the general outline of such a manual are already to be found in Sun's 1959 article "On Value." They were perhaps inspired by the discussion in the Soviet Union of a new edition of the standard economics textbook, *Politicheskaya Ekonomiya: Uchebnik.*

133The reader is referred to two articles which deal with the post-1960 economic debates. Nai-Ruenn Chen, "The Theory of Price Formation in Communist China," *The China Quarterly* (July-September 1966), pp. 35-53, and G. W. Lee, "Current Debate on Profits and Value in Mainland China," *Australian Economic Papers* (June-December 1965), pp. 72-78. Glimpses of the debate may also be obtained from the attack on Sun Yeh-fang by Meng Kuei and Hsiao Lin, "On Sun Yeh-fang's Reactionary Political Stand and Economic Programme," *Peking Review* (October 21 and 28, 1966), and by Yuan En-chen et al., "Resolutely Counterattack Sun Yeh-fang for his Attack on the Party," *Ta-kung Pao* in *URS*, Vol. 44, No. 18 (August 30, 1966), pp. 269-270. Franz Schurmann briefly reviews the debate in his "China's 'New Economic Policy'—Transition or Beginning?" in Choh-ming Li (ed.), *Industrial Development in Communist China*, *op. cit.*, pp. 89-91.

foreigner, were he socialist, fraternal, revisionist, "capitalist of the intermediate zone" (i.e., economically developing and politically noncommitted), or imperialist became for a while the duty of every citizen. The Chinese people's latent ability is enormous. For centuries that ability had been frustrated by foreign ideological models (which, incidentally, the foreigners had discarded at home) and by home-bred philosophies, whether Confucian or Maoist. From time to time the thirst for knowledge unencumbered by normative ballast reasserted itself; such was the case during 1961-63.

VI. SELF-RELIANCE

"We advocate regeneration through our own efforts," wrote Mao. "We hope there will be foreign aid, but we cannot count on it. We rely on our own efforts, on the creative power of the army and the people."[134]

The Soviets were gone, and almost everyone who could possibly have helped, elected, for one reason or another, not to do so. The result, backed by centuries of isolation and illusion, was an inward turning upon one's own resources: self-help and self-reliance, as laudable as they were inadequate to the enormous tasks facing the country. Primary reliance on one's own resources is commendable in that ultimately the job of development cannot be shifted to any significant extent onto foreign shoulders; too much looking outward may sap a country's will, and undermine its resolve to bear the sacrifices which development entails. It has been argued, for example, that U. S. Public Law 480 imports may have adversely affected India's determination to bring about much needed agricultural reforms. Extensive borrowing of foreign technological and economic models may not only be inappropriate to the borrower's economy, but can stunt the growth of native inventiveness, and, by its demonstration effect, raise the level of consumer aspirations above what the economy is at the moment able to provide. The doctrine of self-reliance hinges on the postponement of the revolution of rising expectations; it is part and parcel of a broader philosophy of austerity. On the other hand, failure to make use of foreign technological and scientific advances, to benefit from some measure of derived development will tend to bring about much wasted effort, a rediscovery of things long since known elsewhere, an artificial restriction of developmental inputs. The Chinese government's "greatest fault," wrote one observer, "is its failure to maximize the input of foreign re-

[134] Mao Tse-tung, "We Must Learn to Do Economic Work," *SW*, Vol. III, 2d ed., 1953 (Peking), p. 1015.

sources available for Chinese development—partly out of an innate cultural suspicion of foreigner; partly out of the extraordinary pride and sensitivity of a people who still, emotionally, live in their 'Middle Kingdom' of antiquity; and partly out of ideological zeal which led Mao to break with Russia. In a world in which India is receiving about U.S. $1,000 million a year in foreign aid, China is bravely attempting the road of 'self-reliance.' Unfortunately it is contrary to every fact of modern life to suppose that Chinese development can successfully be promoted from the sidelines of the world technological race."[135] Chinese communism, like its Soviet predecessor, is a ruthless vehicle of modernization, but it is a vehicle which runs on its own narrow tracks, blinds drawn.

The thesis of self-reliance, reiterated many times since 1960, was justified on the doctrinal ground that the objective laws governing the development of things were those in which the internal factors played the decisive dialectical role. Nationalistically, "the guideline of self-reliance gives full expression to our confidence in the great strength, wisdom, and talents of the people and our confidence in their ability not only to liberate themselves, but also to build a good and happy life with their own hands."[136] Internationally, "it is a manifestation of great-power chauvinism to reduce the economy of another country to that of a dependency in the name of 'economic mutual assistance.' International cooperation must be built on the basis of self-reliance."[137] From the standpoint of practical realities, the Chinese after 1960 had little choice but to fall back on self-help and learn from the foreigner only to the extent allowed by the state of their hard-currency holdings and by the willingness of noncommunist countries to enter into a dialogue. Virtue was made of necessity with plenty of precedents drawn from Chinese communist history. "Some comrades," remarked Po I-po, "think we should offer Khrushchev a medal for the spur he gave to our self-reliance."[138] The danger of the self-reliance approach to economic development is that it may foster latent chauvinism and slip into a rejection of all things

[135] Dick Wilson, "China in Perspective," *FEER* (August 27, 1964), p. 374. "We cannot just take the beaten track traversed by other countries in the development of technology and trail behind them at snail's pace." Chou En-lai, "Report on the Work of the Government to the First Session, Third National People's Congress," December 21-22, 1964. *Peking Review* (January 1, 1965), p. 11.

[136] Lu Hsun, "On China's Guideline for Self-Reliance in Socialist Construction," *Ching-chi Yen-chiu*, No. 7 (July 20, 1965) in *SCMM*, No. 488 (1965), p. 2.

[137] Chou En-lai, "Report on the Work of the Government," *op. cit.*, p. 11. Cf. *Communiqué*, Fourth Session, Second National People's Congress (November 17-December 3, 1963), *Peking Review* (December 6, 1963).

[138] In Anna Louise Strong, *Letter from China* (December 30, 1963), p. 3.

foreign. The Chinese have not been able to avoid this. In moments of nationalistic euphoria they denounced not only foreign models but also the achievements of their own precommunist past.

This, however, was not the case in the period 1961-65. During that time the thesis of self-help was interpreted plastically in two main ways. In the first place, it meant belt-tightening and asceticism in the early revolutionary tradition. "Strict economy is essential to the long range national construction and necessary for the revolutionary process. It is also very important currently as we have to get prepared for war and famine."[139] Industry and frugality were praised as "proletarian virtues," and their practice was said to represent true "proletarian style."[140] The emphasis was on economizing, on retrenchment and revolutionary parsimony. But over and above all this there hovered at all times a more subtle notion of poverty as a permanent characteristic of true revolutionaries, a long-term rejection of the gloss and glitter of affluence, inimical to the very substance of the communist vision. Perhaps the distinction between the left's and the right's interpretation of the self-reliance doctrine was that the former saw it as the very cement of the new society, while the latter regarded it as a temporary expedient forced on the leadership by circumstances—some of the left's making, some not. The bureaucratic moderates were more inclined to grant the hypothesis of the common human desire for a better life now, and were more sensitive to the practical difficulties involved in trying to sustain the revolutionary élan by appeals to the nobility of asceticism. Poverty to them was a necessary evil, not a foundation on which to build the new society of the future.

Secondly, self-reliance was not to be confused with autarchy. On the contrary, it fitted in quite well with diversification of markets and sources of supply, and with selective foreign aid to friendly or neutral countries. "The policy of self-reliance is, of course, not a policy that calls for isolation and rejection of foreign aid. . . . However, such economic cooperation must be founded upon the principle of complete equality, mutual benefit, and comradely assistance. . . . As taught again and again by Comrade Mao Tse-tung, the

[139] "Practise Economy for the Revolution," *Chung-kuo Fu-nu* (Women of China), No. 1 (January 1, 1966) in *SCMM*, No. 511 (February 14, 1966), p. 13. Women, incidentally, are an important component of China's labor force, especially in light industry and agriculture. In this respect China's experience is very much unlike India's.

[140] A "Wealth from Waste" campaign to collect scrap metal, rags, waste paper, broken glass, animal bones, discarded rubber, etc., was conducted throughout the country. Articles which could not be reused without processing were purchased exclusively by the Discarded Articles Company; those which could be used again without processing were purchased by the Second-Hand Goods Company.

correct relationship between self-reliance and foreign aid must place primary emphasis on self-reliance and secondary emphasis on foreign aid. . . . [The people] must not look outward, extend their hands, and depend upon other people."[141] Up-to-date chemical plants, airplanes, electronic equipment, refineries, and other installations were imported from the West and Japan; foreign engineers were invited to come and teach their counterparts how to operate the new equipment. In 1964 alone, 71 different varieties of tropical plants were introduced from twelve countries and acclimatized at the South China Subtropical Crop Institute's experimental botanical gardens.[142]

Reports on the attainment of the self-sufficiency objective during the period must be interpreted cautiously. For instance, the 1963 claim of "self-sufficiency in the main" in regard to petroleum may simply have meant that all domestically produced crude oil could be domestically refined. It in no way suggested that domestic supplies of petroleum were adequate either to meet industrial and transportation demand for products or to serve the needs of future development. In fact, at the time the claim was made, China imported about 2 million tons of petroleum products from the USSR, Rumania, and Albania, and discreetly explored the possibility of buying petroleum from Algeria and Kuwait.[143] There is no doubt, however, that during the years 1961-65 the Chinese did design and develop by themselves many types of equipment until then imported from abroad, including blast furnaces, synthetic ammonia plants, and some electronic equipment including analog computers for designing and analyzing automatic control systems. In 1964 domestic industry reportedly supplied 90 percent of the forgings and rolled stock used, as compared with 57 percent in 1957, and 90 percent of "machinery and equipment," compared to 55 percent in 1957. In 1964 for the first time China began producing rolled steel railway wheels and wheel rims, a 12,000-ton (working pressure) forging press capable of forging 200-300 ton steel ingots into heavy machinery parts, steam- and water-driven turbines of 50,000 and 72,500 kilowatts respectively, large mobile cranes (of 350 tons), oil refineries with a capacity of 1 million tons of crude per year, fertilizer plants producing

141 Lu Hsun, *op. cit.*, p. 3. A definition of "self-reliance" may be found in Yung Lung-kwei, "Self-Reliance Has Proved Itself," *China Reconstructs* (April 1966, p. 8).
142 *Peking Review* (March 12, 1965), p. 25.
143 See Jan S. Prybyla, "Communist China's Economic Aid to Noncommunist Asian and African Countries," in Jan S. Prybyla (ed.), *Communism and Nationalism* (University Park, Pa.: Pennsylvania State U., 1969). Also, *Associated Press*, Kuwait, June 7, 1965. The self-sufficiency in petroleum claim was repeated, as latest news, in September 1969.

100,000 tons of nitrogenous fertilizer a year, diesel locomotives, and vertical coalshafts.[144]

All the teaching apparatus in middle schools and college science departments visited by geophysicist C. H. G. Oldham in 1964 were Chinese-made. However, advanced scientific equipment in research institutes had been imported from the USSR, East Germany, Czechoslovakia, Japan, Holland, and Britain.[145]

VII. FOREIGN TRADE: LEANING TO ALL SIDES

The economic new course, for all its insistence on self-reliance, regarded foreign trade as a component part of developmental policy. To promote it, a General Office for Economic Relations with Foreign Countries was established in 1961. The total volume of trade rose steadily after 1961, reaching roughly $4 billion in 1965, or about $5-6 per head of population, a figure lower than that for India or Pakistan. The importance attached to foreign economic contacts during this period (in spite of the modest total and per capita volume) was in contrast to Soviet hesitations on this score at a roughly similar stage of the Soviet Union's economic development. The common denominator of the new policy was balanced diversity, which had three main implications.

The first was the *termination of the 1949-60 policy of "leaning to one side,"* i.e., toward the Soviet Union and other communist countries (Table 9-7). By 1965 China had repaid all debts to the USSR—some $1.7 billion in all. The last loan extended by the Soviets to China was in 1961. Soviet exports to China dropped from $954.5 million in 1959 to a low of $135.2 million in 1964, and imports from China fell from $1.1 billion to $314.2 million in the same period.[146] China's trade turnover with the Soviet Union in 1959 represented about half of the country's total trade turnover; by 1964 this had dropped to 13 percent. In 1959 China's share in the total trade of the Soviet Union was about 20 percent. In 1964 it was less than 4 percent. A year later China moved from sixth to ninth place among the Soviet Union's trading partners. China's 1964 trade will all communist countries was about 35 percent of her total trade. In 1957 it had been over 60 percent. Thus, both from the point of view of

[144]Harald Munthe-Kaas, "China's Mechanical Heart," *FEER* (May 27, 1965), pp. 398-400, 429, 432. At the same time the Chinese contracted for the delivery in 1964-66 of two fertilizer plants from Italy, one ammonia plant from Britain, a petroleum refinery from Italy, an oil cracking plant from West Germany, and a urea plant from Holland.

[145]*FEER* (April 1, 1965), pp. 14-18.

[146]1965 Soviet exports: $191.7 million, Soviet imports: $225.6 million.

TABLE 9-7
Direction of Chinese Communist Trade, 1958-65
(Millions of U. S. dollars)

(1) Year	(2) Total Trade	(3) Trade with Noncommunist Countries	Trade with Communist Countries				
			(4) Total*	(5) USSR	(6) East Europe	(7) Cuba	(8) Far East
1958	3,735	1,385	2,350	1,515	670	—	160
1959	4,264	1,310	2,954	2,055	655	—	244
1960	3,975	1,370	2,605	1,665	640	42	255
1961	3,015	1,335	1,680	919	325	182	257
1962	2,675	1,265	1,410	750	230	171	262
1963	2,755	1,510	1,245	600	225	156	263
1964	3,245	2,120	1,125†	449	245	180	227
1965‡	3,699	2,570	1,129	417	299	213	200

*Including trade with Yugoslavia. (Col. 6 excludes trade with Yugoslavia.)
Far East = N. Korea, N. Vietnam, Outer Mongolia.
†Because of unreliable data on the Far East and Cuba, components do not add up to total by a margin of $24 million.
‡Preliminary estimates.
Note: Figures rounded to nearest $5 million. Because of rounding, components may not add up to the total
Source: Robert L. Price, "International Trade of Communist China, 1950-65," in *An Economic Profile of Mainland China, op. cit.,* p. 584, Tables 9-13.

indebtedness and current trade, the former policy of leaning on socialism to build socialism had come to an end.[147]

The decline in Soviet exports to China until 1964 may be explained by three considerations: (1) the unwillingness of the Soviets to sell certain potentially strategic goods as, for example, petroleum products, aircraft and aircraft components, cobalt, etc.; (2) the disruption of Soviet plant, machinery, and industrial equipment sales in consequence of the withdrawal of Soviet experts and blueprints from China in mid-1960 (Chapter 8); (3) China's attempt to save on imports from the USSR in order to help pay off her debt as rapidly as possible. Underlying it all was China's reluctance to depend too heavily on the USSR for economic goods since, in Chinese eyes, such dependence tended to imply repayment in political goods. *Rodong Shinmon,* organ of the Central Committee of the North Korean Workers' Party, in its issue of September 7, 1964 raised a further

[147]From 1956 until 1965 the Chinese maintained a surplus on their commodity trade with the USSR, this balance being used to amortize economic and military loans received from the Soviets. At its peak (1962) this balance reached $280 million. The increase in Soviet exports to China in 1965 has generally been interpreted as a deliberate effort on the part of the Soviets to bring their trade with China into balance, following the repayment of all debts due to them. In 1965 China's positive balance was only $34 million.

issue—joyfully reproduced by the *Peking Review* eleven days later: "In rendering aid in the rehabilitation and construction of factories, you [the Soviets] furnished us with equipment, stainless steel plate, and other materials at prices much higher than world market prices and took away from us scores of tons of gold, quantities of valuable nonferrous metal and raw materials at prices much lower than world market prices." The work of the Soviet-sponsored Council of Mutual Economic Assistance was described by the Chinese as "an attempt to oppose the independent development of fraternal economies." What the Russians were really after, Peking said, was to reduce these economies to suppliers of raw materials and outlets for Soviet finished goods.

The departure from the policy of leaning to one side was especially marked in the case of machinery and equipment (including complete plants) and petroleum products (Table 9-8). In this instance, however, the decreased reliance on the Soviet Union was not made good to any significant degree by machinery and equipment or petroleum products imports from noncommunist countries. This was due in part to the investment cutback in China in 1961-62, in part to problems involved in obtaining long-term credits outside the communist world, and, to some extent, to the strategically sensitive nature of such items and the resultant reluctance of some Western governments to permit large-scale trade in such goods. The import-substitution effect was presumably another significant factor contributing to the continuing decline in Chinese machinery imports.[148] The one exception was machinery and equipment for the chemical fertilizer industry.

Imports of machinery and equipment from noncommunist countries constituted about 10.1 percent of China's total imports from those countries in 1959, and only 6.5 percent in 1964. Total imports in 1959 from the noncommunist world were about $695 million in 1959, and $1.08 billion in 1964.

By 1965 China had trade relations with 125 countries and regions (including South Africa, to the great annoyance of most African countries). Forty of these had signed intergovernmental trade agreements with Peking. In other cases trade was carried on through informal channels and so-called "friendly firms" in the partners' countries. These were firms with which the Chinese chose to deal (usually through the Chinese Council for the Promotion of International Trade) because of the firms' friendly attitude toward

[148] Answering Soviet charges of unresponsiveness to offers of plant and machinery, the Chinese in 1964 asked the Soviets whether—without the technical specifications and advice needed to put the machines and plant to work—they expected China to buy the machinery merely for display.

TABLE 9-8
Soviet Exports of Machinery and Equipment and
Petroleum Products to China
(Millions of U.S. dollars)

| Year | Machinery and Equipment | | Petroleum Products |
	Total	Complete Plants	
1960	503.9	373.8	113.1
1961	108.1	78.9	120.7
1962	27.3	8.8	79.8
1963	42.2	14.6	60.2
1964	57.6	12.3	21.3
1965	76.2*	3.9	2.2

*Some of the increase may be accounted for by badly needed and long overdue spare parts.
   Source: Robert L. Price, "International Trade of Communist China, 1950–65," in An Economic Profile of Mainland China, op. cit., p. 592, Table 7. Based on official Soviet foreign trade returns. Exports f.o.b.

People's China expressed in the firms' absence of commercial relations with the United States or Taiwan. Frequently the Chinese bent over backward a bit: when they needed equipment unavailable elsewhere, they were willing to deal with dummy friendly firms, knowing that the parent enterprise carried on a lucrative business with the United States and Taiwan. Between 1950 and 1965 the Council for the Promotion of International Trade held 25 economic exhibitions and participated in 67 international fairs in 40 countries. In the same period 11 foreign countries held economic exhibitions in China.

The second major implication of the policy of leaning to all sides was the *stabilization of the pattern of exports and imports*. Large-scale purchases of food grains from abroad became a regular feature of the new course, amounting to about 5.5 million metric tons per year (Table 9-9). A million tons of imported wheat cost the Chinese $50-60 million in hard currencies, so that the annual expenditure on this item ran into some $275-330 million. In 1964 the average freight rate per metric ton was $15.50. The grain exporters (Australia, Canada, Argentina, France, West Germany) extended short-term credits (from six to eighteen months) to help finance shipments, charging an average annual interest rate estimated at 5 percent. Total drawings on grain credits from 1961 through 1964 amounted to $874 million (gross) and $191 million (net, i.e., drawings minus repayments).[149]

[149] An Economic Profile of Mainland China, op. cit., pp. 651, 656.

TABLE 9-9
Communist China's Imports Of Grain
(Thousands of metric tons)

	1961	1962	1963	1964
Argentina				
Corn	45	400	—	—
Wheat	—	186	28	800
Total	45	586	28	800
Australia				
Wheat	2,175	1,142	3,001	1,700
Oats	77	63	—	142
Barley	360	5	—	—
Total	2,618	1,210	3,001	1,842
Canada				
Wheat	1,471	1,948	1,382	1,800
Barley	660	203	24	355
Total	2,131	2,151	1,406	2,155
France				
Wheat	37	405	813	300
Barley	260	124	—	100
Total	297	529	813	400
West Germany				
Wheat	256	258	—	—
Mexico				
Wheat	—	—	—	450
Southern Rhodesia				
Corn	—	54	—	—
South Africa				
Corn	—	27	163	—
USSR				
Wheat	101	110	n.a.	n.a.
Rye	100	247	n.a.	n.a.
Total	201	357	n.a.	n.a.
World total				
Wheat	4,040	4,049	5,224	5,050
Rye	100	247	—	—
Corn	57	481	163	—
Oats	77	63	—	142
Barley	1,286	332	24	455
Grand Total	5,615	5,172	5,411	5,647

Source: Dick Wilson, "China's Trading Prospects," FEER (August 20, 1964), p. 310. Compiled from official partner statistics and news items. 1964 figures from announcements of sales contracts for delivery in calendar 1964. Wheat includes flour at wheat-weight equivalent. R. L. Price, in An Economic Profile of Mainland China, op. cit., p. 601, gives somewhat different figures for Chinese grain purchases from the West.

Grain imports represented about 40 percent of China's annual total imports in value terms, the remainder being accounted for by purchases of chemical fertilizers, jute, cotton, industrial plant and equipment (especially for the chemical fertilizer industry), precision instruments, spare parts, means of transportation, and communications equipment. The Western exporters of these goods extended credits to facilitate the transactions: up to 18 months in the case of fertilizer, up to 5 years in the case of machinery and equipment. Some 13 plants bought by China during this period from Japan (polyvinyl alcohol fiber, acetylene generating, condenser manufacturing), Britain (synthetic ammonia, polyethylene, polyester resin, instruments), West Germany (crude oil cracking and olefin separation, acrylonitrile, air liquefaction, cold strip steel rolling), Sweden (porous silica), Finland, Austria, the Netherlands, and Italy (petroleum refining) were financed in this way.

Following a deterioration during the Great Leap Forward and its immediate aftermath, the balance of payments situation was improved in 1963-64 (Table 9-10). The improvement was due in large measure to substantial earnings from commodity exports. Even so, China's international financial position at the end of the period was still precarious. Gold and hard currency reserves in 1964 were only two-fifths of total merchandise imports compared with the 1957 situation when they were equal to total merchandise imports.

Notice the heavy expenditure on freight and insurance: $365 million in the five years 1958-62 and $145 million in the years 1963-64. Much of this consisted of outlays on ship charters. China's fleet was too small to carry all the goods traded, particularly food grains purchased in distant countries.[150] Hence resort was and continues to be made to foreign vessels flying Greek, Italian, French, Dutch, West German, British, Lebanese, Swedish, Norwegian, and Japanese flags. The use of Soviet and East European ships on the China run fluctuated with the political climate. In 1965 China had charted about 400 ships, totaling 1.4 million tons, some 80 of them in Britain, and another 40 in Scandinavian countries. A number of chartered ships consisted of big bulk carriers and grain-carrying tankers of up to 30,000 ton cargo capacity each.[151] The Chinese drove a hard bargain in a charter market made tight by Soviet bids for ships to carry wheat purchased in Canada and by bids from other quarters to carry grain shipments to India.

The third implication of the policy of leaning to all sides was *trade with and economic assistance to a number of economically underdeveloped countries in Asia and Africa.* All foreign aid has

[150] In 1966 total Chinese oceangoing shipping tonnage was estimated at about 1 million tons, or 150-200 (mostly old, foreign-made) freighters. 95 percent of China's seaborne trade was handled by eight cities (Dairen, Chinhuangtao, Tientsin, Tsingtao, Lienyunkang, Shanghai, Canton—including Whampoa—and Chanchiang). Some 70 percent of the loading and unloading operations were mechanized.

[151] "China Charters," *FEER* (February 10, 1966), pp. 248-249; V. Wolpert, "Grain Shipping—A Tough Problem," *ibid.* (November 9, 1961), pp. 291-292.

TABLE 9-10
Summary of China's Balance of Payments, 1958-62 and 1963-64*
(Millions of U. S. dollars)

	Noncommunist Countries		Communist Countries	
	Credit	Debit	Credit	Debit
	1958-62			
Current account (net)	—	395	1,010	—
Merchandise trade balance . . .	—	350	1,165	—
Freight and insurance	—	290	—	75
Overseas remittances	260	—	—	—
Other transactions (net)	—	15	—	80
Capital and monetary gold (net)	—	60	—	855
Credits and grants extended:				
Net drawings	—	55	—	405
Credits received:				
Drawings	330	—	365	—
Repayments	—	210	—	905
Other transactions (net)	—	125	90	—
Errors and omissions (net)† . . .	455	—	—	155
	1963-64			
Current account (net)	30	—	745	—
Merchandise trade balance . . .	95	—	715	—
Freight and insurance	—	160	15	—
Overseas remittances	120	—	—	—
Other transactions (net)	—	25	15	—
Capital and monetary gold (net)	0	—	—	595
Credits and grants extended:				
Net drawings	—	45	—	190
Credits received:				
Drawings	580	—	—	—
Repayments	—	490	—	430
Other transactions (net)	—	45	25	—
Errors and omissions (net)† . . .	—	30	—	150

*Data are rounded to the nearest $5 million.
†Assumed to be changes in foreign currency balances (noncommunist countries) and clearing balances (communist countries).
Source: Central Intelligence Agency, "Communist China's Balance of Payments, 1950-65," in An Economic Profile of Mainland China, op. cit., p. 628.

political and ideological overtones more or less obvious, and Chinese aid was certainly no exception. "The Chinese leaders," Suslov once said, "represent matters as though the interests of the peoples of Asia, Africa, and Latin America were especially close and understandable to them, as though they were concerned most of all for the further development of the national liberation movements. The facts, however, decisively refute such declarations."[152] One of the reasons

[152] "Report to the Plenary Session of the Central Committee of the Communist Party of the Soviet Union" (February 14, 1964), Pravda (April 3, 1964), pp. 1-8.

TABLE 9-11
Communist China's Loan Commitments
(Millions of U. S. dollars)

Recipient Country	Date	Amount	Drawing Period	Repayment Period
Africa		261.8		
Guinea.	1959	0.5		
	1960	26.0	1961-63	1970-79
Ghana	1961	19.6	1962-67	1971-80
	1964	22.4		
Mali*.	1961	19.6	1962-67	1971-80
Congo (B)	1963	20.0		
	1964	5.2		
Somalia	1963	20.0		
Algeria.	1962	1.8		
	1963	50.0		
Tanzania†	1964	42.5		
Central African Republic	1964	4.2		
Kenya	1964	15.0	1965-69	1975-?
Uganda	1965	15.0		
Middle East		148.4		
UAR‡	1964	80.0	1965-67	1972-81
	1967	10.0		
Syria	1963	16.3		
Yemen.	1958	12.7		
	1959	0.7		
	1963	0.2		
	1964	28.5		
Iraq.	1967	"indefinite"		
Asia		442.9		
Afghanistan	1965	28.0		
Nepal	1956	12.6		
	1960	21.0		
	1961	9.8		
Burma	1961	84.0		
Ceylon.	1958	10.5	1958-62 (1962-67)	1963-72
	1964	4.2	1965-67	
Cambodia.	1956	22.9		
	1960	26.5		
Indonesia	1956	16.2		
	1958	11.2		
	1961	30.0		
	1964	50.0		
	1965	16.0		
Pakistan.	1964	60.0		
	1968	40.0		
Grand Total . . .	1956-68	853.1		

*In 1967 China agreed to design and build a Mali-Guinea railway line. The estimated cost was $100 million.

†In September 1967 China agreed to design and build a 1,000-mile-long Tanzania-Zambia railway, linking Dar-es-Salaam with the Zambian copper belt. The cost of the project was estimated at $275 million.

‡One-third of the $10 million loan was used to pay for 150,000 tons of (Australian) wheat sent by China to Egypt as a "solidarity gift" in the wake of the Arab-Israeli war (June 1967).

Source: Partners' trade statistics and communiqués regarding aid agreements.

for the Chinese foreign aid effort was to show the recipients, the Western "imperialists," and the Soviet "revisionists" that the facts did support these declarations. There was, and is, in China's foreign aid ventures an element of Sino-Soviet competition which came out most clearly in the economic bidding for the favors of such underdeveloped communist countries as Outer Mongolia, North Korea, North Vietnam, and Cuba, but was present in almost every other instance.[153] Since China was still poor and underdeveloped herself, the foreign aid which she gave to others represented for her a burden that was lightened by the expectation of political dividends, careful husbandry of the amount and type of aid extended, and a meticulous selection of beneficiaries. Yet in spite of all the care taken in the selection of foreign aid recipients, there have been surprises and disappointments (e.g., Indonesia, Ghana, Burma).

The pattern of aid which has emerged since 1961 comprised the tying of assistance to the delivery of Chinese goods and services, long-term interest-free (or low interest) loans, and the selection of those aid projects that tended to have the maximum growth impact on the economy of the recipient country. The political timing of loan or grant offers was carefully chosen. Although small compared with the aid programs of Western industrialized countries and the

TABLE 9-12
Communist China's Grant Commitments
(Millions of U. S. Dollars)

Recipient Country	Date	Amount
UAR	1956	4.7
Jordan	1967	60.0
Somalia	1963	3.0
Tanzania	1964	3.0
Kenya	1964	3.0
Ceylon	1957	15.8
	1962	10.5
Total		100.0
Grand total loans and grants, 1956-68.		953.1

Source: as in Table 9-11.

[153] See Jan S. Prybyla, "Soviet and Chinese Economic Competition Within the Communist World," Soviet Studies (April 1964), pp. 464-473, and "Communist China's Economic Aid to Non-Communist Asian and African Developing Countries," in: J. S. Prybyla (ed.), Communism and Nationalism (University Park, Pa.: Pennsylvania State U., 1969). Alain-Gérard Marsot, "China's Aid to Cambodia," Pacific Affairs (Summer 1969), pp. 189-198; Peter S. H. Tang and Joan Maloney, The Chinese Communist Impact on Cuba, Research Institute on the Sino-Soviet Bloc Studies, Monograph Series, No. 12 (Chestnut Hill, Mass.: 1962); Ernest Halperin, "Peking and the Latin American Communists," China Quarterly (January-March 1967), pp. 111-154; "China and Latin America: Peking's Shopping Bag." Economist (October 10, 1964), pp. 136-139.

Soviet Union, China's foreign aid effort has been gradually expanded in some of the world's most sensitive areas. Tables 9-11 and 9-12 show the record from 1956 to 1968.

The following comments on the various items in Tables 9-11 and 9-12 may be useful.

1. The general principles of China's foreign aid policy were set out for foreign consumption by Chou En-lai in Bamako (Mali) in January 1964. This so-called "Eight-Point Charter" insisted that aid should always be mutual, never unilateral, and that it should be without preconditions or privileges which could adversely affect the national sovereignty of the assisted country. Further, economic aid granted by Peking was to take the form of loans free of interest or at nominal interest rates. The avowed objective of such loans, stated Point 4, was to place the assisted countries on the road to independent national development and not to make them dependents of China.[154] The projects financed by the Chinese government were to be those which required the least investment for the quickest results in order to rapidly furnish the governments of the recipient countries with increased revenues. The equipment supplied by China at world market prices was "the best she could produce." Deliveries were accompanied by guarantees to replace any equipment which did not fit the agreed-on specifications. Technical aid was rendered for the purpose of supervising the use of Chinese equipment until such time as the recipients acquired the needed expertise to carry on the job themselves. Finally, experts sent by China were to lead a life the level of which was no higher than that of local technicians. Chinese experts, stated Point 8, claimed no privilege, nor did they expect to enjoy any advantage. These were lofty ideals, easily formulated but often quite unworkable, especially in the instance of a country which repeatedly proclaimed that "politics must take command of economics and not vice versa."[155]

As often happens, the actual implementation of these guidelines

[154] In March 1968 the Soviets charged that Chinese-built factories were intended to make African industry dependent on Chinese raw materials. According to Moscow, the cigarette and match factory built by the Chinese in Guinea was 70 percent dependent on China for tobacco, and completely dependent on China for sulphur and tinfoil. Cf. Jan S. Prybyla, "Communist China's Economic Relations with Africa, 1960-1964," *Asian Survey* (November 1964), pp. 1135-1143; Leon M. S. Slawecki, "The Two China's in Africa," *Foreign Affairs*, Vol. 41, No. 2 (January 1963), pp. 398-409; George T. Yu, "Peking versus Taipei in the World Arena: Chinese Competition in Africa," *Asian Survey* (September 1963), pp. 439-453.

[155] Among many others, see "Politics the Supreme Commander, the Very Soul of Our Work," *Hung-ch'i* editorial, No. 1 (January 1, 1966) in *SCMM*, No. 509 (1966), pp. 1-4; Ko Cheng, "Politics is in Command of Economics, Revolution is in Command of Production," *Peking Review* (July 25, 1969), pp. 5-7.

was less lofty and pure than the statement of intent. At various times, but especially from 1966 onward, Chinese personnel in some aid-receiving countries (e.g., Burma, Egypt, Nepal, Cambodia) acted arrogantly toward their hosts and allegedly interfered in the host countries' internal affairs. Anti-Chinese riots erupted in Indonesia, Ceylon, and Burma. In 1967 the Chinese embassy staff, technicians, and teachers in Burma organized and encouraged provocative actions against that country's government, Peking openly calling for the overthrow of the Burmese Head of State. China also encouraged the Peking-oriented Communist Party of Burma (White Flag) to bring this about. In the ensuing anti-Chinese riots in Rangoon, over 100 Chinese residents were killed. Five hundred Chinese technicians were expelled from the country. During the Cultural Revolution in China (Chapters 11 and 12), Peking attacked Kenya's Minister of Economics, Tom Mboya, branding him an imperialist puppet. In June 1967 Kenya expelled the Chinese ambassador and recalled its representative from Peking. The Chinese also took sides in the Yemen civil war. Chinese technicians, for example, accompanied republican troops sent to relieve Sanaa in February 1968. They helped make the breakthrough possible by throwing a steel span across a damaged bridge at a critical moment. China also trained Kenyan citizens as fighter pilots, without the knowledge or consent of the Kenyan government. The operation was conducted under the cover of the African National Union.[156] Without the knowledge or approval of the Kenyan government, Chinese arms were shipped to Uganda through Kenyan territory in May 1965. President Bourguiba of Tunisia accused China of "inverted racism" and an uncontrolled "folie de grandeur."[157] The government of the Central African Republic broke off diplomatic relations with Peking (January 1966) charging China with the establishment of political indoctrination centers and military training camps for dissident elements on the republic's territory. Similar charges were levelled by the new governments of Ghana (February 1966), Dahomey (January 1966), and the existing governments of the Congo, Niger, Rwanda, and Cameroun.

Where Chinese efforts have been effective, they have centered precisely on the strict and literal interpretation of the Eight-Point Charter. The old Japanese formula of "cheap and good" has been used with notable success in displacing Japanese products from the Yemeni market and in causing problems for Japanese tea in Tunisia and Morocco. Japan and Hong Kong have had to compete hard with Peking's sewing machines, bicycles, textiles, and other light-industry

[156]The news was broken by Kenya's Defense Minister Mungai. See *New York Times* (March 31, 1965), p. 1.
[157]*Realités* (Paris), September 11, 1965.

products (e.g., cement) in much of southeast Asia. Chinese technical assistance, where it has been least resented, has tended to concentrate on teaching the local people how to combine traditional (labor-intensive) and modern (capital-intensive) methods in such areas as irrigation, water conservation, road and trail building, rice cultivation, and public health.

2. The Chinese have been inclined to promise more than they could reasonably be expected to deliver at the present stage of their development. Their foreign aid commitments are notoriously overextended, with unwelcome repercussions on the integrity of their word. On occasion it was not so much a question of exaggerated promises, as of finding mutually acceptable goods that could be used to exhaust the credit lines which China had placed at the disposal of her various partners. As a rule, Chinese assistance was tied to the delivery of Chinese-made goods and services which at times were just not there. At other times China found it difficult to deliver the agreed-on items precisely when needed and according to definite specifications. This was particularly true in 1966-67 when the Cultural Revolution excesses resulted in delays and confusion at Chinese ports, accompanied by the harassment of foreign ships' crews. It is estimated that of the almost $1 billion pledged by China in loans and grants, only about one-third has actually materialized.[158]

VIII. POPULATION RESTRAINT

Before 1949 little was known about the demographic picture of China. There had been no systematic population census, and estimates of population movements were based on sample surveys carried out occasionally and rather haphazardly. The impression obtained from such surveys was that for centuries the increase in population was erratic, suggesting relatively stable birth rates and fluctuating death rates.[159]

In 1953 the communists, with Soviet help, carried out the first fairly scientific population census in China's history. Over 2.5 million enumerators were quickly trained, questionnaires were prepared, and after some nine months of work the results were published on November 1, 1954. They showed a total population of 583 million and indicated a birth rate of 3.7 percent and a death rate of 1.7 per-

---

[158] From 1954 to mid-1967 Soviet economic aid commitments to neutralist developing countries amounted to $4 billion. Actual deliveries were only 40 percent of that sum, or $1.6 billion.

[159] See Ping-ti Ho, *Studies in the Population of China, 1368-1953* (Cambridge, Mass.: Harvard U. P., 1959). A 1930 "census" showed a total population of 475 millions.

cent—that is, a net population increase rate of 2 percent. In spite of many faults, the 1953 census was probably the best one could hope for under the circumstances and it provided a basis for better and bigger censuses to come.[160] None came, however—at least not before 1970. The census should have been repeated in 1963, but was postponed because of economic recession. In 1964 a nationwide count was carried out. It was less systematic and thorough than the 1953 census and the results were not made public.

The 1953 figure is generally accepted as a fairly reliable point of reference, although there has been some argument about the degree of under- or overstatement. It would appear probable that the figure is conservative and that the natural rate of population increase may be somewhat understated.[161]

The Chinese Communists' attitude toward the natural movement of population has shown wide swings from all-out populationism to all-out birth control and back again. These swings are not unrelated to changes in the locus of power within the leadership, the bureaucratic moderates leaning toward family planning (and planning in general), the leftist ideologues toward populationism. The moderates tend to view the problem pragmatically—that is, in terms of per capita food availabilities and the progress of agriculture; the ideologues see it more in terms of the productive powers of the people, and together with Marx, Engels, and Lenin dispute the existence of a universal, invariable law of population.[162] According to the latter position, population headaches are the results of incorrect relations of production (i.e., the wrong sort of institutional arrangements, like capitalism) and not of any natural tendency for population to outgrow the means of subsistence. Given a socialist transformation of the relations of production, the population problem is taken care of by an unprecedented release of productive powers. Until recent years this view was also held by most Soviet demographers, at least in their published writings, but of late a shift toward a more empirical approach to the problem has become noticeable.[163] The academic com-

---

[160]The faults are enumerated by Thomas E. Dow, Jr., in "The Population of China," *Current History* (September 1968), p. 142, and by John S. Aird, *The Size, Composition, and Growth of the Population of Mainland China* (Washington, D.C.: U.S. Bureau of the Census, International Population Statistics Reports, 1961), Series P-90, No. 15, pp. 11-29, and 65-77. The figure of 583 millions excludes Taiwan (8 millions) and overseas Chinese (12 millions).

[161]See John S. Aird, "Population Growth: Evidence and Interpretation," *The China Quarterly*, No. 7 (1961); S. Chandrasekhar, *China's Population* (Hong Kong: Oxford U. P., 1960).

[162]See Harry G. Shaffer and Jan S. Prybyla (eds.), *From Underdevelopment to Affluence: Western, Soviet, and Chinese Views* (New York: Appleton, 1968), Introduction to Chapter 1, pp. 1-4.

[163]*Ibid.*, Chapter 1, pp. 14-30.

munity in China has been divided on the subject roughly along ideological lines. Those like Ma Yin-chú who urged population control,
never openly admitted that socialist China could one day find herself
unable to feed her people. Population restraint was advocated as a
means of enabling people to live better: it would protect the health
of mothers, take a load off the mind of fathers, and give the children
a better opportunity to get educated. Between 1953 and 1968
China's population probably rose by over 200 million. China is a very
young old country, bursting with energy. There is no need to worry,
therefore, about the number of socialists, but rather about their
quality, health and welfare, and the practicalities of coping with
hundreds of millions of restless youngsters. By 1980, given the estimated present rate of increase (between 2 and 2.5 percent per annum), China's population will be about a billion—roughly the same as
the total population of the world a hundred years ago.[164] Unless the
population tide is stemmed or the stagnation of agricultural output
broken, or both, the "vile, low, loathsome mockery of nature and of
mankind" which Malthus described and Marx denounced may yet
rear its head. At the very least, the problem of urban housing and
education will become well-nigh unmanageable.

The zigzag course of Chinese Communist population policy since
1949 may be summarized as follows.

From 1949 until the results of the census became known to the
leadership (late 1953), the leaders' attitude toward population
growth followed the predictable Marxist ideological pattern: the
more socialists the better for mankind. Legal abortion was abolished,
the importation and manufacture of contraceptives prohibited, and
apprehensions about the population-resource balance were dismissed
as so many counterrevolutionary ulterior motives.

The figure of 583 million mouths must have come as something
of a shock to all but the most incorruptible ideologues. At the National People's Congress of 1954, the thesis of population control
was broached for the first time. Then, toward the end of 1956 and
through 1957 (Chapter 7) an all-out birth control campaign was unleashed—crude and, one would think, offensive to the Chinese
peasant's respect for a large family and to his sense of decorum.
Socialist realism was applied to the discussion of the process of
procreation, illustrations were displayed on village walls. Voluntary
sterilization and abortion were legalized and performed virtually free

[164]See John S. Aird, "Population Growth and Distribution in Mainland
China," in *An Economic Profile of Mainland China, op. cit.*, Vol. II,
pp. 341-401; Frederick Nossal, "How Many Chinese?" *FEER* (February 21,
1963), pp. 353-355; Edwin P. Jones, "China's Population: After the Reapprais-
als," *Problems of Communism* (May-June 1964); Roland Pressat, "The Present
and Future Demographic Situation in China," in UNO, *Proceedings of the World
Population Conference*, Vol. II (New York, 1965).

of charge. What the effect of the campaign was on the rural population is far from clear, but there are indications that it was resented
and achieved little or nothing. It may have had some effect in the
cities, but here again the facts are obscure.

In July 1958 the birth control campaign came abruptly to an
end. "The more people we have," wrote *Hung-ch'i*, "the better,
faster, greater, and more economical will be the results of socialist
construction."[165] Unrestrained populationism was again in vogue,
spurred by a rapidly developing labor shortage. Voices advocating
family planning were not altogether stilled, but they cried in the
wilderness.[166]

Populationism collapsed with the Leap. Beginning in 1962 and
through 1965, official attitude veered toward population control
with a difference. Although contraceptive methods, voluntary sterilization, and legalized abortion (if advised and permitted by a recognized physician—free of charge) were reintroduced, and birth control
clinics reopened, the emphasis was on the postponement of marriage
and the spacing out of children. Students on state scholarships, for
example, were not allowed to marry before graduation. In 1963
clothing rations were raised but the rise was tied to population control. Those marrying after the age of thirty were to receive an extra
ration, while the fourth child in a family was to be allotted no
coupons at all. In Shensi (1964) mothers were given maternity supplies (extra food and clothing rations) for the first two children only.
Young people who intended to marry at the minimum legal age (18
for women and 20 for men—see Chapter 3), encountered opposition
from the labor, youth, or Party organization in the place where they
worked or from residents' associations in the district in which they
lived. Since the marriage registry required recommendations from
such organizations or associations before registering a marriage, opposition from these groups could effectively prevent the marriage
from being legally sanctioned. In his interview with Edgar Snow,
Chou En-lai made specific reference to the need to learn population
control techniques from Japan.[167] Chou also reflected sadly that
there was strong reluctance among men to undergo sterilization since

---

[165] *Hung-ch'i*, No. 9, 1958.

[166] For example, Ma Yin-chú who kept up his own population control
campaign in a series of learned papers through March 1960, at which time he was
silenced. On the fluctuations in official population policy, see John S. Aird,
"Population Policy in Mainland China," *Population Studies* (July 1962),
pp. 38-57.

[167] *The New York Times* (February 3, 1964), p. 8. Cf. Derek Davies, "A
New Census," *FEER* (July 9, 1964), p. 42. The planned parenthood policy was
confirmed by Chou En-lai in an interview granted to Felix Greene and published
by the *NCNA* on February 5, 1964. On the procedure for registering marriages,
see "Regulations Governing Registration of Marriage," *NCNA* (Peking), June 1,
1955 and in *SCMP* No. 1062 (June 4-6, 1955), pp. 32-34.

"others will tell such a man that he had been castrated, that he has become a eunuch." To restrict sterilization to women would be socially undesirable, since it would create "an inequality for women." The press, as one, extolled the wisdom and revolutionary virtue of not marrying before the age of thirty for men and twenty-five for women and of having not more than two children. Symbolic marriage postponement heroes were born. Wang Chuan Chuan, for example, the reluctant bride, put off her marriage three times "for production and study," whereby she "correctly handled the relation between marriage, work, and study," and obtained "very good results in the spare-time engineering university." Since all good things come to those who wait, Wang Chuan Chuan "had gloriously attended the Shanghai Municipal Conference of Advanced Collectives and Advanced Workers in Industry and Other Fields."[168] Those who did not conform to the model were denounced. Thus in a letter to the Peking *Kung-jen Jih-pao*, a young reader complained that "since a number of women apprentice workers in the 17-18 age group in our factory appear to be obsessed with their mating problems most of the time, their technical progress has been badly affected."

The post-1960 population control policy was probably aided by the frequent separation of families consequent on large-scale transfers of urban workers to rural areas and the stern disapproval of extramarital relations. Also, many workers in China's factories lived in dormitories, their wives remaining in the villages. The confusion and relaxation of discipline during the Great Proletarian Cultural Revolution (especially between 1966 and 1968) with millions of youngsters out of school, roaming the countryside and invading the cities, may have put a wrench in the family planning policy, but this is no more than a guess. The second wave of urban-rural transfers (late 1968-69) with its accompanying break-up of families, probably helped the cause of birth control again, but at that stage it was not clear what the official policy on population was, or, for that matter, who the officials were.

It would seem that on this very personal question of marriage and sex, the communist state has come up against a passive resistance, which it does not quite know how to handle—in those moments, at least, when it has a population policy. Where bluster,

---

[168]*Chung-kuo Fu-nu* (May 1, 1963). On the post-1960 family planning policy, see "A Silent Campaign for Birth Control," *China Report* (December 1965-January 1966), pp. 5-6; "Youth and the Problem of Marriage," *URS*, Vol. 28, No. 23, and "Birth Control in Communist China," *ibid.*, Vol. 30, No. 11; Dick Wilson, "Counting the Heads," *FEER* (January 6, 1966), pp. 22-23; Colina MacDougall, "Population Policies," *ibid.* (August 9, 1962), pp. 242-243; Amrit Lal, "China's Population Policy," *China Report* (August 1965), pp. 25-28; "Fewer and Better," *FEER* (October 14, 1965), pp. 47-50.

crudity, and decorous persuasion have failed, a long-term, perhaps very long-term change in the people's outlook may yet succeed. Such a change will probably have to await a more widespread urbanization and a substantial increase in living standards, neither of which is on the horizon at this time.

IX. ATTENUATION OF CLASS STRUGGLE

"The bitter cold of the north wind will soon come to an end," wrote Teng T'o in 1962. "In its stead a warm east wind will blow and a thaw will soon set in on this earth."

A period of readjustment and consolidation is one of emergency. The credibility gap has to be closed, confidence restored, disproportions righted. The old methods of mass mobilization no longer work or work less effectively than before, and recourse has to be had to inducement and persuasion. One has to call on all classes in the nation to join in the task of reconstruction.[169] It is especially important to use the abilities and expertise of men whose enthusiasm for socialism is somewhat below par. Battered and frightened, they have to be brought back into the national fold, reassured and comforted, convinced that their less than perfect socialist awareness is now acceptable to the workers' and peasants' state and to the proletariat's vanguard Party. The proof of acceptable ideological remolding, they must be told, resides in their willingness to harness their talents and their energies to the solution of immediate economic, technical, and scientific problems. The nation of peasants and workers is harsh but forgiving, always ready (in times of emergency) to extend a friendly and helping hand to those of its sons who had erred, or intended to err, or who did not intend to err at all, but were convicted of erring all the same. Since alternatives are exiguous, the prodigal sons, as a rule, respond enthusiastically to the offer of class reconciliation. They know they will regret it later, but when one is born into the wrong class and stuck with congenital ideological deficiency, one lives for the fleeting moment. One is even flattered by the attention, glad to contribute to the common weal, vindicated for a while.

During the period 1961-63, but especially during the emergency of 1961-62, the economic policy makers took the stance of class reconciliation, giving semireformed class enemies the benefit of the

---

[169] The policy swings from class witch hunts to interclass cooperation are explained by Donald S. Carlisle in terms of Marxism-Leninism's "exclusivist" (left) and "inclusivist" (right) impulses. See his "The Changing Soviet Perception of the Development Process in the Afro-Asian World," *Midwest Journal of Political Science*, Vol. VIII (1964), in Harry G. Shaffer and Jan S. Prybyla (eds.), *From Underdevelopment to Affluence: Western, Soviet, and Chinese Views* (New York: Appleton, 1968), pp. 119-122.

doubt. "A high class intellectual," Liu reportedly said, "can replace a hundred worker-peasant cadres. . . . We should not be too particular about them."[170] It has already been shown that the moribund "democratic parties" were once again whipped into shape and told to discharge their united front duties. At first they met in self-examination, breast-beating sessions as was their habit, but soon began circumspectly to offer advice. Intellectuals, less-than-red experts, scientists, and technicians found themselves deluged with satisfying work. Wu Han, the historian and Vice Mayor of Peking, called on the intellectuals "with misgivings in their hearts" to go into action: "This door must be broken through," he wrote (February 25, 1961). Those with little ability to verbalize their thoughts—the middle and once rich peasants—went about their private plots quietly, traded their produce on the newly reopened free markets, and made life hard for the local cadres. Since about 20-30 percent of their income was derived from the plots (including most of their cash income), their attitude to the production teams, brigades, and communes was often quite formalistic—that is, indifferent. Unable for the time being to do anything very much about it, the state reciprocated with more leisure time, spring and harvest festivals, rice transplanting festivals—dancing, boat and horse racing, firecrackers, and other light diversions. Photographers were sent out to the communes to take pictures of "team leaders . . . grinning amidst their outsize melons and trailing vines."[171] Shanghai supplied the countryside with 1,200 kinds of cosmetics, including deluxe sets of 28 pieces such as "Twin Sisters" eau de cologne, "lotions to rid a fair face of freckles," cold cream packed in little oyster shells, and other bourgeois appurtenances.[172] The United Front, not heard from during the Grand Leap, was resurrected and declared to be "a magic weapon of the Chinese people for winning victory."[173] Members of the correct classes were urged to unite with the national bourgeoisie while resolutely struggling against them within the elastic bounds of Mao Tse-tung's truth about contradictions among the people. Mao's "one divides into two" was interpreted by some influential Party ideologues as "two combines into

[170] *Liberation Army Literature and Art* (January 25, 1968) in *URS*, Vol. 50, No. 9 (January 30, 1968), p. 129. According to *Jen-min Jih-pao* of April 23, 1968, Teng Hsiao-p'ing put the same thing more metaphorically: "So long as cats, black or white, can catch mice, they are good cats." *SCMP*, No. 4174 (1968), p. 4.

[171] *Peking Review* (December 1, 1961), p. 16. 1961, it should be added, was one of the agriculturally three "bad years."

[172] *Ibid.*, p. 16.

[173] *Hung-ch'i* (June 1, 1961) in *Peking Review* (June 9, 1961), pp. 13-16, and (June 16, 1961), pp. 17-21. Also *Hung-ch'i*, No. 12 (1961) in *Peking Review* (August 25, 1961), pp. 12-18, and (September 1, 1961), pp. 10-14.

one," thus providing a theoretical justification for a lessening of class tension.[174] Overseas Chinese, especially those with substantial foreign currency savings, were warmly welcomed home. Harried by newly emergent, fiercely nationalistic regimes in southeast Asia, overseas Chinese were given special privileges in their native land, allowed to hire household help, provided with newly built apartments, settled in farming colonies in Kwangtung, Fukien, Kwangsi, and on Hainan Island. Their children were accepted in China's schools more readily and with less discipline than the children of residents without foreign currency savings. Thus encouraged, the reconciled class enemies turned against their benefactors: they waved the red flag but in their hearts, we are told, harbored the white flag of reaction. They had "ulterior motives," as the saying goes, and should not have been trusted in the first place. After the September 1962 Plenary Session of the Central Committee, the watchful and ever vigilant masses began to suspect a plot. Their collective will embodied in their Party's directives, they launched a counteroffensive, a massive socialist education drive based on the premise of class conflict. With each passing day the revolutionary wave mounted, incorrect thoughts were chopped off, and the prodigal sons were once again cast out into the darkness.[175]

The process of revolutionary rectification, sponsored by the Party's renascent left wing, is described in the next chapter. But it was not enough. Better was never quite good enough, there was always the nagging suspicion that plots were being hatched in dark corners and that the people's power was being undermined by monsters and ghosts. The flood of socialist consciousness rose to unprecedented heights until it burst all barriers and overwhelmed the nation and the Party, the people and the government, in the Apocalypse of the Great Proletarian Cultural Revolution (Chapter 11). The

[174] On the "one divides into two" versus the "two combine into one" controversy, see Chapter 10 below.

[175] On November 4, 1966 Liu Shao-ch'i, allegedly the main champion of class reconciliation was burned in effigy at a mass rally of the Chengtu Railway Carriage Wheel Factory. His theory of the extinction of class struggle was denounced time and time again. "Picking up the straw effigy by its nose [Mao Lung-chang, and old worker "who has seen our great leader, Chairman Mao"] said: 'Liu Shao-ch'i, you old scoundrel! You babbled that the capitalists had already been thoroughly remolded. Now open wide your dog's eyes, and see if these capitalists who sneaked into the workers' ranks in our factory have ever stopped carrying out counterattacks against the working class?! . . . This old scoundrel only thought of shutting our ears, blindfolding our eyes, and binding our hands and feet with the theory of the extinction of class struggle, so they could easily restore capitalism.' " *Szechuan People's Radio Station* (November 9, 1968) in *URS*, Vol. 53, No. 20 (December 6, 1968), p. 255. Cf. Merle Goldman, "The Unique 'Blooming and Contending' of 1961-62," *China Quarterly* (January-March 1969), pp. 54-83.

struggle between revolutionaries and alleged counterrevolutionaries was, according to the left, a life-and-death struggle, "a relation of one class oppressing another. . . . There can be no other type of relation, such as a so-called relation of equality, or of peaceful coexistence between exploiting and exploited classes, or of kindness or magnanimity."[176]

[176]"Circular of the Central Committee of the Communist Party of China," May 16, 1966.

10 | The Socialist Education Campaign and the Sino-Soviet Dispute, 1963–65

SOCIALIST EDUCATION

The period 1961-65 was one of sharply defined contrasts: caution on the one hand, fire and brimstone on the other. In economics a mild revisionism dominated the scene, an attempt to calculate and to plan within the bounds of a relatively conservative estimation of what was possible. The result was solid if unspectacular progress, with an occasional flourish (nuclear development, chemical fertilizer production). But all this advance took place against a background of revivalist exhortation, to the accompaniment of much ideological drumming. While the country, like the Peking opera, went through elaborate and carefully executed motions, the Great Leapers in the wings carried on something fierce. By 1963 the offstage noises all but drowned out the onstage dialogue. A year later, the extras invaded the stage, argued with the directors, rewrote the lines, and generally lowered the tone of the proceedings. While the going was rough (1961-62) the theme was reconciliation and empathy, a great collective heaving together: forgive, forget, bloom, and contend. Wearied by the physical and emotional outpourings of the Great Leap, the players were saved by the unobtrusive arrival of reason, stern and unbending, but not given to manic depressive cycles. Nursed back to health, the participants in the great drama of socialist construction were again goaded into exultant pirouettes and bitter class struggle "between the two roads."

Up till 1964, percentage production successes were generally attributed to the new course. Beginning in 1964, however, production comparisons were made with the last pre-Leap year (1957), "the eve of China's great upsurge in national construction," the implication being that the 1961-63 achievements were based on the Great Leap Forward. The period of retrenchment was played down and merged into a single whole, a single stage of Red Banner growth.

The so-called "Socialist Education Campaign" (*ssu ch'ing*) was, as we have noted earlier, designed to prevent the essentially revisionist economic course from taking over the nation's superstructure of ideas, its left-socialist culture, and its ascetic, guerrilla-type politics.[1] Its targets were the young successors to the revolution, the revolution's power holders (bureaucrats, technocrats, Party cadres), the intellectuals, middle, upper-middle, and surviving rich peasants, profession-oriented PLA officers, and others. The negative hero was revisionism and economism: the lure of material rewards. Revisionism, said the campaigners, was attended by a host of hangers-on, devils and monsters with ulterior motives, wily, always ready to inject poison into the minds of the people. The whole drama was orchestrated by American imperialism and its lackeys—the Soviet revisionist clique. Confronted with such cunning class enemies, the people had to be alert, vigilant, and politically impregnable. Otherwise the revolution would be undone. Prepared during the September 1962 Tenth Plenary Session of the Eighth Central Committee (at which Mao Tse-tung urged his colleagues not to forget class struggle) and launched in the spring of 1963, the socialist education campaign gathered momentum with each passing year. In 1966 it merged with the Great Proletarian Cultural Revolution (Chapter 11).[2]

But the educational campaign and its successor the proletarian cultural revolution did not—until 1969—manage to take over the economic base of China's society; the leaping was on the whole confined to the cultural and political superstructure. The economic policies and reforms initiated during the period of readjustment, consolidation, filling-out, and raising standards quietly continued on their course. The description given of them in Chapter 9 applies, in the main, to the years 1961-69. There was of course some disruption, but no economic leap forward or backward, no labor mobilization campaigns comparable to those of 1958-59, no fundamental altera-

[1] Some references: "Recent Developments in Socialist Education," URS, Vol. 34, No. 1 (January 3, 1964), pp. 1-12; "Hong Kong Reports on Socialist Education Movement in Communist China," ibid., Vol. 33, No. 9, (October 29, 1963); Richard Baum and Frederick C. Teiwes, Ssu Ch'ing: The Socialist Education Movement 1962-1966 (Berkeley, Calif.: Center for Chinese Studies, Univ. of California, Research Monographs, No. 2, 1968).

[2] Early warning signals could be detected at the end of 1962 when the hero Lei Feng (see below) emerged from anonymity. The real launching of the campaign can, however, be traced to a series of articles published in Chung-kuo Ching-nien Pao from April 2, 1963 onward. The series, addressed to young people in the countryside, was entitled "Talks on Knowledge of Class Struggle in the Rural Areas" and comprised ten "talks." These recounted the history of socialist agricultural reform, the achievements of the Great Leap and the People's Communes, and emphasized the need for class struggle and the holding aloft of the Three Red Banners. After Mao's September 1962 call never to forget class struggle, "deeply alarmed, the monsters and freaks of all descriptions trembled with fright." Yao Wen-yuan, "On 'Three-Family Village'—The Reactionary Nature of Evening Chats at Yenshan and Notes from Three-Family Village," Wen-hui Pao (Shanghai) (May 10, 1966), in The Great Cultural Revolution in China (Hong Kong: Asia Research Center, 1967), p. 109.

tion in the institutional arrangements of the country's economy. After reciting Mao's thoughts, the peasants went back to their production teams and their private plots, perhaps wiser, perhaps less so. The commune remained very much what it had been under the relatively moderate post-1960 regime. There was some reorganization of enterprise management, but in the last analysis the managers still ran their factories, harassed by revolutionary committees and other politico-managerial formations to be sure, but not replaced.

The socialist education campaign of 1963-65, a prelude to the proletarian cultural revolution, comprised a number of subcampaigns. These form the subject of the present Chapter.

CAMPAIGN AGAINST CLASS RECONCILIATION AS PERMANENT FEATURE OF SOCIALIST SOCIETY

"One Divides into Two" versus the "Two Combines into One" Controversy

The negative hero of this campaign was Yang Hsien-chen, a Party intellectual, full member of the Party's Central Committee since 1959, and Head of the Party's Higher School until September 1961. Yang had spent about fifteen years in the Soviet Union, from the early 1930's till the end of World War II. Except for this blot, his credentials were irreproachable.

Yang's mistake was that he set about reinterpreting Mao Tsetung's thesis on contradictions contained in the famous 1937 essay and in Mao's equally significant paper of 1957. The manner in which this reinterpretation was handled and the conclusions drawn failed to receive Mao's approval. We do not have the original text of Yang's philosophical speculations on contradictions, any more than we have the original text of Mao's dissertation on the same subject in 1957. Yang's formulation was apparently contained in a series of lectures and discussions which Yang conducted at the Party School around 1961. From 1961 until early 1964 the issues raised by Yang's theory were hotly debated at the school, finally finding their way into print in May 1964. At that time the *Kuang Ming Daily* carried an article by two of Yang's students who outlined what Yang had taught them. By November more than 100 articles, letters, and comments on the subject had been published. The issue had been thoroughly aired: Mao's interpretation of Mao's thoughts on the subject emerged victorious. Yang disappeared from view.

Quite apart from the substance of the problem, the fact that heretical views were being disseminated by people in high Party positions and trust, convinced those who saw treason and subversion behind every mulberry bush that they had been right all along: the enemy was always lurking in dark places, revisionism had made inroads into the very vitals of the Party State, and hence the thesis of permanent class struggle and revolutionary vigilance was not only correct but indispensable.

The substance of the problem was this. In his work on contradiction, Mao repeated the Marxist tenet that everything in the world contained contradictions. With this position Yang agreed. Next, according to Mao, the contradiction inherent in things took the form of a division of one into two; the two contradictory aspects of the whole were brought out into the open where they struggled, each tending to assume the nature of the other. The result of this struggle of opposites was the emergence of a new entity—a synthesis—whereupon the dialectical process was repeated. Right struggled with wrong, revolution with counterrevolution, proletarian thought with bourgeois thought, socialism with capitalism, and so on. The essence was permanent struggle, permanent revolution—the Dynamo of History. The unity of opposites was temporary at best; opposites could be united only under certain specific conditions.[3] Thus, for example, one might have to ally oneself with the middle and rich peasants in order to resolve the main contradiction between oneself and the landlords. One might unite temporarily with national capitalists to wipe out foreign, bureaucrat, and comprador capital. One could join up with the Kuomintang to defeat the Japanese aggressor. But the unity of opposites was never permanent. The most important thing about contradiction was the division of one into two, not the subsidiary and ephemeral combining of two into one.

Yang thought otherwise. Admittedly, everything in the world contained contradictions: one split into two. However, the most interesting and significant thing about the two sides of the contradiction was what they had in common rather than what separated them. One had to carefully pick out the elements that each side had in common with the other, relegate the differences to the dustheap of History, and reunite the common aspects of the whole. Unity rather than division was the natural order of things: at their origin all things were one. Divided, things were naturally impelled to seek reunification. The essence of the dialectical process was the quest for unity, a permanent striving for oneness and reconciliation that was neither relative nor conditional. In short, the basic issue in dialectics was that two combine into one, smoothly and without struggle. Such a view of the historical process made life a little richer and more humane, a little less bitter and hectic. One could learn even from the revisionists and the bourgeois, work with them hand in hand without fear of

3 "While the identity of opposites is relative, their struggle is absolute." *Hung-ch'i*, No. 12 (1964).

contagion, so long as one distinguished that which complemented and joined from that which separated and could not be united.

Yang was defeated and his ideas were declared to be noxious weeds of bourgeois and revisionist humanism—counterrevolutionary and antisocialist poison. They were, claimed Yang's opponents, the imitations of the shoddy goods peddled by Soviet revisionists who, like Fedoseyev and Mitin, babbled about "the overcoming of opposites through their uniting," and held that under socialism "dialectical opposites, contradictions, turn into differences, and differences merge into unity."[4] "People have come to realize," wrote one exponent of permanent class struggle, "that class struggle will exist for a long time in socialist society and the struggle to promote proletarian ideas and eliminate bourgeois ideas in the ideological and cultural fields will be protracted, complex, and have its ups and downs. It is, therefore, necessary for us to continue steadfastly to follow the direction pointed out by Chairman Mao Tse-tung and take class struggle and the struggle between the socialist and capitalist roads as the lever in our hard and protracted endeavors if we are to carry the socialist cultural revolution to victory."[5]

"THE WHOLE NATION MUST LEARN FROM THE PLA" CAMPAIGN

As the cracks in the Party and government and the mass organizations widened, the People's Liberation Army with its long revolutionary tradition emerged as the one relatively cohesive element in China's society, especially after the purge of P'eng Te-huai and his group (1959) and their replacement by the left-leaning Lin Piao. The "Learn from the PLA" campaign—a multifaced mass emulation drive—represented the left's growing dependence on the army, which became more marked during the Cultural Revolution (Chapters 11 and 12).

There is an old Chinese saying that the three calamities plaguing people are flood, drought, and soldiery. The communists, as we have shown in Chapter 2, made sure that the last of these plagues should be quickly disposed of. The People's Liberation Army was to become a microcosm of the socialist moral order and of proletarian discipline. Their efforts in that direction yielded impressive results. Re-

---

[4] P.N. Fedoseyev, M. B. Mitin in *Voprosy Filosofii* (Moscow), Nos. 3-4 (1962).

[5] Tien Chu, "Fruits of the Cultural Revolution," *Peking Review* (October 15, 1965), p. 6. Yang's transgression, like that of many other intellectual and cultural workers was that he disseminated "abstract humanitarianism which obliterated class struggle" in the guise of historical and dialectical materialism. See "Debate on Philosophical Concepts," in *The Great Cultural Revolution in China* (Hong Kong: Asia Research Centre, 1967) pp. 21-25; "New Polemic on the Philosophical Front," *Peking Review* (September 11, 1964), pp. 9-12.

peatedly the army was subjected to strictly enforced campaigns for the attainment of the "Four Firsts" (putting men before weapons, ideological work before routine political work, political work before other work, and "living examples" before theoretical, "bookish" knowledge). From 1963 onward, conferences of officers and men on this subject multiplied.

During the First Five Year Plan period, on Soviet advice, the PLA was progressively professionalized along Soviet lines. China's experience in the Korean War convinced many high-ranking officers that the old concept of a "democratic" mass army-cum-militia geared to protracted "people's war" could not stand up to the challenge of modern military technology. In February 1955 a set of "Regulations on the Service of Officers" was adopted. The regulations classified officers according to professional specializations, set up stringent criteria of entry into the officers' corps (geared to professional rather than ideological competence), abolished the "supply system" under which officers and men were paid primarily in food and clothing, with a little pocket money for decorous diversion, and substituted for it wages differentiated according to rank and specialization. In effect, the regulations radically altered the formerly "classless" character of the army so as better to prepare the PLA for modern combat. In the summer of 1955, military conscription was introduced. In the autumn, ranks and military titles were instituted.[6]

Those elements in the Party who watched the growing professionalism of the army with misgivings, launched in 1956 a counterattack in the form of a rectification campaign, the objects of which were to curb the trend toward professionalism in the army and stress the old virtues of military classlessness. The drive picked up momentum during the "Antirightist" campaign of 1957 and reached a peak in 1958. After 1960 the campaign ebbed. In 1961 the bureaucratic moderates, technocrats, and professionals moved in again, this time to reduce the PLA's involvement in economic construction and trim the buildup of the people's militia, which had been stepped up during the Great Leap (autumn 1958) under the "Everyone a Soldier" slogan. In the meantime the left opposition seized the army's commanding heights by replacing P'eng Te-huai with Lin Piao and strengthened Party branches at all PLA levels with its own men. The counterthrust gathered force with the launching of the Socialist Education movement in 1963: Party control over the army ("the Party must command the gun") was confirmed in February by a set of "Regulations Concerning Political Work in the Army." A system of

---

[6] Formerly the army was recruited from "volunteers." The annual call up shortly after the reform was estimated at about 750,000 recruits. See Ellis Joffe, "Contradictions in the Chinese Army," *FEER* (July 11, 1963), pp. 123-126, and Alexandra Close, "Old Model Army," *ibid.* (June 17, 1965), pp. 548-550, 579.

dual command (Party-army), and the participation of the army in economic construction was restored.[7] In 1964 the duration of compulsory military service was extended to four years in the army, five years in the air force and the security forces, and six years in the navy; the "politics in command" slogan was given muscle by the multiplication and intensification of political meetings and indoctrination sessions (not less than 30 percent of the soldiers' training time was to be given to political instruction);[8] the "Learn from the PLA" slogan was launched (at a National Conference of Workers in Industry and Communications held in January) and published in *Jen-min Jih-pao* on February 2; and militia forces were brought back to life. Beginning June 1, 1965, military ranks and insignia were abolished. The 1958 "Officers to the Ranks" movement under which every officer was required to serve one month in the year as an ordinary soldier was revived. In a speech celebrating Army Day (August 1, 1965), Vice Premier Ho Lung made it clear that "all questions of major importance [in the army] must be decided by discussion in the Party committee, except in an emergency when a leader has to make a quick decision." In the perspective of the ideologues, the PLA had once again become the model of socialist organization, spunk, and spirit, which the whole nation was urged to emulate.

The emulation drive assumed three main forms: (i) the nation as a whole was to learn from the army as a whole, (ii) various groups in the nation were to learn from various sections of the army, and (iii) individuals were to learn from individual army heroes (moral Stakhanovs).

The Nation Learns from the Army

Emulate the "Five-Good" Fighters. In PLA terminology the "Five-Good" fighters were good in (1) political thinking (that is, thinking like Mao Tse-tung), (2) military skills, (3) the "Three-Eight Working Style,"[9] (4) fulfilling assigned tasks, and (5) physical training. While the whole nation was to follow this general example, the

[7] The National Defense Council included among its members the Ministers of Water Conservancy, Electric Power, State Farms, Land Reclamation, and Forestry, as well as five of the eight Ministers of Machine Building.

[8] A strident call for putting politics in command of economics and all other work was published by the Party's theoretical organ *Hung-ch'i* on March 31, 1964.

[9] The "Three-Eight Working Style" refers to a concept written in Chinese in three phrases and eight additional characters. The "three" refers to the three mottoes: keep firmly the correct political orientation, maintain an industrious and simple style of work, be flexible in strategy and tactics. The "eight" refers to the eight characters which mean unity, alertness, earnestness, and activity (or liveliness). See "Guarantees of New Victories for Socialism," *Peking Review* (January 8, 1965), p. 22.

"Five-Good" was also reinterpreted for the edification of specific groups in the nation. For example, applied to rural commune members, being "Five-Good" meant (1) observing the laws and decrees of the government, (2) protecting the collective, (3) attending to labor, (4) uniting with, and (5) helping other commune members. In principle various economic sectors, schools, research institutes, and so on, could set their own "Five-Good" objectives of struggle in accordance with their own special conditions.[10] Regular study was often included as a sixth good. One offshoot of the campaign was the *Invite the Five-Good Veterans* movement. Potential guests to a village "Five-Good" unit were (1) veterans of the PLA, (2) veteran Party members,[11] (3) veteran village cadres, (4) labor pace and quality setters, and (5) veteran poor peasants. The movement was part of a "Village Education Campaign" described below.[12]

In January 1966, following a Conference on Political Work in the Army, a campaign was set on foot to *Carry Out [Lin Piao's] Five Points*. These were: (1) creatively study and apply the thought of Mao Tse-tung, (2) carry out the "Four Firsts," (3) send leading cadres to basic levels, (4) promote really fine (i.e., politically mature) commanders to key posts, and (5) train hard to master close range and night combat.[13]

Various Groups in Nation Learn from Sections of Army

The Good Eighth Company on Nanking Road. "To counter bourgeois thought, strengthen collectivism, and oppose revisionism" various strata of people were urged to imitate the PLA company which had played a distinguished role in the liberation of Shanghai, and later patrolled the city's main artery, Nanking Road, successfully resisting the lures of neon signs, chrome, and loose women left behind by the retreating bourgeois-imperialist forces. The company returned to its perilous Nanking Road assignment in the autumn of 1956, in the very midst of surging socialist transformation. It never

[10] See, for example, "Penetratively Launching the Emulation Drive for Five-Good Tax Units and Tax Cadres," *Ta-kung Pao* (Peking), January 25, 1964, p. 2 in *URS*, Vol. 35, No. 4 (April 14, 1964), pp. 53-57.

[11] The leftists in the leadership were concerned about the revolutionary stamina of new Party members. At the 40th anniversary of the founding of the Communist Party of China (June 30, 1961) it was noted that the membership of the Party stood at 17 million, 80 percent of the members having joined after 1949, and 75 percent after 1953.

[12] See "Inviting the Five Veterans to Tell Village Histories and Visiting the Elders to Fill in the Family Records," *Chung-kuo Ching-nien Pao*, July 4, 1963, in *URS*, Vol. 34, No. 1 (January 3, 1964), p. 9. Presumably the five good PLA veterans would recount stories of the Long March, the hardships of Yenan, and the uplifting qualities of self-reliance.

[13] The "Five Points" were made public in November 1965.

once flinched or floundered. The company's men were honest. Up to the end of 1962 they returned 1,390 lost articles to the rightful owners, including 87 fountain pens.[14] They were frugal, saving over 80 percent of their pay. They were concerned about public property, protecting it and fixing it up without charge. They maintained high standards of personal physical and moral cleanliness. Their exploits were immortalized in a play which, however, was withdrawn after a short but successful run because of minor ideological deviations in the script.[15]

The Hard-Bone Sixth Company. The Hard-Bone Sixth Company was ideologically superior to the heroes of Nanking Road. The stories told about it were devoid of the personal touch and little acts of individual kindness associated with the Nanking Road people. By all accounts it was a rather priggish outfit, rigorously unbending in its ideology, proletarian determination, and political probity. It had been steeled in the furnace of revolution and had passed the "Four Hard Tests": psychological readiness for war, good soldierly style, good military technique, and strict political and military discipline.

Other exemplary army units were added to the emulation roster from time to time. In 1966, for example, eleven such models were officially recognized.[16]

Individuals Learn from Individual Army Heroes

The hero Lei Feng. The "Learn from Lei Feng" campaign was launched at the end of 1962, but did not really get in stride till February of the following year.[17] By 1965, having apparently done his job as model of Chairman Mao's good fighters, Lei Feng was relegated into the obscurity whence he had come. Lei Feng, the poor man's Mao, according to his official hagiographers, was born in 1939 into a poor peasant family in Hunan. His brother, when just twelve years old, was driven into a factory where "he toiled like a beast of

[14] These were just about the only hard figures issuing from China at this time.

[15] The play was called *On Guard Beneath the Neon Lights* (Peking: FLP, 1966). It was first staged in 1963. The story of the Nanking Road Company was published in the army's newspaper *Liberation Army Daily* on July 23, 1959 and given nationwide publicity during the Socialist Education campaign four years later. See Henry Lethbridge, "Learn from the Army," *FEER* (September 24, 1964), pp. 564-565, and "Sugar-Coated Bullets," *ibid*. (August 1, 1963), pp. 285-287.

[16] The list may be found in *URS*, Vol. 45, No. 18 (December 2, 1966). Another batch of collective and collectively-minded individual heroes made its appearance in the summer and fall of 1969. See *Peking Review*, issues of July-September 1969.

[17] See, Chen Tung-lei, "Lei Feng: A Fine Example of Chinese Youth," *Evergreen* (Peking), No. 2 (April 1963). Cf. Jacques Marcuse, *The Peking Papers* (New York: Dutton, 1967) Chapter 30; *China Pictorial*, No. 4 (1963).

burden" and finally died of consumption in his mother's arms. The mother thereupon hired herself out as a servant to a landlord, and was in due course raped by her employer. Filled with bitter resentment, she hanged herself. Lei Feng became an orphan (his father had earlier been buried alive by Kuomintang troops and Japanese invaders). Young Lei Feng, filled with hatred of the old society, labored to help his poor relatives by tending the landlord's pigs. The landlord's wife beat him on the hand with the back of an axe.[18] In August 1949 Lei Feng was liberated. Filled with hatred of his oppressors and exploiters, he brought living examples to the public trials of landlords. At one such mass rally "he appeared with his scarred hand, and seizing hold of the landlord's wife, poured-out his long pent-up fury on her. This was the first time he was educated in class struggle." There followed a life devoted to the people and the motherland, Lei Feng at all times "brimming over with energy." He enlisted in the PLA, learned how to throw hand grenades with deadly accuracy, and in 1960 was admitted to the Communist Party. His knowledge of Chairman Mao's works increased with each passing day. He kept a voluminous diary (200,000 words) in which, in the tradition of the world's great diarists, he jotted down every detail of his life, explored every cranny of his conscience. "Comrade Lei Feng, born in hard times but brought up in a happy world, was a product of the Party's cultivation. . . . His examples are ready-made for everyone."[19] It was up to all young men and women to examine themselves daily "with Lei Feng as the mirror,"[20] emulate his devotion to duty, zeal for hard work, uncomplaining endurance to hardships, hatred of the enemy, love for the people, selflessness, Red expertise, firm class stand, frugality (all he left behind him were four copiously annotated volumes of the Chairman's works), and devotion to Mao

---

[18] There is some discrepancy in the various accounts of Lei Feng's mauled left hand. *NCNA* on February 3, 1963 claimed that Lei Feng "was stabbed three times in the left hand because he had beaten the landlord's dogs." Chen Tung-lei says that "one day, when cutting firewood in a hill occupied by a landlord, he was caught by the landlord's wife, who wrested the axe from him and struck him on the hand with its back." Whatever the nature of the fine points of detail, the story of Lei Feng's early years is not so far-fetched. Surely it stirred many unhappy memories of wrongs suffered in that oppressed land. Jack Conder and Richard Hughes, two "old China hands" and former residents of Shanghai, describe the Imperial Japanese Army which swept through China in the 1930's as "the foulest and most merciless fighting machine in modern times. . . . [It] slaughtered and raped and burned blindly and indiscriminately. . . ." "A Place in Time," *FEER* (September 11, 1969), p. 659.

[19] Sung Ting-chang (Secretary of the Communist Youth League, Fushun Municipal Committee, Liaoning Province), "How We Launch 'Learn from Lei Feng' Educational Activities," *Chung-kuo Ching-nien Pao* (February 28, 1963), in *URS*, Vol. 31, No. 24 (June 21, 1963), p. 860.

[20] *Ibid.*, p. 860.

Tse-tung whose writings he read, internalized, and knew by heart. On his tattered copies of the Chairman's works, Lei Feng had written: "I will live and die for the people." Reciprocating, Mao himself had written out in his famous calligraphy the rousing slogan: "Learn from Lei Feng" shortly after the young soldier had died for the people, killed by a falling telegraph pole in helping a fellow army driver back up a truck.[21]

The hero Wang Chieh. "Wang Chieh sacrificed himself for his comrades when a package of explosives was accidentally set off during training." This act of heroism took place on July 14, 1964 "while Wang Chieh, squad leader of a PLA engineering company was helping drill militiamen of the Chang-lou People's Commune."[22] Born in 1942 in Shantung Province into a middle peasant family, "the twenty-three year old martyr was a member of the Communist Youth League. He had been elected a Five-Good soldier for three successive years and twice commended for meritorious service. He became a soldier in the PLA in August 1961 and, as extensive extracts from his 100,000-word diary published in the nation's press show, was a highly conscious revolutionary, typical of the finest of the young generation in China today."[23] Wang's case history was all the more interesting and relevant since he had never been oppressed by class enemies and had to overcome his incorrect class background all by himself. *Jen-min Jih-pao* in its editorial of November 8, 1965 called on all young people of China to emulate Wang Chieh's "lofty spirit of wholehearted dedication to the revolution. . . . Fearing neither hardship nor death is a manifestation of the firmness, the fearless spirit, and the revolutionary heroism of the proletariat. It is a mighty spiritual atom bomb. Once this is in the possession of the revolutionary fighters, they will be ever victorious in the fight against the class enemy both at home and abroad, and in the course of socialist construction. . . . [Wang Chieh] used revolutionary theories as his guide to action and revolutionary heroes as examples to learn from. . . . The word 'revolution' was in his heart: the Chinese revolution and the world revolution."[24] Wang was fearless and noble

[21] The unobtrusive cause of death was given later, after much speculation about it in China and abroad. Some thought Lei Feng had died on the Indian battlefront.

[22] "Emulate Wang Chieh, Great Revolutionary Fighter," *Peking Review* (November 12, 1965), pp. 3-4. Cf. *China Reconstructs* (May 1966), pp. 10-13; *URS*, Vol. 41, No. 17 (November 26, 1965), and Vol. 42, No. 7 (January 25, 1966); *China Pictorial*, No. 3, 1966, pp. 28-31 (excerpts from the diary on pp. 30-31); *The Diary of Wang Chieh* is available in English from the *FLP*.

[23] *Peking Review* (November 12, 1965), p. 3.

[24] Lei Feng would have been very much at home with the Good Eighth Company on Nanking Road. Wang Chieh was a hard-boner of the Sixth Company type.

because he had fully mastered the "Four Points of Study." These were: (1) resolutely carry out Chairman Mao's behests, (2) obey Chairman Mao's instructions and fulfill all tasks assigned by the Party, (3) obey Chairman Mao's behests and keep in close touch with reality, and (4) firmly act upon Chairman Mao's words to serve the interests of the people.

The Chinese press cited concrete examples of the way in which the spirit of Wang Chieh inspired assorted representatives of the masses to selfless effort on behalf of the people. The following is a typical instance. Li Chin-shih, a night-soil collector in Canton was discharging his duties one night, when his flashlight fell into the municipal cesspool. To recover the flashlight which had been issued to him by the commune, Li slid down a bamboo pole into the pool and sank into the contents up to his knees. After splashing around for a while, he found the flashlight and proceeded to climb back up the bamboo pole. On the way, however, he was overcome by the effusions, and dropped back into the pool unconscious. By this time, a group of women night-soil workers had gathered around, lowered a ladder, and raised the alarm. At once, night-soil examiner Lu Ping-ch'ang arrived on the scene, went down the ladder, picked up the unconscious Li, passed him on to the women night-soil workers, and overcome by the vile odors, succumbed and fell into the pool. While the now rescued Li was being resuscitated at the local infirmary, Lu lay in the cesspool unattended because in the confusion everyone had assumed that he had climbed out of the hole and gone to the municipal bathhouse for a shower. Fortunately, at this point, a middle-aged man came riding by on his bicycle, looked down into the pool, and at once realized what was going on. "Without uttering a word" he jumped into the cesspool, fished out Lu, and carried him back to safety. In spite of earnest entreaties of the bystanders, he refused to reveal his name, saying that it was a class job which anyone correctly inspired would do anonymously. Later (because someone slyly took down the registration number of the stranger's bicycle) it was discovered that the rescuer was a Party worker in good standing. Li survived, but Lu died. The man on the bicycle was cited as an example of the Wang Chieh spirit.[25]

While Lei Feng and Wang Chieh were the main heroes, there was also presented for the edification of the masses a cast of lesser characters, most of whom, like Lei Feng and Wang Chieh, were assiduous

25 Yang-ch'eng Wan-pao (Canton), November 24, 1965, p. 1, in URS, Vol. 42, No. 7 (January 25, 1966), p. 94. Other hero-imitators included Li K'ang-po from Hupeh Province ("The Heroic Rescue of a Poor Peasant's Child by Pilot Li K'ang-po," Hung-wei Pao, September 22, 1966, p. 1), and Chin Hsi-cheng from Kirin Province. See URS, Vol. 45, No. 11 (Nov. 8, 1966).

diary-keepers. Such, for example, was *Mai Hsien-teh*,[26] a heroic young sailor who, in spite of head wounds, remained at his post during a three-hour battle with ships of Chiang Kai-shek's "pirate gang." *Haterazim*, an Uighur and a member of the PLA, was drowned while trying to save a young man during a flood. His example showed that China's minority nationalities could do noble deeds too, when filled with the spirit of Mao Tse-tung's teachings. Haterazim had testified to that in a lengthy diary. *Chiao Yu-lu*[27] was a little different from the usual run of Maoist characters: he was a Party functionary of middle age who ruined his health proletarianizing the agriculture of Lankao county. His sacrifice (he died of cancer of the liver) showed that older people in positions of authority could set the right example once they had correctly grasped the "Four Points of Study." With all the talk about cadre corruption, the Party apparat could point to Chiao as a symbol of probity and revolutionary devotion to the people's cause. Chiao's last words on his deathbed were addressed to Chairman Mao; they were words of thanks and of regret that death should cut short a man's service to the people.[28] "Under his pillow there were two books, the *Selected Works of Mao Tse-tung* and Liu Shao-ch'i's *How to Be A Good Communist*."[29] *Wang Chin-hsi*, the "Man of Iron," had the distinction of being one of the few heroes who were also alive at the time of their apotheosis. Wang had been a leading driller in the Yumen oilfields in Kansu Province. He and his team went to the newly discovered Taching field (see below, "Production Campaigns") and "pioneered the battle to tap oil. . . . [He and his class brothers] worked, ate, and slept in the open by the first derrick."[30] His determination and ability to take hardship so moved his landlady that she exclaimed: "You must be a man of iron!" Whereupon the whole nation took up this honorable theme because it proved "that by facing contradictions squarely and overcoming all difficulties in the way, the working class is both the maker and the master of history."[31] At the time of his elevation

[26] *China Pictorial*, No. 4 (1966), pp. 8-11.

[27] See, *URS*, Vol. 42, No. 18 (Mar. 4, 1966); *China Reconstructs* (May 1966), pp. 6-9; *China Pictorial*, No. 5 (1966), pp. 1-4.

[28] In the past few years, according to Canton Radio, about 30,000 Canton youths went to take part in agricultural work in rural areas. "They are full of confidence because they have Chairman Mao's works; and they have Lei Feng, Wang Chieh, Chiao Yu-lu, and Mai Hsien-teh as their models." Canton City Service, April 3, 1966, in *News from Chinese Regional Radio Stations* (March 29-April 4, 1966), p. 29.

[29] *China Pictorial*, No. 5 (1966), p. 4. The last was a bad book to have under one's pillow, but at the time Chiao could not know this.

[30] "The Man of Iron—Wang Chin-hsi," *China Reconstructs* (May 1966), pp. 2-4.

[31] *Ibid.*, p. 2.

to the revolutionary Pantheon, Wang was Deputy Director of the Taching oilfields, on a lecture tour of China. "The workers say," Wang lectured, " 'a loose screw, a rusty part, and a leaking valve are all results of wrong ideology.' "[32] "Chairman Mao teaches us to work like an 'ox' in serving the people. . . . For the sake of the Party and the people, I am willing to be an ox for the rest of my life."[33] "Whereas the semi-mythical Lei Feng," wrote Izvestia on May 19, 1967, "dreamed of becoming 'a little rust-proof screw,' the ideal of Iron Wang is the 'humble ox.' 'All my life I have wanted to be an ox,' he is supposed to have said."[34]

THE VILLAGE SOCIALIST EDUCATION CAMPAIGN

Campaign to Spread Mao Tse-tung's Writings in the Countryside[35]

While Liu Shao-ch'i was promoting the distribution of some 12 million copies of his How To Be A Good Communist, an activity for which he was later to be censured,[36] the works of Mao Tse-tung were not lagging far behind. Mao's books had always been a good seller in Communist China, but the real great leap forward in sales occurred after 1964. In the first seventeen years of communist power (1949-66), ten million sets of Mao's Selected Works were published in Chinese; in 1966 and 1967 a total of 35 million sets was scheduled for publication. However, in 1967 the Central Committee considered the original plan inadequate and ordered 80 million sets to be published in that year alone.[37] In 1965 the Ministry of Culture commanded nine publishing houses to print more than 12 million village compendia of the Chairman's thoughts; over 19,000 sales stations for Mao books were set up. Selected readings from the Chairman's works were put out in special versions addressed to cadres (Collection A)

[32] "Excerpts from Lectures by Man of Iron, Wang Chin-hsi," China Pictorial, No. 7 (1966), p. 13.
[33] Ibid., p. 17. A model for children: Huang Chi-kuang. See Huang Chi-kuang: A Hero To Remember (Peking: FLP, 1965).
[34] Izvestia (Moscow), May 19, 1967, p. 2.
[35] On the development of the Mao cult see, "The Tortuous History of the Cult of Mao," China News Analysis, No. 743 (February 7, 1969).
[36] "[An old worker, an ex-army man and Communist Party member] . . . after he had studied the book on 'self-cultivation' [the original essay on which How To Be A Good Communist was based] in 1962, said he was so poisoned by the idea of slavishness peddled by the author that he blindly believed and faithfully carried out whatever the higher authorities told him, never asking whether it was in accord with Mao Tse-tung's thinking." China Reconstructs, October 1967, p. 50. Cf. the hero Chiao Yu-lu who had the book under his pillow at the time of his death.
[37] Jen-min Jih-pao, August 8, 1966 and Wen-hui Pao (Shanghai), January 22, 1967, in: URS, Vol. 44, No. 17 (August 26, 1966), and ibid., Vol. 46, No. 22 (March 17, 1967). Actually (see Chapter 11 below), 86.4 million sets were produced in 1967.

and peasants, workers, and young intellectuals (Collection B). Translations were made into French, German, Spanish, Portuguese, Greek, Russian, Arabic, Swahili, and Braille.[38]

As the campaign to popularize Mao's thought unfolded, accusations were leveled against "various elements in the Party" ("anti-Party black gangsters"), including the former Deputy Director of the Central Committee's Propaganda Department, Chou Yang, for having allegedly sabotaged the publication and dissemination of the Chairman's works. In 1962, for example, only 50,000 sets of the *Selected Works* were printed, while the subversive *The Dream of the Red Chamber* was issued in 140,000 sets; only 72 tons of paper were used for printing Mao literature, and 7,500 tons in producing other books.[39]

The outpouring in print of Mao's political philosophy and poetry, the countless millions of posters, streamers, pamphlets, and tracts must have put considerable strain on the paper industry. The pulping of Liu's works after 1966 and the destruction of the literature of the "anti-Party black gangsters" must have helped some. Other measures taken by the paper industry to keep up with demand included the promotion of papermaking processes using rice and wheat straw, reed grass, sugar cane bagasse, and bamboo. Wood represented only about 20 percent of the raw materials used in paper manufacture.[40] Between 1958 and 1965 at least a dozen paper mills

[38] Between October 1949 and December 1961, Mao's works had been published in fifteen languages, comprising 253 editions of 4.36 million copies. *URS*, Vol. 42, No. 19 (March 8, 1966); *ibid*., Vol. 42, No. 12 (February 11, 1966); *ibid*., Vol. 43, No. 9 (April 29, 1966). English language versions of Communist Chinese publications prepared by the Foreign Languages Press (*FLP*) in Peking were stylistically and grammatically of a high order, given the difficulties inherent in translation from Chinese and the turgid communist prose. Those collaborating in this venture included Israel and Elsie Epstein, Sidney Rittenberg, Revi Alley, Talitha Gerlach, and Gerald Tannenbaum. For an intimate portrait of these people, see Jacques Marcuse, *The Peking Papers, op. cit.*, Chapter 18, and Neale Hunter, "The Three Hundred Percenters," *FEER* (April 11, 1968), pp. 145-147. Mr. and Mrs. Epstein and another member of the group, M. Shapiro, were detained as spies during the Cultural Revolution.

[39] *Jen-min Jih-pao* (August 8, 1966). Most of the other books, it should be added, were commentaries on, repetitions and elaborations of Mao's philosophy. There were also books on mathematics, physics, chemistry, medicine, etc. One physics student at Peking University, after complaining that in the past examinations had been too difficult (resulting in "some class brothers" being thrown out of school) wrote to the *Kuang-ming Jih-pao* (August 9, 1966, p. 3) that in 1960 he was told that "our principal task is to study. If we do not make a success of our study, we have not accomplished the task which the Party assigned to us. Should we further study Chairman Mao's works, we would neglect our proper work." *URS*, Vol. 44, No. 17 (August 26, 1966), p. 251.

[40] China during this period exported paper to Hong Kong, Cambodia, Ceylon, and Malaysia. The United Nations Food and Agricultural Organization put the 1965 domestic Chinese demand for paper and paperboard at 4.5 million metric tons.

were built. As experts in the field, the Chinese contracted to build a paper mill in Burma.

From the standpoint of the promoters, the results of this massive Mao sales campaign were gratifying if judged by the human products publicized in the press. One such alumnus was described by a correspondent in the Soviet newspaper *Pravda*. His dispatch drew on Chinese sources. Little Tsiu Hun, just six years old (three when the sales campaign got in stride), reared from infancy on "the great ideas of Mao Tse-tung . . . knew by the age of four [1965] who is good and who is bad, was aware of what must be loved and what hated. At five [1966] she began to study the works of Mao Tse-tung, and at six could declaim from memory three articles and more than forty sayings of Mao Tse-tung." To reward her diligence she was taken on a tour of enterprises, educational establishments, and military camps in the city of Tsingtao. While looking at the lathes, grasping revolution and promoting production, she was quoted by a Red Guard newspaper as having remarked that "to think of one's family is dogmatism." On the train from Tsinan to Tsingtao she conducted "propaganda of the ideas of Mao Tse-tung among the passengers," to the general delight and edification of those present. In addition to these proselytizing activities, according to *Pravda*, "foul words about Soviet revisionism" poured from the precocious babe's mouth.[41] "The children hate U.S. imperialism very much for its atrocious aggression against Vietnam. They positively support the uncles and aunts in Vietnam in their struggle against American imperialism for national salvation."[42]

The Rural Cadre Rectification Campaign. Some aspects of this campaign had been described in Chapter 9 (the "Four Withs," "Four Clearances," Peasant Associations). All that needs to be done here is to recall that the campaign was probably intended at first to correct real abuses and clear the channels of communication between the basic levels of Party and government organization and the top planning agencies, but that it soon turned into an ideological remolding drive fueled by the fear of revisionism among peasants and lower level cadres in the setting of economic advance.[43] The net effect of the campaign may well have been to make the cadres lose face vis à vis team and brigade rank and file, and so undermine the moderate

[41] *Pravda* (March 11, 1967). Cf. Jan S. Prybyla, "Moscow, Mao, and the Cultural Revolution," *International Review of History and Political Science* (February 1968), pp. 82-92.

[42] *NCNA* (Canton), News Release, No. 4071, May 26, 1965, in *URS*, Vol. 40, No. 1 (July 2, 1965), p. 6.

[43] Liu Shao-ch'i and his wife were later to be repeatedly accused of having tried to keep the Four Clearances movement within the strict bounds of Party discipline and of substituting "sham" Four Clean-Ups for the real Maoist thing.

bureaucrats' effort to clear the ground for the Third Five Year Plan which was due to begin in 1966.

The "How to Spend the Other Eight [Leisure] Hours" Campaign.[44] Launched in early 1964, the campaign set down the following guidelines for the constructive employment of leisure time by peasants, workers, young and old intellectuals, and soldiers.

1. Study Chairman Mao's works and read his poetry.

2. Engage in physical exercise every day. (See below, Campaign for Mass Revolutionary Swimming.)

3. Exchange stories of revolutionary uplift, study the people's misery under the old regime, and compare it with the happy present.

4. Have heart-to-heart chats with friends.

5. Clean up rooms.

6. Wash clothes.

7. Look after children.

The "Four-Anti" Campaign. A special case of the organized leisure drive was a Four-Anti campaign applicable to such folk festivals as the Lunar New Year (renamed "Spring Festival"), Dragon Boat, Harvest Moon, and the socialist holidays of New Year (January 1), Labor Day (May 1), and the Founding of the People's Republic Day (October 1). The idea was to cut down on time taken away from production, curb profligacy, and elevate socialist consciousness. These objectives were summed up in the blanket slogan of "Change Old Habits and Customs, and Replace Old with New," which was also applied to literature and the performing arts. The Four-Anti drive consisted of:

1. Antihomage to deities (gods and buddhas)—lumped together with witchcraft and fortune-telling into the category of feudal prejudices. The ancient custom of paying homage to deities was to be replaced by the paying of respect to revolutionary families and revolutionary martyrs, gatherings of relatives to discuss production plans and ways of raising labor productivity, and by prompt return to work, bodies and spirits invigorated by the holiday activities.[45]

2. Antigift-giving (including mooncake-giving during the Harvest Festival). The idea here was to stamp out bribery and corruption associated with gift-giving to officials.

3. Antiwaste. This comprised a campaign against gambling, pawnshop borrowing, and bourgeois-inspired stretching-out of holidays.[46] Peddlers, small traders, and vagabonds who during the

---

[44] The seven points listed here were sometimes synthesized in so-called "Three Rules of Leisure."

[45] The campaign was also directed against the spread of burial grounds which took up about 2 percent of the villages' farmland.

[46] See *URS*, Vol. 38, No. 11 (Feb. 5, 1965).

holidays tempted peasants and townfolk into games of chance, were registered and in time denied a license to ply their trade. Fortune-tellers were put to productive work. Pawnshops were forbidden to extend loans except against articles of clothing, which were normally in short supply. The traditional three days subtracted from production by Lunar New Year celebrations were telescoped into one day. Transportation was furnished to the merry-makers by the state. Thousands of official story-tellers (many of them high school pupils) spanned out over the countryside.

Under the slogan of changing old habits and customs and re-placing old with new, a campaign was launched in 1964 to *change street names, the names of retail commercial establishments, food dish names "vulgar and pleasant to the ears of the exploiting classes," and even hair styles.* "If a barber is indifferent," said one report on a convention of Canton barbers, "if he takes the attitude that 'I'll give you the haircut you want, so long as you pay for it,' and trims the hair of the customer in a strange style [asked for by the customer], then he is essentially using his hands to propagate bourgeois ideas."[47]

Campaign to Compile Village Histories. Party cadres, members of the Youth League, college students, high school pupils, and members of the PLA were dispatched to the countryside to help the peasants re-write the history of their families, communes, and villages from the standpoint of class struggle and socialist construction.[48] A typical history would cover past wrongs done to the peasants by landlords and rich peasants, the liberation of the poor from oppression by the land reform and subsequent collectivization, the superiority of the people's communes, and a comparison of past and present living standards made from a proletarian standpoint. The compilation of new village histories and organized storytelling did not always meet with unanimous approval. Some people apparently thought that the whole thing was "irrelevant" and a "digression from proper business."[49]

Rural Social Surveys. The basic research for village histories was done by college students who fanned out over the countryside, equipped with copies of Mao Tse-tung's "Postscript to 'Rural Survey,' " collected data and other information helpful in demonstrating the superiority of the present over the past, of how class antagonism

[47] *Yang-ch'en Wan-pao* (Canton), Dec. 5, 1964, p. 1, in *URS*, Vol. 38, No. 2 (Jan. 5, 1965), p. 21.
[48] In the case of industrial workers, the "Three Histories" (*san-shin*) meant histories of families, workshops, and revolutionary struggles.
[49] *Wen-hui Pao* (Shanghai), Jan. 28, 1966, p. 1, in *URS*, Vol. 43, No. 1 (Apr. 1, 1966), p. 7.

made the present possible, the need for continued struggle and vigilance, and the necessity of smashing revisionism, resurgent capitalism, economism, and pure professionalism. In the words of *Jen-min Jih-pao* (July 1964), the surveys and village histories were to be the products of "organizing reminiscence of bitterness and thinking about sweetness to stimulate class feeling."

Politicalization of Experimental Plots and Demonstration Farms. The establishment of experimental plots and demonstration farms (Chapter 9) while apparently agreed to by all factions within the leadership, was viewed with apprehension by the left insofar as it stressed expertise divorced from politics. Beginning in 1965, this shortcoming began to be made good by a drive to extend the acreage of both plots and farms, "democratize" their management through greater participation of poor and lower middle peasants in research and decision making, and by requiring agronomists, botanists, plant pathologists, and other experts to work in the fields part of the time. Parallel with this effort to "solidify political and technical links" went a renewed denunciation of private subsidiary activity and tighter control over rural markets. The high priority accorded to the development of areas of high and stable yields was questioned, and attention shifted to lands tilled by poor and lower middle peasants. Land itself took on the class status of those who worked it.

CULTURAL REFORM

Reform of the Peking Opera

Under the slogan "Replace Old Things with New" a frontal attack was unleashed on the classical repertoire of the Peking opera. The new society, it was argued, had to have its own artistic forms and creations rather than cling to decadent, philistine art inherited from a feudal past. "The criterion for judging a dramatic group or a theatrical worker," wrote the New China News Agency in a November 1963 release, "is chiefly the extent to which they contribute to the service of proletarian politics." Instructions were issued to replace classical plays with plays on modern revolutionary themes and appropriate pressures were exerted on the bureaucracy of culture to speed up the process. Until 1956 there were only a few plays dealing with contemporary subjects.[50]   In 1960, according to one report,

[50] Exceptions to the classical rule: *Bright Skies* (1954), a three-act drama on how a group of doctors and professors shake off their old views of life and the world, including subservience to American influences; *Chu Yuan* (1942), a five-act tragedy on the struggle of the ancient poet with the tyrants of his day. "A sharp satire, though cast in classical mould," on the political situation in China in the early 1940's; *Steeled in Battles* (1955).

97 percent of all the plays staged were classical. In 1962 classical plays represented 100 percent of all productions.[51] 1964 was declared Year of the Drama, in the course of which the metamorphosis of emperors, kings, generals, prime ministers, talented scholars, and beautiful maidens into workers, poor and lower middle peasants, communist youth leaguers, and People's Liberation Army soldiers was to be accomplished. The process known as "weeding through the old [feudalism, capitalism] to let the new [socialism, communism] emerge" was crowned by the Festival of Peking Opera on Contemporary Themes in June 1964. In his speech at the inaugural celebrations, Lu Ting-yi, then Minister of Culture (but subsequently purged), insisted that "the greatest and most glorious task of revolutionary theatrical artists and workers is to educate the present generation and the coming generations, too, to be revolutionary for ever."[52] "All our literature and art," Mao had written, "are for the masses of the people, and in the first place for the workers, peasants and soldiers; they are created for the workers, peasants and soldiers and are for their use."[53]

From September 1964 through September 1965 many plays, motion pictures, novels, and essays were denounced as "poisonous weeds" and "poisoned arrows." They included the film "The Lin Family Shop" produced in 1959 by the Peking Film Studio. The movie had been adapted by Hsia Yen (Vice Minister of Culture since 1954) from a novel by Shen Yen-ping (alias Mao Tun) written in 1932. Shen was relieved of his post as Minister of Culture in 1964, and Hsia was dismissed in April 1965.[54] The charge leveled against the film and its authors and producers was that it glorified the bourgeoisie, vilified the working class, and preached class cooperation. Similar accusations were made against the motion picture "Early Spring in February" (produced in 1963), "Nightless City," "Laying Siege to the City," "The Press Gang" (produced by the People's Liberation Army Film Studios), "Sisters of the Stage," "Red Sun," "Senior Li, Junior Li, and Old Li" (allegedly showing socialism in a gloomy light), and others. Four stage plays, "Hai Jui Dismissed from Office" (by Wu Han, see Chapter 11), "Hsieh Yao-huan," "Li Hui-niang," and "Hai Jui's Memorial to the Emperor," staged respectively in 1961, 1956, 1961, and 1959, came in for

[51] Frederic Kaplan, "China's Directed Drama," *FEER* (June 25, 1964), pp. 634-636.
[52] *Peking Review* (June 12, 1964). Lu was removed from office in 1966 apparently for his lukewarm support of the cultural renovation movement and for failing to carry out Mao's line on culture contained in his *Talks at the Yenan Forum on Art and Literature* (May 1942). See also *A Great Revolution on the Cultural Front* (Peking: FLP, 1965).
[53] *SW*, Vol. III, p. 84.
[54] At the same time (April 1965) another Deputy Minister of Culture, Chen Huang-mei, was fired.

special criticism during the Cultural Revolution (1966). The main charge was that the plays made "veiled criticism of contemporary people with ancient people" and erred ideologically by eulogizing virtues that were above class.[55]

There was a good deal of opposition to the proletarianization of the performing arts. Shen Hsi-hsia, a local Party secretary, allegedly referred to the new plays as being "crude and immature."[56] Lu Ting-yi noted that in recent years "there again appeared a host of ghost operas and other harmful operas on the Peking opera stage. This happened in Peking and also in other cities. With ghost operas appearing in the cities, the villages, too, had them."[57] Liu Shao-ch'i, it was later alleged, "hurriedly traveled north and south of the Yangtse and mustered the small handful of capitalist roaders within the Party to wage desperate struggle against Chairman Mao's proletarian revolutionary line."[58] It was all part of a joint imperialist-revisionist plot to undo the revolution. "The revisionists," wrote *Hung-ch'i*, "lavishly disseminate the bourgeois theory of human nature, humanitarianism, pacifism, and so on and so forth [and] do their utmost to oppose revolution, attack the dictatorship of the proletariat, and besmirch the socialist system."[59]

The new operas and plays (e.g., "The Red Lantern," "Taking the Bandits' Stronghold," "Raid on the White Tiger Regiment," "Comrade You've Taken the Wrong Path")[60] were excellently staged and produced. Their somewhat limited and repetitious content apparently found grudging acceptance among theatergoers.[61] This was not reflected in box office receipts since most theater tickets were normally bought *en bloc* by factories, enterprises, and communes.

[55] See *The Great Cultural Revolution in China* (Hong Kong: Asia Research Centre, 1967), pp. 194-204, and Chiang Ching, *On the Revolution of Peking Opera* (Peking: *FLP*, 1968).

[56] Kaplan, *op. cit.*

[57] "Reform of Peking Opera," in *The Great Cultural Revolution in China, op. cit.*, p. 29. "Some people have asserted that performing such operas [on contemporary themes] means the withering away and death of Peking opera as an art." *Hung-ch'i*, No. 12 (1964).

[58] *Shanghai Radio* (February 10, 1968), in *URS*, Vol. 50, Nos. 13-14 (February 16, 1968), p. 166.

[59] "A Great Revolution on the Cultural Front," *Hung-ch'i* editorial, No. 12 (1964). One of the themes under attack was filial piety and other "trivialities of home life."

[60] Among the new operas available in English translation are: *Raid on the White Tiger Regiment*, *The Red Lantern*, *Shachiapang*, and *Taking the Bandits' Stronghold*. The fifth major opera is *Sea Harbor*. An important theoretical document on the new art and literature is "Comments on Stanislavsky's 'System,'" *Peking Review* (September 3, 1969), pp. 7-13.

[61] One visitor to China described the content of the new operas as "a succession of smug prigs in communion with eternal verities." John Ashdown, "China's Nursed Grudges," *FEER* (April 22, 1965), p. 209. Cf. *URS*, Vol. 40, No. 13 (August 13, 1965).

Reform of Literature

The campaign for a new socialist literature picked up steam after the May 1963 session of the Third National Committee of the All-China Federation of Literary and Art Circles. The do's and don'ts for revolutionary writers may be summed up as follows:

Do	Don't
Portray positive heroes—the makers of History and masters of the new society.	Portray "middle characters," people from among the masses who are neither good nor bad, and both good and bad; the positive and negative in one; the advanced and the backward combined; the strong and the weak all in one.
Write from the standpoint of Marxist ideology, in line with Mao Tsetung's thinking, i.e., from the standpoint of permanent class struggle, and the struggle against revisionism. Enhance the vigilance of the masses.	Write "honestly." "Honesty" in literature is a bourgeois and revisionist subterfuge intended to befuddle the masses. It is the "honesty" of the bourgeoisie: bourgeois humanism, subjectivism, pragmatism, pacifism, individualism, and pursuit of material gain which negate the existence of classes and class struggles by their appeal to "human nature" and "all mankind."
Depict the prerevolutionary past objectively—that is, in dark colors. Be objective about the socialist present and the communist future, that is paint them in bright colors, with the enthusiasm and boundless optimism which they deserve.	Prettify the past and criticize the temporary difficulties of the present. To do this is to act from ulterior motives, and serve the cause of counterrevolution and reaction.
Identify yourself with the broad masses of laboring people; describe their struggles and achievements in socialist construction and in the fight against revisionism. Eulogise the heroism and collectivism of the masses and the power of correct political thought.	Stand aloof from the laboring people and describe the "fate of the individual," "personal happiness" treated in isolation, and the problems and tribulations of individual people unrelated to class stand.
When necessary, use China's (appropriately edited) noble deeds of the past to enhance the picture of China's happy present and glorious prospects.	In the guise of relating stories of misdeeds from China's past, attack the present socialist order.

As during the Great Leap, essays, poems and novels made to the "do" specifications began to flow from writers' pens in a seemingly endless stream.

Encouragement of Mass Singing of Revolutionary Songs

The movement for cultural reform was, in one sense, part of the campaign to teach people how to spend the other eight (leisure) hours in a correct manner. In 1965 a campaign was launched to make people sing songs on contemporary themes in great numbers and, if possible, in unison. "Through mass singing of revolutionary songs, the people's consciousness could be aroused, and all peoples of the whole world could be united to defeat U.S. imperialism."[62] Of the 156 street committees in Shanghai's Yang-Shu-Pu ward, 122 had formed 164 choruses in 1965, with a membership of over 5,500 singers.[63] There was apparently some skepticism on the subject among the masses: some thought the singing drive was "just for fun." Others suggested that "our cultural level is so low, we can't follow the musical notes accurately—we can't sing." Some objected to it because it meant an "additional burden."[64] All these objections and hesitations were, however, cast aside. "Having unified their thinking and coordinated their relations, the cadres were able to solve the contradiction between mass singing and office work."[65] One of the ways in which the contradiction was resolved was by combining the campaign for mass singing with the campaign for organized news-paper reading.[66] "Since the absolute majority of residents . . . attend newspaper reading sessions at a fixed time and place, the promotion of mass singing has thus been able to find fixed time, place, and personnel to pick up practices. Fixed time: newspaper-reading group members go into singing practices before and after their daily reading sessions; fixed place: singing takes place wherever the newspaper-reading session is held; fixed personnel: newspaper-reading group members are at the same time chorus members."[67] Some of the songs recommended bore the following titles: "Song of the Housing Management Workers," "Read Chairman Mao's Books," "To Wear a Flower, Choose the Large and Red One," "When Striking a Wolf, Use a Club," "All Commune Members are Flowers Facing the Sun," "Chairman Mao is the Sun in Our Hearts," "Chairman Mao's Works are like the Sun," "Listen to the Word of the Party."[68]

[62] *Wen Hui Pao* (Shanghai), November 24, 1965, p. 1, in *URS*, Vol. 42, No. 6 (January 21, 1966), p. 79.

[63] *URS*, Vol. 42, No. 6 (January 21, 1966), p. 77.

[64] *Ibid.*, p. 77.

[65] *Ibid.*, p. 79.

[66] Detailed instructions on how to read a newspaper in an organized way were published on June 1, 1966 in Canton's *Yang-ch'eng Wan-pao* (p. 3). See, *URS*, Vol. 45, No. 4 (October 14, 1966), pp. 53-55.

[67] *Wen Hui Pao* (Shanghai), November 24, 1965, p. 1, in *URS*, Vol. 42, No. 6 (January 21, 1966), p. 82.

[68] *Ibid.*, pp. 80, 86. Other important revolutionary songs (available with score in English): "The East Is Red," "Sailing the Seas Depends on the Helmsman," "Battle Song of the Red Guards."

Campaign for Revolutionary Mass Swimming

In June 1965 Mao Tse-tung, then over seventy, swam three times across the Yangtse River at Wuhan in order to demonstrate to the Chinese public (a) that he was in excellent health, contrary to rumors spread from time to time by various unidentified people with ulterior motives, and (b) that swimming trains the body and strengthens will power, both qualities being important for national defense and socialist construction. To drive these points home, Mao wrote at that time his "magnificent and powerful" poem, "Swimming," to the melody of Shui Tiao Keh Tou.[69] In 1957 he swam the Yangtse for the fourth time. And he said: "People say the Yangtse is a very big river; actually there is nothing to be afraid of as regards its size. Isn't U.S. imperialism very big? It turned out to be nothing when we rebuffed it once."[70] Nine years later, when the Party was again threatened by a handful of persons in authority taking the capitalist road and when U.S. imperialism and Soviet revisionism were more than ever showing their paper tiger teeth, Mao plunged into the Yangtse once more. "Chairman Mao Tse-tung, our great leader, once again had a good swim in the Yangtse River, braving wind and waves, on July 16, 1966. . . . Filled with great joy, the people . . . passed the word: 'Our respected and beloved leader, Chairman Mao, is very healthy.' "[71] Not only that, but the Chairman stayed in the water 65 minutes and covered nearly 15 kilometers. "Even the waters of the river seemed to be smiling that day."[72]

Chairman Mao's example stirred up a wave of enthusiasm among the broad masses of the people who thronged both banks of the river. Five thousand of them plunged in at once, including two hundred juveniles ranging in age from eight to fourteen. "Seeing Chairman Mao, the Young Pioneers enthusiastically shouted: 'Long live Chairman Mao!' Beaming with warm smiles, Chairman Mao waved to them and said in an affectionate tone: 'Greetings, children!' "[73]

[69] "Chairman Mao Swims the Yangtse," *China Pictorial*, No. 10 (1966), p. 1.

[70] *Ibid.*, p. 1.

[71] *Ibid.*, p. 1. The news of Mao's July 16 swim was not released by *NCNA* until July 24. Previous to that there was not one word about it in the entire Chinese press.

[72] *Ibid.* This sits badly with "braving wind and waves," but only in formal logic. Cf. "At his advanced age of 73, Chairman Mao goes through swift currents and breaks huge waves in the boisterous Yangste River . . . moving in and out of dangerous waters as if walking on a broad path. So healthy is our respected and beloved leader, Chairman Mao." *T'i-yu Pao* (Peking), July 25, 1966, p. 2, in *URS*, Vol. 44, No. 13 (August 12, 1966). Compare this with the picture of five heads (including Mao's) above calm waters, all mouths closed, published by *China Pictorial*, No. 10 (1966) to commemorate the event.

[73] *China Pictorial*, No. 10 (1966), p. 4.

The result was that "Nieh Chang-hsin, a swimmer from the militia of the Hankow Thermal Power Plant, became so excited . . . that he forgot he was in the water. Raising both hands he shouted: 'Long live Chairman Mao! Long live Chairman Mao!' He leapt into the air, but soon sank into the river again. He gulped several mouthfuls, but the water [in the industrial city] tasted especially sweet to him."[74]

On July 16, 1967, to commemorate Mao's Yangtse swim, 500,000 Chinese men and women plunged into lakes and rivers and swam many miles. Some carried red banners, others placards bearing quotations from the Chairman's works. All revolutionary sportsmen were urged to always "carry a gun in thought."[75]

CAMPAIGN FOR PART-WORK, PART-STUDY SCHOOLS, AND FOR SPARE-TIME EDUCATION AND RESEARCH

What the Maoists called the "struggle between the two roads" was particularly acute in the field of education where the need to build up a pool of scientific and technical manpower and the concept of meritocracy clashed with the extreme left's impatience, egalitarianism, and faith in the force of correct politics. Concentration on academic subjects, basic research, and on reflection undisturbed by immediate involvement in activism, had to contend with political pressures for the application of study to the solution of practical problems of the hour, the ideological imperative of propelling large numbers of the culturally underprivileged but politically elect up the educational ladder in the shortest possible time, and the Marxist-Maoist vision of eliminating the difference between mental and physical labor. What the Party's left feared above all else was a love affair between awakened young minds and pure science to the exclusion of class content. In China's feverish atmosphere, the two approaches to schooling never quite found a common meeting ground; what could conceivably have been regarded as disagreement on techniques of teaching and curriculum development was, in the event, translated into rigid and mutually exclusive ideological positions; where reason could have arbitrated, emotion divided. Dialogue might have produced an interesting educational experiment; instead, dialectics produced conflict. Disagreement became deviation. Dissent in those circumstances was not seen as legitimate scientific questioning, but as a reprehensible activity stemming from moral turpitude and worse.

[74] *Ibid.*, p. 4. See also *URS*, Vol. 43, No. 20 (June 7, 1966).
[75] "Revolutionizing Athletics," *URS*, Vol. 38, No. 7 (January 22, 1965). The young were said to "learn to swim by swimming, learn to make revolution by making revolution."

The struggle between the two roads expressed itself in: (1) stress on speeding up the educational process and quickly raising the number of students at all levels (Maoist position) versus a more relaxed pace, smaller quantity, greater selectivity, and stress on the quality of scientific and technical training, which included borrowing from abroad (moderate bureaucrat and technocrat position); (2) stress on the amalgamation of study and physical labor versus emphasis on "regular" full-time educational institutions; and (3) stress on mass research by the untutored, versus emphasis on research by qualified experts (Cf. Chapters 3, 6, and 8).[76]

1. Speed and Numbers

Table 10-1 shows the "struggle between the two roads" in terms of enrollments of full-time students in and graduates of institutions of higher learning. When the left was clearly in control, the enrollment figures showed a leap forward. Notice particularly the rise of enrollments in the Great Leap years 1958-60, and the subsequent retrenchment.

Figures for primary and middle school enrollments are available up to 1958. The figures for subsequent years are estimates (Table 10-2).

The number of middle and technical middle school graduates from 1949-50 through 1958-59 was about 7.5 millions. Between 1959-60 and 1964-65 the number of those graduates is estimated at about 22 millions.

During the retrenchment period following the Great Leap and at least until 1964, less time was devoted in the schools to political instruction than during the Leap. According to one report, only one

[76] In a letter to *Jen-min Jih-pao* (July 12, 1966), seven students of China's People's University complained about the university's "criminal defects." These included (1) too much reliance on book knowledge, (2) too little emphasis on practical work and social action, (3) too long periods of study and the turning out of graduates at too low a rate, (4) too much "systematic knowledge," which allegedly gave the students headaches and sapped their physical strength (i.e., too much "irrelevant" material which apparently made the students "more muddle-headed after school than before,") (5) too much stress on preparation for personal careers and future material betterment. The plaintiffs proposed (1) cutting university training time by half, (2) more class struggle, activism, and military training, (3) abolition of "bourgeois academic ranks" such as those of professor, lecturer, instructor, etc., (4) more emphasis on the acquisition of knowledge through doing, (5) the abolition of graduate studies except for workers, poor peasants, and former PLA members who had the "correct" class outlook, (6) change of enrollment criteria, emphasis to be shifted from scholastic records to progressive political outlook and class status plus "a certain educational level," (7) the introduction of class struggle as the main subject of study, and (8) the introduction of Mao Tse-tung's books as the main teaching material. See Harald Munthe-Kaas, "Teaching a Lesson," *FEER* (August 4, 1966), pp. 179-182.

TABLE 10-1
Enrollments of Full-Time Students in and Graduates of
Institutions of Higher Learning

Academic Year	Enrollment (thousands)	Index Number (1949-50=100)	Graduates (thousands)
1956-57	403	344	56
1957-58	441	377	72
1958-59	660	564	70
1959-60	810	692	135
1960-61	955 (900)	816	162
1961-62	819 (850)	700	178 (180)
1962-63	820 (750)	700	200
1963-64	(680)		
1964-65	(700)		

Source: Cheng Chu-yuan, *Scientific and Engineering Manpower in Communist China, 1949-1963* (Washington, D.C., National Science Foundation, 1965), p. 74, Table 6 and p. 78, Table 7. *NCNA* (August 26, 1963). Figures in parentheses are estimates of Edwin F. Jones, "The Emerging Pattern of China's Economic Revolution," in *An Economic Profile of Mainland China, op. cit.,* p. 95, Table IV.

TABLE 10-2
Enrollment of Students in Middle and Primary Schools
(Thousands)

Academic Year	Technical Middle Schools Enrollment	Middle Schools Enrollment	Middle and Technical Middle Schools	Primary Schools
1956-57	812	5,165		63,464
1957-58	778	6,281		64,279
1958-59	1,470	8,520		86,400
1959-60			12,900	90,000
1960-61			15,000	85,000
1961-62			13,100	76,000
1962-63			12,000	73,000
1963-64			11,500	76,000
1964-65			12,500	80,000

Sources: Ten Great Years, p. 192; Edwin F. Jones, "The Emerging Pattern of China's Economic Revolution," in *An Economic Profile of Mainland China, op. cit.,* p. 95, Table IV.

hour per week was spent in this way in the schools; one afternoon per week in research laboratories. Quite frequently political knowledge was to be picked up during the students' vacations.[77]

[77]Colina MacDougall, "The Reds and the Experts," *FEER* (February 6, 1964), pp. 310-312. University students in the natural sciences were required to spend 10 percent of their time in political study. *FEER* (April 1, 1965), pp. 14-18.

The increase in the number of high school and university graduates confronted the regime with an employment problem of no
mean proportions, especially during the 1961-62 recession. Apart
from serving as a means toward raising the young people's socialist
consciousness, the massive transfer of young people to the countryside after 1962 may have been intended by the bureaucratic moderates to help ease the unemployment and underemployment problem
among urban youths. "Socialist economies," wrote one student of
the subject, "gravitate toward unemployment, first in agriculture and
later in industry and the government apparatus. The future alternatives are either to accept overt unemployment in the cities or to
transfer underemployment back to agriculture or to the now growing
tertiary sector."[78] The last of these options is not yet open to China.
The massive transfer of youth to the countryside, while it might have
helped solve the problem in terms of numbers, created—as we have
seen earlier—morale problems among the young whose training, in
most cases, could not be related to the jobs available. In 1967 Chou
En-lai complained that Canton was plagued by 30,000 youngsters
who had taken advantage of the Cultural Revolution's (Chapter 11)
injunction to "exchange revolutionary experiences" and returned to
the city from rural areas to which they had been assigned earlier. The
number of such returnees in Shanghai was estimated at 60,000.[79] A
report from Shanghai in July 1969 indicated that 600,000 jobless
youths were roaming the city's streets.[80]

2. Full-Time versus Part-Work, Part-Study Schools

Part-time and spare-time education should normally complement
rather than compete with full-time schooling. However, in China's
ideological setting the two approaches were frequently cast in terms
of contradictions of the "one divides into two" versus "two combine
into one" type. During the 1963-65 period the steady expansion of
universities, colleges, technicums, and other institutes of higher and
middle-level learning was pushed in the midst of rising clamor for the
development of ideologically superior schools in which mental and
physical labor were combined. Liu's attempt to combine the two
approaches was later denounced as a ploy to sabotage Mao's revolutionary line on education.

[78] Carmela Mesa-Lago, *Unemployment in Socialist Countries: Soviet Union,
East Europe, China, and Cuba* (Ph.D. Dissertation, Cornell University, 1968).
Microfilm copies available from University Microfilms, Ann Arbor, Michigan.
[79] P. H. M. Jones, "The Fights Among the Factions," *FEER* (February 1,
1968), p. 189.
[80] *New York Times*, July 19, 1969, p. 5. The youths, deprived of ration
cards, took to crime. See *ibid.*, April 19, 1970, p. 6 for the Canton experience.

Full-time Education. [81] In 1961-65 full-time primary education usually began at the age of seven and lasted six years. Secondary education comprised three types of institutions: middle schools (lower and upper), the term of study being three years in each division; normal schools for training primary school teachers; and professional middle schools, which provided specialized technical training. Higher educational institutions during this period numbered about 400, of which about 20 were universities, another 20 technical universities, and the remainder specialized institutes (agriculture, medicine, engineering, other disciplines and their various subbranches).

Part-Work, Part-Study Schools. [82] These schools (at primary, secondary, and higher levels) combined academic instruction with on-the-job training. They were first introduced by the communes in 1958 and provided agricultural-type education lasting about three years. After the collapse of the Great Leap this type of schooling was deemphasized for a time, only to be revived in 1964 as part of the Socialist Education movement. [83] At that time a number of regular secondary schools were transformed into part-work, part-study institutions. "Varied in organizational forms, some of these schools were run by factories or enterprises either individually or jointly; some had regular links with factories; some were factory-schools-in-one; some had their own small factories or farms; and some arranged for students to do whatever work was available, having themselves no definite places where physical labor could be done." [84] In the countryside (including pastoral regions) the schools were usually under the direction of the production brigades. [85] The syllabus included political affairs, Chinese language, mathematics, industrial or farming techniques—the last taking up about 40 percent of the syllabus time. In the rural schools the teachers were mostly young people who had completed their high school education and returned to the villages under the back-to-the-soil program. They were paid on the basis of work points calculated according to time spent in field labor and on the basis of teaching time rates.

[81] See C. H. G. Oldham, "Science and Education in China," in Ruth Adams (ed.), *Contemporary China* (New York: Vintage, 1966), pp. 281-317.

[82] See, *URS*, Vol. 42, No. 1 (January 4, 1966); *Peking Review* (January 1, 1965), p. 28.

[83] The revival was announced in a Central Committee instruction "On Two Systems of Education and Two Systems of Labor" (August 1964).

[84] "Part-Work, Part-Study System Shows Its Advantages," *Peking Review*, No. 51 (1965); Patricia Penn, "Productive Studies," *FEER* (January 27, 1966), p. 118. At the end of 1964 there were also 10,000 agricultural secondary technical part-work, part-study schools run by local authorities.

[85] In Inner Mongolia the schools were known as part-graze, part-study.

The schools were given output quotas, like ordinary enterprises, the income from the sale of the products going toward the support of the institutions, primarily the payment of tuition fees. The student body was drawn overwhelmingly from among peasants and workers–especially the poor. Thus, for example, 90 percent of the students graduated from the Kwangtung Agricultural Technical School between 1958 and 1964 were of poor and lower-middle peasant origin. In Kiangsu, 98 percent of the enrollment in rural part-work, part-study schools in 1965 came from that socio-economic group.[86] The graduates were expected to go back to the communes whence they had been recruited, and to serve as production team leaders, seed selection specialists, technicians, and research agronomists. In 1965 the enrollment in rural primary part-work, part-study schools was given as 17 millions.

The combination of study and labor was later applied also to medical colleges. Students were invited into operating rooms and from handing instruments to the surgeons, were progressively allowed to make and close incisions, and finally to perform simple operations, long before graduation. After leaving such part-work, part-study schools, many young doctors were sent to the countryside where they trained commune health workers, or so-called "barefoot doctors."[87] This was the culmination of a campaign to (a) send senior medical teams into rural areas for short periods of duty (1965), (b) persuade urban medical and health personnel to settle permanently in the countryside (1966).[38] There was apparently some opposition to the campaign. K'o Lin, First Secretary of the Party's Central Committee at the Chungshan Medical College in Canton and concurrently President of the college, and his deputy Liu Chih-ming, were accused during the Cultural Revolution (1966) of having "stubbornly opposed" the Provincial Party Central Committee's decision to send 60 percent of the college's 1966 graduates to commune clinics and to transfer one-third of the college's personnel to the countryside. "They put professional studies above politics."[89]   K'o and Liu and their "black gang" allegedly held that the application of Mao's thought to medicine brought about calamities.

[86] Kuang-ming Jih-pao (August 8, 1965), p. 2 and NCNA (August 26, 1964), in URS, Vol. 40, No. 21 (September 10, 1965), p. 301. Cf. this with the educational reforms of 1969, Chapter 12 below.

[87] New York Times (March 2, 1969), p. 15. Cf. Chapter 12.

[88] URS, Vol. 38, No. 23 (March 19, 1965); ibid., Vol. 40, No. 19 (September 3, 1965); ibid., Vol. 43, No. 10 (May 3, 1966). Up to April 1965, 1,520 such teams comprising 18,600 medical workers had toured the rural areas. In 1965 a total of 150,000 doctors, nurses, and other medical and health workers were affected by the campaign.

[89] Yang-ch'eng Wan-pao (Canton), July 3, 1966.

If the following extract is representative of what went on, they may well have been right. "A debate was held at the Public Health Bureau for Hosi District of Tientsin on the question of whether politics can cure disease. Some said during the debate that since Taching oilfields gave prominence to politics, petroleum has been produced. Since Tachai production brigade placed politics in command, grain has been turned out. Thus, logically, doctors who put politics above everything else can cure patients. . . . A woman cadre held that a patient who suffered from consumption could cause his lungs to heal if he were good in ideology and politics, and, therefore, happy. . . . The arguments eventually narrowed down to the point that politics cannot replace skill, but must be given command over skill and Mao Tse-tung's thinking must be given prominence."[90]

The part-work, part-study system was, as we have noted, installed not without opposition. Some of the statements on the subject warned against haste, arguing for "five years experimentation, ten years popularization," the "strengthening of leadership," the making of "unified plans," and for "consolidation of what had been achieved."[91]

Spare-time Education. This type of education was distinct from the part-work, part-study schools. It was China's educational extension intended to give workers and peasants schooling after work. The importance of spare-time education was stressed by a Central Committee directive of September 1, 1958; the intent was not only to help people learn to read and write or aid those who had left school, but to turn out a new type of red and expert, collectively minded individual from among the working people. Spare-time education came to the forefront again after 1963. Schools of this type were reestablished first in the urban areas and organizationally were of two kinds: labor academies and spare-time schools run by factories and enterprises. The first type included the Kiangsi Labor Academy founded in 1958 and (in 1964) comprising one college and 46 secondary schools with a total enrollment of 13,000 students; the Shanghai Spare-Time Industrial University founded in 1960, consisting (by 1964) of 83 classes and 7 branch schools with a total enrollment of 4,500 students attending four- to five-year courses in engineering theory and techniques; and the Kwangtung Spare-Time Science and Technology University in Canton founded in 1958, and having a 1964 enrollment of 1,300.[92] By the end of 1965 each

[90] *Jen-min Jih-pao* (March 23, 1966).
[91] *Peking Review*, No. 51 (1965). Cf. "A Significant Development in China's Educational Revolution," *ibid.*, No. 2 (1966).
[92] *NCNA* (August 30, 1964), and "Spare-Time Studies," *FEER* (September 17, 1964), pp. 505-506.

province had one or two such academies. An example of the second type was the Tientsin Municipal Photographic Film Factory Spare-Time School founded in 1958.[93]

Rural spare-time schools were expanded following a State Council Decision on Elimination of Illiteracy (April 1965). Soon afterwards it was reported that nearly 10 million peasants were enrolled in some 10,000 such schools.[94]

Between 1958 and 1962, according to one estimate, 9 million workers learned to read and write in such schools, more than a million completed the equivalent of primary education, 600,000 finished the equivalent of secondary education, and 15,000 finished higher education.[95]

3. The Campaign for Mass Research

It will be recalled that mass research reached its peak in 1958-59 and that for some years thereafter it was in limbo (Chapters 8 and 9). By 1964 it became fashionable once more, but the calls for everyone—especially the poor peasants and workers—to join the ranks of scientists and innovators, were more muted than before. The establishment of research and development departments in farms and industrial enterprises and of specialized research institutes under the Academy of Agricultural Sciences was, after 1963, accompanied by politically motivated mass and spare-time research by workers and peasants on whom the left relied to keep a sharp look-out for any signs of wayward tendencies on the part of the specialists.[96]

PRODUCTION CAMPAIGNS

The common denominator of the Maoist production campaigns after 1964 was (a) renewed stress on quantity of output, and (b) the contention that both quantity and quality were functions of "thinking on a high plane," that is, according to Mao's precepts.

"Quantity," wrote *Hung-ch'i*, "is to be increased in accordance with the standard of quality. [Note the formal adherence to the quality imperative of the new economic policy. Now, however, comes a change in substance] . . . . Where does the high standard of quality come from? It stems from thinking on a high plane. . . . What

[93] The first three labor academies were the Kiangsi Labor Academy already referred to and one academy each in Kirin Province and Sinkiang. See *URS* Vol. 38, No. 10 (February 2, 1965); *ibid.*, Vol. 40, No. 7 (July 23, 1965); *ibid.*, Vol. 45, No. 17 (November 29, 1966).
[94] *NCNA* (February 12, 1965). Cf. *URS*, Vol. 38, No. 21 (March 12, 1965).
[95] C. H. G. Oldham, *op. cit.*, p. 286.
[96] "Agricultural Scientific Research Becoming a Mass Movement in China," *NCNA* (Canton), March 10, 1964; *China Reconstructs*, April 1964.

is thinking on a high plane? It is to hold high the great red banner of Mao Tse-tung's thinking. . . . On the question of raising product quality, our socialist enterprises should take a path totally different from that followed by modern revisionist enterprises. . . . Material incentive is the arch-enemy of quality. The more bonuses and high wages are used as incentives, the more rampant will fraudulent practises become. As a result, product quality will drop. . . . Once man's thinking has undergone changes, he is able to find all the answers. And only then can he create miracles."[97]   There is in this a combination of belief in the corruptibility of man through creature comforts (especially of man in position of power over others) and an ardent faith in man's ability to redeem himself through correct thought allied to labor that is free of personal material aspirations. Quality checks introduced by the new course in 1961-63 (Chapter 9) were replaced in 1964 by the single injunction to learn from the PLA and observe the "Four Strict": strictly carry out instructions of higher levels, fulfill production assignments, be concerned about the quality of products, follow the requirements of various types of work.[98]

The philosophy that economics is the handmaid of politics, and politics is summed up in the thought of Mao, did not go down well with everybody. In the Hengyang Special District some cadres thought that "shouting about politics was useless; production was the real thing." Others said: "production cannot wait one night, but politics can wait a year." The correct answer to this incorrect formulation was that "the theory that 'politics is good if production is good' is actually substituting the production struggle for the class struggle, and covering up the essence of the problem with superficialities. Production must always be based on politics."[99]

The two most important campaigns under this heading were: *Agriculture Learns from Tachai* and *Industry Learns from Taching.*

The village of Tachai (a production brigade at the time of the

---

[97] Su Hsing, "The High Standard of Quality Stems from Thinking on a High Plane," *Hung-ch'i* (January 1, 1966), in *SCMM*, No. 509 (January 31, 1966), pp. 29-32.

[98] *Yang-Ch'eng Wan-pao* (Canton), March 15, 1964, in *URS*, Vol. 40, No. 4 (July 13, 1965).

[99] *Changsha Radio*, April 4, 1966, in *News from Chinese Regional Radio Stations* (March 29-April 4, 1966), p. 12. Cf. the tribulations of "some cadres" in the Chengtung brigade of Hsiatu commune who after being praised for having corrected the tendency of gripping production only and neglecting politics, "thought they would give political and ideological work a break." Immediately work attendance dropped sharply. "There were more who went to the fairs or stayed at home to do housework." Right away the brigade Party cell realized what was amiss. It organized the peasants to study Chairman Mao's works further. As a result "spring farming was pressed forward to a new upsurge." *Hofei Radio* (April 4, 1966), in *ibid.*, p. 2.

campaign) was situated in the Taihang Mountains, Shansi Province. Its population was 83 families. In 1956 the villagers decided to wage a struggle against nature to overcome poverty. "They pledged: 'We'll work for three, five, or even ten years to transform these hills. And if this is still not enough, following generations can continue until the job is finished. We are under the leadership of the Party, we have collective resources, land, rocks, and manpower at our disposal."[100] Using simple tools, they cut into the mountains to build terraces and retaining walls, carried good soil from some distance, raised grain output year after year, and built a 70-kilometer long canal in five years. In 1963 their fields were destroyed by floods. They began all over again. They had high ambition coupled with dauntless revolutionary enthusiasm and perseverance; above all, they were determined to rely on their own strength. When their labors were ravaged by floods, they refused to accept state relief funds. In 1965 their story came to the notice of the authorities; soon the whole country was learning from Tachai. Advanced Tachai-type communes, production brigades, and teams sprang up everywhere; fifty-five Tachai-type farming units were featured at a special exhibition in Peking. Thousands of peasant representatives visited the terraced fields and vowed to catch up with and overtake Tachai. "If the whole country learns from Tachai, what should Tachai do? . . . Tachai must learn from the rest of the country! The question itself is good; the answer even better."[101] To the spirit of perseverance and self-reliance was added the quality of modesty. The campaign lasted about a year.

The Taching oilfield was developed between 1960 and 1963. "The workers and staff at Taching, guided by the great red banner of Mao Tse-tung's thinking, studied Chairman Mao's writings and creatively applied his ideas in their life and work. As a result they burst the fetters of foreign conventions and blazed a path for Chinese methods in prospecting, developing, construction, and production."[102] In 1965 and the following year, Taching gave rise to an enormous literary output; at no time, however, was the field's exact

---

[100] Chin Chi, "Flowering of the Tachai Spirit," *China Pictorial*, No. 2 (1966), pp. 1-4. Cf. *China Reconstructs* (March 1966), pp. 2-11; *URS*, Vol. 38, No. 15 (February 19, 1965).

[101] Chin Nung, "Tachai Learns from the Rest of the Country," *China Pictorial*, No. 3 (1966), pp. 14-17.

[102] *China Pictorial*, No. 7 (1966). Special issue on the Taching oilfield. Taching was also ideologically interesting because it engaged in agricultural production and side occupations thus "reducing the difference between town and country," or, more comprehensively, eliminating the "Three Discriminations"— between town and country, mental and manual labor, factory work and farm work. Japanese correspondents in China (1966-67) reported that the Taching commune had a population of about 200,000. Workers' families cultivated vast tracts of rice and vegetables in order to be self-sufficient in food. See Robert Trumbull (ed.), *This Is Communist China, op. cit.*, p. 128.

location revealed.[103] Like Tachai, the Taching commune was made into a symbol of man's capacity to harness nature to his ends with only an idea, some simple tools, and class resolve to sustain him. The symbol flattered native inventiveness, rejected subservience to foreign models, and scorned faint-heartedness. Taching grew and prospered while all around retrenched, consolidated, readjusted, and filled-out. A refinery was built in eighteen months and oil gushed because the Taching men of iron "relied on Chairman Mao's *On Practice* and *On Contradiction*, and on the concept of one divides into two."[104] Moscow's *Izvestia* put it this way: "The workers bring the state quite large revenues and receive almost nothing in return. In other words, they work under conditions of maximally high returns at minimal wages"[105]—almost, one is inclined to add, as under Stalin in Russia.

The unspectacular, unheroic, often plodding way in which the nation's economic affairs were conducted during the early years (1961-63) of the new course was gradually replaced by ringing phrases and heroic gestures. Below the surface, as we have noted, the change was probably less significant than the press reports, speeches, and parades would lead one to believe. In September 1966 a campaign was launched to "Learn from Drilling Team No. 32111." The men of 32111 were engaged in a test to shut in pressure in a gas well when a seamless pipe on the side of the well burst, causing an explosion and a raging fire in which six of the men died and twenty-one were seriously burned.[106] The heroism, selflessness, and dedication of the team members became the subject of a nationwide emulation drive. An apprentice worker of the 32111 testified to the courage instilled in him in a moment of hesitation by a quotation from the Chairman's treasury of revolutionary wisdom: "At the critical moment, Chairman Mao gave me his instruction, as if talking to me intimately: 'Young fellow, charge! Don't fear death!' "[107] He charged, got badly burned, but accomplished his task.

[103] "The precise location of Taching has not yet appeared on the maps." *Izvestia* (Moscow), May 19, 1967, p. 2.

[104] *China Pictorial*, No. 7 (1966), p. 8.

[105] "What Is the Spirit of Taching?" *Izvestia* (May 19, 1967), p. 2. *Izvestia* continued: "As is known [the Maoists] are striving to free themselves completely from concern for raising the living standard of the popular masses and their everyday life, so that the economized funds may be used to achieve their great-power, nationalistic aims."

[106] *Jen-min Jih-pao* (September 26, 1966), p. 1

[107] *Kung-jen Jih-pao* (October 15, 1966), p. 3, in *URS*, Vol. 45, No. 14 (November 18, 1966). Cf., *China Reconstructs* (January 1967), pp. 26-31 and *China Pictorial*, No. 1 (1967), pp. 14-23. "Hsu Kuang-yi . . . was felled by the poisonous gas fumes after battling for two minutes. . . . The moment Hsu came to, he jumped up and again dashed to the fire site. He seemed to have heard the loving voice of our great leader, Chairman Mao: 'Young fellow, charge! Be resolute and unafraid of sacrifice, and you will surmount every difficulty to win victory!' Hu Teh-ping also fainted at this time." *China Pictorial, loc. cit.*, p. 19.

THE SINO-SOVIET DISPUTE

The quarrel between China and the Soviet Union was, as we have seen earlier (Chapters 3, 8) due to many diverse causes, some of which went far back into the history of Imperial China and Russia, others into the early years of the communist movement in China, while others still, were of much more recent origin. For a while the dispute was carried on by proxy (China employing Albania to do the name-calling),[108] in the third person (that is mainly *via* Yugoslavia described by the Chinese as the very embodiment of revisionism, but also by reference to "some people" who were revisionist or dogmatist, as the case may be), and it was cast in fuzzy metaphysics. Between 1963 and 1965, however, the noise level rose sharply, the issues were more clearly defined, and the dispute shifted from ideological to more mundane issues of interstate relations. To an important degree, the differences between China and the USSR reflected the developmental age gap separating the two communist powers; to some extent they were symptomatic of diverse cultural backgrounds which a commonly shared but differently interpreted Marxist faith was incapable of reconciling.

In an article entitled "Why Khrushchev Fell" published editorially by *Hung-ch'i* on November 21, 1964, the Chinese summarized the reasons which, as they saw it, caused the downfall of the Soviet leader and which by implication were at the core of the Sino-Soviet dispute.[109] Some of these issues are taken up in greater detail below. A number of the ideological differences have been analyzed in earlier Chapters.

The various "bad things" which Khrushchev ("this buffoon on the contemporary political stage") had committed were summed up in his vain opposition to the irresistible forces of history discovered and defined by Marx and Lenin. "This historical trend," the Chinese wrote, "is an objective law which operates independently of man's will and it is irresistible."

Specifically, Khrushchev (and, as it transpired, his successors too):

1. "Railed at Stalin. . . . In opposing Stalin he opposed Marxism-Leninism."

2. "Sought all round cooperation with U.S. imperialism," e.g., in Cuba where his policy combined adventurism with capitulationism (see below).

108 See, William E. Griffith, *Albania and the Sino-Soviet Rift* (Cambridge, Mass.: MIT Press, 1963); Jan S. Prybyla, "Albania's Economic Vassalage," *East Europe* (January 1967), pp. 9-14.
109 *Peking Review* (November 27, 1964), pp. 6-9.

3. Concluded the nuclear test ban treaty—"a pure swindle" (see below).

4. Expounded the theory of the parliamentary road to socialism in capitalist countries.[110]

5. Expounded the theory and practiced the policy of peaceful coexistence of countries with different social systems and sabotaged the national liberation movements. For example, in the United Nations (elsewhere described by the Chinese as a "paper tiger" at the service of U.S. imperialism) he ordered his delegation to vote for the dispatch of forces to the Congo; opposed Algeria's revolutionary struggle by declaring it to be an internal affair of France; stood aloof from the events in the Gulf of Bac Bo (the Tonkin Gulf incident).

6. Cooperated with Tito, the "lackey of U.S. imperialism," "this renegade."

7. Declared Albania to be his "sworn enemy."

8. Harbored an inveterate hatred for the Communist Party of China and tried to subvert socialist China in the following ways:

(a) by "perfidiously" tearing up several hundred agreements and contracts and arbitrarily withdrawing more than one thousand Soviet experts working in China (see Chapter 8);

(b) by engineering border disputes with China as well as subversive activities in Sinkiang (see below);

(c) by backing the "Indian reactionaries" with military aid (see below).

9. Encroached on the independence and sovereignty of fraternal countries under the cover of "mutual economic assistance," which in effect meant that the Soviet Union opposed the independent development of fraternal economies, trying to make these economies into sources of the Soviet Union's raw materials imports and customers for Soviet-made finished products. His model was the capitalist Common Market, which he tried to imitate in the form of the Council for Mutual Economic Assistance (COMECON).[111]

10. Carried on subversive activities against fraternal Communist Parties by:

(a) openly attacking these Parties at Central Committee sessions and Party congresses;

(b) buying over "political degenerates, renegades, and turncoats."

[110] Jan S. Prybyla, "Communism and the Democratic Parliament: A Study in Infiltration Theory and Tactics," *Quarterly Review* (London), January 1957, pp. 72-84.

[111] The Soviet answer to China's oft-reiterated contention that the Council for Mutual Economic Assistance was a tool of Soviet imperialism, was to include Outer Mongolia in the Council in 1962. On COMECON, see Michael Kaser, *COMECON: Integration Problems of the Planned Economies* (New York: Oxford U. P., 1965).

11. Violated the principle of unanimity through consultation among fraternal Parties by:

(a) playing the "patriarchal father Party" role;

(b) convening "illegal international meetings of fraternal Parties to create an open split" (see below).

12. Implemented a series of revisionist policies leading back to capitalism. These included:

(a) abolishing the dictatorship of the proletariat in the name of the "State of the whole people,"[112]

(b) alteration of the proletarian character of the Communist Party of the Soviet Union in the name of the principle of the "Party of the whole people;"[113]

(c) alteration of the proletarian character of the CPSU through its reorganization into "agricultural" and "industrial" branches (this reform was later rescinded by Brezhnev and Kosygin);

(d) practising "a thousand and one ways to switch back to capitalism" under the cover of "full-scale communist construction;"

(e) blind direction of Soviet agriculture and industry which caused "great havoc."

Khrushchev thought, the Chinese alleged, that he was "the hero making history." History proved him to have been wrong.

TERRITORIAL DISPUTES

It was mentioned in Chapter 3 that there exist a number of outstanding territorial issues between China and the Soviet Union. Most of these had been put in cold storage during 1949-60, but they remained at all times politically explosive. China's unease about her minority subjects, especially those inhabiting regions adjacent to the USSR, led to a policy of both forced Sinification and gentle courting, which did not always sit well with those wooed or Hanicized. During the Hundred Flowers interlude of 1957, anti-Han demonstrations erupted in Sinkiang. Peking's dispatch of large numbers of ethnic Chinese to Sinkiang, Inner Mongolia, and Tibet was resented by the native inhabitants: in 1964, for example, the ratio of ethnic Chinese to Kazakhs in Sinkiang was 3:4, and the inflow of Hans continued unabated. By then the natives of Inner Mongolia were outnumbered by immigrant Hans.

In the first six months of 1962 the Soviet Union and China

112 See, "The Program of the Communist Party of the Soviet Union," Adopted by the XXII Party Congress, October-November 1961, in Dan N. Jacobs (ed.), *The New Communist Manifesto and Related Documents* (New York: Harper, 1962), pp. 215-245.

113 *Ibid.*

exchanged harshly worded notes about frontier intrusions, especially in Sinkiang and next door Soviet Kazakhstan. The Sinkiang border had been demarcated in 1860 by the Treaty of Peking at which time the Russians extracted substantial territorial concessions from China both there and in eastern Siberia. More concessions by China followed in 1864. In 1871 the Russians occupied the whole Ili River valley and ten years later incorporated part of the territory by the Treaty of Ili.[114] In 1962 and 1963, as relations between China and the Soviet Union deteriorated, Kazakh uprisings took place in Sinkiang. The September 1963 revolt was bloody. According to Peking, the USSR had "used its organs and personnel in Sinkiang to carry out large-scale subversive activities in the Ili region and enticed and coerced several tens of thousands of Chinese citizens into going to the Soviet Union." The Soviets refused to repatriate the refugees on humanitarian grounds. In reprisal, the Chinese ordered all Soviet consulates in Sinkiang closed. Taking a cue from communist practice in Eastern Europe, the Chinese cleared a broad zone on the frontier to prevent further escapes. Disturbances, however, continued on the Chinese side of the plowed-up strip. Soviet radio stations in Alma Ata, Tashkent, and Frunze broadcast to their Kazakh and Uighur brothers across the border, fostering, the Chinese alleged, secessionist sentiments. In its letter of February 29, 1964, the Chinese Communist Party's Central Committee accused the Soviets of "frequent breaches of the status quo on the border, occupation of Chinese territory, and border provocations." More trouble erupted in Sinkiang in September 1964. In answer to Chinese accusations, the Soviets cited over 5,000 frontier violations allegedly perpetrated by the Chinese in 1962 alone, and charged that in a number of instances the Chinese attempted "to develop some parts of Soviet territory without permission." In February 1964 Soviet and Chinese representatives met in Peking to discuss frontier problems. The talks were held in secret. Later it was learned that they broke down because, as the Soviets put it, "the Chinese representatives showed . . . that the achievement of agreement was not among the plans of the Chinese side. The Chinese delegation tried to question the historically established state frontiers that had been sealed by treaties."[115] The talks were to be resumed on October 15 (the day after Khrushchev's fall and one day before China's first nuclear explosion), but the Chinese refused to take part in them, despite repeated Soviet reminders.

[114] The Soviet-Chinese border in the Far East was given legal status by the treaties of Aigun (1858), Tientsin (1858), and Peking (1860).

[115] Soviet Note to China, March 29, 1969, in *New York Times* (March 31, 1969), p. 16. © 1969 by The New York Times Company. Reprinted by permission.

Instead, according to the Soviets, the Chinese began to build air-fields, roads, barracks, and military depots along the 4,150-mile Sino-Soviet border, glorified the "aggressive raids of Genghis Khan" who was declared an emperor of China, lauded the Manchu emperor Kang-hsi and "Chinese emperors and feudals who pursued a policy of conquests." At the same time they denounced as unequal the treaties imposed on them by Russian czars and feudals. Chinese school texts and other publications were revised, and maps were published "in which vast territories of the Soviet Union were marked as Chinese areas." On certain maps, depicting China at the pinnacle of power, "the border line was drawn in such a way as to incorporate within China, lands in which almost all peoples of Asia and even many European peoples now live."[116]

On September 2, 1964 *Pravda* reacted sharply to Mao's statement made a few months earlier to a visiting group of socialist members of the Japanese Diet, to the effect that the Russians had "grabbed too much territory" not only from China, but from Japan as well (southern Kuriles in 1945). And what, asked Mao, were the Soviets doing in places seized from the East Europeans in 1945? Such talk, *Pravda* argued, was not only unfraternal, but could have "terribly dangerous consequences." China's "provocative calls for frontier re-vision" covered the Soviet Pacific coast, much of eastern Siberia, Kazakhstan, and Kirghizia, or about 1.5 million square kilometers of Soviet territory. Moreover, said *Pravda*, "they [the Chinese] would like to deprive Mongolia [Outer Mongolia] of its independence and make it a Chinese province." In 1964 Chinese guerrillas reportedly infiltrated the Gobi Desert of the Mongolian People's Republic. To forestall any surprises, the leadership of the Communist Party of the People's Republic of Mongolia was quickly cleansed of pro-Chinese elements, and Chinese construction workers in Ulan Bator and along the 23-kilometer highway from Ulan Bator to the Nalaikha coalmines were packed off home (1964) with gifts and flowers.[117] In a series of articles published by the Soviet press, the Chinese Party and government were accused of persecuting national minorities and of running a chain of corrective labor camps in which, among other things, opium poppies were cultivated and smuggled into southeast Asia (cf. Chapter 3). The foreign exchange so obtained (about $500 million) was used, the Soviets said, for "anti-Soviet doping."

116 *Ibid.*, p. 16. © 1969 by The New York Times Company. Reprinted by permission.
117 See L. Delyusin, "Meetings in Mongolia," *Pravda* (March 19, 1965), p. 5. Ever since December 1964, a Mongolian "anti-Party faction . . . tried to cast a shadow on the correct domestic and foreign policies of the [Mongolian] Party and government." *Ibid.* See also "Chinese Personnel Return from Mongolia," *Peking Review* (June 12, 1964), p. 25.

During the Cultural Revolution (Chapter 11) the Chinese were specifically accused by the Soviets of persecuting Tibetans, Uighurs, Kazakhs, Mongols, Chuang, and others, forcing people to eat pork in clear violation of their religious beliefs, gerrymandering ethnic borders, forcing young girls to marry Chinese on the pain of death, and so on. "In their attempt to Sinicize every type of 'tribe,' " wrote *Izvestia* (April 2, 1967), the Maoists "have in point of fact continued the assimilation policy pursued by the Kuomintang." The allegedly rough handling of minorities was linked by Soviet commentators to the Maoists' racism and anti-Sovietism. "Preaching of racial hatred toward 'whites,' " *Izvestia* went on, "which Peking addresses to the Afro-Asian peoples, does not hinder the Maoists from following a policy of intensive discrimination against the fifty-odd non-'white' peoples populating China." Transfers of population from minority areas, the influx of millions of Chinese, the driving of local inhabitants into "lifeless desert," the desecration of mosques, were cited as examples of Mao's "great power" policy and his flaunting of Leninist standards (*Kommunist*, May 1967).[118]

Armed clashes between Soviet border guards and Chinese forces took place on several occasions in 1969. They were given wide publicity in the Soviet and Chinese press.

THE SINO-INDIAN BORDER WAR

On October 20, 1962, after a lengthy period of mounting tension and mutual recrimination,[119] Chinese armies in the North East Frontier Agency (NEFA) and in Ladakh moved against Indian forces, and in a month of fighting drove the Indians to the foothills of Assam. Badly mauled and outflanked, the Indian armies retreated in dis-

---

[118] Some useful references: Daniel Tretiak, "China's New Frontier Trouble," *FEER* (October 10, 1963), pp. 60-62; P. H. M. Jones, "Sinkiang and the Split," *ibid.* (July 23, 1964), pp. 159-160; "Drums Along the Amur," *ibid.* (October 15, 1964), pp. 137-140; "Moscow and the Mongols," *ibid.* (February 17, 1966), pp. 326-328; Jan S. Prybyla, "Unsettled Issues in the Sino-Soviet Dispute," *The Virginia Quarterly Review* (Autumn 1965), pp. 510-524; "The Sino-Soviet Quarrel: A Balance Sheet Since Khrushchev," *Bulletin*, Institute for the Study of the USSR (September 1965), pp. 27-34. The problem of the Amur River Basin was also the subject of bitter disagreement between the two former allies. Joint action by the two countries is needed if the floods which devastate large areas of Soviet territory are to be controlled, and the basin's hydroelectric power potential put to use. The Chinese so far have refused to cooperate, in spite of an ambitious joint exploration and development project drawn up in 1956, and the treaties of 1950 and 1957 which aimed at regulating shipping on the river. On April 19, 1966 China—without advanced warning—promulgated a series of highly restrictive regulations governing foreign ships on border rivers. See Harald Munthe-Kaas, "Amur Amendments," *FEER* (May 26, 1966), pp. 355-358.

[119] See, William E. Griffith, *The Sino-Soviet Rift* (Cambridge, Mass.: MIT Press, 1964), pp. 5-8, and Chapter 4, pp. 56-59.

array, leaving the road to Calcutta open to the Chinese. The invasion probably took place without Moscow's being informed of it beforehand. At first the Soviets showed signs of indecision. Since 1955 Soviet foreign policy had been oriented toward courting India and establishing a "zone of peace" with India as the kingpin. The neutral stance taken by Moscow in October angered both Delhi and Peking; by November 5, in the wake of the Cuban missile crisis, the Soviet position had shifted distinctly in favor of India. A few days later Prime Minister Nehru announced that the Russians would build a MIG fighter factory in India. In the meantime the Soviets sent four MIGs to India in a symbolic gesture of support, and stepped up their exports to that country; on November 18, Czechoslovakia suspended its deliveries of munitions to China. Soviet moral and material backing for "the Indian reactionaries," as Peking put it, was deeply resented in China and contributed to an exacerbation of the Sino-Soviet dispute. While Soviet economic aid to China in the twenty years since the communists seized power came to about $1 billion, aid to India from 1954 through 1965 amounted to $1.02 billion.[120] "The leadership of the CPSU," wrote the Chinese, "has become increasingly anxious to collude with the Indian reactionaries and is bent on forming a reactionary alliance with Nehru against socialist China. The leadership of the CPSU and its press openly sided with Indian reaction, condemned China for its just stand on the Sino-Indian border conflict and defended the Nehru government. Two-thirds of Soviet economic aid to India have been given since the Indian reactionaries provoked the Sino-Indian border conflict. Even after large-scale armed conflict on the Sino-Indian border began in the autumn of 1962, the leadership of the CPSU has continued to extend military aid to the Indian reactionaries. . . . As for their aid to India, here their ulterior motives are especially clear. India tops the list of newly independent countries to which the Soviet Union gives economic aid. This aid is obviously directed against communism, against the people, and against socialist countries. Even the U.S. imperialists have stated that such Soviet aid 'is very much to our [U.S.] interest.' "[121]

[120] Leo Tansky, "Soviet Foreign Aid to the Less Developed Countries," in Joint Economic Committee, United States Congress, *New Directions in the Soviet Economy* (Washington, D.C.: Government Printing Office, 1966), Vol. IV, p. 974.

[121] The first extract is from "The Origin and Development of the Differences Between the Leadership of the CPSU and Ourselves. Comment on the Open Letter of the Central Committee of the CPSU by the Editorial Departments of *Jen-min Jih-pao* and *Hung-ch'i* (September 6, 1963), in *Polemics, op. cit.*, p. 96. The second extract is from "Apologists for Neo-Colonialism," Fourth Comment on the same letter by the same authors, October 22, 1963, in *ibid.*, p. 195.

Having achieved the strategic and political objectives they sought, the Chinese retreated to excellent jump-off positions in NEFA and Ladakh, no doubt content with the embarrassment they had caused in both Moscow and Delhi. China's territorial gains at the expense of India amounted to about 30,000 square miles.

THE CUBAN MISSILE CRISIS[122]

Khrushchev's attempt to introduce nuclear missiles into Cuba (late October 1962) and his subsequent retreat in the face of swift American reaction, contributed to a further worsening of Sino-Soviet state relations. The disagreement over the "paper tiger" nature of nuclear weapons, which had always been there, came into the open in a spectacularly concrete instance. Soviet "adventurism" and subsequent "capitulationism" were linked by the Chinese to the waning in Russia of the revolutionary spirit under the impact of revisionism, and to the emergence of "big-power chauvinism" one manifestation of which was the attempt, jointly sponsored by the imperialists and modern-day revisionists "to bring within the orbit of Soviet-U.S. talks all revolutionary struggles in Asia, Africa, and Latin America." The "prairie fire of national liberation" was to be extinguished by this unholy alliance of the two oldest members of the nuclear club. "The leadership of the CPSU," wrote the Chinese in one of their letters to Moscow, "has become increasingly anxious to strike political bargains with U.S. imperialism and has been bent on forming a reactionary alliance with Kennedy, even at the expense of the interests of the socialist camp and the international communist movement. An outstanding example was the fact that, during the Caribbean crisis, the leadership of the CPSU committed the error of capitulationism by submitting to the nuclear blackmail of the U.S. imperialists and accepting the U.S. Government's demand for 'international inspection' in violation of Cuban sovereignty."[123]

Throughout November 1962 a vast campaign to support Cuba and denounce the United States unfolded through the length and breadth of China. Castro and his new brand of communism were urged to keep up their intransigence in the face of Soviet betrayal, an encouragement to which Castro (whose prestige had been shaken by the Soviets' rapid retreat) responded eagerly, but still within the

122 Some references: Robert F. Kennedy, *Thirteen Days: A Memoir of the Cuban Missile Crisis* (New York: Norton, 1968); David L. Larson, *The "Cuban Crisis" of 1962* (Boston: Houghton, 1963); Henry M. Pachter, *Collision Course: The Cuban Missile Crisis and Coexistence* (New York: Praeger, 1963); William E. Griffith, *The Sino-Soviet Rift, op. cit.,* Chapter 5, pp. 60-63.

123 "The Origin and Development of the Differences Between the Leadership of the CPSU and Ourselves," *op. cit.*, p. 96.

limits of his income. After all, since 1960, Cuba had benefited from sizable Soviet economic assistance, amounting in the period 1960-65 to about $1.1 billion, including the dispatch of some 15,000 Soviet technicians and the training of 4,500 Cuban students in the USSR.[124] Every time the Cubans' neo-Trotskyite, caudillolike, and anarchic propensities manifested themselves too glaringly, the Soviets began talking money. At a secret conference of Latin American Communist Parties held in Havana in November 1964, for example, the Soviet delegation reportedly warned the Cubans against Chinese-inspired and Cuban-tested guerrilla tactics in the underdeveloped countries of the hemisphere. The Eastern Europeans to whom Castro owed another $1 billion also put the Cubans on notice that no pledges of assistance could be made beyond 1964 unless more attention was given in Havana to socialist economic construction, which, in the first place, meant raising the output of sugar.[125]

In 1965-66 the Chinese showed that, poor as they were, they could play the economic pressure game too. In 1965 they had sent 250,000 tons of rice to Cuba—that is, roughly double the amount sold in previous years. The increase, according to Peking, had been specifically asked for by Castro, and there had been no commitment to send this quantity of rice in exchange for about double the amount of sugar in subsequent years. In 1966 the Chinese offered to sell 135,000 tons of rice. In a long speech, Castro conveyed his bitter disappointment with this action, maintaining that according to his understanding China had agreed to exchange 250,000 tons of rice against 500,000 tons of sugar in 1966 as well. The drop in Chinese rice deliveries in 1966 necessitated a cut in Cuba's rice ration from six to three pounds per head per month. The Chinese denied the existence of any such agreement and described Castro's interpretation of the deal as "groundless." It is probably true that China had more sugar than it could use (the 1964 and 1965 sugar harvests had been good) and needed rice both for storage against emergencies and to help North Vietnam. On February 6, 1966 Castro declared that China's action amounted to a "brutal retaliation of an economic nature for purely political reasons." The Chinese retorted that "Castro had added his voice to the anti-China chorus." The revolutionary honeymoon between the two countries was over, at least for the time being. Apart from the sugar-for-rice problem there was also another area of disagreement. The Cubans apparently wished to use a

[124] Leo Tansky, op. cit., p. 964.
[125] Jan S. Prybyla, "Communist China's Economic Relations with Cuba," Business and Society (Autumn 1965), pp. 3-7. Cf. Adrian A. Basora, "Cuba: Castroist Command," in Jan S. Prybyla (ed.), Comparative Economic Systems (New York: Appleton, 1969), pp. 428-441.

10 million pesos balance remaining from a (1960) Chinese loan of 60 million pesos to meet their 1966 trade deficit with China. The Chinese, however, would not go along, arguing that the loan had originally been extended for the purchase of complete sets of equipment and technical aid, and that it had to be used in that way to the last peso. Perhaps they would have relented had Castro shown himself more receptive to their arguments at the Tricontinental Conference held in Havana a few months earlier. Since, however, the Cuban leadership leaned over backward to listen to the Soviet revisionists, the Chinese had no choice but to take such measures as they deemed necessary, including the distribution of propaganda material among Castro's lieutenants. The Cubans found themselves rapidly embroiled in the Sino-Soviet quarrel, a situation which they neither sought nor enjoyed. The solution was to try the old remedy of self-reliance, which meant going out into the sugar cane fields and raising the output of the crop to at least 10 million tons a year. It was a hard blow to Castro's program of diversifying the Cuban economy and to his objective of freeing the country from dependence on a single crop.

THE NUCLEAR TEST BAN TREATY

On July 2, 1963 Khrushchev announced that he was prepared to conclude with the United States and Britain a limited test ban agreement. Three days later, after Khrushchev's well-publicized departure from Moscow, Soviet and Chinese government and Party representatives met in the Soviet capital to try and clarify their differences and perhaps bring the conflicting viewpoints somewhat closer together. The meetings ended on July 20 at Chinese request, without achieving anything constructive. While these sessions were in progress, the Soviets hosted U.S. and British test ban treaty negotiators. On July 25, after ten days of negotiations, the test ban treaty was initialed in Moscow by the representatives of the United States, Britain, and the Soviet Union. By the end of the month Peking had opened an all-out propaganda barrage against the treaty calling the whole affair a "dirty fake," a "sellout," and a "fraud." In the treaty Peking saw an attempt by the Soviet Union in league with the "Western imperialists" to prevent China from obtaining atomic weapons, a manifestation of arrogant big-power chauvinism and capitulationism wrapped in one. While Peking accused Moscow of joining an "alliance against China, pure and simple," Moscow linked China with "a bloc" which, curiously enough, allegedly included Goldwater, de Gaulle, and Adenauer. There is no doubt that the conclusion by the Russians of the test ban treaty aggravated the

Sino-Soviet quarrel by shifting it to the plane of interstate relations and by focusing attention on a narrow range of extremely sensitive issues of national security.

SOVIET ATTEMPTS TO READ CHINA OUT OF THE INTERNATIONAL COMMUNIST MOVEMENT

Before his sudden departure from power, Khrushchev had proposed to call a general meeting of the world's communist parties, the stated purpose of which was to air the movement's outstanding issues, the real object being to line up the various communist parties behind Moscow's position on doctrinal and policy matters and possibly to put China on notice of excommunication. China naturally opposed the convening of such a gathering with all the might and persuasiveness at her disposal. The difficulties which the Soviets faced in bringing the meeting about were considerable. Many of the communist parties of Western Europe were either opposed to the agenda or were hopelessly split between pro-Moscow and pro-Peking factions. Very much the same was true of the communist movements in Asia. Among the Eastern Europeans, the Rumanians showed extreme coolness toward the proposal. Some others were fearful lest the putting of China beyond the pale of world communism result in a reassertion of Soviet hegemony. Khrushchev's successors after a spell of reflection decided to go ahead with the project. In March 1965, after some feverish behind-the-scenes discussions, a preparatory consultative conference was held in Moscow, attended by eighteen parties, of which only two (the pro-Moscow Indian party and the Outer Mongolian party) were from Asia. The meeting, according to *Pravda* (March 12, 1965) considered ways for overcoming disagreements and strengthening the solidarity of the world communist movement. "All the fraternal parties . . . declare[d] their fidelity to the general program formulated at the 1957 and 1960 Moscow conferences . . . [and their resolve to] struggle for universal peace and the peaceful coexistence of states with different social systems." This was, from Peking's viewpoint, not quite in conformity with the facts. For one thing, Peking's interpretation of the 1957 and 1960 Moscow documents was, as we have seen in Chapter 8, at variance with the sense attributed to them by Moscow and the Moscow-aligned parties. The Chinese reaction was scornful in the extreme. The meeting was described by Peking as "schismatic," "illegal," and "divisive," and ridiculed for being "a gloomy and forlorn affair," "neither fish nor fowl." During a trip to Tirana (March 1965) Chou En-lai called it "an extremely serious step to effect an open split in the international communist movement. Strategically this action itself greatly helped U.S. imperialism, no matter how much empty verbiage the successors to Khrushchevism may pour out about unity against imperialism."[126] The explanatory letters sent by the Soviet Communist Party's Central Committee to the Central Committee of the CPC were called by Peking "Orders No. 1 and No. 2 of the CPSU leadership."[127]

The emaciated preparatory conference was to be followed by a full-scale meeting later in the year. This did not come about, however. The idea was revived in November 1966, but again nothing came of it. In February 1968 a series of preparatory meetings began in Budapest: a new date for a get-together was set for October 15, 1968. This was indefinitely postponed by the Soviet invasion of Czechoslovakia. After serious armed clashes on the Sino-Soviet border in March 1969 (the Ussuri River incident) the Soviets again began to work on their friends and allies. They recalled that in November of the previous year a date had been set for the plenary conference (May 1969) and they pressed for final arrangements. A 67-party preparatory commission met in Moscow in March 1969 and after much soul-searching decided to hold another preparatory meeting in May. The long awaited general meeting was scheduled for June 5, 1969 in Moscow.[128] The whole history hardly squared with the Soviet contention that "in today's conditions, the Communist movement has found an excellent form of international solidarity— international conferences conducted in conditions of the full equality and independence of each fraternal party."[129] For their part, the Chinese argued that unity was possible only on the following nonnegotiable conditions which they addressed to the Soviet leadership:[130]

"1. Publicly declare that all orders for convening divisive meetings are wrong and illegal. Openly admit the error of illegally convening the schismatic meeting.

2. Publicly and solemnly admit before the Communists and the people of the world that Khrushchev's revisionism, great-power chauvinism and splittism are wrong.

3. Publicly admit that the revisionist line and program adopted at the 20th and 22nd Congresses of the CPSU presided over by Khrushchev are wrong.

4. Publicly admit that all words and deeds of the leaders of the

---

126 *Peking Review* (April 2, 1965), p. 7.
127 *Ibid.* (March 26, 1965), pp. 19-22. Cf. pp. 6-13.
128 *New York Times* (March 23, 1969), pp. 1, 14.
129 *Pravda* (March 12, 1965), p. 2.
130 "A Comment on the March Moscow Meeting," *Peking Review* (March 26, 1965), p. 13.

CPSU against China, Albania, the Japanese [pro-Peking] Communist Party and other Marxist-Leninist [i.e., pro-Peking] parties are wrong.

5. Publicly pledge yourselves to desist from the error of Khrushchev revisionism and return to the road of Marxism-Leninism and proletarian internationalism and the revolutionary principles [i.e., as understood by Peking] of the 1957 Declaration and the 1960 Statement."

THE VIETNAM CONFLICT

The war in Vietnam which could have become a symbol of international communist resolve and cooperation, in fact, added fuel to Sino-Soviet rivalry and controversy. In addition to all the other points of conflict, Vietnam brought to the surface a more subtle competition for influence in southeast Asia: a three-cornered struggle of new-type empires (the United States, the Soviet Union, and China) to define the borders of their vision of the good life. This unspoken and perhaps even unformulated objective, this trial-and-error demarcation of the frontiers of conflicting perspectives on life, was also present in the Cuban missile crisis and the Indian border war. But in Vietnam its contours were more sharply defined in terms of the psychological tensions, human cost, and material expenditures involved. On the ashes of classical empires, new ones had arisen, competing with one another by different means, confronting one another on the field of battle by proxy. In this triangular storm the Chinese (in spite of serious historical handicaps) posed as the defenders of Asia for the Asians, and not infrequently lumped together in the elastic definition of "Europeans" not only the Americans but all the peoples of the USSR as well. In a more constructive manner, the Chinese economic assistance program to Asian and African countries (discussed in Chapter 9) pursued similar ends.

Soviet, East European, and Chinese economic aid to North Vietnam consisted of grants, long-term loans, and swing credits in support of North Vietnam's recurrent balance of payments deficits. During 1958-60 foreign aid accounted for roughly 20 percent of North Vietnam's budgetary receipts, and for 18.5 percent in the two years 1961-62.[131] The proportion of aid to domestically generated revenue probably rose after the escalation of the Vietnam conflict in 1965. In 1962-64 about 35 percent of North Vietnam's foreign trade turnover was with the Soviet Union (up from just under 5 percent in 1955).

[131] See Prybyla, "Soviet and Chinese Economic Aid to North Vietnam," *China Quarterly* (July-September 1966), p. 90. For background information, see King Chen, "North Vietnam in the Sino-Soviet Dispute, 1962-64," *Asian Survey* (January 1965), pp. 1-11.

The annual balance of trade deficit with the USSR was in the region of $20 million. Soviet aid after 1960 was spent mostly on large industrial projects; Chinese assistance was more concerned with light industry and transportation, while East European aid covered a wide variety of projects including transport, telecommunications, food processing, mining, power, construction, and light industry. Total grants and credits received by North Vietnam from communist countries in 1955 through 1965 came to $832 million, approximately half of this amount consisting of grants, most of which were extended in the period 1955-60.[132] There was a certain complementarity in all this, a socialist division of labor, which, however, revealed many cracks on closer examination. In pursuance of a declared policy of self-reliance (expressing, it may be presumed, a genuine desire on the part of the North Vietnamese to be independent of great powers, especially feuding fraternal ones) the recipients apparently tended to become increasingly sensitive about foreign aid with strings attached to them, whatever the origin. The result was a scorning of expert advice not compensated for by local expertise. In 1963 a Soviet specialist stationed in Hanoi confided in a Western correspondent that "they [the North Vietnamese] no longer permit us to get near the machines which we furnished them with. . . . It is worse here than in China."[133] Chinese specialists probably got a similar reception.

A similar surface complementarity and deeper conflict characterized Soviet and Chinese military aid to North Vietnam. In general, Soviet assistance consisted mostly of rocket and radar installations, antiaircraft artillery, jet fighters, tanks, coastal guns, and warships as well as the training of personnel to man them. China sent assault rifles, carbines, machine guns, grenade launchers, and 81-mm mortars (most of them Soviet-designed and Chinese-manufactured.) The Chinese apparently also helped repair roads, trails, and bridges destroyed by U.S. bombing, and as a bonus urged the creative adoption of Mao's thought on military matters.[134] Both sides, however, eyed each other with suspicion.

In the first place, there was the constant fear in Moscow and Peking that the other side might enter or might already have entered into some sort of agreement with the United States. Soviet ambassador Fedorenko, the Chinese said, "let the cat out of the

[132] Han Van, "Good Use of Valuable Aid from Friendly Countries," *Nhan Dan* (Hanoi), September 8, 1963, p. 3, in *JPRS*, 22041 (1964).

[133] Marcel Giuglaris, "A Journey to North Vietnam," *Konkret* (Hamburg), December 1963, pp. 11-14, in *JPRS*, 5234 (1964).

[134] In mid-1966 an estimated 20,000 Chinese army engineers were thought to be present in North Vietnam. *FEER* (July 7, 1966), p. 23.

bag . . . [when he] linked up the situation in Indochina with the
U.N. 'peace-keeping operations.' "[135] Soviet calls for unity among
the socialist countries for the sake of Vietnam were branded by the
Chinese as "likewise a swindle," and by China's Albanian spokesman
Hoxha as "a mere fraud." What the Soviets were really interested in,
the Chinese thought, was to join in a "love feast" with the United
States, exchange information, extinguish the fires of the people's
wars of liberation, and work in common "against Communism,
against the people, against revolution, and against the national liberation movement for the purpose of maintaining imperialism, revisionism, and reaction everywhere, against all revolutionaries."[136]
Soviet policy was described by Peking as "Three Reconciliations and
One Reduction," namely (1) peace with the imperialists, (2) peace
with reactionaries of various countries, (3) peace with modern revisionists (e.g., Yugoslavia), and—as for the reduction—little support
for and assistance to the revolutionary struggles of oppressed peoples
and nations of the world.[137] For their part, the Soviets were anxious
to find out what the American and Chinese ambassadors were up to
in Warsaw where they held closely guarded talks.[138] The Soviets, in
fact, suggested that for all their inflammatory talk, the Chinese had
agreed not to intervene directly in Vietnam in exchange for a United
States promise not to invade China.[139] They made public the alleged
"Five Major Crimes Committed By Mao Tse-Tung In International
Affairs," namely "(1) He frenziedly attacks the Soviet Union and
other socialist countries. . . . (2) He venomously attacks the Marxist-
Leninist Communist and Workers' parties of all countries. . . . (3) He

[135] *Peking Review* (April 2, 1965), p. 31. "The Soviet Union has always
believed that the UN has been and remains an important international forum,
called upon to play a most important role in the present world order. . . . [It]
has played a definitely positive role in resolving several international problems
and conflicts." V. Mayevsky, *Pravda* (October 24, 1964), p. 3.

[136] "A Comment on the March Moscow Meeting," *Jen-min Jih-pao*
(March 21, 1965), in *Peking Review* (March 26, 1965), pp. 7-13. The proposal
to stop the bombing of North Vietnam was consistently denounced by Peking as
"a joint plot of the Soviet leadership group with American imperialism that
represents an attempt to snuff out the Vietnamese revolution." See *Izvestia*
(March 30, 1967). To which the Soviets replied that for Mao and his clique
"bloodshed passes for supreme virtue." *Ibid.* "The Soviet government," wrote
Jen-min Jih-pao in March 1965, "is servile and obedient to U.S. imperialism."

[137] This charge was made by Liu Ning-yi, Deputy Director of the Foreign
Affairs Office of the State Council in a speech to the National People's Congress
in 1964.

[138] See for example, I. Gavrilov, "Behind the Screen of Secrecy," *Izvestia*
(June 16, 1967), p. 2, and "Deal with the Colonialists," *Izvestia* (June 18,
1967), p. 4.

[139] F. Burlatsky, "Who Welcomes Peking's Line?" *Pravda* (November 2,
1966), p. 2. The article quoted the London *The Statist* to the effect that
"China's contribution [in Vietnam] consists mainly in preventing the delivery of
Soviet arms to the Democratic Republic of Vietnam."

plans to split and undermine the national liberation movement in Asia, Africa and Latin America, pursuing a policy of openly pressuring the developing countries of Asia and Africa. . . . (4) He plans to provoke a U.S.-Soviet and world war. . . . At the Moscow International Meeting in 1957 he openly pressured for a nuclear war which would destroy from one-third to half of mankind. In documents attacking the world communist movement published in April 1960, he continued to call for a nuclear war, which could destroy the entire world. He constantly shouts that the 'atomic bomb is a paper tiger,' that the 'hydrogen bomb is a paper tiger,' that 'atomic and thermonuclear war is not terrible at all.' . . . He has already turned the Sino-Indian border into a major base from which he can stir up international tension and provoke military incidents between states whenever he wants to. He is trying to create a similar situation on the Sino-Burmese and Sino-Nepalese borders. . . . (5) In the economic sphere he is severing ties with the world socialist system and transferring them to the capitalist camp." [140]

Peking charged that the main purpose of Soviet military support for North Vietnam was "to gain the right to have a say, control, and representation on the Vietnam question in the name of aid so as to strike a political deal with the United States." And, the Chinese added, ". . . so far, a great part of the Soviet military equipment supplied to Vietnam consists of obsolete equipment discarded by the Soviet armed forces or damaged weapons cleaned out of warehouses." [141] In a letter circulated by the CPSU among Western European Communist Parties [142] the Soviets revealed that in 1965 alone, their military assistance to North Vietnam amounted to 500 million roubles ($550 million) and that this money was to have been spent on the latest military hardware and to pay for the training of pilots, artillerymen, rocket personnel, tank drivers, and so on. Soviet economic assistance to North Vietnam was reported to have risen from $47.6 million in 1964 to $75 million in 1965.

But there was more trouble. The Soviets accused China of

[140] Wang Ming, *China: Cultural Revolution or Counter-Revolutionary Coup?* (Moscow: Novosti Press Agency Publishing House, 1969), pp. 56-77. Wang Ming *alias* Chen Shao-yu published his pamphlet at the KGB (Soviet secret police)-affiliated Novosti Press Agency. It is among the more hysterical Soviet-sponsored anti-Mao products. Wang Ming, according to *China Reconstructs* (September 1969) "is a renegade, traitor, and lackey of imperialism, revisionism, and reaction with unpardonable crimes."

[141] "How Low Can They Sink?" by Commentator, *Jen-min Jih-pao* (December 23, 1965), in *Peking Review* (January 1, 1966). Earlier the Chinese had charged that "in fact, the new leaders of the CPSU have disclosed the details of their so-called 'aid' to Vietnam to the Americans through various channels." See *Peking Review* (November 12, 1965).

[142] See *Die Welt* (Hamburg), March 22, 1966; *Washington Post* (March 22, 1966), pp. 1 and A 11, and *New York Times* (March 23, 1966), p. 14.

purposely hindering the rail transit of Soviet military materiel to Vietnam through Chinese territory. This was done, Moscow alleged, "under the pretext that the papers for its transit had not yet been filled out and that they [the Chinese] did not know 'whether Vietnam needs this war materiel.' "[143] In its issue of December 10-16, 1965, the Soviet magazine *Za rubezhom* reprinted a *New York Times* report to the effect that China had demanded from the USSR payment in U.S. dollars for the transport of supplies across China to North Vietnam. This accusation brought forth two official Chinese protests, both of which were rejected by the Soviet government.[144] Soviet ships laden with munitions for Hanoi were, according to the Soviets, harassed and delayed in Chinese ports. Soviet planes flying military advisers and technicians to Vietnam were delayed at Peking Airport and made to refuel with all passengers on board. Although Soviet planes were allowed to fly over Chinese territory *en route* to Hanoi, Soviet requests for unrestricted rights to organize a full-scale airlift had allegedly been rebuffed, and each flight had to be specifically cleared by the Chinese authorities. After 1966 Soviet personnel on their way to North Vietnam through China were subjected to refined indignities by Mao's Red Guards and other, as the Russians put it, "organized hoodlums."[145]

KHRUSHCHEV'S PERSONALITY AND THAT OF HIS SUCCESSORS

The tone of the Sino-Soviet polemics has been extremely low. Policy issues and questions of ideological divergence were often discussed in gutter language spiced with personal abuse. The disregard for accepted canons of diplomatic usage must not, by itself, be taken too seriously: revolutionary regimes are not rectory tea parties and the public use of foul words seems to be a part of the joys of remaking the world. Even after fifty years of efforts to smooth out some of the rougher edges of the socialist new man's personality and to acquire a few of the graces of polite society, the Soviets are not averse to reverting on occasion to the primitive revolutionary seman-

143 *Ibid.*

144 *NCNA*, Peking (January 15, 1966). *Pravda* (December 25, 1965) rejected Peking's "smear campaign to discredit Soviet assistance to Vietnam." The Chinese claimed that in the period February through December 1965 they transported 43,000 tons of Soviet military hardware to North Vietnam, a quantity, they said, "far from commensurate" with Soviet capabilities. In the first quarter of 1966, according to Peking, the Soviets asked for a transport capacity of 1,730 railway freight cars for Vietnam aid materiel, but actually used only 556 cars.

145 For further details, see Jan S. Prybyla, "Recent Trends in Sino-Soviet Economic Relations," *Bulletin*, Institute for the Study of the USSR (May 1967), pp. 11-21.

tics of their youth. To do otherwise would be to risk being accused of *embourgeoisement* by those to whom social transformation and proletarian manners are one. It would be to betray Lenin and even Marx in that founder's more irate moods. In addition to substantive issues, the Chinese found Khrushchev personally objectionable, and said so. Khrushchev, in turn, gave as much as he received.[146] Khrushchev's blander successors fared no better. One need not pay the discussants the compliment of reproducing the complete dictionary of fraternal abuse, but a few examples of the type of sentiments aired are instructive if only as a symptom of the failure of Emily Post in Russia and China. In one of their many letters addressed to Moscow, the Chinese called Khrushchev "a Bible-reading and psalm-singing buffoon." In another, he was described as a "Kautsky-type philistine denounced by Lenin." A publisher's note appended to a Chinese edition of Khrushchev's speeches from 1942 to 1953 described the Soviet premier as a "big conspirator, careerist, and double-faced hypocrite in all his ugliness." On occasion, *Pravda* (e.g., September 2, 1964) compared Mao's "expansionist claims" to Hitler's drive for *Lebensraum*, and scorned China's "highfalutin' phrases about revolution." From time to time the Soviet press raised the specter of the "yellow peril." In the famous *Hung-ch'i* editorial of November 21, 1964 entitled "Why Khrushchev Fell," Russia's fallen leader was called an "arch-schemer" who "put the noose around his own neck, dug his own grave." He was a "buffoon on the international political stage," and a "clown." His successors were no better: their "fine words only amounted to selling horsemeat as beefsteak." Their actions were "pure swindle." In "A Comment on the March Moscow Meeting," *Jen-min Jih-pao* (March 21, 1965) accused Brezhnev and Kosygin of having "taken over Khrushchev's revisionism and splittism lock, stock, and barrel," and of having removed their former colleague "not because they had any difference of principle with him, but because Khrushchev had become too odious and had been too stupid in some of his practices, and because Khrushchev himself had become a serious obstacle to the carrying out of Khrushchev's revisionism." The new Soviet leaders were "peddlers of Khrushchev's shoddy goods," ready at a minute's notice to "join in a love feast" with the imperialists. Between October 1964 and August 1966 Brezhnev and Kosygin together with their associates were dubbed a "gang of renegades," a "reactionary hierarchy," a "revisionist clique," "fascist dictators," and much more of the same. Their domestic and foreign policy was described by Peking as a

---

[146] On Khrushchev, see Edward Crankshaw, *Khrushchev: A Career* (New York: Avon, 1966) and George Paloczi-Horvath, *Khrushchev: The Making of A Dictator* (Boston: Little Brown, 1960).

combination of "heinous crimes" and "monstrous deeds." On July 16, 1967, *Jen-min Jih-pao* called them "enemies of the Soviet and the World's people, incorrigible renegades and puppet emperors who have sold themselves to the U.S. imperialist over-lords. . . . Brezhnev and Kosygin, like Khrushchev, are nothing but passing clowns on the stage of history. They will be drowned in the current of the people's revolution." The Soviets, on their side, sneered at Mao's little "red prayerbook" (*Izvestia*, May 26, 1967), his "crude egalitarianism," "utopianism of the petty bourgeoisie," and "arbitrary rule," and denounced the "unbridled Mao Tse-tung hoodlums." The "great-power cult of personality," "antiscientific dogmatism," and Mao's vast "reactionary military coup," the Soviets argued, had nothing to do with socialism as they saw it. Without compassion, Khrushchev sneered at the incompatibility of China's political ambitions and her poverty. At Split in 1963, he told an amused Yugoslav audience that in China "five men share the use of one pair of trousers"[147] and in 1964 entertained the Poles by saying that the Chinese leaders want to "produce belts so that they can tighten their waists."[148] "To regard poverty as an inevitable com-panion of the working people throughout the entire period of socialism, to exalt poverty as all but a blessing is to grossly distort the aims of socialist construction, to concede the progress of material culture altogether to capitalism," wrote *Pravda* (January 14, 1966). "The most important task for a Communist Party," it continued, was "the development of the economy in every possible way."

[147] Quoted by *Yang-ch'eng Wan-pao* (Canton), April 4, 1966, p. 2, in *URS*, Vol. 43 (June 14, 1966).
[148] *Ibid.*

11 | The Great Proletarian Cultural Revolution, 1966–69: The Politics of Upheaval

THE SUPERSTRUCTURE AND THE BASE

The Socialist Education Campaign of 1963-65 prepared the ground for the Great Proletarian Cultural Revolution.[1] The education campaign was, in a sense, a dress rehearsal for and a controlled experiment in cultural rebelling. The Cultural Revolution unleashed by the left-wing faction within the leadership, may be viewed as just another mass campaign, one more example of the way in which Chinese society has been governed since 1949. But it was both something more and something less than the earlier mass upsurges.

Its scope was greater, it lasted longer, it did not try to dissimulate the philosophical and tactical rifts that divided the leaders; it shattered the established structure of the Party and state, bypassed the conventional lines of command, dissolved most of the existing mass organizations, closed down more than 500 newspapers and magazines, dealt a blow to the concepts of authority, professionalism, and elitism measured by conventional educational and achievement yardsticks, and took China out of Sinified Marxism-Leninism-Stalinism into the realm of Mao Tse-tung's vision of a proletarian "left-deviationist" culture where utopian socialism, Proudhon-like anarchism, Trotskyite permanent revolutionary cleansing, and Yenan-type militaristic classlessness coexisted with the gun wielded by the army's left-wing command. It was the dialectical principle in action: supervised anarchy, contempt for rank and authority in the name of a new and stricter order, a downgrading of intellectualism in the cause of an allegedly higher and more ascetic thought, the destruction of the Party for the good of the Party, and of the state on behalf of state power, the ridding of the country of bureaucratic corrup-

[1] See, *CCP Documents on the Great Proletarian Cultural Revolution, 1966-1967* and *The Great Proletarian Cultural Revolution* (Hong Kong: URI, 1967, 1968,). Also by the same publisher, *Documents of the CCP Central Committee, 1956-1968* (1969). Gene T. Hsiao, "The Background and Development of the Proletarian Cultural Revolution," *Asian Survey* (June 1967), pp. 389-404.

tion, patronage, and nepotism by the expedient of appointing friends and relatives to positions of responsibility and trust, a revolution against the old, executed by the young in the service of aged leaders, against entrenched habits of thought for a fossilized belief, for the masses incarnated in the thought of a deified leader, on behalf of a clique.

The Cultural Revolution was also something less than the earlier campaigns, especially the most important of them all, the Great Leap Forward (Chapter 8). At least until 1969, the revolution was largely confined to the "superstructure" of ideas and to the embodiment of those ideas in Chinese society's political power system. It was an enormous palace revolution, a *bouleversement* of the communist establishment from the pinnacle of the Forbidden City down to the tiniest unit of government. It was very largely an urban phenomenon, the full brunt of it bypassing the countryside and hence three quarters of China's population.[2] Unlike the Great Leap Forward, its short-run effects on the institutions of the economy appear to have been marginal. There was some disruption of factory and farm work, an overloading of railroad transport, delays and confusion at the ports, intermittent declines in exports, local inflation, buying sprees, commodity shortages, strikes, passive resistance by workers and managers in league with dissident local Party apparat-men, fistfights, gunfights, and bloodshed. But there was no nationwide breakdown of the economy, such as occurred in 1959-60, no wholesale attempt to put the clock back to 1958 in the crucial matter of economic organization, no concerted attack on the peasants' private plots, no comprehensive Great Leap Forward in production. There were, to be sure, vast movements of population into and out of the cities, exhortations to replace personal material incentives to effort with spiritual boosts inspired by the thought of Mao and personified by model heroes, army contingents, drilling teams, and rural people's communes. There were large-scale campaigns for flood control and water conservation and experiments with new forms of control over enterprises. All this, however, did not add up to a radical overturning of the postulates of the 1961-65 period of reconstruction, consolidation, filling-out, and raising standards, although the investment priorities and developmental strategy of the period were put under severe stress. One gets the impression that beneath all the shouting and pushing, behind the high-flown slogans and ringing phrases, the teenage rampage, the blaring loudspeakers, and the endless repetition of homely parables from the Chairman's selected readings, everyday life in the fields and to a lesser extent on the factory floor went on very

[2] See Harald Munthe-Kaas, "Mao's Pinkish Peasants," *FEER* (December 14, 1967), pp. 479-481.

much as usual. Granted that the usual in Communist China tends to depart from the accepted notions of normalcy, it remains possible that at the basic level there was a remarkable resilience and an ability to adjust to the political hurricanes blowing from Peking. "They don't bother very much about what happens in Peking and they don't care very much about who is in power as long as they leave them alone. People try not to get into trouble with the government; if you don't want to do something the officials tell you to, they come and question you, asking who told you to behave like that, and what are your real thoughts; they go on and on, and it's very bothersome and you can't get rid of them."[3] On September 16, 1967, *Jen-min Jih-pao* remonstrated against the peasants' lack of revolutionary fervor, complaining that when urged to criticize "China's Khrushchev" (Liu Shao-ch'i) they pleaded illiteracy, leaving criticism to those able to read and write. According to the paper, their reaction was: "The Chinese Khrushchev is far from us, and his poison does not reach our little riverside hidden in the mountains. Why waste so much energy on criticizing him?"[4] "People," wrote one eyewitness, "hope that after this campaign [Cultural Revolution] they will have better officials, but they know they won't be perfect and in a few years there'll be another campaign to weed out the bad ones in the new lot."[5] The extent of the peasants' passive resistance to the Cultural Revolution is, of course, difficult to establish with any degree of certainty. This much, however, is clear: the great leap in the superstructure did not develop into another leap in the economic base, at least not by the end of 1969.

REASONS FOR THE CULTURAL REVOLUTION

The Cultural Revolution was the culmination of a long-drawn-out struggle between factions within the Communist Party and government machinery, a struggle fueled by divergent interpretations of Marxism-Leninism, different—often incompatible—ideas on developmental strategy,[6] foreign affairs, military policy, and international relations, varying emphases on the tactics to be adopted toward classes in China's complex society, and other issues of ideology and practice. The growth and gradual exacerbation of these differences

[3] Report from a Hong Kong "overseas Chinese" visitor to a commune in Kwangtung Province. Colina MacDougall, "Bend With the Wind," *FEER* (February 23, 1967), p. 268.
[4] Cited by L. D. Tretiak, "Feeding Revolution," *ibid.* (October 26, 1967), p. 169.
[5] Colina MacDougall, *loc. cit.*, p. 268.
[6] Almost certainly the Third Five Year Plan (1966-70) was at issue. See *Agricultural Machinery Technique* (August 8, 1967), in *URS*, Vol. 49, No. 4 (October 13, 1967), p. 56.

have been traced in the preceding Chapters. Until the latter part of 1965 factional quarrels were conducted with relative decorum within the framework of the Communist Party and state and according to the ground rules of "democratic centralism." Society at large was not taken into the confidence of the in-fighters, dissidents were disposed of quietly, behind thick walls of Party secrecy, the weapons of combat were drawn from the communist establishment's armory of committees, carefully staged and controlled struggle sessions, personal intrigue, organized intimidation, and ritual self-examination. Only the final outcome was publicized, when suddenly an old revolutionary and faithful comrade-in-arms would accuse himself of improbable crimes against the Party, against socialism, and against the people, or would disappear, or be declared an anti-Party bad egg. With an occasional lapse,[7] the quarrels and the washing of unclean linen were exclusive affairs, X-type dramas reserved for ideologically mature audiences only, the populace being nursed on the illusion of the Party's unshakable unity, its monolithic resolve and legitimacy sanctioned by the will of History. Communist tragedies were acted out by members of the elect company in regulation stage settings, in an empty house, the crowd roaring its approval in the streets outside. A chorus of mass organizations, blind and obedient, commented on the happenings, voicing in unison man's ineluctable destiny prescribed by Marxist history. Day after day, for years on end, the show went on in an empty theater. The Cultural Revolution shattered the mystique, thrust open the stage doors, let the crowd in, goaded it on to mount the boards, hopefully in support of the positive heroes, that is those in the limelight of Mao Tse-tung's thought. It was a desperate measure, risky, unpredictable, but satisfying to the masses whose frustration at being kept out so long, and anger with the actors and masters of their lives had reached a point of no return. The masses invaded the hall, rampaged, roared their hatred, ran amok of the play, only to find that they were still, after all, a part of the script, puppets in a vast dialectical drama. The active masses were young and naive, inexperienced, easily engineered, manipulated by this or that faction's invisible hand. The over-thirties milled around in the city squares or lay down on their jobs in the villages on the theory that it was all the same but different, that they had seen it all before, and it was just not worth their while. As will be shown in more detail later, the novel feature of the Cultural Revolution was the resort by the left-wing faction of the leadership to methods of combat not prescribed by Party manuals, its appeal for help to totally new, often obstreperous mass formations outside the Party, its use of the army, and its

---

[7] Eg., resort by the Party's left wing faction to poor and lower-middle peasants' associations.

attack on a recalcitrant Party and government bureaucracy from out-side. Caught by surprise, the right-wing faction tried for a while to wage the struggle according to the well-tested rules of inner-Party maneuverings. It was hampered in this by years of left-wing infiltra-tion and by its very tenuous hold over the mass media. The Right's freedom of movement was restricted by its preference for settling disputes *in camera* and the difficulty of openly challenging the per-sonality of Mao, the symbol of Chinese Communism, the sanctified father figure, elevated over the years to godlike heights where it communed only with Marx, Lenin, and Stalin. Every trite saying of the helmsman had been invested with a depth of meaning, a wisdom, and a sanctity unparalleled in the history of secular leadership. Strik-ing out at this awesome image of man-god was treason, apostasy, and a sure means of courting disaster. And so everyone used Mao, was vocally for Mao, filled with Mao's spirit, inspired by his thought, while pursuing ends the connection of which with the aged leader's philosophy was varied, sometimes doubtful, often nonexistent.

In one important sense, the Cultural Revolution was, therefore, a struggle for succession, a vast insurance operation against future perils. In spite of Mao's geriatrics-defying swims across the Yangtse, his powers were manifestly declining. His disappearance from the political scene was likely to be fraught with heavy consequences. One had to enshrine him, to disembody him, leaving only the pure spirit, so that Mao would live on in his bodily death.[8] It was neces-sary to prove beyond the shadow of a doubt that those who took over the helmsman's job after his physical disappearance were men anointed by him, chosen unequivocally to carry on his tasks. The names of the elect had to be embodied in Party documents, repeated over and over again, engraved on popular memory. Others had to be relegated to outer darkness as enemies not just of the people, social-ism, and revolution, but of the living Mao and his eternal thought. The slate had to be wiped clean of revisionists, indeed, of all accre-tions of the past, so that a new society could be built on Maoist foundations, distilled from Mao's thought. This new proletarian dic-tatorship was to be created *ex nihilo*, a procedure totally foreign to both Marxism and Leninism, and incompatible with the notion of the maturation of dialectical stages.

The Cultural Revolution was also propelled on its wayward course by less lofty motivations. China's ageless tradition of localism played a part in shaping loyalties and in negotiations for positions of

---

[8] "Man obeys Chairman Mao, and earth obeys man." "Hold Aloft the Great Red Banner of Mao Tse-tung's Thought and Topple Completely 'China's Khrush-chev,'" *Rural Youth* (Shanghai), September 10, 1967, in *URS*, Vol. 49, No. 17 (November 28, 1967), p. 229.

strength. Bargains were struck on less than noble terms, a web of competing intrigues was spread over the land. Regional loyalties were put to the test, bread-and-butter promises were made, the pros and cons of future personal advancement were carefully weighed. Nepotism and petty individual jealousies were rampant. As has so often been the case with great historical movements, the whisperings of crafty and vengeful womenfolk seem to have played an inordinately significant part in the proceedings. Mao's wife, Chiang Ching, a small-time movie starlet of the 1930's, emerged as the spokesman for culture in the theater, opera, cinema, and literature, venting her hatreds against intellectual giants who had scorned her in the past. Small, wiry, homely she imposed her petit-bourgeois aesthetic standards on a whole nation, from the thoughts one could entertain to the dress one could wear. Her jealousy of the more refined wife of Liu Shao-ch'i (Wang Kuang-mei) was boundless. She must have savored, and probably inspired, articles and wall posters which described her rival as a "stinking bourgeois apparition."[9] An article in Chiang's favorite aesthetic organ, *Liberation Army Literature and Art* (January 25, 1968) referred to Wang Kuang-mei as China's Khrushchev's "stinking witch." Among the members of the presidium of the Ninth Party Congress, which culminated three and a half years of cultural uproar (April 1969), were the wives of Mao, Lin Piao (Yeh Chun), Chou En-lai (Teng Ying-chao), Kang Sheng (Tsao Yi-ou), and Li Fu-chun (Tsai Chang). Mrs. Mao ranked sixth in the hierarchy at that time, Mrs. Lin twelfth, having risen from complete obscurity. A colorless figure, Lin Piao's wife was distinguished mainly for yell-slogans in support of Chiang Ching at proletarian cultural affairs. Li-Fu-chun and his wife spent some time together with the Chou En-lai's in France in the twenties. Both Mrs. Mao and Mrs. Lin were picked for the 1969 Politbureau. The great Maoist vision of a selfless proletarian society, incorruptible and resting on the dissolution of the individual in the masses, was being created in practice by tawdry little alliances and girls' talk behind the scenes. It was no less tarnished by the continuing presence within the company of utopia

[9] *Rural Youth* (Shanghai), September 10, 1967, in *URS*, Vol. 49, No. 17 (November 28, 1967), p. 225. Cf. this item from *New Peking University*, an undergraduate publication cited in *FEER* (February 23, 1967), p. 271: "On that occasion [Liu Shao-ch'i's visit to Indonesia in 1963] Sukarno and Liu embraced, Karno paid compliments to Wang Kuang-mei and Shao-ch'i to Hartini [Sukarno's wife] . . . Disgraceful! You, the dregs of the Chinese nation, Khrushchev-type venomous snake, creator of Madam Diplomat, who talks of money and friendship!" See also, *Madame Mao—A Profile of Chiang Ching* (Hong Kong: *URI*, 1968); Guy Wint, "Cherchez la Femme," *FEER* (November 23, 1967), pp. 370-373; *URS*, Vol. 53, No. 21 (December 10, 1968). Chiang Ching had on one occasion denounced the American-born Wang Kuang-mei as a spy for the United States.

builders of men known to have opposed the Maoist line and whose survival must have hinged on either their ability to bend with the wind or on compromise deals struck with left-wing enragés. The enragés' delicate nose where questions of class genealogy were concerned, hardly squared with their own predominantly middle class origins: Mao himself was the son of a small landowner; Lin Piao's father was a factory owner; Kang Sheng came from a wealthy landowning family in Shantung. The ideal was far removed from the reality, held together at gunpoint. "Utopian ideals," Djilas, wiser for years of enforced confinement, has said, "the aim of social perfection, are neither realistic nor ultimately humane in practice."[10]

THE PROBLEMS OF QUANTIFICATION AND PERSPECTIVE

Ever since 1959 hard facts about China's economy had become extremely scarce. Official sources, as we have seen, dealt in generalities usually cast in percentage terms and cited only those instances in which success could be claimed. The situation deteriorated gradually in three respects: the amount of quantified information was reduced, sharply so after the autumn of 1965; reading between the lines of official publications became increasingly difficult as the press switched to set phrases, petrified prose, and an unending glorification of the person and mental accomplishments of the Chairman and his "close comrade-in-arms," "vice-commander" Lin Piao; the major national newspapers and journals, repeatedly accused of treasonable practices, were purged of their top personnel, and often shut down, resuming publication only to be vilified for some other deviation.

In August 1967, for example, there was no statistical reporting of any kind from twenty provinces, while percentage claims from regions under Mao-Lin control were fragmentary (usually referring to particular counties, communes, brigades, or plants), and suspect. The editorial boards of the *Peking Daily* (*Pei-ching Jih-pao*), *Peking Evening News* (*Pei-ching Wan-pao*), and *Frontline* (*Ch'ien Hsien*) were dismissed on June 6, 1966. Publication of *Frontline* was discontinued in June, that of the *Peking Evening News* in July, and that of *Peking Daily* on September 3. Teng T'o, a former editor of *Jen-min Jih-pao* was denounced as "chieftain of the black reactionary gang," and accused of "singing the same tune as Khrushchev."[11] The chief editor, Tang Ping-chu was dismissed in January 1967, half the staff was transferred to other jobs, and the offices of the paper were taken

[10] Speech accepting Freedom Award, December 9, 1968, in *Freedom House Newsletter* (February 1969), p. 3.

[11] See *The People's Daily and the Red Flag Magazine During the Cultural Revolution* (Hong Kong: URI, 1969).

over by Maoist revolutionary rebels who quarreled and bickered and
purged themselves ad infinitum. By mid-December 1966 almost all
magazines published by government ministries stopped appearing.
These included *Chinese Light Industry*, *Chinese Finance*, *Rural
Finance*, *Shanghai Machinery*, *Economic Research*, even *Chinese
Sports*. Papers and periodicals put out by mass organizations met a
similar fate (e.g., *Women of China*, whose editor, Tung Pien, was
denounced in July 1966, and the organ of the All-China Federation
of Trade Unions, *Workers' Daily*, closed down on January 3, 1967).
The New China News Agency did not escape either: its director,
Hsiung Fu, was criticized in January 1967 for allegedly having faked
a picture of Mao Tse-tung showing Liu Shao-ch'i standing next to the
helmsman at the October 1, 1966 national day celebrations. In January 1967 Hu Chi, the agency's acting general manager was detained
by the Red Guards. Radio Peking, too, was declared a reactionary
stronghold and taken over by Maoist groups in January 1967. Many
newspapers outside the capital were accused of revisionist deviations,
their editorial boards were purged, and in some instances the papers
ceased to appear. Later, the export of provincial newspapers was
banned, and foreign embassies in Peking—communist and noncommunist alike—were not permitted to receive the provincial press.[12]

The demise of the official press and the replacement of the already small variety of news by reprints from the *Liberation Army
Daily* was accompanied by an explosion of wall posters (*tatse-pao*)
put up by individuals and self-styled revolutionary groups and factions. The poster revolution scaled Himalayan peaks in the autumn
and winter of 1966 and the first six months of 1967. The posters
varied in content and reliability, ranging from the local, trivial, and
petty to the sensational, national, and improbable.[13] For a time the

[12] The restriction followed a ban on Red Guard and Revolutionary Rebel
publications. Shanghai and Canton local papers, however, continued to be smuggled into Hong Kong. Monitoring of provincial radio and television transmissions
went on all around China's borders. See *New York Times*, November 14, 1968,
p. 9. Between 1966 and December 1969 the number of foreign correspondents
in Peking dropped from 40 to 15. As of December 1969 only three correspondents represented the Western and three the Japanese press.

[13] Example of a Red Guard poster photographed in Canton: "To the revolutionary workers of the Nanfong Hotel! The Nanfong Hotel has been often fre-
quented by international friends, and therefore it stinks of bourgeois thinking."
Other *tatse-pao* trivia: "Miss Peng is too feminine and not in step with the new
era!" "Wang goes to the cinema too often." "Chang eats too slowly. Can he not
speed up to get ahead of the times?" "Where was Fang late on Tuesday night?
Was he doing anything which he cannot tell? And with whom?" "Why is Chou
so talkative?" "Why is Ting so silent? Is he not satisfied with the present government?" More serious posters described confessions by public figures, proceedings
of meetings, related news of pitched battles between various factions in various
parts of the country, and so on. See Robert Tung, "The Poster Purgative,"
FEER (September 22, 1966), pp. 556-557. At one juncture, everyone in China
was allegedly instructed to put up at least ten posters a day.

world assisted at the spectacle of a few venturesome foreign correspondents' surreptitiously jotting down and transmitting information on events in China garnered from graffiti scribbled on walls by juveniles. [14] To sort out the wheat from the chaff became the fascinating but difficult task of China watchers the world over. The problem involved not only judgment regarding the reliability of often contradictory information, but the spotting of mistranslations.

Dealing as we are with a titanic struggle between two fragmented, emotionally exalted totalitarian factions given to secrecy and congenital terminological inexactitude, chameleon psychosis, a dialectical conception of life and of personal security, the following outline of what happened in China from the latter part of 1965 to the end of 1969 must be accepted as a first approximation.

CHRONOLOGY

THE PRELIMINARY STAGE: 1963–AUGUST 1965

It is a workable assumption that the left-wing faction within the Chinese Communist leadership saw the collapse of their Great Leap Forward as having been brought about by a combination of (a) insufficient ideological spadework among the masses, (b) opposition from inveterate rightists, right-opportunists, revisionists, and more generally freaks and monsters who had sneaked into the highest offices of the Party and government, and (c) bad weather. There was not too much they could do about the last, except urge continued efforts at flood control and water conservation. They seem, however, to have been persuaded that the first two factors were avoidable and could be eliminated with a dash of *shuo-fu-chiao-yu* (education by persuasion) and a spot of *lao-tung-kai-tsao* (correction through labor). They watched with growing apprehension the inroads into their vision of the new communist society made by the policy of consolidation and filling-out, the spread of the "Three Freedoms and One Contract," the conciliatory attitude toward foreign revisionists, the apparent abandonment by China of the national liberation struggles in Asia and Africa, and the growing preoccupation of peasants, workers, and especially youth with personal advancement and material comfort. To reverse the trend, they inaugurated the Socialist Education campaign, the primary purpose of which was to sweep away old habits and extirpate reactionary bourgeois ideas from the minds of the people, cadres, and government personnel at the middle and lower

[14] But this, too, came to an end. On September 19, 1967 the Peking correspondent of the Japanese Communist Party's paper *Akahata* was roughed up by the wall poster artistes. A few days later *Akahata* called the Maoists "the anti-Party bandit group in Peking."

levels. The Socialist Education campaign may be seen as an attempt to rectify the (a) deficiency which— the leftists thought—had seriously undermined the Great Leap undertaking. [15] The sharpness and indecisive outcome of the conflict within the leadership on the subject of the place of socialist education in consolidation, filling-out, and raising standards may be gathered from the fact that the Third Five Year Plan which should have started in 1963 (by normal political count), or in 1961 (by the Great Leap calendar of "Five Year Plan fulfilled in three years") was not actually announced until 1966, and then only in the most general terms. The intent of the Plan, as we have seen, was to continue the relatively moderate course initiated after the collapse of the Leap, but it is unlikely that the Plan ever existed in detailed form or that (assuming its draft existence) it was consistently applied as a long-range guide to action during the succeeding years.

The Left's counterattack in 1963 had been carefully prepared. Lacking a reliable power base within the Party and governmental bureaucracy, the left-wing faction began, as early as 1959, to seek control of the largest of China's mass organizations, the People's Liberation Army. They correctly surmized that in any future confrontation with opponents (entrenched in the bureaucratic apparatus and the managerial machine) the revolutionary Left would need a reliable and convincing ally able to bring to heel, if need be, recalcitrant Party and state. It was important for the Party—as defined by the Left—to control the gun, even at the risk of producing the opposite result, i.e., of seeing the gun control Mao's Party. The ideology of the Party's Left was, after all, pervaded by the militaristic spirit of the Yenan type, by a barracks-type classlessness understandable to the more reminiscences-prone veterans of the Long March, whose memories of the old days became increasingly one-sided as the years rolled by. [16] If the army of the 1960's could be filled with the spirit of the thirties, which was also that of the Party's Left, the contradiction between the Party and the gun would be resolved. Operating on

[15] "We must pay great attention to the reaction of the superstructure on the economic base and to the class struggle in the ideological sphere. The victory of socialist revolution on the economic and political fronts cannot be consolidated without the victory of the socialist revolution in the ideological sphere." "Never Forget the Class Struggle," *Liberation Army Daily*, editorial, May 4, 1966. Cf. Richard H. Solomon, "On Activism and Activists: Maoist Conceptions of Motivation and Political Role Linking State to Society," *China Quarterly* (July-September 1969), pp. 76-114.

[16] Liao Mo-sha, the former Director of the United Front Work Department of the Party's Peking Municipal Committee was, among others, accused of attacking by parody the communists in the Shensi-Kansu-Ninghsia Border Region, claiming that the region was dominated by corruption and terrorism.

the same ideological wavelength, the new Party and army would become one. Eventually the whole nation would become one with the Party-Army-state.[17]

While (1960-62) the authoritarian moderates were taking over the regular Party and governmental apparatus and tightening their grip on the established mass organizations of workers, youth, women, journalists, writers, artists, and so on, the left-wing began to command the army. An editorial published on August 1, 1966 in the *Liberation Army Daily* (by then firmly in left-wing hands) referred to the "three big struggles with representatives of the bourgeois-military line who had wormed their way into the Party and Army." The first of these struggles took place shortly after the Korean War (1953-54), and the issue was modernization versus the millet-and-rifles concept of the armed forces. The second struggle took place in 1959 at the very moment that the Great Leap policies were showing signs of severe strain. The outcome of this second confrontation was the left-wing's takeover of the army's top leadership, an event crucially important for the future strategy of the Left. P'eng Teh-huai (Defense Minister) and his Chief of Staff, Huang Ko-cheng were, as we have seen (Chapter 8), replaced by the hard-liner Lin Piao. The Leapers lost many key positions of political governance and economic management, retreating to an impregnable "base area"—the army—whence counterattacks could later be launched. The takeover of the army was not, however, complete at first. The purging of the two "persons in authority taking the capitalist road in the army" foreshadowed later similar cleansing of the Party's and government's top echelons, but at that early stage it still left on the middle level of the military establishment some regional commanders whose loyalty to the leftist cause could not be relied on. Even the new appointee to the post of Chief of Staff turned out to have been a capitalist-roader. Lo Jui-ching, who shared this military post with his duties as Secretary of the Communist Party Central Committee's Secretariat,

[17]"The People's Liberation Army is the mighty pillar of the dictatorship of the proletariat. Chairman Mao has pointed out many times: 'From the Marxist point of view the main component of the State is the army.' " Political Report by Lin Piao to Ninth Congress of the CPC, April 1969, *New York Times* (April 29, 1969), p. 12. © 1969 by The New York Times Company. Reprinted by permission. See also Chalmers Johnson, "Lin Piao's Army and Its Role in Chinese Society," *Current Scene*, Vol. 4, No. 7 (July 1966), pp. 1-10; Ralph L. Powell, "The Increasing Power of Lin Piao and the Party-Soldiers, 1959-1966," *China Quarterly* (April-June 1968), pp. 38-65. At the Lushan Plenum (July 23, 1959) Mao had said: "If we deserve to perish, then I will go away, go to the countryside to lead the peasants, and overthrow the government. If you, PLA people, don't follow me, I'll go and find a Red Army. But I think the PLA will follow me." *FEER* (October 2, 1969), p. 30.

vanished from public view in November 1965, was finally purged in late July 1966, and reportedly committed suicide in January 1967.[18] This was the third big struggle within the Left's base area, on the very eve of the launching by the Left of its attack on the—to them deviationist—Party and government.

THE PREPARATORY STAGE: SEPTEMBER 1965–NOVEMBER 10, 1965

Between the second (1959) and third (1965-66) big struggles, the army was subjected to a series of rectification campaigns, presumably directed and staged by Lin Piao and his closest associates. As the army cleansed itself of bourgeois-military and bourgeois-political thinking, it was offered as a model of the new communism, a glowing example of Mao Tse-tung's thought (Chapter 10). Little by little Lin Piao emerged as the executor of Mao's wishes, and the most influential policy maker of the communist Left. Early in 1965 he was promoted to senior vice-premier; in May he proletarianized the army (Chapter 10); in October he circulated his "Long Live the Victory of People's War," a 30,000-character composition that was soon hailed as the Left's new communist manifesto, "the most historic and revolutionary document of this era"; in November he proclaimed his "Five Points," a supplement to his "Four Firsts" of 1960; in December 1965-January 1966 he organized a PLA Conference on Political Work in the Army, and in February "entrusted" Chiang Ching to conduct a Forum on Work in Literature and Art which called for a socialist cultural revolution in the army.[19]

[18] "Mao Tse-tung has used part of the PLA as an instrument of the counter-revolutionary coup and reactionary personal military dictatorship; concentrated part of the PLA on seizing power from the Communist Party and the people's government, killing communists, workers, peasants, and intellectuals; incited one part of the PLA against another part and ordered the PLA to pursue his reactionary policy of 'three supports' and 'two military measures.' . . . The number of generals and admirals of the army, navy, and air force removed from their posts and persecuted, runs, according to incomplete data, from 70 to 80." Wang Ming, "Ten Major Crimes Committed by Mao Tse-tung in China," in *China: Cultural Revolution or Counter-Revolutionary Coup?* (Moscow: Novosti Press Agency Publishing House, 1969), pp. 18-19. The "three supports" meant: (1) support of the Red Guards and Revolutionary Rebels, (2) support of industry, and (3) support of agriculture, which, according to Wang Ming "means the establishment of military control over the country's entire economy." The "two military measures" meant: (1) military administration, i.e., the establishment of military government in towns and the countryside, in factories, offices, and educational establishments, and (2) military training, i.e., the study by one and all, under military supervision, of Mao Tse-tung's thought and the introduction of military drill in schools and higher educational establishments.

[19] "Five Point Principle Guiding the Work of the PLA in 1966," *Peking Review* (January 21, 1966); "PLA Conference on Political Work," *ibid.* (January 21, 1966). On the Forum, see *ibid.* (June 2, 1967). It has been suggested

Between September and early November 1965, events raced to a climax. Mao's renewed call "never to forget class struggle" at the September 1962 meeting of the central committee encountered strong opposition from those who saw in the reminder the signal for a new Leap Forward and who, in view of the escalating Vietnam war, feared China's isolation, which the Left's policies were likely to bring about. On January 4, 1967 Mao was reported to have said that "in September and October 1965 the Central Committee surrendered to revisionism, and I thought that I could not put my ideas into practice in Peking."[20] It is presumed that at that critical moment he hurriedly removed himself to Shanghai, and for some months disappeared from public view. For much of September and all October Peking appears to have been left in control of Liu Shao-ch'i's bureaucratic-moderate faction whose base of operations was the Party's Peking Municipal Committee, the government ministries, the Peking military garrison, the municipal police force, the professionally inclined sections of the PLA's high command (represented by Lo Jui-ching, Wu Fah-hsien, Commander of the Air Force, Li Tso-peng, Deputy Commander of the Navy, and Liu Jen, Political Commissar of the Peking garrison).[21] Outside Peking, the situation was more confused. Indications are that the Liu faction found support in some of the Party's regional bureaus, almost certainly in the Southwestern and Northwestern, and possibly also in the Northern, and among some regional military commanders (e.g., Wang En-mao in Sinkiang, Ulanfu in Inner Mongolia, and Ting Sheng-chien in charge of the Sinkiang Construction Corps).

STAGE THREE: PURGE OF THE PEKING MUNICIPAL COMMITTEE, THE PROPAGANDA APPARATUS, AND THE UNIVERSITIES (NOVEMBER 10, 1965-AUGUST 12, 1966)

On November 10, 1965 a Shanghai paper fired the first salvo heralding a long and bitter battle between the factions. To outside

---

that the relations between Lin Piao and Chiang Ching have not always been cordial. The "Summary [of Chiang Ching's] Forum" was revised three times (allegedly by Mao himself) before being personally transmitted by Lin Piao to the Standing Committee of the Military Commission of the CPC Central Committee. The "Summary" was not made public until June 1967.

[20] *The Cultural Revolution in China* (Keesing's Research Report, New York: Scribner's, 1967), p. 8. The September-October incident referred to, occurred during a meeting of the Politbureau's Standing Committee attended by leading comrades of the Central Committee's Regional Bureaus. There were no *plenary* sessions of the Central Committee from 1962 to August 1, 1966.

[21] Both Wu Fah-hsien and Li Tso-peng, denounced on February 14, 1967, survived the crisis and were listed among the members of the Presidium of the Ninth National Party Congress on April 1, 1969, Wu being listed eleventh.

observers the first burst of fire from the Left appeared innocuous enough. It took the form of a sharp attack against the historian Wu Han by Yao Wen-yuan, editor of the Shanghai *Chieh-fang Jih-pao* and member of the Shanghai Party Municipal Committee.[22] Yao bitterly criticized Wu Han for having in 1961 written a historical play entitled "Hai Jui Dismissed from Office" in which the Ming Dynasty official was portrayed as an opponent of a corrupt court officialdom, unjustly dismissed from office for his pains. The disgrace of Hai Jui was, Wu Han implied, a trumped-up case, a plot hatched by the emperor's sycophants and hangers-on to discredit a noble and righteous servant of the crown. The play, wrote Yao elsewhere, "directed its spearhead against the Lushan [1959 secret Central Committee] meeting . . . with a view to reversing the decisions of that meeting. The clamorous message of the drama was that the dismissal of the 'upright' official Hai Jui, in other words of the right-opportunists, was 'unfair' and that the right-opportunists should come back to administer 'court affairs,' that is to carry out their revisionist program."[23] In short, the apparent innocuousness of the attack on Wu Han's five-year-old historical play was deceptive for two reasons: Wu Han was a vice-mayor of Peking, an influential member of the Party's Peking Municipal Committee, and his play was interpreted in contemporary allegorically factional terms as a move against Mao Tsetung's coterie—Hai Jui, it was alleged, was none other than a thinly diguised P'eng Teh-huai. Hence, by extension, the play was directed against the helmsman himself. That the controversy was not about a deviationist piece of theater became evident in the course of the succeeding months during which a full-scale offensive was launched against practically the whole leadership of the Peking Municipal Party Committee, the mass media, and the universities—all allegedly manipulated by the Liu faction. The revolution was reaching out for victims poised on the top rungs of the leadership ladder, it began to devour its own children. "The higher his position, the greater his

---

[22]"On the New Historical Play, 'Hai Jui Dismissed from Office,' " *Wen-hui Pao* (Shanghai), November 10, 1965. Yao reportedly wrote his review under the "direct guidance of Chiang Ching." See K. H. Fan (ed.), *The Chinese Cultural Revolution: Selected Documents* (New York: Grove Press, 1968), p. 123. A good reference for the Wu Han affair is *Chinese Studies in History and Philosophy* (White Plains, N.Y.: *IASP*) Vol. II, No. 1 (Fall 1968).

[23]Yao Wen-yuan, "On 'Three-Family Village'—The Reactionary Nature of Evening Chats at Yenshan and Notes from Three-Family Village," *Chinese Literature (Chung-kuo Wen-hsueh)*, No. 7, 1966. The author was editor of *Chieh-fang Jih-pao* and the article was originally carried in that paper and *Wen-hui Pao* (Shanghai) on May 10, 1966. He was later appointed to the left wing "Cultural Revolution Group" within the decimated CPC Central Committee, and figured twelfth on the list of dignitaries mounting the rostrum of the Ninth National Party Congress, April 1, 1969.

career," wrote the *Liberation Army Daily*. "The higher his position, the more dangerous."

Yao Wen-yuan linked Wu Han to a "gangster inn" run by Teng T'o, Secretary of the Municipal Committee, Alternate Secretary, Secretariat of the Party's North China Bureau, former editor of *Jen-min Jih-pao* and *Ch'ien Hsien* (*Frontline*), and Liao Mo-sha, Director of the Peking Municipal Party Committee's United Front Work Department.[24] The three were accused of propagating an anti-Party, antisocialist, right-opportunist and revisionist "jumble of trash" in some 150 articles published in the *Peking Evening News*, *Peking Daily*, and *Frontline* from 1961 onward, in columns entitled "Evening Chats at Yenshan" (Teng T'o)[25] and "Notes from Three-Family Village" (Wu Han, Liao Mo-sha). On January 2, 1961 Liao wrote in the *Peking Evening News* that "after the winter drums have sounded, the spring grass begins to grow.... An all-out effort will begin in spring." This was interpreted as a call to revisionism in the wake of the Great Leap, an imitation of the "Hungarian-type" political spring (1956) and the Soviet post-Stalin thaw.[26] There must surely have been persons in even higher authority who with ulterior motives and with treachery in their hearts abetted and protected the black gangster inn of Wu, Teng, and Liao. They were soon exposed. After March 29, 1966 P'eng Chen—the mayor of Peking, member of the Communist Party of China Central Committee and Politbureau, Secretary of the Party's Central Committee Secretariat, Vice-Chairman of the Standing Committee of the National People's Congress,

[24] The first attack on Teng T'o and Liao Mo-sha was made by Kao Chu in an article entitled "Open Fire at the Black Anti-Party and Anti-Socialist Line," *Liberation Army Daily* (May 8, 1966). "Who is this Teng T'o? Investigations have now revealed that he is a renegade." *Hung-ch'i*, No. 7 (1966).

[25] The periodical *Economic Research*, No. 5 (1966) accused Teng T'o of having once said that the people's communes provided the people with only a pot of boiled water and that this boiled water was declared to have been most delicious. Cf. Teng T'o's "Is Wisdom Reliable?" Evening Chats at Yenshan, *Peking Evening News* (February 22, 1962) in *The Great Socialist Revolution in China*, No. 2 (Peking: FLP, 1966), pp. 15-16. At one time, wrote *Pravda* (May 26, 1967), p. 2, Mao issued the slogan: "Tui-chen chu-hsin" officially translated as "seek the new in the old." Now, *Pravda* continued, "a holy war was being waged against all classical literature and art," because "the Chinese classics suggested too many allegories . . . [that] seemed dangerous to the Maoists." The formula "tui-chen chu-hsin" was accordingly retranslated by *NCNA* to mean "reject the old, create the new." To a Chinese this sentence sounds the same as it did before. The words "tui chen" can be understood as "push away the old" or as "push off from the old." "Mao Tse-tung and his group," *Pravda* went on, "evidently believe that this trick will enable them not to lose face."

[26] For a detailed criticism of the Chats, including extensive quotations from the offending articles, see "Teng T'o's Evening Chats at Yenshan Is Anti-Party and Anti-Socialist Double Talk," *Liberation Army Daily* (May 8, 1966) in *The Great Socialist Cultural Revolution in China*, No. 2 (Peking: FLP, 1966), pp. 12-49.

Vice-Chairman of the Chinese People's Political Consultative Conference, and First Secretary of the Peking Municipal Party Committee—vanished into thin air. On June 3, 1966 a laconic statement named Li Hsueh-feng (formerly First Secretary of the North China Bureau) as the new mayor of Peking. A more direct attack on the former mayor followed on June 23. A photograph published in January 1967 showed P'eng Chen wearing a huge placard around his neck, head bowed to the ground. In the small hours of December 4, 1966, P'eng Chen was dragged from his bed by screaming Maoist youngsters, "trembling in every limb and incapable of dressing himself," according to a Red Guard newspaper. On December 12, in company of Lo Jui-ching and others, he was paraded before 100,000 youths in a sports stadium, and again on January 4 and 5, 1967.[27] A major charge leveled against him was that he forbade the Peking papers under his jurisdiction to reprint Yao Wen-yuan's attack on Wu Han's play in November 1965, and had banned the distribution in the capital of all pamphlets printed in Shanghai and bearing the article. In February 1966 he allegedly prepared on behalf of the Central Committee an "Outline Report" which laid down the ground rules of literary criticism, insisting that debates of this kind were to be confined to the academic and aesthetic levels and were not to be used for political ends. Like the good apparat-man that he was, P'eng wanted such discussions to be conducted *in camera*, well out of earshot of the masses.

At last the vigilant masses had found and dragged out the local top person in authority taking the capitalist road: P'eng Chen, protector of the black gangster inn, promoter of peaceful evolution into revisionism, patron of the revisionist Lu Ping (President of Peking University and Secretary of the University's Party Committee), and of other devils and monsters who dared raise their hand against Mao and their voice against Mao's thought. There must, of course, have been other people in even higher positions of authority who were waving the red flag to oppose the red flag. It was only a matter of time before the revolutionary masses exposed them.

Meanwhile the drums of the *Liberation Army Daily* were beating furiously: between February 4 and April 5, 1966 the paper published seven editorials outlining the strategy and tactics of the Cultural Revolution. On April 18 it called for a stepping-up of mass criticism on the cultural front, and followed this up with other orders and instructions to the militants of the Left. At the twentieth meeting of the Standing Committee of the National People's Congress (April 14, 1966), Kuo-Mo-jo, Vice President of the NPC Standing Committee

[27] Red Guard newspaper report, December 15, 1966.

and President of the Chinese Academy of Sciences made a humble self-criticism in which he requested that all his political and literary works be burned.[28] A few weeks earlier, Hsia Yen, Vice Chairman of the All-China Federation of Literary and Art Circles had been denounced for his book "Collected Works on Motion Pictures." On several occasions in May, the *Peking Daily*, *Frontline*, and *Peking Evening News* published self-criticisms and confessions in an effort to stave off further attacks on them. "When we have finished reading your 'self-criticism,' " replied the *Liberation Army Daily*, "we cannot help 'breaking into laughter,' as your Teng T'o put it."[29] On June 6 the editorial boards of all three papers were suspended, the publication of *Frontline* was banned, and a few weeks later the *Peking Evening News* ceased to appear.

Like the Peking mass media, the Peking Party Municipal Committee tried the time-tested tactic of self-evaluation as a way to cool down the political temperature and stem the flood of criticism. It reorganized itself on May 25, but to no avail. On June 3 the Party's Central Committee (or a section of it) was said to have issued an instruction to reorganize the Municipal Committee again,[30] while a *Hung-ch'i* editorial listed ten "crimes against Mao and socialism" said to have been committed by the Peking Committee.[31] The reorganized Committee, in turn, issued an order to reorganize the Party Committee at Peking University which had been under verbal and physical assault since May 25. On that day, one Nieh Yuan-tzu and six others of the Philosophy Department at the University put up a

[28] Kuo Mo-jo survived the storms. In April 1969 he figured among the members of the Presidium of the Ninth National CPC Congress.

[29] *Liberation Army Daily* (May 8, 1966).

[30] Whether the Party's Central Committee actually issued such an instruction is questionable. Probably it came from the left-wing group of the Committee, which gradually began to speak for that body. The existence of such a group "in charge of the Cultural Revolution" within the Central Committee was not, however, revealed until July 10, 1966. As early as February of that year there existed á divided "Group of Five in Charge of the Cultural Revolution" under the deeply split Central Committee. P'eng Chen and the Maoist hard-liner Kang Sheng were among the members. The majority of the group was almost certainly right of center, and as such, unacceptable to the Mao-Lin faction. The group was abolished on May 16, 1966 by a "Circular of the Central Committee of the Communist Party of China" (made public a year later). At that time (May 16) a new Cultural Revolution Group was set up, presumably staffed exclusively by leftists, including Chiang Ching, Chen Po-ta, and Kang Sheng. The new body was directly answerable to the Standing Committee of the Politbureau in which Maoists predominated. This group, too, lost many of its members in the course of the Revolution. On the original group of Five, see Ting Wang, "Plots and Counterplots," *FEER* (January 25, 1968), p. 151.

[31] *Hung-ch'i*, No. 9, 1966, and *Peking Review* (July 8, 1966). The "ten crimes" were earlier enumerated in the May 16, 1966 Circular of the Central Committee. See K. H. Fan, *The Chinese Cultural Revolution: Selected Documents* (New York: Grove Press, 1968), pp. 124-133.

big character poster denouncing the University's President Lu Ping as a "bourgeois royalist," and with him the Vice-President, Chien Po-tsan, P'eng P'ei-yun (Deputy Secretary of the University's Party Committee), and Sung Shuo (Deputy Director in charge of university affairs under the Peking Municipal Committee).[32] It transpired later that the authors of the original big character poster were not only correctly inspired in their literary zeal by Mao Tse-tung's thought, but actually commanded by the helmsman to start a massive poster offensive. Soon the poster-writing urge gripped the masses, and the country was smothered by an avalanche of paper unprecedented in history. As time went on, anyone holding a position of authority was fair game for the wall literati. The poster attack on the University Party machine was accompanied by Left-sponsored demonstrations of the masses, shouting Maoist slogans, beating drums and cymbals, invading the premises, disrupting lectures, parading professors and administrators with placards proclaiming that they were "anti-Party intellectuals." Truckloads of high school students and workers were brought in, lecture halls were turned into dormitories, files were rifled, unacceptable books relegated to the consuming flames of the revolution, and finally the whole works was cordoned off and closed down in order that constructive destruction could have its day. Similar demonstrations were staged outside the Municipal Committee buildings. On June 18, it was announced that the system of admissions to schools and colleges would be revised in the direction of admitting culturally underprivileged but politically enlightened sons and daughters of workers, peasants, soldiers, and revolutionary martyrs.[33] Schools and universities were to fold up until further notice, while the "cultural yoke of the intellectual aristocracy" was being smashed. The moratorium on learning gave students a unique opportunity to participate in street culture, exchange experiences and broaden their horizons by doing. Or as exiled Party member Wang Ming put it, Mao's policy was to prevent "the younger generation of China from becoming knowledgeable people and turn them into a crowd of fools."[34] The entire Young Communist League was

[32] The poster, suppressed by University authorities, was reproduced by *Jen-min Jih-pao* on June 2, 1966 after Mao (June 1) allegedly described it as "the country's first Marxist-Leninist big-character poster." Nieh Yuan-tzu was promoted to the post of Vice-Chairman of the Peking Municipal Revolutionary Committee in April 1967. She was the only (by then veteran) Red Guard identified by Western analysts as having attended the Ninth Party Congress in April 1969. By that time she was a member of the Left establishment.

[33] See, "On Reform of Entrance Examinations and Enrollment in Higher Educational Institutions" (June 17, 1966), *Peking Review* (June 24, 1966). The reform was sparked by a letter (June 6, 1966) sent to the Central Committee and Mao by girls of the senior third grade at Peking No. 1 Girls' Middle School (*Peking Review*, June 24, 1966).

[34] Wang Ming, *op. cit.*, p. 32.

also reformed; Wang Chia-liu, the Deputy Secretary of the League in the Peking Municipal Committee was fired (June 15) and the League's leading organs were disinfected of bourgeois-revisionist and right-opportunist germs. A similar fate befell Fan Hsing, Vice-Chairman of the All-China Journalists' Association, Member of the Executive Committee of the All China Women's Federation, one of the nine Vice-Mayors of Peking, and Director of the *Peking Daily*. These and other comrades, wrote Wang Ming from Moscow, "were without foundation accused of 'counterrevolutionary revisionism,' branded 'traitors' and 'elements against the three' (elements opposing Mao Tse-tung, the Party, and socialism), and subjected to cruel repression, persecution, and insults. Of these some were 'defiled,' and others 'defeated,' still others 'overthrown,' arrested, killed, declared as deserving to be 'burnt alive,' slandered, insulted or publicly humiliated."[35]

Throughout June and July 1966 the public campaign against men in charge of basic Party, governmental, and mass organization organs swelled to a furious pitch. Increasingly the attack came from outside the established communist organizational framework, from youthful "masses" transported hither and thither by trucks and trains, by mushrooming *ad hoc* rebels and other hitherto unknown formations.[36] From the time of the first big character poster it became progressively clear that the Maoist faction had resorted to the streets in order to smash their opponents entrenched within the Party, the government, and the old mass organizations. The whole vast structure of communist power as it existed until then was shaken to its foundations and for a time only the old names remained. Purged, emaciated, swaying, the old organizational empire crumbled, but never quite vanished. Mao, complained Wang Ming from the relative safety of Moscow, "is smashing the Communist Party of China. . . . He has smashed state organs of the democratic dictatorship of the people."[37]

What seems to have been a minority faction (backed by an army that had been four-cleansed before), appealed to the frustrations,

[35] *Ibid.*, pp. 10-11.

[36] In his self-examination (July 9, 1967), Liu Shao-ch'i was said to have stated that "the activities of the Party and of the [Young Communist] League organizations were often aimed at maintaining the old order and at opposing the revolutionary rebel spirit and the revolutionary rebel actions." (June-July 1966). Evidently what Liu's regulars tried to do when faced with an assault by hitherto unknown irregulars was (a) to repress them (via the so-called "work teams"— below, pp. 499-500) and, when this did not work, to (b) save the bureaucratic apparatus by making democratic centralism of the existing Party machinery work according to the book: "On the whole, Party and League members should not hold secret meetings. . . . People outside the Party and League should be invited."

[37] Wang Ming, *op. cit.*, pp. 9, 15.

growing aimlessness, and resentments of China's numerically mighty youth. Sometimes it found grudging support from peasants and workers who surely enjoyed the sight of bureaucrat authority trampled underfoot. There was, however, a limit to worker and peasant support. Although the spectacle of men in possession of absolute power running for their lives, scurrying hither and thither with terror activating their limbs, humiliated by adolescents playing at adults, may have been entertaining to the makers of China's material wealth, they surely harbored a minimum of illusions about the authoritarian hand which manipulated the unruly, obedient youngsters. Slow to stand up in defense of established authority, they were quick to react when their daily rice was directly threatened. In spite of repeated left-wing threats that the Cultural Revolution was on the verge of invading the economic base, the turmoil was for years confined mainly to the superstructure. It was one thing for the leaders to execute improbable dialectical jumps, to squirm and perform leaps forward in political consciousness and ideological awareness; it was quite another to translate these into yet another revolutionary somersault in production relations. The revolutionary breakthrough in China's economy had to come from science and technology, and that was not what the Cultural Revolutionaries had in mind, in spite of their insistence on all knowledge gushing forth from one's ability to declaim passages from Mao's "Three Much Read Articles."[38]

Reputations melted like mud-splattered snow in the spring. On June 30, 1966 *Hung-ch'i* stormed against Chou Yang, Vice-Chairman of the All-China Federation of Literary and Art Circles, Alternate Member of the Party's Central Committee, Deputy Director of the Committee's Propaganda Department, and apparently a "sham leftist and a political thief," "a big red umbrella which covered up all the monsters and demons," an appointee of the black gangster Lin Mohan. On January 3, 1967, *Jen-min Jih-pao* accused him of having plotted for fifteen years to depose Mao by a Hungarian-type revolution. For many years the guardian of Mao's thought, he was now declared "Number One Demon in the Kingdom of Hell" whose thought was "smelly, long, and deep."[39] Less than two weeks before the *Hung-ch'i* attack, Ch'en Ch'i-t'ung (Deputy Director of Culture and Propaganda Departments of the PLA's General Political Department) had been denounced in roughly similar terms by *Jen-min Jih-pao*. After all these years there were traitors everywhere: Lin Mohan, for example, an "accomplice of the black gang" parading as

[38] "In Memory of Norman Bethune," "Serve the People," and "The Foolish Old Man Who Removed the Mountains."
[39] Ma Sitson, former President of the Central Music Academy, in *Life* (June 2, 1967), p. 27.

Deputy Minister of Culture and Deputy Director of the Propaganda Department, and Lu Ting-yi, Minister of Culture since January 1965, Vice Premier since April 1959, Director of the Party's Propaganda Department since 1948, full member of the Central Committee of the Communist Party of China and of the Central Committee's Secretariat. Then there was Li Chi, Director of the Peking Municipal Committee's Propaganda Department, and Tien Han, playwright and reputedly author of the words of "The East Is Red."[40] Lu Ting-yi was replaced on July 10 by Tao Chu (former First Secretary of the Party's South-Central Bureau and Mayor of Canton) as head of the Party's Propaganda Department.[41] But Tao Chu turned out to have been a double-dealer after all: he waved the red flag to oppose the red flag, was uncovered, denounced by wall posters for "building his own independent kingdom," attacked (December 29, 1966), and condemned at a mass meeting of presumably true revolutionaries (January 10, 1967). He was finally replaced by Wang Li, Deputy Editor of *Hung-ch'i*.[42] There was really no knowing who was friend and who was enemy, so wily were the opponents of the revolution. Down came Ho Lu-ting, Director of the Shanghai Music Conservatory, Wang Hsiao-chuan, Head of the Propaganda Department of the

[40] Perhaps the last verse was at issue, and that only in the setting of the Party's destruction in 1966-67. Could there be two suns rising in the East? "What is behind it?" the revolutionary cadres might well ask.

> The East is Red,
> The Sun rises,
> China has brought forth a Mao Tse-tung.
> (*hu er hai yao!*)
> He is the people's great savior.

> Chairman Mao loves the people.
> He is our guide.
> He leads us onward
> (*hu er hai yao!*)
> To build the new China.

> The Communist Party is like the sun.
> Wherever it shines, there is light.
> Where there's the Communist Party
> (*hu er hai yao!*)
> There the people will win liberation!

On April 24, 1970 China launched her first space satellite, a 380-pound device, which orbited the earth every 114 minutes along a trajectory the perigee of which was 263.4 miles and the apogee 1,430 miles. On its course around the planet, the satellite broadcast the music of "The East is Red" (*T'ung Fang Hung*) on a frequency of 20,009 megocycles—*hu er hai yao*!

[41] For a profile of Tao Chu, see *FEER* (October 19, 1967), pp. 126-127. On July 31 *NCNA* announced that General Hsiao Wang-tung was the Acting Minister of Culture. Yen Chin-sheng, another general, became Deputy Minister of Culture about this time.

[42] On December 13, 1966, shortly before his fall, Tao Chu had issued a call to extend the Cultural Revolution to the economy.

Kweichow Provincial Party Committee and Chief Editor of the *Kweichow Daily*, Sun Yeh-fang (October 1966), Director of the Economics Institute of the Chinese Academy of Sciences, Li Meng-wei, Chief Editor of *Yunnan Daily*, the Presidents of Sian, Nanking, Chengtu, Chungking, and Wuhan Universities, Wang Ting-k'un, Deputy Director of the Peking Municipal Committee's Propaganda Department and Deputy Director of the *Peking Daily*, T'ao P'ai, Director of the Propaganda Department, Kiangsu Provincial Committee, and hundreds more. Peng Kang, Rector of Sian University and Secretary of the University's Party Committee was removed, according to the *Shensi Daily* (quoted by *Pravda* on June 26, 1966, p. 4) because he said that "if a man cannot climb a pole and another man reads him a quotation from the Chairman, he still won't be able to climb the pole." Wang Tao, President of Tungchi University in Shanghai was made to mop his room and the school's corridors for the sake of exercise, while devoting the rest of his time to the study of Mao's works.

Insofar as can be determined, until August 1966 the campaign against leading personalities in the Party, government, and mass organizations was, with few exceptions, limited to name-calling and public denunciations in the press and (after May 25, 1966) in wall posters. Men were killed psychologically, not physically. Classroom work was disrupted and offices were lost. Arrests, however, were few, there was relatively little physical violence, probably much panic and deft footwork among office holders, an almost desperate bending with the chilling gust of ideological wind. All this lends weight to the belief that until August the opposing forces were very much in balance, the victims of the verbal denunciations being able to hold onto their persons if not always their jobs.[43]

Based on Shanghai, after their setback at the September-October meeting, the Lin-Maoists' first task was to discredit their opponents barricaded in the Peking Party and governmental machine.[44] This

---

[43] Ma Sitson, former Director of the Central Music Academy, in his account of the Cultural Revolution, gives one clue. Until August, Liu Shao-ch'i and his group were apparently able to protect some of the persons in authority by the expedient of sending them away for "study training" to various places of forced residence (e.g., the Socialist Institute in Peking) where they were, at least, protected from the mob by army units. The study training consisted of writing big-character posters, reading Mao's literature, and holding endless discussion meetings. See Ma Sitson, "Cruelty and Insanity Made Me a Fugitive," *Life* (June 2, 1967), pp. 27-28.

[44] The Shanghai Municipal Party Committee, however, turned out to have been full of traitors too. "In Shanghai, Ch'en P'i-hsien, Ti-ch'iu, Yang Hsi-kuang, and other scoundrels, using their official power, have opposed Chairman Mao's revolutionary line and suppressed the proletarian revolutionaries." *Radio Shanghai* (February 10, 1968), in *URS*, Vol. 50, Nos. 13-14 (February 16, 1968), p. 176. While Mao, Lin, and their people were plotting in Shanghai, Ch'en, unsure of the direction events would take, prudently took sick leave from the Shanghai Committee.

appears to have been the meaning of the Shanghai press and *Liberation Army Daily* campaign of November 1965 through April 1966. The next task was to gain control of the Peking mass media and their overseer, the Peking Municipal Party Committee. To accomplish this, two generals loyal to the Lin-Mao group (Yang Cheng-wu and Yang Yung)[45] were reportedly dispatched to the capital in May. In a way yet to be explained in detail, they took over the editorial offices of *Jen-min Jih-pao*, fired the Liu men from the boards of the major Peking papers, seized the radio station and the offices of the NCNA, and saw to it that the clean-ups by the masses in the university were not interfered with by right-opportunist stratagems.

Taken aback, the Liu faction mounted an elaborate holding operation, using all the tools and tactics of the Party's machinery. Officials under left-wing attack were advised to put up self-accusation posters and retreat to supervised work and study havens where they remolded themselves by reading the Chairman's literary masterpieces and pondered the revolutionary ramifications of such immortal phrases as "in a class society everyone lives as a member of a particular class," and "in this world things are complicated and are decided by many factors."[46] Work teams were dispatched by the Party center to investigate the Party and state organs under attack as well as their attackers, and find out what was going on in the schools. Members of the teams mingled with student extremists and nonstudents brought into the schools by army trucks, assured one and all that the Party was mindful of their problems and ever attentive to their demands, promised reforms, and tried to channel the mounting wave of hysteria into approved channels. In the process they apparently tread hard on many leftist toes and waved the red flag while opposing the red flag.[47] Subsequently, in a last-minute attempt at participatory democratic centralism, large numbers of high Party and government officials (including Liu and Chou En-lai) toured the provinces, visited universities, press bureaus, Party and government departments, explained the correct position as they saw it, were heckled and insulted by the audiences, and bit by bit lost the

[45] General Yang Yung, appointed Commander of the Peking Military Region, was reportedly dismissed in February 1967 for "breach of Party discipline." Former Defense Minister P'eng Teh-huai was arrested at Chengtu on December 24, 1966.

[46] *Quotations from Chairman Mao Tse-tung* (Peking: FLP, 1966).

[47] Hans Granqvist in his *The Red Guards: A Report on Mao's Revolution* (New York: Praeger, 1967), p. viii, claims that the work teams went about their business with such brutality that they caused a deep reaction which may have been a contributing factor in the emergence of the Red Guards. For a verbatim account of a Work Team session at the Peking College of Construction Engineering on August 4, 1966, attended by Liu Shao-ch'i, see *Collected Works of Liu Shao-ch'i, 1958-1967, op. cit.*, pp. 345-355. It is a most instructive document showing the Party structure tottering under the onslaught of young rebels, the confusion of the Party brass faced with a totally new phenomenon.

mystique and prestige of their exalted office.[48] All the while, Mao and Lin sat in seclusion on the Olympian heights, watching the tigers fight.[49] At the Central Committee meeting in August 1966, Mao Tse-tung opined that 90 percent of the investigating teams had committed serious ideological, political, and class errors.[50] The teams were trimmed at the end of July and jettisoned in August. The regular Party's attempt to take over the Cultural Revolution by playing the rectification game according to democratic centralist rules had failed. By then the leading apparat men and apparat intellectuals had suffered a massive loss of face by means to which they had not been accustomed.

In June Liu Shao-ch'i, the leader of the majority opposition, apparently decided that the time had come to get rid of the Chairman by the accepted procedure of summoning the right kind of plenary session of the Party's Central Committee.[51] To accomplish this he needed cooperation from the Party's Secretary General, Teng Hsiao-p'ing, who accordingly became the object of assiduous courting by Liu's men. In the second half of June, P'eng Chen, by then already ousted from the reorganized Peking Municipal Committee, reportedly toured the northwest and southwest seeking support for the impending coup among the members of the Party's regional bureaus.[52] His mission met with some success. At the end of the month and in early July, Central Committee members began to converge on the capital from all over the country. These reportedly included Ulanfu, the leader of Inner Mongolia, Li Chien-chuan (Polit-

---

[48] The original work team dispatched to Peking's Tsinghua University was dismissed by the revolutionary students and left-wing sympathizers.

[49] Mao disappeared from public view from November 1965 till early May 1966. It was his longest retreat. In early spring 1966 he was reportedly seen in Shanghai.

[50] The charge was repeated by Chou En-lai on August 22, 1966 in a speech at Tsinghua University.

[51] In his self-examination (July 9, 1967) Liu said that "for some time prior to July 18 last year [1966], the daily work of the Party Central Committee was in my charge in the absence of Chairman Mao. The conditions of the Great Cultural Revolution in various respects in Peking were regularly reported at meetings of the Central Committee over which I presided. These meetings made some wrong decisions, approved or agreed to some wrong suggestions" Liu also admitted having made "a mistake in line and orientation while guiding the Great Proletarian Cultural Revolution" during fifty days after June 1, 1966, i.e., throughout the crisis period of June-July 20, described here. SCMP, No. 4037 (October 9, 1967), pp. 1-7.

[52] Wall posters in Peking on April 17 accused Liu of having plotted with P'eng to oust Mao through a military coup. The coup was allegedly planned for February 1966. Liu, according to these reports, had made a number of trips to Sinkiang where he tried to enlist the armed support of Wang En-mao. Similar charges, slightly more veiled, were made by Jen-min Jih-pao on April 17, 1967, against P'eng Chen. The coup rumor was reportedly denied by Chou En-lai and Kang Sheng on April 28, 1967.

bureau member since 1958), and Li Po-hua (Secretary of the Eastern Bureau).[53]

On July 28 Mao, Lin, and their supporters arrived by air from Shanghai. Dissident sections of the army were brought to heel, and on August 1 the Eleventh Plenary Session of the Central Committee opened in Peking and struggled on for twelve days in a setting increasingly unfavorable to the Liu faction.[54] The meeting was packed with Red Guards and other "representatives of the revolutionary masses" who attended in the capacity of observers without voting rights. Their observation was intended to intimidate the anti-Maoist members of the Central Committee into adopting the Maoist line.[55] On the fifth day Mao, with his own hand, wrote a big character poster: "Bombard the Headquarters," which foreshadowed the events of the eighth day on which the session adopted the so-called "Sixteen Points Concerning the Great Proletarian Cultural Revolution." On August 12 the Central Committee issued a communiqué. To celebrate the event, a mass rally was held on August 18 in Tien An Men square attended by over a million people. Major speeches were made by Lin Piao, Chou En-lai, and Chen Po-ta, all members of the left-wing faction. The Chairman was there, smiled, waved to the jubilant masses, but did not speak. In the official listing of leaders at the rally, Liu Shao-ch'i had dropped from his usual second to eighth place, Teng Hsiao-p'ing retained sixth place, Lin Piao rose from seventh to second place, Tao Chu, Chen Po-ta, and Kang Sheng emerged from relative obscurity to occupy respectively the fourth, fifth, and seventh places. Marshal Chu Teh dropped from fourth to ninth place, and P'eng Chen, P'eng Teh-huai, and Liu Po-cheng were not listed among the top twelve.[56]

Between August 18 and November 23[57] Mao met the masses eight times in the square, reviewing a total of eleven million

[53] Ulanfu was accused by wall posters in January 1967 of opposing Han migration into Inner Mongolia, supporting "Mongolia for the Mongols," and launching his troops against cultural revolutionaries. He was dismissed on April 13, 1967.

[54] "During the latter part of the Plenum the question of our mistakes was brought up for discussion, which was followed by the election of members of the Standing Committee of the Central Committee." Liu Shao-ch'i, "Self-Criticism," *op. cit.*, p. 363.

[55] This was revealed by two Hong Kong communist papers, *Wen Hui Pao* (November 24, 1968) and *Ta Kung Pao* (December 3, 1968). Red Guards and other pro-Maoists were admitted to the Central Committee session probably on the fifth day and thereafter.

[56] "At the Plenum Comrade Lin Piao was unanimously recommended as Chairman Mao's first assistant and successor. Comrade Lin Piao is better than I in every respect." Liu Shao-ch'i "Self-Criticism," *op. cit.*, p. 363.

[57] Note that November 23 was the day on which the first known public attack was made on Liu Shao-ch'i and Teng Hsiao-p'ing, thus giving the Red Guards something new and absorbing to do.

youngsters, or roughly half the university and high school students in China. Each time he waved and smiled, but did not open his mouth. Others spoke for him, his quotations spoke for him, his past deeds, but not the Chairman himself. While the country screamed itself hoarse, the helmsman stood at the helm, or at any rate somewhere near it, and kept his counsel in awesome, distant majesty. When rumors began to circulate that he was a prisoner of this or that faction, senile, paralyzed, and sick, he would take a swim in the Yangtse, and the people would shout: "Our respected and beloved leader, Chairman Mao, is in such wonderful health! Long live Chairman Mao! A long, long, long life to him!"[58]

The Sixteen Points and the communiqué are instructive documents.[59] They suggest that although the plenary session had removed the immediate danger to the Chairman's authority and had strengthened the hand of the left-wing extremists, the authoritarian apparat-men were far from beaten. In fact, it must have become quite clear to the radicals that, do what they might, they could not win a decisive victory within the existing framework of Party and state. If they were to carry the Cultural Revolution "through to the end," as the saying goes, they would have to step up the assault on the Party-State from outside, use hitherto unexplored or insufficiently explored channels of class struggle, stir up the masses even more, and equip them with new organizational weapons. "Trust the masses, rely on them and respect their initiative. Cast out fear. Don't be afraid of disturbances. . . . Let the masses educate themselves in this great revolutionary movement and learn to distinguish between right and wrong and between correct and incorrect ways of doing things. Make the fullest use of big-character posters and great debates to argue matters out . . ."[60]

[58] Such a ritual swim took place in July 1966 at the height of the intra-Party crisis, after Mao had been out of public view for some time. Cf. Chapter 10. On October 1, 1969 Mao reappeared on the Tien An Men Square rostrum, after a four-and-a-half-months retreat during which rumors about his health had been circulated by Moscow.

[59] Decision of the Central Committee of the Chinese Communist Party Concerning the Great Proletarian Cultural Revolution (Adopted on August 8, 1966), (Peking: FLP, 1966), and Communiqué of the Eleventh Plenary Session of the Eighth Central Committee of the Communist Party of China (Peking: FLP, 1966). "Who gave Mao Tse-tung the right to convene the so-called 11th and 12th 'plenary meetings of the CCCPC'? No matter how much he tries to use the signboards 'CPC' and 'CCCPC' to mask his real face, all his actions betray him as an anti-Communist from head to toe. His group is incontestably an anti-Communist clique." Wang Ming, op. cit., p. 12.

[60] Decision, loc. cit., pp. 4-5 (Point 4). Cf. "Revolutionary Big-Character Posters Are 'Magic Mirrors' That Show Up All Monsters," Jen-min Jih-pao (June 20, 1966) in K. H. Fan (ed.), The Chinese Cultural Revolution, op. cit., pp. 308-310.

The trouble, however, was that the masses were not homogeneous, that they bickered and quarreled among themselves as masses will, and that collective wisdom did not always work, because collective wisdom is a convenient abstraction the arithmetic of which has not been convincingly explored. "In such a great revolutionary movement, it is hardly avoidable that [the masses, especially youngsters] should show shortcomings of one kind or another; however, their general revolutionary orientation has been correct from the beginning." [61] To people endowed with progressive ideological insight the question "Who are our enemies? Who are our friends?" presented no problems. But because the masses were frequently being misled by "ideological pickpockets" in authority (taking the capitalist road), there was confusion, and often real revolutionaries were taken for counterrevolutionaries. These evil persons in authority "resorted to such tactics as shifting the targets for attack and turning black into white in an attempt to lead the movement astray." [62] "They have puffed up the arrogance of the bourgeoisie and deflated the morale of the proletariat. How poisonous!" [63] It was inconceivable that some masses should think differently from the right-thinking masses, unless they had been misled, stabbed in the back, led astray by rightists, demons, freaks, and monsters. "At present,this resistance is still fairly strong and stubborn." [64] There was much uncertainty about who was in charge, a possibility of repeated reversals in the struggle. All of which demanded revolutionary determination, daring, and perseverance. However, "when there is a debate, it should be conducted by reasoning, not by coercion or force." [65] "Criticism of anyone by name in the press should be decided by the Party Committee at the same level, and in some cases submitted to the Party committee at a higher level for approval." [66] "As regards scientists, technicians, and ordinary members of working staffs, as long as they are patriotic, work energetically, are not against the Party and socialism, and maintain no illicit relations with any foreign country, we should in the present movement continue to apply the policy of 'unity, criticism, unity.' Special care should be taken of those scientists and scientific and technical personnel who have made contributions [e.g.,

---

[61] *Decision, loc. cit.*, p. 2 (Point 2).
[62] *Ibid.*, p. 4 (Point 3).
[63] Mao Tse-tung, "Bombard the Headquarters: My Big-Character Poster" (August 5, 1966), *Peking Review* (August 11, 1967).
[64] *Decision, loc. cit.*, p. 2 (Point 2).
[65] *Ibid.*, p. 6 (Point 6).
[66] *Ibid.*, p. 10 (Point 11).

nuclear scientists?]. Efforts should be made to help them gradually transform their world outlook and their style of work." [67]

There is in the document an eye-catching dichotomy between revolutionary nonchalance and caution; between praise of the "revolutionary young people, previously unknown . . . courageous . . . daring . . . vigorous . . . and intelligent," and warnings against youthful overexuberance attributable to the intrigues of elusive ghosts and monsters; between time-tested procedures for settling grievances (Party bodies) and new cultural revolutionary groups, committees and congresses;[68] between disinfecting the cadres and distinguishing the good from the comparatively good, both from those who had committed serious mistakes but had not turned into antisocialist rightists, and all three from "the small number of anti-Party, antisocialist rightists;" [69] between calls for a thorough educational reform "beginning with simplifying complicated material" plus short courses, and an insistence that the students' "main task is to study;" between petit-bourgeois conceptions of culture and of knowledge, and fear that the cultural goings on might leave China with only a spiritual atom bomb, the "pillar supporting the heavens," that is, the red plastic-covered edition of *Quotations from Chairman Mao Tse-tung*;[70] between grasping revolution and promoting production: "if the masses are fully aroused and proper arrangements are made, it is possible to carry on both the cultural revolution and production without one hampering the other, while guaranteeing high quality in all our work."[71]

For all its strident calls to usher in a new world, the *Decision* is a compromise document, witness to yet another stalemate within the leadership. Compared with 1961-63 there is a redistribution of influence, the left renascent, semantically jubilant. There are only losers, but no real victors.[72]

[67] *Ibid.*, p. 11 (Point 12). A nuclear device was exploded on December 24, 1966. It was reportedly technologically unsuccessful, the "dirtiest" to-date. The explosion emitted materials associated with an H-bomb: U-235, U-238, and lithium-6. According to C. H. G. Oldham, the guidelines laid down by Point 12 were in all likelihood not upheld in subsequent months. "Science for the Masses?" *FEER* (May 16, 1968), pp. 353-355.

[68] *Decision*, pp. 8-9 (Point 9). Note here the nostalgic reference to the model of the Paris Commune of 1871.

[69] *Ibid.*, p. 8 (Point 8).

[70] Put out by the General Political Department of the PLA in 1964; mass produced after August 8, 1966.

[71] *Decision*, p. 12 (Point 14).

[72] "The 11th Plenary Session of the CPC Central Committee," commented *Pravda* (November 27, 1966), "officially confirmed the great power anti-Leninist course of Mao Tse-tung and his group." The rejection of the élite nature of the Communist Party was described by the Soviets as Mao Tse-tungism, an "arrogant attempt to proclaim Mao Tse-tung's views as the pinnacle of Marxism."

STAGE FOUR: THE RED GUARDS (AUGUST 1966-EARLY 1967)

This time, however, the Lin-Mao Left was not content to let matters rest. It had its opponents on the run, not defeated but in disarray. The big character poster at Peking University and the great indoor debates had shaken many a stout person in authority. "I was confused," Liu Shao-ch'i kept saying in his self-criticism. "I was gripped by fear and confusion . . . I vacillated." An old Maoist military precept has it that when the enemy retreats the revolutionaries attack. If they do not attack, the enemy reforms and strikes back. Already in the last days of May, when truckloads of youngsters, mostly high school pupils, were brought in to orchestrate the struggle sessions against the University's Party Committee and the Peking Municipal Party machine, a new, rather loose formation began to emerge. It was given the name of Red Guards (*Hung-wei-ping*) and its birthplace seems to have been a middle school attached to Tsinghua University. [73] While school was out for the duration, the youngsters played revolutionary hookie, tasting the joys of seeing how their mentors run. The Left's calls for educational reform were to their liking: what was the use of cramming all that complicated verbiage that the academic authorities passed off as knowledge, when, after all the hard obstacles had been negotiated, one ended up in a people's commune doing a job that, as likely as not, would not have the slightest connection with one's training. There was also evidence that the treatment of students by Party and school authorities had often been harsh and arbitrary. [74] One might just as well learn by heart the 300-odd pages of the Chairman's sayings, and skip the rest.

The Decision of the Eleventh Plenary Session of the Central Committee said that "many new things have begun to emerge in the Great Proletarian Cultural Revolution. The cultural revolutionary groups, committees, and other organizational forms created by the masses in many schools and units are something new and of great historical importance. . . . They are an excellent bridge to keep our Party in close contact with the masses. They are organs of power of the proletarian cultural revolution." [75] The Red Guards were at first thought of as one of these new organs of power. At the mass rally in Tien An Men square on August 18, Mao put on a red armband, a magnanimous gesture signifying his approval of the Red Guard

[73] See Anna Louise Strong, *Letter from China*, No. 41 (September 20, 1966).

[74] See, for example, the so-called "incident of 600 work-study students" from Canton who shortly after entering the dual system of education in 1964 were summarily dismissed, sent home or to state farms for self-remolding. *URS*, Vol. 50, No. 3 (January 9, 1968).

[75] *Decision, op. cit.*, p. 8 (Point 9).

movement. By August 20 the urge to consolidate and expand this "reliable reserve of the PLA," as it came to be called, gripped the masses of eight- to twenty-year olds. They began to converge on Peking—the center of revolutionary struggle—to see their leader and swap revolutionary experiences mainly by reciting in unison the Chairman's words and waving the little red book. Classrooms, lecture halls, railroad stations, public buildings, and other places not directly relevant to the cultural cause were commandeered to house the youthful wayfarers, many of whom rapidly developed a liking for city lights and the exhilarating experience of power, and refused to go back whence they had come. The cost of keeping the Red Guards housed, fed, and mobile was to be borne, albeit reluctantly, by municipal and provincial authorities. The burden to Canton was estimated at 250,000 yuan per day (November 1966), not counting the cost of urban transportation provided "free" on presentation of a student card. In addition to food and free lodging, the Guards were supposed to receive half a yuan per day while on active cultural duty. Under the banner of making revolution, the movement of young people to the countryside, which had engaged the energies of decision makers for years, was being reversed. The slogan "From the commune to the commune" lost its meaning when the whole nation—with Peking as its core—became one vast commune. In intervals between their various cultural activities, the Red Guards were kept busy denouncing themselves, exploring by doing, finding out who was their enemy and who was their friend, and attending monster rallies in the square. Rally followed rally, with the Chairman, decked out in an army uniform passing the Guards in review, waving benevolently, saying nothing. The sight of the helmsman, perched on top of an army jeep, surrounded by his close comrades-in-arms and followed by carloads of PLA brass indistinguishable from common soldiers, was enough to send the Red Guards rampaging through the dens of ghosts and monsters inhabiting the socialist superstructure. Probably apocryphal sayings of the Chairman were sufficient to trigger cultural fads of phenomenal dimensions. "What is your name?" the Chairman was reported asking a young Red Guard girl. "Ping Ping," (Civic Virtue), she replied. "Your name—Ping Ping," came the immortal advice, "is too feminine. Revolution cannot be carried out civilly. [76] You must

[76] "A revolution is not a dinner party, or writing an essay, or painting a picture, or doing embroidery; it cannot be so refined, so leisurely and gentle, so temperate, kind, courteous, restrained and magnanimous. A revolution is an insurrection, an act of violence by which one class overthrows another." Mao Tse-tung, "Report on An Investigation of the Peasant Movement in Hunan" (March 1927), SW, Vol. I, p. 28.

call yourself Yau Wu (Be Martial)," which she did forthwith. And many thousands emulated her example.

The Red Guards' cultural activities escalated from enmity toward everything faintly bourgeois and revisionist to attacks on specific "capitalist roaders" and revisionists in Party and government offices, from innuendos to the naming of individual victims, from the general to the particular. In the course of this ascent, the movement developed splits, its rowdiness grew, and ideological commitments got enmeshed in a web of personal vendettas. The general rule seems to have been that admission to the ranks was to have been governed by a "Five Pure Classes" test. Red Guard membership was open to children of workers, poor and lower-middle peasants, soldiers, "good" Party officials, and revolutionary martyrs (i.e., those who had suffered at the hands of the Kuomintang or the Kuomintang's imperialist overlords). [77] In actual practice, however, the descendants of bourgeois classes, of "comparatively good" Party officials, and even of those who had committed "serious mistakes" without sliding into anti-Party, antisocialist rightism or right-opportunism, were considered for membership, once they denounced their class origin and manifested convincing revolutionary zeal and proletarian vigilance. Given the intellectual maturity of the judges, the process of selection for admission into the elite corps ("Mao's little stormtroopers," as the Soviets called them), was bound to generate frictions, intolerance, jealousies, in short, a teenage bedlam with which the old men at the top knew not how to cope. They had brought into being a sorcerer's apprentice whose feverish activity on behalf of the Maoist vision had in the end to be stopped by recourse to the timeless magic of the gun. The permanent ad hoc committee of children and adolescents lacked the organizational cohesion one generally expects of communist mass movements. An attempt to set up a central Red Guard headquarters ended in failure almost as soon as it was tried. There seems to have been a contradiction there

---

[77] Later, as factionalism within the young rebel ranks grew into anarchy, it became extremely difficult to define a martyr. In Canton, for example, the "Red Flag" faction composed mainly of students, fought another faction, composed of young workers, in a series of bloody encounters known as "the August [1967] massacre." Four months later, the Red Flag people complained that their slain comrades were being vilified: "Those who hid themselves in gutters during the August storm are making a lot of noise now. They babble: 'Those who died in the August violent struggle lost their lives for the faction; their death was lighter than the feathers of sparrows.'" This, the Red Flag people said, was a denigration of revolutionary martyrs. Red Guard tabloid, *Cultural Revolution Critic* (Canton), January 1968, in *URS*, Vol. 50, Nos. 11-12 (February 9, 1968), p. 158. See also John Israel, "The Red Guards in Historical Perspective: Continuity and Change in the Chinese Youth Movement," *China Quarterly* (April-June 1967), pp. 1-32.

between defiling some authority and accepting any authority, a defiance of social structuring when sponsored anarchy was so much sweeter. In opening wide the dam of pent-up youthful frustrations, the left-wing social engineers had underestimated the youth's propensity for playpen cruelty and overestimated the privileged young people's presumed drive toward an ascetic community of men and women bound by a common desire to see the world improved. Perhaps the leaders' memories had failed them. The noble aspirations of their own youth were given too much weight; the execution of those ideals through highly structured and repressive forms of social organization was seen as the aberration of a "handful." From a perspective of half a century, the aspirations may have appeared purer and nobler than they actually had been. To give the totalitarian leftists credit where credit is due, one could argue that they fell victim to their wishful recollections. As adults brought up in a hard school, they were not far off on their demography: they appealed to the largest age bracket of China's society. Yet they seemed to have erred in their estimation of the numerically superior youths' ability to unify and better the land.

Given a free hand, the youngsters succumbed to ideological frenzy. Nominally instructed but practically unrestrained by Chen Po-ta's Cultural Revolution Group within the Central Committee of a Party, which, they were told, was full of a handful of saboteurs, the revolution's first generation went on a simulated revolutionary spree, the likes of which had rarely been seen. Flapper girls, Hong Kong-type barbers, "social youths," reactionary street names, intellectuals (standing on stools, wearing the white cap of humility, bowing to their pupils' demands, cleaning out rest rooms, begging for forgiveness) were all subjected to a vast cleaning operation. Inspired by the thought of "the greatest Marxist-Leninist of our era," [78] the builders of new China smashed the remaining church windows, insulted the few surviving nuns,[79] demanded that all personages of bourgeois background get out of Peking, ordered the better restaurants to serve only cheap meals, pushed old men and women through jeering crowds, dragged out art objects from private homes, smashed them and set them afire, made bonfires of books,[80] closed

[78] Lin Piao, Foreward to the second edition of *Quotations from Chairman Mao Tse-tung* (Peking: *FLP*, December 16, 1966).

[79] *New York Times* (September 1, 1966), p. 3.

[80] "[Mao] has banned the reading of Marxist-Leninist literature. He burns progressive Marxist-Leninist literature." Wang Ming, *op. cit.*, p. 9. Cf., Anatoly Kuznetsov's account of the burning of books in the Soviet Union in 1937 and the continuing control of creative activity by people who are ignorant, cynical, and removed from literature. *Time* (August 8, 1969); *New York Times* (August 17, 1969). Cf. Julia Wang, *A Study of the Criteria for Book Selection in Communist China's Public Libraries, 1949-1964* (Hong Kong: *URI*, 1968).

Peking's cemetery for foreigners, and renamed it "anti-imperialist, anti-revisionist orchard," and generally, in the words of one Hong Kong observer, gave vent to "an emotional pressure that existed in private households, in government offices, and, in fact, throughout the nation."[81]

"Beating drums and singing revolutionary songs, detachments of Red Guards are out in the streets doing propaganda work, holding aloft big portraits of Chairman Mao, extracts from the Chairman's works, and great banners with the words: 'We are the critics of the old world; we are the builders of the new world.' They have held street meetings, put up big-character posters and distributed leaflets in their attack against all the old ideas and habits of the exploiting classes. . . . Shop signs which spread odious feudal and bourgeois ideas have been removed, and schools tainted with feudalism, capitalism, or revisionism or which had no revolutionary significance have been replaced by revolutionary names. The service trades have thrown out obsolete rules and regulations. . . . [In Shanghai the Red Guards] have taken down all the imperialist signs from walls and removed the bronze lions outside one of the big buildings. The revolutionary workers and staff of Shanghai barber shops have adopted revolutionary measures in response to the proposals of the Red Guards: they no longer cut and set hair in the grotesque fashions indulged in by a small minority of people; they cut out those services especially worked out for the bourgeoisie, such as manicuring, beauty treatments, and so on. . . . In Lhasa, the city's streets have been bubbling with excitement. . . . Carrying big portraits of Chairman Mao, displaying declarations of war on the old world, and beating drums and gongs, hundreds of Red Guards and revolutionary students and teachers of the Tibetan Normal School and the Lhasa Middle School took to the streets in a vigorous offensive to destroy the 'four olds'—old ideas, old culture, old customs, and old habits. . . . They proposed that literary and art groups forbid the performance of operas and plays which reek of imperialism and feudalism."[82]

Apparently the Red Guards did not limit themselves to beating drums: they beat people too, and were, in turn, beaten up by them.

[81] Robert Tung, "The Sins of the Capitalists," *FEER* (September 8, 1966), p. 441. Cf. *New York Times* (August 27, 1966), pp. 1, 11, reporting on *Radio Peking* broadcast monitored in Tokyo. See also *New York Times* (September 5, 1966), pp. 1-2.

[82] "Red Guards Destroy the Old and Establish the New," *Peking Review* (September 2, 1966). On August 25 the Guards reportedly sacked the principal temple in Lhasa and destroyed all religious effigies. *The Cultural Revolution in China* (Keesing's Research Report), *op. cit.*, p. 19. See also Hans Granqvist, *The Red Guard: A Report on Mao's Revolution* (New York: Praeger, 1967), Chapter 5.

As the frenzy mounted, reports started coming in from the provinces of torture administered to Party officials (e.g., in Anwhei, November 11, 1966) and of rising opposition to the youngsters' revolutionary tantrums, from workers, peasants, less exalted youths, Party cadres, and others. In February 1967 and the following months, the Soviet press described the cultural activities of the Red Guards as "organized violence and savage hooligan revelry," [83] called the PLA's reliable reserve "pogromists" who delighted in "anti-Soviet bacchanals," talked of "acts of banditry," "farcical Hung-wei-ping trials" and "hooligan escapades," "Chinese thugs," "witches' sabbaths," and predicted that the "Hung-wei-ping will disappear, leaving only a faint smudge on the history of the 1960's." [84] In answer to which, according to the Soviets, the Chinese "showered filth upon our people and its Party." [85] On July 16, 1966, as a sample of things to come, *Jen-min Jih-pao* referred to the Soviet leadership as a "revisionist clique," a "bunch of renegades" (also a "gang" and a "handful" of renegades) "more disgusting and shameless than . . . Khrushchev." [86]

The first peak of Red Guards' revolutionary exuberance was apparently reached in the five days of August 24-28, 1966. On the latter date, *Jen-min Jih-pao* began to throw cold water on the youngsters. It called on them to behave properly, carry out the revolution through to the end by peaceful means, and learn discipline from the PLA. Immediately, posters began to appear acknowledging mistakes and excesses and vowing to reform, but the rampage went on. Mass rallies kept the Guards busy, but also whipped up their thirst for more flesh and blood victims. On September 7 *Jen-min Jih-pao* told the Guards to suspend their activities and lend a hand with the autumn harvest, but apparently to no avail. On November 17 the Guards were told that they could no longer live off the largesse of the Party-State, that they should stop coming to Peking and declog the railroads needed for economic construction and preparation for war. Nothing much happened. On December 5 the youngsters were ordered to get out of Peking by the 21st of the month, but they stayed. To lighten the burden on the railroads and temper the young people in the hardships of revolution, the Guards

[83] USSR Ministry of Foreign Affairs, Note to the Chinese Embassy in Moscow protesting against attacks on the Soviet Embassy staff in Peking, *Pravda* (February 9, 1967), p. 5.

[84] *Izvestia* (February 8, 1967), p. 2; *Pravda* (February 9, 1967), p. 5; *Pravda* and *Izvestia* (June 22, 1967), p. 3; *Pravda* (February 20, 1967), p. 3; *Izvestia* (May 5, 1967), p. 3.

[85] *Pravda* and *Izvestia* (February 16, p. 3, and February 17, pp. 2-3, 1967).

[86] *Peking Review* (July 21, 1966), pp. 9-11.

were told by Lin Piao (November 3) to stage little Long Marches, the sort of thing their elders had done under much more adverse circumstances thirty-odd years earlier. Groups of young people wearing red armbands, carrying flags and large pictures of Mao Tse-tung, reciting the Chairman's words, and waving their little red books, could be seen marching hither and thither—mainly toward Peking—over country roads, making revolution. In October 1966 the campaign against the four olds began to lose momentum, the noise level subsided somewhat as the Red Guards searched for new revolutionary peaks to scale.

On November 23 the Red Guard movement found something new to do. The fierce struggle going on at the top of the communist pyramid burst into the open. The Guard organization in Peking University published on that day a pamphlet calling for the dismissal of Liu Shao-ch'i and Teng Hsiao-p'ing as "leaders of the anti-Party group." The demand was repeated in posters. The accusations leveled against the two top persons in authority were quite specific, detailing all sorts of alleged crimes committed by the accused as far back as 1945 and 1956. The information had clearly been leaked to the poster writers by other high persons in authority bent on getting rid of the two leaders. Other posters (December 26-27) revealed that Liu had made a public self-criticism on October 23 before a Work Conference of the Party's Central Committee, and that his self-criticism ("I must have committed right-inclined opportunism") was superficial and insincere.[87] The self-criticism implicated Teng Hsiao-p'ing, Chen Yun, and others, and expressed repentance for sending out the work teams "to monopolize the mass movement." "I was gripped by the fear of confusion, great democracy, rebellion of the masses against us, and uprisings of counterrevolutionaries."

The big game hunt was on. It was open season on topmost Party persons in authority who were by now deprived of their organizational foothold.[88] In June and July Mao's "swimming fish"—dissidents without a regular organization, with only the authority of the Chairman and the strong arm of the PLA to back them—were caught by Liu's work teams. They were, in Liu's words, "encircled and attacked . . . branded as 'counterrevolutionaries,' 'rightists,' 'sham leftists,' 'swimming fish,' etc."[89] Now the reverse

[87] Liu's self-criticism may be found in *Collected Works of Liu Shao-ch'i, 1958-1967* (Hong Kong: URI, 1968), pp. 357-364.

[88] "Black Hand Huang said: 'If a certain organization exists, then I exist; if a certain organization dies, I die also.' This black devil only had half of it right." *Kiangsi People's Radio* (January 25, 1967) in *URS*, Vol. 50, No. 8 (January 26, 1968), p. 117.

[89] Liu Shao-ch'i's "Self-Examination," in *SCMP*, No. 4037 (October 9, 1967), pp. 1-7.

was the case: the swimming fish were pursuing the sharks. Arrests, seizures, kidnappings, Hung-wei-ping trials, public confessions and self-examinations by hitherto untouchable leaders followed in rapid succession.[90] Liu Shao-ch'i and Teng Hsiao-p'ing criticized themselves at a Central Committee Work Session on October 23. Since this was deemed insufficient, Ch'i Pen-yu addressed eight questions to the Head of State and published them in Jen-min Jih-pao on April 1, 1967.[91] Between April 3 and 10 three mass rallies were organized in Peking to denounce Liu's alleged towering crimes, his rightist deviation, and the plot he had allegedly hatched up to bring about a capitalist restoration in China. Liu's answer to the eight questions appeared on wall posters in early August. It, too, was judged superficial. On July 9 Liu made another self-examination and probably many more thereafter.

In the meantime the teenage Red Guards ignoring—probably on reliable authority—repeated pleas to go back home, roamed the streets screaming for vengeance. They held demonstrations denouncing Liu as "the top Party person in authority taking the capitalist road," "the No. 1 rightist and counterrevolutionary," and "China's Khrushchev"; accused Teng of being the No. 2 Party person in authority taking the capitalist road, and demanded that a special session of the National People's Congress be summoned forthwith to remove both No. 1 and No. 2 from their posts. The Guards were ready to "drag them out" and do whatever was necessary to sterilize them in the heat of revolution. It has been suggested that Liu's and Teng's life was saved by the moderating influence of Chou En-lai whose access to Mao was probably equal to that of Lin Piao and the fiery Chiang Ching. Liu's wife, Wang Kuang-mei, was subjected to refined indignities. She reportedly admitted having committed a multitude of political errors—duly recounted by wall posters—and ascribed them to capitalist influences and her bourgeois education.[92] In April and May 1967 many articles and editorials were published in

[90] "According to incomplete data, the number of people persecuted, arrested, and physically annihilated by Mao Tse-tung and his group in the course of the 'cultural revolution' exceeded five million long ago." Wang Ming, op. cit., p. 42.

[91] The eight questions ranged from Liu's alleged deviations at the outbreak of the Sino-Japanese war, through "sabotage of the socialist education movement," to errors allegedly committed during the Cultural Revolution. The questions may be found in Collected Works of Liu Shao-ch'i, 1958-1967, op. cit., p. 368.

[92] Wang Kuang-mei reportedly toured the country during the "Four Clean-Ups" movement (Chapter 9), apparently in an attempt to keep the clean-ups within Party channels. Already at that time the movement was slipping out of the authority faction's fingers.

leading newspapers bringing to the attention of the masses more and more evidence concerning the crimes of the fallen leaders. [93]

P'eng Chen was arrested on December 4, 1966; paraded before 100,000 jeering adolescents on December 12. Lo Jui-ching, caught by Lin's troopers in July, was rearrested by Mao's Guards on December 20. On the same day, Lu Ting-yi and Yang Shang-kun (an alternate member of the Central Committee's Secretariat) were put under arrest. On January 3, 1967 it was officially reported that Chou Yang had been put under lock and key. On January 4 and 5, P'eng, Lo, Lu, and Yang were subjected to mass insults at Red Guard struggle sessions. They bowed their heads and humbly confessed their sins. P'eng Teh-huai was caught in Chengtu on December 24, 1966.[94] On January 3, 1967 the Red Guards arrested Po I-po, Vice Premier and Chairman of the State Economic Commission who, behind the backs of the masses and under the cloak of socialist planning, had for years been laying the foundations of capitalism in China. They dragged him from Canton to Peking, and displayed him there before the masses as an example of a particularly vicious anti-Party, antisocialist, rightist counterrevolutionary capitalist roader. Ch'en P'i-hsien, First Secretary of the Party's Shanghai Municipal Committee was subjected to two self-examinations, both of which were declared sham, double-dealing, and filled with ulterior motives.

Communist China's top strategist, leader of the 1934 Long March, Marshal Chu Teh, was toppled because he had been an "ambitionist" and was associated with P'eng Teh-huai. However, Chu Teh reemerged on January 25, 1969, no worse for wear, at a reception given by Mao for revolutionary fighters. Marshal Ho Lung was denounced for being an "ambitious gangster." Yang Yung, a general, was reportedly fired for having tried to fire General Hsiao Hua. In January the Cultural Revolution Group in the army was thoroughly reorganized. The leaderships of the air force and army academies were condemned for having prevented cadets from demonstrating in support of Mao.

"Mao Tse-tung and his group," commented *Pravda*, "are launching new attempts to establish a dictatorship of personal power in the country."[95] The "chief obstacles on this path," according to *Pravda*,

[93] "Evidence of the Crime of the No. 1 Person in Authority Taking the Capitalist Road in Advocating the System of Capitalist Exploitation," *Jen-min Jih-pao* (April 15, 1967); *Peking Review* (April 21, 1967); "Betrayal of Proletarian Dictatorship Is Essential Element in the Book on 'Self-Cultivation,' " *Hung-ch'i*, editorial (May 8, 1967).

[94] J. D. Simmonds, "P'eng Te-huai: A Chronological Re-Examination," *China Quarterly* (January-March 1969), pp. 120-138.

[95] "Situation in CPR Becomes Heated," *Pravda* (April 14, 1967), p. 5.

were the Communist Party and true communists "who regard the Party not as an instrument for establishing the arbitrary rule of a small handful of politicians." The Cultural Revolution was "coming more and more to resemble a reactionary military coup."

THE FIFTH STAGE: REVOLUTIONARY REBELS, REVOLUTIONARY VIOLENCE, REVOLUTIONARY COMMITTEES, ECONOMISM AND FACTIONALISM (EARLY 1967-AUGUST 1967)

Having cleared the decks of top persons in authority taking the capitalist road, the Cultural Revolution began to tackle the economic base of China's society. At the time of the autumn harvest, Chou En-lai had instructed the Red Guards to keep their reforming zeal away from the farms. But on December 26, 1966 and again on January 1, 1967 *Jen-min Jih-pao* issued a call for the revolutionary takeover of factories, farms, mines, and other enterprises where rightists, right-opportunists, and capitalist roaders allegedly held sway. The transition from the superstructure—i.e., the realms of Party and government affairs and of cultural activity in the widest sense—to the economic base of China's society, that is toward seizure of the economic apparatus, from ideas about policy to the actual formulation of policy, was an important event in the development of the Cultural Revolution. Until that time the effectiveness of Mao's thought had been tested primarily in realms that eluded quantification. After January 1967 it began to be tested in terms of tons of steel produced, bushels of wheat grown—in short, in terms of "concrete" economic variables. At that point the Cultural Revolution began to directly affect the livelihood of the workers and peasants; it was no longer a power struggle at the top which most people only read about in the papers and wall posters.

The transition from superstructure to base was not smooth or even: there were orders and counterorders, attacks and retreats reflecting the shifting power balance at the top, the strength of the opposing forces at the local level, time of year (e.g., before or after harvest), and other factors. The revolutionary pendulum swung from the left to right as confusion and unrest grew progressively worse. There were signs that as the year dragged on, what remained of the center began to lose control over events in the provinces; the specter of national disintegration, civil war, and local warlordism once again haunted China.

From the immense confusion of those times it is possible to extract a number of guideposts. They are: (1) the emergence of the so-called "Revolutionary Rebels," (2) economism, (3) strikes, sabotage, slowdowns in the economy and physical violence in the cities and the countryside, (4) the establishment of "Revolutionary Committees" based on "Three-Way Alliances" (also called "Three-In-One Combinations"), and (5) pervading it all, "bourgeois and petty bourgeois" factionalism.

Revolutionary Rebels

The Red Guards were used to knock down the established order ("Suspect all, overthrow all") and create a revolutionary ferment as a prelude to the takeover of power over the economy and politics of the country by the Left faction centering on the Central Committee's Cultural Revolution Group and the army's Left-wing command. The Red Guards, however, consisted mostly of children who could hardly have been entrusted with the actual exercise of authority over the economy and state of affairs of the country. In spite of repeated attempts to bring the Red Guard movement under some sort of central control, give the movement an organizational structure, in spite of rhetoric about its being the emerging organ of proletarian power, it must have been clear to the sponsors that sooner or later the children would have to go back to school and that their usefulness as instruments of revolutionary transformation was strictly limited. They could destroy the old but could hardly be entrusted with running the complex machinery of the state or govern the economy. In the process of sweeping away the old superstructure of ideas and with it the men in charge of ideas, the Red Guards splintered into an incredibly large number of factions, trading insults and accusations, and wallowing in personal animosities that in time overshadowed issues of a higher, ideological order. The children's crusade had sooner or later to be brought to an end, and replaced by a crusade of adults.

The instruments chosen by the Mao-Lin group to bring about actual seizure of the economic apparatus were revolutionary groups consisting of revolutionary workers, peasants, and "good" cadres. They were to take over enterprises, offices, factories, mines, and farms in order to implement the Maoist economic program of "grasping revolution and promoting production," emphasizing moral incentives, production leaps, self-reliance, income equality, and the creative wisdom of the unlettered. The name given to these revolutionary groups was "Red Rebels" or more commonly "Revolutionary Rebels." The rebels first came into prominence as agents of power seizure at the base, in early January 1967. On January 3 a communiqué by the Chinese Association of Revolutionary Rebels announced the seizure of the All-China Federation of Trade Unions and of its organ the *Workers' Daily*. That the Revolutionary Rebels were thenceforth to become the main agents of the Cultural Revolution (gradually displacing the Red Guards) became evident between January 9 and 20. On January 9 the Shanghai Workers' Revolutionary Rebel General Headquarters consisting of no less than 31 revolutionary rebel organizations, issued an "Urgent Notice" informing the masses that they had taken over the Party and municipal government of the city, thrown out many of the former government's decrees, and dealt a crushing blow to the reactionary bourgeois line. How much of what the urgent notice said was true to the fact and how much of it was bravura, is difficult to say. There were, in fact, five power seizures before power was finally seized, and even then no one was quite sure. Subsequent events in Shanghai and elsewhere lead one to think that the opposition to the rebels had probably been much stronger than the notice conveyed.[96] Antirevolutionary revolutionary rebels soon sprang up in the city and elsewhere, vying for influence. " 'Rebels,' 'rebels'—all traitors, special agents, spies, black hands, capitalist roaders have put up the banner 'Support the Rebels,' sneaked into the mass organizations, and turned out to be qualified 'rebels'!"[97] The policy was to do unto others lest they do unto you. Everyone had a fifty-fifty chance of being exposed as a villain, since by definition villains existed everywhere. On January 20 another urgent notice was issued, this time by an outfit naming itself the Shanghai Peasant Revolutionary Rebel Organization. It heralded the extension of the revolutionary rebel form of organization to the countryside. On January 11 the Mao-Lin group in Peking sent a "Message of Greetings to Revolutionary Rebel Organizations in Shanghai," and followed this up with a "Letter to Poor and Lower-Middle Peasants and Cadres at All Levels in Rural People's Communes All Over the Country" (February 20). Both documents conveyed the Left's official approval of the revolutionary rebel way to communism. The message spoke of a "new counterattack of the bourgeois reactionary line" and of the "brilliant example" set by the Shanghai rebels for the working class and all laboring people. The working class and the laboring people, however, were not greatly taken by the rebels. Fearing for their livelihood and unconvinced by the ascetic philosophy of the Maoist Left, they rebelled against the rebels. In fact, the emergence of the Shanghai revolutionary rebels

[96] On the Shanghai events see "The Experience of the Shanghai January Revolution," *URS*, Vol. 50, No. 2 (January 5, 1968).

[97] "The Ex-Central-South Bureau Must Be Thrown Into Great Confusion," by "Facing the Battlefield with a Smile" Revolutionary Committee of Chungshan University, *Chung-ta Chan-pao* (Canton), January 11, 1968, in *URS*, Vol. 50, No. 7 (January 23, 1968).

organization culminated weeks of bitter strife between workers, many Party cadres, and managers on the one side, and the heralds of the new world on the other.

Economism[98]

The weapon allegedly used by the followers of the Liu faction was "economism," an appeal to the workers' and peasants' understandable desire for an improvement in their living conditions threatened by the concepts and actions of the Left. Taking a cue from Mao's reflection that "we should support whatever the enemy opposes and oppose whatever the enemy supports," Party and government apparat-men encouraged the workers and peasants to take advantage of the recolutionary ferment, travel a bit at the state's expense, go to Peking to present their case, push for higher wages, take in a little sightseeing on the way, and—like the Red Guards— "exchange revolutionary experiences," "rebel and take part in violent struggle." At the Malu People's Commune in Chaiting *hsien*, for example, 900 participants in a production brigade meeting adjourned to go to the county seat and "rebel" in the Party Municipal Committee. The deputy brigade chief was quoted as telling the peasants that "it is more profitable to rebel in the municipal committee than to engage in production. Each person can get six big pieces of bread a day in addition to the opportunity for sightseeing."[99] "The enemy," wrote *Hung-ch'i* on January 12, 1967, "has deceived many people with their economism. They increased wages and benefits, gave out money and goods. They incited the workers to leave their working posts and to stop working. Railway communications were disrupted. This is economism: disregard for the interests of the state, sabotage of socialist ownership."[100]

Having watched millions of Red Guards travel free on the railways, the railway workers decided to do the same. For two days the railway system of China came to a standstill. Sporadic strikes on the railroads continued through January, especially around Shanghai, where work stoppages in support of wage demands occurred ever since mid-December. Bloody fighting between railwaymen and Revolutionary Rebel groups was reported from the city on January 8, and admitted by Peking Radio a few days later. Restiveness among railway workers erupted again in late summer 1967 and in winter 1967-68.[101] Although, as we have seen, the Rebels claimed to have

[98] Cf. Chapter 12 below.
[99] Hsiao Ai, "Internal Struggle Hurts Peking's Economy," *Chinese Communist Affairs* (April 1967), pp. 21-22.
[100] *China News Analysis*, No. 648 (1967), pp. 4-5.
[101] *Ibid.*, No. 698 (March 1, 1968).

taken control of Shanghai on January 9, fighting, strikes, and other disturbances continued until early February. On February 6 a Paris Commune-type committee was said to have been constituted to govern the unruly city. Several days later, the commune was denounced in Peking wall posters because it had not been approved by Mao and because it represented dangerous "federalism." It was reorganized shortly thereafter into a "revolutionary committee."[102] On March 18 the Central Committee was still writing urgent letters calling on workers to resist (with the PLA's help) anarchism, selfishness, bourgeois "small group mentality," economism, and other evils, and to work eight hours a day, reserving their free time for revolutionary cultural activity and on the spot exchange of experiences.[103] Apparently misled by rightists and other persons in authority, the workers had cut off Shanghai's water and electricity supply, extracted cash from relatively cooperative managements, went on a buying spree suggestive of loss of confidence in the currency, and hampered work in the port.[104] The Revolutionary Rebels' "Urgent Notice" of January 9, ordered the "circulating funds of all government offices, organizations and enterprises . . . [to be] frozen. . . . This [was to] be effected by the financial organizations at the municipal level and at all other levels under the joint supervision of the Revolutionary Rebel groups and the revolutionary masses."[105] The Notice called on all Shanghai workers traveling throughout the country to stop exchanging revolutionary experience and "to return

---

[102] "At the time when the 38 organizations were holding a meeting to draft a document for the establishment of the 'Shanghai People's Commune,' 25 other organizations were found also holding a meeting for the establishment of a 'New Shanghai People's Commune.' . . . It seemed that two factions would be formed." Chang Ch'un-ch'iao in URS, Vol. 50, No. 2 (January 5, 1968), pp. 21-22.

[103] "Letter from the Central Committee of the CPC to Revolutionary Workers and Staff and Revolutionary Cadres in Industrial and Mining Enterprises Throughout the Country," March 18, 1967. Describing the power seizure in Shanghai, Chang Ch'un-ch'iao, Deputy Head of the Central Cultural Revolution Group said: "The seizure of power occurred many times in Shanghai. . . . One day, some 40 [Revolutionary Rebel] organizations might be represented at the [joint Revolutionary Rebel] conference, and on the next day, over 100. . . . Nobody knew who was who. . . . We were very busy and rather confused." URS, Vol. 50, No. 2 (January 5, 1968), pp. 19-20. Tsao Ti-chiu and Chen Pi-hsien, for example, had formed in January 1967 a "rebel command" within the Shanghai Workers' Revolutionary Headquarters, which, as it transpired a year later, was neither rebel nor a command, and worst of all, it was not revolutionary.

[104] Shanghai banks reportedly paid out money on demand—10 million yuan in one day alone.

[105] "Urgent Notice," op. cit. "Matters related to the adjustment of wages, back payment of wages and material benefits, shall in principle be dealt with at a later stage of the movement."

to Shanghai immediately, so that . . . the 1967 production plans can be overfulfilled."

Krasnaya Zvezda (the organ of the Soviet army) commented on February 28, 1967 that "in rejecting the experience of the USSR and other socialist countries, the CPC leaders declared economic construction a secondary matter and have deprived their people of the prospects and great blessings socialism brings." The workers' natural and understandable demands for better living conditions, the paper continued, were regarded by Peking's Leftists as "the gravest crime," "100 percent counterrevolutionary revisionism," "a dagger used to kill people without bloodshed," "an opium that is poisoning the people." In a spell of forgetfulness of the Soviet Union's not so distant Stalinist past, *Krasnaya Zvezda* analyzed the material condition of the Chinese people in the following terms: "The material circumstances of the Chinese people have deteriorated. Suffice it to say that in the past ten years the real wages of workers in China not only have not increased, but have even declined. Many Chinese workers receive extremely low wages, subsist on wafers made out of chaff, are unable to replace their outdoor clothes (often cotton) for several years on end, and live in debt. New steps to reduce wages have already been taken in the course of the current 'Cultural Revolution.' This was expressed in the abolition of bonuses for the overfulfillment of production assignments."[106] The preaching of a philosophy of poverty was combined with an "adventurist economic policy."[107]

One of the accusations made against Liu Shao-ch'i was that in conversations with foreign guests he had "babbled": "The final goal of the Chinese Communist Party . . . is to build up China, ensure that China will be an independent country and a sovereign state, and improve the livelihood of the people. . . . What we mean by improving the livelihood of the people is to improve people's economic life and cultural life in the realization of socialism and communism." *Liberation Army Literature and Art*, Lin Piao's and/or Chiang Ching's semimonthly, combated this counterrevolutionary view of China's socialist destiny in its issue of January 25, 1968: "In popular language [to improve the people's livelihood] means to enjoy eating,

[106] "What Lies Behind the Struggle Against 'Economism'?" *Krasnaya Zvezda* (February 28, 1967), p. 3. The term "economism" was first applied to certain Russian Marxists who around 1900 held that Marxism's main preoccupation was struggle for better living conditions for the workers, and that political struggles took second place.

[107] "Marxism has always characterized preachings of crude egalitarianism and calls for the preservation of poverty and for 'equality' on a backward economic basis, as reactionary petty-bourgeois utopias." T. Timofeyev, "Scientific Socialism and Petty-Bourgeois Ideology," *Pravda* (October 24, 1966), pp. 2-3.

drinking, playing around, and seeking pleasure. This is utterly absurd and reactionary! . . . How can there be a communist society enjoying eating, drinking, playing around, and seeking pleasure?"[108]

Economism spoke more convincingly to the workers and peasants than all the fuss about the correct proletarian line in the opera. Even the model fighters of Taching succumbed to the lures of gain: on January 10, Chou En-lai complained that 10,000 Taching heroes had let the oil gush unattended while they traveled to Peking to exchange revolutionary experiences.[109] Even a year later, the black wind of counterrevolutionary economism was still blowing strong in Hunan, Anhwei, Hopei, Kwangtung, and Inner Mongolia. The new revolutionary leaders of Inner Mongolia, for example, were said to have fallen prey to laziness: "Some play poker or majong deep into the night."[110] Absenteeism, slackness on the job, and apathy became common throughout China. The attitude of indifference toward work persisted into 1969. In Chekiang, farmers were getting ready for the Lunar New Year without heed to the country's enormous effort at the revolutionary transformation of the four olds: "They kill pigs, buy fish, prepare the new year's rice cake, arrange days of rest, visit relatives." One family was cited as having prepared 200 pounds of food for the celebrations.[111] Tu Kuei, the hero of the "Paupers' Co-op" and head of the model Hsipu Production Brigade, Tsunhwa *hsien*, Hopeh Province, distinguished peasant leader of a micro Tachai, was found by an investigating PLA officer to have been really "a local agent of China's No. 1 capitalist roader." When the Cultural Revolution began he had said of the Chairman's works: "What's the good of reading that stuff? Why not get more sleep?" He had also refused to give his donkey to the collective in 1952 and had sold chestnuts for private profit during the Great Leap.[112]

Reports from the countryside indicated strong resistance to

---

[108] "Soviet Union's Khrushchev said: 'Our communism is beef cooked with taro.' China's Khrushchev said in a more civilized manner: 'Our communism is to improve people's livelihood,' and 'on the average each may have his ration of 2,000 catties of grain.' Actually he meant nothing more than 'rice plus pork.' " *Liberation Army Literature and Art*, January 25, 1968, in *URS*, Vol. 50, No. 9 (January 30, 1968), p. 126.

[109] On Taching economism see *China Pictorial*, No. 2 (1969), pp. 26-31. A three-way revolutionary committee (see below) was not formed there until May 31, 1968.

[110] *China News Analysis*, No. 695 (1968): *Inner Mongolian PBS* (January 23, 1968). The No. 4 issue of Canton's *August 1 Combat Bulletin* (January 1968) said of the Canton rebels that "everyone feels that the situation is boring and knows not what to do."

[111] *China News Analysis*, No. 695 (1968): *Chekiang PBS* (January 18, 1968).

[112] See Richard Baum, "A Parting of Paupers," *FEER* (January 4, 1968), pp. 17-19.

endemic stoicism, the Red Guards, Revolutionary Rebels of all hues, and to the collective principle itself. Many peasants deserted their communes and traveled about the country exchanging revolutionary experiences, while allegedly "taking part in violent struggle." Others began parceling out communal property among themselves, roughed up "good," "moderately good," and "bad" cadres alike, neglected tools and machinery, raided food stocks, failed to collect manure for the collective fields, sold livestock, seed, and farm implements on the open market, divided the proceeds among themselves, wrangled over land boundaries, chopped down trees, evaded or avoided payment of the agricultural tax, tried to get out of selling produce to the state, extracted cash advances against future deliveries of industrial crops, and "lay down in the fields" at harvest time.[113] In short, they succumbed to the three slogans of rural economism: "Share out all and eat up all; retain more, sell less; share out more and store up less."[114]

To counter the wave of economism among the peasants and assure essential food supplies, the army was called out to help the peasants with the harvest, protect commune and state property (especially storage bins and farm tool sheds), and prevent the peasants from traveling and paying too much attention to their private plots. Army units were ordered to assume control of all wheat stocks in the main ports, suggesting a history of looting.

More than the "handful of persons" in ultimate authority, factionalism among the masters from the top down, made economism possible.[115] What strikes one in reading the mass of conflicting reports about the cultural goings-on is not so much the desperate seriousness of the leaders, their fuming and fulminating, their calls for revolutionary vigilance and their near paranoic fear of ghosts and demons lurking everywhere; rather it is the good-natured going about their business of the peasants and workers, deftly grasping and hanging onto every little freedom presented to them by the confusion at the top, whipping the devil of diktat round the village maypole, trading, slaughtering pigs, making rice cakes, visiting with friends, and roughing up Red Guards and Revolutionary Rebels of all factions whenever they interfered too much with the really serious business of wresting from nature a modest living.

Rural cadres deprived of clear-cut orders and backing from the center, easily and perhaps even enthusiastically submitted to peasant manipulations. Work points were accorded more generously and pri-

---

[113] *China News Analysis,* No. 691 (January 12, 1968). Cf. Prybyla "The Economic Cost" [of the Cultural Revolution], *Problems of Communism* (March-April 1968), pp. 1-13.

[114] *Chengtu Radio* (November 20, 1968).

[115] On the phenomenon of factionalism, see below, pp. 531-534.

vate plots grew in size. Small-scale but satisfying private initiative flourished beyond the reach of the enragés. Some enterprising souls even cashed in on the recurrent shortage of Mao buttons as their own special little contribution to the revolutionary upsurge. The cellular character of Chinese society reasserted itself with the breakdown of central authority and the complicity of local officials. An underground private industrial and handicraft system came into being, producing and distributing textiles, leather goods, hardware, glassware, electrical equipment, bricks, tiles, cement, and an array of other goods. Underground construction teams did good business in private contracting jobs. The raw materials needed were acquired or filched from state enterprises and peasants through free-lance middlemen. Private business in wheat, rice, cotton, and edible oils thrived in the economic base, while the superstructure was being cleansed of bourgeois and petit-bourgeois conceptions to the accompaniment of lofty slogans and the beat of the East Is Red. It is not unreasonable to speculate that the sloganeers had met their match in the imperturbable passivity of the people who in their millenial experience had seen ruling dynasties come and go, and whose memories of the Great Leap Forward were not obscured by dialectical ex-post rationalizations.

Revolutionary Violence

Physical violence erupted sporadically and reportedly took heavy toll of life. The peak of violence was probably reached in the early months and in the summer of 1967. During this period wall posters in Peking and other cities, Revolutionary Rebel and Red Guard newspapers, and on occasion the national and provincial press and radio reported battles between Maoists and their opponents, among Mao's opponents, among Maoists, between workers and students, among workers, among students, between peasants and Red Guards, between Red Guards and the PLA, and even among detachments of the PLA. The violent turmoil was directly related to the call of December 26, 1966 to extend the revolution to farms, factories, and enterprises. The revolutionary pendulum swung sharply from right to left (December 1966-January 1967), then to the right again (February 1967, later called the month of the "right adverse current"), then— during the summer—very far to the left (period of the "extreme left deviation"), a little to the right (September 1967-March 1968), and to the left again (April 1968). In January 1967, Po I-po (Chairman of the State Economic Commission) had reportedly tried to commit suicide as did Teng Hsiao-p'ing and Yang Hsiu-fen (Chief Justice of the Supreme Court).

Fighting between workers and Red Guards and among Red Guards and Revolutionary Rebels was reported from Canton in January and February 1967, the adversaries raiding the army's arsenals for weapons. Heavy fighting and "bloody incidents" occurred in Shanghai during this time; near anarchy reigned in Nanking. Peasants beat up Red Guards in Anhwei. There was violence in Honan and Heilungkiang where workers and peasants attacked Revolutionary Rebels. Bloodshed was reported daily from almost every province. The worst incidents apparently occurred in Sinkiang, Inner Mongolia, and Tibet. At the new town of Shihotze (Sinkiang) some 10,000 anti-Maoists, including demobilized soldiers who had been settled in the area, attacked pro-Mao factions with army support. One report indicated that General Wang En-mao's dissident forces comprised seven of the eight regular army divisions in Sinkiang, in addition to about 20,000 former soldiers organized in a so-called "8/1 Field Army."[116] It was also hinted that a Kazakh Liberation Army, some 60,000 strong, staffed with refugees from Sinkiang, was directing anti-Mao guerrilla operations out of Alma Ata (USSR) under the command of Zunum Taipov, a former MVD man who in 1958 had been Deputy Chief of Staff of the Sinkiang Military Region and had defected to the Soviet Union in 1962. Wang En-mao, who re-emerged as one of the 170-odd Presidium members of the Ninth National Party Congress in April 1969, held a trump card which for some years he played with consummate skill: the nuclear testing site at Lop Nor and some of China's major oil fields were in his province. Wang was violently denounced by Red Guards in Sinkiang and Peking in 1967. But a little later (September 1968) he was named third ranking Vice-Chairman of the province's revolutionary committee. Still later he was removed from that post and replaced by Lung Shu-chin from Hunan.[117]

The anti-Maoist movement in Sinkiang was fed by resentment against the excesses of the Red Guards, the wrecking of Moslem mosques and the humiliation of Moslem religious personages, the

[116] P. H. M. Jones, "Sensitive Sinkiang," *FEER* (February 9, 1967), pp. 189-191. See also June Dreyer, "China's Minority Nationalities in the Cultural Revolution," *China Quarterly* (July-September 1968), pp. 96-109.

[117] See *New York Times* (January 17, 1969), p. 4. The Sinkiang Revolutionary Committee denounced Wang in 1968 for his alleged "mountain-stronghold mentality" and for his attempts to carve out for himself an "independent kingdom." He was also said to have "fabricated orders from the central authorities" to promote his own ends. However, Wang was among the distinguished military leaders who attended a reception given by Mao on January 25, 1969 for 40,000 revolutionary activists in Peking's Great Hall of the People. The guest list included Chu Teh, Nieh Jung-chen (Head of the Science and Technology Commission in charge of nuclear research), Yeh Chien-ying, Liu Po-cheng, and Su Yu, all three military leaders since the nineteen-twenties.

restlessness of the young members of the Sinkiang Construction Corps (many of them natives of Canton, Shanghai, and other eastern cities), and the dissatisfaction of former soldiers who had been invited to settle in the region, often presumably against their will. Wang En-mao and his deputy traveled to Peking to negotiate with the faction-torn helmsmen and helmswomen of the revolution. On February 25, 1967 (i.e., during what was later called the "right adverse current"), Chou En-lai implored one and all to put an end to the Cultural Revolution in Sinkiang in order not to fall into the "trap of Soviet revisionism." But things picked up again in May when Wang started putting the heat on local Maoists while publicly expressing loyalty to the Chairman and wholehearted support for the Cultural Revolution.

There was grave trouble in Tibet where opposition to Red Guard excesses raised the specter of yet another rebellion. The Guards had ordered Tibetans to cease and desist from all religious practices, take down prayer flags, burn all joss sticks. They invaded the monasteries, beat up the monks, burned sacred images, desecrated what could not be physically destroyed. According to Chou En-lai, 100,000 lamas enthusiastically engaged in supervised production activities as a means of spiritual salvation and correct moral rebirth. The resentment against these measures reached such proportions that full-scale war seemed inevitable. This was apparently too much for General Chang Kuo-hua, regional commander of the PLA forces charged with the security of this strategically sensitive territory. On February 9, 1967, he reportedly moved against the Maoist youngsters who had "seized power" in Lhasa, arrested 400 of them and manhandled the rest. Airborne forces dispatched from Peking to help the Maoists soon found themselves fighting Chang's troops. Bloody battles, daily executions, and refined cruelties continued through April. In May, Chang was transferred to head the Chengtu region of Szechwan Province. He survived the twists and turns of the revolution, and together with Wang En-mao reemerged at the Ninth Party Congress in April 1969, just as if nothing had ever happened. One prominent victim of the Tibetan anarchy was the Panchen Lama who, following the Dalai Lama's exile, nominally assumed the spiritual headship of Tibet on behalf of Peking. The Panchen Lama had opposed Maoist policies in Tibet, especially the recruitment of monks for productive activities under the supervision of the masses. He was stripped of all his offices and disappeared from public view (February 1967).

Revolutionary violence was reported from Inner Mongolia where troops loyal to deposed General Ulanfu turned on the Maoists and for a time (mid February 1967) reportedly took control of the region.[118] As in Tibet, troops loyal to the Lin-Mao faction had to be dispatched from Peking, and bitter fighting ensued.

The situation in Heilungkiang, another sensitive area and key industrial region, was extremely confused. In January the army apparently wavered, supporting anti-Maoist forces on at least one bloody occasion.

And so it went throughout the country. In February a shift seemed to have occurred in what power there still was at the bickering summit. From Peking came orders, instructions, injunctions, messages, plans, urgent notices, all aimed at restoring a measure of calm and order, stressing discipline and organization, condemning sectionalism and splittism, calling on students to go back to their schools and make revolution in the classrooms under PLA supervision, insisting that the PLA pull itself together and encourage all the warring factions to put aside their differences. A *Hung-ch'i* editorial of February 1, 1967 suggested that revolutionaries of all hues try a modified united front approach toward leading Party cadres, who, it was said, could not all be bad. Arbitrary arrests, the "dragging out" of offensive persons, seizure of property, house searches, and many other favorite pastimes of the Red Guards and Revolutionary Rebels were banned—at least on paper. On February 23, 1967 Chou En-lai deplored the public humiliation of the former Minister of the Coal Industry, Chang Lin-chih, who died following his interrogation by the masses. Yao Yi-lin, the Minister of Commerce, was granted a leave of absence to rest and recuperate after being manhandled and morally mauled by Mao's youngsters. The Red Guards were ordered to stop stomping through the country in imitation of the classic Long March. At the end of February and in early March schools were reopened, but attendance was spotty at best. In spite of the white gauze masks worn by the revolutionary youngsters, there was talk of epidemics as the adolescents carried with them more than germinating ideas. On March 10 it was forbidden to put up big character posters that divulged state secrets, Party documents, and speeches by top Party persons still in authority. By then the question was who was in authority? The "adverse current" of February 1967 was later ascribed mainly to the machinations of Vice-Premier T'an Chen-lin. It was allegedly intended to reverse the denunciations of Liu Shao-ch'i and Teng Hsiao-p'ing. According to the Left's spokesmen Chen Po-ta, Chiang Ching, and Kang Sheng, the "adverse February current" meant: "persistently supporting the Liu-Teng line and pointing the spearhead at the proletarian headquarters headed by Chairman

---

[118] Paul Hyer and William Heaton, "The Cultural Revolution in Inner Mongolia," *China Quarterly* (October-December 1968), pp. 114-128.

Mao and with Vice-Chairman Lin as its deputy leader when the Great
Proletarian Cultural Revolution entered the stage of power seizure,
denying the achievements of the Red Guards and the Great Proletarian Cultural Revolution, and launching a new attack against the Cultural Revolution Group headed by Chen Po-ta and Chiang Ching."[119]

It is likely that the shift in influence toward the right was not
unconnected with the state of China's agricultural arts and the impending spring activity in the fields. The "February right-adverse
current" was short-lived. As soon as the sowing and the planting had
been done, revolutionary fever rose again. A second wave of violence
swept the country during the summer months of 1967, and the
turmoil was worse than ever. This time the extreme left elements of
the left-wing faction had their field day. The top men associated with
this particular outburst were Wang Li, Kuang Feng (a former editor
of *Hung-ch'i*), and Chi Pen-yu, all members of the Cultural Revolution Group, Chiang Chin'g's ideological colleagues, "small lizards
and evil agents of China's Khrushchev," as it transpired later. By the
end of August, China was on the brink of civil war; in some localities
civil war was actually in full swing. Attacks on Liu Shao-ch'i became
more virulent than before: his philosophy was described as "cannibal-
istic," his voice was that of "vampires" and "parasites," his soul was
"bourgeois" and "filthy." (*Hung-ch'i*, April 2, 1967). Low-level
speech poured forth in all its four character ugliness throughout
April, May, June, July, and August. Yet a few weeks earlier Mao
Tse-tung, himself a poet and a man charged by history with attending
to the birth of new revolutionary aesthetics, criticized (or at least
was said to have criticized) some of the poster language and many of
the photographs displayed by the builders of China's communist
future as lacking in artistic merit and short on good taste. On February 26 Mao said that some of the revolutionary wall literature was of
"a very low level."

The summer months saw fierce fighting in almost every province
and autonomous region of China. Only one serious incident is recounted here: the Wuhan revolt.[120]

The triple city of Wuhan, comprising Hankow, Hanyang, and
Wuchang in Hupeh Province, is an important industrial center with a
population of over 2 million. It boasts the only rail and road bridge
over the Yangtse River for hundreds of miles, and by virtue of this

---

[119] *URS*, Vol. 53, No. 24 (December 20, 1968).

[120] For a review of armed uprisings and factional battles elsewhere during
this time, see Keesing's Research Report, *The Cultural Revolution in China* (New
York: Scribner's, 1967), pp. 50-52, 55-58. According to Hsieh Fu-chih, between
April 30 and May 10, 1967, there were 130 armed incidents in Peking, resulting
in 63,500 casualties. See *FEER* (February 1, 1968), p. 184.

fact is a vital north-south traffic link. Soviet arms for North Vietnam passed across the bridge. In March 1967 the administration of the city was nominally taken over by local army units headed by General Chen Tsai-tao, flanked by Chung Han-hua, Second Political Commissar, and Wang Jen-chung, First Secretary of the Central-South Bureau and First Political Commissar of the region. General Chen proclaimed his loyalty to Mao Tse-tung. He apparently found it difficult to govern the city because of the existence there of many rival organizations whose propensity to splinter and abuse each other was limitless. A complicated struggle developed during the spring and early summer months, in the course of which hundreds of people were killed and over two thousand factories and workshops were affected. Traffic over the Chanchiang bridge was interrupted on a number of occasions.

Faced with imminent chaos, Chen Tsai-tao backed the largest and, as it turned out, most conservative faction, the "One Million Heroes" composed of industrial workers allied with peasant formations and elements of the local militia.[121] Toward the end of July the Peking Lin-Mao faction sent two emissaries to Wuhan to mediate the differences which threatened the city and province with civil war. The emissaries (Hsieh Fu-chih and Wang Li) were detained and beaten up by anti-Maoists and at least one of them (Wang) was reportedly paraded through the city wearing a dunce's cap. Chou En-lai flew to Wuhan to negotiate for the release of Hsieh and Wang, and narrowly missed being arrested. On July 22 the two emissaries, somewhat worse for wear, returned to Peking having apparently been released through the personal intervention of General Chen. The release of the emissaries was followed by heavy fighting between Lin-loyal parachute troops and gunboats sent to the city, and local troops supported by security forces and sections of the population.[122] On August 4 Canton Radio reported that Wuhan's hospitals were filled with wounded soldiers. Although it was claimed that a Maoist administration was in charge of the city and province after August 1, heavy fighting apparently continued both in the city and throughout the province as late as August 15. The Wuhan incident

---

[121] Militia forces seemed in general to have given support to the more moderate factions. In Szechwan the militia became a powerful local army under the name of the "Industrial Army."

[122] "At the close of July 1967 [Mao Tse-tung] sent paratroops and warships to strike at the garrison of the Wuhan Military District and to take bloody retribution against the working people of Wuhan. He followed this up by sending the 40th and 47th Armies and another five divisions against the revolutionary workers and revolutionary military units in Canton, causing enormous bloodshed among the revolutionary masses with such heavy weapons as artillery, tanks and so forth." Wang Ming, *op. cit.*, pp. 5-6.

had shown that there was disaffection, or at very least disorientation in the army and that anti-Maoist forces could count on widespread popular support.[123]

In September 1967 the revolutionary pendulum swung to the right again. The summer excesses were roundly denounced as left-extreme deviation, the "small lizards and evil agents" Wang Li, Kuang Feng, and Chi Pen-yu were removed from the Cultural Revolution Group, and the task of rebuilding the country's civil administration began under the supervision of an imperfectly loyal army.[124] The autumn harvest was approaching and the more exciting but economically negative cultural activities had to be called off, or at least suspended for the time being.

Revolutionary Committees: Three-in-One Combination

The multiplication of groups claiming to exercise power in the name of Mao Tse-tung's revolutionary proletarian line was not only intellectually confusing but downright unworkable and prejudicial to the orderly conduct of economic affairs. Since late 1965 the revolution seemed to have been running in circles. At some time or other just about everyone fell victim to its tantrums, yet in the end the same actors reappeared, familiar faces smiled from the rostrums, the same old voices called on the people to be vigilant. True, many people formerly in top authority vanished into outer darkness, but at the middle and lower levels of the rambling power structure the survival rate was amazingly high. Perhaps in the long run the principal victims of the upheaval were the young whose credulity and inexperience had been used to the full by hardened manipulators behind the scenes. Youthful ideals, hope, and aspirations had been dashed to the ground, trampled upon by the inexorable need of society to survive as a structured whole, perhaps a little more intolerant and rigid than before. "As soon as disorder is turned into order," said Chou En-lai, "production can quickly pick up and rise."[125]

So the little long mini-marchers were marched by the PLA back into their classrooms where they read and reread the Chairman's works, with peasants and soldiers acting as intellectual mentors.[126] Those with an obstinate liking for the outdoors were harnessed to

---

[123] See Harald Munthe-Kaas, "Problems for the PLA," *FEER* (October 5, 1967), pp. 39-43; William Whitson, "The Field Army in Chinese Communist Military Politics," *China Quarterly* (January-March 1969), pp. 1-30.

[124] Wall posters in Peking on October 17, 1967 described Wang Li as a "Taiwan spy."

[125] Speech at Wuhan on October 9, 1967, quoted by *FEER* (October 19, 1967), p. 125.

[126] On this see Harald Munthe-Kaas, "The Wrong Idea," *FEER* (December 14, 1967), pp. 469-470. Cf. Chapter 12 below.

the loading and unloading of ships on the waterfront and to other activities of a manual character. The revolution ceased to be fun and games and became the hard-nosed drudgery of economic construction: up at six, toil at the lathe and the mine face, with Mao study for recreation.

While the youngsters were cleared off the streets and highways of China, the adults set about rebuilding the machinery of government. One thing the Cultural Revolution had shown was that the adults' views on how social engines should be put together were quite divergent but fairly evenly balanced. One could not settle the differences by resort to arms, even though one had tried, because as soon as an armed confrontation occurred the contending sides split and splintered, fought among themselves while fighting each other, confused and demoralized the army, and ended up almost exactly where they had begun.

The compromise solution consisted in the establishment of new organs of provincial and municipal administration called "Revolutionary Committees." These were to be based on a triple alliance or "three-in-one combination" of Revolutionary Rebels (that is, "leaders of revolutionary organizations who truly represented the masses," as well as "up-and-coming" representatives of the revolutionary masses, i.e., young people, former Red Guards, etc.),[127] rehabilitated Party cadres (that is, "the majority of cadres who had proved to be good or comparatively good"), and representatives of the PLA. Nominally the three participants in the committees were to be equal, but in practice the representatives of the army came to be more equal than the other two. The reason was simple: there was no such thing as a coherent Revolutionary Rebel community—there were only factions ready at the drop of a hat to fly at each other's throats, compete with each other for the distinction of being the most revolutionary, and accuse each other of revolutionary deficiencies. Nor was there any such thing as a clear-cut no-nonsense good or comparatively good cadre community. Cadres vied with each other for the honor of being classified as good or comparatively good, denounced each other; some were rehabilitated in February, only to be found bad in March, comparatively good in April, and sent down to the country for remolding in May. Thus neither the Rebels nor the rehabilitated cadres could govern the country by themselves. The three-in-one combination was designed to bring them together under army supervision, if not in perfect harmony, at least with a minimum

[127]"In this Great Proletarian Cultural Revolution, the shortcomings and errors of the leaders of revolutionary mass organizations who truly represent the masses are a question of one finger among ten, and a problem that arises in the course of progress." *Hung-ch'i*, No. 5 (1967).

of bloodshed. By virtue of this function, the army became the *de facto* ruler of China.[128] The best that could be said for the army was that it (a) remained the only organized social body in the midst of chaos, (b) was less split than other social formations, (c) had a sense of duty, and (d) possessed the argumentative power of the gun. With occasional lapses and a compromise here and there struck between independent-minded regional commanders and the Lin-Mao center, the PLA could, on the whole, be counted on by the Left and even more by the slightly right-of-left pragmatists among the leftists.[129]

Throughout 1967 (but especially after September of that year) and until September 1968, the PLA set about the arduous task of "spontaneously" creating Revolutionary Committees in the twenty-eight administrative regions of China. It was tough going. The way in which the three-way alliances were spontaneously set up seems to have been through "democratic mass consultations" between warring Rebel and cadre factions sponsored by the army. Democratic consultation usually meant that the local PLA authorities picked Rebels and cadres most likely to meet with the least resistance from the masses, and that having picked them, the army protected them from the fickle mood and angry temper of the masses. Some committees were "preparatory" and "provisional" for months on end; other were "permanent" only to fall apart, be reorganized, fall apart again, be reconstituted with different personnel, sometimes by different army commanders.[130] It was a makeshift arrangement, which seemed to satisfy nobody, but it was the best the Cultural Revolution could come up with, somewhat against its will and its original intent. This stroke of organizational genius was, of course, attributed to Mao.

The first intimation that after experimenting with Red Guards, Revolutionary Rebels, Paris-type communes, and other forms of power-wielding, the correct form of power seizure was to be that of the revolutionary committees, came from Shansi on January 14, 1967.[131] The Shansi experience was commented on by the Central Committee, or what was left of it, in a broadcast from Peking on January 30. Something similar happened in Heilungkiang on the

---

[128] *The Hunan Daily* put it this way: "In essence, the state is the army . . . . The army is the center of centers and the key of keys." See *FEER* (April 17, 1969).

[129] See, "PLA Soldiers in Politics," *China News Analysis*, No. 751 (April 4, 1969).

[130] At a meeting held in Sinkiang in March 1969, Li Chuan-chun, a Vice-Chairman of the region's Revolutionary Committee revealed that the region was not yet "all Red" and that it had to be made all Red "at an early date." Tibet at that time was not all Red either. See *New York Times* (March 30, 1969), p. 4.

[131] "Shansi Revolutionary Rebel General Headquarters' Public Notice No. 1," *Peking Review* (February 3, 1967).

same day. On February 10 the Heilungkiang model was analyzed by *Jen-min Jih-pao* which on that occasion used the term "three-in-one" for the first time. The scriptural authority for the three-in-one combination was found in Mao's 1929 essay "On Correcting Mistaken Ideas in the Party."[132] On February 24, 1967 a three-in-one revolutionary committee was set up in Shanghai and was soon hailed as another model of correct power seizure emanating from the Shanghai January Revolution. Thus theory and practice were combined and offered as examples for other troubled cities and provinces to emulate. It took Tientsin another nine months to settle down, however: its democratic consultations did not spontaneously produce a three-in-one revolutionary committee until December 6, 1967.

By November 1, 1967 there was a grand total of eight such committees (six provincial, including Inner Mongolia's formed that day, and two municipal, Shanghai and Peking) out of a possible twenty-eight. Between January 1967 and January 1968 only nine committees were established: in the provinces of Shansi, Heilungkiang, Shantung, Kweichow, and Tsinghai, the autonomous region of Inner Mongolia, and in the municipalities of Shanghai, Peking, and Tientsin. This left more than two-thirds of the country without provincial, autonomous region, or municipal government, or with government organs unacceptable to the Lin-Mao-Chiang Ching group.[133] Twelve committees were set up between January and April 1968 (most of them relatively conservative) and three more were created in May. The Party's Ninth National Congress was postponed until such time as a country-wide democratic consultation was certain to produce the correct representation rather than unpleasant surprises. This state of affairs was not reached until April 1969, although by September 1968 the spontaneous process of forming revolutionary three-in-one committees throughout the country had been completed. The Ninth Congress was almost eight years late by the Party's official count, but eight years is as nothing in the majestic sweep of history.

Factionalism

The Cultural Revolution was plagued from the beginning by what came to be euphemistically called "bourgeois and petty-bourgeois factionalism." It was described by those in authority (but presumably not, or not yet, taking the capitalist road) as "the placing of

---

[132] *SW* (Peking: *FLP*, 1964), Vol. 1, pp. 105-116. Significantly, this article was republished by *Jen-min Jih-pao* on January 28, 1967. Mao's essay attacked "ultrademocracy" as a leftist deviation which tended to wreck Party organization.

[133] Note that by mid-February 1968 only five of the original seventeen members of the Cultural Revolution Group were still around.

personal gain and the benefit of small groups above everything, show-ing groupism, sectarianism, and mountain-topism, anarchism, out-ward attention to the Chairman's instructions but inner resistance, etc., in action." It was, in fact, an incredibly complex splintering of the contending forces, rampant petty jealousies, personal and group score-settling, which as time went on had less and less to do with ideology and more and more with a confused, compassless compul-sion toward activism. The bitter wrangling of men at the top seeped down into the very marrow of society. The destruction of the au-thority of some leaders eroded respect for all authority, since au-thority in People's China, the people were told, went hand in hand with a propensity for treason, untrustworthiness, personal ambition, ulterior motives, black-handedness, and plain unreliability.

By mid-1967 all sense of direction and purpose seemed to have been lost. There was uncertainty about what to rebel for and whom to rebel against: it was everyone for himself and devil take the hind-most. Even the PLA, as we have seen, did not escape the contagion, On March 7, 1968 the Acting Chief of Staff, Yang Cheng-wu, was seen at a public rally, a pillar of revolutionary will. A few days later he was sacked from his post in company with the Political Commis-sar of the Air Force, Yu Li-chin, and the Commander of the PLA's Peking garrison, Fu Chung-pi. According to Chiang Ching, Yang had been an "ambitious man." Later it came out that, in fact, he was a traitor who had tried to seize power from Chiang Ching and her oft-purged group. There were dark hints that some other persons in authority had plotted with Yang.

Reference to Mao's quotations failed to clarify the faction-ridden issues. The helmsman's words were taken out of context, and even in context they were often platitudinous. "Communists," said the Chairman, "must always go into the why and wherefore of things, use their own heads to carefully think over whether or not it cor-responds to reality and is really well founded." He also said: "Grasp class struggle and all problems can be solved." That was not much of a help. Pregnant with elusive meaning, the words were learned by heart, but failed to arrest the mounting wave of anarchy.[134] In 1967 Chang Chun-chiao, Deputy Director of the Cultural Revolution Group, tried to clarify the problem: "All [Mao's] works," he said, "are not of the kind you can comprehend after one reading. Even repeated readings do not guarantee understanding." All the more, one should add, since such understanding depended on who at the particular moment was in the power saddle, in charge of interpreta-tion.

[134] "Anarchism is a punishment for factionalism" *Anhwei Radio* (Febru-ary 15, 1968) in *URS*, Vol. 50, No. 18 (March 1, 1968).

The conjunction of factionalism at the top of society, stresses at the bottom, and the difficulty inherent in understanding the Chairman's guiding thoughts, even after repeated readings, spawned revolutionary upmanship on a scale hitherto inexperienced. "To unite," went the slogan, "you must admit to our faction that you are wrong because our faction is more revolutionary than yours."[135] The harassed PLA officer sent to investigate a reported power struggle in the model Hsipu Production Brigade (the "Paupers' Co-op") early in 1967, wrote to his superiors (who hopefully were still in place): "Both Wang Kuo-fan (the Commune's Director) and Tu Kuei (the Brigade Chief) are Party persons in authority. But which of them is taking the capitalist road?"[136] A Red Guard transcript of a reception given by the "central leaders" (Chen Po-ta, Chiang Ching, Kang Sheng) to representatives of the masses from Szechwan (March 15, 1968) records Kang Sheng's analysis of one particular situation: "In the course of struggling against former Party Secretary Li Ching-chuan, the 'Hung-cheng' group was actually struggling against Liu Chieh-ting and Chang Hsi-ting. Such a lack of distinction between friend and foe is impermissible!"[137]

Memories of bloody skirmishes between splinter groups rankled on: "Debts of blood must be repaid with blood!" proclaimed one Canton faction after it had been coaxed by the PLA into sharing power with those who a few months earlier had thinned its ranks with the gun. By September 1967 the question was posed whether China was governable otherwise than on an ad hoc regional basis. The answer was to institutionalize the revolution with the assistance of the army. But no sooner was this relatively pragmatic course implemented, than the extreme Left was on the move again, and factionalism became a virtue overnight. On May 1, 1968, *Hung-ch'i* wrote in its editorial: "Apart from uninhabited deserts, wherever there are groups of people, they are invariably composed of the left, the middle, and the right. This will still be the case after ten thousand years." Whether factionalism was right or wrong depended on the factions' class content.

Many of the larger factions were well organized on paramilitary principles. They were directed by central committees, possessed a network of lower echelon subcommittees, departments of propaganda, finance, and organization, printing presses turning out tabloid publications, special "fighting corps," weapons (seized from or sup-

---

[135] See *URS*, Vol. 50, No. 8 (January 26, 1968), and No. 18 (March 1, 1968).

[136] Richard Baum, "A Parting of Paupers," *FEER* (January 4, 1968), pp. 17-19.

[137] *FEER* (October 3, 1968), p. 75.

plied by the PLA or the militia), representatives in Peking, couriers, liaison men, and even clandestine radio stations. There were "conservative" factions composed of senior Party cadres, skilled workers, intellectuals, some students, and peasants, and there were "radical" factions composed of unskilled workers, contract laborers, disgruntled ex-servicemen, ex-students doing manual work, lower level teachers and cadres, and others who had a stake in change.[138]

STAGE SIX: REVOLUTIONARY PAUSE (SEPTEMBER 1967-MARCH 1968)

From September 1967 to April 1969 the army made efforts to bring into being revolutionary committees to replace the old organs of Party and state power. During this period the revolutionary committees devoted their energies to internal struggles pitting the Left authoritarians against Right and middle-of-the-road authoritarians in the name of Mao Tse-tung's thought, "the Marxism-Leninism of the present era." On the whole the "leaders of revolutionary organizations truly representing the masses" and the "up-and-coming revolutionaries," young devotees of Chen Po-ta and Chiang Ching fared less well than the old apparat-men whose Marxism-Leninism was rooted in a Stalinist predilection for centrally imposed order and whose talent lay in playing the old rules of the game. It was a period of revolution through the committee in preparation for the long-awaited Ninth Party Congress. However, the task of committee building was interrupted for a while by a Left revival (March-July 1968), so that it seems advisable to divide the period into two parts. From September 1967 to March 1968 the work of administrative reconstruction was carried on with relative calm, the army exercising its authority firmly if cautiously.

On August 25, 1967 Mao Tse-tung personally instructed the masses to "Support the Army and Cherish the People,"[139] a slogan chiseled out jointly by the State Council, the Military Affairs Commission, and the Cultural Revolution Group. One of the ways to support the army was not to steal arms and equipment from it. An order to that effect was issued on September 5, 1967. If some semblance of order was to be restored and the revolution was to be grasped, carried through to the end while promoting production, the army had to be protected from public censure by bad elements, counterrevolutionaries, black gangsters, and other agents of China's Khrushchev posing as leaders of the revolutionary mass organiza-

---

138 See *FEER 1969 Year Book*, pp. 142-145.
139 See *Peking Review* (January 28, 1968), pp 9-10; *ibid*. (February 9, 1968), pp. 13-14; *China Pictorial*, No. 2 (1969), pp. 32-36.

tions. If sacking of military personages was to be done, it was up to the true revolutionaries to do it, even if it was not always easy to identify these.[140]

The campaign was to be concretely carried out through the conclusion of "Support the Army and Cherish the People Pacts . . . from top to bottom and bottom to top." One item in such pacts was the prohibition of verbal and physical attacks on the PLA, such attacks having tended to sap the army's morale and undermine its prestige. "The great People's Liberation Army is the mainstay of the dictatorship of the proletariat," even if "in certain places, some comrades in local army units . . . commit temporary mistakes in giving their support because of the intricate and complex conditions of class struggle."[141] The army was to set an example in loving the people by modestly learning from the masses. If disputes arose as to who was to be counted among the people, they were to be settled through "democratic mass consultations"—a not overly helpful guideline for harassed local army commanders. "All revolutionary comrades must keep a cool head and not get confused."[142] The army was to continue promoting three-way alliances, play a key role in the formation of revolutionary committees based on such three-in-one combinations, but at the same time it was to lean toward the revolutionary Left, which, however, was by no means unequivocally defined. "We must support all revolutionary organizations. Favoring one while becoming estranged from another, cannot be allowed. Nor is it permissible to support one against another. It is also wrong to support whatever you do if you are the Left. Instead we should support all words and deeds that conform to Mao Tse-tung's thought."[143]

The army was to assist in economic work and provide leadership in offices, schools, organizations, communes, and enterprises whenever necessary. In fact, the army was to do almost everything from tilling fields to administering and defending the country, with only the vaguest of central guidelines to help it steer clear of possible charges of revisionist deviation.

Later—in the fall of 1968—Mao Tse-tung's Thought Propaganda Teams composed of veteran factory workers and peasants came to the army's aid in defining what the Chairman's thought on this or that concrete subject really was, but since the teams survived only because the army backed them up and, in fact, was part of them,

---

[140] By October 1967, in China's 13 military regions, 8 army Political Commissars and 4 area commanders had been relieved of their functions.

[141] *Hung-ch'i*, No. 5 (1967).

[142] *Hung-ch'i*, No. 5 (1967). Cf. "Earnestly Implement the Principle of 'Supporting the Left, But Not Any Particular Faction,' " *Peking Review* (February 2, 1968), pp. 8-9.

[143] *Liberation Army Daily*, editorial (January 28, 1968).

the uncertainty surrounding correct interpretations of Mao's thought remained as acute as ever. And yet the Chairman's typical" latest directives" were clear enough. He said: "Historical experience merits attention. Line and viewpoint must be talked over constantly and repeatedly. It won't do to talk them over with only a few people; they must be made known to all the revolutionary masses."[144] The Support the Army part of the campaign was, no doubt, intended to stem growing popular resentment against the all-pervading role of the armed forces in the life of the country, amounting to an all-out military dictatorship. The wily class enemy, it was said, resorted to sugar-coated bullets under the guise of supporting the army: he tempted the soldiers with "money and women."[145]

STAGE SEVEN: OPENING TO THE LEFT (MARCH 1968-JULY 1968)

The moderate trend dominated by the PLA from September 1967 was abruptly reversed in March 1968 when a flurry of left-wing activity produced new conflicts and factional disputes. The following events were among the more significant:

1. Dismissal of Acting Chief of Staff, Yang Cheng-wu, Air Force Political Commissar, Yu Li-chin, and Peking Garrison Commander, Fu Chung-pi (end of March 1968).

2. Rise in the influence of Chiang Ching who at the May Day celebrations in Peking was catapulted from nineteenth to ninth place in the official hierarchy. Miss Chiang's mediocre taste in art and literature found expression in a flood of portraits of the Chairman in various saintly poses, and in a pedestrian literary output consisting mainly of worn revolutionary phrases.[146]

3. Renewed wall-poster attacks on Vice Premiers Nieh Jung-chen, Tan Chen-lin, and Li Fu-chun.

4. Insistence that the army's role in the revolutionary committees be trimmed and that greater voice be given to Revolutionary Rebels.

5. Calls for intensification of the class struggle.[147]

6. Support for "proletarian factionalism." "We oppose bourgeois factionalism precisely in order to safeguard the factionalism of the proletarian revolutionaries."[148]

7. Formation of left-leaning revolutionary committees in Shensi, Liaoning, and Szechwan (May).

[144] *China Pictorial*, No. 2 (1969).
[145] *China News Analysis*, No. 744/745 (February 14, 1969), p. 3.
[146] See "Beaux Arts," *China News Analysis* (January 17, 1969).
[147] See *Peking Review* (May 10, 1968), pp. 11-14.
[148] "Make a Class Analysis of Factionalism," *Hung-ch'i* Commentator, *Jen-min Jih-pao* (April 27, 1968) in *Peking Review* (May 10, 1968), pp. 3-4.

8. Renewed violence during the summer, especially intense in Kwangsi and Kwangtung, possibly also in Tibet, Sinkiang, and Chekiang.

9. Temporary (June-July) halt to the formation of revolutionary committees in a number of sensitive areas, especially Fukien, Kwangsi, Yunnan, Tibet, and Sinkiang.

There were, however, signs that the Left was weaker and more weary than a year earlier and that it was rapidly losing support in a nation tired of anarchy and factionalism.

THE EIGHTH STAGE: PREPARING FOR THE NINTH NATIONAL PARTY CONGRESS (JULY 1968-APRIL 1, 1969)

In July 1968 the power vacuum in Peking began to be filled again, mostly it would seem, by Left moderates and army pragmatists. In the provinces a crackdown began on feuding factions, the extreme Left beating a hasty retreat. "Spontaneously and voluntarily," Red Guards and other Left organizations were dismantled province by province. Many leaders of revolutionary organizations truly representing the masses and large numbers of up-and-coming revolutionaries were sent to work on PLA farms and to other places of intellectual remolding. The young, Mao told student representatives on July 27-28, had let him down; they were no longer to bask in the warm rays of the Red sun. Absolute obedience to the PLA became the order of the day once again, and the leading revolutionary role of the working class was given prominence. The Party apparatus at the provincial and lower levels was slowly and painfully being rebuilt on new foundations, which on closer examination were not so new after all.

Mao Tse-tung Thought-Propaganda Teams[149]

Beginning in late July 1968 and modeled on an earlier PLA experiment, a new formation came into being, the purpose of which was to explain to the masses the correct meaning of the Chairman's instructions and so crack down on factionalism through "struggle-criticism-transformation."[150] The "Mao Tse-tung Thought Propa-

[149] See *URS*, Vol. 53, No. 19 (December 1968); "Anniversary of Entry of Working Class Into Realm of Superstructure," *Peking Review* (August 1, 1969), pp. 3-7.

[150] "Struggle-criticism-transformation" meant that one should (1) set up Mao Tse-tung thought-study classes and pay particular attention to class struggle, (2) guard against class enemies trying to usurp leadership, (3) encourage the masses to expose and accuse hidden enemies, (4) drag out hidden and obvious class enemies and discredit them, (5) define the line of attack so as not to dislocate production while keeping the problem in historical perspective, which

ganda Teams" consisted of veteran factory workers and soldiers, or
veteran poor peasants and soldiers who soon fanned out over the
country, penetrating every school, hospital, government office, "and
other spheres of the superstructure." The first team was introduced
into Peking's Tsinghua University in August, and into the city's two
other major universities shortly thereafter.[151] To commemorate the
event, Mao sent the Tsinghua team a gift of mangoes. Soon artificial
mangoes became the symbol of the Cultural Revolution, next only to
the book of quotations and Mao buttons. Factories, schools, and
other institutions displayed bowls of mangoes in prominent places,
and visitors bowed before them. Everyone, including the most extreme ex-Red Guards, was to learn from the teams. In Szechwan,
membership in the teams was said to have numbered about a million;
in Kwangtung, 50,000 factory workers and 280,000 peasants were
harnessed to this task; in Hopei (population 44 million) over
22.5 million peasants attended Mao thought classes during the winter
of 1968-69; in the country as a whole, team members were estimated
to have numbered nearly 10 million. Although the movement was
nationwide, it was apparently most marked in the industrialized
provinces and in areas and institutions in which the interpretation of
the Chairman's instructions had been most confused in the past. The
stress from then on and until further notice was not on the young
up-and-coming, who in spite of their simulated Long Marches had
disappointed the Chairman, but on the experienced working class.
"Our country," Mao had said, "has 700 million people, and the
working class is the leading class. It is essential to bring into full play
the leading role of the working class in the Great Cultural Revolution
and in all fields of work. For its part, the working class should always
raise its political consciousness in the course of struggle." It was the
last injunction which may have worried the working class and spoiled

---

enabled one to distinguish antagonistic contradictions from contradictions
among the people, (6) promote the great alliance, oppose factionalism and the
"theory of many centers." (1) through (4) look like left-wing positions. (5) and
(6) are more right-inclined. See "The Process of 'Struggle-Criticism-Transformation' in Rural Areas," *Chinese Communist Affairs: Facts & Figures*. Vol. II,
No. 8 (February 5, 1969), pp. 6-9.

[151] Hsu Teh-hsiu, "After the Mao Tse-tung's Thought Propaganda Team
Entered Tsinghua University," *China Reconstructs*, January 1969, pp. 4-6. "I am
the daughter of a poor peasant," wrote the author. "I gave a talk [to the young
people brought up in the new society] using my own blood-and-tears experience
as a kind of living teaching material. . . . Tears streamed down the cheeks of
many veteran workers and students as I told my story" (pp. 5-6). Cf. "The
Dilemma of Workers' Propaganda Teams on the Cultural Front," *URS*, Vol. 56,
No. 4 (July 11, 1969). "At present, comrades of our workers' propaganda team
[at Futan University] are required to learn the abilities of using Mao Tse-tung's
Thought to distinguish the direction of the wind." *Shanghai Radio* (July 7,
1969) in *ibid.*, p. 54.

its satisfaction at being selected to lead the struggle against higher wages and for longer working hours.

To supply the teams and Mao Tse-tung study classes with reading materials, 86.4 million sets of the *Selected Works of Mao Tse-tung* were published in 1967 in addition to 350 million copies of *Quotations from Chairman Mao Tse-tung*, 47.5 million copies of *Selected Readings* from the Chairman's works, and 57 million copies of the Chairman's poems. "Printing workers said: Every extra set of the *Selected Works of Mao Tse-tung* is so much added strength to the world revolution and another spiritual atom bomb of incomparable strength. . . . Let the brilliant thought of Mao Tse-tung light the whole world," they said.[152] By the end of 1968, 740 million copies of the *Quotations* and 150 million sets of Mao's *Selected Works* had been printed.[153]

Campaign to Purify Class Ranks

The Mao Tse-tung Thought Propaganda Teams and "Leadership Core Groups" within the Revolutionary Committees were instrumental in pushing forward a campaign to clean out class ranks in preparation for the establishment of a new revolutionary Party based on the thought of Mao Tse-tung. Those to be cleaned out were the "Seven Black Elements": former landlords, former rich peasants, former capitalists, rightists, counterrevolutionaries, bad elements, and black gangsters. The campaign gathered momentum in the autumn and winter 1968, but as almost all the earlier Cultural Revolution movements it, too, had its snags. It was not always clear who was a counterrevolutionary or a black gangster for that matter. Former landlords, capitalists, and rich peasants were more readily spotted, but even here there was some difficulty since many of them had managed to get themselves reclassified under the Liu regime, some succeeded in having their dossiers destroyed during the more anarchic months of the revolution, others had had their verdicts reversed during the February 1967 "right adverse current." Frequently the reason for classifying a man as counterrevolutionary, black gangster, or bad element was quite simply a personal grudge by someone in temporary authority. Most often, however, the predominantly conservative Revolutionary Committees interpreted the vague instructions from Peking in an anti-left sense and came down hard on the extremists. Many ultra-revolutionary former Red Guards and other leftists fared badly in the cleaning process. The usual penalty was forced labor in a remote frontier region or work in the victim's place of residence under the supervision of the masses. Pri-

---

[152] *Peking Review* (January 3, 1968), p. 15.
[153] *China News Analysis*, No. 744/745 (February 14, 1969), pp. 7-13.

son terms were not uncommon. Death sentences carried out on the spot following struggle and accusation sessions have also been reported.[154] In some localities the army resorted to "Workers' Provost Corps," conservative-oriented public security bodies, to enforce law and order and weed out troublemakers.

That Peking was worried about the new organs of people's power and not quite sure how the Chairman's strategy was being interpreted in the provinces, was revealed in the 1969 New Year's editorial published jointly by *Jen-min Jih-pao* and the *Liberation Army Daily*: "*Ssu-ch'ao*, the non-proletarian class trend . . . finds channels of representation in the very heart of the leading organs [Revolutionary Committees] and jams up the process of the strategy laid down by Chairman Mao."[155] In a speech to students of Nanking University and the Nanking Engineering Institute on June 11, 1968, Hsu Shih-yu, the Commander of the Nanking Military Region said: "You must set up Revolutionary Committees quickly, and when they have been set up, our troops will be withdrawn. (The audience: 'Please don't take them away!') They cannot be withdrawn at present, of course, because you are still fighting one another."[156] The precise place of the Revolutionary Committees in the new Party structure was far from clear and possibly the subject of acrimonious debate among the central leaders. "In planting so-called 'revolutionary committees,' " wrote Wang Ming from his Moscow exile, "Mao Tse-tung counted on creating a weapon of his personal military dictatorship. Their paramount task is to persecute and annihilate Communists, Communist Leaguers, revolutionary servicemen and foremost workers, peasants, and intellectuals. As soon as a so-called 'revolutionary committee' was set up, Hung-wei-pings led by the chairman of the 'revolutionary

---

[154] See *New York Times* (December 8, 1968), p. 7. On August 25 Yao Wen-yuan, whose article criticizing Wu Han was the opening salvo of the Cultural Revolution, published an essay denouncing the Red Guards and ordering them to submit to discipline.

[155] *China News Analysis*, No. 739 (January 10, 1969), p. 5. In Ningpo, a city in Chekiang, a December 1968 report spoke of a reactionary trend which spread word that there never had been an "adverse February [1967] current." "They wickedly say that the February Counter-Current is in the Party Central, not in Ningpo." *Ibid.*, p. 6. Cf. *ibid.*, No. 749 (March 21, 1969). "The proletarian revolutionaries in the wine, salt and tobacco company exposed how the former Party secretary and manager had pretended to be mad during every political campaign, and how he had gone even more crazy when the battle call was sounded to clean up the class ranks. . . . They also exposed that there was nothing wrong with him most of the time. Through investigations inside and outside, they discovered that he was a veteran traitor who had been concealed for over twenty years." *Kweiyang Radio*, December 13, 1968, in *FEER* (December 26, 1968), p. 716. It is reasonable to argue that the individual in question may in reality have been badly rattled by every political campaign, the rattle assuming psychotic dimensions during the battle call to clean up the class ranks.

[156] *FEER* (October 13, 1968), p. 74.

committee' publicly smashed the signboards of the local CPC committee and of the people's committee. This was followed by the publication of notices ordering all officials of local Party organizations and Communists as well as cadres of the organs of power to register at the 'revolutionary committee' within three days and await further sanctions. Arrest, exile, imprisonment or murder awaited many of those who registered and also those who did not register but were later discovered."[157]

Rebuilding the Party Apparatus

A step on the road to Party rebuilding was the secret "extended" Central Committee meeting (Twelfth Extended Central Committee Plenum) held in Peking reportedly from October 13 through 31, 1968. The word "extended" meant that the meeting was attended by various "progressive elements" who were not regular members but were granted full voting rights. It is possible that these progressive elements included a number of military men whose views were relatively conservative. That at least was the impression one got from the inconclusive communiqué issued by the meeting, a subdued document, which apart from a violent attack on Liu Shao-ch'i did not say very much.[158] Liu was stripped of all positions inside and outside the Party—an illegal procedure, since the Chief of State's removal from government offices could be finalized only by the National People's Congress. The ousting of Liu was generally interpreted as a symbolic gesture toward the extreme Left, which apart from this appeared to have gained very little from the extended plenum. A nationwide Liu denunciation campaign was immediately launched. Fifteen million people in Peking, Shanghai, and Tientsin, and another 100,000,000 in provincial capitals and smaller towns were said to have celebrated the event with gongs, drums, cymbals, and fireworks. That Liu was a scab who hated the people was witnessed to, among others, by the crew of the warship "Loyang." In 1958 Liu visited the ship for four hours "only." "When a fighter poured a glass of water for him, Liu Shao-ch'i immediately gave a hint to a member of his entourage to throw it out and bring him a glass of 'Ever Safe' drinking water which they had specially brought with them from Hangchow."[159]

[157] Wang Ming, *op. cit.*, pp. 16-17. For a more optimistic view, see "Three Strands of Rope Tightly Twisted Into One," *Peking Review* (July 18, 1969), pp. 11-14.

[158] The extended plenum decided "to expel the renegade, traitor, and scab Liu Shao-ch'i from the Party once and for all." In the meantime, Liu and his wife lived in the Chung-nan-hai district of Peking reserved for high Party and government officials. They were protected from rampaging mobs by a divisional force of the PLA's special police guard.

[159] *China Pictorial*, No. 2 (1969), p. 9.

The extended Central Committee discussed the calling of the Ninth Party Congress and approved the completed new structure of Revolutionary Committees. It probably also addressed itself to the continuing strife within many of the committees and to the formulation of the Party's new draft constitution.[160]

A copy of the draft constitution became available in the West early in January 1969 and was published in the New York Times on January 8. Compared with the 1956 Constitution, the new charter was short and imprecise. The Party was no longer declared to be the Party of the working class with ties to intellectuals and other patriots; it was thenceforth "the political Party of the proletariat . . . composed of advanced elements of the proletariat," that is, "workers, poor peasants, lower-middle peasants, revolutionary servicemen, and other revolutionary elements who have reached the age of eighteen." The document omitted all references contained in the earlier constitution to the identity of interests between the Party and the people, and failed to mention the objective of unifying the broad masses of the people.[161] Instead of secret ballot elections to Party bodies at all levels, the new draft constitution stipulated that "leading organs of the Party at all levels [were to be] produced through democratic consultation and election."[162] The National Party Congress and the Central Committee produced by it were to remain the nominally highest Party organs, but the Congress was to meet every five years instead of annually as provided by the 1956 Constitution. Nothing was said about how frequently the Central Committee was to meet. The Plenary Session of the Central Committee was to produce a Politbureau and a Standing Committee of the Politbureau as well as the Chairman and Vice Chairman of the Central Committee. There was no mention of the Party's Secretariat or the Secretary General.

The Constitution also made provision for local Party congresses at the *hsien* level and above (and, in the case of the PLA, at the

[160] "The decision of the so-called '12th Extended Plenary Meeting of the CPC' was published recently in Peking. This, as everybody knows, was a plenary meeting without the participation of the overwhelming majority of members and alternate members of the CCCPC. Instead, it was attended by members of the so-called 'Group for the Cultural Revolution Affairs,' representatives of the Hung-wei-pings and tsao-fans [Revolutionary Rebels], of the provincial 'revolutionary committees,' and of military leaders favored by Mao Tse-tung. Incidentally, Mao Tse-tung granted all of them the 'right of a casting vote' of members of the CCCPC." Wang Ming, *op. cit.*, p. 13.

[161] An omission partly made good by the reprinting in the winter of 1968 of Mao's March 1949 "Report to the Second Central Committee Plenum" in which unity was a major theme. See also "The Rehabilitation of the Chinese Communist Party," *URS*, Vol. 56, No. 3 (July 8, 1969).

[162] A *Hung-ch'i* editorial (No. 4, 1968) repudiated the "blind faith in elections as a form of conservative thinking." The elections had been unanimous in any case.

regimental level and above) to be held every three years instead of annually as provided by the earlier document, but did not elucidate the relationship between those bodies (and the Party committees issuing from them) and the Revolutionary Committees. The idea was probably for the Revolutionary Committees to take an active part in producing (presumably through democratic consultation) Party Leadership Core Groups which, in turn, would be responsible for reexamining Party membership, summoning Party congresses, and setting up provincial and other Party committees. The draft constitution named Lin Piao Mao Tse-tung's successor, and proclaimed the thought of Mao to be the Marxism-Leninism of the present era. With minor modifications, the draft was adopted by the Ninth National Party Congress in April 1969 (Chapter 12 and Appendix 1).

The Ninth National Party Congress (April 1-25, 1969) was a murky affair.[163] Its opening date was not announced beforehand and its exact location in Peking was not revealed. These details, however, did not deter hundreds of thousands of citizens from jubilantly celebrating its advent with gongs, cymbals, and firecrackers. "Chairman Mao Tse-tung and his close comrade-in-arms, Comrade Lin Piao, mounted the rostrum at 5 p.m. sharp," to be greeted by the assembled delegates with "prolonged, thunderous applause." "The delegates cheered most enthusiastically."[164] The Chairman acknowledged the welcome by giving an "extremely important speech," the substance of which was not revealed except for one sentence. "We hope," said Mao, "that the present Congress will be a congress of unity and a congress of victory and that, after its conclusion, still greater victories will be won throughout the country."[165] "The delegates unanimously expressed with elation their determination to respond to the great call of Chairman Mao. With full confidence they declared: . . . 'Under the direct leadership of Chairman Mao, our Congress has been going on very smoothly and in great unity, and it is very fine.' "[166] There were 1,512 delegates on hand, compared to 1,021 at the First Session of the Eighth Congress in 1956. In the course of a public discussion sponsored by the Peking press in 1967, it had been suggested that to make the gathering really popular and fully participatory, the congress should be attended by 10,-000 people who "would fill the Great Hall of the People to capac-

---

[163] *Moscow Radio* commentator Boris Kuznetsov, described the congress as "a secret funeral held in silence." Cf. "Moscow's Comment on the Maoist Ninth CCP Congress," *Chinese Communist Affairs: Facts and Figures*, Vol. 2, No. 15 (May 14, 1969), pp. 17-20.

[164] "Press Communiqué of the Secretariat of the Presidium of the Ninth National Congress of the Communist Party of China," April 1, 1969.

[165] *Ibid.* (April 14, 1969).

[166] *Ibid.*

ity." The proposal was adopted by the Central Committee on November 27, 1967, but nothing more was heard of it.[167]

The 1,512 delegates were a politically ill-assorted lot, even though they had been picked by democratic consultations. They were described by the official communiqués as "industrial workers in factories, mines, and other enterprises . . . poor and lower-middle peasants in people's communes, and delegates of women Party members on all fronts . . . veteran fighters of the Red Army . . . as well as new fighters . . . [and] delegates from among Red Guards who [were] attending a Party congress for the first time."[168] As a matter of fact, a close analysis of the 176-member Presidium of the Ninth Congress, revealed the following. (a) Fifty-eight percent of the old Central Committee members were missing, suggesting that the "handful of Party persons in authority taking the capitalist road" was a majority handful. (b) About 40 percent of the Presidium members were army people, including 11 (out of a possible 13) regional PLA commanders, all of them chairmen or vice-chairmen of Provincial Revolutionary Committees.[169] (c) Thirty-eight Presidium members could not be positively identified by Western experts.[170] (d) The balance was about evenly divided between old Party hands and newly emergent "revolutionaries" of the Chen Po-ta, Chiang Ching, Kang Sheng breed. (e) There was only one Red Guard representative who could be positively identified—Nieh Yuan-tzu of the Tsinghua big character poster fame, and she had joined the ranks of the Left establishment two lunar years before. All in all, the student Red Guards who had responded to the Chairman's call in the hour of need, were underrepresented at the Congress. Their utopian idealism and chronic factionalism had little to contribute to an assembly devoted to unity.[171] (f) The coterie of 14 men and women around Mao

167 John Gittings, "Through a Glass Darkly," FEER (April 17, 1969). In the latter part of 1967 the Central Committee issued two documents in preparation for the Ninth Congress. These were: "Notification Concerning Seeking Opinion on the Problem of the Ninth CPC National Congress," and "Circular Concerning Seeking Opinion on Holding the Ninth CPC National Congress." See Jen-min Jih-pao, Hung-ch'i, and Liberation Army Daily joint New Year 1968 editorial on this subject.

168 "Press Communiqué of the Secretariat of the Presidium of the Ninth National Congress of the Communist Party of China" (April 1, 1969).

169 In his April 1 political report, Lin Piao reminded the assembled delegates that the "People's Liberation Army is the mighty pillar of the dictatorship of the proletariat. Chairman Mao has pointed out many times: 'From the Marxist point of view, the main component of the state is the army.' "

170 These probably included some workers and model poor and lower-middle peasants and middle-rank Party cadres and PLA men—perhaps even a veteran Red Guard or two.

171 Cf. "Children Feeling Pressure in China," New York Times (April 27, 1969), p. 8.

included two wives, one ghost writer, one former Mao bodyguard, and one professional propagandist. Among the top 24 members of the Presidium were a number of survivors of the old Politbureau who had been frequently criticized during the Cultural Revolution. They included the Foreign Minister Chen Yi, the Party's Vice-Chairmen Tung Pi-wu and Chu Teh, Vice Premiers Li Fu-chun and Li Hsien-nien, and four PLA generals, Liu Po-cheng, Hsu Hsiang-chien, Nieh Jung-chen, and Yeh Chien-ying. Of the former 97 Central Committee members, 60 had been publicly attacked during the Cultural Revolution and 50 failed to show up in public since late 1966. (g) The low priority assigned by the Congress to economic matters was evidenced by (i) the omission from the agenda of any discussion of the economic plan, (ii) the presence on the Presidium of only two economic planners, Li Fu-chun and Li Hsien-nien (in nineteenth and twenty-first places respectively).

The Congress listened to a political report by Lin Piao,[172] which "summed up the basic experience of the Great Proletarian Cultural Revolution, analyzed the domestic and international situation and put forward the fighting tasks of the Party. Comrade Lin Piao's report was warmly welcomed by the delegates and punctuated by prolonged applause and cheers."[173] Beginning April 2, all delegates held group discussions. Not surprisingly, they "expressed their warm support for [Chairman Mao's extremely important speech]," denounced right and left opportunism and the bankrupt headquarters of Liu Shao-ch'i, analyzed the Party's 48-year-old history, "conscientiously discussed again and again the political report made by Vice-Chairman Lin Piao, paragraph by paragraph and sentence by sentence," and found that the report "summarized all that they want to say, and that the more they read this report, the happier they feel, the more they read it, the more it warms their hearts."[174]

The new Central Committee which emerged from the Congress was an ideologically and temperamentally curiously mixed group. It consisted of 170 full members and 109 alternates, compared with 97 full members and 73 alternates in the previous Central Committee. The authoritarian pragmatists emerged stronger than they had entered the Congress, but failed to displace the most vociferous Maoists. Thirty-five of the original 176 Congress Presidium members

[172] Lin's report was released by *NCNA* on April 28. For excerpts see *New York Times* (April 28, 1969), p. 14, and (April 29, 1969), p. 12. Also, *China Reconstructs* (July 1969), pp. 11-31.

[173] "Communiqué" (April 1, 1969).

[174] "Communiqué" (April 14, 1969). See "An Analysis of the CCP Ninth Central Committee," *Chinese Communist Affairs: Facts and Figures*, Vol. 2, No. 15 (May 14, 1969), pp. 9-13.

(all but one lower level Maoists)[175] failed to obtain posts on the New Central Committee. Of the New Central Committee members, 141 were old hands picked from outside the Congress Presidium: including about 60 military men and a smattering of Party and government bureaucrats who had weathered the cultural storms. These included Wang En-mao—of Sinkiang fame—and Yu Chiu-li, the highly criticized Minister of Petroleum Industry, Admiral Wang Hung-kun, and Generals Wang Shu-sheng, Wang Hsin-ting, Kuang Jen-juing, and Peng Shao-hui.

The delegates also "conscientiously discussed the draft of the revised Constitution of the Communist Party of China, chapter by chapter and article by article," and found it to their unanimous liking. What they liked best of all was that the document "clearly stipulated that Comrade Lin Piao is the successor to Chairman Mao."[176] At an April 14 plenary session "the great leader Chairman Mao made an extremely important and inspiring speech. Comrade Lin Piao made an important speech." Others "also spoke." The Lin Piao report and the Constitution were adopted. In the meantime, "the whole nation has been in jubilation. Hundreds of millions of revolutionary people of all nationalities held grand parades and meetings to celebrate the convening of the Congress."[177] Foreign Party representation at the Congress was practically nonexistent.

To guide the Party and the revolutionary people through the twists and turns, and ups and downs, the shoals and perils of revolutions to come, the Congress laid down a clear directive: "In solving a problem, we should note both its positive and negative aspects; when taking notice of one main tendency, we should also pay attention to the other tendency, which may be covered up; we must take full notice and get firm hold of the main aspects and at the same time solve problems of the minor aspects one by one. Leading comrades at all levels must understand the whole situation, be good at grasping typical examples, sum up experience, closely follow the trends, do their work in a deep-going and meticulous way, and overcome the tendency of falling into generalities."[178]

The Congress sent warm regards to patriotic overseas Chinese and patriotic compatriots in Hong Kong and Macao, to compatriots in

[175] The one top level casualty was Jen Jung, Political Commissar of the Tibet military region.

[176] "Communiqué" (April 14, 1969). For an analysis of the new constitution see, Chinese Communist Affairs: Facts & Figures, Vol. 2, No. 15 (May 14, 1969), pp. 6-8, and "A Comparison Between CCP's Old and New Constitutions," China News Analysis, No. 757 (May 16, 1969), pp. 1-4.

[177] Ibid. Mao's April 14 extremely important and inspiring speech was not published.

[178] "Communiqué" (April 24, 1969).

Taiwan, warm and militant salute to the Albanians and to the revolutionary people of the five continents. Warm and militant salute was also sent to the Vietnamese people. It had harsh things to say about the "sugar-coated bullets of the bourgeoisie and its attempts to corrupt and split [the] Party and the revolutionary ranks," about "modern revisionism with the Soviet revisionist renegade clique as its center," and about "imperialism headed by the United States." The Congress expressed its determination to liberate Taiwan and "defend the sacred territory and sovereignty of [the] great motherland" against the "schemes, sabotage, and shameless aggression by U.S. imperialism, Soviet revisionism, and the reactionaries abroad, and all the schemes and sabotage by domestic reactionaries," who presumably were no small handful.

The mountain of the Great Proletarian Cultural Revolution gave all indications of having given birth to a mouse. Things would never be quite the same again, but they were not all that different either. The great and abiding problem of the economy received the scantiest of attentions. The working class, the poor and lower-middle peasants, and the people of all nationalities were to persist in building socialism "independently and with initiative in our own hands and through self-reliance, and by going all out, aiming high, and achieving greater, faster, better, and more economical results." They were to grasp revolution and promote production and other work in preparedness against war. Because it was a congress of unity, it displayed a tendency to fall into generalities, and really did not take account of one tendency while paying attention to the other tendency, which was probably covered up. It failed to take notice and get firm hold of the main aspects and at the same time to solve problems of the minor aspects one by one. Because it was a congress of victory, it neglected to take note of the bothersome problems of the economic base and answer the question of what to do about the loss of two years of formal education for all those spirited youngsters. It wished the Chairman a long life—a long, long life to him. It sensed that if this wish were not to come true, there would have to be more mass democratic consultations, and that there would probably be some first-rate turmoil in spite of the clearly stipulated condition that Comrade Lin Piao was the successor of Chairman Mao. The earthly condition of the Chairman hung heavily over the Congress.

On April 28 the Central Committee picked a 21-man Politbureau and a Standing Committee of five.[179] The five were Mao Tse-tung,

[179] See "An Analysis of the Politbureau of the 9th CCP Central Committee," *Chinese Communist Affairs: Facts and Figures*, Vol. 2, No. 15 (May 14, 1969), pp. 1-3.

Lin Piao, Chen Po-ta, Chou En-lai, and Kang Sheng with the official order of precedence applying only to the first two. The former Standing Committee had seven members, enlarged to ten during the Cultural Revolution. The former Politbureau had 17 members, and 6 alternates, later enlarged to 21. Chen Yi and Chen Yun (an economic planner) were not included in the new Politbureau, nor was Li Fu-chun. All of them were formerly members of that body. However, Mrs. Lin Piao (Yeh Chun) and Mrs. Mao (Chiang Ching) made it,[180] as did two veteran military leaders (Yeh Chien-ying and Liu Po-cheng), Chu Teh (one of the founders of the PLA and the object of numerous attacks during the Cultural Revolution), and a number of other military leaders including Air Force Commander Wu Fa-hsien, Chiu Hui-tso (Director of the Army Service and General Rear Department), and Yung-sheng (the army's Chief of Staff, attacked during the Cultural Revolution). All in all, nine out of the 21 Politbureau members were military men. With the exception of Li Hsien-nien, there were no economists of rank on either body.

[180] "Comments on the Modesty of Mao Tse-tung and his Family," *Moscow Radio*, December 7, 1968, in *Chinese Communist Affairs: Facts and Figures*, Vol. 2, No. 6 (January 8, 1969), pp. 18-19.

12 | The Cultural Revolution and the Economy

The striking fact which emerges from a reading of Chinese literature in the years 1966-69 is the silence on the great economic issues facing the country. Throughout the Cultural Revolution the space devoted by Chinese publications to the economy was minimal. What little information was given, took the form of appeals to grasp the revolution thriftily and promote production,[1] clarion calls to put politics in command of economic work, assurances that the situation was excellent, very good or comparatively good,[2] examples of how Mao Tse-tung's thought could inspire men to superhuman effort, move mountains, change the course of rivers, and better men's minds. The usual percentage claims were released from time to time, veiled threats were made against economic saboteurs and others who despite repeated warnings persisted in bourgeois-inclined errors. But all this did not add up to much hard information about how the economy was faring, which way it was going, and what kinds of priorities it was adhering to. It was far from clear who, if anyone, was in charge. The overwhelming preoccupation was with the superstructure of ideas and with political power play. The fact that the Cultural Revolution affected primarily the superstructure of China's society, that it concentrated on the cities, and that it unfolded in a period of relatively propitious weather, leads one to suspect that the rural economy continued to function, if not smoothly, at least without major country-wide breakdowns. Some of the temporary disruptions have been mentioned earlier (Chapter 11). They seem to have affected primarily industry, transportation, and distribution, and were serious enough at the time.[3]

But the kind of superstructural disturbances caused by the Cul-

[1] That is, make revolution in one's own locality and in one's spare time.

[2] "In his latest instructions, the great leader Chairman Mao pointed out: 'The situation of the Great Proletarian Cultural Revolution throughout the country is not just good, it is excellent. In a few more months the situation will become better still.' " *Peking Review* (February 23, 1968), p. 17.

[3] See Prybyla, "Communist China: The Economy and the Revolution," *Current History* (September 1968), and "China's Economy: Balance Sheet After Twenty Years," *ibid*. (September 1969).

tural Revolution are bound to have longer-run consequences which it is difficult to predict, much more quantify at this stage. Some of them may turn out to be positive: for example, the shock administered to the new priestly class of Party officials and government bureaucrats, the challenge to the sanctity of the Party, the demonstrable proof of the wrath of a people aroused and of the almost infinite diversity that exists under the surface of a totalitarian society, the condition of relative freedom brought about by confusion at the center and by a loosening of the center's control over the grass roots of society,[4] the continuing preoccupation with the poor, an almost pathetic striving for popular participatory democracy vitiated by the totalitarian temper, a yearning for equality among the people wrecked by the dogmatic conviction that some people are more equal than others and that some people are not people at all. There will also be negative consequences. What China needs and what it probably wants above all else—semantic heroics notwithstanding—is to free itself from the clutches of poverty. Economic development, however, does not fare well on political slogans and permanent superstructural upheaval.

INDUSTRY

The greatest dip in industrial production seems to have occurred in 1967. Western estimates pointed to a drop of between 15 and 20 percent in industrial output in 1967 compared with the previous year.[5] Speaking before 10,000 activists gathered in Peking on April 2, 1968, Chou En-lai admitted that "planned targets had not been realized [in 1967] and output figures for many products were lower than those of 1966." The *coal* industry appeared to have been the most affected by "anarchism," i.e., idleness, absenteeism, disregard for working hours, slackness, and so forth. It is possible that coal output in 1967 declined by as much as 20-25 percent from the level of 1966, or to about 190 million tons. Since coal supplied 90 percent of China's energy consumption, the troubles of the coal-mining sector must have had adverse repercussions on almost every department of the industrial economy, the more so since *railroad transportation* was seriously disrupted in the summer and early fall

---

[4] A small but interesting example of this withering away of central authority has been the alacrity with which the overworked urban masses abandoned compulsory morning physical exercises that used to be collectively engaged in by the people in the small hours of the morning. See "The Peking Way of Life," *New York Times Magazine* (June 1, 1969).

[5] *Quarterly Economic Review: China, Hong Kong, North Korea. Annual Supplement 1969*, p. 6.

of 1967 until, that is, the establishment of military control over the railways. On July 25, 1968, Kang Sheng lectured Kwangsi revolutionaries representing "two factions' mass organizations" in the following terms: "The railway lines [in Kwangsi] ceased operation for more than two months. I will ask you now: Do you or do you not support the Vietnamese in their struggle against the U.S.? (Mass: we do!). Now that the supplies to aid Vietnam have been seized [over 100,000 cases of them] the railways stop operation. Who is happy about that? The U.S. imperialists! The Soviet revisionists! The traitors and special agents! They are all happy!"[6] The army was also apparently sent into the mines and steel mills in 1968 to forestall a major breakdown of the economy.[7] Phenomenal percentage increases in coal output were reported in the latter part of 1968; they could be explained only in terms of recovery from very low output levels.[8] Shensi reported a 50 percent increase in coal production between June and July 1968, Kwangtung 51 percent during the same period. In some Yunnan mines damaged by the 1967 factional fighting, output had risen 2.8 times in December 1968 compared with November. Coal shortages and labor troubles affected the *steel* industry in 1967 and the early months of 1968. The iron and steel industry comprising some 20 large plants in southern, central, and northeastern China turned out an estimated 15.5 million tons of pig iron and 12 million tons of crude steel in 1967.[9] These estimates appear to be on the high side.

Relatively few capital expansions were reported from the steel sector during the Cultural Revolution. The one exception was a rolling mill at Paotow commissioned in the early months of 1969. But Paotow failed to report any output data throughout 1968. Instead it reported continuing purges of "latent class enemies" and "double-dealers" among managers and workers, the establishment of Revolutionary Committees, but only in about 80 percent of the factories and mines belonging to the Paotow Iron and Steel Corporation, the

[6] "Instruction by Leaders of the CPC Central Committee and the Central Revolutionary Group at Reception of Comrades of Two Factions' Mass Organizations and Army Cadres from Kwangsi," July 25, 1968, East Hall of the Great Hall of the People, Peking, in *URS*, Vol. 53, No. 9, p. 102.

[7] A report from Shanghai said that "with the ardent help of the Liberation Army stationed in the plants," a great production effort was made in the usually slack months of June to August (1968). *Jen-min Jih-pao* (September 2, 1968), p. 3.

[8] Average monthly increases in industrial production (1968) in the reporting provinces and sectors work out at about 20 percent. In Shensi industrial production in the summer of 1968 was reported to have grown by 100 percent. See *China News Analysis*, No. 741 (January 24, 1969).

[9] The estimated crude steel output for 1966 was 12.2 million tons. See *New York Times* (May 23, 1967), p. 6, based on Hong Kong reports.

stationing of troops and paramilitary worker formations in the mills, and other revolutionary gossip of like kind. It would appear, in fact,that very little industrial capital construction was undertaken during the Cultural Revolution. Only in the latter part of 1968 and early 1969 was it possible to detect an upturn in industrial construction with the announced opening at Funchun of a hydroelectric power station with an annual capacity of 900 million kwh, a large (100,000 tons annual capacity) nitrogenous fertilizer plant, a diesel locomotive repair works, a few small fertilizer, chemical, and machine tools plants, a new bridge over the Yangtse, and the launching of a 10,000-ton freighter. Even in 1969, however, abandoned and half-finished industrial construction projects could be seen up and down the country, the slogan still was "make revolution thriftily,"[10] and the main emphasis was on repair and adaptation of existing plant and equipment. Although the working class was once again declared to be the vanguard of the revolution, economic policy was in the melting pot, there seemed to have been no clear guidelines, and references to the Third Five Year Plan were ritualistic, few, and far between. Occasionally economic policy statements sounded like a throwback to the Great Leap years: there was talk (1969) of a "new flying leap," about a "revolution in the economy," and about politics in command of economics. But still the leap did not develop; the only jump was from low production levels.

China's pride, the *petroleum* industry, had also suffered during the cultural turmoil. Economism at Taching had already been mentioned. The unsettled state of affairs in Sinkiang (Karamai fields) must also have affected crude oil production. There were persistent reports of trouble at the Lanchow refinery. Western estimates pointed to a drop of 10-15 percent in oil output in 1967 compared with 1966, i.e., a 1967 output of 8.5-9 million tons (about 10 million tons in 1966). By 1969 crude oil production had recovered to an estimated annual rate of 12 million tons, up 4 million tons from precultural revolution (1965) levels. There must have been a decline in *cement* production in 1967-early 1968 of at least 20 percent from 1966). Reports from one major plant in Anhwe indicated that output rose by 78 percent from August 1968 to September of that year, by 69.3 percent from September to October, and by 24.3 percent from October to November, suggesting a very low starting point for these leaps. 1966 cement output was estimated at about 12 million metric

[10]Throughout 1968 and 1969 appeals were made to save on coal, electricity, oil, paper, paint, dyestuffs, cotton cloth, fertilizer, rubber, building materials, packaging materials, agricultural implements, and so on. See *URS*, Vol. 50, No. 23 (March 19, 1968).

tons, compared with about 10 million tons a year later.[11] Workers were said to have abandoned their posts in the first half of 1967; they "destroyed equipment and installations." [12] Physical confrontation—reportedly broken up by the PLA—occurred in the Peking cement plant in July 1968. It is possible that the disruption of railroad transportation and the drying up of Agricultural Bank credit affected chemical fertilizer production in the smaller plants, while worker stoppages reduced output in the larger ones. Throughout 1968 and 1969 peasants were urged not to depend too heavily on chemical fertilizers and to go in for organic manure "in a big way." In the spring of 1968 Chou En-lai admitted that fertilizer supplies had fallen by 50 percent from previous years' levels.

Consumer goods production probably suffered, although it is difficult to say how severely. Vague claims were made in 1968 that the previous year's output of a number of consumer goods exceeded the levels of 1966. These claims could not be substantiated.[13] The only consumer goods which undoubtedly broke all records were plastic covers for Chairman Mao Tse-tung's works, Mao badges, and paper for printing the Chairman's sayings and poems. "Reports of fulfillment of the 1967 state plans ahead of schedule have been coming in from an increasing number of enterprises and areas," stated the Peking Review on January 3, 1968. "The workers and staff charged with the glorious task of producing paper for printing Chairman Mao's works and portraits have surpassed their target. The output of red plastic covers for Chairman Mao's works and of Chairman Mao's badges has greatly exceeded the plan." [14] Delays in distribution and sudden shortages were reported from a number of cities in 1967 and 1968.

Nuclear development, primarily with military applications in view, was pushed ahead. Reference to an unsuccessful test in December 1966 has already been made (Chapter 11, footnote 69). Another test having a yield of three megatons (equivalent to three million tons of TNT) was carried out on December 27, 1968. Further tests were conducted on September 23 and 29, 1969, the first involving an underground explosion in the low-intermediate range, the second a

[11] An Economic Profile of Mainland China, op. cit., Vol. I, p. 25; Quarterly Economic Review: China, Hong Kong, North Korea. Annual Supplement 1969, p. 7.

[12] Anhwe Radio (December 8, 1968) in China News Analysis, No. 741 (January 24, 1969), p. 6.

[13] Such claims were made for salt, clocks, watches, toothpaste, synthetic detergents, egg products, wines, spirits, clothing, headgear, footwear, hardware, leather goods, printing ink, fountain and ballpoint pens. Peking Review (January 3, 1968), p. 45.

[14] Cf. URS, Vol. 53, No. 18 (November 29, 1968).

three megaton device exploded in the air. The tests, besides being ascribed to the invincible thought of Mao Tse-tung, were said by the New China News Agency to have provided encouragement and support for various revolutionary peoples struggling against U.S. and Zionist aggression. On April 24, 1970 (see Chapter 11) a 380-pound earth orbiting satellite was successfully launched from a site believed to be located near Shuang-cheng-tze in western Inner Mongolia, some 400 miles northwest of the nuclear center of Lanchow. It was believed in Western intelligence circles that, given the booster rocket needed to place such a payload in orbit, China was capable of deploying a medium range (ca. 1,000 miles) ballistic missile by 1975 at the latest. The Soviet Union's Sputnik I (launched on October 4, 1957) weighed 184 pounds. The first U.S. satellite (January 31, 1958) weighed 30 pounds. Japan's 50-pound satellite—denounced by Peking as a first attempt to "unleash wars of aggression"—was launched in February 1970.

The need to *disperse industry* throughout the country in preparation for war against U.S. imperialism, Soviet social imperialism, or both, was stressed throughout 1969. With a view to preparedness against war, "every area, province and city [was to] pay attention to rational geographical distribution and appropriate multi-purpose development of industries in line with Chairman Mao's instruction: 'Various localities should endeavor to build up independent industrial systems. Where conditions permit, coordination zones, and then provinces, should establish relatively independent but varied industrial systems.' " *Hung-ch'i*, which commended this course of action under the signature of the Peking Municipal Revolutionary Committee (October 14, 1969), made it clear that in the event of such a war, the Chinese people would "have many big and small reliable industrial bases which provide [them] with more room for maneuver, so that all parts of the country can fight the war on their own, become impregnable, wipe out the enemy, and win victory." All parts of the country could not only fight the war on their own, they would also have to pay for their industries on their own. More precisely, local industries—small power stations, fertilizer plants, agricultural tool and repair shops—would be set up with commune funds, and the payroll of their workers would be met from the same source.

THE "ANSHAN CONSTITUTION"

From late July 1968 onward, emphasis was placed on Chairman Mao's so-called "Anshan Constitution" which outlined the Cultural Revolution's approach to the management of industry. The document was reportedly drawn up by Mao himself for the Anshan iron and steel works and was to serve as a model charter for all of China's industries. The pillars of the Anshan Constitution were (1) politics in command of all work, (2) worker participation in management and management participation in physical labor (i.e., workers and officials were periodically to change places), (3) worker innovation, and (4) abolition of "reactionary rules and regulations." The document was anti-intellectual and antiexpert in spirit, Maoist in its emphasis on the inventive capacity of the masses and in its scorn for material incentives, lumped together with other reactionary rules and regulations.[15]

A rural variant of the Anshan Constitution was the "Tachai Work Point System" under which commune members' performance was to be measured not only or even mainly by the amount of work done, but by the degree of the workers' revolutionary spirit. The old piece-work rate system was to be replaced by periodic awards based on scales established by revolutionary pace-setters.

"BETTER TROOPS, SIMPLER ADMINISTRATION"

The slogan was launched reportedly by Mao himself in the spring of 1968 and soon everyone was saying: "It is fine that the revolutionary committees carry out 'better troops and simpler administration.' It brought us the work style of the Eighth Route Army."[16] The idea was to struggle against overstaffed departments, superfluous personnel, bureaucratic habits of mind, the expert-above-the-masses mentality, and other manifestations of the new class, while saving the state money. The concrete expression of better troops and simpler administration was the dispatch of large numbers of cadres, managers, technicians, experts, bureaucrats, officials, and others to the countryside where they modestly learned from the masses of poor and lower-middle peasants. Lingpao *hsien* in Honan Province served as model. It had fostered revolutionary consciousness of its administrative personnel and improved its managerial work by sending 80 percent of its cadres to work on farms. The model was emulated by many provincial revolutionary committees, which by July had

[15] Earlier in the year Chou En-lai went on record as opposing excessive demands on experts' time. The Minister of the Petroleum Industry, Yu Chiu-li, Chou said, should not be asked to go for criticism more than three times a week since he was needed for consultations, and too much communion with the masses might undermine his health. Yu, as we have seen (Chapter 11) made it to the new Central Committee in April 1969. On the general problem of restoring and maintaining industrial labor discipline, see "Workers and Discipline," *China News Analysis*, No. 769 (August 15, 1969).

[16] *China Reconstructs*, February 1969, pp. 39-41. Cf. "Cadres Should Go Among the Masses," *Jen-min Jih-pao* editorial (November 19, 1967) in *Peking Review* (November 24, 1967), pp. 6-9.

instituted a rotating system under which one-third of their members labored on farms or in factories at any one time. Lower-level revolutionary committees followed suit. Some sent 20 percent of their managerial personnel to the farms, others as many as 80 percent. The bureaucrats carted manure for at least three months before returning to their desks. To make sure that the instruction was properly understood and carried out, the Chairman issued another latest directive on October 4, 1968. It was based on the experience of the Heilungkiang Revolutionary Committee's Liu Ho commune in Chingan *hsien*, which on May 7, 1968 had formed a "May 7th Cadre School." The school represented a creative embodiment of "Better Troops and Simpler Administration." The cadres labored in the fields for long periods of time: the bad ones permanently, the good and comparatively good ones for two or three months in the year.[17] Soon the movement was transformed into a mass exodus from the cities, for in addition to adult cadres, young educated people were caught in the swell.

BACK TO THE SOIL MOVEMENT

"The educated youth," said Mao, "must go to the villages and accept re-education from the poor and lower-middle peasants. The cadres and others in the cities must be persuaded to send their children to the villages when they have finished study in lower and higher middle schools and in the universities; they must be moved to do so. The comrades in the villages must welcome them."[18] "Resounding cheers burst forth throughout the country."[19] The comrades in the villages who had enough problems without having to take care of millions of educated youths (who despite their cheering "lived bodily in the countryside but had their hearts in the cities"),[20] followed the Chairman's latest teaching in their own way. "In accordance with this great teaching of Chairman Mao, the poor and lower-middle peasants in Huining county welcomed the educated young people and town residents who have come to settle in the countryside. The first thing they do is to present the newcomers with the treasured red books of Chairman Mao."[21]

After the Chairman had informed the young educated people that they had disappointed him (July 27-28, 1968), the movement to

[17] *URS*, Vol. 53, No. 11 (November 5, 1968).
[18] "Chairman Mao Tse-tung's Most Recent Teaching" (December 21, 1968), *Jen-min Jih-pao*, Dec. 22, 1968, p. 1.
[19] *China Pictorial*, No. 4 (1969), p. 41; *ibid.*, No. 3 (1969), pp. 18-21.
[20] *New York Times*, April 6, 1969, p. 7, reporting on *NCNA* February 1969 dispatch; © 1969 by The New York Times Company. Reprinted by permission.
[21] *China Pictorial*, No. 4, 1969, p. 4 (photo caption).

send the young to the countryside got in stride. In the latter part of 1968 and early 1969, some 20-25 million people, most of them youthful, were shepherded out of the cities. Besides the Chairman's disappointment, there were other more cogent reasons for the exodus. The second half of 1968 and the year 1969 looked very much like 1961-62 from the standpoint of rehabilitating the economy. It was a period of consolidation and filling out. The influx of people into the cities during the Cultural Revolution (including large numbers of peasants)[22]   produced urban unemployment and the concomitant problem of "social, nonlaboring" (i.e., unemployed) youth. Millions of youngsters had been out of school for two years, tasting the joys and sorrows of making revolution but not promoting production very much. For many of them continuation of formal education seemed pointless, all the more since new curricula had not yet been fully worked out and many teachers had left their profession for safer jobs. The state of the economy was such as to raise apprehensions even among the most ardent revolutionaries at the center. It seemed wiser to revolutionize the young by contact with the soil ("political camping") than by giving them a free hand to write posters, handbills, and tabloids. The workers, too, were unwilling to put up with any more nonsense from the youngsters. A Right reaction gradually set in. The workers and peasants concerned with making a living, hence with a measure of stability, were given pride of place backed by appropriate reprints from the Chairman's more moderate works.[23]

EDUCATION

"Carrying their manure baskets, students arrive at school."[24]

"To accomplish the proletarian revolution in education," the Chairman said in one of his latest directives, "it is essential to have working class leadership; the masses of workers must take part in this revolution and, in cooperation with Liberation Army fighters, form a revolutionary three-in-one combination with the activists among the

[22] Chou En-lai: "The peasants who went to the city should return. . . . The PLA will persuade the peasants to return to their countryside and resume production." Peking meeting, July 25, 1968, in *URS*, Vol. 53, No. 9, p. 107.

[23] E.g., Mao's "Report to the Second Plenum of the Central Committee of the CPC" (March 1949), reprinted by all major papers in December 1968. The report reads like a Liuist document. It speaks of the economic necessity for private capitalism to coexist and expand with the socialist sector and of the need to "unite with as many as possible of the urban petty bourgeoisie and national bourgeoisie."

[24] *China Reconstructs*, February 1969 (photo caption). Cf. *Peking Review* (November 24, 1967), pp. 9-10.

students, teachers, and workers in schools and colleges, who are determined to carry the proletarian revolution in education through to
the end. The workers' propaganda teams should stay permanently in
the schools and colleges, take part in all the tasks of struggle-criticism-transformation there, and will always lead these institutions. In
the countryside, schools and colleges should be managed by the poor
and lower-middle peasants—the most reliable ally of the working
class."[25]

The first item on the agenda of the Cultural Revolution, it will be
recalled, was to downgrade "bourgeois intellectuals and bourgeois
academic authorities," who, like the Party cadres, had taken on airs
and isolated themselves from the masses contrary to Mao's teachings
on the class character of art, literature, science, and technology. The
second item of the cultural drive was to close down all schools. Now
the Chairman's latest instruction showed how a totally new culture
could be built on China's cultural wasteland. The instruction contained all the basic ingredients of educational reform. Resounding
cheers and thunderous applause greeted the master plan, and everyone said that the Chairman's latest directive was fine.

The first ingredient of Mao's educational reform was the substitution of the Chairman's works for the numerous, irrelevant, complicated, and long-winded works of the bourgeois academic authorities.
The latter tended to confuse people because they were not easily
assimilable by poor and lower-middle peasant intellects and because
they surrounded the life of the mind with an aura of mystery. The
thought of Mao Tse-tung (spelled Mao Tsetung since April 1969)[26]
was to form the core of the new curriculum at all levels. It is difficult
to say how thoroughly this was carried out. A report from one
school in Kweichow Province showed that Mao thought study took
up 58 percent of the curriculum time, and "basic subjects" 21 percent.[27]

The second ingredient of Mao's educational reform was the sub-

[25] *China Reconstructs* (February 1969), p. 2. The directive was said to have
been based on the Chairman's earlier latest directive of May 7, 1966, which said
"While their [the students'] main task is to study, they should in addition to
their studies learn other things, that is, industrial work, farming, and military
affairs. They should also criticize the bourgeoisie. The period of schooling
should be shortened, education should be revolutionized, and the domination of
our schools by bourgeois intellectuals should by no means be allowed to continue." Cf. "Two Examples of Maoist Education Reform in Cities," *Chinese
Communist Affairs: Facts & Figures*, Vol. 2, No. 9 (February 19, 1969),
pp. 16-20.

[26] To make the spelling of Marxism-Leninism-Mao Tsetung thought look less
cumbersome than Marxism-Leninism-Mao Tse-tung thought. "At least," exclaimed one Hong Kong China watcher, "we used to have non-events to write
about—all we have now are non-non-events."

[27] *FEER* (December 5, 1968), p. 521.

stitution of the worker (or poor and lower-middle peasant) Mao Tse-tung thought propaganda teams for bourgeois academic authorities who had formerly directed and supervised the schools. The teams were to stay in the schools permanently to make sure that the process of struggle and criticism produced the correct transformation.

The third ingredient was to substitute workers and poor and lower-middle peasants for the former bourgeois-inclined teachers, and to recruit, where possible, student and teacher activists to do the teaching. The new worker-peasant-activist teachers were to become one with the peasant and worker masses in a three-in-one combination. Concretely, they were to be paid like industrial workers or like commune members on the basis of Tachai-type work points, presumably calculated by the propaganda teams.[28] Another concrete manifestation of the triple alliance was the combination of study and manual labor. Education was to be applied rather than theoretical, relevant to the immediate needs of the economy.

The fourth ingredient was to make the nation's school system an integral part of the life (and finances) of the farm and factory. Primary and secondary schools were to be turned over to factories, enterprises, and (in the countryside) production brigades. In this way both ideological and state financial objectives would be achieved, the burden of educational expenditure being shifted onto the economy's basic production units. Hopefully, some of the outlay would be recovered from the students' labor contribution to the units' income.[29] The poor and lower-middle peasants could say: "Our school

[28] Sample of the educational reform given by the *China Reconstructs* (February 1969) language instruction corner (p. 47). Literal translation from the Chinese: "Guanghui People's Commune's poor (and) lower-middle peasants manage commune schools. All people recommended old poor peasant Chen Kai-wan [to] be teacher, go lecture [on] water rice sow seeds. Chen Kai-wan first talked for whom to sow seeds. He said: 'In old society we for landlords sowed seeds, planted fields, one year toiled to end, still no rice went down cooking pots. Now [we] are for revolution, for [the] country, for socialism sow seeds! Afterwards he only began lecture [on] sow seeds technique. Lecture finished after, he immediately took students to fields to go work, taught them how [to] sow seeds." Cf. "Some Tentative Programs for Revolutionizing Education," *Peking Review* (November 17, 1967), pp. 9-11; "Great Changes in Futan University Under the Leadership of the Working Class," *ibid.* (August 15, 1969), pp. 16-19. "School Management by Poor and Lower-Middle Peasants as Shown by the Practice of Three Production Brigades in the Educational Revolution," *Jen-min Jih-pao* (October 28, 1968) in *Chinese Education*, Vol. 1, No. 3 (Fall 1968), pp. 3-14. No wonder many students became apathetic and at least as disillusioned with the Chairman as the Chairman was with them. See "Apathy Reported in China Schools," *New York Times* (October 12, 1969), p. 8. See also Appendix B.

[29] Considering that the farming sector probably suffered from surplus labor, the marginal productivity of the newcomers was likely to have been zero.

has not cost the state a cent." Those quoted by the national press did just that.

The system was to be made more democratic in a class sense by abolishing entrance examinations and age restrictions, and lowering or dispensing with tuition fees. It was found that many poor rural families could not afford the old school fees, modest as these had been, and that consequently many farm youths had remained illiterate despite the phenomenal successes claimed by earlier anti-illiteracy campaigns. Needy families were to receive allocations from the communes' general fund to help them pay for such items as children's clothing. It remained problematical, however, whether the general funds of most communes would be in a position to sustain such expenditures.

There is little doubt that the educational system of Communist China was in need of reform and that the ingrained habits of centuries had to be changed. As in many developing countries, there was a tendency for educated people to spurn physical labor and look down on laboring people. The danger that the system was producing a new elite class divorced from the everyday realities of society was probably quite serious. Some of the reform proposals advanced by various institutions during the educational campaign sounded like pages out of John Dewey. Here is one, submitted by the Peking Teachers' University in November 1967: "Examinations," it said, "are aimed to promote study. They should not be a test of memory, but of the power of reasoning. Mechanical repetition of teaching material should be opposed. Students should be encouraged to study creatively, to apply what they have learned, and to expound their own ideas. There should not be too many examinations and an end should be put to surprise tests. Examinations may be done away with altogether in some subjects. Examinations may take various forms: students may be given a choice of questions to answer; they may be allowed to use textbooks, notes, and reference materials during examinations; or they may be examined while engaged on some practical work. Examinations should be so designed as to give full play to the students' ability to reason things out. They should be allowed to discuss the questions together and use reference books."[30] The trouble with the proposal was that it was made in a society in which the reference books, the notes, and textbooks were written by one author, the discussions had to conform to the class line, and the answers had to be "Three Loyal": loyal to Chairman Mao Tse-tung, to his thought, and his proletarian revolutionary line. The democratic educational reform was doomed from its inception by the totalitar-

[30] *Peking Review* (November 17, 1967), p. 11.

ian spirit which animated it and the intolerant political system in which it was to be implemented.

PUBLIC HEALTH

One of the by-products of two years of turmoil and mass migrations was a decline in the people's health and at least a partial breakdown of the public health service. In this area, as we have seen, Communist China had in the past made substantial progress. Travelers in China's larger cities reported in 1968 and 1969 that rubbish had been left to pile up in the streets for weeks on end, and that in some localities night-soil collections had been suspended. There was a spread of communicable diseases, reportedly an alarming increase in the incidence of cerebral and spinal meningitis. It was thought in some quarters that the "Asian flu" epidemic which swept through the world in the autumn and winter of 1968 originated on the mainland of China, having first been carried to Hong Kong by Kwangtung Chinese who crossed the border back and forth. The problem was not made any easier by the suspension of classes in medical schools and by the hospitals' and clinics' preoccupation with making revolution to the detriment of disease prevention and cure.

Early in 1968 the China Medical College (formerly the Rockefeller Institute) came under attack for alleged bourgeois proclivities.[31] Its admissions policy, it was said, was too restrictive, its graduate program too long and too narrowly professional. The institution was too heavily oriented toward large urban hospitals, paying little heed to the needs of the rural areas. Students of peasant and worker origin were discriminated against,[32] their academic failure rates were inordinately high. There was too much emphasis on examinations and grades; too little attention was paid to the students' revolutionary quotient, even less to political study and activism. Far too few students and professors were assigned to serve in the countryside where in addition to alleviating pain they could learn from the poor and lower-middle peasants and acquire knowledge of acupuncture. Students, it was said, had no voice in the development of the curriculum. The proposed reform of the China Medical College served as model for a nationwide campaign to shorten the period of medical training, reduce theoretical content, instill practical experience into

[31] *Jen-min Jih-pao* (February 24, 1968), p. 4.
[32] According to the *Peking Review* (April 26, 1968, pp. 16-18), of the new students enrolled in Peking between 1959 and 1962, only 5 percent came from worker and peasant families. Roughly one-third of students of worker and peasant origin enrolled in 1961 as transfer students, were dismissed within two years. Half of them were Communist Party members.

the curriculum, abolish professional entrance examinations, and replace them with political recommendations and ideological means
tests, specialize in diseases common to the rural areas, and replace
the "Three Bigs" (big universities, big cities, big hospitals) with the
"Three Smalls" (small schools, small towns, small clinics). In the
First Medical College of Shanghai, according to *Jen-min Jih-pao*,
nurses operated under the new dispensation. They were so skilled
that even brain operations were entrusted to them.[33] In the hospital
in Anhwe, separate surgery and medicine departments were reportedly abolished, and all doctors were required to do everything.[34]
Large numbers of doctors were sent to settle permanently in the
countryside.[35]

COOPERATIVE MEDICAL SERVICE

The reform of medical schools was part of a drive to focus medical work and public health services on the countryside. The blueprint
for a cooperative medical service in the countryside was developed
by the PLA and the revolutionary committee of a county in Hopei
Province and published in *Jen-min Jih-pao* in early December 1968.
Under the plan, each commune member was to pay 1 yuan per year
to cover costs of operating the commune clinic. The commune contributed 10 fen (1/10 yuan) per person from the common fund. The
state contributed nothing. Each commune member was also to pay a
very small registration fee (5 fen) on each visit to the clinic. The
doctors in the Hopei clinic were young peasants ("barefoot doctors")[36] with three years primary education and some training in
traditional Chinese medicine obtained at the local county town. Of
the twelve doctors, all but two were attached to production brigades
(i.e., worked part-time in the fields) and were paid on the basis of
work points earned, most of the earnings being in kind. The two
remaining doctors received regular salaries. The chronically ill were

[33] *Jen-min Jih-pao* (July 9, 1968), p. 2. See, "Health for the Millions,"
China News Analysis, No. 738 (January 3, 1969).
[34] *Anhwe Radio* (December 2, 1968) in *China News Analysis*, No. 738 (January 3, 1969), p. 5.
[35] Janet Salaff, "Physician Heal Thyself," *FEER* (October 31, 1968),
pp. 291-293; Kuo Shu-su, "Using Materialist Dialectics to Cure Common Diseases," *Peking Review* (September 3, 1969), pp. 12-14, 18: "The contraction
and relaxation of muscles are two aspects of contradiction."
[36] The first "barefoot doctors" emerged in the suburbs of Shanghai during
the Great Leap years. They usually received basic medical training of about
2-3 months' duration from graduates of city medical schools sent to the countryside. See, "The System of 'Cooperative Medical Care' in Mainland Rural Areas,"
Chinese Communist Affairs: Facts and Figures, Vol. 2, No. 6, (January 8, 1969),
pp. 15-18.

excluded from the Hopei plan. In a discussion of the system launched by *Jen-min Jih-pao* on December 5, 1968, four questions were asked: (1) What was to be done if the money collected through annual members' contributions, registration fees, and commune subsidy from the general fund proved insufficient? (2) How was the cost of drugs to be covered? (3) If only two doctors were to be permanently on duty in the commune clinic, would they be able to cope with the work? (4) Were the descendants of the "four elements" (landlords, rich peasants, counterrevolutionaries, bad elements) to be allowed to join the system?[37]

Fantastic results were reported from all parts of the country, as health teams combined labor with the application of Mao Tse-tung's thought in the prevention and cure of disease, including malignant tumors. "Marvels of world medical history" were allegedly performed by barefoot doctors equipped with the correct ideology.[38] "Under the guidance of the great thought of Mao Tse-tung, the Mao Tse-tung's thought medical team of the Chinese PLA Unit 3125, treated 105 students of the Fuhsien School for Deaf-Mutes in Liaoning Province, enabling all of them to recover their hearing and speaking faculties. Now everyone of them can cheer 'Long live Chairman Mao!' and recite quotations from Chairman Mao."[39]

AGRICULTURE

Until late 1968 the countryside had been left more or less alone by the Cultural Revolution. The weather in 1967 was good. It was poor, but not disastrously so, in 1968.[40] Central controls over commune economy had been weakened and the peasants apparently profited from this to relax and engage in a little economism on the side. Throughout 1967 and to some extent in 1968 and 1969, the state found it difficult to extract from the peasants its full quota of compulsory deliveries of produce and to collect the full amount of

[37] *China News Analysis*, No. 738 (January 3, 1969), pp. 6-7. Note that the fifth element, the rightists, is missing. Note also that question (4) refers only to the children of the four elements, not to the four elements themselves. Presumably the latter were automatically excluded from the plan. Cf. "A Cooperative Medical Service Greatly Welcomed by Poor and Lower-Middle Peasants," *Peking Review* (January 17, 1969), pp. 4-8.

[38] See, for example, *China Pictorial*, No. 8 (1968) and "Cooperative Medical Service Is Fine!" *ibid.* No. 4 (1969), pp. 23-25.

[39] "Mao Tse-tung's Thought Opens New Road to the Curing of Deaf-Mutes," *China Pictorial*, No. 3, 1969, p. 28. Cf. "Foreign Friends Acclaim Mao Tsetung Thought for Lighting Up the 'Forbidden Zone' of Deaf-Mutes," *Peking Review* (August 15, 1969), pp. 20-21. For another sample, see Appendix B.

[40] Drought in the north and heavy rains in the south reportedly occurred at crucial periods during 1968.

agricultural tax.[41] Troubles on the railways hampered the smooth flow of food from the farms to the cities, but no widespread or severe shortages were recorded, although local disruption of food distribution, especially in the more remote provinces, may have been common. There occurred a steady drift of peasants into the cities that was not reversed until the second half of 1968. Many of the town-bound migrants had their travel and incidental expenses paid for by disaffected rural cadres. The 1967 harvest was at first said to have been greeted with "lively rejoicing," and the harvest itself was officially declared to have been excellent—later scaled down to "rather good."[42] Grain output was said to have shown "fairly big increases compared with 1966."[43] Output of cotton was reportedly good,[44] as was that of oil-bearing crops, sugar beet, sugar cane, bast fiber crops, tobacco, and livestock. The 1968 grain output was probably a little below 1967 levels—only six provinces reported increases over the previous year and there were insistent warnings against "overeating" and eating meat every day. Wheat purchases from Canada in the two years 1966 and 1967 amounted to 235 million bushels at an estimated cost to China of $106 million (25 percent payable in cash, the balance due in 18 months with interest). Wheat purchases in 1968 were probably in the region of 5 million tons. Most of the foreign wheat was probably used to feed the army and the cities, a portion being reserved for export to Albania and North Vietnam. Contracts with Canada and Australia specified delivery of about 4 million tons of wheat in 1969.

Estimated domestic food grain output in 1966 through 1968 is shown in Table 12-1.

Although these estimates represent not more than general orders of magnitude, it is fairly certain that there had been neither a significant decline in food grains output nor an important improvement compared with the last pre-Cultural Revolution year 1965. In fact, output was almost exactly where it had been in 1957, the last year for which meaningful official figures are available.

As the Cultural Revolution ebbed in the cities, a crackdown began in the countryside. Mao Tse-tung's thought propaganda teams

---

[41] According to the *NCNA*, 1968 procurements in twenty principal wheat-growing regions were better than in 1967. In some localities, however, communes reportedly understated their harvest results, chaff was added to rice delivered to the state, and there was a lack of enthusiasm for autumn sowing.

[42] L.D. Tretiak, "Lively Rejoicing," *FEER* (January 4, 1968), pp. 5-6.

[43] See, "China Reaps All-Round Record Harvest," *Peking Review* (January 3, 1968), pp. 43-45. Cf. "Agriculture 1967," *China News Analysis*, No. 691 (January 12, 1968).

[44] "Tremendous Development in China's Cotton Industry," *Peking Review* (September 26, 1969), pp. 19-21.

TABLE 12-1
Estimated Output of Food Grains, 1966–68
(Millions of Metric Tons)

1966	1967	1968
175–180	187–200	ca. 180

Sources: Hong Kong estimates for 1966; The Economist Intelligence Unit, London, *Quarterly Economic Review: China, Hong Kong, North Korea. Annual Supplement 1969*, p. 5. Taiwan estimates for 1967 range from 160 to 170 million metric tons.

fanned out over the provinces, the language of the Great Leap filled the Peking—and especially the Shanghai—press, material incentives and private plots were vigorously denounced. The campaign to restore discipline in the countryside took several forms.

1. Peasants were urged to emulate the Tachai spirit, work primarily for the good of the cause, and adopt the Tachai work point system of remuneration in which revolutionary consciousness paid off more handsomely than mere slogging for material reward.

2. The peasants were told to be "Three Loyal," that is, as we have seen (p. 560 above)—loyal to Chairman Mao, to Chairman Mao's thought, and to Chairman Mao's proletarian revolutionary line. Such loyalty involved active participation in

3. The process of purifying class ranks in the countryside by means of criticism-struggle-transformation. It meant, above all, dragging out hidden class enemies who, in spite of twenty years of proletarian vigilance by the dictatorship of the proletariat, had managed to conceal their family backgrounds and forge family records.

4. The state's treasury having been strained by two years of cultural activity, industrial strife, administrative confusion, and planlessness, the slogan of commune financial self-reliance was revived, and the peasants were instructed to pay for their own medical insurance, schools, and agricultural machinery stations.[45] In addition, the peasants were expected to absorb millions of presumably reluctant and resentful town dwellers—house them, feed them, and find work for them to do. In spite of injunctions to the comrades in the villages

[45] A movement to turn state-run agricultural machinery stations over to the communes began in earnest in 1967. It will be recalled that the question of who was to control (and pay for) these centers was one of the issues in dispute between the Liu and Mao leadership factions. It was reported that by the end of 1967 all communes in Hupeh had taken charge of the stations. The transfer implied putting tractor drivers, mechanics, and the administrative staffs of the machine stations on the commune payroll. The Taching system of remuneration may have alleviated somewhat the material burden on the communes, but whether it made for better machinery utilization remains an open question.

to welcome the new arrivals, frictions between villagers and towns-people-turned-peasants were probably frequent and the resulting con-tradictions quite antagonistic. In line with the poor and lower-middle peasants' promotion to the rank of revolutionary avant-garde, tough and self-reliant, the villagers were told not to look for agricultural credit to the state, but rather to supply it from their own savings.

5. Production teams which under the Liu-influenced policy of 1961-65 had assumed the principal responsibility for basic produc-tion planning and income distribution, saw their prerogatives curbed in the autumn of 1968 and early 1969.[46] The idea seemed to have been to supersede the teams by production brigades, move toward "great production brigades," and eventually to the communes, thus reversing the 1961-65 trend of "Filling-Out and Raising Standards."

6. The size of private plots was to be reduced. The exact inter-pretation of this directive was difficult to determine. During the period of feverish cultural activity in the cities and in the Party apparatus, the peasants surreptitiously enlarged their family holdings. The campaign against private plots might have been not much more than a drive to shrink the swollen plots back to regulation size.

7. Water conservation. The Great Leap Forward, it will be re-called (Chapter 8) was heralded by an immense drive to conserve and contain water. The Cultural Revolution in the countryside was similarly announced by a stepped-up effort to build dikes, irrigation canals, and reservoirs. Neglected in 1967 and 1968, the water conser-vation campaign picked up momentum in the winter and spring 1968-69. More than 37 million people were reportedly digging irriga-tion ditches and building dikes in eleven provinces. In the Pearl River delta alone, over 5,000 water-control projects were said to have been completed in the winter. In Hunan, tens of thousands of real and transfer peasants dug a canal 330 feet wide, 2 miles long and 25 feet deep in 50 days. The canal bypassed a bend in the Yangtse River. In Kiangsi Province, 40,000 water conservation projects were completed in a matter of months, "revolutionary settlers" from the cities ac-counted for the bulk of the labor force put at 3.5 million people. In Kiangsu, 2.5 million regular and transplanted peasants did the same thing.[47] By promoting production in the countryside, the former Red Guards, teachers, doctors, young revolutionaries, old counter-revolutionaries, Revolutionary Rebels, less than comparatively good Party cadres and officials were grasping revolution in a concrete way. In the meantime in the cities, a new generation of Red Guards was being brought up: three- to seven-year-olds were organized in teams to propagate the thought of Mao Tse-tung on street corners. In Pe-

[46] See *New York Times* (February 23, 1969), p. 7.
[47] *New York Times* (March 23, 1968), p. 11; *Quarterly Economic Review: China, Hong Kong, North Korea*, No. 2 (1969).

king alone, 1,300 such teams were said to have been brought into being in the early months of 1969. They quoted the Chairman at passersby unaware of the fact that their elder brothers who had done that very thing a year or two earlier were at that moment grasping revolution and promoting production down on the farm. There was a Fourierist touch to these armies of youngsters performing menial labor; a Kafkaesque denouement to their revolutionary zeal.

8. At the end of 1967 the movement for popular innovations and mass farm tool reform was resuscitated. Almost like during the Great Leap Forward, the poor and lower-middle peasants were harnessed to the task of technical and scientific invention, which they performed with statistical gusto.[48]

FOREIGN TRADE

The Cultural Revolution had no noticeably adverse effect on China's foreign commerce in 1966. There was, however, some decline in exports, especially to hard-currency areas, resulting in a trade deficit of about $50 million. In 1967 this trend continued, the trade deficit rising to an estimated $200 million. The drop in exports was probably traceable to disruptions at Chinese ports (especially in 1967) and to confusion on the railroads. The fall in trade in 1968 was less rapid than expected. Japanese exports to China (mainly steel) rose by 13 percent during the year, and Canadian exports (mainly wheat) showed an upward trend.

The 1961-65 geographical pattern of trade was maintained. Total turnover with communist countries in 1966 amounted to about $1,150 million, falling to $865 million in 1967 (the greatest decline being registered in China's trade with the USSR). Turnover with Western countries was $3,160 in 1966, and $3,200 in 1967.

In 1965 through 1967 China bought some gold on the London market: $99 million in 1965, $37 million in 1966, and $137 million in 1967. The 1965 and 1966 purchases were probably made as a hedge against the expected devaluation of the pound. China did not join in the rush on gold at the end of 1967 and in early 1968.[49]

[48] Cf. Chapter 8 above. See "The Lowly Are the Most Intelligent," *China Pictorial*, No. 3 (1969), pp. 37-39, and *URS*, Vol. 50, No. 22 (March 15, 1968).

[49] Some further reading on the Cultural Revolution and the economy: Dwight H. Perkins, "Economic Growth in China and the Cultural Revolution (1960-April 1967)" *China Quarterly* (April-June 1967), pp. 33-48; Cheng Chouyuan, "The Cultural Revolution and China's Economy," *Current History* (September 1967), pp. 148-154, 176-177; Colina MacDougall, "Pie in the Sky," *FEER* (June 26, 1969), pp. 706-708; Leo A. Orleans, "Evidence from Chinese Medical Journals of Current Population Policy" *China Quarterly* (October-December 1969), pp. 137-146.

13 | The China After Mao

"The Master said: The phoenix does not come: the river gives forth no chart. It is all over with me." But Confucius erred. The heavens did intend him to play the sage's part, and his thought influenced twenty-five centuries of man. The new Master said: "Everyone should create several successors. Do not simply behave in accord with your own interest, as if the world would stop going around when you are gone. There is nothing to fear about death. Is not Marx dead? . . . But we should prepare successors for the next three generations." The new Master also spoke of preparing to meet God and of the young successors who had disappointed him. The phoenix did not come, the river gave forth no chart.

Whether, in spite of the absence of such portents, the thought of Mao has about it the touch of immortality is a question which none but the most ardently faithful Maoist would dare answer. But how is he to be found for sure? Have not many who called themselves the followers and disciples of Mao turned out to be scabs and renegades, red of mouth and white of heart? Have not the chosen young successors fallen prey to the lures of petty bourgeois factionalism and antirevolutionary anarchism? Has not the working class itself yielded to the attractions of material reward, refusing to "create wealth with political awareness, not money"? The young have trickled away from contact with the soil and communion with poor and lower-middle peasants, toward the neon signs and the Nanking Road whenever the opportunity presented itself. And have not the leaders failed to live up to the high standards of probity and moral rectitude which they urged on others? They have had their affair of the necklace, their tawdry *cherchez la femme* (in the Politbureau), their proletarian salons in which an aging actress set the tone and laid down the rules for opera, theater, and literary creativity. They have lived off their Long March reputations, nibbled away at past glories, bickered over socialist construction and the nature of contradictions, until nothing was left of the myth of unshakable unity. They have compressed thirty centuries of intrigue into two decades and built on shaky ethical foundations a monument to the future society of moral stimulation. On the ashes of a totalitarian bureaucratic Party they erected a sprawling myth of Mao: "Oh Chairman Mao, Chairman Mao! ... You have summed up the experience and lessons of the international communist movement and led 700 million people to a completely new stage of socialist revolution. ... You told us: 'I give you my firm support!' ... You grasped the newborn thing of exchanging revolutionary experience on a big scale. ... Where is the greatest revolutionary of the present era? He stands by our side and before our eyes, and he is our most respected and beloved great leader Chairman Mao!"[1]

"An important achievement of the Twentieth Congress of the Communist Party of the Soviet Union," said the renegade, scab, and capitalist-roader Teng Hsiao-p'ing, "lies in the fact that it showed us what serious consequences can follow from the deification of the individual. Our Party has always held that no political parties and no individuals are free from flaws and mistakes in their activities. ... Our Party abhorrs the deification of the individual. ... Likewise, it has been against exaggerating the role of leaders in works of art and literature."[2] Teng, of course, was taking liberties with the truth: Communist Parties have been known to accommodate themselves to personality cults of incredible proportions. In fact, they often became mere shadows of the cult, as did the Chinese Party after 1965. A "personality cult" does not stop at the person of the leader. It extends to his thought, thus hoping to span the generations.

What the communists found facing them when they came to power were centuries of economic neglect and thousands of years of a unique and almost unchanging culture. To scale the formidable mountain of economic retardation required not only policy but faith. To overcome cultural immobility, called for an upheaval in the superstructure, a constant churning of ideas or, as Mao saw it, a permanent cultural revolution. The communism of Mao's conception was not so much an upsurge of economic development as an explosive growth of the human spirit, a broadening of men's horizons, the creation of a collective being. Material growth would inevitably follow, but it was never to be allowed to corrupt the soul; its tentacles of comfort and leisure were to be strictly disciplined in the collective interest. The new society emerging from continuous mass struggles would be democratic in the sense that heaven is democratic: a communion of beings in the state of highest perfection bathing in the rays of an eternal truth. There would be broad discussions and mass consultations, the outcome of which would be obvious and

[1] "A New Era of Vigorously Establishing the Complete Ascendancy of Mao Tse-tung's Thought," *Peking Review* (December 9, 1966), p. 15.

[2] Eighth Party Congress, September 1956.

natural in a communist Enlightenment sense. There would be equality and all-roundedness, each atomistic unit a microcosm of the collective whole. There would be no domineering, no bureaucrats, no apparatus, no classes, no toadying sycophants, pedants, and villainous tyrants, only a willing, self-imposed discipline, a compulsive merging of individual interest in the communal will. On the basis of such superstructure the Marxist economic base of society would grow and prosper. The attainment of this vision demanded qualities of character in the leaders worthy of a Buddha, combined with the wrath and asceticism of a John the Baptist. It was, perhaps, asking too much of millions of men whose earthly condition placed them beyond the pale of absolute purity and destined them to pass their lives in a state of tolerably normal perfection, with all the backsliding that this implies. In the event, neither the people nor their high priests have lived up to expectations.

The Great Leap Forward hurled millions of people against the barrier of economic backwardness on the assumption that the people had been spiritually readied for the task by earlier mass campaigns, notably by the little big leap of 1956. Formally, from the standpoint of property relations, the superstructure was equal to the job: it had been collectivized, then swiftly communized. But, as it turned out, the essential ingredient of the superstructure—a fired-up revolutionary spirit—was lacking. The leap in property relations failed to bring about an equally startling jump in the material-technical base of the economy, just as Marx had implied. The traitors and black hands within the leadership, the rightists, "rotten sensualists," and capitalist-roaders had argued that the Leap had put the Maoist ox before the Marxist cart, that the development of the material productive forces should precede not follow the radicalization of production relations. They had little trust in spiritual rebirth as agent of a revolutionary transformation of the economic base of society. They approached the problems of revolution dogmatically, like scholars whose thought was petrified by constant scanning of the texts, like old women with bound feet, un-Lenin-like. They, a handful but a big one, failed to set the correct example of courage, confidence, imagination, and élan. Cemented in emotionally irrelevant issues of policy, they were paralyzed by conservative notions of the people's material welfare as this related to output and labor productivity. They babbled about working hours, pensions, periods of rest, and wage incentives, and were blind to the limitless possibilities of correct politics outlined and explained in the works of Mao. Lacking in faith, the handful failed to see that the Chinese revolution was a spiritual phenomenon, that it had succeeded thus far in the teeth of incalculable adversity by reason of its inner strength, resilience, and determination. A further nurturing of these qualities was a prerequisite for raising the revolution to new heights and carrying it through to the end. Such, broadly, was the Maoist interpretation of the events of 1958-60.

On this interpretation, the task ahead was not to develop the base step by step, as the apparat-men—revisionists one and all—had argued before and after the Great Leap score was in, but to fashion new, bigger, and better revivalist clean-ups, deep-plow the people's mind, change the people's habits, instill the masses with the revolutionary spirit; in short, profoundly alter the cultural make-up of Chinese society, beginning with the cities where the dangers of material debasement were the greatest, fanning out into the countryside, sweeping away all obstacles, right up to the Party itself if need be.

This vast cultural revolution had not only to rid the nation of old, die-hard revisionists and unreformable elements inherited from the past, but to ensure that the new generation on the threshold of adult life be knowledgeable in the letter and filled with the spirit of Mao Tse-tung's thought. The new generation had been born and raised in time of peace. It had not known the hardships of prerevolutionary years which tempered a man. One had to simulate hard times by denying the young the modest dividends of progress, furnish them with manure baskets and other appurtenances of poor peasant culture, and send them off to where the going was the roughest. One could use the young, as one had used the private sector, to destroy the old. "Revolutionaries are Monkey Kings," wrote the Red Guards of Tsinghua University on June 24, 1966, "their supernatural powers far-reaching and their magic omnipotent, for they possess Mao Tse-tung's great invincible thought. We wield our golden rods, display our supernatural powers and use our magic to turn the old world upside down, smash it to pieces, pulverize it, create chaos, and make a tremendous mess, the bigger the better!"[3] The price of smashing the old was disorder, factionalism, and disarray verging on anarchy and civil war; "certain signs of disunity within the revolutionary ranks," as the Maoists put it. During the turbulent process of creating that "newborn thing," a social conscience, the old-line cadres were loath to discipline the masses for fear of making right-opportunist mistakes for which they would have to pay later. The veil of authority and respectability had been torn from their faces. The masses had a field day: some rampaging, others traveling, some playing majong deep into the night. Soldiers argued with their commanders, students

[3] Quoted in *FEER* (October 2, 1969), p. 34.

talked back to their teachers, workers failed to clock in on time, peasants lay down in the collective fields or tended to their private plots with a single-mindedness unusual in the annals of Utopia builders. Within the confines of the Mao myth, China exploded in all its youthful diversity, making the foreign barbarians think that it was falling apart, when it was only reliving—in an instant—thousands of years of its history.

In the end the Party disappointed Mao, the government bureaucracy disappointed Mao, and the young disappointed him too. Only the army remained, and it also had disappointed Mao now and then. One by one the myths of revolutionary righteousness, rule by persuasion, unity and mass enthusiasm faded away. In the loneliness of his grand design, the Master stood alone. The phoenix did not come, the river gave forth no chart. But it was not all over with him yet.

Bereft of a Party and a government, his mass organizations dissolved, he set about institutionalizing his thought once more, implanting it on the base of China's society. To give frame to the spirit of his vision, Mao entwined the country in a net of revolutionary committees and self-sufficient communes in which workers, peasants, soldiers, and intellectuals were to perform one another's jobs in turn, where peasants ran small factories, health clinics, and schools (see Appendix B), and urbanites plowed the fields and modestly learned the things all new socialist men should know. The kingpin of the system was moral incentive, the turning out of material goods with little material reward and much spiritual uplift. The core of moral incentive was correct politics, internalized and taken on faith. With consummate skill, Mao choreographed his revolutionary minuet: two steps forward, one step back; now spirit and struggle, now hard-headed policy; a little turmoil, and a pinch of planning. The known canons of civil rule, Mao seemed to be saying, did not apply to a vast, underdeveloped land, weighed down with a millenial tradition and peopled by the very young whose numbers rose vertiginously. Totally new ways of conducting the business of such a society had to be found. A single injection of revolution followed by decades of administrative bureaucracy would not do. The magic of revolution had to be made permanent, the drama of seizure of power had to be replayed over and over again, allegiance to the center had to be sought in a complete abnegation of the self, which would enable the center to devolve policy-making authority onto local communes and revolutionary committees in the knowledge that these communes and committees would automatically and without prodding act as the center would. If, during the interval between experiment and perfection, moral correctives were needed, the PLA would take care of that. Democratic centralism was organizationally redefined, but by the end of 1969 it was still not clear what precisely was the role of the Party in the new scheme.

Mao's disappearance from the stage will leave a void which his thought and its present organizational extensions may find it diffi-cult to fill. The latest instructions will no longer come from the living Mao, but from his continuators who, at least for a time, will speak in the name of Mao. The revisionists, the apparat-men thirsting for revenge, the lumpen bureaucrats and office-wallahs, the PLA, the left groupies, and, above all, the restless young are in the wings, anx-iously watching and waiting. The ghosts and monsters of cupidity, personal ambition, score-settling, and fatigue are there too. As late as July 1969 they burst upon the scene in Taiyuan in a frenzy of petty bourgeois factionalism. Only the intervention of the PLA's moral disincentives prevented the situation from getting out of hand. More important perhaps, the common human desire for a better life now, clamored for recognition. Indications were that it would not be exor-cised by dialectical squirming or the promise of betterment in the future conditional. Ominously, the two experiments in pure Mao-ism—the Great Leap Forward and the Cultural Revolution—have ap-parently failed to lift China out of the morass of poverty nor have they brought about a moral rebirth on a scale that would guarantee the coming of Mao's vision. Agriculturally and (barring certain sub-sectors) industrially, China in 1969 was not much better off than in 1957, the last year of the apparat-based First Five Year Plan. More than a decade of potential growth was squandered in ideological muscle-flexing, fritted away in politically-induced business cycles. The turmoil of 1967 may have been as much a manifestation of the regime's failure to move the country away from the hunger margin as of Maoist intent. There has been a net gain in the public expression of China's underlying diversity and in the exteriorization of leader-ship tensions. This, however, was not enough to answer the problem raised in Chapter 1: how to adequately feed, clothe, house, and keep in good health (and good temper) a population which increases by over 200 million every fifteen years.

The country is in flux. There are no clear trends on which reason-ably accurate predictions could be made. If such trends do, in fact, exist, the outside world is not allowed to detect them. All one can say is that with Mao's death China will reach yet another momentous turning point in her history and that the most exciting annals remain to be written. The present rejection of policy as a right-opportunist deviation cannot perhaps go on for long. Reliance on the power of the spirit to produce policy may yet turn out to have been a mirage. "The Master said: I once spent a whole day without food and a whole night without sleep, in order to meditate. It was no use. It is better to learn."

The Constitution of the Communist Party of China*

CHAPTER I GENERAL PROGRAMME

The Communist Party of China is the political party of the proletariat.

The basic programme of the Communist Party of China is the complete overthrow of the bourgeoisie and all other exploiting classes, the establishment of the dictatorship of the proletariat in place of the dictatorship of the bourgeoisie and the triumph of socialism over capitalism. The ultimate aim of the Party is the realization of communism.

The Communist Party of China is composed of the advanced elements of the proletariat; it is a vigorous vanguard organization leading the proletariat and the revolutionary masses in the fight against the class enemy.

The Communist Party of China takes Marxism-Leninism-Mao Tsetung Thought as the theoretical basis guiding its thinking. Mao Tsetung Thought is Marxism-Leninism of the era in which imperialism is heading for total collapse and socialism is advancing to worldwide victory.

For half a century now, in leading China's great struggle for accomplishing the new-democratic revolution, in leading her great struggle for socialist revolution and socialist construction and in the great struggle of the contemporary international communist movement against imperialism, modern revisionism and the reactionaries of various countries, Comrade Mao Tsetung has integrated the universal truth of Marxism-Leninism with the concrete practice of revolution, inherited, defended and developed Marxism-Leninism and has brought it to a higher and completely new stage.

Comrade Lin Piao has consistently held high the great red banner of Mao Tsetung Thought and has most loyally and resolutely carried out and defended Comrade Mao Tsetung's proletarian revolutionary

---

*Adopted by the Ninth National Congress of the Communist Party of China on April 14, 1969.

line. Comrade Lin Piao is Comrade Mao Tsetung's close comrade-in-arms and successor.

The Communist Party of China with Comrade Mao Tsetung as its leader is a great, glorious and correct Party and is the core of leadership of the Chinese people. The Party has been tempered through long years of class struggle for the seizure and consolidation of state power by armed force, it has strengthened itself and grown in the course of the struggle against both Right and "Left" opportunist lines, and it is valiantly advancing with supreme confidence along the road of socialist revolution and socialist construction.

Socialist society covers a fairly long historical period. Throughout this historical period, there are classes, class contradictions and class struggle, there is the struggle between the socialist road and the capitalist road, there is the danger of capitalist restoration and there is the threat of subversion and aggression by imperialism and modern revisionism. These contradictions can be resolved only by depending on the Marxist theory of continued revolution and on practice under its guidance. Such is China's Great Proletarian Cultural Revolution, a great political revolution carried out under the conditions of socialism by the proletariat against the bourgeoisie and all other exploiting classes.

The whole Party must hold high the great red banner of Marxism-Leninism-Mao Tsetung Thought and lead the hundreds of millions of the people of all the nationalities of our country in carrying on the three great revolutionary movements of class struggle, the struggle for production and scientific experiment, in strengthening and consolidating the dictatorship of the proletariat and in building socialism independently and with the initiative in our own hands, through self-reliance and hard struggle and by going all out, aiming high and achieving greater, faster, better and more economical results.

The Communist Party of China upholds proletarian internationalism; it firmly unites with the genuine Marxist-Leninist parties and groups the world over, unites with the proletariat, the oppressed people and nations of the whole world and fights together with them to overthrow imperialism headed by the United States, modern revisionism with the Soviet revisionist renegade clique as its centre and the reactionaries of all countries, and to abolish the system of exploitation of man by man on the globe, so that all mankind will be emancipated.

Members of the Communist Party of China, who dedicate their lives to the struggle for communism, must be resolute, fear no sacrifice and surmount every difficulty to win victory!

CHAPTER II MEMBERSHIP

ARTICLE 1

Any Chinese worker, poor peasant, lower-middle peasant, revolutionary armyman or any other revolutionary element who has reached the age of 18 and who accepts the Constitution of the Party, joins a Party organization and works actively in it, carries out the Party's decisions, observes Party discipline and pays membership dues may become a member of the Communist Party of China.

ARTICLE 2

Applicants for Party membership must go through the procedure for admission individually. An applicant must be recommended by two Party members, fill out an application form for Party membership and be examined by a Party branch, which must seek the opinions of the broad masses inside and outside the Party. Application is subject to acceptance by the general membership meeting of the Party branch and approval by the next higher Party committee.

ARTICLE 3

Members of the Communist Party of China must:

(1) Study and apply Marxism-Leninism-Mao Tsetung Thought in a living way;

(2) Work for the interests of the vast majority of the people of China and the world;

(3) Be able at uniting with the great majority, including those who have wrongly opposed them but are sincerely correcting their mistakes; however, special vigilance must be maintained against careerists, conspirators and double-dealers so as to prevent such bad elements from usurping the leadership of the Party and the state at any level and guarantee that the leadership of the Party and the state always remains in the hands of Marxist revolutionaries;

(4) Consult with the masses when matters arise;

(5) Be bold in making criticism and self-criticism.

ARTICLE 4

When Party members violate Party discipline, the Party organizations at the levels concerned shall, within their functions and powers and on the merits of each case, take appropriate disciplinary measures—warning, serious warning, removal from posts in the Party, placing on probation within the Party, or expulsion from the Party.

The period for which a Party member is placed on probation shall not exceed two years. During this period, he has no right to vote or elect or be elected.

A Party member who becomes politically apathetic and makes no change despite education should be persuaded to withdraw from the Party.

When a Party member asks to withdraw from the Party, the Party branch concerned shall, with the approval of its general membership meeting, remove his name from the Party rolls and report the matter to the next higher Party committee for the record. When necessary, this should be made public to the masses outside the Party.

Proven renegades, enemy agents, absolutely unrepentant persons in power taking the capitalist road, degenerates and alien class elements must be cleared out of the Party and not be readmitted.

CHAPTER III ORGANIZATIONAL PRINCIPLE OF THE PARTY

ARTICLE 5

The organizational principle of the Party is democratic centralism.

The leading bodies of the Party at all levels are elected through democratic consultation.

The whole Party must observe unified discipline: The individual is subordinate to the organization, the minority is subordinate to the majority, the lower level is subordinate to the higher level, and the entire Party is subordinate to the Central Committee.

Leading bodies of the Party at all levels shall regularly report on their work to congresses or general membership meetings, constantly listen to the opinions of the masses both inside and outside the Party and accept their supervision. Party members have the right to criticize Party organizations and leading members at all levels and make proposals to them. If a Party member holds different views with regard to the decisions or directives of the Party organizations, he is allowed to reserve his views and has the right to bypass the immediate leadership and report directly to higher levels, up to and including the Central Committee and the Chairman of the Central Committee. It is essential to create a political situation in which there are both centralism and democracy, both discipline and freedom, both unity of will and personal ease of mind and liveliness.

The organs of state power of the dictatorship of the proletariat, the People's Liberation Army, and the Communist Youth League and other revolutionary mass organizations, such as those of the workers, the poor and lower-middle peasants and the Red Guards, must all accept the leadership of the Party.

ARTICLE 6

The highest leading body of the Party is the National Party Congress and, when it is not in session, the Central Committee elected by it. The leading bodies of Party organizations in the localities, in army units and in various departments are the Party congresses or general membership meetings at their respective levels and the Party committees elected by them. Party congresses at all levels are convened by Party committees at their respective levels.

The convening of Party congresses in the localities and army units and their elected Party committee members are subject to approval by the higher Party organizations.

ARTICLE 7

Party committees at all levels shall set up their working bodies or dispatch their representative organs in accordance with the principles of unified leadership, close ties with the masses and simple and efficient structure.

CHAPTER IV CENTRAL ORGANIZATIONS OF THE PARTY

ARTICLE 8

The National Party Congress shall be convened every five years. Under special circumstances, it may be convened before its due date or postponed.

ARTICLE 9

The plenary session of the Central Committee of the Party elects the Political Bureau of the Central Committee, the Standing Committee of the Political Bureau of the Central Committee and the Chairman and Vice-Chairman of the Central Committee.

The plenary session of the Central Committee of the Party is convened by the Political Bureau of the Central Committee.

When the Central Committee is not in plenary session, the Political Bureau of the Central Committee and its Standing Committee exercise the functions and powers of the Central Committee.

Under the leadership of the Chairman, the Vice-Chairman and the Standing Committee of the Political Bureau of the Central Committee, a number of necessary organs, which are compact and efficient, shall be set up to attend to the day-to-day work of the Party, the government and the army in a centralized way.

CHAPTER V PARTY ORGANIZATIONS IN THE LOCALITIES AND THE ARMY UNITS

ARTICLE 10

Local Party congresses at the county level and upwards and Party congresses in the People's Liberation Army at the regimental level and upwards shall be convened every three years. Under special circumstances, they may be convened before their due date or postponed.

Party committees at all levels in the localities and the army units elect their standing committees, secretaries and deputy secretaries.

CHAPTER VI PRIMARY ORGANIZATIONS OF THE PARTY

ARTICLE 11

In general, Party branches are formed in factories, mines and other enterprises, people's communes, offices, schools, shops, neighbourhoods, companies of the People's Liberation Army and other primary units; general Party branches or primary Party committees may also be set up where there is a relatively large membership or where the revolutionary struggle requires.

Primary Party organizations shall hold elections once a year. Under special circumstances, the election may take place before its due date or be postponed.

ARTICLE 12

Primary Party organizations must hold high the great red banner of Marxism-Leninism-Mao Tsetung Thought, give prominence to proletarian politics and develop the style of integrating theory with practice, maintaining close ties with the masses of the people and practising criticism and self-criticism. Their main tasks are:

(1) To lead the Party members and the broad revolutionary

masses in studying and applying Marxism-Leninism-Mao Tsetung Thought in a living way;

(2) To give constant education to the Party members and the broad revolutionary masses concerning class struggle and the struggle between the two lines and lead them in fighting resolutely against the class enemy;

(3) To propagate and carry out the policies of the Party, implement its decisions and fulfil every task assigned by the Party and the state;

(4) To maintain close ties with the masses, constantly listen to their opinions and demands and wage an active ideological struggle within the Party so as to keep Party life vigorous;

(5) To take in new Party members, enforce Party discipline, constantly consolidate the Party organizations and get rid of the stale and take in the fresh so as to maintain the purity of the Party ranks.

Samples of New Educational Materials and Healing Techniques Emerging from the Great Proletarian Cultural Revolution

1. *Example of new teaching material on arithmetic from Yuehchin Brigade, Chinchiapa Commune, Wuchiang County, Kiangsu Province.* The material was prepared by Chi Fu-ching, a commune member of poor peasant origin. Reprinted from "Some Problems in Arithmetic," *China Pictorial*, No. 8 (1969), pp. 38-39 (full text).

"Before liberation, there were altogether six in my family. Working as hired hand for a landlord, I had to cultivate 15 *mou* of land, and reaped about 620 *jin* of grain per *mou* a year. The landlord, who was more deadly than a poisonous snake, did everything he could to exploit us poor and lower-middle peasants. It was made clear beforehand that he was to pay me eight *piculs* of rice a year as wages. But charging me for this, that, and the other as he willed, in the end he meted out to me only six and a half. It was impossible to support a family on that, and we lived like beasts of burden. At the time, in our Hsitsun Village and its neighborhood, there were 13 hired hands and four girl children were forced to be child brides.

The east is red; the sun rises. Chairman Mao led us in overthrowing the three big mountains. We have become masters in our own country and our lives improve with each passing day. We should never forget that it was the Communist Party which emancipated us poor people and that it was Chairman Mao who brought us happiness. But the arch renegade Liu Shao-ch'i desperately tried to drag us back onto the capitalist road, and we are determined to fight him with all our might.

Now, let us calculate the following:

1. What was the total number of hired hands and child brides in Hsitsun Village and its neighborhood before liberation?
2. How many *jin* of grain was poor peasant Chi Fu-ching able to grow by laboring for a year?
3. The landlord gave Chi Fu-ching only 6.5 *piculs* of rice (one *picul* of rice equals 200 *jin* of grain) as wages. How many *jin* of grain did Chi Fu-ching get after a year's labor? How many *jin* of grain did exploitation by the landlord amount to? What percentage of the total output of grain did exploitation by the landlord amount to? And what percentage of the total output did Chi Fu-ching, who had toiled the year round, receive as wages?

2. *Overcoming the Sequelae of Infantile Paralysis.* Reprinted from *China Pictorial*, No. 9 (1969), pp. 32-35 (abridged).

In August last year, revolutionary medical workers of the PLA No. 208 Hospital relying on the invincible Mao Tsetung Thought, succeeded in curing Chang Kuei-chih, a young woman worker who had been paralyzed for four years and diagnosed by the reactionary bourgeois medical "authorities" as "incurable." As the good news spread, other paralytics came to the hospital from all parts of the country, full of hope. Most were diagnosed as suffering from the after-effects of infantile paralysis.

The sequelae of infantile paralysis had long been considered as "irremediable." Now, a serious test faced the revolutionary medical workers, whether to push the class brothers out of the door, or to tackle this difficult problem in the interest of the people.

The hospital's Party committee considered that in order to cure the after-effects of infantile paralysis, it is necessary first of all to cure the ideological "after-effects" on the medical workers of the poison of the counterrevolutionary revisionist line pushed by the big renegade Liu Shao-ch'i in medical and health work. Therefore it organized the medical workers to intensively study Chairman Mao's series of brilliant instructions on medical and health work and to go among the workers and poor and lower-middle peasants to investigate and study the history of the struggle between the two lines in medical and health work. Cherishing profound proletarian class feeling, they looked at the victims crippled by the after-effects of infantile paralysis, and listened to accusations from the patients and their families. These vivid lessons on the two-line struggle filled them with revolutionary ardor. They solemnly pledged to the great leader Chairman Mao:

"Chairman Mao! Ah, Chairman Mao! We are the people's army, loyal fighters defending your revolutionary line. The people's needs are our fighting order. We are determined to restore more sick class brothers to health so that they can closely follow you in making revolution. . . ."

Enduring acute pain, they tried the big acupuncture needles out on their own bodies. Their thighs became swollen, and their eyes were red after sleepless nights. But the revolutionary medical workers armed with Mao Tsetung Thought regarded this as pleasure and happiness. They said: "To defend Chairman Mao's revolutionary line, we are willing to acupuncture our legs to pulp. . . ."

Through repeated practice on their own bodies, they eventually created advanced experience in the use of a new acupuncture therapy to treat the after-effects of infantile paralysis. Now, the overwhelming majority of the more than 6,000 patients treated show marked improvement, and victims who had been crippled or paralyzed for several years or even more than a decade can stand up again and take part in socialist revolution and socialist construction.

Table of Measures

1 mou	=	1/5 hectare, 1/6 acre
1 catty (*shih chin*)	=	1/2 kilogram, 1.1023 pound
1 picul (*shih tan*)	=	50 kilograms, 0.0492 long ton
1 li	=	1/2 kilometer, 0.3107 mile

Index

Name Index

Adams, R., 94n
Adenauer, K., 467
Aebi, A., 283n
Agarwala, A. N., 329n
Aird, J. S., 416n, 417n
Allen, G. C., 58n
Alley, R., 437n
Ames, E., 116n
Armstrong, J. A., 28n
Ashbrook, A. G., 47n
Ashdown, J., 381n, 395n, 443n
Ashton, J., 339
Atwater, E., 90n

Baratz, M. S., 130n
Barnett, A. D., 2n, 14n, 28n, 79n, 80n, 89
Basora, A. A., 466n
Bauer, P. T., 115n
Bauer, R. A., 116n
Baum, R., 424n, 520n, 533n
Baykov, A., 166
Bereday, G. Z. F., 90n
Bergson, A., 114n, 116n, 132n, 135n
Bernstein, E., 330
Bernstein, T. P., 46n
Bethune, N., 496n
Blaustein, A. P., 8n, 26n, 28n, 85n, 95n, 98n
Bochenski, J. M., 15n
Bombelles, J. T., 111n
Bourguiba, H., 413
Bradley, M. E., 114n
Brandt, C., 15n, 105n
Brennan, C., 378n
Brezhnev, L., 460, 475, 476
Brodersen, D., 116n
Brzezinski, Z. K., 15n
Buchan, A., 29n
Buchanan, K., 383, 384n
Buck, J. L., 35n, 36, 347n
Bukharin, N. I., 363

Burki, S. J., 348
Burlatsky, F., 472n

Carin, R., 266n
Carlisle, D. S., 22n, 419n
Casella, A., 380n
Castro, F., 465, 466, 467
Chai, Chien-hua, 398
Chandrasekhar, S., 415n
Chang, Ch'un-ch'iao, 518n
Chang, Ho, 271n
Chang, Hsi-ting, 533
Chang, Hsueh-liang, 105
Chang, J. K., 53n, 54n
Chang, Kuo-hua, 524
Chang, Kuo-tao, 310n
Chang, Lin-chih, 277, 525
Chang, Ling, 398
Chang, Po-chun, 248n
Chang, P. H., 260n
Chang, Wen-tien, 333
Chang, W. Y., 380n
Chao, Chung, 191n
Chao, Kang, 93n, 121, 141, 307n
Chao, Kuo-chun, 158n, 161n, 286n, 292n
Ch'en, Ch'i-t'ung, 496
Chen, Feng-tung, 273n
Chen, Huang-mei, 442n
Chen, K., 470n
Chen, Kai-wan, 559n
Chen, Ko-fun, 59
Chen, Nai-Ruenn, 7n, 8n, 37n, 52n, 53n, 59n, 60n, 63n, 75, 81n, 86, 117, 121, 122, 127n, 133n, 134, 135, 141n, 166, 167n, 177, 205n, 207n, 210, 337, 340n, 398n
Ch'en P'i-hsien, 498n, 513, 518n
Chen, Po-ta, 25n, 37n, 493n, 501, 508, 525, 526, 533, 534, 544, 548
Chen, S. H., 242n, 245n, 259n, 283n

Subject Index